Cultural Anthropology

A Perspective on the Human Condition

Canadian Edition

Cultural Anthropology

A Perspective on the Human Condition

Emily A. Schultz   Robert H. Lavenda   Roberta Robin Dods

OXFORD
UNIVERSITY PRESS

OXFORD

UNIVERSITY PRESS

70 Wynford Drive, Don Mills, Ontario M3C 1J9
www.oupcanada.com

Oxford University Press is a department of the University of Oxford.
It furthers the University's objective of excellence in research, scholarship,
and education by publishing worldwide in

Oxford   New York
Auckland Cape Town Dar es Salaam Hong Kong Karachi
Kuala Lumpur Madrid Melbourne Mexico City Nairobi
New Delhi Shanghai Taipei Toronto

With offices in
Argentina Austria Brazil Chile Czech Republic France Greece
Guatemala Hungary Italy Japan Poland Portugal Singapore
South Korea Switzerland Thailand Turkey Ukraine Vietnam

Oxford is a trade mark of Oxford University Press
in the UK and in certain other countries

Published in Canada
by Oxford University Press

Library and Archives Canada Cataloguing in Publication

Schultz, Emily A. (Emily Ann), 1949–
Cultural anthropology : a perspective on the human
condition / Emily A. Schultz, Robert H. Lavenda & Roberta
R. Dods.—1st Canadian ed.

Includes bibliographical references and index.
ISBN 978-0-19-542601-4
1. Ethnology–Textbooks. 2. Ethnology–Canada–Textbooks.
I. Lavenda, Robert H. II. Dods, Roberta R. III. Title.

GN316.S38 2009   306   C2009-901061-5

Cover image: Shahn Rowe/Getty Images

This book is printed on permanent acid-free paper ∞.

Printed and bound in the United States of America.

2 3 4 — 12 11 10 09

Brief Contents

Contents

Part One
The Tools of Cultural Anthropology

Chapter 1

The Anthropological Perspective on the Human Condition   2

Chapter 2

Fieldwork   25

Part Two

The Resources of Culture

Chapter 3

Chapter 4

Chapter 5

Chapter 6

Part Three
The Organization of Material Life

Chapter 7

Chapter 8

Part Four
Alliances for Living: Relationships

Chapter 9

Chapter 10

Part Five
From Local to Global

Chapter 11

Chapter 12

Chapter 13

Chapter 14

Maps

Preface

In the Moroccan Sahara just north of the Algerian border is the Erg Chebbi: a sea of shifting sand where the dunes can reach heights of 150 metres. It was here that the cover photo was taken. Dressed in the indigo blue associated with the Tuareg—a Berber people who have lived as nomadic pastoralists in the Western Sahara for thousands of years—a descendant of an ancient culture uses a new window on the world while his camel, the time-honoured 'ship of the desert', waits in the background. Around the globe today traditional peoples are incorporating modern technologies into age-old ways of life.

From the Author

This edition of *Cultural Anthropology* situates students in a Canadian world view informed by a concern for social justice within a discussion of the discipline of anthropology, specifically cultural anthropology. To better fit the pedagogical structure of Canadian universities, this edition has been reorganized into 14 chapters without jeopardizing the conceptual integrity of Schultz and Lavenda's original text. Each chapter begins with a Chapter Outline and Learning Objectives and then concludes with Key Terms, Chapter Summary, Critical Thinking Questions, and Suggested Readings augmented with Related Websites. This challenges students to integrate learned concepts while providing them with a 'window' to a wider world of inquiry.

We begin Chapter 1 with a discussion of anthropology and its four traditional sub-fields, as well as what could effectively be considered its fifth sub-field: applied anthropology. The theme of applied anthropology in its various forms (e.g., medical anthropology) echoes throughout this text. We continue with an introduction to cultural anthropology—the central topic of this text—and its scope and goals. Further, we explain the concept of *culture* and examine the recent critique of its use within a wider historical perspective as forms of inquiry and explanation and emerge with an understanding of the efficacy of the concept of *holism*. We also introduce *fieldwork* as a methodology and its resulting reportage, *ethnography*, and conclude with a discussion of *ethnocentrism*.

In Chapter 2, we examine ethnographic fieldwork in detail, comparing and contrasting three forms of ethnographic research and offering insight into preparing for 'the field', forms of data collection, professional ethics, and culture shock. An explanation of the dialectic of fieldwork considers the roles people play when acting as an anthropologist's guide in the fieldwork situation, accounts for the effects of fieldwork on all involved, and reinforces an appreciation of anthropological knowledge and its open-ended nature.

Our focus in Chapter 3 is on colonialism, capitalism, and the concept of modernity, from a historical viewpoint, which contributes to the introduction of the idea of political economies. Here, we place anthropology as a 'player' in the colonial encounter.

We then critique the development and use of various classification systems with the *Culture Areas* concept, as used in North America, comparing and contrasting it to earlier systems. In conclusion, we reflect on post-colonial realities as a counterpoint and a challenge.

Understanding language in a theoretical and practical way is our objective in Chapter 4. Here, we discuss the relationship between language and culture and the importance of symbolic representation. We then introduce some of Charles Hockett's *design features* followed by an overview of the components of language and context of usage (phonology, morphology, syntax, semantics, pragmatics, and ethnopragmatics). We also consider linguistic inequality and areas of negotiated meaning exemplified by pidgin languages and conclude with a brief statement on the dialectic between experience and language and the creation of ambiguity in symbolic systems, given that reflexive consciousness 'makes human's aware of alternatives'.

In the next chapter we explore how individual psychology is situated in the context of a symbolic, cultural world, starting with how we perceive the world and how we recognize experience as useful *schemas*, which are then organized into *prototypes*—manageable, meaningful categories of experience. Learning how to look at the world is important in this process. We then link cognitive capacities—'a nexus of relations between the mind at work and the world in which it works'—to a discussion of intelligence, cognitive (learning) styles, reasoning, and logic. In Chapter 5, we also examine culture bound forms of intelligence testing, as well as emotion as the product of the dialectic between bodily arousal and cognitive interpretation mediated by, and embedded within, a cultural matrix. Here, we distinguish socialization from enculturation and emerge from this discussion to consider the *self* and how this 'entity' interprets the world and, specifically, how the *self* survives in the face of violence and trauma.

In Chapter 6, we present *play*—like language—as an open system. Play allows us to communicate about communicating (*metacommunication*) and allows us to see how it can provide an entrée to meaningful reflexivity. From play, we move on to discuss *sport* as embedded in the prevailing social order—providing serious metaphors—and then on to *art* as play that produces significant *transformation-representation*. *Myths* as charters for social action and providers of stories of truth lead to *ritual* as a culturally defined schema that brings *text* and *performance* together, which can result in the integration of play and ritual as complementary forms of metacommunication.

In Chapter 7 we consider the seemingly simple, yet actually complex, subject of world view in the context of key metaphors. We explore the role of metaphor, metonymy, and symbolic thought and comment on the anthropological analysis of religion within the context of world view. Secularism is considered. As we come to understand world views as instruments of power, we also come to understand how key metaphors and world views are maintained and modified in a world of change.

With our understanding of the importance of symbols, in Chapter 8 we turn to social organization and patterns of human interdependence, with an emphasis on multi-causal factors to explain the complexities of human social relations. We consider coercion and persuasion, with respect to the exercise of *power*, as well as forms of domination. Discussing how people bargain for reality, and use history as prototypes for action and change, results in thinking about the power of negotiating the meaning of history and tradition.

In Chapter 9, we begin with a consideration of subsistence strategies that focuses on economics. We present the relationship between production, distribution, and consumption and compare and contrast internal (needs) and external (resources) explanations of consumption patterns. We also explore the cultural and symbolic nature of consumption in the dialectic between the meaningful and the material and then elucidate distribution and exchange at local and global levels by examining various forms of exchange—from reciprocity to market to marketplace.

In Chapter 10 we analyze the complexities of human relationships, beginning with human beings as biological organisms that are dimorphic in morphology—male and female. We also analyze other possible outcomes of biology in a cultural context, which leads to a discussion of *gender role*s and the many ways that various cultures define these roles. From this, we turn to what determines relatedness and group membership and therefore consider how sex and gender are manifest in *kinship* since the importance of *descent* and extended kin, in some cultures, is significant. We then compare and contrast kin-based versus non-kin-based societies and conclude with an appreciation for the nuances of the dimensions of group life.

In Chapter 11 we ask: What is *marriage* in a cross-cultural perspective? We discuss marriage as a social process in the context of economic exchange and then explore dimensions of family life. Through this, we come to appreciate the interconnections of brothers and sisters in many cultures. With respect to situations of international migration, we analyze families in a historical and transformative context. Cross-cultural analysis allows us to understand the adaptability and flexibility of marriage in the context of sexual practices and the construction of relationships. Thus, we also include new forms of family (based on gay and lesbian unions) in the discussion. To conclude, we consider aspects of sexuality and power.

In Chapter 12, we delve into social inequality and explore the multi-dimensional nature of inequality as well as *class-stratified* societies and class mobility. We also present examples of *caste* and how, in India, class (economic) is also a factor within and between castes (religious). We then survey the discredited concept of *race* and its manifestation in today's world. How race became a social divide is an ethical consideration, not only for anthropologists. We then reflect upon *ethnicity* and how it is defined and conclude with an examination of what constitutes a *nation*, what a national identity is, and how it may manifest in *nationalism*.

We explore the emergence of the *global world* in Chapter 13. In the context of the history of the development of political economies, we consider globalization and the pressures on nation-states as new cultural processes emerged and continue to emerge. A key issue is the challenge of human rights in a 'globalized' world and we discuss cultural imperialism, cultural hybridization, and cosmopolitanism as responses to this challenge.

In the concluding chapter, we present the idea that anthropology encompasses so much more than what students will learn in a classroom. It is about the lives and worlds of the people who gift us with their world views. Anthropology is a portal to effective global citizenship in a world of uncertainty. It offers perspective and a way to develop awareness (reflexivity) in order to confront issues and challenge views on freedom and constraint.

A Final Note

Each new edition of *Cultural Anthropology* has moved forward in some small and/or large way to illuminate the trends of the discipline. What has been constant, however, has been the book's core value: a respect for students. Like Schultz and Lavenda, I, too, take students seriously. I believe that students have the capacity to read and think as involved adults. It has been my experience using this book over the years that students are happy to be seen as capable of the reflexivity the book espouses. They may, as the original authors note in an earlier edition, sometimes complain about and sometimes struggle with the content and concepts. Nonetheless, I have found they are charmed into learning as they come to appreciate that the text grounds them in an intellectual, emotional, and practical (as Schultz and Lavenda note) perspective that finds resonance in their—quite substantial—understanding of the world. What we offer are the tools for analysis. Inevitably, students appreciate how this book, and anthropology as a subject, situates them in a world of change and challenges them to be concerned citizens of that world.

Acknowledgements

At the outset, I want to thank the people I met and worked with in the field who gifted me with their friendship and insights into their lives. They have been my true teachers, and their kind involvement has been a sacred gift. As this book has always inferred, such generosity helps us face the world with humility while the study of anthropology situates us in a world of analysis that fosters the development of humble concern and deep hope. None of this could be possible without the kindness of others.

I would like to thank Schultz and Lavenda for providing the foundation upon which the first Canadian edition of *Cultural Anthropology* was built.

The work would not have proceeded without the exceedingly positive relationship that I developed with my editors at Oxford University Press. Here, I note two people specifically: Peter Chambers, Developmental Editor, Higher Education Division; and Amanda Maurice, Assistant Editor, Higher Education Division. Peter worked with me from the outset and got us all through what was at times a difficult process of making a book 'Canadian' while keeping the tone of the original authors. And Amanda—as my copy editor—well, who could have asked for such a happy happenchance that we would work so well together to get the text neat and tidy!

All the people that Schultz and Lavenda thanked in previous editions have their place in this edition as well. And to this list, I add a special thanks to my immediate colleagues at the University of British Columbia Okanagan for their input, several of whom provided their insights here in this edition.

Last, I want to thank my husband, Wayne Dods, for his patience when I needed his listening skills.

The author and the publisher would like to thank the following reviewers, whose thoughtful comments and suggestions helped shape this new edition.

Steven Ferzacca, Lethbridge University
Diana French, University of British Columbia
Dawn Grimes-MacLellan, St Mary's University
Carlota McAllister, York University
David Ryniker, University of British Columbia
Alan Smart, University of Calgary
Susan Walter, St Mary's University

Roberta Robin Dods

From the Publisher

To think globally but act locally has become one of the mantras of the modern environmental movement. The phrase, however, applies just as surely to the textbook you are now reading. Anthropology is a global discipline, taking as its subject nothing less than human nature, human society, and human history. But the research and theory that inform an anthropological understanding of the world are in many cases intensely local, concerned with concrete details of how humans act within a specific cultural, historical, and social context.

So it is with this book. This first Canadian edition of *Cultural Anthropology: A Perspective on the Human Condition* builds upon the solid foundations of Emily A. Schultz and Robert H. Lavenda's original text, while introducing issues and examples that not only make the subject come alive for Canadian students but also demonstrate the breadth and depth of anthropological research being carried out in this country.

Key Features

Key features of *Cultural Anthropology*, Canadian Edition, include:

- **Broad theoretical coverage.** As it has evolved, anthropology has been shaped by a variety of theoretical perspectives. The authors discuss cutting-edge theories that reflect the most recent trends in the discipline, while also acknowledging anthropology's rich and complex history.

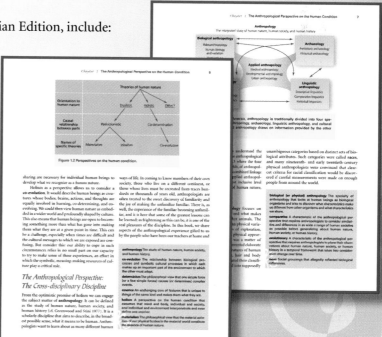

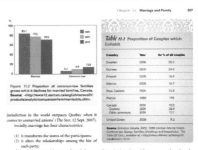

- **Unique Canadian content.** A wide variety of Canadian examples, illustrations, and issues are integrated throughout the book. The result is a text that reflects the nature of anthropology as a global discipline that encompasses unique Canadian contributions.

In Their Own Words

- **'In Their Own Words' boxes.** Short commentaries from experts in the field provide students with alternative perspectives on key issues and also furnish insight into what it means to be an anthropologist.

EthnoProfiles

- **'EthnoProfiles'.** To provide context, summaries of relevant geographic, demographic, and political information, as well as area maps, are provided for societies discussed at length in the text.

- **Vibrant four-colour design.** A wealth of photos, illustrations, graphs, and tables help bring anthropology alive for readers.

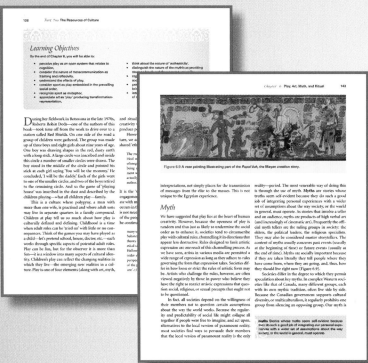

• **Fresh treatment of standard topics.** The authors help make standard topics more interesting by considering new and different perspectives. For instance, coverage of play, art, myth, and ritual is presented in a framework that highlights cultural creativity.

• **Wide array of learning tools.** Learning objectives, critical thinking questions, annotated suggestions for further reading, lists of related websites, and a variety of boxed features help summarize key concepts and support student learning.

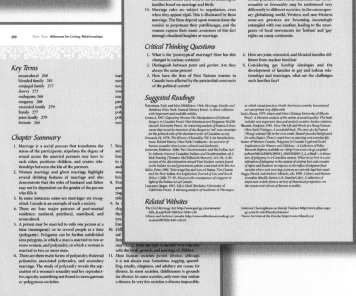

• **Extensive ancillary package.** Both instructors and students will benefit from the exceptionally rich supplemental package accompanying the text, including a student study guide, PowerPoint slides, instructor's manual, and test bank.

Part One

The Tools of Cultural Anthropology

In Part One we explore the ways we try to come to know our world by considering various modes of explanation, anthropology—specifically cultural anthropology—as a form of inquiry and a way of knowing, culture and the culture concept with fieldwork as a method of data collection, and the historical context for how anthropologists have attempted to make sense of human cultural diversity.

Chapter 1

The Anthropological Perspective on the Human Condition

Chapter Outline

Learning Objectives

By the end of Chapter 1, you will be able to:

- define anthropology's aims and scope of study,
- explain culture as a concept within anthropology,
- distinguish cultural anthropology as a sub-field of anthropology,
- articulate connections and relationships between the four major sub-fields of anthropology in North America,
- explain the world views of dualism and holism

and show ways that the conflict between them has shaped anthropology,
- contrast optimistic and pessimistic versions of cultural determinism,
- describe how fieldwork and ethnographies are used in cultural anthropology, and
- explain the relationship between cultural relativism and ethnocentrism and give examples of both.

Explanations of the Human Condition

Dualistic, Idealistic, and Materialistic Explanations of Our World

What is the world like? And what is the human condition within the world? Indeed, does it make sense to speak of a *single* 'condition' shared by all human beings? Members of all societies pose questions like these. And all societies develop their own answers. If asked what they believe about human nature, for example, many North Americans would answer that human nature has two parts: *mind* and *matter*, *soul* and *body*, or *spirit* and *flesh*. The belief that human nature, or reality as a whole, is made up of two radically different yet equal forces is called **dualism**. For millennia, from the time of the Greek philosopher Plato (428–347 BC) onward, people of the Western tradition have debated the importance of each half of human nature with each person made up of an earthly material body inhabited by a mind whose true home is the realm of ideal forms. According to Plato (Figure 1.1), the drama of human existence consists of the internal struggle between the body (drawn naturally to base, corruptible matter) and the mind or soul (drawn naturally to pure, unchanging forms). Christian theology later incorporated the view that each human being consists of a soul that seeks God and a physical body that is tempted by the material world. This view of earthly life as a struggle between spirit and flesh is sometimes called *conflict dualism*.

Figure 1.1 According to Plato (428–347 BC), the drama of human existence consists of the dualistic struggle between the body and the mind.

Subsequently, Platonic and Christian theories of human nature came to emphasize that although human beings are equipped with material bodies, their true nature is spiritual, not material; the body is a material impediment that frustrates the full development of the mind or spirit. This view is known as **idealism**. Conversely, it is possible to argue that material activities of our physical bodies in the material world make us who we are. From this perspective, human existence

dualism The philosophical view that reality consists of two equal and irreducible forces.

idealism The philosophical view (dating back as far as Plato in Western thought) that ideas—or the mind that produces such ideas—constitute the essence of human nature.

becomes the struggle to exercise our physicality as fully as we can; to put spiritual values above bodily needs would 'go against human nature'. This view is known as **materialism**.

Idealism and materialism are both forms of **determinism**: idealists claim that human nature is *determined by* the causal force of mind or spirit; materialists argue that human nature is *determined by* the causal force of physical matter. In both cases the goal is to strip away attributes of the thing we are examining that seem extraneous or unnecessary in order to reveal an unchanging core or **essence** that is unique and defining to things of the same kind (whether those are chairs, cows, ideas, or people). Many debates in Western philosophy about human nature have assumed that our species has an essence but have disagreed about just what that essence is. Dualism, idealism, and materialism can be understood as attempts by some Western thinkers to pinpoint the essence of what it means to be human.

Other thinkers argued that human beings come into the world with *no fixed essence*. For them, we are shaped by various forces we encounter throughout our lives. But what those forces might be, how many there are, and which of them is the most powerful, remain part of the debate. Some nineteenth-century thinkers argued that the most powerful material forces that shape human nature were to be found in the surrounding *natural environment*. Rich soil, a temperate climate, drought, and the absence of animals amenable to domestication are examples of the environmental factors understood to shape past and present societies and, ultimately, their inhabitants' sense of who they were, indeed are. Followers of Karl Marx (1818–83), by contrast, argued that forces shaping human beings' self-understanding were rooted in social relations shaped by the mode of economic production (from the German *Produktionsweise* meaning 'the way we produce things') that sustained a society. Because different groups, or *classes*, played different roles in that production process, members of each group would develop a different sense of what life was all about. An extreme idealist reaction against such materialist thinking, influential in cultural anthropology, has argued that human beings have no fixed essence when they come into the world, but they become different kinds of human beings as a result of the particular ideas, meanings, beliefs, and values that they absorb as members of particular societies (see Benedict 1934).

A serious conceptual difficulty for some scholars is the way in which the apparently optimistic, 'liberating' assumption that 'frees' our species from the burden of being born with a fixed essence regularly turns into a pessimistic account. Humans come to be portrayed as passive, pliable creatures who are *wholly* molded by the forces of the natural environment, the socio-historical environment, the cultural environment, or something else. Thus, according to these scholars, the open possibilities with which we begin are inevitably closed down tight as human possibilities are overwhelmed by environmental determinism, socio-historical determinism, or cultural determinism.

Holistic Explanations

Many anthropologists have long argued that there is another point of view on the human condition that is less distorting than dualism, less simplistic than idealism or materialism, and that does not reduce human beings to passive lumps of clay molded by totalitarian forces completely beyond their control. The anthropological point of view called **holism** assumes that no sharp boundaries separate mind from body, body from environment, individual from society, my ideas from your ideas, or their traditions from our traditions (Figure 1.2). Rather, holism assumes that mind and body, body and environment, and so on, interpenetrate and even define each other. Anthropologists who have struggled to develop this holistic perspective on the human condition have made a contribution of unique and lasting value. Holism holds great appeal for those who seek a theory of human nature that is rich enough to do justice to its complex subject matter. Thus the whole (i.e., a human being, a society, a cultural tradition) is greater than the sum of its parts, and human beings are what they are because the mutual shaping of genes and culture and experience has produced something new, something that cannot be reduced to the materials used to construct it. Similarly, a society is not just the sum of the behaviours of its individual members. Instead, human beings living in groups become different kinds of creatures. They are so deeply affected by shared cultural experiences that they become different from what they would have been had they matured in isolation. Geertz notes that human beings raised in isolation would be neither failed apes nor 'natural' people stripped of their veneer of culture; they would be 'mental basket cases' (1973: 40). Social living and cultural

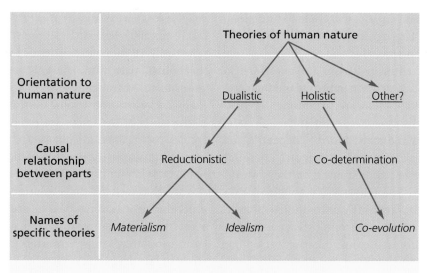

Figure 1.2 Perspectives on the human condition.

sharing are necessary for individual human beings to develop what we recognize as a *human* nature.

Holism as a perspective allows us to consider a **co-evolution**. It would describe human beings as creatures whose bodies, brains, actions, and thoughts are equally involved in learning, co-determining, and co-evolving. We could then view human nature as embedded in a wider world and profoundly shaped by culture. This also means that human beings are open to becoming something more than what has gone into making them what they are at a given point in time. This can be a challenge, especially when times are difficult and the cultural messages to which we are exposed are confusing. But consider this: our ability to cope in such circumstances relies in no small part on our capacity to try to make sense of these experiences, an effort in which the symbolic, meaning-making resources of culture play a critical role.

The Anthropological Perspective: The Cross-disciplinary Discipline

From the optimistic promise of holism we can engage the subject matter of **anthropology**. It can be defined as the study of human nature, human society, and human history (cf. Greenwood and Stini 1977). It is a scholarly discipline that aims to describe, in the broadest possible sense, what it means to be human. Anthropologists want to learn about as many different human

ways of life. In coming to know members of their own society, those who live on a different continent, or those whose lives must be recreated from traces hundreds or thousands of years old, anthropologists are often treated to the sweet discovery of familiarity and the joy of making the unfamiliar familiar. There is, as well, the experience of the familiar becoming unfamiliar, and it is here that some of the greatest lessons can be learned; as frightening as this can be, it is one of the real pleasures of the discipline. In this book, we share aspects of the anthropological experience gifted to us by the people who have been our teachers at home and

anthropology The study of human nature, human society, and human history.

co-evolution The relationship between biological processes and symbolic cultural processes in which each makes up an important part of the environment to which the other must adapt.

determinism The philosophical view that one simple force (or a few simple forces) causes (or determines) complex events.

essence An unchanging core of features that is unique to things of the same kind and makes them what they are.

holism A perspective on the human condition that assumes that mind and body, individual and society, and individual and environment interpenetrate and even define one another.

materialism The philosophical view that the material activities of our physical bodies in the material world constitute the essence of human nature.

away in the hope that you, too, will come to find pleasure, insight, and self-recognition from an engagement with a shared humanness.

It is true that anthropologists are not alone in focusing their attention on human beings and their creations. Human biology, literature, art, history, linguistics, sociology, political science, economics—all these scholarly disciplines and many more—concentrate on one aspect of human life or another. Life and its origins is a topic for those in 'hard' sciences as they investigate the dynamics of the universe (cf. Shapiro 2007). And as Darnell notes, anything can be anthropology if only one views it from the anthropological perspective (2001: 24). This anthropological perspective, unique in the social sciences, draws on the findings of these other disciplines and attempts to fit them together with its own findings in order to understand how these data collectively shape human life. Anthropologists are convinced that explanations of human activities will inevitably be superficial unless they acknowledge that human lives are always entangled in complex and fluid patterns of work and family, power and meaning. Nevertheless, because unanticipated constraints and opportunities emerge out of these entanglements, the 'whole' of human life is always greater than the sum of its 'parts'. This holistic point of view recognizes that so long as they are alive, individuals and societies always remain open to influences and opportunities that may take them beyond what they are at the present moment or what they have been in the past.

To generalize about humanity requires evidence from the widest possible range of human societies. Thus, in addition to being holistic, anthropology is a **comparative** discipline. The caveat here is that *comparative* does not mean it is the study of the *exotic*, the *primitive*, or the *savage*, all terms that anthropologists reject. It is not enough, for example, to observe only our own social group, discover that we do not eat insects, and conclude that human beings as a species do not eat insects. When we compare human diets in different societies, we discover that insect-eating is quite common and that our North American aversion to this practice is specific to our own society. Thus the word *comparative* is denotative of the challenge of gathering data from many cultures so we may come to informed and testable hypotheses about what it means to be human and to see what, if anything, can be said about the human condition that might be

valid across space and over time (synchronically and diachronically). Such analyses are situated in data from potentially all human societies as well as all periods of the human past, from the emergence of human-like primates in Africa some five million years ago, to the present. Consequently, some anthropologists specialize in the study of the biological evolution of the human species, paying attention not only to the study of human origins but also to the patterns of biological variation in living human populations; others study past cultures.

If we understand that evolution as a concept represents change over time, then human societies and cultures may also be understood to have evolved. Still one of anthropology's most important contributions to the study of human evolution has been to demonstrate the critical differences that separate *biological evolution* (which concerns the resources for human development provided by our genes and other elements that make up our physical bodies and how these bodies respond to environmental *circumstances*, as Darwin would term it) from *cultural evolution* (which concerns beliefs and behaviours we incorporate into human development through the experiences of teaching and learning). This distinction remains important as a way of demonstrating the fallacies and incoherence of arguments that assert that everything people do or think can be explained biologically, for example, in terms of their 'race' or their 'sex'. Because anthropologists are interested in documenting and explaining change, the anthropological perspective is **evolutionary** at its core. Anthropologists' involvement in all aspects of the study of the evolution of human beings and their cultures is so very important today as we move into an era when even our biological being can be altered through the agencies of our biological technologies. In the 1970s there was an undergraduate course at the University of Toronto called *Sociology of the Possible*. The required readings were all in the genre of science fiction—much of which has since become science fact. Consider this: through this perspective, movies such as *Blade Runner* (based on *Do Androids Dream of Electric Sheep?* [1968] from the sci-fi pen of Philip K. Dyck) become warnings of who will be classified as human in a world where 'made-to-task', 'best-by-date' biological androids are designed for profit motive in a corporate factory-lab. In this world of change anthropologists can be the agents of understanding and social action.

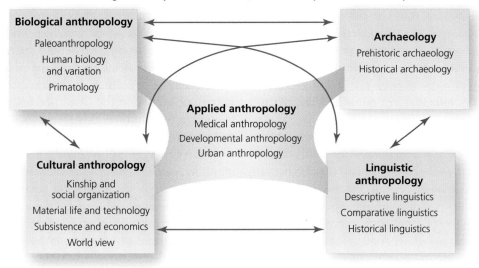

Anthropology
The integrated study of human nature, human society, and human history

Figure 1.3 In North America, anthropology is traditionally divided into four specialties: biological anthropology, archaeology, linguistic anthropology, and cultural anthropology. Applied anthropology draws on information provided by the other four specialties.

The diverse ways we come to understand the meaning of being human through the anthropological perspective can be seen in Figure 1.3 where the four traditional sub-disciplines, or sub-fields, of anthropology show their integration and their combined linkage to the relatively recent addition of applied anthropology. This illustrates that at the most inclusive level anthropology is the holistic study of human nature, human society, and human history.

Biological Anthropology

Biological (or **physical**) **anthropology** focuses on human beings as living organisms and what makes us different from or similar to other animals. The nineteenth-century interest in human physical variation was a by-product of centuries of exploration, when tremendous variation in the physical appearance of peoples around the world was a matter of comment. Physical anthropologists invented elaborate techniques to measure observable features of human populations including skin colour, hair and body type. This 'scientific' evidence facilitated their classification of all the peoples of the world into supposedly

unambiguous categories based on distinct sets of biological attributes. Such categories were called **races**, and many nineteenth- and early twentieth-century physical anthropologists were convinced that clear-cut criteria for racial classification would be discovered if careful measurements were made on enough people from around the world.

biological (or physical) anthropology The specialty of anthropology that looks at human beings as biological organisms and tries to discover what characteristics make us different from other organisms and what characteristics we share.

comparative A characteristic of the anthropological perspective that requires anthropologists to consider similarities and differences in as wide a range of human societies as possible before generalizing about human nature, human society, or human history.

evolutionary A characteristic of the anthropological perspective that requires anthropologists to place their observations about human nature, human society, or human history in a temporal framework that takes into consideration change over time.

races Social groupings that allegedly reflected biological differences.

This early interest in racial classification in physical anthropology did not take place in a social and historical vacuum. It fit into important social and historical processes during that period. The peoples whom physical anthropologists were trying to assign to racial categories were in most cases non-European peoples, peoples coming under increasing political and economic domination by colonizing European and European ancestry capitalist societies (a sobering discussion of the Americans in 1491 can be found in Mann 2005). These peoples differed from 'white' Europeans not only because of their darker skin colour but also because of their unfamiliar languages and customs, and, because in most cases, they possessed technologies that were no match for the might of the industrialized West. As a result, racial membership was understood to determine not just outward physical attributes of groups but their mental and moral attributes as well. Races were ranked in terms of these attributes. Not surprisingly, 'white' Europeans and North Americans were seen as superior, and the other races were seen to represent varying grades of inferiority. In this way, the first physical anthropologists helped develop theories that would justify the social practice of **racism**: the systematic oppression of members of one or more socially defined 'races' by another socially defined 'race' that is justified in terms of the supposed biological superiority of the rulers and the supposed biological inferiority of those they rule. This was the basis for the policies implemented by the Canadian government that resulted in Native residential schools. Chrisjohn and his colleagues wrote that these schools destroyed the circles of life and life-affirming metaphors of unity and wholeness, substituting instead Euro-Canadian 'circle games' of the 'empty non-existence of zero' (1997: 115).

With changes in method and theory in the early twentieth century, based on principles of holism, physical anthropologists began to measure numerous internal features of populations, such as blood types, that they added to their calculations. The more they learned about the biological attributes of human populations, the more they realized that races with distinct and unique sets of such attributes simply did not exist.

Thus they concluded that the concept of 'race' did not reflect a fact of nature but was instead a cultural label invented by human beings to sort people into groups. Anthropologists like Franz Boas (1858–1942),

for example, who in the early 1900s founded the first department of anthropology in the United States at Columbia University, had long been uncomfortable with racial classifications. Boas and his students devoted much energy to debunking racist stereotypes, using both their knowledge of biology and their understanding of culture. As the discipline of anthropology developed in the United States, students were trained in both human biology and human culture to provide them with the tools to fight racial and ethnic stereotyping. This became the general program of study in North American departments. Rejecting the racial thinking of the nineteenth century, many modern anthropologists who study human biology prefer to call themselves **biological anthropologists** and focus on patterns of variation within the human species as a whole.

Some biological anthropologists, such as Biruté Galdikas from Simon Fraser University and Lisa Gould from the University of Victoria, work in the field of **primatology** (the study of the closest living relatives of human beings, the non-human primates). Others, such as the University of Alberta's Pamela Willoughby, work in the field of **paleoanthropology** (the study of fossilized bones and teeth of our earliest ancestors) and human skeletal biology (measuring and comparing the shapes and sizes—or morphology—of bones and teeth using skeletal remains from different human populations). Newer specialties focus on human adaptability in different ecological settings, on human growth and development, or on the connections between a population's evolutionary history and its susceptibility to disease. Forensic anthropologists, as noted below in the applied anthropology discussion, use their knowledge of human skeletal anatomy to aid law enforcement and human rights investigators. Molecular anthropologists trace chemical similarities and differences in cells, tissues, and organs; what they have learned about the immune system, for example, has enabled them to contribute actively to AIDS research. In recent years, new analytic techniques such as biostatistics, three-dimensional imaging, and electronic communication and publishing have revolutionized the field. In all these ways, biological anthropologists can illuminate what makes human beings similar to (and different from) one another, other primates, and other living organisms (Boaz and Wolfe 1995; Weinker 1995).

Archaeology

Archaeology, another major specialty within anthropology, is the study of the human past through the analysis of material remains (Figure 1.4). Depending on the locations and ages of archaeological sites, archaeologists may also have to be experts on various technologies and environmental as well as economic indicators (plant and animal remains). Archaeologists frequently work in teams with other scientists who specialize in specific areas of research. Their findings complement those of paleoanthropologists and indeed sometimes become common interest, as with Maxine Kleindienst and her work on the Dakhleh Oasis Project (directed by Anthony J. Mills) in Egypt (see EthnoProfile 1.1: Dakhleh). For example, archaeological information about successive stone-tool traditions in a particular region may correlate with fossil evidence of prehistoric human occupation.

Scientific dating techniques allow archaeologists to make hypotheses about the age, territorial ranges, and patterns of socio-cultural change in ancient societies, thus tracing the spread of cultural inventions over time and space. Sabloff tells us that archaeology is an 'action' science in the modern world as it 'can play helpful roles in broad, critical issues facing the world today . . . [informing] in general about lessons to be learned from the successes and failures of past cultures and [thus] provide policy-makers with useful contexts for decision-making in the world today. . .' (2008: 17). In such a context, archaeology becomes applied anthropology as we will discuss later!

Linguistic Anthropology

Perhaps the most striking cultural feature of our species is **language**: the system of arbitrary vocal symbols we use to encode our experiences of one another and the world. Many early anthropologists were the first researchers to transcribe non-Western languages and to produce grammars and dictionaries of those languages (Figure 1.5). Language loss is also a concern (see Abley 2005). Contemporary linguistic anthropologists and their counterparts in sociology (called *sociolinguists*) study the way language differences frequently correlate with differences in gender, race, class, or ethnic identity.

Linguistic anthropology has become so highly specialized that modern linguistic anthropologists are deeply trained in both linguistics and cultural anthropology, and, equally, many cultural anthropologists receive linguistics training as part of their professional preparation. Linguistic anthropologists are applied anthropologists in some instances, working to maintain endangered languages, attempting to bring an understanding to all of us of the nature of language and our links to our cultural identity.

Figure 1.4 Archaeologists working in the Roman forum, Italy. Archaeologists study the human past through the analysis of material remains.

archaeology The study of the human past involving the analysis of material remains left behind by earlier human societies.

biological anthropologists Anthropologists who specialize in the study of patterns of biological variation within the human species as a whole.

language The system of arbitrary vocal symbols we use to encode our experiences of the world and of one another.

linguistic anthropology The specialty of anthropology concerned with the study of human languages.

paleoanthropology The search for fossilized remains of humanity's earliest ancestors.

primatology The study of non-human primates, the closest living relatives of human beings.

racism The systematic oppression of one or more socially defined 'races' by another socially defined 'race' that is justified in terms of the supposed biological superiority of the rulers and the supposed biological inferiority of those they rule.

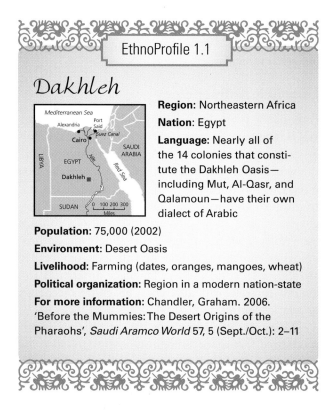

EthnoProfile 1.1

Dakhleh

Region: Northeastern Africa

Nation: Egypt

Language: Nearly all of the 14 colonies that constitute the Dakhleh Oasis—including Mut, Al-Qasr, and Qalamoun—have their own dialect of Arabic

Population: 75,000 (2002)

Environment: Desert Oasis

Livelihood: Farming (dates, oranges, mangoes, wheat)

Political organization: Region in a modern nation-state

For more information: Chandler, Graham. 2006. 'Before the Mummies: The Desert Origins of the Pharaohs', *Saudi Aramco World* 57, 5 (Sept./Oct.): 2–11

Cultural Anthropology

Now we come to the central topic of this book and situate ourselves in **cultural anthropology**, sometimes called *socio-cultural anthropology*, *social anthropology*, or *ethnology*. It focuses on sets of learned behaviours and ideas that human beings acquire as members of society. Because people ordinarily take their culturally shaped beliefs and behaviours for granted, anthropologist Michael Herzfeld has suggested that cultural anthropology might be usefully defined for us as 'the study of common sense' although 'sense' as a concept is neither common to all cultures nor particularly sensible to anyone unfamiliar with its specific cultural context (2001: 1).

Because people everywhere use culture to adapt to and transform everything in their wider world, the field of cultural anthropology is vast. Cultural anthropologists tend to specialize in one domain of human cultural activity or another. Some study the ways particular groups of human beings organize themselves to carry out collective tasks, whether economic, political, or spiritual. This focus within cultural anthropology bears the closest resemblance to the discipline of sociology and from it has come the identification of anthropology as one of the social sciences. In fact, sociology and anthropology developed during the same period of the late nineteenth and early twentieth centuries and thus share some similar interests in social organization. However, anthropological interest in comparing different forms of human social life sets it apart from sociology. Transcending the racism of the nineteenth and early twentieth centuries, modern anthropologists are concerned with studying *all* human societies, doing research in urban and rural settings around the world, including their own. They reject, as noted earlier, the labels *civilized* and *primitive* for the same reason they reject the term *race* since these concepts carry offensive connotations and are inadequate to the task of helping us make sense of the everyday realities of human life.

In recent years, cultural anthropologists have studied contemporary issues of gender and sexuality, transnational labour migration, urbanization, globalization, and the resurgence of ethnicity and nationalism. Other cultural anthropologists have investigated the patterns of material life found in different human groups. Among the most striking are worldwide variations in clothing, housing, tools, and techniques for getting and preparing food and making material goods (Figure 1.6).

Figure 1.5 On the road to Mouk territory in Papua New Guinea. William Thurston with his friend Avel, a Lusi speaker, who acted as guide and introduced Thurston and Rick Goulden to the community where they collected material on the Mouk language. Picture taken by Rick Goulden, 1981.

Cultural anthropologists, like archaeologists, interested in material life describe the natural setting for which technologies have been developed and analyze the way technologies and environments shape each other.

With the post-colonial and neo-colonial era upon us, cultural anthropologists have begun to investigate the ways non-Western peoples have responded to the political and economic challenges of colonialism and the capitalist industrial technology that came with it. The study of the impact of Western technologies has shown the creative and unanticipated ways peoples use things such as popular media and cybertechnology, including applications such as Internet, e-mail, and instant messaging, to make sense of their own local cultural context and situate it in a wider world.

As cultural anthropologists have become increasingly aware of the socio-cultural influences that stretch across space to affect local communities, they have also become sensitive to those that stretch over time. As a result, many contemporary cultural anthropologists make serious efforts to place their cultural analyses in detailed historical contexts. These anthropologists often work closely with archaeologists and historians who have related interests. Many anthropologists study language, music, dance, art, poetry, philosophy, religion, or ritual in other societies, and they share the results of their research not only with other anthropologists but also with specialists in the disciplines of fine arts and humanities.

Cultural anthropologists, no matter what their area of specialization, ordinarily collect their data during an extended period of close involvement with the people in whose way of life they are interested. This period of research is called **fieldwork**. Its central feature is the anthropologists' involvement in the everyday routine of those among whom they live. This methodology is called **participant-observation**. People who share information about their lives with anthropologists have traditionally been called **informants**; however, today some prefer to describe these individuals as *respondents*, *teachers*, or simply '*the people I work with*' because these terms emphasize a relationship of equality and reciprocity. Regardless of the term used, fieldwork is a period when the anthropologist receives one of the most meaningful gifts that any human can receive—entry into the lives of others. This gift is part of an act of reciprocity. The reciprocal relationship is built by

Figure 1.6 Cultural anthropologists investigate worldwide variations in clothing, housing, tools, and techniques for getting and preparing food—such as this Bedouin woman making bread—and making material goods.

participating in social activities. The negotiation of the meaning of the observed occurs with the informant or teacher. Participant-observation requires that the anthropologist engage in what is termed *reflexivity*—thinking about why and how one thinks about specific things—as we will see later.

One of the most important things cultural anthropologists do is write about what they have learned. Sometimes they document the lives of the people they

cultural anthropology The specialty of anthropology that shows how variation in the beliefs and behaviours of members of different human groups is shaped by sets of learned behaviours and ideas that human beings acquire as members of society—that is, by culture.

fieldwork An extended period of close involvement with the people in whose language or way of life anthropologists are interested, during which anthropologists ordinarily collect most of their data.

informants People in a particular culture who work with anthropologists and provide them with insights about their way of life; also called *respondents*, *teachers*, or *friends*.

participant-observation The method anthropologists use to gather information by living as closely as possible to the people whose culture they are studying while participating in their lives as much as possible.

work with on video. The use of 'shadow catching' technology has a long history in the discipline and dates back to the earliest period of photography in the nineteenth century. It has been an invaluable record, even if flawed, because of its incorrectly assumed neutral stance (Ball and Smith 1992). However, sometimes the pictures say more about the photographer than his or her subject, as illustrated by some of Franz Boas's pictures (Figure 1.7), taken for the US National Museum, and the Edward Curtis movie *In the Land of the War Canoes* (1914).

Ethnography, a central form of anthropological writing, is a description of 'the customary social behaviours of an identifiable group of people' (Wolcott 1999: 252–3); **ethnology** is the comparative study of two or more such groups. Thus, cultural anthropologists who write ethnographies are sometimes called *ethnographers*, and anthropologists who compare ethnographic information on many different cultural practices are sometimes called *ethnologists*.

Applied Anthropology

Applied anthropology could be termed *action* anthropology. Anthropological information is put to practical use to propose solutions to pragmatic and, frequently, serious social and cultural problems. Currently, perhaps those who have the highest general public profile are forensic anthropologists, such as Simon Fraser University's Mark Skinner, who work on highly publicized

Figure 1.7 Franz Boas demonstrates a position in the Kwakiutl Hamatsa dance ritual, as he observed it at Fort Rupert, British Columbia, in 1894.

crime cases and genocide investigations (Figure 1.8). Other areas of application are also important, as seen in some of these examples:

- using a culture's ideas about illness and health to introduce new public health practices in a way that makes sense to, and will be accepted by, adherents of that culture;
- taking the knowledge of traditional social organization to ease the problems of refugees trying to settle in a new land;
- integrating traditional and Western methods of cultivation to help farmers increase their crop yields; and
- studying the effects of different technologies on the environment to find ways of bringing Western and non-Western knowledges together in order to create sustainable technologies that minimize pollution and environmental degradation.

Anthropologists become advocates/activists, using their ethnography skills as a way of drawing public attention to the plight of the people they study, to seek social justice, to fight discrimination, or to support human or cultural rights. This is particularly the case with First Nations land claims and public policy issues in Canada (Hedican 2000).

Many anthropologists believe that applied work can be done within any of the four traditional fields of anthropology, and this is very much so. However, an increasing number of anthropologists have come to view applied anthropology as a separate field of professional specialization (see Figure 1.3). Thus more universities in Canada and the United States have begun to develop courses and programs specifically in applied anthropology.

Anthropology and the Concept of Culture

The central concept in anthropology has been the idea of **culture** as a marker of our humanness. This can be seen in a historical perspective, such as when Edward Tylor defines culture as 'that complex whole which includes knowledge, belief, art, morals, law, customs, and any other capabilities and habits acquired . . . as a member of society' (1958 [1871]: 1). Later definitions are more or less refinements or elaborations of this theme. Of course in Tylor's time it was believed that humans alone 'owned' the cultural experience. Increasingly we have been challenged by the studies of other primates (Fouts 1997), indeed other mammals. What has emerged is the understanding that we have been the most effective developers and users of culture in shaping our societies and transforming the physical world.

Undoubtedly the most profound impact on human nature and human society has been the emergence of culture, and the most profound impact on anthropology has been the development of the culture concept. Human beings are more dependent than any other species on learning for survival because we come into the world so physically underdeveloped, having long infancy and childhood stages. Thus, we have come to use our large and complex brains to learn what we need to know to survive. This is the primary focus of childhood and can be a lifelong challenge.

From the anthropological perspective, culture is central to explanations of why we are what we are and why we do what we do. Anthropologists have been able to show that members of a particular social group behave in a particular way *not* because the behaviour was an inevitable result of their biology but because they observed other people and copied what they did. Interestingly, anthropologists were able to demonstrate the power of culture precisely because they were

also knowledgeable about human biology. Scholars who were trained in both areas came to understand how genes and organisms work and were acquainted with comparative information about a wide range of human societies. As a result, they became more realistic in evaluating the ways that biology and culture contribute to any particular form of human behaviour. Indeed, most anthropologists reject explanations of human behaviour that force them to choose between biology and culture as the cause. Instead, they prefer to emphasize that human beings are **bio-cultural organisms**. Our biological make-up, the outcome of developmental processes to which our genes and cellular chemistry contribute in fundamental ways, also contributes to our capacity to create and use culture. Conversely, our survival as biological organisms depends upon learned ways of thinking and acting that help us find food, shelter, and mates and that teach us how to rear our children. Other living species learn, but because our brains are apparently capable of open symbolic thought and our hands are capable of manipulating matter, powerfully or delicately, we interact with the wider world in a way that is distinct from any other species.

Being capable of open symbolic thought entails the development of the skills to use symbols. A **symbol** is something that stands for something else. For example, various alphabets (Latin, Cyrillic, Hebrew, Arabic, and Greek) symbolize the sounds of different spoken languages. The sounds themselves are symbols, and they stand for meanings a speaker tries to express. The fact that we can translate from one language to another

Figure 1.8 A forensic anthropologist works on a mass grave in Guatemala.

applied anthropology Using information gathered from the other anthropological specialties to solve practical cross-cultural problems.

bio-cultural organisms Organisms (in this case, human beings) whose defining features are co-determined by biological and cultural factors.

culture Sets of learned behaviours and ideas that humans acquire as members of society. Humans use culture to adapt to and transform the world in which we live.

ethnography An anthropologist's written or filmed description of a particular culture.

ethnology The comparative study of two or more cultures.

symbol Something that stands for something else.

suggests that the same or similar meanings can be expressed by different symbols in different languages. Or, as Shakespeare noted in *Romeo and Juliet*, 'a rose by any other name would smell as sweet'. However, language is not alone in the use of symbols. Everything we do in society has a symbolic dimension, from how we conduct ourselves at the dinner table to how we bury the dead.

Culture's beginnings are deep in time and can perhaps be glimpsed among Japanese macaque monkeys who invented the custom of washing sweet potatoes and among wild chimpanzees who invented techniques to crack open nuts or to gain access to termites or water (Boesch-Ackerman and Boesch 1994; Wolfe 1995: 162–3). Our primate ancestors surely shared similar aptitudes when they started walking on two legs over five million years ago. Two and a half million years later, their descendants were making stone tools, and through human paleontology and archaeology we can follow our cultural path to the silicon chip. Thus, as Potts puts it, 'an evolutionary bridge exists between the human and animal realms of behaviour' (1996: 197). Potts urges us to think of the modern human capacity for culture not as a uniform monolith but rather as a structure whose various pieces were added at different times in our evolutionary past (Figure 1.9). The foundation of culture, he proposes, contains five elements:

(1) *transmission*, copying behaviour by observation or instruction;

(2) *memory*, because traditions cannot develop unless the new behaviour is remembered;

(3) *reiteration*, the ability to reproduce or imitate behaviour or information that has been learned;

(4) *innovation*, the ability to invent new behaviours; and

(5) *selection*, the ability to select which innovations to keep and which to discard.

To this Potts adds three elements that evolved later and made human culture possible:

(6) *symbolic coding*, or *symbolic representation*, something we share with other species, in particular the great apes;

(7) *complex symbolic representation*, the ability to communicate freely about the past, the future,

and the invisible. On a very complex level this ability distinguishes human language, for example, from the vocal communication systems of apes although we now know that apes can remember complex symbolic structures and can hold information on remote things. But biological anthropologist Terrence Deacon argues that evolution produced in *Homo sapiens* a brain 'that has been significantly overbuilt for learning symbolic associations' such that 'we cannot help but see the world in symbolic categories' (1997: 413, 416). Moreover, the enormous adaptive value of complex symbolic representation for our ancestors appears to have created a new set of selective pressures that favoured genetic changes that improved our brain's symbolic capacities. Put another way, culture and the human brain *co-evolved*, each furnishing key features of the environment to which the other needed to adapt (Deacon 1997: 44; Odling-Smee 1994); and

(8) *institutional development*, the creation of complex and variable forms of social organizations

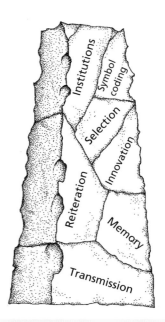

Figure 1.9 The modern human capacity for culture did not appear all at once; rather, the various pieces that make it up were added at different times in our evolutionary past.

unique to our species. As a result, for *Homo sapiens* culture has become 'the predominant manner in which human groups vary from one another . . . it *swamps* the biological differences among populations' (Marks 1995: 200). We are truly bio-cultural organisms.

Culture is not completely reinvented by each generation. It is learned from other members of the social groups to which we belong although we may modify this heritage in response to changed circumstances. Therefore, culture is shared as well as learned and can be adapted to meet present or future needs. Many of the things we learn, such as table manners, what is good to eat, and where people are supposed to sleep, are never explicitly taught. Rather, they are absorbed in the course of daily practical living. Such learning is sometimes called *habitus* since it is rooted in habitual behaviour. Cultural traditions always encompass the varied knowledges and skills of many different individuals. Thus we participate individually with different cultural skill sets within an encompassing cultural identity that, as a collective, allows us as a group, or subsets of the group, to accomplish beyond our individual limitations.

Human cultures also appear patterned; that is, related cultural beliefs and practices repeatedly show up in different areas of social life. Cultural patterns can be traced over time: that English and French are widely spoken in Canada (whereas Fulfulde, a language spoken in West Africa, is not) is connected to the colonial conquest and domination of Canada by speakers of English and French. Cultural patterns also vary across space. In Canada, for example, the English of Newfoundland and Labrador differs from the English of southwestern Quebec, and the various dialects used by various First Nations communities, in rhythm and vocabulary. Indeed, in the First Nations example,

Research involving Indigenous peoples outside of Canada emphasizes the influences of Indigenous language learning and cultural aspects of language socialization on English conversational style and dialect. Dialect learning and features of language mediated interaction using varieties of the dominant language have implications for education, developmental assessment, early intervention, cultural preservation, and justice issues. There is an emerging awareness that the heritage languages, language socialization,

and cultures of Aboriginal peoples living in Canada influence the ways in which Aboriginal children and families use English, as well as their experiences within dominant culture institutions such as schools. (Bernhardt, Ball, and Deby 2007)

Because of this patterned cultural variation, anthropologists frequently distinguish different 'cultural traditions' from one another. Although distinguishing different cultural traditions can be useful as a kind of shorthand, it is important to remember that the boundaries between cultural traditions can be very fuzzy, ultimately resting on someone's judgment about how different one set of customs is from another. Indeed, customs in one area of a culture may contradict customs in another area, as when religion tells us to share with others and economics tells us to look out for ourselves. In addition, people have always borrowed cultural elements, and many now refuse to be limited by cultural practices of the past. And then there is the question of 'Traditional Culture'—what of the past do specific peoples want to protect, maintain, or retrieve? (Note Regna Darnell, *In Their Own Words.*) Worldwide this is a fundamental dilemma for peoples who have not fared well under colonization and in the Canadian context for First Nations peoples. Ron Ignace's interview with Noel Dyck illustrates this critique from a First Nations perspective. Some anthropologists and museums, he notes,

don't seem to understand that we still exist as a people, that we adapt and change, and we have the right to adapt and change, while still maintaining some of our principles that were tried and true over the years. Particularly principles that are necessary for survival as a people. . . . When I walk into a museum, . . . you never get the social dynamism of the culture and how the culture has grown and changed and adapted over the years. (Ignace et al. 1993: 168–9)

Anthropology and Culture/cultures: Critique and Response

The culture concept anchored the anthropological perspective and illuminated the human condition in powerful ways. Amazingly this powerful idea of *Culture* became the most contested concept of contemporary anthropology and in the 1970s and 1980s it came under criticism as the basis for the perceived problems of lingering racism. What once was 'a shared discourse in anthropology . . . [a] common link among anthropology's sub-disciplines', no longer existed and there emerged a 'growing intellectual fragmentation [that] has . . . led to greater specialization of each field . . .' (Yengoyan 1986: 368). Essentially culture as our 'most cherished' concept and our subject matter, Yengoyan emphasizes, became neither a point of departure nor a point of convergence. Essentially the critique centres on the use of the term *cultures* rather than *Culture*. In this critique the human species as a whole can be said to have *Culture* as a distinguishing attribute, but actual human beings would only have access to particular human *cultures*, either their own or others'. While by and large those who 'write against culture' (Abu-Lughod 1991) continue to defend the validity of *Culture* as a concept, they object to the use of the term *cultures* as it is used to refer to particular, learned *ways of life* belonging to specific groups of human beings.

The controversy is heated because many anthropologists have viewed the plural use of the culture concept as not only analytically helpful but as politically progressive. Their view reflects a struggle that developed in nineteenth-century Europe: supporters of the supposedly progressive, universal civilization of the Enlightenment, inaugurated by the French Revolution and spread by Napoleonic conquest, were challenged by inhabitants of other European nations, who resisted both Napoleon and the Enlightenment in what has been called the Romantic Counter-Enlightenment. Romantic intellectuals in nations like Germany rejected what they considered to be the imposition of 'artificial' Enlightenment *civilization* on the 'natural' spiritual traditions of their own distinct national *cultures* (Kuper 1999; Crehan 2002). This political dynamic, which pits a steamroller civilization against vulnerable local cultures, carried over into the usage that later developed in anthropology, particularly in North America.

In Their Own Words

Invisible Genealogies

Regna Darnell speaks to the concepts of 'tradition' and 'traditional' culture.

'Traditional' culture is a moving target, always changing and adapting to new circumstances. It is located in the contemporary practices of the communities whose interests and concerns direct the work of anthropologists. The label 'traditional' is used with considerable rhetorical force in contemporary Native American communities and in their interactions with non-Native institutions and individuals. 'Tradition' does not imply returning to some idealized pure culture that existed before Columbus spearheaded the invasion of the 'new' world. Native Americans recognize that their societies, like those of white people, whether in Europe or America, have changed in 500 years; all peoples have a history in which living traditions are continuously invented and reinvented.

   This discourse is, of course, very different from the non-Americanist one about 'invented traditions' that somehow lack authenticity because they are continually

constructed by contemporary communities, often without attention to the scientific authority of the anthropologist to define their culture. In my view, anthropologists, in the field and in their writing alike, must respect both the cultural heritage and the contemporary practice of the peoples with whom they work. 'Tradition', in such a discourse, refers to that which is continuous with the past, in line with the practices and values of a moral community. Native people themselves can and should define what is traditional within their own communities. They do so in terms of innovations that serve to maintain the identity of the community and its members in relation to their collective histories and personal agencies. 'Tradition', in Native American terms, holds much of the meaning that 'culture' embodies for anthropologists. If it is invented, we must celebrate its creativity and adaptability under conditions of change. That anthropologists sometimes produce alternative interpretations for other purposes is, of course, another matter.

Source: Darnell, Regna. 2001. *Invisible Genealogies: A History of Americanist Anthropology* (Lincoln: University of Nebraska Press), 16–17.

The decades surrounding the turn of the twentieth century marked the period of expanding European colonial empires, as well as westward expansion and consolidation of control in North America by European settlers. At that time, the social sciences were becoming established in universities, and different fields were assigned different tasks. Anthropology was allocated what Trouillot (1991) has called *the savage slot*—that is, the so-called primitive world that was the target of colonization. Anthropologists thus became the official academic experts on societies whose members suffered appalling racist denigration as 'primitives' and whose ways of life were being undermined by contact with Western colonial 'civilization'. And rightly, anthropologists were determined to denounce such practices and to demonstrate that the 'primitive' stereotype was false.

Some found inspiration in the work of English anthropologist E.B. Tylor who, as we noted earlier, had defined 'culture or civilization'. His definition had the virtue of blurring the difference between 'culture' and 'civilization', and it encouraged the view that even 'primitives' possessed 'capabilities and habits' that merited respect. Thus, in response to stereotypes of 'primitives' as irrational, disorganized, insensitive, or promiscuous, anthropologists like Franz Boas and Bronislaw Malinowski were able to show that, on the contrary, so-called *primitives* possessed 'cultures' that were reasonable, orderly, artistically developed, and morally disciplined. The plural use of culture allowed them to argue that, in their own ways, 'primitives' were as fully human as 'civilized' people.

By the end of the twentieth century, however, the plural use of culture began to appear pernicious rather than progressive. To some, the boundary that was once thought to protect vulnerability now looked more like a prison wall, condemning those within it to live according to 'their' culture just as their ancestors had done, like exhibits in a living museum, whether they wanted to or not. Critics argue that the plural concept of culture not only highlights the differences between groups of people, but it also assumes that group members uncritically accept those differences, want to preserve them, and naturally view cultural change as the loss of authenticity. Consequently, if group members disagree with one another publicly, import ideas or practices from other societies, or challenge traditional ways by, for

example, protesting against social inequality, they may be condemned by insiders and outsiders alike as flirting with cultural treason. It is this 'totalitarian' concept of culture (Hann 2002: 260) that is the problem: it seems to endorse an oppressive kind of cultural determinism.

Anthropologists Michel-Rolph Trouillot and Adam Kuper agree that for anthropologists to continue to use *culture* as a part of their professional analytic vocabulary risks lending credibility to the way the concept has been used to oppress rather than to liberate. This is a serious statement and we must, as anthropologists, be constantly vigilant that oppression is not the outcome of our work. Allowing or facilitating any outcomes of oppression from our research is a betrayal of the great gift of 'self' made, to us and through us to the world, by individuals and cultures in which we have conducted fieldwork.

Ortner notes that the essence of the critique was that in the atmosphere of post-colonialism 'many ethnic groups, and many contemporary post-colonial intellectuals, react very strongly against being studied as specimens of cultural differences and otherness'. Thus the critique of racism was not infrequent. However, Ortner continues by stating that it is not an issue of 'banishing' the culture concept but rather of 'reconfiguring this enormously productive concept for a changing world, . . . a changing landscape of theoretical possibilities . . .' (1999: 8). What she calls for are three 'imperatives':

(1) 'To the move to reduce difference . . . add the move to exoticize and objectify the culture of the ethnographer, placing it in the same analytic framework. . . . In other words, maintain a strong presumption of cultural difference but make it do new things' (8).

(2) In what she terms of the 'most profound importance', emphasize the issue of meaning-*making*. 'It is central to questions of power and its effects. The idea that symbolic constructions of meaning are actively made by real historical actors [is important] . . . to the fundamental assumption that people are always trying to make sense of their lives, always weaving fabrics of meaning, however fragile and fragmentary . . .' (8–9), however desperate their circumstances.

(3) '[S]ituate cultural analysis within and, as it were, beneath larger analyses of social and political events and processes. . . . [It] can no longer . . . be an end in itself . . .' (9).

Attempts by anthropologists to deal with these complications will be a focus in future chapters, especially in our discussions of anthropological approaches to ethnicity and nationalism (Chapter 12), globalization (Chapter 13), and democracy and multiculturalism (Chapter 14).

The Challenge of Differences

The same objects, actions, or events frequently mean different things to people within different cultures. In fact, what counts as an object or event in one tradition may not be recognized as such in another. Even within a single cultural tradition, the meaning of an object or an action may differ depending on the context. Quoting philosopher Gilbert Ryle, anthropologist Clifford Geertz notes that 'there is a world of difference between a wink and a blink, as anyone who has ever mistaken one for the other has undoubtedly learned' (1973: 6).

Thus, human experience is inherently ambiguous. To resolve the ambiguity, experience must be interpreted. Human beings turn to their own cultural traditions in search of an interpretation that makes sense and is coherent. They do this daily as they go about life among others with whom they share traditions. But this interpretive activity does not cease at the boundary of their own culture. Self and other need not belong to the same society or share the same traditions, and yet this interpretive activity continues. Serious misunderstandings may arise when two individuals are unaware that their cultural ground rules differ. At this point, the concepts of ethnocentrism and cultural relativism become relevant.

Ethnocentrism is the term anthropologists use to describe the opinion that one's own way of life is natural or correct, indeed the only way of being fully human. Ethnocentrism is one solution to the inevitable tension between one cultural self and another cultural self. It reduces the other way of life to a distorted version of one's own (see Miner 1956).

The members of one society may go beyond merely interpreting another way of life in ethnocentric terms. They may decide to do something about the discrepancies they observe. They may conclude that the other way of life is wrong but not fundamentally evil and that the members of the other group need to be converted to their own way of doing things. If the others are unwilling to change their ways, however, the failed attempt at conversion may enlarge into an active dualism: we versus they, civilization versus savagery, good versus evil. The ultimate result may be war and *genocide*—'ethnic cleansing'—the deliberate attempt to exterminate an entire group based on race, religion, national origin, or other cultural features. Such assumed differences could be used as an excuse for economic and political gains by one faction over another. This has been a problem of recent history, from Yugoslavia to the continuing Darfur tragedy. What has changed since Jonathan Swift published *A Modest Proposal* in 1729?

Here is an important question: Is it possible to avoid ethnocentric bias? A holistic approach to relationships between us and others, both across and within cultural traditions, holds promise. But so too does our lifelong ability to learn—if we honour this potential in ourselves and others. People with a cultural background very different from your own may help you see possibilities for belief and action that are drastically at odds with everything your tradition considers possible. By becoming aware of these unsuspected possibilities, you become a different person. In effect you may have been gifted with an 'Aha!' moment. People from the other cultural background are likely to be affected in the same way. None of you will be the same again.

Learning about other cultures is at once enormously hopeful and immensely threatening. Once it occurs, we can no longer claim that any single culture has a monopoly on truth and that the truth embodied in any cultural tradition is bound to be partial, approximate, and open to further insight and growth.

Cultural Relativism

Anthropologists must come to terms with the consequences of learning about cultural differences as they do their fieldwork. One result has been the formulation of the important, although now debated, methodological concept of **cultural relativism**. Boas taught that relativism was the considered response to racism and prejudice and the outcomes of such perspectives. One of his students, Ruth Benedict, commented that all cultures are 'equally valid patterns of life, which mankind has created for itself from the raw materials of existence'. Considered definitions of cultural relativism have varied over time as different anthropologists have tried to draw conclusions based on their own experience of other ways of life. One definition that attempts a holistic approach is: '[Cultural relativism involves] understanding another culture in its own terms sympathetically enough so that the culture appears to be a coherent and meaningful design for living' (Greenwood and Stini 1977: 182). According to this definition, the goal of relativism is understanding. For example, cultural relativism demands that we try to understand how genocide could develop in a society.

Recent episodes in central Europe and Rwanda prove, tragically, that genocide did not end with the defeat of Nazi Germany in World War II. The Holocaust was intimately related to certain cultural patterns and historical processes that were, and perhaps are yet seen in the issues of Muslim immigration, deeply rooted in German, and European, society. Answering questions on the causes of the Holocaust involves investigating the historical roots of anti-Semitism and nationalism in Germany (Figure 1.10).

A relativistic understanding of events such as mass genocides accomplishes several things. It can make the Holocaust, and more recent genocides, somewhat comprehensible, even coherent. It reveals, to our horror, how the persecution and murder of human beings can appear perfectly acceptable when placed in a particular context of meaning. One thing that this relativistic understanding does not do, however, is allow us to excuse or condemn mass killers for what they did, or are doing, on the grounds that it was all due to their culture. For many people, a deterministic interpretation would be preferable: for some, it would absolve such killers of any blame because they had no choice but to do what their culture dictated; for others, it would absolve noncombatants of blame—after all, if a culture had led to the genocide, then responsibility for its horrors would lie squarely on the people of that culture.

These attempts to contain evil genocide by placing blame on one group of people or another are understandable. To leave matters here is to give an incomplete account of complex historical phenomena. And to call any incomplete account *relativistic*, as some critics have done, is to vulgarize the holistic understanding of cultural relativism that makes a complex historical explanation possible.

To accept the argument that 'their' culture made them do it is to accept cultural determinism. Cultural determinism requires us to accept three assumptions about human nature and human society:

(1) that cultures have neat boundaries between them and are sealed off from one another;
(2) that every culture offers people only one way to interpret experience (that cultures are monolithic and permit no variety, harbour no contradictions, and allow no dissent); and
(3) that people living in these closed cultural worlds are passively molded by culture, helpless to resist indoctrination into a single world view, and incapable of inventing alternatives to that view.

Figure 1.10 The Holocaust Memorial in Berlin commemorates the genocide of six million European Jews during World War II. Was the Holocaust due to the perversion of German morality by a charismatic madman who wished to rule the world, or was it rooted in long-standing social, historical, and cultural patterns?

cultural relativism 'Understanding another culture in its own terms sympathetically enough so that the culture appears to be a coherent and meaningful design for living.'

ethnocentrism The opinion that one's own way of life is natural or correct and, indeed, is the only true way of being fully human.

But the lived human experience undermines all three of these assumptions. Cultures are not sealed off from one another. Their boundaries are fuzzy, and people with different cultural backgrounds regularly exchange ideas and practices. Cultures are not monolithic. Even without the alternatives introduced from the outside, every culture offers a variety of ways to interpret experience, although official sanction may be given only one. Finally, human beings are not passive lumps shaped unresistingly to fit a single cultural mold. There is no such thing as a single cultural mold in a society acquainted with variety, and in a society where options exist, choices must be made.

Understanding something is not the same as approving or excusing it. We may be repelled by unfamiliar cultural practices when we first encounter them. Sometimes when we understand these practices better, we change our minds. We may conclude that the practices in question are more suitable for the people who employ them than our own practices would be. We might even recommend that they be adopted in our own society. But the opposite may also be the case. We may understand perfectly the cultural rationale behind such practices as slavery, infanticide, headhunting, or genocide—and still refuse our approval. We may not be persuaded by the reasons offered to justify these practices, or we may be aware of alternative arrangements that could achieve the desired outcome using less drastic methods. Moreover, it is likely that any cultural practice with far-reaching consequences for human life will have critics as well as supporters within the society where it is practised. This is certainly the case in North American societies where such sensitive topics as abortion, capital punishment, or same-sex marriage have been and continue to be discussed in many contexts.

Cultural relativism makes moral reasoning more complex. It does not, however, require us to abandon every value our own society has taught us. For each of us, our culture, like every other culture, offers more than one way of evaluating experience. Exposure to the interpretations of an unfamiliar culture forces us to reconsider the possibilities our culture recognizes in light of new alternatives and to search for areas of intersection as well as areas of disagreement. What cultural relativism does discourage is the easy solution of refusing to consider alternatives from the outset. Also, it does not free us from sometimes facing difficult choices between alternatives whose rightness or wrongness is

less than clear-cut. In this sense, 'cultural relativism is a "tough-minded" philosophy' (Herskovits 1973: 37). Rosaldo (2008) comments that

> Relativism . . . argues for engagement, for dialogue between cultures. This is not the kind of easy cosmopolitanism that implies enormous privilege—the capacity, for example, to spend three days in the Bali Hilton. It's a deeper form of knowing that entails some recognition that I am one among others. I'm not the centre of the universe.

Culture, History, and Human Agency

The human condition is rooted in time and shaped by history. As part of the human condition, culture is also historical, worked out and reconstructed in every generation. As paleoanthropologists have shown, the human species is itself a product of millions of years of evolution. Hence, human history is an essential aspect of the human story.

Anthropologists sometimes disagree about how to approach human history. Nineteenth-century thinkers such as Herbert Spencer argued that the evolution of social structures over time was central to the study of the human condition. Other anthropologists, sensitive to the excesses of people like Spencer, were not interested in change over time. In the 1930s, A.R. Radcliffe-Brown justified this lack of interest by pointing out that in societies without written records, knowledge about past life is non-existent; any attempt to reconstruct such past life would be an unfounded attempt at 'conjectural history'.

Other anthropologists had no interest in history for a different reason. Western capitalist culture, with its eye on the future and its faith in a theme from the Enlightenment—progress—has had little use for the past. It is therefore no wonder that some anthropologists built clockwork models of social structures that could be trusted to run reliably without 'losing time'. In these models, human beings and societies are both likened to machines. If a living organism is used as the model of society, and if organisms are nothing but machines, then a machine model of society with individuals as robot-like moving parts is not at all far-fetched. One can think here of the Charlie Chaplin movie *Modern Times* (1936) as emblematic of such a view (Figure 1.11).

A holistic and dialectical approach (the assessment of counter points of view) to human history, however, rejects these clockwork models. Our bio-cultural heritage has produced a living species that uses culture to surmount biological and individual limitations. The result has been the emergence of creatures who are capable of studying themselves and their own bio-cultural evolution.

But just how free from limitations are humans? Opinion in Western societies often polarizes around one of two extremes: either we have *free will* and may do just as we please or our behaviour is completely determined by biology or society. Many social scientists, however, are convinced that a more realistic description of human freedom was offered by Karl Marx, who wrote, 'Men make their own history, but they do not make it just as they please; they do not make it under circumstances chosen by themselves but under circumstances directly encountered, given, and transmitted by the past' (1963: 15). As humans we regularly struggle, often against great odds, to exercise some control over our lives. We are *agents*, but agents who cannot escape from the cultural and historical contexts within which we act (Figure 1.12). We must frequently select a course of action when the 'correct' choice is unclear and the outcome uncertain. Some anthropologists even liken our existence to a minefield that we must painstakingly try to cross without blowing ourselves up. It is in such contexts, with their ragged edges, that we as human beings make

Figure 1.12 Mohawk protestors from the Bay of Quinte successfully shut down Highway 401, one of Canada's busiest highways, as part of their protest of a housing development near Deseronto, Ontario, in 2007.

interpretations, formulate goals, and set out in pursuit of them. A holistic, dialectical approach to the human condition recognizes the existence and importance of **human agency**—the stuff of our dreams and the realm of our potential for growth.

The Promise of the Anthropological Perspective

The anthropological perspective on the human condition is not easy to maintain. It forces us to question the common-sense assumptions with which we are most comfortable. It only increases the difficulty we encounter when faced with moral and political decisions. It does not allow us an easy retreat to ethnocentrism when the going gets rough. For once we are exposed

Figure 1.11 When we say that we are only cogs in a machine or talk about status and roles as interchangeable parts, we are using machine metaphors.

human agency The exercise of at least some control over their lives by human beings.

to the kinds of experiences that the anthropological undertaking makes possible, we are changed—for better or worse. We cannot easily pretend that these new experiences never happened to us. Once we have had a genuine glimpse of the other as human beings equal to ourselves, there is no going back, except in bad faith.

So, anthropology is guaranteed to complicate your life. Nevertheless, the anthropological perspective can give you a broader understanding of human nature and the wider world—of society, culture, and history—and thus help you construct more realistic and authentic ways of coping with those complications.

Key Terms

anthropology 5
applied anthropology 12
archaeology 9
bio-cultural organisms 13
biological anthropologists 8
biological (or physical) anthropology 7
co-evolution 5
comparative 6
cultural anthropology 10
cultural relativism 18
culture 12
determinism 4
dualism 3
essence 4
ethnocentrism 18
ethnography 12

ethnology 12
evolutionary 6
fieldwork 11
holism 4
human agency 21
idealism 3
informants 11
language 9
linguistic anthropology 9
materialism 4
paleoanthropology 8
participant-observation 11
primatology 8
races 7
racism 8
symbol 13

Chapter Summary

1. The belief that human nature has two parts is known as *dualism*. Mind–matter dualism is deeply rooted in Western thought, dating back to figures such as Plato.

2. Idealism reduces human nature to ideas or the mind that produces them. Materialism reduces human nature to genes, hormones, or biology. Biological determinism, environmental determinism, and historical determinism are all forms of materialist determinism.

3. The most extreme position against the various forms of materialist reductionism—cultural determinism—argues that the ideas, meanings, beliefs, and values that people learn in society determine their behaviours. Optimistic versions of cultural

determinism hold out the hope that we can change these determining agents and make ourselves whatever we want to be. Pessimistic versions conclude that 'you are what you are conditioned to be', something over which you have no control.

4. In preference to dualism, anthropologists have suggested holism, which assumes that objects and environments interpenetrate and even define each other. Thus, the whole is greater than the sum of its parts. Human beings and human societies are open systems that cannot be reduced to the parts that make them up. The parts and the whole mutually define or co-determine each other and co-evolve.

5. Anthropology is a scholarly discipline that aims to describe, in the broadest sense, what it means

to be human. To achieve this aim, anthropologists have developed a perspective on the human condition that is holistic, comparative, and evolutionary. Because human beings lack instincts that automatically promote our survival, we must learn from other members of our society what we need to know to survive. For this reason, the concept of culture is central to the anthropological perspective.

6. In North America, anthropology is usually considered to have four major specialties: biological anthropology, archaeology, linguistic anthropology, and cultural anthropology. Some anthropologists consider applied anthropology to be a separate sub-field of professional specialization.

7. Biological anthropology began as an attempt to classify the world's populations into different races, an undertaking that some people used to justify the social practice of racism. By the early twentieth century, however, most anthropologists had rejected racial classifications as scientifically unjustifiable. Since the early twentieth century, anthropologists have used information about human biology and human culture to debunk racist stereotypes.

8. Modern anthropologists who are interested in human biology include biological anthropologists, primatologists, and paleoanthropologists. Cultural anthropologists study human diversity by focusing on sets of learned behaviours and ideas that human beings acquire as members of different societies. Because anthropology is comparative, research is done in Western and non-Western settings alike. Anthropological linguists study linguistic diversity in different human societies, relating various forms of language to their cultural contexts.

9. Archaeology is a cultural anthropology of the human past, but the material remains archaeologists recover can be of value to biological and cultural anthropologists.

10. Linguistic anthropologists try to understand language in relation to broader cultural, historical, and biological contexts. They study the connections between language and social identity, language acquisition, sign language, and challenges to communication across linguistic barriers. Recent work focuses on the way political relationships influence language use.

11. Through fieldwork, cultural anthropologists gain insight into another culture both by participating with their informants in social activities and by observing those activities as outsiders. Ethnographies are published accounts of what was learned during fieldwork. Ethnology involves comparing ethnographic information from two or more different cultures. Because human experience is often ambiguous, adaptation requires cultural interpretation, which is a constant, necessary process, whether it is an attempt to understand people or symbols within one's own culture or those of another culture.

12. Applied anthropologists use information gathered from the other anthropological specialties to solve practical problems in areas such as health care and economic development.

13. Most anthropologists emphasize that human beings are bio-cultural organisms whose biological make-up allows us to make and use culture. As a result, human beings have produced a tremendous variety of distinct cultural traditions.

14. Many anthropologists have criticized the use of the term *cultures* to refer to particular, learned ways of life belonging to specific groups of human beings. Critics argue that the plural concept of culture seems to endorse an oppressive kind of cultural determinism, but many groups have incorporated the plural use of culture into their own self-definitions, which other anthropologists defend as valuable and progressive.

15. Ethnocentrism is a form of reductionism. Anthropologists believe it can be countered by a commitment to cultural relativism, an attempt to understand the cultural underpinnings of behaviour. Cultural relativism makes moral decisions more difficult because it requires us to take into account many things before we make up our minds. Cultural relativism does not require us to abandon every value our society has taught us; however, it does discourage the easy solution of refusing to consider alternatives from the outset.

16. Human history is an essential aspect of the human story, a dialectic between biology and culture. Culture is worked out over time and passed on from one generation to the next. Because human beings have the power to act in their own interests, the story of our species also involves human agency.

Critical Thinking Questions

1. Using the concepts of idealism and materialism, how would you develop definitions of what it means to be human? How deterministic are these definitions?

2. Distinguish between *Culture* and *cultures*. Why has this distinction become contentious in anthropology, and what is the suggested resolution to this problem?

3. Consider the concept of holism. How does anthropology use this as a methodology as well as a concept? Can holism succeed in anthropology without cultural relativism?

4. How do the four original sub-disciplines of anthropology contribute to an understanding of humans? How does the fifth way of applied anthropology add to this anthropological perspective, and what would you consider its ethical position in anthropology?

Suggested Readings

Ashmore, Wendy, and Robert J. Sharer. 2000. *Discovering Our Past: A Brief Introduction to Archaeology*, 3rd edn (New York: McGraw-Hill). *An engaging introduction to the techniques, assumptions, interests, and findings of modern archaeology.*

Feder, Kenneth L. 2002. *Frauds, Myths and Mysteries: Science and Pseudoscience in Archaeology*, 4th edn (New York: McGraw-Hill). *An entertaining and informative exploration of fascinating frauds and genuine archaeological mysteries that also explain the scientific method.*

Gamst, Frederick, and Edward Norbeck. 1976. *Ideas of Culture: Sources and Uses* (New York: Holt, Rinehart & Winston). *A useful collection of important articles about culture. The articles are arranged according to different basic approaches to culture.*

Marks, Jonathan. 2002. *What It Means to Be 98% Chimpanzee: Apes, People, and Their Genes* (Berkeley: University of California Press). *A lively and provocative text by a molecular anthropologist who explains what can and cannot be concluded from the fact that the genomes of chimpanzees and humans are nearly identical.*

Ortner, Sherry. 2006. *Anthropology and Social Theory: Culture, Power, and the Acting Subject* (Duke University Press). *So you want to be an anthropologist? This is a must read either now or when you are in an advanced theory course!*

Relethford, John. 2003. *The Human Species: An Introduction to Biological Anthropology*, 5th edn (New York: McGraw-Hill). *An excellent, clear introduction to biological anthropology.*

Skinner, M., and K. Bowie. 2008. 'Forensic Anthropology: Canadian Content and Contributions', in *Handbook of Forensic Anthropology and Archaeology*, eds S. Blau and D.H. Ubelaker (California: Left Coast Press). *As the title indicates, this is a handbook for the practising forensic anthropologist.*

Voget, Fred. 1975. *A History of Ethnology* (New York: Holt, Rinehart & Winston). *A massive, thorough, and detailed work. For the student seeking a challenging read.*

Watson, Patty Jo. 1995. 'Archaeology, Anthropology, and the Culture Concept', *American Anthropologist*, New Series, 97, 4 (Dec.): 683–94. *How an anthropologist/archaeologist evolved in her thinking about the nature of the subject of her discipline and her specialty within that discipline.*

Related Websites

Applied Anthropology: http://www.thecanadianencyclopedia.com/index.cfm?PgNm=TCE&Params=A1ARTA0000237

Canadian Archaeological Association: http://www.canadianarchaeology.com/

Hidden from History—The Canadian Holocaust: http://www.hiddenfromhistory.org/

Parks Canada: http://www.pc.gc.ca/progs/arch/index_e.asp?sec=1&doc=0

Patty Jo Watson—An Intellectual Biography: http://www.utexas.edu/courses/wilson/ant304/biography/arybios97/gebhardbio.html

Residential Schools: http://archives.cbc.ca/society/education/topics/692/; http://www.cbc.ca/canada/north/story/2008/04/02/north-schools.html; http://www.cbc.ca/canada/story/2008/05/16/f-faqs-residential-schools.html

Society for Applied Anthropology: http://www.sfaa.net/

Chapter 2

Fieldwork

Learning Objectives

By the end of Chapter 2, you will be able to:

- consider the endeavour of ethnographic fieldwork,
- outline forms of data collection,
- detail the process of preparing to do fieldwork from graduate school to the field itself,
- understand the importance of professional ethics,
- identify with the difficulties of culture shock,
- compare and contrast three modes of ethnographic research,

- recognize the agency of both anthropologist and informant in the dialectic of fieldwork,
- consider the effects of fieldwork on all involved, and
- appreciate the utility of anthropological knowledge and its open-ended nature.

By deliberately bringing people from different cultural backgrounds together, ethnographic fieldwork makes (mis)understandings and surprises likely. Many people around the world find something unusual about ethnographic fieldwork. Here is someone who shows up in a community, plans to be there for a year or more, claims to be interested in their way of life, and then spends all of his or her time observing, talking to people, and taking notes! And yet the great gift is given: people give of themselves and their resources, sharing their families and friendships, homes and food, as well as insights into their lives and their culture. This can be a very humbling experience. Fieldwork, as an endeavour, not only broadens anthropological understandings of cultural worlds but also regularly transforms the self-understandings of anthropologists, the people with whom they work, and, ultimately, the discipline of anthropology itself. Thus all emerge changed in essential ways. However, it is important to reflect on the fact of change and remember that researchers get to go home, and the people they study *are* at home and have to live with what the researcher may have transformed. There is, then, the incredible responsibility of behaving ethically in seeking and accepting the gift. In this chapter, we consider the fieldwork experience.

A Meeting of Cultural Traditions

In addition to participant-observation, anthropologists also gather data by conducting interviews, administering surveys, and consulting published literature and archives relevant to their research. Sometimes questionnaires and psychological tests are part of their fieldwork, but they never rely solely on such methods because, by themselves, the information they produce cannot be contextualized and may be highly misleading. But participant-observation, which relies on face-to-face contact with people as they go about their daily lives, was pioneered by cultural anthropologists and remains characteristic of anthropology as a discipline. It allows anthropologists to comprehend what people say and do in the wider context of social interaction and cultural beliefs and values. Participant-observation is perhaps the best method available to scholars who seek a holistic understanding of culture and the human condition.

The Fieldwork Experience

For many cultural anthropologists, ethnographic fieldwork is the quintessential anthropological experience. Sometimes field experience begins in undergraduate or early graduate studies, when students work on research projects or in field schools run by established anthropologists. An extended period of fieldwork is the final phase of formal anthropological training, but most anthropologists hope to incorporate additional periods of field research into their subsequent careers.

Beginning anthropologists usually decide during graduate school where and on what topic they wish to do their research. Success depends on being able to obtain permission to work in a particular place, such as approvals from academic and government offices in the host country, and acceptance from the people who will be participants in the study. This was not always the case as, in the past, the people who were to be studied did not always know an anthropologist was on the way. Arriving in Pond Inlet in 1963, Matthiasson notes, 'No one in the settlement knew of my impending arrival although I was equipped with an Explorer's and Scientist's licence properly signed by the appropriate officials in Ottawa—a bureaucratic prerequisite for research in the Northwest Territories' (1992: 13). Today this would never do! The funds to support one's research need to be sought.

Getting grants from private or government agencies involves, among other things, persuading them that your work will focus on a topic of current interest within anthropology and that it is connected to their funding priorities. As a result, 'field sites end up being defined by the cross-hatched intersection of visa and clearance procedures, the interests of funding agencies, and intellectual debates within the discipline and its sub-fields' (Gupta and Ferguson 1997: 11). Since funds are finite, not all topics of current interest can be funded, and so some anthropologists pay for their research themselves by getting a job in the area where they want to do fieldwork or by supplementing small grants out of their own pockets.

Professional voluntary associations like the Canadian Sociology and Anthropology Association (CSAA) and the American Anthropological Association (AAA) offer guidelines for research. The *Statement of Professional Ethics* from the CSAA states, 'Sociologists and anthropologists, when they carry out research, enter into personal and *moral relationships* with those they study, be they individuals, households, social groups, or corporate entities' (1994: s.5; italics added). Similarly, the AAA's *Code of Ethics* states that 'Anthropological researchers have *primary ethical obligations* to the people, species, and materials they study and to the people with whom they work' and must 'do everything in their power to ensure that their research does not harm the safety, dignity, or privacy of the people with whom they work, conduct research, or perform other professional activities' (1998: III, A.1, A.2; italics added). Foremost are moral and ethical obligations.

Sadly enforcement can be difficult except for the fact that in Canada the *Tri-council Policy Statement* (TCPS) dominates in ethical consideration. It is this document that informs the Research Ethics Boards (REB) of all federally funded institutions as 'These Agencies will consider funding (or continued funding) only to individuals and institutions that certify that they comply with this Policy regarding research involving human subjects' (CIHR, NSERC, SSHRC 1998). Policies evolve from the problems, constraints, and considerations that arise from fieldwork. Mike Evans, from his Island Cache research in British Columbia, addresses the problem of voice and representation within the constraints of confidentiality for informants as outlined in the *TCPS*. (Note Mike Evans, *In Their Own Words*.)

Evans, like all anthropologists, feels strongly that informants have the right to protect their identities. Indeed, the need for protection is paramount when informants belong to marginal and powerless groups that might suffer retaliation from more powerful members of their society and external controlling agencies. However, Evans emphasizes that in certain situations, such as community centred research when informants wish to express their identities and ideas, anthropologists need to work in other forms of ethnographic writing. Here the anthropologist serves primarily as translator and editor of the voices and opinions of individual informants (see also Keesing 1983; Shostak 1981). Increasingly, anthropologists working in their own societies write about their fieldwork both as observers and as members of those societies (see, e.g., Foley 1989; Kumar 1992).

Classic anthropological fieldwork emphasized working 'abroad'—that is, doing fieldwork in societies that were culturally and geographically distant from that of the ethnographer. This orientation bears undeniable traces of its origins under European colonialism, but it continues to be a valuable means of drawing attention to ways of life and parts of the world that elite groups in powerful Western nations have traditionally dismissed and marginalized. More recent discussions of anthropological fieldwork have drawn attention to the significance of working 'at home'—including paying attention to the forms of social differentiation and marginalization present in the society to which the ethnographer belongs. This orientation has the virtue of emphasizing ethnographers' ethical and political accountability to those among whom they work, especially when anthropologists are members of the groups they study. Such an orientation incorporates traditions of anthropological research that have developed in countries like Mexico, Brazil, India, and Russia, where fieldwork at home has long been the

In Their Own Words

Ethics, Anonymity, and Authorship in Community Centred Research Or Anonymity and the Island Cache

Mike Evans is Associate Professor and past Canada Research Chair in World's Indigenous Peoples in Community, Culture, and Global Studies at the University of British Columbia Okanagan. Currently, he is Head of the Unit.

Since its introduction in 1998 the *Tri-council Policy Statement* on *Ethical Conduct for Research Involving Humans* (hereafter referred to as the 'Tri-council policy' or just the 'policy') has had more and more impact on social science research in Canada. All across the country 'Research Ethics Boards' have been set up, and the eight central principles of the Tri-council guidelines now set the terms of reference for almost all university associated research with people.

On the surface, there is little to quarrel with in the policy itself. There have been increasingly audible mutterings in the hallways of the academy about the way the guidelines have been interpreted and enforced by various Research Ethics Boards, but not particularly about the guidelines themselves. The eight central principles are:

(1) Respect for Human Dignity
(2) Respect for Free and Informed Consent
(3) Respect for Vulnerable Persons
(4) Respect for Privacy and Confidentiality
(5) Respect for Justice and Inclusiveness
(6) Balancing Harms and Benefits
(7) Minimizing Harm
(8) Maximizing Benefit

Respect, clearly a good thing, figures prominently. But, by way of example of why the uniform application of these principles is problematic, I would like to talk about . . . contemporary community centred research and the way the Tri-council policy is having some impacts that are, contrary to its central principles, not particularly respectful. . . . Community centred research is just that, a research process that is both located at the community and one that centralizes community concerns and participation. The central question . . . is: Can community centred research be respectfully undertaken while embracing the notion of anonymity of research participants?

* * *

Respect for Privacy and Confidentiality

. . . I will concentrate on some of the tensions between acknowledgement and anonymity in contemporary social science research—and especially community centred research. . . .

Tri-council policy enshrines 'Respect for Privacy and Confidentiality' as one of its eight central principles. In the introduction of the ethics document, the following can be found:

> Respect for human dignity also implies the principles of respect for privacy and confidentiality. In many cultures, privacy and confidentiality are considered fundamental to human dignity. Thus, standards of privacy and confidentiality protect the access, control, and dissemination of personal information. In doing so, such standards help to protect mental or psychological integrity. They are thus consonant with the values underlying privacy, confidentiality, and anonymity respected. (CIHR, NSERC, SSHRC 1998)

On the surface, there is very little to disagree with here. However, I want to question the statement that confidentiality (anonymity) protects mental or psychological integrity. Confidentiality and anonymity can be quite valuable in protecting people in research involving psychological experiments or quantitative sociological surveys where there is absolutely no cost to the research, or it is essential to the validity of the research paradigm. In qualitative branches of sociology, history, anthropology, or Indigenous studies, and especially in the context of much community centred research, anonymity can obscure community authority and voice, and the intent of the principle above is undone. In fact, misplaced confidentiality can 'disappear' people and communities. . . .

Section 3 of the Tri-council policy deals specifically with issues of confidentiality and anonymity. Nowhere in this section, or for that matter anywhere else in the document, does a research participant's right to be recognized as the source of information get any ink. The document does deal very carefully with how to maintain confidentiality in the context of primary research and secondary data use. But except where information is collected individually and then aggregated (i.e., in quantitative research such as a demographic survey), confidentiality in a community is a much bigger problem than using pseudonyms or anonymity can accommodate. When talking about oral history and/or contemporary social issues, anonymity might protect people from outsiders, but less dependably from people within the community. This is especially a problem when there is an explicit commitment on the part of the researchers to make research results available to as wide a cross-section of the community as possible. . . . The same might be said of whole communities—i.e., the practice of assigning pseudonyms to communities only protects the community from people who don't care to do the little bit of digging required to figure out the real community identity. As researchers struggle to make research community centred—increasing the participation of community in setting research questions, undertaking the research itself, and producing community accessible research products—confidentiality becomes more and more difficult to maintain and more and more costly (in terms of other values like representation, authority, and voice) to the communities.

Are confidentiality and privacy moot? No. Contemporary community centred research agendas must recognize that anonymity is not a panacea for maintaining ethics and must not (to make a hybrid of two metaphors of common anatomical reference) become a Band-Aid that protects institutional butts while leaving community ones exposed. This may be an especially poignant issue when it comes to Indigenous communities who have suffered expropriation of various types. But if one goes to Section 6 of the Tri-council policy, a section that deals directly with Aboriginal persons, you will find what is basically a call for participatory research without any reconsideration of the issues of anonymity.

What then? How does this affect 'science', as it surely does? I mean to imply that the content of research needs to be tested against the protection of (more positively, the benefit to) 'mental or psychological integrity', and I would add social integrity, of communities. For many people this might be heretical, tantamount to censorship—certainly and explicitly what I am saying means that some things might simply not be researchable in some contexts (of course the Tri-council policy has the same implications). I do not mean to suggest that difficult issues should be avoided in, or by, any community (though I do mean to state plainly that some issues should be addressed in terms of intervention and community activism rather than as research problems). Against the loss of research results in the issue of benefits, the benefits to communities that come of effective participatory research, truly community centred research projects, and research results that community members can interpret, own, and in which they see themselves reflected and named. Anonymity is not, at least not always, the best route to ethical research. The challenge is to do research and to produce research results that are ethical in content and structure rather than structure alone.

Source: Evans, Mike. 2004. 'Ethics, Anonymity, and Authorship in Community Centred Research Or Anonymity and the Island Cache', *Pimatisiwin: A Journal of Aboriginal and Indigenous Community Health* 2, 1 (spring): 60–75.

norm. In the twenty-first century, these developments are helping create 'decolonized anthropology in a deterritorialized world' that will be enriched by varied contributions of anthropologists trained in different traditions, working at home and abroad, who seek to forge 'links between *different* knowledges that are possible from different locations' (Gupta and Ferguson 1997: 35, 38).

Anthropologists who work among remote peoples in rain forests, deserts, or tundras may need to bring along their own living quarters. In other cases, an appropriate house or apartment in the village, neighbourhood, or city where the research is to be done becomes the anthropologist's home.

In any case, living conditions in the field can provide major insights into the culture under study. Early in their stay, it is not uncommon for fieldworkers to feel overwhelmed by the need to adjust to local water, food, and climate. Many anthropologists encounter plants, animals, insects, and diseases with which they have had no previous experience. Physical and mental dislocation and stress can be expected. This is **culture shock**.

Further, certain risk factors need to be considered. Nancy Howell, professor *emerita* from the University of Toronto and a demographer very much involved with

culture shock The feeling of physical and mental dislocation/discomfort a person experiences when in a new or strange cultural setting. It can manifest most deeply on returning 'home', with home seeming exceedingly strange after extended stays in the fieldwork situation.

anthropological research in areas such as Botswana (Figure 2.1), has explored some of these risk factors. She has observed:

> Anthropologists need to be mentally prepared to cope with . . . risks (diseases, criminal and political threats, vehicle accidents, etc. . . .) to their health and safety and to the health and safety of . . . others who accompany them on field trips. We don't need to write the kind of guidebook that systematically warns about sunburn, jet lag, and the inoculations needed in various countries. . . . What is needed for anthropology is the sensitizing to the hazards that are likely to be encountered, systematic sharing of experiences with hazards in the field, the best available advice on prevention and responses when they are encountered, and some mental rehearsals of what to do under those circumstances. (1988: 786–7)

In addition, there are cultural differences—which is why fieldworkers came to the field. Yet the immensity of what they will encounter is difficult for them to anticipate. Initially, just getting through the day—finding a place to stay and food to eat—may seem an enormous accomplishment. With time, however, the great process of human survival begins to assert itself: they begin to adapt. The rhythms of daily activity become

Figure 2.1 Elephants on a road in Botswana. Many anthropologists encounter plants, animals, insects, and diseases with which they have had no previous experience. The physical and mental dislocation and stress they may experience in the fieldwork situation is called *culture shock*.

familiar. Their use of the local language improves. Faces of the local inhabitants become the faces of neighbours. Incredibly, the time comes when they are able to turn their attention to their research.

Modes of Ethnographic Fieldwork: A Short History

When anthropology began to take on its own identity as an intellectual discipline during the nineteenth century, it aspired to be scientific. Anthropology still aims to be scientific in its study of human nature, human society, and human history. For several decades, however, scientists, philosophers, historians, and increasing numbers of social scientists have been re-examining some deeply rooted assumptions about what science is and how it works. This research effort has challenged many popular understandings about science. One outcome of this work has been the demonstration that the so-called hard sciences (such as physics, chemistry, and biology) and the so-called soft sciences (such as psychology, sociology, and anthropology) actually have more in common with each other than previously recognized (e.g., Barad 1999; Pickering 1995). Another outcome has been to show that there are actually a variety of scientific methods that have been developed to produce reliable knowledge in different scientific disciplines that focus on different aspects of the world (e.g., Knorr Cetina 2000). Therefore we can study an infinite number of 'logically possible worlds' (Popper 1979: 39) using diverse methodologies. What is important, according to Cohen (1994: 6), is that each inquiry has its own integrity, internal coherence, and results that can be 'tested'.

These developments intersect in important ways with the efforts anthropologists have made over the years to understand the scientific status of the fieldwork tradition based on participant-observation. This research strategy came into its own in the early decades of the twentieth century in the work of pioneer ethnographers such as Bronislaw Malinowski (who, it is often said, invented long-term participant-observation based fieldwork), Franz Boas (who based much of his fieldwork on the Kwakiutl in British Columbia), Boas's best-known student Margaret Mead (who, on her own admission, 'escaped' Boas's control by going on fieldwork in the South Pacific), and Frank G. Speck (who worked with the Algonquians of eastern Canada [1914–31]). Since that time, the conditions within which fieldwork has been carried out have changed, and anthropologists have been prompted to rethink and revise their basic views about fieldwork in terms of its scientific status and as a form of human interaction. Three modes of ethnographic fieldwork have developed over the last hundred years: the positivist approach, the reflexive approach, and multi-sited fieldwork.

The Positivist Approach

The traditional method of the physical sciences, which early social scientists tried to imitate, is often called *positivistic science*. Its proponents based their view of science on a set of principles most fully set out in the writings of a group of influential thinkers known as *positivists*, who were active in the late nineteenth and early twentieth centuries, though refers back to French philosopher Auguste Comte (1798–1857) and his 'positive philosophy'. Today, **positivism** has become a label for a particular way of looking at and studying the world scientifically.

First, positivists are committed to explaining how the material world works in terms of material causes and processes that we can detect using our senses. Second, to achieve this goal, positivists are also committed to a separation of facts from values as part of scientific methodology. This is justified on the grounds that facts relate to the nature of physical, material reality—what *is*—whereas, in their view, values are based on speculation about what *ought to be*. To the positivist, scientific research is concerned only with the former. As a result all valid scientific inquiry, from subatomic structure to genetic engineering to in vitro fertilization or human sexual response, should be understood as different aspects of a single, disinterested quest for knowledge, a quest that cannot be compromised simply because it offends some people's moral or political sensibilities. The truth remains the truth whether people like it or not, whether it conforms to their idea of what is good and proper or not. These examples point to a third feature of positivism: the conviction that a single scientific method can be used to investigate any domain of reality, from planetary motion to chemical reactions to human life. The most ambitious positivists are convinced that all scientific knowledge will ultimately be unified in a 'theory of everything'.

The traditional goal of the positivist program has been to produce **objective knowledge**, knowledge about reality that is true for all people, in all times and places. Positivist science has been viewed as the route to that objective knowledge, precisely because of its disciplined determination to describe the way the material world actually is, unobscured by any webs of meaning and value that human beings might ascribe to it.

Applying Positivist Methods to Anthropology

For the positivist, the prototypical research scenario involves a physical scientist in a laboratory. This prototype creates obstacles for those who study human life by means of participant-observation in a natural setting. Early cultural anthropologists were aware of these obstacles, and they tried to devise ways to get around them. Their first step was to approximate lab conditions by testing hypotheses in different cultural settings. These settings were carefully selected to exhibit the same range of variation, naturally, that a laboratory scientist could create artificially. As a result, the field could be seen as a living laboratory. Each research setting would correspond to a separate experimental situation, a method called *controlled comparison*. Margaret Mead used this method in the 1930s when she studied four different societies in an attempt to discover the range and causes of gender roles (Figure 2.2).

Anthropologists like Mead were encouraged by the enormous successes that the physical scientists had attained by following these principles. It must be noted that Freeman (1999) has criticized Mead's field methodology, noting that it did not meet even the most fundamental tenets of the positivist approach. From the mid-nineteenth to the mid-twentieth centuries, positivistically inclined anthropologists recorded the ways of life of peoples their contemporaries had neither heard of nor cared to know. Rejecting the slipshod, impressionistic work of an earlier period, they attempted to produce accounts of other cultures that were systematic

objective knowledge Knowledge about reality that is absolute and true for all people, in all times and places.

positivism The view that there is a reality 'out there' that can be detected through the senses and that there is a single, appropriate scientific method for investigating that reality.

Figure 2.2 Participant-observation has long been a hallmark of research in cultural anthropology, whether in the 1920s with Margaret Mead on the island of Samoa (left) or in the 1980s with Naomi McPherson in Papua New Guinea (above).

and accurate, and they more or less succeeded although they were sometimes accused of insensitivity.

Anthropologists found themselves confronting a paradox. Although they regularly developed close personal ties to the people among whom they worked, defending their full humanity to outsiders and sometimes intervening on their behalf with the government, none of this showed up in their ethnographies. Instead, they wrote as if they had been invisible observers recording objective facts about a way of life in which they were not personally involved. This stance was anything but true because of the nature of participant-observation.

Questioning the Positivist Approach

The 1960s and 1970s marked a turning point in anthropological understandings of fieldwork. Many assumptions about the way the world worked were called into question, including the nature of scientific inquiry. Anthropologists began to reconsider the ethics and politics of positivist science in general and of participant-observation in particular. In the 1970s and 1980s anthropologists began to write ethnographies highlighting the ways their own involvement with others in the field had contributed to the growth of cross-cultural knowledge. They were able to show how different observers, working from different assumptions, often produce different knowledges about the same society. At the same time, differently situated

fieldworkers also draw similar conclusions, which allows them to link their work in productive ways.

Consider the fieldwork of Bronislaw Malinowski and Annette Weiner in the Trobriand Islands, carried out nearly 60 years apart. Malinowski and Weiner were anthropologists of different nationalities and different genders working in different villages with different informants during different historical periods. Weiner made an important contribution to our understanding of Trobriand life by describing and explaining activities involving Trobriand women's 'wealth' that were absolutely central to the continued healthy functioning of Trobriand life—but about which Malinowski had written nothing (see Chapter 9). Weiner might have published her findings by declaring that Malinowski had got it wrong. But this route did not appeal to her primarily because, as she alluded, he got so very much right. Malinowski's own preoccupations led him to write about aspects of Trobriand life different from those that interested Weiner. As a result, he left behind a portrait of Trobriand society that Weiner later felt obliged to supplement. Nevertheless, much of Malinowski's work remained valid and insightful to Weiner. In tribute to him, she quoted long passages from his ethnographies (see Weiner 1976; 1988; see also EthnoProfile 9.1: Trobriand Islanders).

Closer attention was paid to the ethical and political dimensions of the relationships that anthropologists developed with their informants. Since the 1960s there has been a re-examination of the laboratory model of fieldwork. In the physical sciences it is fairly easy to justify a hierarchy elevating the inquiring intelligence of scientists over their subject matter. It seems difficult to imagine the ethical obligations that a geologist might have to a mineral.

Matters are otherwise when human beings are the subject. Anthropologists cannot avoid the realization of shared commonalities based in our humanness. We *do* have ethical obligations to other human beings; political factors *can* complicate the relationships ethnographers are able to develop with informants. Further, informants may be as eager to learn about the anthropologist as the anthropologist is to learn about them. First, though, scientific accuracy requires anthropologists to regard themselves as human beings, not as impersonal recording machines. Additionally, there is a need to acknowledge that appropriate human involvement with informants is central to cross-cultural understanding.

Questioning positivist science is not taken lightly. Those who do are often accused of abandoning scientific discipline entirely, allowing material facts to be obscured by their own individual, *subjective* values and preferences. However, the point is that observation 'has a subjective component by virtue of the observer's taxonomic decision to recognize certain distinctions' (Allen and Hoekstra 1991: 49); so, in effect, it is not necessarily value free.

So, does the rejection of positivism turn fieldwork into just one person's subjective impressions of other people? Most anthropologists would answer with a firm *no* because fieldwork is a *dialogue* between ethnographers and their informants. Ethnographers engage in real, literal conversations with their informants in order to learn about their ways of life. These dialogues are often patient and painstaking collaborative attempts to sort things out, to piece things together. When successful, the outcome is a new understanding of the world that both anthropologist and informant can share. This means that field data are not subjective but *intersubjective*: they are the product of long dialogues between researcher and informant. The focus of fieldwork is the range of **intersubjective meanings** that informants share. This is what participant-observation is all about.

The Reflexive Approach

The intersubjective meanings on which informants rely are public, not private. Informants take them for

Figure 2.3 Anthropologists use different technologies for different research purposes. Anthropologist Ryan Cook videotapes the spectators and ritual performers at the Popocatepetl volcano in Mexico.

granted, but they may not be obvious to an outsider. In order to make these meanings explicit, anthropologist and informant together must occasionally step back from the ordinary flow of daily life and examine them critically. They must think about the way members of the culture normally think about their lives. This thinking about thinking is known as **reflexivity**; thus, fieldwork in cultural anthropology is a reflexive experience. Reflexive fieldwork retains a respect for detailed, accurate information gathering (Figure 2.3), but it also pays explicit attention to the ethical and political context of research, the background of researchers, the full partnership of informants, and the collaborative relationships that produce anthropological knowledge. It is important to note that the assumptions embedded in this approach have been under criticism recently, and most centre on the reliability of self-reports as to positionality (research subjectivity) since 'consideration of the possibility of reliable self-reports leads to skepticism rather than confidence' (Salzman 2002).

Nonetheless, reflexive fieldwork can take into consideration a broader range of contextual information than positivistic fieldwork. But consideration of

---

intersubjective meanings The shared, public symbolic systems of a culture.

reflexivity Critically thinking about the way one thinks; reflecting on one's own experience.

these factors is seen to be essential in order to produce knowledge about human beings that is scientifically valid. To approach human beings as objects, lacking the same inquisitive intelligence as the scientists who study them, is to mischaracterize the subject matter of anthropology. To objectify human beings and disregard ethical consideration or to mute political sensitivity is to wilfully suppress key aspects of the very human situation under investigation. Thus, ethnographers have come to recognize that the reliability of their knowledge of other cultures depends on explicit recognition of the ethical and political dimensions of fieldwork. Ethnographic knowledge shaped by reflexivity becomes *situated knowledge* (Haraway 1991). The 'situating' to which Haraway refers involves making explicit exactly who you are as an ethnographer, i.e., your gender, nationality, political preference, class/ethnic/educational backgrounds, and so forth.

It is precisely these kinds of factors that will shape the distinctions made by ethnographers. This will outline the structure of relationships with informants. For example, in some societies, being a female ethnographer may bar you from studying certain social activities that are central to the ongoing viability of the local culture. Such an ethnographic account of that culture is bound to be partial and could be seen as a weakness under the test of 'scientific objectivity'. Nevertheless, the ethnographer's ability to present a detailed and accurate account of what she was able to learn, together with an explicit acknowledgement of its limitations (based on who she is, what she is competent to write about, and what she is permitted to study) can be seen as far more reliable because it accurately reflects the objective fact that she did not talk to everybody or see everything. This becomes situated knowledge by refusing to make sweeping generalizations about an entire social group on the basis of clearly defined partial knowledge. Far from making ethnographic knowledge subjective, however, reflexivity generates what philosopher of science Sandra Harding calls *strong objectivity*, which she contrasts with *weak objectivity* produced by traditional positivistic approaches (1991: 149ff.). We would argue that the best ethnographies have always been reflexive, whether or not the ethnographers realized it. Ethnographic understanding of Trobriand culture is richer and more reliable when the partial, situated knowledges of Malinowski and Weiner are acknowledged and juxtaposed.

The commitment to reflexivity means anthropologists are scientifically obligated to make public the way in which they gather data. Some anthropologists have argued that they must also share their conclusions with their informants and include their informants' reflections on those conclusions in their published ethnographies. Bettylou Valentine, for example, persuaded several of her informants in Blackston, US, to comment on her manuscript before publication. She visited them for lengthy discussions and found that, in general, they agreed with her conclusions. In the published volume, Valentine states her own conclusions, and she dedicates space for her informants' voices in the final chapter. Valentine's ethnography presents a vivid example of the open-endedness of the dialogue between anthropologist and informant: no single interpretation of human experience is final. This kind of mutual reflexivity is at the heart of anthropological knowledge and recognizes that 'tomorrow' situated knowledge may be positioned in new worlds of meaning.

The Dialectic of Fieldwork: Interpretation and Translation

Fieldwork is a risky business. Fieldworkers not only risk offending their informants by misunderstanding their way of life, but they also face the shock of the unfamiliar and their own vulnerability. Indeed, they must embrace this shock and cultivate this vulnerability if they are to achieve any kind of meaningful understanding of their informants' culture. They resist ethnocentric impulses by recalling 'that if what we observe appears to be odd or irrational, it is probably because we do not understand it and not because it is a product of a "savage" culture in which such nonsense is to be expected' (Greenwood and Stini 1977: 185).

Anthropologist Michael Agar uses the expression 'rich points' for unexpected moments when problems in cross-cultural understanding emerge. The phrase is apt because it portrays these moments as opportunities for insight. Agar observes that rich points, the words or actions that signal the gaps between the anthropologist's out-of-awareness assumptions about how the world works and those of the local people, are the raw material of ethnography. As he says, 'it is this distance between two worlds of experience that is exactly the problem that ethnographic research is designed to locate and resolve' (1996: 31). That the anthropologist doesn't understand what's going on is the anthropologist's problem, not the local people's, and the anthropologist has to discover the context for the action and then take that discovery to the world in which it occurs to see if it fits more broadly.

Interpreting Actions and Ideas

How does one go about interpreting the actions and ideas of other human beings? We need a form of interpretation based on reflexivity rather than objectivity. In *Reflections on Fieldwork in Morocco* (1977), Paul Rabinow addresses this problem. He suggests that what we require has already been set forth in the philosophy of French thinker Paul Ricoeur:

> Following Ricoeur, I define the problem of hermeneutics (which is simply Greek for 'interpretation') as 'the comprehension of the self by the detour of the comprehension of the other'. It is vital to stress that this is not psychology of any sort. . . . The self being discussed is perfectly public. . . . [It is] the culturally mediated and historically situated self which finds itself in a continuously changing world of meaning. (1977: 5–6)

In the field, then, interpretation becomes a task of coming to comprehend the *cultural self* by the detour of comprehending the *cultural other*. In other words, the anthropologist's understanding of the cultural other is intersubjectively constructed, using elements drawn from the cultural systems of anthropologist and informant alike. As we come to grasp the meaning of the other's cultural self, we simultaneously learn something of the meaning of our own cultural identity. Anthropologist and informant engaged in participant-observation do share one thing: the fieldwork situation itself. However, anthropologists must never develop hubris in assuming that they and their informants share complete understandings. The gulf between self and other may seem, and indeed sometimes is, unbridgeable since each is essentially situated in a different context as 'apart from' and 'a part of' the culture under study.

Anthropologist and informant find themselves in physical proximity, observing and discussing the same material activities. At first, they may talk past one another, as each describes these activities from a different perspective using a different language. However, all cultures and languages are open enough to entertain a variety of viewpoints and a variety of ways to talk about them. Continued discussion allows anthropologist and informant to search for areas of intersection for understanding and describing the same behaviour. Any intersection, however small, can form the foundation on which anthropologist and informant may then build a new intersubjective symbolic language. This process of building a bridge of understanding between self and other is what Rabinow refers to as 'the **dialectic of fieldwork**' (39). Both fieldworker and informant begin with little or nothing in the way of shared experience that could allow them to figure one another out with any accuracy. But if they are motivated to make sense of one another and willing to work together, steps toward understanding and valid interpretation—toward recognition—can be made.

Traditional fieldwork often begins with collecting data on kinship relations in the host society. A trained anthropologist comes to the field with certain ideas about kinship in mind. These ideas derive in part from the anthropologist's own experience of kinship in his or her own culture. They are also based on research and theorizing about kinship by other anthropologists. As the fieldworker begins to ask informants questions on kinship, he or she may discover that the informants have no word in their language that accurately conveys the range of meaning carried by the term *kinship*. This does not mean that the anthropologist must give up. Rather, the anthropologist must enter into the dialectic process of interpretation and translation.

The process works something like this:

- The anthropologist poses a question about kinship using the term in the informants' language that seems to come closest to kinship in meaning.
- The informants do their best to interpret the anthropologist's question in a way that makes sense to them. That is, each informant has to be reflexive, thinking about how people in his

dialectic of fieldwork The process of building a bridge of understanding between anthropologist and informant so that each can begin to understand the other.

or her society think about a certain domain of experience.

- Having formulated an answer, the informant responds to the anthropologist's question in terms he or she thinks the anthropologist will understand.
- Now it is the anthropologist's turn to interpret this response, to decide whether it carries the kind of information he or she was looking for.

In the dialectic of fieldwork, both anthropologist and informant are active agents. Each party tries to figure out what the other is trying to say. If there is goodwill on the part of both, each party also tries to provide responses that make sense to the other. As more than one anthropologist has remarked (see, e.g., Crick 1976; Rabinow 1977), anthropological fieldwork is <u>translation</u>. Translation is complicated and tricky, full of false starts and misunderstandings. Moreover,

the informant is just as actively engaged in translation as the anthropologist. As time passes and the partners in this effort learn from their mistakes and successes, their ability to communicate increases. Each participant learns more about the other: the anthropologist gains skill at asking questions that make sense to the informant, and the informant becomes more skilled at answering those questions in terms relevant to the anthropologist. The validity of this ongoing translation is anchored in the ongoing cultural activities in which both anthropologist and informant are participant-observers. Out of this mutual activity comes knowledge about the informant's culture that is meaningful to both anthropologist and informant. This is new knowledge. Knowledge of the culture is a hybrid that emerges from the collaboration of anthropologist and informant, who create a world, usually thin and fragile, of common understandings and experiences.

Informants are equally involved in this dialogue and may end up learning as much or more about

In Their Own Words

Some Biased Remarks on Interpretism

Contemporary anthropologists come from many places other than Canada or Europe. Anthropologist Roberto da Matta explores what it means for him to be a Brazilian anthropologist working in Brazil.

In order to grasp deep motivations in ethnographic styles, one has to deal with how Natives are represented as 'others'—as different, as distinct—in divergent national contexts. In Brazil, the 'other' is incarnated by a small Native population, scattered in the empty Amazon and Central Brazil, a population generically called by the name 'Índio' (Indian). But the 'Indian' is not alone, for with the category 'Negro' they form the basis of a singular and intriguing view of the immediate human diversity for Brazilians. The 'Negro' (who is fundamentally the ex-slave) is an intrinsic element of Brazilian social structure, haunting with his massive presence the 'whiteness' of a bourgeois lifestyle. The

'Indian' is an outsider, giving rise to the romantic fantasies of the noble savage who has to be either isolated and protected from the evils of civilization or be eliminated from the national landscape for incapacity to take part in modern progress.

In this context, to be with 'Indians' is, for a Brazilian anthropologist, more than having the opportunity of living with another humanity. It is also to have the privilege of getting in touch with a mythical other. And by doing so, have the honour of being the one to overcome all manner of discomforts in order to describe a new way of life in the midst of Brazilian civilization. Thus, for Brazilian anthropologists, 'to be there' is also an opportunity of being a witness to the way of life of a different society. This is particularly true when that way of life runs the risk of succumbing to a contact situation that is brutally unequal in political terms.

Source: da Matta, Roberto. 1994. 'Some Biased Remarks on Interpretism', in *Assessing Cultural Anthropology*, ed. Robert Borofsky (New York: McGraw-Hill), 119–32.

anthropologists as anthropologists learn about them. But it is important to emphasize that in field situations the dialogue is initiated by anthropologists. They come to the field with their own sets of issues and concerns, which are determined not by the field situation but by the discipline of anthropology itself (see Karp and Kendall 1982: 254). This continues to be true even when anthropologists find that their research project is changing direction in response to developments at the field site. Furthermore, when anthropologists are finished with a particular research project, they are free to break off the dialogue with informants and resume discussions with fellow professionals. The only link between these two sets of dialogues—between particular anthropologists and the people with whom they work, and among anthropologists in general—are the anthropologists themselves.

Professional colleagues have relied on fieldworkers to speak for informants, traditionally assuming that informants would not speak for themselves. In recent years, however, members of Indigenous societies have begun to speak powerfully on their own behalf, as political advocates, lawyers, organizers, and professionals. Although language and other barriers may prohibit informants from speaking directly to an audience of professional scholars, their voices and messages are important (see Evans 2004). Nonetheless, fieldwork involves differences of power, most particularly when the anthropologist is seen as representative of the dominating culture. This is difficult to escape in the present circumstances of globalization. There is, then, a heavy burden of responsibility on researchers because the privilege of being gifted with the knowledge of the other, and the rights the other confers through that gift, comes with serious obligations. As noted at the beginning of this chapter, anthropologists are accountable not only to their informants but also to the discipline of anthropology that has its own theoretical and practical concerns and ways of reasoning about ethnographic data. For these reasons, Appadurai calls for a 'deparochialization of the research ethic' involving a collaboration with colleagues outside centres of dominance (mostly Western academic and government institutions) who often lack the kinds of institutional resources and professional experience that Western scholars take for granted. With the right support, such colleagues could become equal partners in 'a conversation about research' in which they 'bring their own ideas of what counts as new knowledge', as well as their own ideas of how to measure the researcher's accountability, to those among whom they work (2002: 281).

Consider da Matta's 'Situation of the Brazilian Anthropologist' and the serious resonances for Canadian researchers when confronting the 'mythical other'. As inheritors of *terra nullius*, the colonial concept of the 'empty land' (here substitute McGregor's 'view from the fort' [1985] for da Matta's 'empty Amazon and Central Brazil'), we have engaged the 'mythical other' and the 'noble savage' as we studied 'new' cultures while essentially seeing them as representative of an earlier stage of human evolution. Here was a serious area of concern, an area of self-examination with respect to professional and personal ethics (see Liebersohn 1994). But is there more to be done than being a 'witness'? Hastrup and Elsas (1990) address this issue. From their fieldwork with the Arhuacos of the Sierra Nevada of northern Colombia, they came to examine the concept of the anthropologist as advocate, noting:

> Even this is ambiguous in anthropology, however, because in anthropological discourse there is no sharp division between 'self' and 'other'; these are categories of thought rather than objective entities. The anthropological advocate therefore cannot claim to plead the cause of 'an Other' in any direct manner; . . . There is a continuum of anthropological interest from the countering of Western, colonial ethnocentrism by providing systematic knowledge about other cultures to the active pleading of the cause of a particular ethnic group vis-à-vis a government (Van Esterik 1985). In principle this continuum leaves no anthropologist untouched by the problem of advocacy. . . . When anthropologists use their knowledge for a particular cause, they can be charged with furthering 'the colonial processes still at work by stealing crucial decisions and political initiatives from Indigenous peoples' (Henriksen 1985: 124–5). . . . Anthropology is, so to speak, born of the cultural encounter, and anthropological practice always involves some kind of representation of 'others'. There is, however, an inherent dilemma in anthropological advocacy. Anthropology is concerned with context rather than interest, while advocacy means making a choice among interests within the context. (1990: 302, 303, 307)

The Dialectic of Fieldwork: Examples

Nita Kumar is an anthropologist from Delhi, India, who chose to do fieldwork in her own country, in a region very different from the one where she grew up:

> Banaras was such a mystery to me when I arrived there in 1981, ironically *because* I was an Indian and expected to have a privileged insight into it. In fact, from Banaras I was *thrice* removed: through my education and upbringing, than which there is no greater molder of attitudes; by language and linguistic culture; and by region and regional culture. (1992: 15)

Although her social connections smoothed the way for her in official circles, she had no special advantage when trying to make contact with the artisans in Banaras whose way of life interested her (Figure 2.4).

Finding informants and establishing a rapport with them has always been seen as an indispensable first step in fieldwork, but there are no foolproof procedures that guarantee success. In her fieldwork memoir, *Friends, Brothers, and Informants* (1992), Kumar shares the four failed attempts she made to contact weavers. In her first attempt, the weavers turned out to have well-established ties to rickshaw pullers and taxi drivers who regularly brought tourists to visit their shop and buy souvenirs. Not wishing to become just another business contact, she left. Her second attempt was with the Muslim owner of a weaving establishment whose suspicions of her motives caused her to turn elsewhere. Her third attempt was made through a sari salesman who took her to a market where silk weavers sold their wares. Unfortunately for her, he would periodically announce to all assembled who she was and invite weavers to come up and speak with her, a procedure she found deeply embarrassing. Her fourth attempt followed the accidental discovery that two members of a family selling firecrackers were also weavers. When she was invited to see one brother's loom, however, she grew 'uncomfortable with all the

Figure 2.4 Prayer and worship on the Ganges, Banaras, India.

Figure 2.5 Summer in the traditional lands of the Utku Inuit in Nunavut.

obvious evidence of bachelor existence and their readiness to welcome [her] into it. . . . [She] just went away and never came back' (99). On her fifth attempt, a silk-yarn merchant introduced her to weavers living in a government-subsidized housing project next to his house. In the home of a weaver named Shaukatullah, surrounded by members of his family, she finally found a setting in which she felt welcome and able to do her work. 'In a matter of weeks I was given the status of a daughter of Shaukatullah' (105). That status was not only important to Kumar's research, but it was also a congenial status to her, one with which she was familiar.

Jean Briggs is an anthropologist who was also adopted by a family of informants. Briggs worked among the Utkuhikhalingmiut (Utku, for short), an Inuit group in Canada (see Figure 2.5; see also EthnoProfile 2.1: Utkuhikhalingmiut [Utku Inuit]). There were several steps her informants took in order to figure her out once she took on the role of daughter in the home of her new 'father', Inuttiaq, and 'mother', Allaq: 'From the moment that the adoption was settled, I was "Inuttiaq's daughter" in the camp. [They] drilled me in the use of kin terms appropriate to my position, just as they drilled [Inuttiaq's] three-year-old daughter, who was learning to speak' (1980: 46). The context of their interactions had clearly changed as a result of the adoption, and Briggs's family had new expectations both of Briggs and of themselves: 'Allaq, and especially Inuttiaq . . . more and more attempted

to assimilate me into a proper adult parent–daughter relationship. I was expected to help with the household work . . . and I was expected to obey unquestioningly when Inuttiaq told me to do something. . . . Inevitably, conflicts, covert but pervasive, developed' (47).

Briggs found herself feeling increasingly uncomfortable and began to analyze her situation. She began to realize that part of the problem had to do with differences between her ideas of how parents ought to relate to their daughters and Utku beliefs on this matter. She also experienced contradictions between her roles as daughter and anthropologist. The dialectic of fieldwork aided her understanding of the meaning of those roles in her own culture. Moreover, Briggs was not the only person who had to be reflexive. Her Utku informants were forced to reconsider how they had been dealing with her since her arrival. As she was able to reconstruct it, their understanding of her went through three stages. At first, her informants thought she was strange,

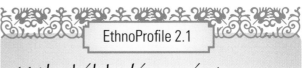

EthnoProfile 2.1

Utkuhikhalingmiut
(Utku Inuit)

Region: North America

Nation: Canada (Nunavut); The area between Franklin Lake and Chantrey Inlet (Tariunnuaq) on the east side of Adelaide Peninsula

Language: Utkuhikhalingmiut, or the Utku Inuit (*the people of the place where there is soapstone*), are speakers of the dialect of Inuktitut called Utkuhiksalingmiutitut

Population: 35 (1970)

Environment: Tundra

Livelihood: Seasonal fishing, hunting, and gathering

Political organization: Communal, with hunting territories

For more information: Briggs, Jean. 1970. *Never in Anger: Portrait of an Eskimo Family* (Cambridge, MA: Harvard University Press); 2000. 'Emotions Have Many Faces: Inuit Lessons', *Anthropologica 42*, 2

anomalous. After her adoption, they saw her as educable. But when a communication breakdown occurred, they concluded that she was 'uneducable in important ways . . . a defective person' (60–1). Unlike Kumar, Briggs found that assuming the role of daughter was uncomfortable. While it initially provided her with an opportunity to 'fit into' the community she was studying, it also posed challenges to the very continuation of her fieldwork.

Briggs's experience among the Utku illustrates how, despite strenuous efforts at mutual understanding and translation, the dialectic of fieldwork is not always smooth and how, despite one's best efforts, the ethnographer may fail to perceive how the same behaviour in different cultural circumstances can be interpreted differently. Briggs understood from her informants that anger was dangerous and must never be shown. She also became aware of the various ways her informants diverted or diffused angry feelings. Nevertheless, she remained ignorant of the full power of this value in Utku culture until she found herself having seriously violated it.

A few summers before Briggs's arrival, sportsmen from Canada and the United States began to fly into the inlet where her informants lived. Once there, they borrowed canoes belonging to the Utku. Although there had at one time been several usable canoes in the community, only two remained when Briggs arrived. That summer some sportsmen borrowed one canoe but ran it onto a rock. They then asked the Utkus if they could borrow the remaining canoe, which happened to belong to Inuttiaq.

Briggs was annoyed that their carelessness had led to the ruin of one of the last two good canoes. Because canoes are used for getting food and are not pleasure craft, the loss had serious economic consequences for her informants. When the outsiders asked to use the last canoe afloat, Briggs 'exploded'. She lectured the sportsmen about their carelessness and insensitivity and explained how important canoes were to the Utku. Then, remembering Inuttiaq's often-repeated admonition never to lend his canoe, she told the sportsmen that the owner of the remaining canoe did not want to lend it. When Inuttiaq insisted that the canoe be lent, she was not only surprised, she was shocked.

But this was only the beginning. Briggs discovered that following her outburst, her informants seemed to turn against *her* rather than the sportsmen. 'I had spoken

unbidden and in anger. . . . Punishment was a subtle form of ostracism. . . . I was isolated. It was as though I were not there. . . . But . . . I was still treated with the most impeccable semblance of solicitude' (56–7). Briggs discovered just how much at odds her breaking point was with Utku cultural style. This breach might well have ended her fieldwork if a Westernized Utku friend, Ikayuqtuq, had not come to her rescue. 'I had written my version of the story to Ikayuqtuq, had told her about my attempt to protect the Utku from the impositions of the *kaplunas* [white men] and asked her if she could help to explain my behaviour to the Eskimos' (58). Ikayuqtuq did write to Allaq and Inuttiaq, although the letter did not arrive until three months later. During that time, Briggs seemed to be frozen out of Utku society.

Once the letter arrived, everything changed. Briggs's friend had found a way to translate her intentions into terms that Allaq and Inuttiaq could understand. As Briggs recalls, 'the effect was magical'. Inuttiaq began to tell the others what a dangerous task Briggs had taken on to defend the Utkus against the white men. The ice melted. And Briggs knew that relationships had been restored (and perhaps deepened) when Inuttiaq called her *daughter* once again.

The struggle that ensued when Briggs tried to be a good Utku daughter stems in part from what happens when ethnographers struggle to keep the full expression of their own cultural selves in check, in an effort to avoid offending their informants. The situation is complicated by the fieldworker's imperfect awareness of the sort of behaviour that is likely to offend informants. As a result, the fieldworkers have frequently felt that their motto ought to be 'The informant is always right.' Many fieldworkers therefore forbid themselves to express anger, disgust, or disagreement. But this behaviour is likely to cause problems. After all, what sort of person is always smiling, never angry, without opinions? Anthropologists who refuse to challenge or be challenged by their informants dehumanize both themselves and their informants. Clearly, it takes a good deal of diplomacy to walk the fine line between ethnocentrism and depersonalization. Sometimes, as in Briggs's case, this may not be possible, and the fieldwork itself may be put in jeopardy.

These examples of ethnographic fieldwork illustrate, each in its own way, the effects of reflexive awareness on the production of anthropological knowledge by means of participant-observation rooted in the dialectic of fieldwork. These commitments also affect the kinds of ethnographies anthropologists write. Unlike earlier ethnographies committed to the positivist approach, in reflexive ethnographies the presence, personalities, and voices of ethnographers and informants alike become vivid elements. All these accounts highlight the complications and misunderstandings that are a regular part of the dialectic of fieldwork. This seems to mark a clear advance over positivistic ethnographies. As a result, each account can lay claim to strong objectivity.

In other ways, however, modern fieldwork is very much an inheritance from Malinowski and Boas. That is, all ethnographers engage in what remains the most common form of fieldwork in anthropology: 'the intensively-focused-upon single site of ethnographic observation and participation' (Marcus 1995: 96). Much valuable work of this kind continues to be done. But changes in the world as a whole in recent decades have led many anthropologists to undertake fieldwork projects that include more than a single site.

Multi-sited Fieldwork

Some of the factors pushing toward multi-sited fieldwork came from within anthropology and related social sciences as they responded to wider social and political changes. In 1974, sociologist Immanuel Wallerstein published a highly influential two-volume study called *The Modern World System* in which he argued that the rise and expansion of the European capitalist economy between 1450 and 1750 had incorporated vast regions of the world into a world system held together by the market. This had important implications for anthropologists, for he argued that many parts of the world where anthropologists worked had been remade to occupy specialized niches within the capitalist world system. Thus, anthropological attempts to account for the current beliefs and practices of small-scale societies in these parts of the world could not ignore the historical impact upon them of world-system influences such as European colonialism.

Wallerstein's work was followed by anthropologist Eric Wolf's monumental *Europe and the People without History* (1982). Wolf's title is to be taken ironically: the non-European people about whom he wrote were, in his view, very much involved in the history of European expansion. Tracing some of the same world-system interconnections discussed by Wallerstein, Wolf regularly abandoned the abstract view of the overall system in order to focus on the historical ethnographic details of specific societies affected by that system. Thus, in Wolf's discussion, Indigenous peoples of North America appear as actors creatively coping with the challenge of the fur trade and European settlement, developing some of their characteristic forms of social organization.

Wallerstein's and Wolf's influence on ethnographers was profound. Marcus notes that single-site fieldwork continued, but it was now conceived from the perspective of the world system (1995: 96). Anthropologists began to supplement their own data-gathering with archival research that allowed them to situate the society they encountered historically, and they began to rethink existing social arrangements and cultural understandings as the products of *active response* to outside pressures rather than as timeless practices. Such work reanimated their awareness of the *lack* of isolation of the societies they studied, both in the past and in the present, and reinforced their awareness of their informants' agency that had been emphasized in the reflexive approach. The result was that neat boundaries between particular societies and the larger world system, of which they were parts, began to dissolve as ethnographers were contextualizing their own field data in the context of places and processes that stretched far beyond their original field site. By the early 1990s, after the break-up of the Soviet Union, the somewhat successful move of capitalism into China, and the extraordinary surge of migrants around the world because of war and economic dislocation, all traditional boundaries seemed on the verge of dissolution. This is more so the case as we move into the second decade of the twenty-first century. Fundamentalist activists, frequently described and actualized as terrorists, attempt to redefine political, ethnic, linguistic, economic, and religious boundaries while Western capitalists work at actualizing their 'bottom lines', expanding their access to dwindling resources and creating markets for 'new and improved products'. (Note Benjamin R. Barber, *In Their Own Words*.)

Thus in the years since Wallerstein's world system was proposed, the 'system' no longer seems so systemic, and the attention of many anthropologists has shifted to mapping the disconnected, fragmentary cultural processes in a disorganized, globalized world. These are the issues with which all contemporary ethnographic fieldwork must somehow come to terms.

How do you proceed with fieldwork then? For increasing numbers of anthropologists, the answer is **multi-sited ethnography**, which focuses on cultural processes that are not contained by social, ethnic, religious, or national boundaries. The ethnographer follows the process from site to site, often doing fieldwork in sites and with persons that were traditionally never subject to ethnographic analysis. As Marcus describes it, 'Multi-sited research is designed around chains, paths, threads, conjunctions, or juxtapositions of locations' as ethnographers trace 'a complex cultural phenomenon . . . that turns out to be contingent and malleable as one traces it' (1995: 105–6). Like all good researchers working on complex issues, multisited ethnographers follow *people*, *things*, *metaphors*, *plots*, and *lives* (107).

The Effects of Fieldwork

The Effects of Fieldwork on Informants

Fieldwork changes both anthropologists and informants. What kinds of effects can the fieldwork experience have on informants? Anthropologists have not always been able to report on this as the effects may take many years to manifest. In other cases, it becomes clear in the course of fieldwork that the anthropologist's presence and questions have made the informants aware of their own cultural selves in new ways that are both surprising and uncomfortable.

Rabinow, who worked in Morocco, recalled some cases in which his informants' new reflexivity led to unanticipated consequences (Figure 2.6). One key

In Their Own Words

Jihad vs McWorld

Political scientist Benjamin R. Barber describes the conflict between tribalism and globalism.

Just beyond the horizon of current events lie two possible political futures—both bleak, neither democratic. The first is a retribalization of large swaths of humankind by war and bloodshed: a threatened Lebanonization of national states in which culture is pitted against culture, people against people, tribe against tribe—a Jihad in the name of a hundred narrowly conceived faiths against every kind of interdependence, every kind of artificial social cooperation and civic mutuality. The second is being borne in on us by the onrush of economic and ecological forces that demand integration and uniformity and that mesmerize the world with fast music, fast computers, and fast food—with MTV, Macintosh, and McDonalds pressing nations into one commercially homogenous global network: one McWorld tied together by technology, ecology, communications, and commerce. The planet is falling precipitantly apart *AND* coming reluctantly together at the very same moment.

These two tendencies are sometimes visible in the same countries at the same instant: thus Yugoslavia, clamouring just recently to join the New Europe, is exploding into fragments; India is trying to live up to its reputation as the world's largest integral democracy while powerful new fundamentalist parties like the Hindu nationalist Bharatiya Janata Party, along with nationalist assassins, are imperilling its hard-won unity. States are breaking up or joining up: the Soviet Union has disappeared almost overnight, its parts forming new unions with one another or with like-minded nationalities in neighbouring states. The old interwar national state based on territory and political sovereignty looks to be a mere transitional development.

The tendencies of what I am here calling the forces of Jihad and the forces of McWorld operate with equal strength in opposite directions, the one driven by parochial hatreds, the other by universalizing markets, the one recreating ancient sub-national and ethnic borders from within, the other making national borders porous from without. They have one thing in common: neither offers much hope to citizens looking for practical ways to govern themselves democratically. If the global future is to pit Jihad's centrifugal whirlwind against McWorld's centripetal black hole, the outcome is unlikely to be democratic. . . .

Source: Barber, Benjamin R. 1992. 'Jihad vs McWorld', *Atlantic Monthly* 269, 3 (Mar.): 53–65, available at: <http://www.globalissues.org/Geopolitics/WarOnTerror/McWorld.asp>.

Figure 2.6 Paul Rabinow's reflections on his fieldwork experiences in a Moroccan village much like this one led him to reconceptualize the nature of anthropological fieldwork.

informant, Malik, agreed to help Rabinow compile a list of landholdings and other possessions of the villagers of Sidi Lahcen Lyussi (see Map 2.2). As a first step in tracing the economic status of the middle stratum in society, Rabinow suggested that Malik list his own possessions. Malik appeared to be neither rich nor poor; in fact, he considered himself 'not well-off'.

> As we began to make a detailed list of his possessions, he became touchy and defensive. . . . It was clear that he was not as impoverished as he had portrayed himself. . . . This was confusing and troubling for him. . . . Malik began to see that there was a disparity between his self-image and my classification system. The emergence of this 'hard' data before his eyes and through his own efforts was highly disconcerting for him. (1977: 117–18)

Malik's easy understanding of himself and his world had been disrupted, and he could not ignore the disruption. He would either have to change his self-image or find some way to assimilate this new information about himself into his old self-image. In the end Malik managed to reaffirm his conclusion that he was not well-off by arguing that wealth lay not in material possessions alone. Although he might be rich in material goods, his son's health was bad, his own father was dead, he was responsible for his mother and unmarried brothers, and he had to be constantly vigilant in order to prevent his uncle from stealing his land (117–19).

The Effects of Fieldwork on the Researcher

What does it feel like to be in the field, trying to figure out the workings of an unfamiliar way of life? What are the consequences of this experience for the fieldworker? Graduate students in anthropology who have

multi-sited ethnography Ethnographic research on cultural processes that are not contained by social, ethnic, religious, or national boundaries in which the ethnographer follows the process from site to site, often doing fieldwork in sites and with persons that were traditionally never subject to ethnographic analysis.

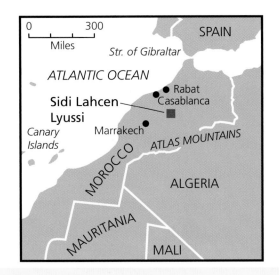

Map 2.2 Sidi Lahcen Lyussi

not yet been in the field often develop an idealized image of field experience: at first, the fieldworker is a bit disoriented and potential informants are suspicious, but uncertainty soon gives way to understanding and trust as the anthropologist's good intentions are made known and accepted. The fieldworker succeeds in establishing a rapport. In fact, the fieldworker becomes so well loved and trusted, so thoroughly accepted, that he or she is accepted as an equal and allowed access to the culture's secrets. Presumably, all this happens as a result of the personal attributes of the fieldworker. If you have what it takes, you will be taken in and treated like one of the family; if this doesn't happen, you are obviously cut out for some other kind of work.

But much more than the anthropologist's personality is responsible for successful fieldwork. Establishing a rapport with the people being studied is an achievement of anthropologist and informants *together*. Acceptance is problematic even for the most gifted fieldworkers. After all, fieldworkers are usually outsiders with no personal ties to the communities they research. According to Karp and Kendall (1982), it is not just naive to think that the locals will accept you as one of them without any difficulty, but it is also bad science. It is remarkable that anthropologists—trained by experienced fieldworkers—can still be seduced by such an idealized image.

Rabinow recalled the relationship he formed with his first Moroccan informant, a man called Ibrahim,

whom he hired to teach him Arabic. Rabinow and Ibrahim seemed to get along well together, and, because of the language lessons, they saw each other a great deal, leading Rabinow to think of Ibrahim as a friend. When Rabinow planned a trip to another city, Ibrahim offered to go along as a guide and stay with relatives. This only confirmed Ibrahim's friendliness in Rabinow's eyes. But things changed once they arrived at their destination. Ibrahim told Rabinow that the relatives with whom he was to stay did not exist, that he had no money, and that he expected Rabinow to pay for his hotel room. When Rabinow was unable to do so, however, Ibrahim paid for it himself. Rabinow was shocked and hurt by this experience, and his relationship with Ibrahim was forever altered. Rabinow remarks: 'Basically I had been conceiving of him as a friend because of the seeming personal relationship we had established. But Ibrahim, a lot less confusedly, had basically conceptualized me as a resource. He was not unjustly situating me with the other Europeans with whom he had dealings' (1977: 29).

Rabinow's experience illustrates what he calls the *shock of otherness*. Fieldwork institutionalizes this shock. Having to anticipate culture shock at any and every turn, anthropologists sometimes find that fieldwork takes on a tone that is anything but pleasant and sunny. For many anthropologists, what characterizes fieldwork, at least in its early stages, is the anxiety of an isolated individual with nothing familiar to turn to, no common sense on which to rely, and no relationships that can be taken for granted.

The move to multi-sited fieldwork can bring additional anxieties. Marcus (1995) notes that the special value of single-sited fieldwork comes from its ability to offer insights that can only come from long-term, intense involvement in a single locale, which would seem to suggest that it is not the kind of research strategy best suited to investigating 'global' phenomena. However, attempting to carry out multi-sited fieldwork appears to dilute the intensity of involvement, depth of understanding, and insight fieldworkers develop with their informants in each site studied. Further, some activist anthropologists who use their ethnography to draw public attention to the plight of those whose lives they study see multi-sited research as undercutting their political commitments to their primary informants.

Marcus recognizes these drawbacks but does not see them as fatal. Even multi-sited fieldwork is usually based in one primary site; its major innovation involves doing fieldwork in additional sites and bringing information from all these sites together in a single study that argues for their relationships 'on the basis of first-hand ethnographic research' (100). However, concerns about the way multi-sited ethnography may dilute one's ability to adopt an unequivocal position as defender of a single group is an issue with no easy resolution. Multi-sited ethnography is a form of fieldwork that highlights the multi-centred, complex conflicts of the contemporary world in which clear-cut 'good guys' and 'bad guys' are increasingly hard to identify. When individuals legitimately claim, or are accorded, multiple identities, some of which conflict, innocent 'identity politics' become impossible (Haraway 1991: 192). For example, to defend the views of working-class women in a single site is to downplay or ignore the points of view of unemployed women; it may gloss over differences *among* those women based on class, 'race', ethnicity, or religion, and it ignores entirely the points of view of men. Moreover, the spread of industrial capitalism across the globe means that the growth of an urban immigrant workforce in one place is probably connected to a lack of employment somewhere else. Multi-sited ethnography offers the possibility of juxtaposing more than one place, more than one time, and more than one point of view, thereby bringing to light connections among them that would otherwise remain unsuspected.

Re-studies (same place, different time; thus diachronically multi-sited) of traditional societies alert us to the nature of our changing world. For example, there is a

> break in the ability to write about such traditional topics as religion as if they were a stable source of values and social integration. Werbner's (1991) and Honwana's (1996) accounts of the attempt to reshape the social integrative uses of witchcraft in southern Africa in the aftermath of civil war are poignant examples. So, too, are Hutchinson's (1996) account of the Nuer after years of civil war trying to deal with new modalities of killing that cannot be publicly acknowledged and Daniel's (1996) accounts of the psychodynamic inability to recall to memory the witnessing of the torture of kin and friends in Sri Lanka. (Fischer 1999: 471)

Indeed, Fischer challenges us to go beyond the multi-sited research modality—to go to the heart of the changes in our world—when he calls attention to three key overlapping arenas that should be of concern to anthropologists:

(1) the centrality of science and technology;
(2) decolonization, post-colonialism, and the reconstruction of societies after social trauma; and
(3) the role of the new electronic and visual media (458).

He notes that contemporary ethnographic practice must be part of reworking traditional notions of comparative work for a world that is increasingly aware of difference.

> No longer is it possible to speak of modernity in the singular. . . . [the term] *alternative modernities* acknowledges the multiple, different configurations that modernities have taken and the recognition that modernization and globalization are not homogenizing processes. . . . It challenges old area studies frameworks, as well as old-style social theory, and requires re-studies of canonic anthropological societies, to provide a sense of the transformations of the past century, as well as new ways of doing fieldwork, engaging colleagues and interlocutors in new relationships. . . . (470–2)

Examples of this kind of ethnography will appear throughout the book and are the core of the discussions to follow.

The Humanizing Effects of Fieldwork

Anthropological knowledge is the fruit of reflexivity produced by the mutual attempts of anthropologist and informant to understand each other. As a result, anthropological knowledge ought to be able to provide answers to questions about human nature, human society, and human history. Good ethnography offers readers the extraordinary opportunity to experience 'the others' as human beings while learning about their lives. This privileged position is an experience that comes neither easily nor automatically. It must be cultivated, and it requires co-operation between, and effort from, one's informants and oneself. We have made an important first step if we can come to recognize, as Rabinow did, that 'there is no primitive. There are other [people] living other lives' (1977: 151). Everyone lives in their own modernity—their own place—in this world we share.

Multi-sited ethnography can complicate the picture by simultaneously offering rich, fieldwork-based

In Their Own Words

The Skills of the Anthropologist

Anthropologists cannot avoid taking their own cultural and theoretical frameworks into the field. However, as Stephen Gudeman observes, fieldwork draws their attention in unanticipated directions, making them aware of new phenomena that constantly challenge those frameworks.

According to the accepted wisdom, poets should be especially facile with language and stretch our vision with freshly cut images. Historians, with their knowledge of past events, offer a wise and sweeping view of human change and continuities. Physical scientists, who have analytical yet creative minds, bring us discoveries and insights about the natural world.

What about anthropologists? Have we any finely honed talents and gifts for the world?

Because anthropology is the study of human life, the anthropologist needs to know a little something about everything—from psychology to legal history to ecology. Our field equipment is primitive, for we rely mainly on the eye, the ear, and the tongue. Because ethnographers carry few tools to the field and the tools they have can hardly capture the totality of the situation, the background and talents of the researcher strongly determine what is 'seen' and how it is understood. But the field experience itself has a special impact, too. I studied economic practices in Panama because I was trained to do so, but the field research forced me to alter all the notions I had been taught. Most of them were useless! Anthropologists try to open themselves up to every facet of their field situation and to allow its richness to envelop them. In this, the tasks of the anthropologist are very unlike those of

the normal laboratory scientist: the anthropologist can have no predefined hypothesis and testing procedures. The best equipment an ethnographer can possess is a 'good ear' and patience to let the 'data talk'.

This is not all. In the field, anthropologists carry out intense and internal conversations with themselves. Every observation, whether clearly seen or dimly realized, must be brought to consciousness, shuffled about, and questioned. Only by recognizing and acknowledging their own incomprehension can anthropologists generate new questions and lines of inquiry. In the solitude of the field, the anthropologist must try to understand the limits of her or his knowledge, have the courage to live with uncertainty, and retain the ambition to seize on openings to insight.

But field studies constitute only a part of the total research process. Once home, the field notes have to be read and reread, put aside, and then rearranged. The anthropologist is a pattern seeker, believing that within the data human designs are to be found. The task is like solving a puzzle, except that there is no fixed solution and the puzzle's pieces keep changing their shapes! With work and insight, however, a picture—an understanding or an explanation—begins to emerge.

Eventually, the results of all these efforts are conveyed to others, and so anthropologists also need to have expository skills and persuasive powers, for they have to convince others of their picture and their viewpoint about how cultures and social lives are put together.

Source: Gudeman, Stephen. 1990. 'The Skills of the Anthropologist', guest editorial in *Cultural Anthropology: A Perspective on the Human Condition*, 2nd edn, eds Emily Schultz and Robert Lavenda (St Paul: West), 458–9.

portraits of 'other people living other lives' and by demonstrating, moreover, that members of these groups share important cultural commitments. In the best ethnographic writing we can grasp the humanity—the greed, compassion, suffering, pleasure, confusion, and ambivalence—of the people who have granted the anthropologist the privilege of living with them for an extended period of time. It may also become more natural for us to talk about cultural differences by saying 'not "they", not "we", not "you", but some of us are thus and so' (Smith 1982: 70).

The Production of Anthropological Knowledge

If anthropological knowledge is the intersubjective creation of fieldworker and informant together, so too are the facts that anthropologists collect. The dialectic of fieldwork, however, often involves extended discussions about just what counts as 'the facts'. We can follow anthropologist David Hess and define **fact** as a widely accepted observation, a taken-for-granted item of common knowledge (1997: 101–2). Ethnographers' field notebooks will be full of facts collected from different informants, as well as facts based on their own cultural experiences and professional training. But what happens when facts from these various sources contradict one another?

Facts turn out to be complex phenomena. On the one hand, they assert that a particular state of affairs about the world is true. On the other hand, reflexive analysis has taught us that *who* tells us that *x* is a fact is an extremely important thing to know. This is because facts do not speak for themselves. They speak only when they are interpreted and placed in a context of meaning that makes them intelligible. What constitutes a cultural fact is ambiguous. Anthropologists and informants can disagree; anthropologists can disagree among themselves; informants can disagree among themselves. The facts of anthropology exist neither in the culture of the anthropologist nor in the culture of the informant. 'Anthropological facts are cross-cultural because they are made across cultural boundaries' (Rabinow 1977: 152). In short, facts are not just out there waiting for someone to come along and pick them up. They are made and remade

- in the field,
- when fieldworkers re-examine field notes and reflect on the field experience,
- when the fieldworkers write about their experiences or discuss them with other anthropologists, and
- when fieldwork is redone to mark the changes that have occurred.

For Bradburd, fieldwork begins with 'being there'. But simply being there is not enough. As he puts it,

> my experiences among the Komachi shaped my understanding of them, and that part of field experience consists of a constant process of being brought up short, of having expectations confounded, of being forced to think very hard about what is happening, right now, with me and them, let alone the thinking and rethinking about those experiences when they have—sometimes mercifully—passed. (1998: 161–2; see Map 2.3)

After all, fieldwork is field*work*—there are notes to be taken, interviews to be carried out, observations and interpretations to be made. There is also the

Map 2.3 Komachi

transformation of the experience of being there into what Bradburd calls 'elements of an understanding that is at once incomplete and impossible to complete, but also wonderfully capable of being improved' (164). According to Wolcott, it is what ethnographers do with data—

> making considered generalizations about how members of a group tend to speak and act, warranted generalizations appropriate for collectivities of people rather than the usual shoot-from-the-hip stereotyping adequate for allowing us to achieve our individual purposes (1999: 262)

—that makes fieldwork experience different from just experience and turns it into ethnography. Multi-sited fieldwork elaborates upon and further complicates this experience because it involves being 'here and there'. In the course of the movement from site to site, new facts come into view that would otherwise never be known, adding a further layer to the thinking and rethinking that all fieldwork sets in motion. What happens if you

> **fact** A widely accepted observation, a taken-for-granted item of common knowledge. Facts do not speak for themselves; only when they are interpreted and placed in a context of meaning do they become intelligible.

find that your activism in support of the urban poor at one site works against the interests of the Indigenous people you have supported at a different site? 'In conducting multi-sited research,' Marcus says, 'one finds oneself with all sorts of cross-cutting commitments' that are not easily resolved. Unlike positivists, however, who might have found 'refuge in being a detached anthropological scholar', Marcus suggests that the multi-sited journey will itself shape the 'circumstantial activism' of ethnographers doing fieldwork in a variety of sites. 'If that sounds contradictory or ambivalent, it is nevertheless faithful to key features of the contemporary world in which we all live' (1995).

Anthropological Knowledge as Open-ended

We have suggested that there is no such thing as purely objective knowledge and that when human beings are both the subject and the object of study, we must speak in terms of reflexivity rather than objectivity. Cultivating reflexivity allows us to produce less distorted views of human nature and the human condition, and yet we remain human beings interpreting the lives of other human beings. We can never escape from our humanity to some point of view that would allow us to see human existence and human experience from the outside. Instead, we must rely on our common humanity and our interpretive powers to show us the parts of our nature that can be made visible.

Since there truly is 'no primitive', no subsection of humanity that is radically different in nature or in capacity from the anthropologists who study it, then the ethnographic record of anthropological knowledge is perhaps best understood as a vast commentary on human possibility. As with all commentaries, it depends on an original text—in this case, human experience. But that experience is ambiguous, speaking with many voices, capable of supporting more than one interpretation. Growth of anthropological knowledge is no different, then, from the growth of human self-understanding in general. It ought to contribute to the domain of human wisdom that concerns who we are as a species, where we have come from, and where we may be going.

Like all commentaries, the ethnographic record is and must be unfinished: human beings are open systems, human history continues, and problems and their possible solutions change. There is no one true version of human life. For anthropologists, the true version of human life consists of all versions of human life.

This is a sobering possibility. It makes it appear that 'the anthropologist is condemned to a greater or lesser degree of failure' in even trying to understand another culture (Basham 1978: 299). Informants would be equally condemned to never fully know their own way of life. And the positivistic orientation resists any admission that the understanding of anything is impossible. But total pessimism does not seem warranted. We may never know everything, but it does not follow that our efforts can teach us nothing. 'Two of the fundamental qualities of humanity are the capacity to understand one another and the capacity to be understood. Not fully certainly. Yet not negligibly, certainly. . . . There is no person on earth that I can fully understand. There is and has been no person on earth that I cannot understand at all' (Smith 1982: 68–9).

Moreover, as our contact with the other is prolonged and as our efforts to communicate are rewarded by the construction of intersubjective understanding, we can always learn more. Human beings are open organisms, and we have a vast ability to learn new things. This is significant, for even if we can never know everything, it does not seem that our capacities for understanding ourselves and others is likely to be exhausted any time soon. This is not only because we are open to change but also because our culture and our wider environment can change, and will continue to do so as long as human history continues. The ethnographic enterprise will never be finished since change and how it manifests within cultures is also a concern of our work.

Key Terms

Chapter Summary

1. Anthropological fieldwork traditionally involves extended periods of close contact with members of another society. This form of research is called *participant-observation.*

2. The nineteenth century saw the birth of positivistic science in Western thought. Early anthropologists who wanted to be scientific attempted to adapt positivism to their needs. They adopted a view of controlled laboratory research as the prototype of scientific investigation and attempted to apply the prototype to the field situation. In this way, highly accurate data were systematically collected in many parts of the world.

3. When human beings study other human beings, research is coloured by the context and cultural presuppositions of both the anthropologists and the people they study. If the objects of anthropology are human beings, scientific accuracy requires that we relate to them as human beings. Successful fieldwork involves anthropologists who think about the way they think about other cultures. Informants must also reflect on the way they and others in their society think and try to convey their insights to the anthropologist. This is basic to the reflexive approach to fieldwork.

4. The dialectic of fieldwork is a reflexive interchange between anthropologist and informant. It is a collaborative undertaking involving dialogue about the meaning of experience in the informant's culture. Fieldworkers and informants working together construct an intersubjective world of meaning.

5. Learning about another culture is often greatest following a rupture of communication between anthropologist and informant. Ruptures occur when current intersubjective understandings prove themselves inadequate to account for experience. A rupture always carries the possibility of bringing research to an end. But when the reasons for the rupture are explored, and explanations for it are constructed, great insights are possible.

6. In recent years, a number of anthropologists have undertaken fieldwork projects that include more than a single site in an attempt to acknowledge the lack of isolation of the societies they studied. Multi-sited ethnography focuses on cultural processes that are not contained by social, ethnic, religious, or national boundaries, and the ethnographer follows the process from site to site.

7. Fieldwork has the potential to change informants and researchers in unpredictable ways. Some anthropologists work with their informants to effect social change; however, others argue that anthropologists' main task is to clarify how people in particular places, at particular moments, engage with the world.

8. Because the world is changing and cultures are challenged by change, ethnographic practice must be part of reworking traditional notions of comparative work for a world that is increasingly aware of difference.

9. Because cultural meanings are intersubjectively constructed during fieldwork, cultural facts do not speak for themselves. They speak only when they are interpreted and placed in a context of meaning that makes them intelligible. Multi-sited fieldwork complicates this because it involves the anthropologist in cross-cutting commitments in different contexts.

10. The ethnographic record of anthropological knowledge is perhaps best understood as a vast unfinished commentary on human possibility. We may never learn all there is to know, but we can always learn more.

Critical Thinking Questions

1. Although participant-observation is considered a central methodology for ethnographical data collection, consider alternative methods anthropologists could use. How are they different from participant-observation in the type of data they are suited to?

2. Have you considered how and why you think in a specific way about people and things? When your observations are challenged, do you try to analyze how you have reached your conclusions? Now consider reflexivity and its use to the anthropologist.

3. Three modes of ethnographic fieldwork have been developed over the last hundred years: the positivist approach, the reflexive approach, and multi-sited fieldwork. What are the positive features of each approach? Would you expect different results from each?

4. Anthropological professional organizations and government-fund granting agencies have codes of conduct. Why are such moral and ethical obligations a critical part of fieldwork, specifically, and anthropology, generally?

Suggested Readings

Bradburd, Daniel. 1998. *Being There: The Necessity of Fieldwork* (Washington, DC: Smithsonian Institution Press). *An engaging personal study of how the many seemingly small details of experience during field research add up to anthropological understanding.*

Kumar, Nita. 1992. *Friends, Brothers, and Informants: Fieldwork Memoirs of Banaras* (Berkeley: University of California Press). *A moving and thought-provoking reflection on the experience of fieldwork in the author's own country but in a culture quite different from her own.*

Lévi-Strauss, Claude. 1974. *Tristes Tropiques* (New York: Pocket Books). *Originally published in French in 1955, this book (with an untranslatable title) is considered by some to be the greatest book ever written by an anthropologist (although not necessarily a great anthropology book). This is a multi-faceted work about voyaging, fieldwork, self-knowledge, philosophy, and much more. It is a challenging read in some places but highly rewarding overall.*

Liebersohn, Harry. 1994. 'Discovering Indigenous Nobility: Tocqueville, Chamisso, and Romantic Travel Writing', *American Historical Review* 99, 3 (June): 746–66. *A discussion of the development of the construct of the noble savage.*

Nurse, Andrew. n.d. '"Their Ancient Customs Are Gone": Anthropology as Cultural Process' (Mount Allison University), available at: <http://www.mta.ca/faculty/arts/canadian_studies/anurse/Draft%20Ancient%20Customs.pdf>. *Examines the cultural significance of Canadian anthropologist Marius Barbeau's representation of First Nations in his ethnographic research.*

Rabinow, Paul. 1977. *Reflections on Fieldwork in Morocco* (Berkeley: University of California Press). *An important, brief, powerfully written reflection on the nature of fieldwork. Very accessible and highly recommended.*

Salamone, Frank A. 1979. 'Epistemological Implications of Fieldwork and Their Consequences', *American Anthropologist*, New Series, 81, 1 (Mar.): 46–60. *How do we manage as both the social scientist based in specific 'approaches' and the active fieldworker where various unexpected things may arise, some seriously counter to our expectations?*

Valentine, Bettylou. 1978. *Hustling and Other Hard Work* (New York: Free Press). *An innovative, provocative study of African American inner-city life. Reads like a good novel.*

Related Websites

American Anthropological Association (AAA): http://www.aaanet.org/

Canadian Institutes of Health Research, Natural Sciences and Engineering Research Council of Canada, Social Sciences and Humanities Research Council of Canada (CIHR, NSERC, SSHRC): http://www.pre.ethics.gc.ca/

Canadian Sociology and Anthropology Association (CSAA): http://www.csaa.ca/

Chapter 3

Anthropology in History and the Explanation of Cultural Diversity

Chapter Outline

- Learning Objectives
- Capitalism, Colonialism, and 'Modernity'
- Anthropology and the Colonial Encounter
- Toward Classifying Forms of Human Society
- Key Terms

- Chapter Summary
- Critical Thinking Questions
- Suggested Readings
- Related Websites

Learning Objectives

By the end of Chapter 3, you will be able to:

- outline the nature of capitalism,
- detail the process of colonialism,
- critique the concept of modernity,
- understand the idea of a 'political economy',
- consider the role of anthropology in the colonial encounter and its analysis,

- begin to assess various classification systems and the forms of human society,
- assess an attempt at an alternative in the use of culture areas in the North American context, and
- think about post-colonial realities in a world of similarities and dissimilarities.

Central to third-century BCE Chinese scientific thought was the Five Element theory. Each element (wood, metal, fire, water, earth) fit into a relational structure that allowed it to 'conquer' its predecessor (think of the game *rock, paper, scissors* where physical characteristics define the outcome). The rationale was a logical typology situated in a circular sequence of everyday scientific facts: 'Wood conquers Earth because, presumably, when in the form of a spade, it can dig up earth; again, Metal conquers Wood since it can cut and carve it; Fire conquers Metal for it can melt or even vaporize it; Water conquers Fire because it can extinguish it; and, finally, Earth conquers Water because it can dam it and contain it' (Ronan and Needham 1978: 151). This typology was also considered significant with respect to social order and therefore it was useful for retrodiction (historical explanation) and for prediction (future planning). 'The Five Elements gradually came to be associated with every conceivable category of things in the universe that it was possible to classify in fives' (153) such as the seasons, the points of the compass, tastes, smells, numbers, kinds of musical notes, heavenly bodies, planets, weather, colours, body parts, sense organs, affective states, and human psychological functions. It also included the periods of dynastic history, the ministries of government, and the styles of government. In effect it was, as will be seen later, what anthropologists call a *key metaphor*—central to a world view. As with any apt metaphor or good scientific theory, Ronan and Needham conclude,

> these correlations met with criticism, sometimes severe, because they led to many absurdities. . . . Yet in spite of such criticisms, it seems that in the beginning

these correlations were helpful to scientific thought in China. . . . it was only when they became over-elaborate and fanciful, too far removed from the observation of Nature, that they were positively harmful. (156–7)

This resulted in a paradigm shift (Kuhn 1962). Like the Chinese sages, anthropologists in the nineteenth century first sorted human cultures into different categories based on what they believed to be their similarities and differences. Over time, the purposes and the categories have been modified in ways that reflect changes in the wider world, changing research interests among anthropologists, and critical analyses of disciplinary origins. This chapter looks at these developments.

Canadian institutions were somewhat late to the game although cultural research had been conducted in Canada since the nineteenth century. Sir Daniel Wilson (1816–92) is illustrative of this period (Figure 3.1). Later, A.G. Bailey's research of French–Indian contact (1969 [1937]) shows the mettle of what Canadian anthropology was to become. Bailey was influenced by his association with Thomas McIlwraith (Figure 3.2), who founded the first department of anthropology in Canada at the University of Toronto in 1936. Bailey's research 'prefigures . . . the development of American Indian ethnohistory' (Trigger 1975) and was special to the University of Toronto—and the Canadian—setting, finding favour with the '[American] fieldwork-orientated Boasians and the [British] social anthropologists of the 1930s' (1975). Three major anthropological schools of thought came to influence the development of Canadian anthropology: American, British, and French. Thus our proximity to the United States, our British ties, and,

Figure 3.1 Sir Daniel Wilson is considered by many the first professional scholar in Canadian archaeology and ethnography.

Figure 3.2 Thomas McIlwraith, like A.G. Bailey, was interested in ethnology and how Canadian Native peoples were affected by change.

most specifically for universities in French Canada, our French intellectual heritage were central to the process. Remembering that no tradition lives in isolation and each can influence another, this convergence may have been serendipitous for anthropology in Canada, a happy happenstance of time and place. It produced flexibility, starting with the exemplar of Bailey that has been productive for Canadian researchers.

It is the paradox of the human condition: by paying attention to some parts of the physical world and ignoring others, cultural traditions are formed. Traditions lock us into sets of relationships that we may not easily abandon. Indeed, these relationships can and do exert a determinant pressure on our future choices. Both the internal tradition of the group itself and external, sometimes unpredictable, encounters with other human groups need to be considered. It is the interplay of forces shaping human society and human history that create the dynamic of a culture. When we further situate the discipline of anthropology within the social and historical contexts that have shaped its development, we also gain a clearer understanding of the kinds of situated knowledge anthropologists have

developed. We contextualize anthropologists in their respective social and historical contexts.

Capitalism, Colonialism, and 'Modernity'

In *Europe and the People without History* (1982) Eric Wolf discusses modes of production and the relationships of peoples as **capitalism**, an economic system dominated by a supply and demand market designed to create capital and profit, emerged as a global force. Challengingly, a problem that Wolf identifies is: 'The tacit anthropological supposition that [Indigenous] people . . . are people without history', which 'amounts to the erasure of 500 years of confrontation, killing, resurrection, and accommodation' (1982: 18). If, as Wolf contends, anthropologists are the children of an imperialist/capitalist parent, what is our legacy?

capitalism An economic system dominated by a supply and demand market designed to create capital and profit.

Subsequent to the Age of Enlightenment at the height of nineteenth-century European colonial expansion, and in the division of labour between the new social sciences, anthropology was assigned 'the savage slot' as its 'field' of inquiry. In North America this meant the Indigenous inhabitants of the continent. They occupied what was characterized by Europeans as emergent borderlands along the edge of the province of the 'civilized'. These borderlands took on different properties for Euro-Americans and Euro-Canadians. For Americans it became a frontier, a battle line over which the Native 'other' would first be transported and later met with armed, face-to-face confrontation while Euro-Americans lived out their 'manifest destiny'. For the developing Euro-Canadian world view, it was an edge as well, not to a new frontier but to a vast and frightening, essentially empty wilderness. This was a wilderness where Aboriginal peoples became shadows in a land of liminality in the Canadian context. Posed by Northrop Frye as the 'riddle of unvisualized land . . .' (1971: 201), this dangerous wilderness was a place of fact and fancy seen in written descriptions of explorers and discussed as a cardinal truth in our literary tradition. Indeed, Margaret Atwood remarked that the 'central symbol . . . is undoubtedly Survival, *la Survivance . . .*' (1972: 32) and this is the survival of 'the land, the climate . . . [a] spiritual survival . . .' (33). It is McGregor's 'view from the fort' (1985: 5), the observance, without contemplative engagement, of the world beyond the safety of the Euro-Canadian enclave. This wilderness then became the 'field' of the emerging Canadian anthropology.

The themes played in North America can be seen in variations in all colonial contexts, from South America to Africa, Australia, New Zealand, the South Pacific, and Asia. Indeed, there have been ramifications felt from the colonial aspirations and Enlightenment ideas of progress held by Europeans, even into what we consider our 'modern' era. The genesis of ideas for westward expansion out of Europe dated to the reign of Elizabeth I, when Hakluyt the Younger's *Discourse of Western Planting* of 1584 (Rich 1961a: 4) presented America as a potential source of fresh resources and a distant place to effectively 'dump' redundant or troublesome populations. Of course in Tudor and Stewart times, and subsequently, population displacement became an issue as the structure of human/land relationships and the landscape itself were altered both literally and metaphorically in what has come to be called the Early Modern Period in Britain. In 1606 King James I of England granted a new warrant to the Virginia Company, essentially a cadre of gentlemen entrepreneurs, to establish a settlement in the New World. Like many other ventures founded on British royal letters patent based on the assumption of *terra regis*, such as the Rupert's Land enterprise dating from 1670 that granted most of northern North America a similar venture— the Hudson's Bay Company (Figure 3.3)—the assumed objectives were the exploitation of Indigenous resources and the continued exploration for a route to the Far East or the 'Passage' to the South Sea (56). Of course there were two vital differences between the Virginia and Rupert's Land enterprises:

(1) The Hudson's Bay Company was ALL about commerce, for although their Charter gave equal weight to trade and colonization, the Company, with a unified vision maintained over 200 years, traded (55). On the other hand, the Virginia Company's Jamestown Island included colonization with commerce to graft upon the wild the tame although the profits were to accrue to the folks back home.

(2) The Hudson's Bay Company endeavour required the participation, albeit manipulated, of Indigenous peoples while the Jamestown enterprise dealt with Indigenous peoples as troublesome and mostly expendable threats to the safety of colony property and colonist life.

These early voyagers 'knew virtually nothing of the Native languages of the Americas, even as they freely translated them' (Cheyfitz 1991: xv) with seeming accuracy that was a mere fiction of power. Language, as we will see in Chapter 4, was a key element of the process of colonization. Indeed, on this topic Cheyfitz continues:

> What the English and Europeans could not achieve in actuality they achieved textually . . . [through] early narratives: the translation of the Indians into proper English. . . . these narratives became models of actuality, models for legal decisions in which the Indians were literally forced to speak proper English, to speak, that is, whether they could speak English or not, in the letter of a law that recognized only the terms of property. (10)

Figure 3.3 The Hudson's Bay Company was an enduring presence in the lives of many Indigenous peoples in Canada. A group of Inuit from the Belcher Islands of James Bay stand in front of an HBC store in 1946.

Thus the translation had commenced of North American oral kin-based societies into English of the Early Modern Period variety on its way to a capitalist vocabulary. Translation errors abound from Jamestown to Wounded Knee, from the American Marshall decision of 1823 (10–11) to the Canadian Marshall decision of the 1990s, both court decisions on Indian land claims. And of course translation errors were not unique to the Americas with perhaps the most notorious being the series of events that led to the death of Captain Cook in Owhyhee (Hawaii) when 'ye Natives' manifested 'insolence' (Sahlins 1995: 84). Cook died without ever truly understanding the dangerous position he had attained in the cultural constructs of a specific society although Sahlins attributes his death more to hubris than linguistic incompetence (228).

The Key Metaphor of Capitalism

Fundamental to these enterprises was and remains what has become capitalism—company enterprises with shareholders under government letters patent or warrants. On capitalism Wolf comments that 'The guiding

fiction . . . [and] one of the key tenets . . . is that land, labour, and wealth are commodities, that is, goods produced not for use but for sale' (1969: 277). The world is a market, and everything within the world has, or should have, its price. Capitalism very much became a key metaphor. However, it is no longer unambiguously aligned to a specific cultural tradition but permeates the lives of everyone.

The genius of capitalism has been the thoroughgoing way in which those committed to the marketing metaphor have been able to convert anything that exists into a commodity; they turn land into real estate and material objects into inventory. They can also attach price tags to ideas (copyright laws) and even to human beings (patents on genetic materials). In the Americas the forced labour enslavement of Natives by the British was characterized in euphemistic terms of 'population recruitment' (Bailyn 1986), but we should note that regardless of their origin, Native or 'imported', all slaves shared one thing—they were considered 'first and foremost a commodity . . . chattel, totally in the possession of another person . . .' and they were used 'for private ends' (Kopytoff and Miers 1977: 3). Even human beings who were not slaves were nevertheless reduced to their labour power by the capitalist market and became worth whatever price the laws of supply and demand determined; thus, human beings were also turned into objects, and labour became a commodity along with beans and cotton. Even when people function as buyers in the market, their actions are supposed to be governed by maximizing utility. They should buy cheap, sell dear, and not allow any personal or social considerations to divert their attention from the bottom line.

To be sure, complex commercial activity was not invented by Western capitalists. Stratified societies always devised sophisticated socio-economic systems. Trade, money, and markets became highly developed. Elites in such societies were well prepared to take advantage of new economic opportunities offered by Western entrepreneurs, often helping establish capitalist practices in their own societies and benefitting as a result. However, the consequences of capitalism were often negative for ordinary members of these societies, who lost many traditional socio-economic supports.

Capitalism was even more devastating in small-scale societies. Members of these societies saw their land turned into a commodity for sale on the capitalist market. They experienced the devaluation of their traditional social identities based on descent, alliance, and residence and the erosion of traditional obligations that protected them from destitution—they experienced **colonialism**. European conquest of non-Western societies created colonial empires in two historical phases:

(1) Spain, Portugal, and Holland, with colonies paying tribute to the empire through trading companies; and

(2) England and France, with 'plantations' and colonization based on industrial capitalism (Gledhill 1994: 74).

To function intelligibly within the capitalist world order, colonized peoples had to begin seeing the world as a storehouse of potential commodities. Much of recent world history can be usefully viewed as a narrative of non-Western responses to this New World view and the practical actions it encouraged and justified. Some people's responses were enthusiastic, others were resentful but accommodating, and still others were violent in repudiation or took action to protect themselves.

Responses to European Colonialism: The Fur Trade in North America

The modern First Nations populations of northern boreal Canada, like American Aboriginal populations, have been through social, cultural, and environmental disruptions with appalling consequences in the historic past. It has been a journey of both immense tragedy and tremendous courage and along the way many compromises were made as a direct and sometimes needed response to changed circumstances. The consequences of these disruptions can be seen in the modern circumstances of northern peoples today. The major interjection of northern life came from the fur trade. This was an international trade of longstanding and pre-contact European economic competition (Wolf 1982: 158ff.). In North America the 'winners' in all of this were the British—they outmanoeuvred and/or defeated both the Dutch and the French for control of resources—mostly beaver (*Castor canadensis*). Beaver were not only a keystone species but were a feature of the key metaphor of many Algonquian peoples (Dods 2003; 2007; Overholt and Callicott 1982: 74–5). At contact this seemed to be an inexhaustible resource, as the estimate of beaver

numbers at 60×10^6 to 400×10^6 indicates (Naiman et al. 1986: 1254). However, by the nineteenth century in areas such as northern Ontario, this animal was extinct. The capitalist response to declining resources was to open new territory—they moved on. In places like northwestern Ontario it meant a change in food strategies (Rogers and Black 1976). The 'fish and hare' period, 1880–1920, was a response to widespread starvation but is considered to have begun earlier 'in the Osnaburgh House area during the 1820s—and somewhat later to the north of that area—in response to certain environmental changes' (1976: 13). Bishop (1973) considers this post-contact collapse of the food chain to be the precipitating circumstance for the elaboration of the Windigo complex, the fear of cannibals and cannibalism. This complex, first seen in documents dating from the early nineteenth century (Bishop 1970: 8), has been interpreted by modern psychologists as a psychosis. However, Bishop (1973) considers this to be the direct result of protein starvation. His interpretation is somewhat supported by work done with Arctic peoples (Lapland, Siberia, North America). Here 'hysterical fits' and 'periodical madness' are reported (extending to Eskimo dogs) but interpreted as a lack of minerals or vitamins, in particular a low level of calcium 'which is essential for the nervous system' (Høygaard 1941: 72).

Additionally, as seen in other areas of the Americas and elsewhere, disease played a significant role in the alteration of population patterns and social cohesion. The high mortality rate 'devastated and decimated some groups, modifying social organizational features and ecological relationships . . .' (Bishop 1981: 45). Further, Trigger notes that 'failure to cope with epidemic diseases led to a spiritual crisis . . .' (1981: 36). This did not stop in the twentieth century. Consider Norway House in northern Manitoba in 1918–19 during the Spanish flu pandemic. They lost 18 per cent of their adult population (ages 20–64) in the span of six weeks. This is comparable to the 3 per cent of Indigenous populations affected during that same year (Herring 1994: 96). 'Its key position in the fur trade network and frequent contact with locations to the west, northwest, northeast, and south, left it particularly vulnerable to imported micro-organisms' (97). Ray notes the location of settlements with respect to active trade routes as a central factor in the infection rate for Indigenous peoples in the nineteenth century (1976: 156).

The Slave and Commodities Trades

While the fur trade unfolded in the north, the slave trade and the trade in commodities such as sugar and cotton accompanied the rise of capitalist industry in the south. Now these things were connected in the emerging world markets as social life throughout the world was reshaped to market 'demands'. The slave trade dominated commerce between Europeans and coastal Africans by the eighteenth century. The nature of the merchandise sought for this trade—people—had a devastating effect on the societies of the African hinterland, whose members were captured and sold to meet European demand. But the slave trade did not alter social relations in Africa alone. In the New World it profoundly reshaped the lives of both local Indigenous peoples and European colonists. The growth of plantation economies in areas that had been used by hunters, gatherers, or small-scale farmers altered the local ecology as well as local society. And the wealth produced in these economies transformed both the local gentry and the European nations who claimed sovereignty over them. As a result, Africa, the Americas, and Europe became inextricably intertwined in one another's fate.

Colonialism and 'Modernity'

What is 'modernity'? Its prototype was the European industrial city although it should be noted that the city did not have to be in Europe. Consider the colonial city and how it differed from the great Indigenous cities of pre-contact times. The colonial city in which capitalist transactions centred was 'a conquered place' (Gilsenan 1982: 197). Colonial administrators, merchants, and local elites united in such places to defend their joint interests against those who remained in outlying areas—the 'others' of the hinterland, a hinterland soon to be coveted for its resources, thus potential commodities. Systems set up by colonial authorities to extract raw materials disrupted Indigenous communities and created new ones. The mining towns of southern Africa, for example, are outgrowths of this process. Labour for such enterprises was recruited, sometimes by force, from local populations. Little by little, in an effort to streamline the system of colonial exploitation, society was restructured.

In the colonial context, 'modernity' has often been understood as nothing more than adopting the practices and world view of Western capitalism. As a result, the so-called backward rural peoples often turned out to be either those who escaped capitalism's embrace or those who actively opposed it. For many of them, the colonial city and the life it represented symbolized everything that was wrong with the colonial order. At times of crisis in contemporary Muslim societies, for example,

> the modern city is itself called in question, taken to symbolize forces of oppression or a non-Islamic way of life. . . . For radical and millennial groups the city is a home of unbelief, not of sober, textual Islam. The true believer should, in an image that has great historical resonance, go out from the city, leave as the Prophet Muhammad did the hypocritical and unbelieving citizens of Mecca. (214)

The Colonial Political Economy

Because the colonial order focused on the extraction of material wealth, it might be said that its reason for existence was economic. Economically, it linked communities and territories that in many cases had led a fairly autonomous existence before colonization. Yet this new economic order did not spring up painlessly by itself. It was imposed and maintained by force. For that reason, many anthropologists describe the colonial order as a **political economy**—a holistic term that emphasizes the centrality of material interest in the organization of society and the use of power to protect and enhance that interest. The colonial political economy created three kinds of links:

(1) connecting conquered communities with one another within a conquered territory,
(2) different conquered territories with one another, and
(3) all conquered territories with the country of the colonizers.

Wolf describes a particularly striking example of this connection: silver, mined in Spanish colonies in America, was shipped to a Spanish colony in Asia—the Philippines—where it was used to buy textiles

colonialism The cultural domination of a people by larger, wealthier powers.

political economy A holistic term that emphasizes the centrality of material interest (economy) and the use of power (politics) to protect and enhance that interest.

from the Chinese (1982: 153) for the European market that in turn used it to trade in North America.

Colonial enterprises drew labour from neighbouring regions. For example, in African mining, Indigenous Africans were recruited from some distance; money earned in one area was thus remitted for the economic support of families in another area. Such linkages did not come about spontaneously and their emergence in this example is very telling. In the beginning, Africans were still largely able to guarantee their own subsistence through traditional means. They were unwilling to work for wages in the mines except on a short-term basis. Therefore, profitability in mining required that African self-sufficiency be eliminated so that Africans would have no choice but to work for whatever wages mine owners offered. This goal was achieved in two ways:

(1) Taxes were imposed on conquered African populations, but the taxes could only be paid in cash.

(2) The colonial government deliberately prevented the growth of a cash economy in African areas. Thus, the only way Africans could obtain the cash to pay their taxes was by working for wages in the mines.

Of course colonial administrators were generally convinced that the work of empire would benefit those they dominated—if not now, then in the future. However, we can note here the Canadian example of 'good' outcomes that support the counter view that any benefits could accrue to a dominated and exploited people.

In the socially constructed landscapes of the colonized, Canadian Native peoples were forcibly sent to residential schools (Figure 3.4) where their life-affirming metaphors of unity and wholeness were usurped, as we noted earlier (Chrisjohn et al. 1997: 115). Such schools are seen by First Nations peoples as factories of cultural genocide designed by the Government of Canada to eliminate the 'Indian Problem' one way or another, once and for all (42). Or as Morris noted in 1877, 'let us have a wise and paternal Government . . . doing its utmost to help and elevate the Indian population who have been cast upon our care [doing] . . . our duty by the red man' (296–7); here, succinctly stated, is the 'white man's burden'! First Nations peoples have noted that the actual agenda was the 'good' Indian and of course they sardonically observe that the only good Indian is a dead Indian, 'Not dead physically, but dead spiritually, mentally, economically, and socially' (Waubageshig 1970: vi) since

Figure 3.4 Native parents camp by a residential school to visit their children, Birtle, Manitoba, 1904.

the 'problem' was (and is) that there were (and are) Aboriginal owners (and their legal descendants) inhabiting the land to which the Europeans wished to lay claim. . . . genocide of Aboriginal peoples grew out of [a] . . . need to extinguish Aboriginal title to the land without violating the letter and spirit of established British policy. (Chrisjohn et al. 1997: 51–2)

The spirit of the Enlightenment was humanist, and its primary goal was to come to an understanding of the 'moral, genetic, and historical unity of mankind' (Mafeje 1976: 310), and this would be the mandate of the 'father' of American anthropology, Franz Boas. However, this intellectual environment also provided the rationale for the development of the notion of the 'civilizing mission' of Europeans. This was pervasive in the nineteenth century and became 'a rationalization of more mundane things such as economic plunder, political imposition, and other inhuman practices' (1976). Indeed, Lukács has called the capitalist era the *imperialist era* (1971).

Women and Colonization

Ethnographic data show that colonial conquest did not affect all groups in the same ways. Women were one such group. We will see in Chapter 9 that Trobriand women of New Guinea suffered no loss of status under colonial rule (see EthnoProfile 9.1: Trobriand Islanders). Baule women of Ivory Coast in western Africa were less fortunate (see EthnoProfile 3.1: Baule).

In pre-colonial Baule society, production centred on two products: yams and cloth (Etienne 1980). Gifts of yams and cloth consolidated marriages, and both sexes worked together in the production of each. Yet the relations of production assigned men responsibility for yams and women responsibility for cloth. Men's traditional control over yams was an outgrowth of the sexual division of labour; men cleared and prepared farm plots for planting although the women tended the crops. Similarly, women controlled cloth because they raised the cotton and spun the thread from which it was woven although the men did the actual weaving. Both yams and cloth were indispensable for subsistence as well as for exchange in various traditional social contexts. As a result, the balance of power between men and women was highly egalitarian.

France colonized the Ivory Coast in 1893. In 1923, in Baule territory, the French built a textile factory that sold factory-spun thread for cash (Figure 3.5). Baule men with cash could therefore buy their own thread, and they, not their wives, would control any cloth woven from it. French colonial administrators also encouraged Baule farmers to plant new varieties of cotton as a cash crop. Baule women had traditionally practised crop rotation with the yams and cotton. Now the fields were devoted to growing only the new cotton. This industrial crop required new farming techniques, but for a variety of reasons those techniques were taught to Baule men. Consequently, women's cotton production was reduced considerably. Now women had to work in their husbands' cash-crop fields and the traditional yam plots. The agricultural work for women increased, and they had less time to spin traditional thread.

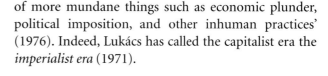

EthnoProfile 3.1

Baule

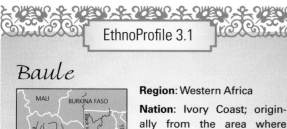

Region: Western Africa

Nation: Ivory Coast; originally from the area where the Koussou Dam was built (1971), resulting in the relocation of 75,000 Baule to the forests southwest of the country; nearly one-third of the remaining 1.5 million Baule have left their traditional homelands because of poor harvest

Language: Baule are one of the Fante-Akan speaking peoples and make up 20 per cent of the population of the Ivory Coast

Population: 2,760,000

Environment: Savannah

Livelihood: Farming (yams in particular), coffee, cocoa, and cloth production

Political organization: In the pre-colonial period, no state and no clear stratification; today, part of a modern nation-state

For more information: Vogel, Susan M. 1997. *Baule: African Art, Western Eyes* (New Haven: Yale University Press)

Figure 3.5 Factory production has displaced traditional household-based production of cloth, not just among the Baule of Ivory Coast but throughout Africa. Pictured here are women working in a textile factory in southern Africa.

The colonial government required men to pay their wives' taxes in cash, a move that seemed to justify the right of Baule men to control the production of crops that could be sold for cash. Under colonial rule, cash-cropping became increasingly important. As a result, Baule women found that their traditional autonomous rights to use their husbands' land for their own production gradually eroded, and they became increasingly dependent on their husbands' arbitrary generosity.

There is a final irony in this series of developments. By the 1970s, many Baule women had become wage labourers in the textile factory in order to earn cash to buy their own cloth, which they could then control. They were aware of the loss of status and power they had suffered over the years, and their discontent had undermined traditional Baule marriage. Etienne reported that

> The wife–husband production relationship has become a constant source of conflict. Because the production relationship has always been the foundation of marriage, and because cloth and cash now tend to be the measure of a husband's affection and respect, the whole personal relationship is also conflict-laden. Inevitably, many women prefer to remain unmarried and all seek to acquire their own cash. (1980: 231)

In this way, the traditional Baule mode of production was transformed by contact with the capitalist market. The previously egalitarian relations of production linking women and men (husbands and wives) were destroyed.

Anthropology and the Colonial Encounter

This section's title has been borrowed from the title of a book edited by anthropologist Talal Asad (1973). It is important because it is the first high-profile work by an anthropologist to consider the connections between anthropology and colonialism. Two decades after its publication, Asad addressed the evidence and conclusions that could be drawn from this exercise in disciplinary self-scrutiny. Although charges have been made, from those within and outside the discipline, that anthropology was nothing more than a form of 'applied colonialism', there is little evidence that this was the case, and for two reasons:

(1) anthropological findings were too specialized to be used by colonial administrators, especially compared to the enormous amount of information supplied to them by merchants, missionaries, and other government functionaries; and

(2) colonial governments were preoccupied with day-to-day concerns of administration and, for them, social change involved the adjustment of conquered peoples to life under colonial rule; thus the research that would let them rule with as little difficulty as possible was of interest.

European anthropologists sometimes played an equivocal role in the colonial setting; they were valued for the expert knowledge they could provide, but they were also viewed with suspicion because their expert knowledge might easily contradict or undermine administrative goals. But even for anthropologists, whose goal was to resist or mitigate the effects of colonial rule on subject peoples, the colonial context itself constituted a space within which anthropologists were obliged to manoeuvre. Therefore, Asad emphasizes, 'the process of European global power has been central to the anthropological task of recording and analyzing the way of life of subject populations' and therefore must be recognized as having been 'always part of the reality anthropologists sought to understand, and the way they sought to understand it' (2002: 134).

One way of coping with colonial power was to address it indirectly. For example, in the mid-twentieth

Figure 3.6 Beverley Jacobs, Head of the Native Women's Association of Canada, and Phil Fontaine, Assembly of First Nations Chief, shown here in the House of Commons on 11 June 2008 alongside former residential school students, await Prime Minister Stephen Harper's official apology.

century, a number of North American anthropologists also tried to clarify what their role should be in the expanding world of capitalist colonialism. Two documents (Redfield et al. 1936; Broom et al. 1954) bracket the period that Bohannan and Plog (1967: x) called the *high period* of the study of culture. The anthropologists involved promoted an impartial and scientific program of research that would discover the laws of culture change. They had a broad view of culture change. The anthropologists did not see themselves supporting any particular political position in advocating that culture change be approached in this way; however, they were sympathetic to the plight of colonial subjects. Melville Herskovits, in particular, was outspoken in his defence of the right of Indigenous African peoples to control their own destinies.

In the years following World War II, European colonial powers were increasingly forced to come to terms with colonial subjects who rejected the role they had been forced to play as students of civilization. The colonial order was no longer a given, and its ultimate benevolence was sharply questioned. This critical attitude persisted after independence was granted to most European colonies in the 1950s and 1960s. It became clear that formal political independence could not easily undo the profound social and economic entanglements linking the former colonial territories to the countries that colonized them. The persistence of ties in the face of political sovereignty came to be called **neo-colonialism**.

The study of neo-colonialism led to a new awareness of just how strongly the fate of colonies and the fate of the colonizers continued to be mutually interdependent. Recognizing the strength of this interdependence, scholars began to offer new explanations for the 'underdevelopment' that characterized the new nations in what came to be known as the Third World. However, now we have what is termed the 'Fourth World'—subjugated original peoples struggling in ex-colonial or neo-colonial settings—to add to the analysis. The realities of the remains of colonialism will be addressed in subsequent chapters. As Canadians we cannot be smug. We only have to read the newspaper or watch the evening news to know that the aspirations of the First Nations peoples of Canada have yet to be addressed in an adequate way. An excellent resource on these issues is the Assembly of First Nations (AFN) website, and especially interesting is their 2007 response to Bill C-44, the Canadian government's proposal to change section 67 of the Canadian Human Rights Act. And the residential school ramifications continue to be a central problem, both of reconciliation and redress, regardless of the latest apology in Parliament (Figure 3.6).

neo-colonialism The persistence of profound social and economic entanglements linking former colonial territories to their former colonial rulers despite political sovereignty.

In Their Own Words

The Anthropological Voice

Anthropologist Annette Weiner (1933–97) traces the history of anthropological challenges to colonialism and Western capitalism, pointing out why the perspective of anthropologists has so often been ignored.

Colonialism brought foreign governments, missionaries, explorers, and exploiters face to face with cultures whose values and beliefs were vastly different. As the harbingers of Western progress, their actions were couched in the rhetoric of doing something to and for 'the Natives'—giving them souls, clothes, law—whatever was necessary to lift them out of their 'primitive' ways. Anthropologists were also part of the colonial scene, but what they came to 'do' made them different from those who were carrying out the expectations of missions, overseas trade, and government protectorates. Anthropologists arrived in the field determined to understand the cultural realities of an unfamiliar world. The knowledge of these worlds was to serve as a warning to those in positions of colonial power by charging that villager's lives were not to be tampered with arbitrarily and that changing the lives of powerless people was insensitive and inhumane, unless one understood and took seriously the cultural meanings inherent in, for example, traditional land ownership, the technologies and rituals surrounding food cultivation, myths, magic, and gender relations.

All too often, however, the anthropologist's voice went unnoticed by those in power, for it remained a voice committed to illuminating the cultural biases under which colonialists operated. Only recently have we witnessed the final demise of colonial governments and the rise of independent countries. Economically, however, independence has not brought these countries the freedom to pursue their own course of development. In many parts of the world, Western multinational corporations, often playing a role not too dissimilar from colonial enterprises, now determine the course of that freedom, changing people's lives in a way that all too often is harmful or destructive. At the same time, we know that the world's natural resources and human productive capabilities can no longer remain isolates. Developed and developing countries are now more dependent on one another than ever before in human history. Yet this interdependency, which should give protection to Indigenous peoples, is often worked out for political ends that ignore the moral issues. Racism and the practice of discrimination are difficult to destroy, as evidenced by the United States today, where we still are not completely emancipated from assumptions that relegate blacks, women, Asians, Hispanics, and other minorities to second-class status. If we cannot bridge these cultural differences intellectually within our own borders, then how can we begin to deal politically with Third World countries—those who were called *primitives* less than a century ago—in a fair, sensitive, and meaningful way?

This is the legacy of anthropology that we must never forget. Because the work of anthropology takes us to the neighbourhoods, villages, and campsites—the local level—we can ourselves experience the results of how the world's economic and political systems affect those who have no voice. Yet once again our voices too are seldom heard by those who make such decisions. Anthropologists are often prevented from participating in the forums of economic and government planning. Unlike economists, political scientists, or engineers, we must stand on the periphery of such decision-making, primarily because our understanding of cultural patterns and beliefs forces on others an awareness that ultimately makes such decisions more formidable. . . .

Source: Weiner, Annette. 1990. 'The Anthropological Voice', guest editorial in *Cultural Anthropology: A Perspective on the Human Condition*, 2nd edn, eds Emily Schultz and Robert Lavenda (St Paul: West), 392–3.

Toward Classifying Forms of Human Society

Now we can draw several conclusions, both about the peoples among whom anthropologists first worked with and about the kinds of anthropological research they conducted.

- All peoples live in their own modernity. Therefore the societies studied by anthropologists were not and are not leading timeless, unchanging ways of life unaffected by the presence of others. Cultural patterns have been affected everywhere by the arrival of Europeans or the transformations of the world set in motion by the spread of European capitalism and colonialism.

- Many groups have shaped new identities and devised new social forms to deal with the effects of contact and conquest. These new social forms sometimes drew on very ancient traditions, reworked to meet the demands of new experiences. Additionally, ways of life that were invented long ago continue to prove their worth or are being reintroduced today. Sometimes, ancient modes of living are falling before the advance of Western technology and the rigours of market capitalism (see, e.g., Lee 2002; 1992a; 1992b). Far from being static survivors of a timeless past, these people are actively coping with contemporary problems and opportunities. They are not without history. However, their recent history is deeply entangled with the European conquests and the outcomes.

- Colonial empires have been replaced by the empires of transnational corporations. The effects supersede much of the colonial experience and all local peoples, us included, have to devise new forms of recourse to challenge the agents of such change.

Evolutionary Typologies: The Nineteenth Century

Anthropologists, like all children of the Age of Enlightenment, liked to devise **typologies**, the classifications of variation. This was thought to facilitate the study of similarities and differences in cultural and social responses. We will briefly examine some of these typologies, how the colonial context of ethnographic research shaped the most influential, and how they fell out of favour.

Each system of classification reflects the attributes believed to be most significant by its creator. Therefore, different assessments can lead to different classifications. In the pervasive nineteenth-century Western view, certain features came to set apart Europeans from the various peoples they conquered. They identified these differences between themselves and others as *deficiencies*: lack of a state, lack of sophisticated technology, lack of organized religion, and so

forth, much along the lines of discussion in Hobbes's *Leviathan* (1651). Western industrial capitalist society became the universal 'yardstick'. This spoke directly to the cross-cultural experience that Western nations were having with non-Western peoples. For example, a colonial functionary eager to establish a smoothly working trading post and anxious to maximize profits in the fur trade would be most aware of the facets of a people's life that kept him from reaching his goals. How do you 'pay' for beaver pelts when the 'sellers' are not interested in money? Europeans faced with such practical problems were bound to see life outside Europe in terms of a series of deficiencies compared with what they could count on in their home country.

More philosophical nineteenth-century observers pondered why there should be such deficiencies in the more provincial areas of Europe and societies beyond Europe. As they sat in their libraries studying the reports of travellers and missionaries, as well as history, they learned that many of the social and technological patterns they took for granted had not always existed, even in Europe. If they went back far enough, beyond the Middle Ages, perhaps they would discover that their more distant ancestors had lived much the same way as many peoples of America or Africa. Indeed, Julius Caesar had painted a picture of Indigenous life in early Europe that resembled the contemporary customs of Indigenous Americans and Africans; this view was reinforced as archaeologists discovered ancient artifacts presumably made by the primitive ancestors of modern Europeans.

Thus, the experience of social change, together with historical and archaeological evidence of past social change, was suggestive. Perhaps the ways of life of the non-Western peoples they were reading about were similar to, and even repeats of, the ways of life of European generations long past. That is, perhaps the West had already moved through *stages* of history in which ways of life had been the same as those of contemporary non-Western societies. According to these scholars, if non-Western societies were left to themselves and given enough time, they would make the same discoveries and social changes as western Europe.

typologies Classification systems based on systematic organization into *types* on the basis of shared attributes.

This way of thinking about social and cultural change has been called **unilineal cultural evolutionism** (Figure 3.7). It reached its most elaborate development in the nineteenth century, when ideas of social Darwinism were generally popular. Unilineal cultural evolutionism was used to explain the widespread cultural diversity that Europeans had been finding since the Age of Exploration. Purportedly, it accounted for this diversity by arguing that different kinds of societies represented different stages of societal evolution through which every human society either had passed or would pass if it survived. Unilineal cultural evolutionists viewed their own late nineteenth-century European capitalist industrial society as the most advanced stage of cultural evolution. Living societies that had not already reached this level were seen as primitive relics of the stages the West had already left behind.

For insight we consider two unilineal cultural evolutionary schemes:

(1) the Three Age System (from European archaeology), and
(2) the Ethnical Stages of the American Lewis Henry Morgan.

Figure 3.7 E.B. Tylor (1832–1917), one of the founders of anthropology in Great Britain, was convinced that societies moved through a series of unilineal stages.

C.J. Thomsen's systematic, 1836 study of artifacts in the Danish National Museum became his *Three Age System* and popularized ideas on social evolution not long before Darwin published his first book on biological evolution, *The Origin of Species* (1859). Based on the raw materials from which tools had been made, Thomsen proposed that Europeans had passed through three technological stages or 'ages': the Stone Age, the Bronze Age, and the Iron Age. Later the Stone Age was subdivided into the Paleolithic (Old Stone Age—itself divided into Lower, Middle, and Upper divisions), Mesolithic, and Neolithic (New Stone Age).

However, the most influential cultural typology came in *Ancient Society: Researches in the Lines of Human Progress from Savagery through Barbarism to Civilization* (Morgan 1877). Morgan outlined three 'ethnical periods'. The first two, 'Savagery' and 'Barbarism', were also subdivided into Lower, Middle, and Upper categories and were defined by technological attributes, in particular food acquisition technologies. One striking feature, however, effectively kept 'Civilization' for Europeans alone—the use of the phonetic alphabet. *Ancient Society* was based in equal parts on Morgan's mid-nineteenth-century in-field observations of the Iroquois of the Finger Lakes District of New York, the emerging concepts of evolution (biological and cultural), and the ideas of progress from the Age of Enlightenment. In effect it was an attempt at 'anthropological' synthesis of the evolutionary stages of human society. The importance of this book cannot be overemphasized. Engels, in *Origin of the Family, Private Property and the State* (1972 [1884]), was greatly influenced by, and drew upon, this work. Well into the twentieth century, Morgan's classification, because of its link through Engels to Marxism, was *au courant* in some sectors of the academic world. For example, Morgan was the main and, indeed, sometimes the only authority cited in the cultural analysis found in Chinese archaeological reports well into the 1970s. In the Americas, Morgan gained renewed immediacy in the 1940s and 1950s with the unilineal evolutionary approaches of Leslie White, the rebellious intellectual son of Boas.

Such stages were used to justify racist ideas. Equally distinguished were those who had 'stagnated', in effect the cultural 'back-sliders' as well as those that were 'eminently gifted' (de Gobineau 1967 [1915]: 27). Racial inferiority, de Gobineau opines, 'is shown, not only by defeat, but also by the lack of the attributes that may be seen in the conquerors' (31). He asks: if all men are brothers and the brain of the Huron Indian is the same as that of an Englishman or a Frenchman, 'Why then, in the course of the ages, has [the Huron] not invented printing or steam power?' (37), neglecting to note that printing was actually the invention of a group classified as Upper Barbarians—namely the Chinese! But of course we can sardonically note that the evidence was there in the advances that Europe had experienced since antiquity. These were seen to be unique, unmatched by social changes in other civilizations, which were understood to be declining. That decline seemed proven when representatives of Western civilization found they could conquer the rulers of such civilizations, as the English had done in India or the Dutch in Bali. The labels of unilineal evolutionism remained part of the vocabulary of anthropology for many years. Malinowski, for example, was quite comfortable sometimes referring to the inhabitants of the Trobriand Islands as *savages*. Indeed, as reported in the *Globe and Mail* (18 July 2007: L6), the British based Association of Social Anthropologists and the activist group Survival International have initiated a campaign to 'challenge racist descriptions' in the press, citing the CBC, among others, for using 'Stone Age' in their coverage of contemporary peoples. Anthropologists find such approaches to the classification of forms of human society to be inadequate—indeed, misleading. But both of these schemes continue to resonate and their continued popularity among ordinary members of Western societies is neither surprising nor difficult to understand: they offer seemingly coherent frameworks for classifying all societies.

Social Structural Typologies: The British Emphasis

Although unilineal cultural evolutionism may have justified the global ambitions of Europe and made colonial rule appear inevitable and just, it was inadequate for meeting the practical needs of colonials once they were in power. Most of Africa and much of Asia, which until then had remained nominally independent, were divided up among European powers. At the same time, the United States and Canada assumed a similarly powerful and dominating role in their relationships with the Indigenous peoples of North America.

Effective administration of subject peoples required accurate information about them. For example, one goal of a colonial administrator in Africa was to keep peace among the various contending groups. The administrator needed to know how those people were accustomed to handling disputes. Most colonies included several societies with various customs for dispute resolution, and administrators had to be aware of their similarities and differences in order to develop successful government policies. Colonial officials also planned to introduce certain elements of European law and political economy uniformly throughout the colony. Common examples were commercial laws permitting the buying and selling of land on the open market. They also tried to eliminate practices like witchcraft accusations or local punishment for capital crimes. Reaching these goals without totally disrupting life in the colony required first-hand understanding of local practices. The earlier 'armchair anthropology' approaches, based on reading reports from distant places, were wholly incapable of providing that understanding.

These changes in the relationships between the West and the rest of the world fostered the development of an altered anthropological research paradigm based on detailed information on more societies. This led to a dissatisfaction with grand generalizations about cultural diversity and change. This altered perspective was the outcome of improved scholarship and better scientific reasoning, driven by the changes taking place in the world. Unsettled conditions had made such work difficult in earlier times. But under the colonial 'peace', anthropologists found that they could carry out long-term fieldwork, even with colonial governments supporting their research when it was seen as 'scientific' and contributing to effective colonial rule. This did not mean that anthropologists who carried out fieldwork under colonial conditions supported colonialism. To the contrary, their sympathies often lay with the colonized peoples with whom they worked. For example, Evans-Pritchard, who

unilineal cultural evolutionism A nineteenth-century theory that proposed a series of stages through which all societies must go (or had gone) in order to reach civilization.

worked in central Africa for the British government in the 1920s and 1930s, saw himself as an educator of colonial administrators. He tried to convey to them the humanity and rationality of Africans. His goal was to combat the racism and oppression that seemed an inevitable consequence of colonial rule. Consequently, colonial officials were often wary of anthropologists and distrustful of their motives.

Colonial officials quickly learned that administering their rule would be easier if they could rely on traditional leaders as intermediaries to keep the peace among their people (Figure 3.8). Thus the British policy of *indirect rule* was developed. How could anthropologists contribute to the effectiveness of indirect rule? Perhaps the information on the traditional political structures of different groups might offer insights into the best way to adapt indirect rule to each group. As a result, anthropologists—especially British ones—developed a new way of classifying forms of human society. Their focus was on the **social structure**, especially the political structure, of groups under colonial rule. That British anthropologists came to call themselves *social anthropologists* reflects these developments.

In 1940, in a classic work on African political systems, Fortes and Evans-Pritchard distinguished between *state and stateless societies*. This distinction had some similarity to Morgan's ethnical periods but was neither a connotation nor a denotation of 'progress' in the discussion of the two political systems.

Thus the productive emphasis on contemporary social structures emerged and questions of evolution and social change were superseded by concerns about the enduring traditional structures of the societies in which anthropologists worked. A detailed knowledge of social structures supposedly allowed anthropologists to identify the social type of any particular society. These types were treated as unchanging. They were compared for similarities and differences, and out of this comparison emerged a new classification of social forms.

The Classification of Political Structures

An example of a typical social-structural classification is shown in Figure 3.9. Here, the major distinction is between *centralized* and *uncentralized* (*egalitarian*) political systems. It appears that only the labels have

Figure 3.8 Colonial officers often relied on traditional rulers to keep the peace among their subjects through traditional means. This 1895 photograph shows the British governor of the Gold Coast (seated on the right) together with a contingent of Native police.

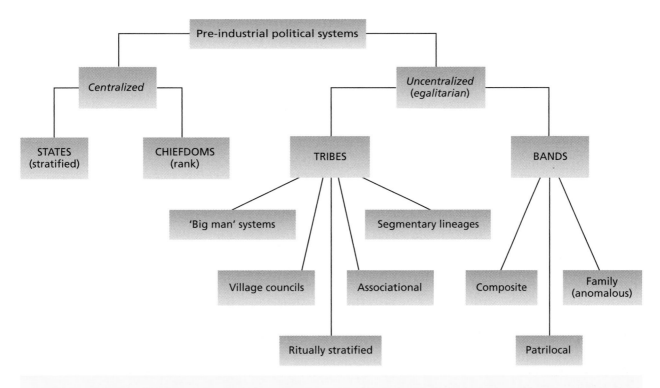

Figure 3.9 A typical classification of forms of human society. **Source:** Lewellen 1983: 16.

been changed from Fortes and Evans-Pritchard's distinction between state and stateless societies. However, we can note that uncentralized societies are now distinguished in positive terms. In uncentralized systems there is no distinct, permanent institution exclusively concerned with public decision-making, and groups (and perhaps even individuals) within these systems enjoy relative autonomy and equal status and are not answerable to any higher authority.

In this typology, uncentralized political systems can be divided into two types:

(1) **Band**: a small social group whose members neither farm nor herd but depend on wild food sources. Lewellen refers to three subtypes of a band, including the *family band* (1983: 26).

(2) **Tribe**: a group that lies somewhere between a band and a centralized political system. A tribe is generally larger than a band and has domesticated plants and animals, but its political organization remains largely egalitarian.

Lewellen also identifies five subtypes of a tribe but comments that they hardly exhaust the variety of social arrangements that tribes display (26).

Centralized political systems differ from uncentralized systems because they have a central, institutionalized focus of authority such as a chief or a king. Some members of centralized societies have greater wealth, power, or prestige than other members. Thus

band The characteristic form of social organization found among foragers; a small group of people, usually with less than 50 members. Labour is divided according to age and sex, and social relations are highly egalitarian.

social structure The enduring aspects of the social forms in a society, including its political and kinship systems.

tribe A form of social organization generally larger than a band; members usually farm or herd for a living. Social relations in a tribe are relatively egalitarian, although there may be a chief who speaks for the group or organizes group activities.

hierarchy is an evident characteristic. Centralized systems are divided into two types:

(1) **Chiefdom**: usually only the chief and the chief's family are set above the rest of society, which remains fairly egalitarian.
(2) **State**: different groups suffer permanent inequality of access to wealth, power, and prestige, which signals the presence of social stratification.

Lewellen's typology did not attempt to make any hypotheses about evolutionary relationships. Tracing change over time was not its purpose. Instead, the focus is on structural similarities and differences observed at one point in time. This is not accidental. Remember that classifications of this kind were made in response to practical needs in European colonies. Colonial rulers assumed that they were *civilized* and that their colonial subjects were *primitive*, but they cared little about matters such as the origin of the state. The pressing questions for them were more likely 'How do African states work today?' and 'What do we need to know about them to make them work for us?'

Structural-functional Theory

The theories of British social anthropologists dealt with how particular social forms function from day-to-day in order to reproduce their traditional structures. Such **structural-functional theory** was perhaps most highly developed by A.R. Radcliffe-Brown in the 1930s and 1940s. Social anthropologists began to ask: Why do things remain the same rather than change? For example:

- Why do some social structures last for centuries (the Roman Catholic Church) and others disappear quickly (the utopian communities of nineteenth-century America, such as the Shakers)?
- Why did some societies abandon foraging for agriculture thousands of years ago, while others are still hunting and gathering in the twenty-first century?

Both kinds of questions are needed since the emphasis on social stability tends to downplay or ignore questions of change, and the emphasis on social change tends to downplay or ignore questions of stability.

This new focus in British social anthropology has produced a succession of non-evolutionary classifications of human social forms. As data on more and more varieties of social structure grow, however, these typologies seem to overflow with more and more subtypes. It is not surprising that some anthropologists question the point of it all.

Attempting to Do without Typologies: Culture Area Studies in America

Similarly, American anthropologists became dissatisfied with unilineal evolutionism. The most significant figure was Franz Boas. Boas and his students worked primarily among the Indigenous peoples of North America, collecting more and better data about these societies, especially data relating to the histories of individual groups. The First Nations peoples of the west coast of Canada contributed significantly to the development of the Boasian theoretical approach.

These researchers found that change had not progressed through uniform stages for all these societies. For example, two societies with similar forms of social organization might have arrived at that position through different historical routes: one through a process of simplification, the other through a process of elaboration. Therefore, *historical particularism*—the study of cultures in their own historical contexts—was the appropriate approach.

Boas emphasized that many seemingly new cultural forms were actually borrowed from neighbouring societies. He and his followers were quick to note that if cultural borrowing, rather than independent invention, played an important role in culture change, then any unilineal evolutionary scheme was doomed. However, a focus on cultural borrowing also emphasized the porous boundaries around different societies that made such borrowing possible.

The view of society that developed in North America was, consequently, quite different from the one that developed in Great Britain. Boas and his followers rejected the cultural evolutionists' view of societies as isolated representatives of universal stages, closed to outside influences, responsible for progressing or failing to progress. Critical of the structural-functional view of societies as bounded, *atemporal* social types, they saw social groups as fundamentally open to the outside world. Change was considered more a result of idiosyncratic borrowing from neighbours than of inevitable, law-governed *progress*. Therefore, the Boasians focused their attention on patterns of cultural borrowing, a form of research called *cultural area studies*. They developed lists of **culture traits**, or features characteristic of a particular group: a particular ritual, for example, or a house style. They then determined how widely those cultural traits had spread into neighbouring societies. A **culture area** was defined by the limits of borrowing, or the *diffusion*, of a particular trait or set of traits. Ironically the idea itself actually diffused from Mason (1896; 1902) to Wissler (1914) to Kroeber (1939) and then to Harold Driver's *North American Indians* (1961), used for many years in Canadian universities (see Map 3.2). Indeed, Driver's book had the distinguishing feature of page after page of maps of specific culture trait distributions.

Thus 'timeless' classificatory schemes, like those of social anthropologists, were of limited value because of the assumption that societies were clear-cut entities with internally consistent social structures. But societies perpetually open to cultural borrowing make it impossible to describe their structures in unambiguous terms. Area studies created cultural classifications

that were either broader than an individual society (culture areas) or narrower than an individual society (culture traits). The end product was a list of traits and a map of cultural areas in which the traits could be found. Societal boundaries were ignored. But did this mean the analysis was typology-free? Far from it! Since culture areas are based on shared attributes, they are a form of typology but with dimensions not found in earlier attempts at classification.

Post-colonial Realities

Then the world changed again. World War II was closely followed by the break-up of European colonial empires in Africa and Asia and by the civil rights movements in Western democracies focused on issues of race, gender, and sexual orientation. Former colonies were now independent states. Their citizens rejected the traditional Western view of them as savages or barbarians.

Political realities thus created for Westerners new experiences of the 'other' that made the pretensions of unilineal evolutionism beyond plausible. Additionally, the leaders of new states began to frame a national consciousness, pulling together supposedly disparate peoples within their borders. This effort made the structural focus of pre-independence social anthropologists seem increasingly misguided. It showed that the traditional societies anthropologists had been studying had not, in fact, been structurally separate even under colonialism. Decolonization forced anthropologists to pay direct attention to colonialism as a form of political domination that eliminated the autonomy of

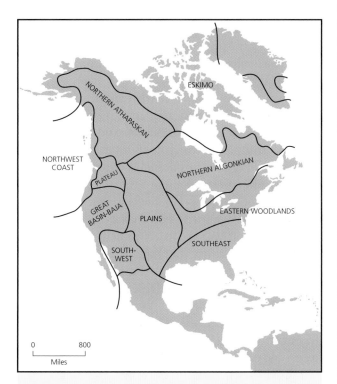

Map 3.2 This map shows the Native American culture areas for North America, north of Mexico.

chiefdom A form of social organization in which the leader (a chief) and the leader's close relatives are set apart from the rest of the society and allowed privileged access to wealth, power, and prestige.

culture area The limits of borrowing, or the *diffusion*, of a particular cultural trait or set of traits.

culture traits Particular features or parts of a cultural tradition such as a dance, ritual, or style of pottery.

state A stratified society that possesses a territory that is defended from outside enemies with an army and from internal disorder with police. A state, which has a separate set of governmental institutions, designed to enforce laws and collect taxes and tribute, is run by an elite that possesses a monopoly on the use of force.

structural-functional theory A position that explores how particular social forms function from day-to-day in order to reproduce the traditional structure of the society.

Figure 3.10 Since the beginning of the twenty-first century, increasing numbers of anthropologists have been coming from regions of the world outside the West. Sri Lankan anthropologist Arjun Guneratne converses with some of his informants in Nepal.

Indigenous social groups and forcibly restructured them into subordinate positions within a larger entity.

At the same time, anthropologists with roots in the non-Western world began to add their voices to those of Western anthropologists (Figure 3.10). They remain highly critical of the cultural stereotypes institutionalized by unilineal evolutionism and structural-functionalism since 'ranking' typologies have not disappeared altogether in contemporary cultural and social anthropology.

Studying Forms of Human Society Today

Some anthropologists, especially those interested in political and economic issues, continue to find typologies useful but opinions differ greatly among contemporary anthropologists. Still, most would agree that an emphasis on cross-cultural similarities or differences is intimately related to the type of questions anthropologists are framing and the theoretical approaches they apply.

For example, let us turn again to Lewellen's classification of social types. How meaningful is it? What does it reflect? Lewellen argues that it is designed to reflect structural, organizational similarities and differences. To defend such criteria, he employs a metaphor:

Two houses built of different materials but to the same floor plan will obviously be much more alike than two houses of the same materials but very different designs (say, a townhouse and a ranch house). . . . In short, a house is defined in terms of its organization, not its components, and that organization will be influenced by its physical environment and the level of technology of the people who designed it. (1983: 17)

Lewellen assumes that structural similarities and differences are both significant and *obvious*, seemingly affiliating him with the British social anthropology tradition. Thus, for Lewellen, the materials out of which the houses are made can safely be ignored. Sometimes this may work. So then, is a house's organization manifested in the floor plan of the builder or in the way the various rooms are *used* regardless of floor plan? Is a bedroom still a bedroom, whether in a townhouse or a ranch house, when the people living in that house use it to cook in? Does a family's ideas about how living space should be used change when the family moves from a thatched hut to an apartment with wooden floors and plaster walls?

Would the similarities and differences that seemed obvious to many political anthropologists in the British tradition seem so sharp to an anthropologist interested in classifying the ways different societies make a living? As we shall see, anthropologists interested in making such a classification employ concepts like *subsistence strategy* or *mode of production* to order their typologies, focusing on the strategies and technologies for organizing the production, distribution, and consumption of food, clothing, housing, tools, and other material goods. Defining different domains of relevance always results in different typologies.

Since the end of colonialism, anthropologists have had to contend with new forms of classification. During the Cold War (1948–89), a new set of categories came into existence that classified these states into the First ('developed') World, the Second ('communist') World, the Third ('underdeveloped') World, or the Fourth ('neo-colonial') World. Anthropologists adjusted to this transmuted context; many of them eventually became highly critical of the way 'development' and 'underdevelopment' were understood and addressed by scholars and government officials alike. With the passing of the Cold War, these distinctions have become even more problematic, more so as the world has become polarized along the lines of fracture between capitalist and fundamentalist religious ideologies since 9/11.

Sometimes it is easy to emphasize the shortcomings of past classificatory schemes in anthropology, regardless of the important lasting contributions they have made. Despite its excesses, unilineal cultural evolutionism highlights the fact that cultures change over time and that our species has experienced a broad sequence of cultural developments. Structural-functionalist typologies may seem overly rigid and static, but the structural-functionalist ethnographies show just how intricate the social institutions and practices of so-called simple societies can be. The culture area studies of the Boasian school de-emphasize societal boundaries while illustrating that Indigenous peoples have never been unthinking slaves to tradition. On the contrary, they have been alert to their surroundings, aware of cultural alternatives, and ready to adopt new ways from other people when it has suited them.

A focus on 'developed' and 'underdeveloped' societies may have raised more problems than it solved, but it was in the very attempt to explain why those problems existed that new anthropological understandings were achieved. Finally, it is the continuing cultural creativity of all human beings in all societies that keeps anthropologists especially busy today. Virtually all of the familiar anthropological classifications are dropping away as anthropologists explore the effects of globalization on all people, in all places.

Key Terms

band 67
capitalism 53
chiefdom 68
colonialism 56
culture area (diffusion) 69
culture traits 69
neo-colonialism 61

political economy 57
social structure 66
state 68
structural-functional theory 68
tribe 67
typologies 63
unilineal cultural evolutionism 64

Chapter Summary

1. Modern Western history has been characterized by the rise of capitalism. The key metaphor of capitalism is that the world is a market and everything within the world—including land, material objects, and human beings—can be bought and sold. Such a view was unknown in non-capitalist societies before Western contact, even in those with highly developed economic institutions. To function intelligibly within the capitalist world order, colonized peoples had to begin seeing the world as a storehouse of potential commodities.

2. Non-Western societies have not escaped the historical forces that have influenced everyone else. Many of the groups anthropologists studied were relatively recent creations, forged in the course of commercial and political contacts between Indigenous populations and Europeans. The societies that survive today show that conquered peoples can actively cope with the challenges and opportunities offered by such contacts to reshape their social identities.

3. The European capitalist penetration of non-Western societies was frequently followed by political conquest, which then reshaped those societies in ways that promoted economic exploitation. Colonial empires drew together economically and politically vast and previously unconnected areas of the world. Indigenous peoples lost their autonomy and were reintegrated as component groups within a larger, new colonial political economy.

4. The context of European colonialism was an ever-present reality within which anthropologists were obliged to manoeuvre. Many hoped that the dismantling of colonial empires after World War II would restore sovereignty and dignity to colonized peoples. However, independence did not free former colonies from deeply entangling economic ties with their former masters. These entanglements have, in some cases, persisted for over 100 years and are called *neo-colonialism*.

5. A survey of the forms of human society identified by anthropologists over the past century and a half can illuminate the historical circumstances surrounding contact between anthropologists and their informants. Each classification depends on identifying those societies that are most distinct from one another based on certain criteria and then sorting known societies by their resemblance to these exemplars. Depending upon an anthropologist's analytical purposes, the same social forms can be classified in different ways.

6. The earliest important anthropological typology of forms of human society was proposed by unilineal cultural evolutionists in the nineteenth century. They tried to explain contemporary cultural diversity by arguing that different kinds of societies existing in the nineteenth century represented different stages of societal evolution. Every human society either had passed or would pass through the same stages.

7. Anthropologists doing research in colonial settings in the first half of the twentieth century collected a vast amount of detailed, accurate information about aspects of Indigenous life, which colonial administrators hoped would help them to be more effective rulers. Their research focused on social structural similarities and differences observed at a single point in time.

8. Following Boas, North American anthropologists rejected unilineal cultural evolutionism on the grounds that societies could easily borrow cultural forms from one another, thus skipping supposedly universal evolutionary stages. Consequently, the aim of much research shifted to making lists of culture traits and mapping the culture areas through which they had spread as a result of cultural borrowing.

9. Since the end of colonialism, new classifications have appeared, such as the Cold War division of nation-states into First, Second, Third, and Fourth worlds and the contrast between 'developed' First World societies and 'underdeveloped' Third World societies. While some anthropologists were dissatisfied with these distinctions, they have become increasingly problematic since the end of the Cold War.

10. Although some anthropologists still find some typologies useful for investigating particular kinds of issues, classifying forms of human society is not an ultimate goal for most anthropologists today. The fuzziness of category boundaries reminds us that taxonomies are human constructions, not pure reflections of objective reality. With the increasing importance of anthropological studies of globalization since the end of the Cold War, many kinds of traditional classifications are dropping away.

Critical Thinking Questions

1. Outline the three major schools of anthropological thought that came to influence the development of anthropology in Canada. Why do you suppose this was the way anthropology developed in Canada? Discuss in a speculative way how these differences influenced later relations with Indigenous peoples in Canada and the United States.

2. In the beginning of British colonial North America there were two early capitalist ventures, one in Virginia and one in Rupert's Land. What were the crucial differences between these two enterprises?

3. There have been criticisms of the roles anthropologists played under colonial rule. How could anthropologists contribute to the effectiveness of indirect rule?

4. How would you distinguish between *centralized* and *uncentralized* (*egalitarian*) political systems?

5. How did Fortes and Evans-Pritchard distinguish between state and stateless societies? Compare and contrast their approaches to Morgan's ethnical periods.

Suggested Readings

Barnard, Alan. 2000. *History and Theory in Anthropology* (Cambridge: Cambridge University Press). *A recent, concise overview of the history of anthropological ideas, tying together developments on both sides of the Atlantic.*

Driver, Harold E. 1961. *Indians of North America* (Chicago: University of Chicago Press). *A comprehensive overview of Indigenous traditional life in North America.*

Kroeber, Alfred. 1939. 'Cultural and Natural Areas of Native North America', *University of California Publications in American Archaeology and Ethnology* 38: xii (Berkeley: University of California Press). *Also issued in hard cover as a separate book.*

Kuhn, Thomas. 1962. *The Structure of Scientific Revolutions,* 1st edn (Chicago: University of Chicago Press). *A seminal work on the way paradigms are called into question, challenged, and then changed.*

Lewellen, Ted. 1993. *Political Anthropology,* 2nd edn (South Hadley, MA: Bergin & Garvey). *Contains much useful information about the different kinds of societies that different scholars have identified.*

Quimby, G.I. 1954. 'Cultural and Natural Areas before Kroeber', *American Antiquity* XIX, 4: 317–31. *An overview of the development of the culture area concept.*

Weatherford, Jack. 1988. *Indian Givers: How the Indians of the Americas Transformed the World* (New York: Fawcett Columbine).

———. 1991. *Native Roots: How the Indians Enriched America* (New York: Fawcett Columbine).

———. 1994. *Savages and Civilization* (New York: Random House). *All three of these books are engaging accounts of the consequences of contact between the Old World and New World in the past and in the present.*

Wolf, Eric. 1982. *Europe and the People without History* (Berkeley: University of California Press). *A classic text about the connection of European expansion to the rest of the world. This work also discusses the effect of European contact on Indigenous societies.*

Related Websites

A Brief History of Anthropology at the University of Toronto: http://chass.utoronto.ca/anthropology/history.htm

Assembly of First Nations (AFN): http://www.afn.ca/

Association of Social Anthropologists of the UK and Commonwealth: http://www.theasa.org/

Survival International: http://www.survival-international.org/

Part Two

The Resources of Culture

The next four chapters focus on a range of human capacities that lie at the centre of human cultural creativity, flexibility, and diversity. Human beings survive in a material world by means of open, flexible symbolic patterns that assign meanings to various aspects of that world. As a result, human beings never confront the material world directly but always through a web of meanings of their own creation. Cultural meaning is perhaps most directly encountered in language, but it is also revealed in habitual patterns of thought and action and is at its most elaborate in those creations that Westerners traditionally call *art*, *myth*, *ritual*, and *world view*. Because the dependence of the human species on culture for survival is total, a proper awareness of the depth, breadth, and complexity of human culture is, from the anthropological perspective, indispensable for an adequate understanding of the human condition.

Chapter 4

Language

Learning Objectives

By the end of Chapter 4, you will be able to:

- consider the relationship between language and culture,
- outline the design features of language,
- situate language in a context,
- understand the importance of linguistic relativity,
- identify the components of language,
- think about linguistic inequality,
- consider negotiated meaning using Pidgin languages as an example, and
- explore the linkages between language and truth.

The system of arbitrary vocal symbols human beings use to encode and communicate their experiences of the world and of one another is called **language**. It is a unique faculty that sets human beings apart from other living species. It provides basic tools for human creativity, making the cultural achievements that we view as monuments to our species' genius possible. And yet, despite all that language makes possible, its tools are double-edged. Language allows people to communicate with one another, but it also creates barriers to communication. One major barrier is linguistic diversity (Figure 4.1). There are some 3,000 mutually unintelligible languages spoken in the world today. Why should there be such barriers to communication? This chapter explores the ambiguity, limitations, and power of human language.

Language and Culture

Human language is a bio-cultural phenomenon. The human brain and the anatomy of our mouth and throat make language a biological possibility for us. At the same time, every human language is clearly a cultural product. It is shared by a group of speakers, encoded in symbols, patterned, and historically transmitted through teaching and learning, thus making communication possible.

Anthropological Interest in Language

Language is of primary interest to anthropologists for at least three reasons:

(1) Anthropologists often do fieldwork among people whose language is different from their own. In the past these languages were often unwritten and had to be learned without formal instruction.

(2) Anthropologists can transcribe or tape-record speech and thus lift it out of its cultural context to be analyzed on its own. The grammatical intricacies revealed by such an analysis suggested to many that what was true about language was true about the rest of culture. Indeed, some schools of anthropological theory have based their theories of culture explicitly on ideas taken from **linguistics**, the scientific study of language.

(3) Most important, all people use language to encode their experiences, to structure their understanding of the world and of themselves, and to engage with one another.

By learning another society's language, we learn something about its culture as well. In fact, learning another language inevitably provides unsuspected insights into the nature of our own language and culture, often making it impossible to take language of any kind for granted.

As with the culture concept, the concept of language has regularly involved a distinction between *Language* and *languages*. *Language* with a capital *L* (like *Culture* with a capital *C*) was viewed as an abstract

language The system of arbitrary vocal symbols we use to encode our experiences of the world.
linguistics The scientific study of language.

Figure 4.1 Language, like universal symbols, allows people to communicate with one another, but language can also create barriers to communication.

property belonging to the human species as a whole, not to be confused with the specific *languages* of concrete groups of people. This distinction initially enabled the recognition that all human groups possessed fully developed *languages* rather than 'primitive', 'broken', or otherwise defective forms of vocal communication. Today, however, linguistic anthropologists realize that totalitarian views of 'languages' can be as problematic as totalitarian views of 'cultures'. The difficulties associated with demarcating the boundaries between one language and another, or with distinguishing between dialects and languages, become particularly obvious in studies of pidgins and creoles, as we will see.

It remains useful, however, to distinguish *language* from *speech* and *communication*. We usually think of spoken language (speech) when we use the term *language*, but we can communicate through codes, such as Morse code, or sign languages, such as Canadian or American Sign Language (CSL/ASL), all non-spoken media. Interestingly CSL and ASL were only two of several 'signed' languages. Canadian anthropological linguist William Thurston has observed that, for a time, SEE (Signed Exact English) and MEE (Manually Encoded English) were designed to submerge CSL and ASL, much in the way Native languages, such as Cree or Mohawk, were violently discouraged in residential schools in Canada—for assimilation and the convenience of the dominant sector of society. This has now been eclipsed with the acceptance of CSL/ASL as a language—indeed one that is more related lexically to

French if anything. Of course, this example suggests that language and its use can be a human rights issue.

Human communication can be defined as the transfer of information from one person to another, which can take place without the use of words, spoken or otherwise. People communicate with one another non-verbally all the time, sending messages with the clothes they wear, the way they walk, or how long they keep others waiting.

In fact, even linguistic communication depends on more than words alone. Native speakers of a language share not just vocabulary and grammar but also a number of assumptions about how to speak that may not be shared by speakers of a different language. Students learning a new language discover early on that word-for-word translation from one language to another does not work. Sometimes there are no equivalent words in the second language; even when there are, a word-for-word translation may not mean in language B what it means in language A. For example, when English speakers have eaten enough they say 'I'm full.' This may be translated directly into French as *Je suis plein*. To French speakers, this sentence (especially when uttered at the end of a meal) has the nonsensical meaning 'I am a pregnant [male] animal.' Alternatively, if uttered by a man who has just consumed a lot of wine, it means 'I'm drunk.'

Speaking a second language is often frustrating and even unsettling; someone who once found the world simple to talk about suddenly turns into a babbling fool. Studying a second language, then, is less a matter of learning new labels for old objects than it is of learning how to identify new objects that go with new labels. The student must also learn the appropriate contexts in which different linguistic forms may be used. Knowledge about context is cultural knowledge. The linguistic system abstracted from its cultural context must be returned to that context if a holistic understanding of language is to be achieved.

Talking about Experience

Language, like the rest of culture, is a product of human attempts to come to terms with experience. Each language, having the ability to change and adapt, is adequate for its speakers' needs, given their particular way of life. Speakers of a particular language tend to develop larger vocabularies to discuss those aspects of life that are important to them. Thurston notes that some languages such as Salish, San, and Kartvelian are phonetically much more complex than Cree, Swahili, or Turkish; that European or Australian languages are morphologically more complex than Mandarin; and that English is lexically more complex than most other languages, while Javanese (see Map 4.1) and Malagasy are socio-linguistically more complex than Cree of Lusi. So all languages are complex although their complexity may manifest in different areas. Further, all languages ever studied are equal in their open potential for expression. You can talk about anything in any language—it may be easier to talk about some items of Western culture, such as software, in a Western language and easier to talk about *mana* in Hawaiian than in English, but it is possible nonetheless. Just as there is no such thing as a 'primitive' human culture, there is no such thing as a 'primitive' human language.

Traditionally, languages are associated with concrete groups of people called *speech communities*. Nevertheless, because all languages possess alternative ways of speaking, members of particular speech communities do not all possess identical knowledge about the language they share nor do they all speak the same way. Individuals and subgroups within a speech community make use of linguistic resources in different ways. Consequently, there is a tension in language between diversity and commonality. Individuals and subgroups attempt to use the varied resources of a language to create unique, personal voices. These efforts are countered by the pressure to negotiate a common code for communication within the larger social group. In this way, language is produced and reproduced through the activity of its speakers. Any particular language that we may identify at a given moment is a snapshot of a continuing process.

There are many ways to communicate our experiences, and there is no absolute standard favouring one way over another. Some things that are easy to say in language A may be difficult to say in language B, yet other aspects of language B may appear much simpler than equivalent aspects of language A. For example, English ordinarily requires the use of determiners (*a, an, the*) before nouns, but this rule is not found in all languages. Likewise, the verb *to be*, called the *copula* by linguists, is not found in all languages although the relationships we convey when we use *to be* in English may still be communicated. In English, we might say 'There *are* many people in the market.' Translating this sentence into Fulfulde, the language of the Fulbe of northern Cameroon, we get *Him'be boi 'don nder luumo*, which, word-for-word, reads something like 'people-many-there-in-market' (Figure 4.2). No single Fulfulde word corresponds to the English *are* or *the*.

Design Features of Human Language

In 1966, anthropological linguist Charles Hockett listed 16 different **design features** of human language that in his estimation set it apart from other forms of animal communication. Six of these design features seem especially helpful in defining what makes human language distinctive: openness, displacement, prevarication, arbitrariness, duality of patterning, and semanticity.

Map 4.1 Java

design features Those characteristics of language that when taken together differentiate it from other known animal communication systems.

Figure 4.2 *Him'be boi 'don nder luumo.*

Openness, probably the most important feature, is the ability to talk about the same experiences from different perspectives, to paraphrase using different words and various grammatical constructions. Indeed, it means that the experiences themselves can be conceived, labelled, and discussed differently. Thus no single perspective would necessarily emerge as more correct in every respect than all others.

For example, compare spoken human language to the vocal communication systems (or *call systems*) of monkeys and apes. Anthropologist Terrence Deacon (1997) points out that modern human beings still possess a set of six calls: laughing, sobbing, screaming with fright, crying with pain, groaning, and sighing. These calls, together with gestures and the changes in speech rhythm, volume, and tonality that linguists call *speech prosody*, all appear to have co-evolved alongside our use of language, which is probably why they integrate with one another so smoothly when we speak. Deacon emphasizes, however, that primate call systems ranging from 15–40 calls, depending on species, do *not* map onto any of the elements of human language and are even controlled by different parts of the brain. They are produced only when the animal finds itself in specific situations such as the presence of food or danger; friendly interest and the desire for company; the desire to mark its location; or to signal pain, sexual interest, or the need for maternal care. For these reasons, the call systems of non-human primates are said to be *closed* when compared to open human languages.

Closed call systems also lack *displacement*, our human ability to talk about absent or non-existent objects and past or future events as easily as we discuss our immediate situations. As Thurston noted in a recent conversation,

> displacement allows us to communicate about things that are not here and now; it also allows us to talk with great precision about things that do not exist, like unicorns. The important thing here is that it permits the extension of linguistic creativity to such phenomena as narrative, religion, rhetoric, politics, poetry, history, and science itself. For me, that's why displacement is so important.

Although non-human primates clearly have good memories, and some species such as chimpanzees seem to be able to plan social action in advance (such as when hunting for meat), they cannot use their call systems to this extent. It is here, Thurston continued, that we can include something not found in Hockett's discussion of design features. Thurston noted that the use of language (or even protolinguistic symbols like those demonstrated for the apes) provides the detachment of volition from expression. 'That is, by using a symbol, the individual can refer to an entity without necessarily being emotionally involved with it.' In effect this is a displacement of affect.

Perhaps the most striking consequence of linguistic openness is the design feature *prevarication*. Hockett remarks: 'Linguistic messages can be false, and they can be meaningless in the logician's sense' (1966). Not only can people use language to lie but also to form statements that are grammatically correct but that are semantic nonsense. For example, Chomsky's 'Colourless green ideas sleep furiously' (1957: 15). This is a grammatical sentence on one level—the right kinds of words are used in the right places—but on another level it contains multiple contradictions. The ability of language users to prevaricate—to make statements or ask questions that violate convention—is a major consequence of open symbolic systems.

Closed call systems also lack *arbitrariness*, the lack of a transparent connection between the form (features of expression) of a symbol and its function/meaning.

Arbitrariness is evident in *duality of patterning*. Human language, Hockett claimed, is patterned on two different levels: sound and meaning. On the first level, the small set of significant sounds, or *phonemes*, are symbols that act as the expressive medium (form/signal/signifier) of other symbols, namely *morphemes*.

Phonemes, in themselves, have no 'meaning' in the sense of referential or lexical meaning. But on the second level of patterning, grammar puts the sound units together according to an entirely different set of rules: the resulting sound clusters are the smallest meaning-bearing units of the language: morphemes (e.g., */boi/* refers to a young male).

But the principle remains the same: units at one level, patterned in one way (sounds), can be used to create units at a different level, patterned in a different way (morphemes, or units of meaning). The rules governing morphemes, in turn, are different from the rules by which morphemes are combined into sentences, which are different from the rules combining sentences into discourse. With *semanticity* we have a very simple concept: language *means* things, or as Ferdinand de Saussure (1993), the 'father' of twentieth-century linguistics, would say, 'the signifier stands for the signified', and the connection between the two is arbitrary. To rephrase and expand on this, form does stand for a function, and this is certain in specified contexts (Pike 1943; 1967). Thus the association of linguistic signals with aspects of the social, cultural, and physical world of a speech community become significant because people use language to refer to and make sense of objects and processes in the world. Nevertheless, we need to remember that linguistic descriptions of reality are always selective, highlighting some features of the world and downplaying others. For example, a trained primatologist would distinguish apes (like chimpanzees) from monkeys (like baboons) and both apes and monkeys from prosimians (like lemurs) (Figure 4.3). By contrast, a person with no special knowledge of primates might use the words *monkey* and *ape* interchangeably to refer to chimpanzees and might never have heard of prosimians. Each speaker links the same words to the world in different ways.

Language and Context

Anthropologists are powerfully aware of the influence of context on what people choose to say. Years ago, for example, studies of child language amounted to a list of errors that children make when attempting to gain what Chomsky calls **linguistic competence**, or mastery of adult grammar. Today, however, linguists study children's verbal interactions in social and cultural contexts and draw attention to what children can do very well.

Figure 4.3 Distinct from apes and monkeys, Lemurs are prosimians found only on the island of Madagascar. Lemurs may have floated there eons ago on 'rafts' of vegetation and evolved in isolation over thousands of years.

From an early age they appear to communicate very fluently, producing utterances which are not just remarkably well-formed according to the linguist's standards but also appropriate to the social context in which the speakers find themselves. Children are thus learning far more about language than rules of grammar. [They are] acquiring communicative competence. (Elliot 1981: 13)

Communicative competence, or mastery of adult rules for socially and culturally appropriate speech, is a term coined by American anthropological linguist Dell

communicative competence A term coined by anthropological linguist Dell Hymes to refer to the mastery of adult rules for socially and culturally appropriate speech.

linguistic competence A term coined by linguist Noam Chomsky referring to the mastery of adult grammar.

Hymes (1972). As an anthropologist, Hymes objected to Chomsky's notion that linguistic competence consisted only of being able to make correct judgments of sentence grammaticality (Chomsky 1965: 4). Hymes observed that competent adult speakers do more than follow grammatical rules when they speak. They are also able to choose words and topics of conversation appropriate to their social position, the social position of the person they are addressing, and the social context of interaction.

For example, consider the issue of using personal pronouns appropriately. For native English speakers, the problem almost never arises with regard to pronoun choice because we address all people as 'you'. But any English speaker who has ever tried to learn French has worried about when to address an individual using the second-person plural (*vous*) and when to use the second-person singular (*tu*). To be safe, most students use *vous* for all individuals because it is more formal and they want to avoid appearing too familiar with native speakers whom they do not know well. But if you are dating a French person, at which point in the relationship does the change from *vous* to *tu* occur, and who decides? Moreover, sometimes—for example, among university students—the normal term of address is *tu* (even among strangers); it is used to indicate social solidarity. Native English speakers who are learning French wrestle with these and other linguistic dilemmas. Rules for the appropriate use of *tu* and *vous* seem to have nothing to do with grammar, yet the choice between one form and the other indicates whether the speaker is someone who does or does not know how to speak French.

Linguistic Relativity

During the first half of the twentieth century, two American anthropological linguists noted that the grammars of different languages often described the same situation in different ways. Edward Sapir and Benjamin Whorf concluded that language has the power to shape the way people see the world. This claim has been called the **linguistic relativity principle**, or the Sapir–Whorf hypothesis. This hypothesis has been highly controversial because it is difficult to test and the results of testing have been ambiguous.

The so-called strong version of the Sapir–Whorf hypothesis is also known as *linguistic determinism*. It is

a totalitarian view of language that reduces patterns of thought and culture to the patterns of the grammar of the language we speak. If a grammar classifies nouns in gender categories, for example, linguistic determinism concludes that speakers of that language are forced to think of males and females as radically different kinds of beings. By contrast, a language that makes no grammatical distinctions on the basis of gender presumably trains its speakers to think of males and females as exactly the same. If linguistic determinism is correct, then a change in grammar should change thought patterns: if English speakers replaced *he* and *she* with a new, gender-neutral, third-person singular pronoun such as *te*, then, linguistic determinists predict, English speakers would begin to treat men and women as equals.

There are a number of problems with linguistic determinism. In the first place, there are languages such as Fulfulde in which only one third-person pronoun is used for males and females, (*o*); however, male-dominant social patterns are quite evident among Fulfulde speakers. In the second place, if language determined thought in this way, it would be impossible to translate from one language to another or even to learn another language with a different grammatical structure. Because human beings do learn foreign languages and translate from one language to another, the strong version of the Sapir–Whorf hypothesis cannot be correct. Third, even if it were possible to draw firm boundaries around speech communities (which it isn't), every language provides its native speakers with alternative ways of describing the world. Finally, in most of the world's societies, monolingualism is the exception rather than the rule, yet people who grow up bilingual do not also grow up schizophrenic, as if trying to reconcile two contradictory views of reality (Figure 4.4). Indeed, bilingual children ordinarily benefit from knowing two languages; they do not confuse them, they can switch readily between them, and they even appear to demonstrate greater cognitive flexibility on psychological tests than monolinguals (Elliot 1981: 56).

In the face of these objections, other researchers offer a 'weak' version of the Sapir–Whorf hypothesis that rejects linguistic determinism but continues to claim that language shapes thought and culture. Thus, grammatical gender might not determine a male-dominant social order, but it might facilitate the acceptance of such a social order because the to rules for combining sounds into words and words into sentences. Whorf believed that grammar needed to be thought of in broader terms (Schultz 1990), but he died before working out the theoretical language to describe such a level.

Components of Language

Linguistic study involves a search for patterns in the way speakers use language; linguists aim to describe these patterns by reducing them to a set of rules called a **grammar**. Over time linguists came to recognize a growing number of components that form part of the grammar of any language. The most widely acknowledged components of language are phonology, morphology, syntax, semantics, and pragmatics.

Phonology: Sounds

The study of the sounds of language is called **phonology**. The sounds of human language are special because they are produced by a set of organs, the speech organs, that belong only to the human species. The actual sounds that come out of our mouths are called *phones*, and they vary continuously in acoustic properties. As speakers of a particular language, however, we hear all the phones uttered by fellow speakers within a particular range of variation as functionally equivalent *allophones* of the same *phoneme*, or characteristic speech sound in the language. Part of the phonologist's job is to map out possible arrangements of speech organs or acoustic perception that human beings may use to create and understand the sounds of language. Another part is to examine individual languages to discover the particular sound combinations they contain and the patterns into which those sound combinations are organized. No language makes use of all the many sounds the human speech organs can produce, and no two languages use exactly the same set. Canadian English uses only 38 sounds (more or less depending on the dialect). Most

Figure 4.4 People who grow up bilingual do not also grow up schizophrenic, as if trying to reconcile two contradictory views of reality.

grammatical distinction between *he* and *she* might make separate and unequal gender roles seem 'natural'. *Because many native speakers of English also are strong promoters of gender equality, however, the shaping power of grammar would seem far too weak to merit any scientific attention.*

Neither Sapir nor Whorf favoured linguistic determinism. Sapir argued that language's importance lies in the way it directs attention to some aspects of experience rather than others. He was impressed by the fact that 'it is generally difficult to make a complete divorce between objective reality and our linguistic symbols of reference to it' (1966 [1933]: 9, 15). Whorf's views have been more sharply criticized by later scholars. His discussions of the linguistic relativity principle are complex and ambiguous. At least part of the problem arises from Whorf's attempt to view grammar as the linguistic pattern that shapes culture and thought. Whorf's contemporaries understood grammar to refer

grammar A set of rules that aims to describe the patterns of linguistic usage observed by members of a particular speech community.

linguistic relativity principle A position associated with Edward Sapir and Benjamin Whorf that asserts that language has the power to shape the way people see the world.

phonology The study of the sounds of language.

work in phonology has been done from the perspective of the speaker who produces, or articulates, the sounds of language using the speech organs.

Although all languages rely on only a handful of phonemes, no two languages use exactly the same set. That is, the range of variation among phones, mentioned above, may be organized into different phonemes in different languages. Furthermore, different speakers of the same language often differ from one another in the way their phonemes are patterned, producing 'accents', which constitute one kind of variety within a language. This variety is not random; the speech sounds characteristic of any particular accent follow a pattern. Speakers with different accents are usually able to understand one another in most circumstances, but their distinctive articulation is a clue to their ethnic, regional, or social class origins.

Morphology: Word Structure

Morphology is the study of how words are put together. The study of the Indigenous languages of North America by linguistic anthropologists like Sapir and Whorf revealed many kinds of word structures that were not found in European languages.

What is a word? English speakers tend to think of words as the building blocks of sentences and of sentences as strings of words. But words are not all alike: some words (*book*) cannot be broken down into smaller elements; even though we might think that *boo* is a word, the remaining *k* is not. The word *bookworm*, however, can be broken down into *book* and *worm*. The puzzle deepens when we try to translate words from one language into another. Sometimes expressions that require only one word in one language (*préciser* in French) require more than one word in another (*to make precise* in English). Other times, we must deal with languages whose utterances cannot easily be broken down into words at all. Consider the utterance *nikookitepeena* from Shawnee (an Indigenous North American language), which translates into English as 'I dipped his head in the water' (Whorf 1956: 172). Although the Shawnee utterance is composed of parts, the parts do not possess the characteristics we attribute to words in, say, English or French (Table 4.1).

To make sense of the structure of languages such as Shawnee, anthropological linguists needed a concept that could refer to both words (like those in the English sentence above) and the parts of an utterance that could not be broken down into words. This led to the development of the concept of *morphemes*, traditionally defined as the minimal units of meaning in a language. The various parts of a Shawnee utterance can be identified as morphemes, and so can many English words. Describing minimal units of meaning as morphemes and not as words allows us to compare the morphology of different languages.

Morphemic patterning in languages like Shawnee may seem hopelessly complicated to native English speakers, yet the patterning of morphemes in English is also complex. Why is it that some morphemes can stand alone as words (*sing*, *red*) and others cannot (*-ing*, *-ed*)? What determines a word boundary in the first place? Words, or the morphemes they contain, are the minimal units of meaning. Thus, they represent the fundamental point at which the arbitrary pairing of sound and meaning occurs.

Syntax: Sentence Structure

A third component of language is **syntax**, or sentence structure. In languages like English, for example, rules governing word order cannot explain what is puzzling about the following English sentence: 'Smoking grass means trouble'. For many native speakers of Canadian English, this sentence exhibits what linguists call

Table 4.1 **Morphemes of Shawnee Utterance and Their Glosses**

ni	*kooki*	*tepe*	*en*	*a*
I	immersed in water	point of action at head	by hand action	cause to him

structural ambiguity. That is, we must ask ourselves what kind of *trouble* is involved: the illegal act of smoking grass (marijuana) or the danger of a prairie fire? In the first reading, smoking is a gerund, a noun derived from a verb (the act of smoking); in the second, it is a participle, an adjective derived from a verb (grass which is smoking).

We can explain the existence of structurally ambiguous sentences if we assume that the role a word plays in a sentence depends on the overall structure of the sentence in which the word is found and not on the structure of the word itself. Thus, sentences can be defined as ordered strings of words, and those words can be classified as parts of speech in terms of the function they fulfill in a sentence. But these two assumptions cannot account for the ambiguity in a sentence like 'The father of the girl and the boy fell into the lake.' How many people fell into the lake? Just the father or the father and the boy? Each reading of the sentence depends on how the words of the sentence are grouped together. Linguists discovered numerous other features of sentence structure that could not be explained in terms of morphology alone, leading to a growth of interest in the study of syntactic patterns in different languages. Although theories of syntax have changed considerably since Chomsky's early work, the recognition that syntax is a key component of human language structure remains central to contemporary linguistics.

Semantics: Meaning

Semantics, the study of meaning, was avoided by linguists for many years because *meaning* is a highly ambiguous term. What do we mean when we say that a word or a sentence means something? We may be asking about what each individual word in the sentence means, or what the sentence as a whole means, or what I mean when I utter the sentence, which may differ from what someone else would mean even if uttering the same sentence.

In the 1960s, a formal analysis of semantics was prompted by Chomsky's argument that grammars needed to represent all of a speaker's linguistic knowledge, including word meanings, as sets of abstract rules. Formal semanticists focused attention on how words were linked to each other within a language, exploring relations such as *synonymy*, or 'same meaning' (*old* and *aged*); *homophony*, or 'same sound,

different meaning' (*would* and *wood*); and *antonymy*, or 'opposite meaning' (*tall* and *short*). They also defined words in terms of *denotation*, or what they referred to in the 'real world'.

The denotations of words like *table* or *chair* seem fairly straightforward, but this is not the case with words like *truth* or *and*. Moreover, even if we believe a word can be linked to a concrete object in the world, it may still be difficult to agree on exactly what the term should refer to. (We saw this earlier when we discussed Hockett's design feature of *semanticity*.) Formal semantics studies the meaning relations among the words of a language as they might appear in a dictionary, whereas semanticity refers to the way actual speakers use those words to talk about things in the world. And, as Hockett stressed, the link between the vocabulary items in a dictionary and objects in the world is open, never determined once and for all.

This suggests that meaning must be constructed in the face of ambiguity. Formal semantics, however, tries to deal with ambiguity by eliminating it, by 'disambiguating' ambiguous utterances. To find a word's 'unambiguous' denotation, we might consult a dictionary. According to the *Oxford English Dictionary* (*OED*), for example, a pig is 'An omnivorous, domesticated even-toed ungulate derived from the wild boar *Sus scrofa*, with a stout body, sparse bristly hair, and a broad flat snout for rooting in the soil, kept as a source of bacon, ham, pork, etc. Also with distinguishing word to specify the breed.' A formal definition of this sort does indeed relate the word *pig* to other words in English, such as *cow* and *chicken*, and these meaning relations would hold even if all real pigs, cows, and chickens were wiped off the face of the earth. But words also have *connotations*, additional meanings that derive from the typical contexts in which they are used in everyday speech. In the context of anti-war demonstrations in the 1960s, for example, a 'pig' was a police officer.

From a denotative point of view, to call police officers *pigs* is to create ambiguity deliberately, to muddle

morphology In linguistics, the study of the minimal units of meaning in a language.
semantics The study of meaning.
syntax The study of sentence structure.

rather than to clarify. It is an example of **metaphor**, a form of figurative or non-literal language that violates the formal rules of semantic denotation by linking expressions from unrelated domains of meaning (e.g., law enforcement and livestock). Metaphors are used all the time in everyday speech, however. Does this mean, therefore, that people who use metaphors are talking nonsense? What can it possibly mean to call police officers *pigs*?

We cannot know until we place the statement into some kind of context. If we know, for example, that protesters in the 1960s viewed the police as the paid enforcers of racist elites responsible for violence against the poor, and that pigs are domesticated animals, not humans, who are often viewed as fat, greedy, and dirty, then the metaphor 'police are pigs' begins to make sense. This interpretation, however, does not reveal the true meaning of the metaphor for all time. In a different context, the same phrase might be used, for example, to distinguish the costumes worn by police officers to a charity function from the costumes of other groups of government functionaries. Our ability to use the same words in different ways (and different words in the same way) is the hallmark of openness, and formal semantics is powerless to contain it. This suggests that much of the referential meaning of language escapes us if we neglect the context of its use.

Pragmatics: Language in Contexts of Use

Pragmatics can be defined as the study of language in the context of its use. Each context offers limitations and opportunities concerning what we may say and how we may say it. Everyday language use is thus often characterized by a struggle between speakers and listeners over definitions of context and appropriate word use.

Formal linguistic pragmatics developed during the 1970s and 1980s; it has been described as the 'last stand' of formal linguists who wanted to explain speech entirely in terms of invariant grammatical rules (Hanks 1996: 94). Indeed, both language use and context are narrowly defined in formal pragmatics, bearing only on those uses and contexts that are presumably common to all speakers of all languages, a problematic assumption. Formal pragmatics more closely resembles formal logic than patterns of everyday language use.

Michael Silverstein (1976; 1985) was one of the first linguistic anthropologists to argue that the referential meaning of certain expressions in language cannot be determined unless we go beyond the boundaries of a sentence and place the expressions in a wider context of use. Two kinds of context must be considered. *Linguistic context* refers to the other words, expressions, and sentences that surround the expression whose meaning we are trying to determine. The meaning of *it* in the sentence 'I really enjoyed it' cannot be determined if the sentence is considered on its own. However, if we know that the previous sentence was 'My aunt gave me this book for my birthday', we have a linguistic context that allows us to deduce that *it* refers to 'this book'. *Non-linguistic context* consists of objects and activities that are present in the situation of speech at the same time we are speaking. Consider the sentence, 'What is that on the door?' We need to inspect the actual physical context at the moment this sentence is uttered to find the door, find what is on the door, and thus give referential meaning to the word *that* (Figure 4.5). Furthermore, even if we know what a door is in a formal sense, we need the non-linguistic context to clarify what counts as a door in this instance (e.g., it could be a rough opening in the wall).

By forcing analysts to go beyond syntax and semantics, pragmatics directs our attention to **discourse**, which is formally defined as a stretch of speech longer than a sentence united by a common theme. Discourse includes a spoken one-word greeting, a series of sentences uttered by a single individual, a conversation among two or more speakers, or an extended narrative. Many linguistic anthropologists accept the arguments of Mikhail Bakhtin and Valentin Voloshinov (see, e.g., Voloshinov 1986 [1929]) that the series of rejoinders in conversation are the primary form of discourse. In this view the speech of any single individual, whether a simple 'yes' or a book-length dissertation, is only one rejoinder in an ongoing dialogue.

Ethnopragmatics

Linguistic anthropologists analyze the way discourse is produced when people talk to one another. But they go far beyond formal pragmatics, paying attention not only to the immediate context of speech, linguistic and non-linguistic, but also to broader cultural contexts that are shaped by unequal social relationships and rooted in history (Brenneis and Macauley 1996; Hill and Irvine

Figure 4.5 To answer the question 'What is that on the door?', we need to inspect the physical context of the door and determine what *that* refers to.

1992). Duranti calls this **ethnopragmatics**, 'a study of language use that relies on ethnography to illuminate the ways in which speech is both constituted by and constitutive of social interaction' (1994: 11). Such a study focuses on *practice*, human activity in which the rules of grammar, cultural values, and physical action are all conjoined (Hanks 1996: 11). Such a perspective locates the source of meaning in everyday, routine social activity, or habitus, rather than in grammar. As a result, phonemes, morphemes, syntax, and semantics are viewed as linguistic resources people can make use of, rather than rigid forms that determine what people can and cannot think or say.

If mutual understanding is shaped by shared routine activity and not by grammar, then communication is possible even if the people interacting with one another speak mutually unintelligible languages. All

they need is a shared sense of 'what is going on here' and the ability to negotiate successfully who will do what (234). Such mutually co-engaged people shape *communicative practices* that involve spoken language but also include values and shared habitual knowledge that may never be put into words. Because most people in most societies regularly engage in a wide range of practical activities with different subgroups, each one will also end up knowledgeable about a variety of different communicative practices and the linguistic habits that go with them. For example, a university student might know the linguistic habits appropriate for the dinner table, classroom, dormitory, worship services, and her part-time job. Each set of linguistic habits she knows is called a *discourse genre*. Because our student simultaneously knows a multiplicity of different discourse genres she can use in speech, her linguistic knowledge is characterized by what Bakhtin called *heteroglossia* (1981).

For Bakhtin, heteroglossia is the normal condition of linguistic knowledge in any society with internal divisions. Heteroglossia describes a co-existing multiplicity of linguistic norms and forms, many of which are anchored in more than one social subgroup. Because we all participate in more than one of these subgroups, our language use is complex, even if the only language we know is English! Our capacity for heteroglossia is another example of Hockett's linguistic openness: it means that our thoughts and speech are not imprisoned in a single set of grammatical forms as linguistic determinists argued. Indeed, if our university student reflects on the overlap as well as the contrasts between the language habits used at the dinner table with those used in the dorm, she might well find herself raising questions about what words really mean. To the extent, however, that her habitual ways of speaking are deeply rooted in

discourse A stretch of speech longer than a sentence united by a common theme.

ethnopragmatics 'A study of language use that relies on ethnography to illuminate the ways in which speech is both constituted by and constitutive of social interaction.'

metaphor A form of thought and language that asserts a meaningful link between two expressions from different semantic domains.

pragmatics The study of language in the context of its use.

Figure 4.6 Although nominal power rests with Samoan chiefs, when village elders meet in the *fono*, titled orators like this man from the island of Tutuila tend to direct its proceedings.

One of the most obvious ways that context influences speech is when speakers tailor their words for a particular audience. Advertising agencies, for example, are notorious for slanting their messages to appeal to the people they want to buy their clients' products or services. Duranti learned that a sense of audience is highly cultivated among the professional orators who argue cases before the titled people, called *matai*, who regularly meet in the Samoan village council, or *fono* (Figure 4.6) (see EthnoProfile 4.1: Samoa). Orators make use of a discourse genre midway in formality between everyday speech and ceremonial speech. Because the *fono* renders judgments that assign praise and blame, the main struggle between orators for different sides is 'often centred on the ability to frame the reason for the meeting as involving or not involving

EthnoProfile 4.1

Samoa

Region: Oceania

Nation: Independent State of Samoa (Western Samoa 1914–97)

Language: Samoan people are one-half of the Samoan speakers of the world. This language is of the Malayo-Polynesian family, part of the Austronesian languages

Population: 214,265 (92.6 per cent Samoan) with 75 per cent living on the main island of Upolu

Environment: Tropical

Livelihood: Horticulture of tropical and subtropical crops, fishing, wage labour in capital

Political organization: Ranked, with linguistic markers for high- and low-status people; now part of a modern nation-state

For more information: Duranti, Alessandro. 1994. *From Grammar to Politics: Linguistic Anthropology in a Western Samoan Village* (Berkeley: University of California Press); Mead, Margaret. 1928. *Coming of Age in Samoa* (New York: Morrow); Freeman, Derick. 1983. *Margaret Mead and Samoa* (Cambridge: Harvard University Press)

everyday routine activity, they may guide the way she typically thinks, perceives, and acts. And to that extent, linguistic relativity may be seen to operate on the level of discourse (Hanks 1996: 176, 246; Schultz 1990).

A practice approach to language use aims to show how grammar, human action, and human values are all inextricably intertwined. But this does not mean that formal grammar can be ignored. As Hanks puts it, 'The system of language does have unique properties, and we do better to recognize this than to try to pretend it isn't so' (1996: 232). Each language, as a system, has a particular set of formal possibilities that can be mobilized as resources when people talk to one another. At the same time, 'context saturates linguistic forms, right down to the semantic bones' (142). Meaning is the outcome, thus, both of the formal properties of language uttered and the contextual situation in which it is uttered. And context always includes understandings about social relationships and previous history that may never be put into words.

certain key social actors' (Duranti 1994: 3). Of all the grammatical resources used by orators, one particular form called the *ergative Agent* most attracted Duranti's attention.

In semantic terms, an ergative Agent can be understood as a 'wilful initiator of an event that may be depicted as having consequences' for either an object or a passive recipient of the event (125). In Samoan, ergative Agents are marked by the preposition *e*, to distinguish them grammatically. Other forms of agency are marked by different prepositions: for example, *i* or *ia* frames the human agent as the source of the transaction rather than as its wilful initiator; the possessive marker *o* or *a* attached to an agent focuses attention not on the possessor but on the object possessed, that is, on John's *food* rather than on *John's* food. These ways of framing agency in grammatical terms are common in the *fono*, as disputants argue over who should be held accountable for some act. Possible agents include God, particular individuals, or groups. It is perhaps not surprising that the speaker who produced the highest number of ergative Agents in his speech was the senior orator who ran the meetings and often served as prosecutor. 'Powerful actors are more likely to define others as ergative Agents when they want to accuse them of something. Less powerful actors can try to resist such accusations by suggesting alternative linguistic definitions of events and people's roles in them' (133). In all cases, final judgments are the outcome of talk but of talk saturated with socio-political awareness and deeply rooted in local historical context.

Pidgin Languages: Negotiated Meaning

The Samoan village *fono* is a setting in which speakers and listeners are able, for the most part, to draw upon knowledge of overlapping language habits in order to struggle verbally over moral and political issues. In some instances, however, potential parties to a verbal exchange find themselves sharing little more than physical proximity to one another. Such situations arise when members of communities with radically different language traditions and no history of previous contact with one another come face to face and are forced to communicate. There is no way to predict the outcome of such contact on either speech community, yet from these new shared experiences, new forms of practice, including a new form of language—**pidgin**—may develop.

'When the chips are down, meaning is negotiated' (Lakoff and Johnson 1980: 231). The study of pidgin languages is the study of the radical negotiation of new meaning, the dialectical production of a new whole (the pidgin language) that is different from and reducible to neither of the languages that gave birth to it. The shape of a pidgin reflects the context in which it arises—generally one of colonial conquest or commercial domination. Vocabulary is usually taken from the language of the dominant group, making it easy for that group to learn. Syntax and phonology may be similar to the subordinate language (or languages), however, making it easier for subordinated speakers to learn. Morphemes that mark the gender or number of nouns or the tenses of verbs tend to disappear (Holm 1988).

Pidgins are traditionally defined as reduced languages that have no native speakers. They develop in a single generation between groups of speakers of distinct native languages. When speakers of a pidgin language pass that language on to a new generation, linguists usually refer to the language as a *creole*. The creolization of pidgins involves increased complexity in phonology, morphology, syntax, semantics, and pragmatics, such that the pidgin comes to resemble a conventional language.

This traditional view suggested to Bickerton (1981) that the way in which pidgins form could shed light on the universal biological bases of human language. He found that Hawaiian Pidgin English differed in many ways from Hawaiian Creole, which descended from it. Because, in his view, none of these differences could be connected to any of the languages available to those who invented Hawaiian Creole, he concluded that they were produced by the innate linguistic 'bio-program' of the creole creators, and he claimed that these same forms could be found in other unrelated creoles as well.

Other students of pidgins and creoles tried to test his hypothesis. While their work did not confirm his

pidgin A language with no native speakers that develops in a single generation between members of communities that possess distinct native languages.

views, it did reveal other important data. One discovery was that the old distinction between pidgins and creoles was more complex than previously thought. In the Pacific, for example, linguists have discovered pidgin dialects, pidgin languages used as main languages of permanently settled groups, and pidgins that have become native languages. Moreover, creolization can take place at any time after a pidgin forms, creoles can exist without having been preceded by pidgins, pidgins can remain pidgins for long periods and undergo linguistic change without acquiring native speakers, and pidgin and creole varieties of the same language can co-exist in the same society (Jourdan 1991: 192ff.). In fact, it looks as if heteroglossia is as widespread among speakers of pidgins and creoles as among speakers of other languages.

More information has been gathered about the historical and socio-cultural contexts within which pidgins first formed. Here as elsewhere in linguistic anthropology, the focus has turned to practice. Awareness of heteroglossia in pidgin/creole speech communities has led to the redefinition of a pidgin as a shared secondary language in a speech community, where speakers also use some other main language in smaller groups, and a creole as a main language in a speech community, whether or not it has native speakers. According to the new view, creolization is likely when pidgin speakers find themselves in new social contexts requiring a new language for *all* the practical activities of everyday life; without such a context, it is unlikely that creoles will emerge (196).

Viewing pidgin creation as a form of communicative practice means that attention must be paid to the role of pidgin creators as agents in the process (Figure 4.7). As we negotiate meaning across language barriers, it appears that all humans have intuitions

Figure 4.7 Tok Pisin, a pidgin language that developed in New Guinea following colonization by English speakers, has become a major medium of communication in New Guinea.

about which parts of our speech carry the most meaning and which parts can be safely dropped. Neither party to the negotiation, moreover, may be trying to learn the other's language; rather, 'speakers in the course of negotiating communication use whatever linguistic and socio-linguistic resources they have at their disposal until the shared meaning is established and conventionalized' (200).

Linguistic Inequality

Pidgins and creoles are far more complex—and the result of far more active human input—than previously thought, which is why they are so attractive to linguists and linguistic anthropologists as objects of study. Where they co-exist, however, alongside the language of the dominant group (e.g., Hawaiian Pidgin English and English), they are ordinarily viewed by members of society as defective and inferior languages. Such views can be seen as an outgrowth of the situation that led to the formation of most of the pidgins we know about: European colonial domination. In a colonial or post-colonial setting, the colonizer's language is often considered to be superior to pidgin or creole languages, which the colonizers characterize as broken, imperfect versions of their own language. The situation only worsens when formal education, the key to participation in the European dominated society, is carried out in the colonial language. Speakers of a pidgin or creole or Indigenous language who remain illiterate may never be able to master the colonial tongue and may find themselves effectively barred from equal participation in the civic life of their societies.

To take one language variety as the standard against which all other varieties are measured might be described as linguistic ethnocentrism, and such a standard may be applied to any language, not just pidgins and creoles. This is one kind of linguistic inequality: making value judgments about other people's speech in a context of dominance and subordination. A powerful example of the effects of linguistic inequality is found in the history and controversies surrounding African American English in the United States.

Language Habits of Change and Loss

Although, seemingly, this is an example that only has meaning for students that are 'American' rather than

'Canadian', it is in effect an issue that needs to be considered in any community where specific forms of a language emerge or evolve. African American English (AAE) now permeates certain areas (not confined to African American communities or the United States) of the entertainment industry and has reached into mainstream sectors of the wider North American, indeed world, use of English. This is to be expected in any 'living' language: invention, borrowing, evolution. And the history of the English language shows that it has always moved with its time. In the 1960s, some psychologists claimed that African American children living in urban areas of the northern United States suffered from linguistic deprivation. They argued that these children started school with a limited vocabulary and no grammar and thus could not perform as well as Euro-American children in the classroom—that their language was unequal to the challenges of communication. Sociolinguist William Labov and his colleagues found such claims incredible and undertook research of their own (Labov 1972), which demonstrated two things:

(1) they proved that the form of English spoken in the inner city was not defective pseudo-language, and
(2) they showed how a change in research context permitted inner-city African American children to display a level of linguistic sophistication that the psychologists had never dreamed they possessed.

When African American children were in the classroom (a Euro-American dominated context) being interrogated by Euro-American adults about topics of no interest to them, they said little. This did not necessarily mean, Labov argued, that they had no language. Rather, their minimal responses were better understood as defensive attempts to keep threatening Euro-American questioners from learning anything about them. For the African American children, the classroom was only one part of a broader racist culture. The psychologists, due to their ethnocentrism, had been oblivious to the effect this context might have on their research.

Reasoning that reliable samples of African American speech had to be collected in contexts where the racist threat was lessened, Labov and his colleagues conducted fieldwork in the homes and on the streets of the inner city. They recorded enormous amounts of speech in African American English produced by the same children who had had nothing to say when questioned in the classroom. Labov's analysis demonstrated that AAE was a variety of English that had certain rules not found in Standard English. This is a strictly linguistic difference: most middle-class speakers of Standard English would not use these rules but most African American speakers of AAE would. However, neither variety of English should be seen as 'defective' as a result of this difference. This kind of linguistic difference, apparent when speakers of two varieties converse, marks the speaker's membership in a particular speech community. Such differences can exist in phonology, morphology, syntax, semantics, or pragmatics. Indeed, similar linguistic differences distinguish the language habits of most social subgroups in a society, like that of Canada or the United States, that is characterized by heteroglossia.

Consider the issue of First Nations and Aboriginal language retention in Canada (Figure 4.8). Many communities are struggling to retain original languages, some having been pushed to extinction or near extinction by the residential school experience where use of original languages was firmly and sometimes violently discouraged. English became the language of domination and the medium of remembrance of the residential school experience. Many First Nations communities are engaged in programs to retain and/or recall and teach their languages. 'Memory needs a place, a context. Its place, if it finds one that lives beyond a single generation, is to be found in the stories that we tell. . . . [and it is this] art of memory . . . rooted in a land alive with geographical mnemonics . . .' (Kenny 1999: 421, 425) that remains important in the recall, teaching, and retention of language, as demonstrated in the work of the linguistic anthropologist Christine Schreyer. Further, language learning becomes one route to healing the injured individual and group who have suffered loss through the colonial process—it is the process of recalling memory. Thus this speaks to the study of **language ideology**: ways of representing the intersection 'between social forms and forms of talk' (Woolard 1998: 3). While the study of language ideology discloses speakers' sense of beauty, morality, or basic understandings of the world, it also provides

evidence of the ways in which our speech is always embedded in a social world of power differences. Language ideologies are markers of struggles between social groups with different interests, revealed in what people say and how they say it. The way people monitor their speech to bring it into line with a particular language ideology illustrates that language ideologies are 'active and effective . . . they transform the material reality they comment on' (11). In settings with a history of colonization, where groups with different power and different languages co-exist in tension, the study of language ideologies has long been significant (16). The skills of linguistic anthropologists especially suit them to study language ideologies because their linguistic training allows them to describe precisely the linguistic features (e.g., phonological, morphological, or syntactic) that become the focus of ideological attention, and their training in cultural analysis allows them to explain how those linguistic features come to stand symbolically for a particular social group.

Language Habits of Women and Men

Differences in language habits not only distinguish ethnic groups from one another but also distinguish the speech habits of women and men. Indeed, one of the early objections to work on African American English was that it focused on the discourse genres of men only. Since the 1970s, the language habits of African American women and girls have figured in numerous studies, to which Morgan's work is a recent contribution (see, e.g., Morgan 1995: 336ff.).

Sociolinguist Deborah Tannen (1990) gained much popular attention in the media with her study of speech patterns of men and women in the United States. Tannen focuses on typical male and female styles of discourse, arguing that men and women use language for different reasons: men tend to use language as a competitive weapon in public settings, whereas women tend to use language as a way of building closeness in private settings. Tannen shows what happens when men and women each assume that their rules are the only rules without realizing that the other gender may be defining appropriate language use from a different perspective. For example, when a husband and wife get home from work at the end of the day, she may be eager to talk while he is just as eager to remain silent. She may interpret his silence as a sign of distance or coldness and be hurt. He, by contrast, may be weary of the day's verbal combat and resent his wife's attempts at conversation, not because he is rejecting her personally but because he believes he has a right to remain silent.

Language and Truth

For Thomas Kuhn, a philosopher of science, metaphor lies at the heart of science, and changes in scientific theories are 'accompanied by a change in some of the relevant metaphors and in corresponding parts of the network of similarities through which terms attach to nature' (1979: 416). Kuhn argues that these changes in the way scientific terms link to nature are irreducible to logic or grammar. 'They come about in response to pressures generated by observation or experiment'—that is, by experience and context. And there is no neutral language into which rival theories can be translated and subsequently evaluated as unambiguously right or wrong (416). Kuhn asks the question, 'Is what we refer to as "the world" perhaps a product of mutual accommodation between experience and language?'

If our understanding of reality is the product of a dialectic between experience and language (or, more broadly, culture), then ambiguity will never be permanently removed from any of the symbolic systems that human beings invent. Reflexive consciousness makes humans aware of alternatives. The experience of doubt, of not being sure what to believe, is never far behind.

This is not merely the experience of people in Western societies. Evans-Pritchard (1963) describes the same sort of disorientation among the Azande of central Africa (see EthnoProfile 7.1: Azande). The Azande people are well aware of the ambiguity inherent in language, and they exploit it by using metaphor (what they call *sanza*) to disguise speech that might be received badly if uttered directly. For example, 'A man says in the presence of his wife to his friend, "Friend, those swallows, how they flit about in there." He is speaking about the flightiness of his wife and in case she should understand the allusion, he covers himself by looking up at the swallows as he makes his seemingly innocent remark' (1963: 211). Evans-Pritchard later observes that *sanza*

> adds greatly to the difficulties of anthropological inquiry. Eventually the anthropologist's sense of security is undermined and his confidence shaken. He learns the language, can say what he wants to say in it, and can understand what he hears, but then he begins to wonder whether he has really understood . . . he cannot be sure, and even they [the Azande] cannot be sure, whether the words do have a nuance or someone imagines that they do. (228)

However much we learn about language, we will never be able to exhaust its meanings or circumscribe its rules once and for all. Human language is an open system, and as long as human history continues, new forms will be created and old forms will continue to be put to new uses.

Figure 4.8 John Steckley, an anthropologist based in Toronto, is the world's last known Huron-language speaker. Huron language and history has been his focus for more than 30 years.

language ideology Ways of representing the intersection 'between social forms and forms of talk'.

In Their Own Words

The Round Robin Healing Circle

Christine Schreyer writes on her initial field experience and one of the programs to retain the Tlingit language.

On 25 June 2005, I arrived in Whitehorse, Yukon, for the very first time. I had come to begin my doctoral research with the Taku River Tlingit First Nation, located in Atlin, British Columbia, and the following morning I set out on the two-hour drive down the Alaska Highway to Jake's Corner, Yukon, and then turned down the windy, gravel mountain road to Atlin. When I arrived in town, I managed to get a hold of someone who could give me directions to the Five Mile reserve where the majority of the Taku River Tlingit community members currently live, five miles south of town, and to the Round Robin Healing Circle family camp [Figure 4.9]. I would be spending two weeks living there on my own whilst getting to know the community and working on a volunteer project. When I finally managed to find my way to the camp, I was warmly welcomed by Louise Gordon, her family, and friends and promptly set up in one of the wall tents at the camp. The camp is used by Louise and her family for sustainable activities such as fishing, nature walks, and berry picking,

as well as for community events such as culture camps. The volunteer project I would be working on with Louise and the Taku River Tlingit First Nation community was a Tlingit language board game for language revitalization. The Tlingit language is an endangered language, and within their community there are less than five elders who are fluent in the language, and no children learn Tlingit as their mother tongue. The game, now titled *Haa shagóon ítx yaa ntoo.aat* (or 'Travelling Our Ancestors' Paths') incorporates knowledge about subsistence practices, such as those practised at the Round Robin Healing Circle family camp, including words for resources and place names in the Tlingit language. The game was created with the help of Louise's grandmother, Antonia Jack, who had travelled Atlin Lake in 1999 to record the Tlingit place names so that her children, grandchildren, and great-grandchildren could learn the names of the places that are part of their heritage. The game is used in language revitalization programs within the community, and allows for children and adults to learn the language while having fun and interacting together.

Source: Schreyer, Christine. 2009. 'The Round Robin Healing Circle', guest editorial.

Figure 4.9 Round Robin Healing Circle family camp in Atlin, British Columbia, 26 June 2005.

Key Terms

communicative competence 81
design features 79
discourse 86
ethnopragmatics 87
grammar 83
language 77
language ideology 92
linguistic competence 81
linguistic relativity principle 82

linguistics 78
metaphor 86
morphology 84
phonology 83
pidgin 89
pragmatics 86
semantics 85
syntax 84

Chapter Summary

1. Language is a uniquely human faculty that both permits us to communicate and sets up barriers to communication. It is a part of culture that people use to encode their experiences, structure their understanding of the world and of themselves, and to engage with one another. The study of different languages reveals the shared nature of language and culture and the contextual assumptions that speakers make and use.

2. There are many ways to communicate our experiences, and there is no absolute standard favouring one way over another. Individual efforts to create a unique voice are countered by pressures to negotiate a common code within the larger social group.

3. Of Charles Hockett's 16 design features of language, six are particularly important: openness, displacement, prevarication, arbitrariness, duality of patterning, and semanticity.

4. Early linguistic anthropologists like Edward Sapir and Benjamin Whorf suggested that language has the power to shape the way people see the world. This is called the *linguistic relativity principle*.

5. Today formal linguistic analysis is usually divided into five specialties: phonology, the study of the sounds of language; morphology, the study of the minimal units of meaning in a language; syntax, the study of sentence structure; semantics, the study of meaning; and pragmatics, the study of language in the context of its use. These formal analyses, however, often more closely resemble formal logic than patterns of everyday language use.

6. Ethnopragmatics pays attention both to the immediate context of speech and to the broader contexts that are shaped by unequal social relationships and rooted in history. It locates meaning in routine practical activities, which turn grammatical features of language into resources people can use in their interactions with others.

7. Because linguistic meaning is rooted in practical activity, which carries the burden of meaning, the activity and the linguistic usage together shape communicative practices. Different social groups generate different communicative practices. The linguistic habits that are part of each set of communicative practices constitute discourse genres. People normally command a range of discourse genres, which means that each person's linguistic knowledge is characterized by heteroglossia.

8. The study of pidgin languages is the study of the radical negotiation of new meaning. In pidgins, two groups of language speakers who come in contact (often as a result of colonization or commercial domination) invent a new language different from either parent language. Pidgin languages exhibit many of the same linguistic features as non-pidgin languages. Studies of African American English illustrate the historical circumstances that can give rise to creoles and also provide evidence of the ways in which our speech is always embedded in a social world of power differences. Linguists and anthropologists have described differences in the gender-based communicative practices of women and men.

Critical Thinking Questions

1. Distinguish between phonemes and morphemes. Considering sociolinguistics, how do the use of phonemes and morphemes distinguish regional and socio-economic accents in the Canadian context?
2. Are all aspects of the design features of language used only by humans?
3. What are the processes of language change? How has language evolved in your lifetime?
4. Discuss the loss of languages and the struggle for language retention/learning in First Nations communities. Can programs for language retention play a role in reconciliation?
5. What makes Canadian English Canadian? Is it the Standard English of all of Canada, and is it stable or subject to change?
6. Consider words for various colours and shades of colour. How would you classify the colours of a rainbow? Is such a system of classification a cross-cultural phenomenon? Is it even consistent within your own linguistic community?

Suggested Readings

Akmajian, A., et al. 2001. *Linguistics*, 5th edn (Cambridge, MA: MIT Press). *A fine introduction to the study of language as a formal system.*

Brenneis, Donald, and Ronald K.S. Macauley, eds. 1996. *The Matrix of Language* (Boulder, CO: Westview Press). *A wide-ranging collection of essays by anthropologists studying linguistic habits in their socio-cultural contexts.*

Lakoff, George, and Mark Johnson. 1980. *Metaphors We Live By* (Berkeley: University of California Press). *An important, clear, and very accessible book that presents a radical and persuasive view of metaphor.*

Salzmann, Zdenek. 1998. *Language, Culture, and Society: An Introduction to Linguistic Anthropology*, 2nd edn (Boulder, CO: Westview Press). *An up-to-date and thorough text on linguistic anthropology.*

Smitherman, Geneva. 1977. *Talkin and Testifyin: The Language of Black America* (Detroit: Wayne State University Press). *An engaging introduction to black English vernacular, for native and non-native speakers alike, with exercises to test your mastery of the grammar of African American English.*

Related Websites

Franglais: http://www.yrad.com/franglais/

Language and Gender: http://www.kichu.com/elp/gender.html

Language Ideology and Language Education: http://www.languages. ait.ac.th/hanoi_proceedings/tollefson.htm

Newfoundland Word Game: http://www.nfld.com/nfld/other/ words/word.html

Semiotics for Beginners: http://www.aber.ac.uk/media/Documents/ S4B/sem07.html

Tok Pisin: http://www.calibercreations.com/pisin/; http://www.abc. net.au/ra/png/pnghome.htm

Culture and Individuals

Learning Objectives

By the end of Chapter 5, you will be able to:

- understand how perception organizes information,
- recognize that prototypes are central to the way meaning is organized,
- appreciate that cognition is 'a nexus of relations between the mind at work and the world in which it works',
- comprehend that emotion can be understood as the product of a dialectic between bodily arousal and cognitive interpretation,

- consider that the sources of motivation are embedded within a cultural matrix,
- distinguish between socialization and enculturation,
- consider what sort of entity is a *self*,
- identify how violence and trauma affect and are interpreted by the *self*, and
- realize that individual psychology is situated in the context of culture.

We do not all learn the same things, even if we live in the same society. This is because our learning is socially and culturally shaped by differences in status and experience. Patterns and variations in patterns can be detected; thus anthropologists are interested in cultural learning by individuals. Historically, psychological anthropology addressed this phenomenon by seeking answers for a series of persistent questions: 'What characteristics of our species are found in all times and places? What features are limited to specific groups of humans? How can we best take account of individual uniqueness?' (Bock 1994: ix).

Bock notes that 'An anthropology that takes account of individuals must make use of ideas from neighbouring disciplines' (ix), primarily from different kinds of psychological theories. To some extent this has involved anthropological adoption and cross-cultural evaluation of a series of different theoretical orientations in psychology as these succeeded one another historically. For example, some of the first twentieth-century anthropologists to take an interest in psychological matters, such as Margaret Mead and Bronislaw Malinowski, were influenced by the psychology of Sigmund Freud and attempted to test in non-Western settings certain Freudian ideas about personality development based on social relations in late nineteenth-century Viennese society.

These early studies initiated a pattern of analysis that has remained central to much psychological anthropology: that of critically examining universal statements about human nature produced by Western psychologists, especially those based on assumptions about how people in Western societies are supposed to be. This critical role is especially important in those situations where researchers make extreme claims about all members of the human species. Such claims frequently get publicity and tend to generate controversy. Early tests of Freudian theory are a good example. Is the pattern of early childhood development described by Freud universal in all human groups—'found in all times and places'? Or, conversely, is it an example of 'individual uniqueness', characteristic perhaps of individuals with disturbed childhoods but not of everyone else?

In North American Euro-ancestry societies, claims about universal human psychology compete with assertions of individual uniqueness. One of the most deeply entrenched forms involves opposing 'biology' to 'culture' as alternative, mutually exclusive explanations for some particular aspect of human psychological functioning. Such extreme claims and counterclaims never seem to be resolved, perhaps because they are too crude to illuminate much lasting interest in human psychology.

Most psychological anthropologists would agree that human beings are bio-cultural organisms. But finding a way to explain the connection between human biology and human culture that avoids an either–or option is often elusive. It is for this reason, as Bock says, that anthropologists have typically concentrated on 'the intermediate zone of group differences' where it becomes possible to identify relationships between specific features of a given culture and specific individuals (ix). This sort of demonstration has done a great deal to undermine ethnocentric prejudices, such as the assumption that all people are (or ought to be) 'just like us' or that some of us are 'rational' while others are 'irrational'.

One of the more promising directions recognized by Bock, and taken by some psychological anthropologists in recent years (e.g., Ingold 2000), has been influenced by the work of developmental psychologist Susan Oyama (1985). Now becoming known as Developmental Systems Theory (DST), this perspective has made great strides in rethinking the relationship between evolving species and the development of individual members of those species. DST recognizes that a developing organism is subject to many environments, identifiable at different levels of analysis, as it lives out its life cycle. From their perspective, a proper account of development requires taking into account the reciprocal influences of organisms and their environments at all steps in this ongoing process. It involves recognizing, furthermore, that environments as well as genes are passed on from parents to offspring, from the cytoplasm of the mother's egg to the cellular products produced within the developing embryo, to the mother's uterus, to the postnatal setting that provides (or fails to provide) the amounts and kinds of resources the organism needs to continue to develop.

Social, economic, and political environments thus become relevant factors shaping individual development for human beings, and enduring features of socially constructed environments get passed on to subsequent generations as faithfully as genes, thus influencing the developmental trajectory of future life cycles and, potentially, evolutionary selection pressures that impinge on the species itself. Human beings live in social groups that intensively rework their material environments; bequeath social, economic, and political resources to subsequent generations; and so shape the directions of their lives in decisive ways. Much recent work by psychological anthropologists implicitly, if not explicitly, adopts the DST approach in addressing various issues in human psychology.

Because of its wide variety of research problems and theoretical orientation, the field of psychological anthropology is not easy to summarize. However, Bock groups the work of psychological anthropologists into three basic areas of human experience: perception, cognition, and motivation (x). We will look at each area in turn.

The evidence overwhelmingly sustains the view put forth in our discussion of language: like language, human psychology is an open system. Thus if no one way of thinking or feeling is obligatory, then any particular way of thinking or feeling is shaped by factors encountered in the course of development. Human psychology routinely develops in the context of culturally shaped activities that draw our attention to some parts of the world while ignoring others. What we think or feel about something depends greatly on what we have learned to pay attention to in the past and the values we have learned to associate with it. As a result, different groups in a society—with different histories and experiences—are likely to develop unique points of view, pay attention to different things, and feel differently about them. When we learn from this culturally shaped experience, we can use pre-existing categories to help us interpret new experiences. This is a version of the linguistic design feature called *displacement*. All our senses can play tricks on us, moreover, and if they are artful enough people can trick other people into perceiving something that 'does not exist'. Thus, *prevarication* is a built-in feature of general human psychological processes, just as it is of language.

Human psychological processes are also heavily influenced by symbols. Language and visual perception, for example, both require human beings to construct symbolic representations of their experiences in order to make sense of them. As a result, the meaning of what we see, touch, smell, taste, or hear depends on context. As with language, two contexts are normally invoked: the *immediate* context of the perception itself and the *displaced* context stored in memory and shaped by culture. The 'same' object can mean different things in different contexts. Consider what seeing a butcher knife means (1) lying on a cutting board in your kitchen next to a pile of mushrooms or (2) wielded by an intruder who has cornered you in your kitchen.

Perception

Studies of perception flourished in the 1950s and 1960s and the results remain significant in correcting persistent misunderstandings about the way human perception works. **Perception** can be defined as the 'processes by which people organize and experience information that is primarily of sensory origin' (Cole and Scribner 1974: 61). It links people to the world around them or within them: we perceive size, shape, colour, pain, and so on.

Much like opposing biology and culture, intellect and emotion have referred to the two principal ways in which perceptions might be dealt with: rationally and logically, or passionately and intuitively. Anthropologists and some psychologists suggest that this approach is highly problematic. Particularly troubling is the traditional split between reason (Spock) and emotion (Kirk), which has often been accompanied by the overvaluing of one at the expense of the other. Particularly problematic is any assumption that perception occurs in a culture-free vacuum. In this anthropologists have always insisted that 'culture enters into every step of the perceptual process, initially by providing patterned material for perception . . . and later, through verbal and non-verbal means, by suggesting (or insisting on) the proper labelling of and responses to perceived patterns' (Bock 1994: xi).

Chunks of experience that appear to hang together as wholes, exhibiting the same properties in the same configuration whenever they recur, are called **schemas**. As human beings grow up, they gradually become aware of the schemas that their culture (or subculture) recognizes. Such schemas are often embedded in practical activities and labelled linguistically, and they may serve as a focus for discourse. People living in North America, for example, cannot avoid a schema called *Christmas*, a chunk of experience that recurs once every year. The Christmas schema can include features like cold and snowy weather and activities like baking cookies, singing carols, going to church, putting up a Christmas tree, and buying and wrapping gifts. In the experience of a child, all these elements may appear to be equally relevant parts of a seamless whole. It may take time and conditioning for Christian parents to persuade children what the 'true meaning of Christmas' really is: struggling with the secularization and commercialization of an essentially religious holiday. Non-Christians living in predominantly, if only nominally, Christian societies must also come to terms with this schema and may struggle to explain to their children why the activities associated with Christmas are not appropriate for them.

People take for granted most of the schemas that their culture recognizes, using them as simplified interpretive frameworks for judging new experiences as typical or not, human or not (D'Andrade 1992: 48). Schemas thus become **prototypes**. Prototypes appear to be central to the way meaning is organized in human language. Words refer to typical instances, typical elements or relations, and are embedded in genres of discourse associated with routine cultural practices.

When we organize on the basis of prototypes, however, the categories we use have fuzzy boundaries (openness) because our experiences do not always neatly fit our prototypes. Is a library a prototypical library when it contains fewer books than DVDs, videotapes, and electronic databases? In a case like this, suggests linguist R.A. Hudson (1980), a speaker must simply recognize the openness of language and apply linguistic labels creatively. Similarly, when confronted with novel perceptions, experiences for which no ready-made cultural interpretation is at hand, thinking and feeling human beings must extrapolate creatively to make sense of what is going on around them.

Traditional positivist science only recognizes the evidence of our five senses. As such, a suitably objective observer should be able to see and describe the world as it truly is. If other people describe the world differently, then their perceptions must in some way be distorted. Either they are not being objective or their ability to discriminate among sensations is impaired, or they are attempting to trick and mislead. However, most modern researchers are far less certain about what perception entails. True, our perception is sometimes impaired, either for physical reasons (we aren't wearing our glasses) or because our observations aren't disinterested (our child's forehead feels cool because we are afraid he or she might have a fever). And people do sometimes play jokes on one another, insisting that they have seen things they really have not seen. But what about people whose physiological equipment is functioning properly, who have no stake in the outcome, who are not trying to deceive, and yet who perceive things differently?

Classic research on variations in perception attempted to relate people's descriptions of their experiences, or their performances on psychological tests, to their understandings of *context*. The question is: What is their social and/or cultural position as an observer? For example, non-literate South African miners were tested using

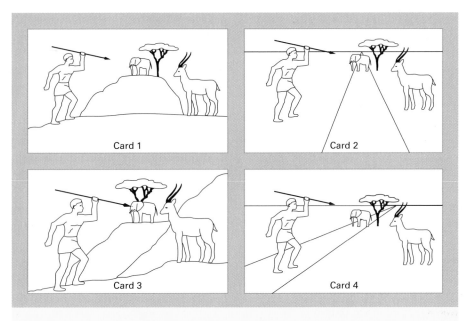

Figure 5.1 Pictures used for the study of depth perception in Africa.

two-dimensional line drawings of three-dimensional objects (Figure 5.1). The test results indicated that the miners consistently interpreted the drawings in two dimensions. When asked at which animal the man was pointing his spear on Card 1, subjects would usually respond 'the elephant'. The elephant is, in fact, directly in line with and closest to the spear point in the drawing. However, the elephant ought to be seen as standing on top of the distant hill if the subjects interpret the drawings three-dimensionally. Did their responses mean that they could not perceive in three dimensions?

J.B. Deregowski devised the following test: he presented different African subjects with the same drawings, asked them to describe what they saw, and was then given two-dimensional verbal reports. Next, he presented the same subjects with the line drawings in Figure 5.2. This time, he asked his subjects to construct models based on the drawings using materials he provided. His subjects had no difficulty producing three-dimensional models.

In these tests, the 'correct' solution depended on the subject's mastery of a Western convention for interpreting two-dimensional drawings and photographs. For the drawings in Figure 5.1, the Western convention includes assumptions about perspective that relate the size of objects to their distance from the observer. Without such a convention in mind, it is not obvious

that the size of an object has any connection with distance. Far from providing us with new insights about African perceptual abilities, perhaps the most interesting result of such tests is what they teach us about Western perceptual conventions. That is, drawings do not necessarily speak for themselves. They make sense to us only once we accept certain rules for interpreting them (Cole and Scribner 1974). And we need to remember that *perspective* in Western drawing is a relatively recent 'invention', and thus through openness our conventions changed.

Illusion

If you examine Figure 5.3, you will see that marks on a piece of paper can be ambiguous. The signals we receive from the outside world tend to be open to more than one interpretation, be they patterns of light and dark striking our retinas; smells, tastes, shapes, or words. The contrast between literal and metaphorical

perception The 'processes by which people organize and experience information that is primarily of sensory origin'.

prototypes Examples of a typical instance, element, relation, or experience within a culturally relevant semantic domain.

schemas Patterned, repetitive experiences.

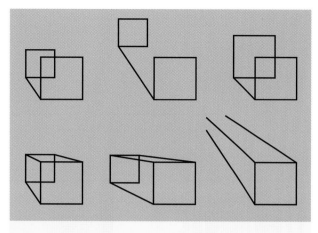

Figure 5.2 Drawings used for the construction of models in the depth perception test in Africa.

language is not unlike the contrast between reality and illusion as it relates to perception. In both cases, knowledge of context permits us to distinguish between the literal and the metaphorical, the real and the illusory.

Richard Gregory (1983), a cognitive psychologist, thinks illusions are produced by *misplaced procedures*: perfectly normal, ordinary cognitive processes that have somehow been inappropriately selected and applied to a particular set of visual signals. Thus perceptions are symbolic representations of reality, not direct samples of reality. Perceivers must often work very hard to make sense of the visual signals they

receive. When they are wrong, they are subject to illusion. Consider the visual illusion Gregory calls *distortion*: what you see appears larger or smaller, longer or shorter, and so on, than it really is. Look at the Ponzo illusion in Figure 5.4. Typically, the upper parallel line appears to be longer than the lower one when in fact they are equal. The standard explanation of this illusion is that we are looking at a two-dimensional drawing but interpreting it as if it were in three dimensions. In other words, the Ponzo illusion plays on our ability to see three-dimensional space in a two-dimensional drawing. The shapes trick us because they are very similar to what we perceive when we stand on a railroad track and look toward its vanishing point on the horizon. The Africans in Deregowski's test did not attempt to interpret the Ponzo-like lines on Card 2 of Figure 5.1 as representations of three-dimensional reality. On the contrary, they seemed to work very hard to keep the relationships between objects in two dimensions, even if this meant that the sizes of the objects themselves appeared distorted. When we compare the Western interpretation of the Ponzo illusion with the African interpretation of the pictures in Figure 5.1, we

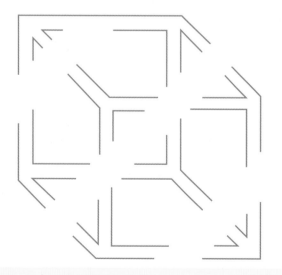

Figure 5.3 Ambiguous marks.

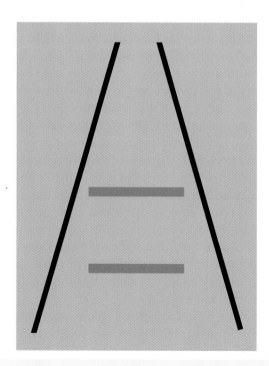

Figure 5.4 An example of distortion: the Ponzo illusion.

discover something important: both sets of drawings are ambiguous, and both are potentially open to distortion; how people interpret them depends on pre-existing experiences and cultural conventions.

Anthropologist Colin Turnbull worked among the Mbuti of the northeastern Democratic Republic of the Congo (Zaire) for many years (see Figure 5.5; see also EthnoProfile 5.1: Mbuti [Bambuti]). He discovered that people who live all their lives in a dense forest have no experience of distance greater than a few feet and are therefore not accustomed to taking distance into consideration when estimating the size of an object in the visual field. Turnbull took one of his informants, Kenge, on a trip that brought them out of the forest and into a game park. For the first time in his life, Kenge faced vast, rolling grasslands nearly void of trees. Kenge's response to this experience was dramatic: 'When Kenge topped the rise, he stopped dead. Every smallest sign of mirth suddenly left his face. He opened his mouth but could say nothing. He moved his head and eyes slowly and unbelievingly' (Turnbull 1961: 251). When Kenge finally saw the far-off animals grazing on the plain, he asked Turnbull what insects they were. When told that they were buffalo, Kenge laughed and accused Turnbull of lying. Then he strained to see

EthnoProfile 5.1

Mbuti
(Bambuti)

Region: Central Africa

Nation: Ituri Forest (70,000² miles) in the northeastern Democratic Republic of the Congo (Zaire)

Language: Mbuti, or the Bambuti, are actually three distinct cultures differentiated by the dialects they speak: Balese (Efŭ people), Bira (Sua people), and Mangbetu (Aka people)

Population: 30,000–40,000

Environment: Dense tropical rainforest with a two-month dry season

Livelihood: Hunting and gathering

Political organization: Traditionally, communal bands of seven to 30 families (average 17 families with 15–60 members); today, part of a modern nation-state

For more information: Turnbull, Colin. 1961. *The Forest People* (New York: Simon & Schuster); 1983. *The Mbuti Pygmies: Change and Adaptation* (New York: CBS College Publishing)

better and inquired what kind of buffalo could be so small. Later, when Turnbull pointed out a fishing boat on the lake, Kenge scoffed at him and insisted it was a piece of floating wood (252).

Visuality: Learning to Look

Susan Vogel has studied the sculpture of the Baule people of Ivory Coast since the early 1970s (see Ethno-Profile 3.1: Baule), and her research taught her that looking and seeing are culturally learned modes of sensory perception (1997: 108–11). She uses the term **visuality** to refer to the ways that individuals from

Figure 5.5 A Mbuti pygmy mother paints her daughter's face with a black juice from the gardenia fruit called *kangay*, used for staining the body or for drawing patterns on bark cloth. About every three months the clan moves to a new site where the women erect sapling and leaf huts.

visuality The ways that individuals from different societies learn to interpret what they see and to construct mental pictures using the visual practices that their own cultural system favours.

different societies learn to interpret what they see and to construct mental pictures using the visual practices that their cultural system favours. Vogel notes that, for the Baule, objects are powerful and affect the people who see them. Spiritually significant objects, which include much of what Westerners would call *sculpture*, are thus potentially dangerous. 'Even an inadvertent glimpse of a forbidden object can make a person sick, can expose them to huge fines or sacrifices, or can even be fatal' (110).

Vogel observed that, for the Baule, looking is the most important of all perceptual activities: seeing something is potentially more significant and more dangerous than touching, eating, or drinking something. There is an explicit etiquette governing how one ought to look at things, and staring is highly disapproved of. It is disrespectful for younger people to look directly at their elders, for example (110), and the rules for looking actually limit the 'visibility' of sculpture. For example, Western worshippers in a medieval Christian cathedral might gaze directly and intently at the altar, paying special attention to the elaborate painting or sculpture with which it has been adorned. For the Baule, however, analogous behaviour would be highly improper:

> If someone stopped and looked for a whole minute at the altar erected in plain view in Nguessan's courtyard, they would be called before the chief to explain. The fact that the altar stands in a public place, where a hundred people pass daily, does not mean it can be stared at. In fact the only motives for looking hard at such an object would be malevolent: a desire to kill someone in the courtyard, or to nullify the altar's powers. The stare itself is not the means of achieving either of these ends; it merely accumulates information for later use. (111)

Speakers of a language shape its vocabulary to reflect their cultural preoccupations. This can be seen in the ways Baule speakers talk about visuality. There are four words in the Baule language for looking and seeing. These terms distinguish among objects that anyone can look at, objects that must never be deliberately looked at, and all degrees in between (91).

(1)   The most common verb translated as 'to look' is *nian*, which can also mean 'to watch'. It connotes intentional watching, and is used for watching mask dances intended for entertainment and for watching television.

(2)   The noun *nyin* means 'a stare' or a good hard look. The phrase *nyin kpa*, 'a real stare', is used to describe looking at a useful decorated object with no sacred meaning.

(3)   The noun *kanngle* means 'evil looks from the corner of the eye'.

(4)   *Nian klekle* means 'to look clandestinely', to 'cast a rapid glance' (91).

The most awesome objects and events—the men's sacred masks, divination dances, and funerals—are not spoken of with any of those words. 'One never says one has seen or looked at these potent things; one merely says *N'wo se bo*, "I went to the funeral", or *N'su ko awebo*, "I went to the divination dance" (92).'

Life is lived knowing that sculptures—powerful objects—are present but cannot be examined, cannot be looked at closely. As a result, when these objects are visible, even though they are incompletely seen, they make an extraordinary impression on people who use memory and imagination to construct lasting images in their minds, remembering their experiences of seeing sculpture in great detail for the rest of their lives. Such experiences make powerful contributions to the perception of a particular Baule world view.

Cognition

The study of illusion demonstrates that there can be a gulf between what we see and what we know, what we perceive and what we conceive. In everyday life, these discrepancies seem to be manageable: there is coherence between perceptions and conceptions. Moreover, because our link with the world is a dialectical one, there is no sharp boundary between what we perceive and what we conceive. Not only can new perceptions lead us to modify our conceptions (i.e., we learn), but new conceptions can also lead us to perceive aspects of the world around us that we didn't pay attention to before. We are active meaning-makers, internally negotiating our experiences. As a result, **cognition** is perhaps best understood as 'a nexus of relations between the mind at work and the world in which it works' (Lave 1988: 1).

The study of cognition began in the 1960s with growing interest by anthropologists in the ways different peoples classified cultural knowledge. An interesting and comprehensive review of the early application of theories of cognition can be found in Roy D'Andrade's book *The Development of Cognitive Anthropology* (1995). Chapter Five on folk taxonomies gives us insight into shared salient cognitive features and of particular use here are the early studies of *ethnobotany* and *ethnozoology*. Using the language of their informants, anthropologists were effectively doing *ethnoscience*—finding the **taxonomies** used for specific things and the **generics** used to lump things into categories.

> Taxonomies use relations between *kinds of things* which have been recorded into 'configurational attributes'. A *collie* is a kind of *dog*, and 'dogginess' is a configurational attribute—a configuration of large numbers of attributes 'recorded' and 'chunked' into a single gestalt of 'dogginess'. By virtue of being a *kind of dog*, collies 'inherit' all the recorded attributes that make up the chunked quality of 'dogginess'—nose, tail, yelp and all. (D'Andrade 1995: 93)

Eventually pursuing links between language and culture, researchers moved beyond classifying different parts of the natural world and came to focus on the many other ways of 'labelling' the social and cultural worlds of their informants. Recently, cognitive anthropologists have become more interested in the mental processes people use to make sense of their experiences in the world.

Cognitive Capacities and Intelligence

What makes it possible for human beings to receive signals from the outside world (or from within our own bodies) and then interpret those signals in a way that makes appropriate action possible? One traditional answer has been that every person either possesses at birth or develops over time certain basic cognitive capacities. At one time, these hypothetical capacities were thought of as substances or properties, and the goal of psychological testing was to measure how much of each cognitive capacity an individual had. Consequently, intelligence has traditionally been 'measured' using an 'instrument' called the *intelligence test*; the 'amount' of intelligence measured is assigned a number called the *Intelligence Quotient*, or *IQ*. In the past, some researchers were quick to equate differences in performance on intelligence tests with differences in intelligence. Today, such a reductionist approach is subjected to intense scrutiny.

If it is difficult to identify and measure cognitive capacities in individuals, it may be impossible to do so for entire groups. Michael Cole is a scholar who has spent several decades trying to combine psychology and anthropology in his own work (Cole 1994: 329). Beginning in the 1960s, he and Sylvia Scribner developed extensive experience in cross-cultural psychological testing. In their fieldwork, they repeatedly encountered situations in which the same psychological test produced results that differed between Western and non-Western subjects. They rejected the idea that non-Western subjects were less intelligent because outside the laboratory setting, in the routine contexts of everyday life, their informants' intelligence and full humanity were obvious.

So why do intelligent informants often perform poorly on psychological tests? In the work of the Russian psychologist Lev Vygotsky, Cole and Scribner (1974) found an approach that pointed toward an answer. Vygotsky distinguished between elementary cognitive processes and the higher systems into which these processes are organized. **Elementary cognitive processes** include the ability to make abstractions, to categorize, to reason inferentially, and so forth. All humans without intellectual cognitive impairment are equipped with these abilities. Different cultures, however, organize these elementary processes into different **functional cognitive systems**. Culture also assigns different functional systems to different tasks in different contexts. There are different ways of defining tasks; once tasks are defined, there are different strategies for carrying them out, and routine strategies for carrying

cognition (1) The mental process by which human beings gain knowledge, and (2) the 'nexus of relations between the mind at work and the world in which it works'.

elementary cognitive processes The ability to make abstractions, reason inferentially, categorize, and perform other mental tasks common to all humans without intellectual cognitive impairment.

functional cognitive systems Culturally linked sets of cognitive processes that guide perception, conception, reason, and emotion.

generics Refers to an entire group, kind, or class in a general or inclusive way.

taxonomies Schemas that sort groups of things (taxonomic units) into subgroups (*taxa*) in a way that the subgroups are mutually exclusive. Thus, all subgroups share the defining characteristic of the group but at least one characteristic that makes them exclusive to their subgroup. Taxonomies usually result in an arrangement that has a hierarchical structure.

out (or refusing to carry out) tasks cannot be separated from the broader cultural and political contexts in which people live. As a result, administering an adequate psychological test starts to look as difficult as doing good anthropological fieldwork, with the same rewards and pitfalls.

Cognitive Style

Cognitive style refers to a recurring pattern of perceptual and intellectual activity. Cultures provide people with a range of cognitive styles that are appropriate for different cognitive tasks in different contexts. Psychological anthropologists have attempted to compare cognitive styles cross-culturally. Some have argued that the styles of individuals and of groups can be located on a continuum between a global style and an articulated style. People who use a **global style** tend to view the world holistically; they first see a bundle of relationships and only later see the bits and pieces that are related. They are said to be *field dependent*. By contrast, people who use an **articulated style** tend to break up the world into smaller and smaller pieces, which can then be organized into larger chunks. They also tend to see a sharp boundary between their own bodies and the outside world. People using an articulated style are able to consider whatever they happen to be paying attention to apart from its context and so are said to be *field independent* (Cole and Scribner 1974: 82).

Originally, most people in Western societies were thought to be field independent, whereas most people in most non-Western cultures were thought to be field dependent. However, more detailed research shows that these generalizations are misleading. For instance, the preferred cognitive style of an individual often varies from task to task and from context to context. People who use articulated styles for some tasks also use global styles for other tasks. In fact, they may bring a range of different styles to bear on a single task.

Research by Jean Lave and her colleagues (1988) demonstrated that middle-class North Americans are not field independent in all contexts, even when the task involves mathematics, which would seem to be the most field independent of all cognitive activities. Lave and her associates wanted to test the widespread assumption that cognitive style does not vary across contexts. In particular, they wanted to find out whether ordinary people use the same mathematical skills in the supermarket and the kitchen that they use in the classroom. As part of the research, subjects were given a pencil-and-paper math test to determine how well they could solve certain problems in a school-like context. Researchers also observed how the same subjects used mathematics while making buying decisions at the grocery store. Finally, the subjects were presented with paired grocery items and asked to calculate the best buy.

The results were surprising. First, the subjects averaged only 59 per cent correct on the pencil-and-paper test but achieved averages of 98 per cent on the supermarket experiment and 93 per cent on the best-buy experiment. Second, the researchers found that the high scores on the last two experiments were achieved with very little reliance on mathematics taught in school. Many observers would have expected subjects trained in formal mathematics to rely on its infallible methods to help them make wise economic decisions. On the contrary, the test results suggest that shoppers were better able to make wise economic decisions using informal calculation strategies. The three most common informal strategies were *inspection* (recognizing that one item was both lower in price and larger in volume), *best-buy calculations* (comparing two quantities and two prices first and choosing the better value), and a *difference strategy* (deciding whether a marginal difference in quantity was worth the marginal difference in price) (Lave 1988: 107ff.).

Lave notes that some psychologists would conclude from these results that there was something primitive or illogical about the informal strategies—and, by extension, about the people who used them (see, e.g., Lave 1988: 79ff., 107ff.). In the terms we used earlier, these strategies are all closer to the global, field-dependent end of the cognitive-style continuum. Should we conclude, therefore, that ordinary middle-class North Americans fail to think rationally when they shop for groceries? This conclusion is contradicted by the experimental evidence showing that the shoppers' informal strategies were exceptionally accurate. In addition, shoppers did occasionally use formal mathematics as an alternative to the other informal strategies, but they did so only when the numbers for quantity and price were easy to transform into unit–price ratios. This did not happen very often, however, because units and prices in supermarkets are often given in prime numbers, making rapid mental calculation tedious and complicated. Rather than waste time dividing $5.27 by 13 ounces to obtain the price per ounce, the shoppers preferred to rely on other calculation strategies (Figure 5.6).

This last observation points to a major difference between 'school' math and 'grocery store' math. In school, the only purpose of a mathematical exercise is to obtain a single correct answer. 'The puzzles or problems are assumed to be objective and factual. . . . Problem solvers have no choice but to try to solve problems, and if they choose not to, or do not find the correct answer, they "fail"' (Lave 1988: 35). Matters are otherwise outside the classroom. Shoppers do not visit supermarkets as an excuse to practise formal mathematics; they go to buy food for their families. Consequently, the choices they make are influenced not merely by unit–price ratios but by the food preferences of the other family members, the amount of storage space at home, the amount of time they can spend shopping, and so on. In the supermarket, as Lave puts it, '"problems" are dilemmas to be resolved, rarely problems to be solved' (20). Formal mathematical calculations and knowledge of what costs less per unit may help resolve some dilemmas, but in other cases they may be too troublesome to bother with, or even irrelevant. Shoppers, unlike students in the classroom, are free to abandon calculation, to use means other than formal mathematics to resolve a dilemma (58).

One feature all Lave's subjects shared was the knowledge that pencil-and-paper tests in school-like settings required an articulated, field-independent

Figure 5.6 Shoppers often rely on informal mathematical strategies to calculate the best buy because numbers for quantity and price are not often easy to transform into unit–price ratios.

style. In non-Western societies, attending a European- or American-style school seems to impart the same knowledge to non-Western people. But even Western subjects may reserve that cognitive style for the classroom, preferring a variety of more global strategies to resolve the dilemmas of everyday life. We have seen how some of these dilemmas can be generated by a lack of fit between the background information we take for granted and sensory signals that are ambiguous. This lack of fit may be between, say, our family's food preferences and confusing price–ratio information on two products we are comparing. It may be between our expectation that straight edges are normally continuous and surprising gaps in our visual field. In any case, our awareness of the cognitive dilemmas we face should make us more sympathetic to cognitive 'errors' we see being made by people from different cultures who may be employing different cognitive styles.

These studies reinforce the conclusion that competent members of all societies employ a range of cognitive styles. We cannot speak of abstract thinking and concrete thinking as mutually exclusive. Anthropologists have found that many non-Western peoples are not used to thinking about things without relating them to some kind of context. Members of those societies can learn to use a context-free cognitive style if they attend school, but this does not mean that they never use abstract categories outside the classroom. As Lave's research demonstrates, the full range of her shoppers' calculating skills were displayed only when she studied mathematics in the supermarket rather than in the classroom and became aware of the range of factors in addition to price that influenced buying decisions.

Consider Levinson's (1998) work on viewpoint-dependent (relative/flexible) and viewpoint-independent (absolute/fixed) systems. 'A system of fixed orientations

articulated style A way of viewing the world that breaks it up into smaller and smaller pieces, which can then be organized into larger chunks. People who use such a style consider whatever they happen to be paying attention to apart from its context. They are said to be field independent.

cognitive style Recurring patterns of cognitive activity that characterize an individual's perceptual and intellectual activities.

global style A way of viewing the world that is holistic. People who use such a style first see a bundle of relationships and only later see the bits and pieces that are related. They are said to be field dependent.

is a social fact . . . that is arbitrary . . . whose existence constrains individuals. It can be learned only through communication. To use it requires constant background computations of a specialized sort that members of other communities may not indulge in at all' (20). Thus, cross-cultural research in cognition is a delicate business. For the researcher, the first trick is to devise a test that will give people who use different cognitive styles an opportunity to show what they know and what they can do. The researcher must also discover whether different groups of subjects share the same understanding of tasks they are being asked to perform. In recent years, a number of researchers have worked to develop methods to assess cognition that are not bound to the traditional psychological testing laboratory or to the classroom.

Reason and the Reasoning Process

From the earliest days of the West's discovery of other societies, there has been a debate about the extent to which non-literate non-Western peoples might be said to possess reason. Rooted in the context of Western colonialism, this debate was rarely disinterested, for domination by Europeans was often justified on the grounds that those dominated were irrational. Faced with this problematic history, how might anthropologists study rational thinking? Most cognitive psychologists have adopted Jerome Bruner's famous definition of **thinking** as 'going beyond the information given'. This means that thinking is different from remembering (which refers to information already given) and also from learning (which involves acquiring information that was not given beforehand). Going beyond the information given thus implies a complex interrelationship between information already at hand and the cognitive processes of the person who is attempting to cope with that information. This definition highlights the 'nexus of relations between the mind at work and the world in which it works'. Thinking is open and active, and it has no predetermined outcome.

Culture and Logic

One set of cognitive tests has to do with verbal reasoning ability. These tests present subjects with three statements in the form of a syllogism—for example, 'All men are mortal, Socrates is a man, therefore Socrates is mortal.' The first two propositions are called the *premises*, and the third statement is the *conclusion*. For

a syllogism to be sound, the conclusion must follow from the premises.

Syllogistic reasoning is enshrined in Western culture as the quintessence of rational thought. Some researchers suggested that the rational capacities of non-Western peoples could be tested using logical problems in syllogistic form. Presumably their rationality would be confirmed if they could deduce correctly when the conclusion followed logically from the premises and when it did not.

Cole and Scribner presented logical problems involving syllogistic reasoning to their Kpelle subjects in Liberia (see Map 5.2). Typically, the logical problem was embedded in a folktale-like story. The experimenter read the story to the subjects and then asked them a series of follow-up questions designed to reveal whether the subjects could draw a correct conclusion from the premises given.

Here is one story Cole and Scribner prepared: 'At one time Spider went to a feast. He was told to answer this question before he could eat any of the food. The question is: Spider and Black Deer always eat together. Spider is eating. Is Black Deer eating?' (1974: 162). Given the two premises, the conclusion should be that Black Deer is eating. Now consider a typical Kpelle response to hearing this story:

> Subject: Were they in the bush?
>
> Experimenter: Yes.
>
> Subject: Were they eating together?
>
> Experimenter: Spider and Black Deer always eat together. Spider is eating. Is Black Deer eating?
>
> Subject: But I was not there. How can I answer such a question?
>
> Experimenter: Can't you answer it? Even if you were not there, you can answer it. (Repeats the question.)
>
> Subject: Oh, oh, Black Deer is eating.
>
> Experimenter: What is your reason for saying that Black Deer was eating?
>
> Subject: The reason is that Black Deer always walks about all day eating green leaves in the bush. Then he rests for a while and gets up again to eat. (Cole and Scribner 1974: 162)

The subject's answer to the question and subsequent justification for that answer seem to have nothing whatsoever to do with the logical problem the subject is being asked to solve.

In Their Own Words

A Place for Memory

Michael Kenny from Simon Fraser University in Vancouver discusses residential schools to which First Nations children were sent.

Boarding schools were seen as a practical necessity if Indian children were to be acculturated to the new European order. Government and church authorities thought it best for children to be taken away from their families and cultural milieu so that they could be 'civilized', meaning that they would be taught to work and to be good Christians. While the Nazi concentration camp guards regarded Jewish inmates as *Urgeziefer* (vermin), Native children often remember being regarded as dumb, dirty, lousy Indians. Seen in a certain light, the schools were a Dickensian horror: squalid, oppressive, and violent.

The Canadian Federal Government has responsibility for Native affairs. Given the vast size of the country, underfunding, and the absence of constitutional barriers limiting sectarian involvement in public education, the Canadian state in effect farmed Indian education out to the churches and most particularly to the Roman Catholic Church (the United Church of Canada and the Anglican Church were also involved, among others). The schools were often highly regimented, a discipline of much work and, at least at first, little play, insufficient food, and a high mortality rate—particularly from tuberculosis—brought about by the harsh and overcrowded conditions. Children were taken from their families, sometimes with consent, sometimes coercively. While in school, boys were separated from girls, sibling from sibling. The speaking of Indigenous languages was prohibited, and little place made for Native culture.

This widely shared school experience has in recent times led to a sense of collective victimization and, inversely, to renewed self-assertion among Canadian Native peoples: 'The residential school issue has united Native people across Canada like no other issue in recent history.' But the way in which the residential school story has come to be told is a sign of *our* times. Sexual abuse allegations about what went on in the schools have multiplied, accompanied by numerous confessions and convictions, extending even to a Roman Catholic bishop: 'What people make of their places is closely connected to what they make of themselves as members of society.' What Native peoples now make of the residential schools has been accompanied by a sea-change in political consciousness.

It is now possible to speak of a Residential School Syndrome, of Native people as its survivors, and of what Euro-Canadians tried to do to them as 'cultural genocide'. Political and therapeutic discourse have become thoroughly intertwined around the central metaphor of 'healing'. It is said that, as the white world tried to deny Native history, so recovery of the hidden history of the residential schools affirms the persistence and constitutional status of the First Nations as a necessary step toward the restoration of integral personal and cultural identity. One such account actually attempts to drop the 'healing' metaphor since, in the view of its authors, it tends to psychologize what is at root a political issue. What happened in the schools was not the product of an honest mistake on the part of misguided churches and a paternalistic government; instead, it was attempted genocide, as defined by the UN Genocide Convention—an Indian Holocaust. . . .

Source: Kenny, Michael G. 1999. 'A Place for Memory: The Interface between Individual and Collective History', *Comparative Studies in Society and History* 41, 3 (July): 420–37.

The experimenters devised this story the same way schoolteachers devise mathematical word problems. That is, the contextual material is nothing more than a kind of window dressing. Schoolchildren quickly learn to disregard the window dressing and seek out the mathematical problem it hides. In the same way, the Kpelle subjects hearing the story about Spider and Black Deer were supposed to demonstrate logic by disregarding the contextual material about the feast and

seeking out the syllogism embedded within it. However, Kpelle subjects did not understand that they were being

syllogistic reasoning A form of reasoning based on the syllogism, a series of three statements in which the first two statements are the premises and the last is the conclusion, which must follow from the premises.

thinking An active cognitive process that involves 'going beyond the information given'.

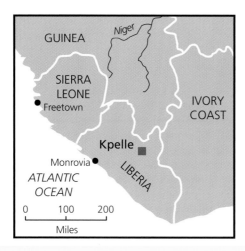

Map 5.2 Kpelle

read this story in a testing situation for which considerations of context or meaningfulness were irrelevant. In the preceding example, the subject seemed to have difficulty separating the logical problem both from the introductory material about the feast and from the rest of his experiential knowledge.

Cole and Scribner interpreted their subject's response to this problem as being due not to irrationality but to a 'failure to accept the logical task' (162). In a follow-up study, Cole and Scribner discovered that Kpelle high-school children responded 'correctly' to the logical problems 90 per cent of the time. This suggests a strong correlation between Western-style schooling and a willingness to accept context-free analytic tasks in testing situations (164).

But this is not all. David Lancy, one of Cole and Scribner's colleagues, discovered that Western-style syllogisms are very similar to certain forms of Kpelle riddles. Unlike syllogisms, however, those riddles have no single 'logically correct' answer. 'Rather, as the riddle is posed to a group, the right answer is the one among many offered that seems most illuminating, resourceful, and convincing as determined by consensus and circumstance. This emphasis on edification as a criterion for "rightness" is found in Kpelle jurisprudence as well' (Lancy, cited in Fernandez 1980: 47–8). In other words, the 'right' answer cannot be extracted from the form of the riddle by logical operations. Rather, it is the answer that seems most enlightening and informative

to the particular audience in the particular setting where the riddle is posed. Also, it reinforces the concept of consensus—inclusion of all in the process—thus making problem solving a group activity thereby creating group ownership of not just the problem but the solution. There is no reason to doubt that all humans come equipped with the same elementary cognitive processes: the ability to make abstractions, to create conceptual categories, and to reason inferentially. The difficulty is to understand how these elementary cognitive processes are put to work within culturally shared schemas to produce different, functional cognitive systems known as **reasoning styles**.

Emotion

Psychological anthropologists who try to define emotion in cross-cultural terms run into a familiar problem: they discover not just that different cultures talk about emotion in different languages but also that not all languages possess a term that might be translated as *emotion*. To get out of this tangle, they have tried to develop a theory of cognitive functioning that accounts for the experiences that some cultures recognize as emotional.

We return to Western dualism where reason and thought are associated with the mind and emotion with the body. Any attempt to explain emotion must deal with the nature of the bodily arousal we associate with it. But there is more to emotion, as commonly understood, than mere bodily arousal. Recall the butcher knife scenario referred to earlier. What do we feel when we see a butcher knife sitting beside mushrooms on a cutting board in our kitchen? What do we feel when we see that same knife in the hands of an intruder bent on attacking us? The knife alone does not trigger our feeling. The context in which we encounter the knife is equally important. The context itself can be ambiguous, and our emotional experience changes as our interpretation of the context changes.

Emotion engages both bodily arousal and cognitive interpretation. Cognitive psychologist George Mandler suggests that bodily arousal can trigger an emotional experience by attracting our attention and prompting us to seek the source of arousal (Mandler 1975: 97). Conversely, a particular interpretation of our experience can trigger bodily arousal. Arousal may heighten or diminish depending on how we interpret what is happening around us.

Mandler's discussion of emotion, like Cole and Scribner's discussion of cognition, describes emotions as *functional systems*. Each links elementary processes that involve the body's arousal system to other elementary processes that play a role in the construction of perception, conception, and reasoning. 'Emotions are not something that people "have"; they are constituted of people's states, values, and arousals' (Mandler 1983: 151). Approaching emotion from this perspective accomplishes three things:

(1) it integrates mind and body in a holistic fashion;

(2) it acknowledges ambiguity as a central feature of emotional experience, just as we have argued it is central to linguistic, perceptual, and conceptual experience; and

(3) it suggests how different cultural interpretive frameworks might shape not only what we think but also what we feel.

Therefore, **emotion** can be understood as the product of a dialectic between bodily arousal and cognitive interpretation. It is comprised of states, values, and arousals.

Why should we experience emotion at all? The role of emotion in human life may be rooted in the evolutionary history of a highly intelligent species that is capable of thinking before acting. Bodily arousal alerts us to something new and unexpected in our environment, something that does not easily fit into any conventional schema. Once our attention is caught in this way, the rest of our cognitive processes can focus on the interrupting phenomenon. From this perspective, a person would be foolish to ignore his or her 'gut feelings' when trying to sort out a confusing experience. Indeed, the 'gut feelings' are usually what alert us to confusion in the first place. The need of whole-body experience for understanding also becomes more comprehensible. Mandler notes, 'Just telling people what a situation is going to be like isn't enough, and it isn't good enough training when you encounter the real situation' (1983: 152). Generations of new spouses, new parents, and anthropological fieldworkers can testify to the overwhelming truth of this statement.

In sum, we experience bodily arousal when our familiar world is somehow interrupted. Such arousal may either fade away or develop into an emotional experience depending on the meaning we assign to it. Possible meanings arise out of cultural interpretations of recurring experiential schemas. We should not be surprised to find some overlap in the categories of feeling recognized by different cultures. After all, certain experiential schemas that interrupt the familiar world—birth and death, for example—are human universals. At the same time, we should expect that the wider cultural context will, in each case, modify the perspective from which such experiences are understood and, thus, the categories of feeling associated with them.

Emotion in an Eastern African Culture

David Parkin (1984) has studied the cultural construction of emotion among the Giriama of coastal Kenya (see Map 5.3). We must explain several features of Giriama thinking before considering their understanding of what we call *emotion*. First, the Giriama theory of human nature does not recognize a mind–body dualism of the Western sort. Indeed, the Giriama are unwilling to set up sharp, mutually exclusive oppositions of any kind when discussing human nature. Parkin tells us that such behaviour as spirit possession, madness, hysteria, witchcraft, persistent violence, drunkenness, and thieving are explained

> as the result of what we might call imbalances in human nature. . . . I call them imbalances because the Giriama do not believe that a person can be intrinsically or irredeemably evil: at some stage, usually remarkably quickly, he will be brought back into the fold, even if he subsequently leaves it again. A large number of terms, roughly translatable as greed, lust, envy, jealousy, malice, resentment, anger, are used to refer to these imbalances of character and the accompanying behaviour. (1984: 14)

emotion The product of a dialectic between bodily arousal and cognitive interpretation. It is comprised of states, values, and arousals.

reasoning styles How we understand a cognitive task, how we encode the information presented to us, and what transformations the information undergoes as we think. Reasoning styles differ from culture to culture and from context to context within the same culture.

Map 5.3 Giriama

As with Westerners, the Giriama associate different feelings with different parts of the body. In the West, people conventionally connect the brain with reason and the heart with emotion. For the Giriama, however, the heart, liver, kidneys, and eyes are the seat of reason and emotion. Although the Giriama may distinguish thinking from feeling in discussing the actual behaviour of real people, they nevertheless presume a common origin for both (17). Indeed, the Giriama framework for understanding human cognition has much in common with the anthropological perspective described throughout this chapter.

What about particular emotions? Although the categories of feeling recognized by Giriama overlap in some respects with the experiences labelled by English terms for emotions, Parkin suggests that there are important differences that stem from the nature of the schemas that Giriama culture conventionally recognizes and from the prototypical thoughts and feelings that are appropriate to those schemas. Consider what the term *utsungu* means as a label for a category of feeling:

> *Utsungu* means poison, bitterness, resentment, and anger, on the one hand, but also grief on the other. It is the feeling experienced at a funeral of a loved or respected relative or friend. A man or woman is grieved at the loss but also bitter that it has happened at all, and angry with the witch who caused the death. Since the witch will be made to pay, the sentiment carried with it both the consequences of the loss of a dear one and the intention to avenge his or her death. (118)

In Western societies, people also feel 'grief' at the death of a loved one. But the prototypical Western experience of grief does not contain the additional meaning involving anger at witchcraft and the desire for vengeance. Perhaps one would have to be a Giriama—or have lived in another culture in which witchcraft was understood as the usual cause of death and in which such wrongful death could be avenged—to experience the emotional configuration that Parkin describes.

Motivation

Perception and cognition are psychological processes that acquaint us with the inner and outer 'worlds' of our experiences and assist us in making sense of those worlds. But human life involves activity, agency: we set goals and pursue the means to achieve them. Even when those goals and means are culturally prescribed, we have to be induced to accept them as valid and important enough to take them on and make efforts to accomplish what our culture values. Anthropological approaches to motivation have always embedded the sources of motivation within a cultural matrix. In the early years of the discipline, when Freudian theory was influential, many psychological anthropologists accepted Freud's idea that all human beings were motivated to seek pleasure in a world that frequently made that goal unattainable. Freud spoke of two basic kinds of 'instincts', the erotic and the aggressive, which were present in all human beings. Unregulated pursuit of satisfaction of these instincts would lead to social chaos. Thus, culture entered the picture as a set of humanly invented arrangements that allowed these otherwise destructive instincts to be curbed or channelled into socially useful activities (Bock 1994: xii).

However, many anthropologists have found speaking of 'instinct' to be unhelpful, particularly when the culturally defined goals which people pursue in different societies seem so different from one another that tying these goals to the same instinct is implausible. In the 1930s, Ruth Benedict argued that each culture had its own set of motives, its own models of ideal behaviour, which members of a particular society adopted and which motivated them to pursue some kinds of behaviours rather than others. More recently, in work like that of Catherine Lutz, anthropologists have focused on how people interact with one another and how they talk about those interactions, in an attempt to uncover the local 'ethnopsychology of motives' (Bock 1994: xii–xiii). This, in turn, requires close attention to the social and cultural contexts in which individuals learn to interact with other members of their society, learn to understand the local discourse about vice and virtue, and come to terms with these practices and values when attempting to exercise their own agency. That is, the mainsprings of motivation are to be uncovered in the study of socialization and enculturation.

The Process of Socialization and Enculturation

Children use their own bodies and brains to explore their world, but other people in their lives are actively working to steer their activity and attention in particular directions. Consequently, their exploration of the world is not merely trial and error: the path is cleared by others who shape their experiences—and their interpretations of their experiences—for them.

Two terms in the social sciences refer to this process of culturally and socially shaped cognitive development. The first, **socialization**, is the process of learning to live as a member of a group. This involves learning how to interact appropriately with others and how to cope with the behavioural rules established by the social group. The second term, **enculturation**, refers to the cognitive challenges facing human beings who live together and must come to terms with the ways of thinking and feeling that are considered appropriate in their respective cultures. Becoming human involves both these processes, for children learn how to act, think, feel, and speak at the same time as they participate in the joint activities carried out by social groups to which they belong. We will use the term *socialization/enculturation* to represent this holistic experience.

Anthropologists need a theory of cognitive development that is holistic; therefore, many psychologists and anthropologists have been attracted to the ideas of George Herbert Mead (1863–1931) and, more recently, to the work of Lev Vygotsky (1896–1934). Although both men were contemporaries, Vygotsky's work has only recently become influential in the West. Before his early death, Vygotsky helped found a major school of Soviet psychology that continues to thrive. The writings of this *socio-historical school* have inspired some of the most interesting recent research in cognitive anthropology.

For Mead and Vygotsky alike, human life is social from the outset. As Vygotsky wrote, 'The social

dimension of consciousness is primary in time and in fact. The individual dimension of consciousness is derivative and secondary' (1978: 30). Like Vygotsky, Mead (1934) believed that human nature is completed and enhanced, not curtailed or damaged, by socialization and enculturation. Indeed, the successful humanization of human beings lies in people's mastery of symbols, which begins when children start to learn language. As children come to control the symbolic systems of their cultures, they gain the ability to distinguish objects and relationships in the world and come to see themselves as objects as well as subjects.

Mead's analysis focused primarily on face-to-face interactions, but anthropologists need a theoretical framework that goes beyond such interactions. Here Vygotsky's work is important because his understanding of context goes beyond Mead's. Vygotsky wanted to create a psychology that was compatible with a Marxian analysis of society. His ideas are far from doctrinaire; indeed, during the Stalin years in Russia his work was censored. At the same time, his orientation directed attention to the social, cultural, and historical context in which face-to-face interaction is embedded.

Vygotsky's theoretical contributions of the distinction between elementary cognitive processes and functional cognitive systems is useful in anthropology because it provides a way of describing the similarities and differences observed when we compare how people from different cultures think and feel. These differences have implications for cognitive development as well. The functional systems employed by adult members of society must be acquired during childhood. For Vygotsky, acquisition takes place in a context of face-to-face interactions between, typically, a child and an adult. When children learn about the world in such a context, they are not working on their own; on the contrary, they are learning about the world as they learn the symbolic forms (usually language) that others use to represent the world.

enculturation The process by which human beings living with one another must learn to come to terms with the ways of thinking and feeling that are considered appropriate in their respective cultures.

socialization The process by which human beings as material organisms, living together with other similar organisms, cope with the behavioural rules established by their respective societies.

This learning process creates in the child a new plane of consciousness resting on the dialogue-based, question-and-answer format of social interaction. From this, Vygotsky inferred that our internal thought processes would also take the format of a dialogue. Mead suggested something similar when he spoke of every person as being able to carry on internal conversations between the *I* (the unsocialized self) and the *me* (the socially conditioned self). Only on this basis can an individual's sense of identity develop as the self comes to distinguish itself from the conversational other.

One interesting Vygotskian concept is the *zone of proximal development*, which is the distance between a child's 'actual development level as determined by independent problem solving' and the level of 'potential development as determined through problem solving under adult guidance or in collaboration with more capable peers' (Vygotsky 1978: 86). Psychologists everywhere have long been aware that children can often achieve more when they are coached than when they work alone. Western psychologists, with their individualist bias, have viewed this difference in achievement as contamination of the testing situation or as the result of cheating. Vygotsky and his followers see it as an indispensable measure of potential growth that simultaneously demonstrates how growth is rooted in social interaction, especially in educational settings (Moll 1990). The concept of the zone of proximal development enables anthropologists and comparative psychologists to link cognitive development to society, culture, and history because practices of coaching or formal instruction are shaped by social, cultural, and historical factors (Figure 5.7). To the extent that these factors can vary, we can expect cognitive development to vary as well.

Is Cognitive Development the Same for Everyone?

Most theories, including Mead's, portray cognitive development as a progression through a series of stages. With the exception of Vygotsky's theory, these theories ordinarily assume that the stages are the same for all human beings or at least all human beings in a particular society. A Vygotskian perspective helps us explain not only cross-cultural differences in development but also differences in the cognitive development of different subgroups in a single society.

Figure 5.7 A Japanese woman and child at the Sanja festival in Tokyo, Japan. Practices of coaching or formal instruction are shaped by social, cultural, and historical factors.

For example, from their birth in 1973 through the late 1980s, a sample of 4,299 children were followed by a team of Cuban researchers who periodically collected information on their cognitive, social, economic, physical, and academic development (Gutierrez Muñiz, Hurtado, and Beatón 1997). The researchers identified a series of correlations between levels of education, wage employment, living standards, and health of mothers and levels of development and achievement of the children. Put in Vygotskian terms, the data show that the zone of proximal development is greater for children of mothers with higher levels of education and participation in the paid workforce than it is for children of mothers with lower educational levels who do not work outside the home. These findings contradicted popular beliefs that the children of educated working

In Their Own Words

Blood and Nerves Revisited

Dona L. Davis discusses concepts of menopause and how these concepts changed with the changing realities of life in outport communities in Newfoundland as the cod fishery disappeared.

In *Blood and Nerves: An Ethnographic Focus on Menopause* (1983) (based on fieldwork in the 1970s), I dutifully recorded symptom and attitude data but was able to show with ethnographic data that women's experience of menopause was not adequately captured by medical models and methods of understanding. There were a number of reasons for this and all were rooted in the collective nature of life in the local community. Women's knowledge about menopause was based in lived experience. It was embedded in and conditioned by the day-to-day dynamics of social interaction. Knowledge of the body came from observations of behaviour, through the oral transmission of shared experience, and an intimate, long-term knowledge of each other. Moreover, folk idioms of nerves and blood dominated the local systems of meaning and encapsulated all talk about health-related phenomena. Complex and polysemic, these idioms shaped and governed women's discourse about symptoms in light of increasingly wider and mutually encompassing social milieus such as a shared and valued local history and pride in an occupational/fisher identity.

My challenge in *Blood and Nerves* was to depict the dynamic nature of nerves and blood as exact/inexact and individual/collective phenomena, and as metaphors that both elaborated and condensed the life experiences of fisher people in a small face-to-face community. . . .

When I came back to the community for a second period of fieldwork in 1989–90, it soon became obvious to me that the once-popular focus among women on nerves and blood had become trivialized and that those who persisted in these complaints were ridiculed as old fashioned and backward. With increased literacy and greater, although problematic, access to medical services, these idioms had given way to a more biomedically informed discourse about the body. To state the crux of it, in the 1970s talk about the body was talk about everything else, whereas in 1989 talk about the body had become talk about the body. . . . Yet during my fieldwork in the 1990s, I was witness to and cognizant of changes to which the women themselves were not especially aware. In my view, a dramatic difference had emerged as folk idioms were superseded by medical models. The once collective, public body with its permeable and multiple boundaries had become bounded and private. The markedly different experiences and characteristics of menopause for the cohorts of women who entered middle age during the 1970s and 1990s cannot just be attributed to global and wider forces like the mass media, education, modernization, or increased access to medical services. The privatization of the body must be understood in terms of the changed exigencies of daily life in the local community whose ramifications have dramatically affected village women and men of all ages. . . . The extended family and village-wide patterns of visiting have declined, as people become less willing to share diminishing resources. The practice of limiting family size to one or two children and divorce and separation have further reduced in size and fragmented local families, as has the out-migration of young people. A sexual antagonism has also emerged that pervades the community. No one talks about good hard-working women and men any more. Instead, tales of violent confrontations and sexual scandals dominate village discourse. The interests of men are pitted against those of women in a variety of arenas such as who has priority on make-work projects, who controls domestic and public spaces of the community, and who has what rights and responsibilities over children of divorced or unmarried parents. These changes have undermined what was once a collective community, privatizing both households and the individuals who live in them.

With these changes comes the demise of older women as a moral force in the community. Middle-aged women in the 1990s are seen as out-of-sync with the times, products of another era with little of value to pass on to the younger generations who are more highly educated, more material-minded in their values, and who see themselves as 'liberated' and who eschew the values of self-sacrifice and stoic endurance. Locals now look to the wider middle and working classes of Canada for their role models [as] they . . . come to terms with an internal and external morale that devalues them as archaic survivors of a defunct fishery.

Source: Davis, Dona L. 1997. 'Blood and Nerves Revisited: Menopause and the Privatization of the Body in a Newfoundland Post-industrial Fishery', *Medical Anthropology Quarterly* 11, 1: 3–20.

mothers would suffer as a result of their mothers' activities (Beatón, personal communication).

Carol Gilligan (1982) carried out a comparative study on the moral development of women and men in North American society. She argues that middle-class boys and girls begin their moral development in different socio-cultural contexts. Boys are encouraged from an early age to break away from their mothers and families and make it on their own. In this context, they learn that independence is good, that dependency is weakness, and that their first duty is to themselves and what they stand for. By contrast, girls mature in a socio-cultural context in which their bond to their mothers and families is never sharply ruptured. They learn that connection to others is good, that the destruction of relationships is damaging, and that their first responsibility in any difficult situation is to ensure that nobody gets hurt.

Gilligan did not adopt a Vygotskian perspective in this study, although she was influenced by Mead. But the Vygotskian concept of the zone of proximal development provides a useful tool for describing how the differential moral development of boys and girls is accomplished. In Vygotskian terms, the moral development of boys and girls proceeds in different directions because boys and girls are coached differently by more mature members of society. That is, when faced with the same dilemmas but unsure of how to act, boys are encouraged to make one set of choices, girls another. In this way, each gender category builds up a different set of schemas as to what constitutes the 'good'. As a result, North American men and women consistently see one another acting immorally. For example, when men and boys try to be true to themselves and strike out on their own, women and girls may condemn such action as being highly destructive to personal relationships. When women and girls try to encourage intimacy and closeness, men and boys may view such ties as confining and repressive.

Like Vygotsky, Gilligan situates the development of moral reasoning in socio-cultural and historical contexts. She argues that men are able to present their moral perspective as universally correct because men as a group hold power over women as a group in North American society. As women gain power, however, their 'different voice' may acquire more legitimacy, and the culturally embedded paths of moral development may themselves be altered.

Personality/Self/Subjectivity

Socialization and enculturation produce a **self** capable of functioning successfully in society. But what sort of entity is a self? Many Western psychologists have assumed that the mature self was a bounded, independent, self-contained entity with a clear and non-contradictory sense of identity that persisted through time. Anthropologists working in other societies, however, often found that the development of such an independent self was not recognized as the goal of socialization and enculturation. On the contrary, socialization and enculturation were often designed to shape selves that did *not* think of themselves as independent and self-sufficient; the mature individual was one motivated to look out for others, work for the well-being of the family or the lineage rather than in pursuit of his or her own individual self-interest.

Early psychological anthropologists often spoke of individual **personality** rather than the self; this is seen in the name adopted by the early *culture and personality school* of the mid-twentieth century. Bock points out that in such formulations,

> personality involves the relative *integration* of an individual's perceptions, motives, cognitions, and behaviour within a socio-cultural matrix (the subjective view of this unity is more often referred to as the *self*). The importance of consistent social feedback to individual functioning has been demonstrated. . . . Personality is thus revealed as part of a dynamic interactive system between a human organism and its physical–social environment. (1994: xiv)

Many psychological anthropologists, including Bock himself, have argued that an individual's personality, understood in this way, is not merely a reflection of a culturally ideal type, but is regularly shaped by such factors as 'the individual's position in the social structure, including his or her social class, gender, occupational role, and even birth order. . . . These quasi-universal structural constraints cut across conventional divisions into "cultures" and even nations' (xiv).

The notion of an integrated personality, or self, harks back to Enlightenment ideas; as a result, it is hardly surprising that the postmodern critique of Enlightenment ideas questioned the existence of integrated, harmonious personalities or selves. Attention began to be paid to the different dimensions of one's personality or self that were activated (or de-activated) in different contexts, and people began to speak of 'decentred' selves as the norm rather than the exception. The idea of a centred, integrated self was viewed as an illusion or an effect of powerful political ideologies that worked to mask the heterogeneity and contradictory features of individual experience. Contemporary scholars in many fields continue to disagree about the extent to which anyone's self is integrated or coherent, and few anthropologists would defend an unreflective Enlightenment view of the self. In psychological anthropology, this has led to the shift of focus we see in the work of Lutz, for example: rather than attempt to relate an individual's behaviour to internal experiences of the self, attention is focused on social discourse about people's behaviour. This suggests that 'culture is (largely) created by people in the discourse justifying their behaviour as rational and moral' (Bock 1994: xv). But anthropologists who recognize the uneven and contradictory features of individual self-experience also often draw attention to the attempts individuals make. In the most difficult or bewildering situations in a disorderly world, and even if our understandings are inevitably imperfect and partial, we struggle to find patterns and strive to achieve ordered, coherent understandings of the world and of ourselves.

Many psychological anthropologists and others have come to speak not of individual personality or individual self but of individual **subjectivity** as 'the felt interior experience of the person that includes his or her positions in a field of relational power' (Das and Kleinman 2000: 1). To think of individuals as *subjects* has much to recommend it in a postmodern climate. It points to individual agency with each of us as the initiating subject of our actions. However, individual agency is not absolute since our agency is circumscribed by various limitations that result from the deployment of social, economic, and political power in the societies in which we live. These limitations may be greater or lesser, depending on social variables such as class, gender, occupation, or birth order. That is, we are *subject to* the workings of institutionalized power in the various *subject positions* we occupy. The fact that all people in all societies occupy a variety of different subject positions reflects our 'decentred' selves: a particular individual may, in different contexts, be positioned in terms of gender, ethnicity, occupation, class, or some combination of these positions. At the

same time, however, all of us can potentially play the insights gained from each subject position against the others and thus gain a measure of reflexive awareness and understanding of our own situations.

Individual subjectivity is heavily influenced by socialization and enculturation. But social and cultural expectations are sometimes overturned by experiences that intrude on predictable daily routines, and these, too, will have a powerful role in shaping the subjectivities of the individuals who are affected. Among the most powerful experiences are those occasioned by structural violence and social trauma, two areas of social suffering that have unfortunately become all too prevalent in recent times. Processes of globalization, which displace populations or shape the contexts that allow their governments to oppress or persecute them, have themselves become all too frequent in the late twentieth and early twenty-first centuries. For those who live under such disordered circumstances, orderly, harmonious daily life is not taken for granted. A number of anthropologists have turned explicitly to the investigation of the sources of social suffering and the consequences of such suffering for individual subjectivity. Although the world's attention is usually drawn to large-scale *traumatic violence* that erupts in civil wars or other forms of armed conflict, anthropologists have also pointed to less spectacular forms of *structural violence* that in their own way are responsible for severe social suffering. As we look at each in turn perhaps we should consider our responses to such violence. Here, Susan Sontag's *Regarding the Pain of Others* (2004) places us in a 'society of spectacle' where we should attempt to remember that 'Compassion is an unstable emotion. It needs to be translated into action, or it withers.'

Structural Violence

Paul Farmer is an anthropologist and medical doctor who has worked in Haiti since 1983 (see Map 5.4; Figure 5.8). His activities as a physician have exposed him

personality 'The relative integration of an individual's perceptions, motives, cognitions, and behaviour within a socio-cultural matrix.'

self The result of the process of socialization/enculturation for an individual.

subjectivity 'The felt interior experience of the person that includes his or her positions in a field of relational power.'

to extreme forms of human suffering that are part and parcel of everyday life for those at the bottom of Haitian society. As he points out, 'In only three countries in the world was suffering judged to be more extreme than that endured in Haiti; each of these three countries is currently in the midst of an internationally recognized civil war' (Farmer 2002 [1996]: 424). But if the suffering of poor Haitians is not the outcome of the traumatic violence of war, it can be described as a consequence of another form of violence: structural violence. **Structural violence** is violence that results from the way that political and economic forces structure risk for various forms of suffering within a population. Much of this suffering is in the form of infectious and parasitic disease. But it can also include other forms of extreme suffering such as hunger, torture, and rape (424). The operations of structural violence create circumscribed spaces in which the poorest and least powerful members of Haitian society are subjected to highly intensified risks of all kinds, increasing the likelihood that sooner or later they will experience one or more varieties of social suffering. The structural aspect of this violence is important to emphasize since the attention of most Western outside observers, even those who want to alleviate suffering, is often trained on individuals and their personal experiences, with the resulting temptation to blame the victims for their own distress.

Farmer's work as a physician allowed him to see first-hand the suffering of poor Haitians he knew, and his work as an anthropologist allowed him to link that

Figure 5.8 Dr Paul Farmer with an AIDS patient at Clinique Bon Sauveur in Haiti.

suffering to economic and political structures in Haitian society that are often invisible in local situations but that can be revealed through careful analysis. Farmer begins by offering the biographies of two young Haitians he treated, one a woman and one a man. Both died young, the woman of AIDS and the man of injuries inflicted on him in the course of a beating by the police. As he says, these two individuals 'suffered and died in exemplary fashion', and he shows how the combined forces of racism, sexism, political violence, and poverty conspired 'to constrain agency' and 'crystallize into the sharp, hard surfaces of individual suffering' (425).

Acéphie Joseph was the woman who died of AIDS at age 25, in 1991, one of the first in her rural village, 'the latest in a string of tragedies that she and her parents readily linked together in a long lamentation, by now familiar to those who tend the region's sick' (426). Her parents had been prosperous peasant farmers selling produce in village markets until 1956, when the fertile valley in which they lived was flooded after a dam was built to generate electricity. They lost everything and became 'water refugees' forced to try to grow crops on an infertile plot in the village where they were resettled. Acéphie and her twin brother were born in the village and attended primary school there. Farmer writes that Acéphie's 'beauty and her vulnerability may have sealed her fate as early as 1984' (426). She began to help her mother carry produce to the market along a road that went past the local military barracks, where soldiers liked to flirt with the passing women, and one

Map 5.4 **Haiti**

soldier in particular approached her. 'Such flirtation is seldom unwelcome, at least to all appearances. In rural Haiti, entrenched poverty made the soldiers—the region's only salaried men—ever so much more attractive' (427). Although Acéphie knew he had a wife and children, she nevertheless did not rebuff him; indeed, he visited her family, who approved of their liaison. '"I could tell that the old people were uncomfortable, but they didn't say no . . . I never dreamed he would give me a bad illness . . . it was a way out, that's how I saw it"', Acéphie explained. Only a few weeks after the beginning of their sexual relationship, the soldier died, and Acéphie sought training as a cook in order to qualify for work as a servant in the city, for she had no other viable alternative. Eventually she found work as a maid and began a relationship with a young man, who drove a bus, whom she planned to marry. After three years as a maid, Acéphie became pregnant, and went home to her village to give birth, but she had a very difficult delivery, and when she finally sought medical help for a series of infections, she was diagnosed with AIDS. Following her death, her father hanged himself.

Chouchou Louis grew up in a village on the Central Plateau of Haiti. He attended primary school briefly and then worked with his father and older sister to raise produce after his mother died. In the 1980s, times were especially difficult under the repressive dictatorship of Jean-Claude Duvalier. Those Haitians who tried to flee by boat to the United States were termed *economic* rather than political refugees; a 1981 treaty between Duvalier and President Ronald Reagan ensured that such refugees would be promptly returned to Haiti. By 1986, a pro-democracy movement had grown powerful enough in Haiti to force Duvalier to leave the country, but he was replaced in power by the military. The US government hoped that this military government would bring democracy and supplied it with over $200 million in aid. But poor peasants like Chouchou Louis and his family saw little difference between the military rulers and the dictator they had replaced because peasants continued to be subject to violence at the hands of soldiers. An election in 1990 brought the popular leader Father Jean-Bertrand Aristide to power with over 70 per cent of the vote, but in 1991 he was ousted in a coup. Anger in the countryside at this coup 'was soon followed by sadness, then fear, as the country's repressive machinery, dismantled during the seven

months of Aristide's tenure, was hastily reassembled under the patronage of the army' (429). Soon thereafter Chouchou was riding in a truck when he made a remark about the poor state of the roads that might have been interpreted as a veiled criticism of the coup. On the same truck was an out-of-uniform soldier who, at the next checkpoint, had Chouchou dragged from the truck and beaten. Although he was let go, he lived in fear of another arrest, which came several months later, with no explanation, when he was visiting his sister. He was taken to the nearest military checkpoint and tortured. After three days he was dumped in a ditch, and the following day Farmer was brought in to treat him, but his injuries were too severe. He died three days later.

Acéphie and Chouchou are individuals, and so it is natural to ask how representative their experiences might be. Farmer's experience among many poor women with AIDS allowed him to recognize that all of their cases, including Acéphie's, showed 'a deadly monotony'. The women he interviewed 'were straightforward about the non-voluntary aspect of their sexual activity'. They had been driven to it by poverty (431). Similarly, Chouchou was only one of more than 3,000 Haitian civilians, most of them poor peasants, who were killed after 1991 by military or paramilitary forces. Thus, Farmer concludes, 'the agony of Acéphie and Chouchou was in a sense, "modal" suffering. In Haiti, AIDS and political violence are two leading causes of death among young adults' (431). And all this suffering and death was the outcome of structural violence: all the key events that contributed to their deaths, from the flooding of the valley to the funding of the Haitian army, were the consequences of human agency which, in turn, severely circumscribed the agency of Acéphie and Chouchou no matter what they did. Farmer identifies specifically the relations of power in which each of them was embedded, for these contributed to the likelihood that their suffering and death would take the forms it took. For example, 'gender helps explain why Acéphie died of AIDS, whereas Chouchou died from torture' (433). Race or ethnicity helps explain why

structural violence Violence that results from the way that political and economic forces structure risk for various forms of suffering within a population.

illness is more likely to be suffered by the descendants of enslaved Africans, and social class helps explain why they were more likely to be poor.

> These grim biographies suggest that the social and economic forces that have helped to shape the AIDS epidemic are, in every sense, the same forces that led to Chouchou's death and to the larger repression in which it was eclipsed. What is more, both were 'at risk' of such a fate long before they met the soldiers who altered their destinies. *They* were both, from the outset, victims of structural violence. (431)

Trauma

Incidents of warfare, genocide, ethnic cleansing, and other forms of large-scale, collective violence were distinctive features of the twentieth century, leading not only to widespread death but also to the disruption of social institutions, the destruction of economic and political arrangements, and the displacement of surviving populations into unfamiliar and often hostile new settings. These developments have not been ignored by anthropologists, many of whom have collaborated with specialists in other disciplines to investigate the causes of these events and to help treat the victims. In approaching this topic, some have chosen to speak in terms of **trauma**: 'events in life generated by forces and agents external to the person and largely external to his or her control and specifically to events generated in the setting of armed conflict and war', including such phenomena as 'separation and loss, imprisonment and exile, threats of annihilation, even death and mutilation' (Apfel and Simon 2000: 103). Apfel and Simon distinguish these sorts of experiences from the less devastating 'ordinary traumas' or 'necessary losses' that all people are likely to face, 'such as the birth of a sibling, natural death of a parent or sibling, divorce, illnesses, and accidents, whether man-made or natural' (103).

Anthropologists investigating the causes and consequences of such large-scale trauma regularly work together with other specialists, including psychoanalysts like Apfel and Simon because such phenomena are so complex. Large-scale collective violence has complex causes involving psychic, social, political, economic, and cultural factors, and aims to destroy not just individual psychological functioning but also the physical body and the social order. Individual and cultural factors together bring about the trauma and are equally implicated in the ways in which survivors come to deal with trauma's aftermath (Suárez-Orozco and Robben 2000: 1). This means, of course, that attempts to reduce explanations of large-scale collective forms of violence to either 'nature' or 'culture' are bound to be inadequate. Like Bock, Suárez-Orozco and Robben seek analysis in the intermediate zone 'somewhere between those two analytical dead ends' (2). For example, attributing large-scale, collective forms of violence to some innate *individual* capacity for violence ignores the many differences between small-scale, face-to-face violent interchanges and the massing of armies and technology to wreak havoc on an 'enemy' that is often not known personally. To grasp the complexities involved requires 'processual multi-level approaches' that combine 'solid understandings of the inner psychic processes as well as the social and cultural contexts of large-scale violence and trauma' (4).

Western scholarly and medical understanding of large-scale trauma developed over the course of the twentieth century. Phenomena called *shell shock* or *battle fatigue* were first identified in some soldiers during World War I (Figure 5.9). Although initially these soldiers were vilified as cowards who were morally corrupt, some researchers, including anthropologists W.H.R. Rivers and Abram Kardiner, eventually proposed that the suffering these soldiers experienced could not be attributed to individual psychological or moral deficiency, but needed to be seen as a consequence of the trauma inflicted by battlefield experience itself. The commitment in World War II to 'total war' made the destruction of civilian populations and support structures as important, or more important, than the destruction of soldiers on the battlefield. 'The number of civilian casualties went from 5 per cent in the First World War and 50 per cent in the Second World War to over 80 per cent in the Vietnam War' (Suárez-Orozco and Robben 2000: 15). After World War II, attention was for the first time directed to the massive trauma to which civilians had been subjected, with particular attention focused on the experiences of those who survived Nazi concentration camps. Suárez-Orozco and Robben note that the pioneering work by psychoanalyst Bruno Bettelheim, for example, highlighted the 'complex social dynamics between perpetrators

Figure 5.9 World War I Canadian soldiers are brought to the Field Dressing Station at Vimy Ridge, April 1917.

and victims of violence' (17), but these dynamics were neglected in the aftermath of the Vietnam War, in which the focus was on identification and treatment of roughly one-third of individual veterans suffering from what was officially designated as 'post-traumatric stress disorder' (PTSD) in 1980 (20).

Suárez-Orozco and Robben emphasize the importance of promoting effective forms of healing among those who suffer such massive trauma, but they also note that societies as well as individuals need to heal. In both cases, successful healing seems to require the re-establishment of 'basic trust': individuals need to find ways to trust other individuals, but all survivors also need to be able to find ways to develop trust in the institutions of their society, which are also implicated in the management of (or in failing to manage) collective violence. Some dimensions of healing can be successfully promoted by the efforts of psychiatrists and medical specialists who focus on individuals; for example, interpreting the suffering of Vietnam-era veterans in medical terms, as PTSD, acknowledged

that the veterans' suffering was not a consequence of their own personal defects but had to be traced to the trauma they had experienced in war. At the same time, medicalization of PTSD and a continuing focus on individuals diverts attention away from the sociocultural dimensions of such trauma. 'Combat trauma shatters the meaningfulness of the self and the world, and makes its sufferers put their bodies and minds on constant alert for any possible attack. They become distrustful of others, their own memories, and visual perceptions' (Suárez-Orozco and Robben 2000: 20). The taken-for-grantedness of everyday social life is destroyed, allowing 'the uncanny'—'the dread and horror of social violence'—to become a recurring and unassimilable feature of their lives.

trauma 'Events in life generated by forces and agents external to the person and largely external to his or her control and specifically to events generated in the setting of armed conflict and war.'

Those who experience such traumas are faced with an unbelievable and unreal reality that is incompatible with anything they knew previously. As a result, they can no longer fully believe what they see with their own eyes; they have difficulty in distinguishing between the unreal reality they have survived and the fears that spring from their own imagination. . . . When one experiences the uncanny . . . what has been hidden becomes visible, what is familiar becomes strange and frightening. (Gampel 2000: 49–50)

We all experience a mild form of 'the uncanny' when we find ourselves in more manageable situations of ambiguity, for example, when learning a new language or becoming acquainted with new foods or new customs. The cultural shock of fieldwork is more jarring, but still manageable by most anthropologists. So too living in another society, whether as a tourist or student or immigrant, can be a struggle but may involve less trauma if the experience was chosen and the individuals involved are surrounded by supportive economic, social, and political institutions: anthropologists who study migration have been able to document such cases, some of which we will look at in more detail in later chapters. But 'the uncanny' experienced by war refugees, concentration camp survivors, or victims of state repression is more intense. 'We feel safe when we exist in a constantly affective background, in a constant social context. The feeling of uncanniness overwhelms us when we are thrust into a fragmented, violent social context, one without any continuity and which transmits extremely paradoxical messages' (55). The response of individuals to these experiences varies, however. For survivors of Nazi death camps, trauma was often severe and affected the children of survivors in ways that were often not made explicit but were revealed in such behaviours as parental anxiety and over-protectiveness. Psychoanalysts can be effective in helping those who suffer from such experiences, but many believe it is naïve and overly optimistic to imagine that total 'cure' is possible (Langer 1997). Other survivors exhibit (and pass on to their children) a remarkable resiliency, 'the capacity to survive violence and loss, and moreover, to have flexibility of response over the course of a life time' including 'a sense of agency and a sense of capacity to choose—among courses of action and among conflicting moral values' (Apfel and Simon 2000: 103).

Still, in other cases, however, collective trauma can produce far more troubling responses. Some traumatized persons and groups turn to 'hatred and violence as ways of coping with traumatic wounds' (102). Vamik Volkan has described one way in which this can happen, in terms of what he calls a group's *chosen trauma*. A chosen trauma arises, Volkan argues, from experiences of collective violence and loss that survivors are unable to mourn. This can lead to a collective focus on the group's past experiences of victimization or humiliation, and the entire identity of the group's members may come to centre on the chosen trauma. Moreover, the chosen trauma can be passed on to subsequent generations along with the expectation that it is up to them to right past wrongs, using violence if necessary. 'While the group does not consciously choose to feel victimized, it does choose to psychologize losses and to transform them into powerful cultural narratives which become an integral part of the social identity' (Suárez-Orozco and Robben 2000: 23). Volkan studied Christian Serbs, who elaborated and passed on for hundreds of years their chosen trauma: the loss of their empire to the Ottoman Turks in the early 1500s. Although this chosen trauma was not always in the forefront of Serbian actions during those centuries, it remained a powerful cultural resource which Slobodan Milosevic and his cronies successfully exploited for their own political purposes in the 1990s, as the former Yugoslavia broke apart (23).

The power of chosen traumas derives in large part from the fact that they remain unmourned, thus cutting off possible forms of social and cultural healing that can rebuild trust in social institutions. Suárez-Orozco and Robben note, for example, that 'institutional acknowledgement—in the form of "truth" commissions and reparations (monetary and symbolic)—and justice—in the form of trials of perpetrators—can begin partially to restore the symbolic order that is another casualty of the work of violence' (2000: 5). These kinds of institutional acknowledgements, most often initiatives taken on the level of the nation-state (as in post-apartheid South Africa), may coincide with more local actions designed to reduce the trauma of massive social disruption, through healing rituals and other collective symbolic activities designed to aid recovery and rebuild social trust (22, 24).

The residential school trauma of First Nations peoples in Canada can be seen in a similar context. (Note Michael Kenny, *In Their Own Words*, above.) Today the Canadian federal government is moving to compensation and various forms of reconciliation. But consider this within the context of the above discussion—perhaps healing does not emerge when the members of the dominant sector of society are not perceived to be engaged in the process and the conditions resulting from the original trauma are restructured into other sectors of the lives of the oppressed.

Individual Psychology and Context

Cross-cultural studies of human psychological functioning all stress the vital importance of *context*—not just the immediate context of the laboratory situations or fieldwork encounters but also the displaced context of culture and history that may be invisible in local settings but present in people's habits of thought and feeling. Sometimes, however, contextual factors are obvious. When administering a psychological test on visual illusions to the Fang in Gabon, for example, James Fernandez (1980) discovered that many questioned his explanation of the 'real' reason behind such a bizarre activity as psychological testing. Years of colonial domination and exploitation at the hands of outsiders made their suspicions of the anthropologist's motives far from irrational.

Contextual factors shape human experiences in subtle ways as well, contributing to nuanced, holistic ethnographic understandings of other ways of making meaning. An excellent description of this kind of holistic experience is given by anthropologist Michael Gilsenan (1982), who worked for a time among urban Muslims in Cairo, Egypt (see Map 5.5). Gilsenan spent many hours with his informants observing their prayers in the local mosque. Along the inside wall of the mosque were verses from the Quran shaped out of bright green neon tubing. Green is the colour of the prophet Muhammad, so finding that colour used prominently in mosque decoration is not surprising. However, Gilsenan's experiences in Western culture did not include schemas in which neon lights and serious worship went together, and for several months the neon interfered with his attempts to assume a properly reverential attitude. Then one day, Gilsenan reports, 'I turned unthinkingly away from the swaying bodies and the rhythms of the remembrance of God and saw, not neon, but simply greenness. . . . No gaps existed between colour, shape, light, and form. From that unreflecting and unsuspecting moment I ceased to see neon at all' (1982: 266).

Nothing had happened to Gilsenan's eyes or his other senses, which continued to receive the same signals they had always received, but the meaning of the signals had been altered. Gilsenan's experience in the mosque situated neon light within a new schema, and his growing familiarity with that schema made the neon seem more and more natural. Eventually, Gilsenan was noticing only the colour green. He was still able to report, of course, that the green light was produced by green neon tubing; however, that fact seemed irrelevant given the new schema he used to interpret his experience.

These transformations of perception and understanding remain mysterious, but they seem to occur whenever we have an insight of any kind. Insights, like apt metaphors, reshape the world for us, throwing new aspects into sharp focus and casting other aspects into the background. Our ability to achieve insights, like our ability to create apt metaphors, remains the most central and most mysterious aspect of human psychological processes.

Map 5.5 Cairo

Key Terms

Chapter Summary

1. Anthropologists have long been interested in cultural learning by individuals. They have tried to find out what all members of our species have in common, what features are limited to specific groups of humans, and how individual uniqueness might be understood. This effort has involved co-operation with other disciplines, such as psychology. Often anthropologists have tested universal assumptions about human psychology in different cultural settings and have found them to be problematic.

2. The field of psychological anthropology is complex and difficult to summarize but can be grouped into three basic areas of human experience: perception, cognition, and motivation. Research overwhelmingly sustains the view that human psychological processes are open to a wide variety of influences.

3. Human psychological perception always takes place in a cultural context. Researchers use concepts like schemas and prototypes to describe some of the ways in which meaning is mapped onto our experience. Classic research on cross-cultural variations in perception showed that variation in responses to psychological tests depended on the meanings subjects brought to the testing situation, especially whether they understood the tests the same way Western subjects typically understood them.

Alternative understandings are possible because of the ambiguity of many perceptual signals, a phenomenon that is illustrated in the study of visual illusions. In addition, looking and seeing are culturally learned modes of sensory perception, as illustrated in Vogel's study of Baule visuality.

4. Human beings are active meaning-makers, striving to make sense of our experiences, which is a focus of anthropological studies of cognition. Their research has been critical of so-called intelligence tests on which non-Western subjects performed poorly because outside the laboratory setting the same individuals' intelligence and full humanity were obvious. Today, it is unclear exactly what the results of intelligence tests represent. Consequently, research has shifted its focus to cognitive processes and the way these are organized into culturally shaped functional systems.

5. Some anthropologists argue that people in different cultures have different cognitive styles that can be located on a continuum ranging from global style at one end to articulated style at the other. Research suggests that the same individual may use a global style for some tasks and an articulated style for others. In everyday situations, the goal of cognition is not to solve a problem by finding the single

correct answer. Instead, people try to resolve dilemmas in a way that allows them to get on with life.

6. Several attempts have been made to measure the levels of rational thinking in non-Western populations. The results are problematic. Rational thinking is not the same as logic. Formal Western logic is better understood as a learned reasoning style characteristic of Western culture. Rules of Western logic can be useful, but other logics may be equally valid in other societies—or on other occasions in Western societies—when contextual factors are vital and must be taken into consideration.

7. Our emotions, like our thoughts, are not just something we have; they are culturally constructed of our state of mind, our cultural interpretations, and our levels of bodily arousal. Different cultures recognize different domains of experience and different categories of feeling as being appropriate to these domains. For this reason, it is often difficult to translate the language of emotion from one culture to another.

8. Anthropological approaches to motivation have always embedded the sources of motivation within a cultural matrix. Finding the notion of 'instinct' to be unhelpful, anthropologists have had greater success in studying the culturally defined goals which people pursue in different societies.

9. The mainsprings of motivation are to be uncovered in the study of socialization and enculturation. Humans must learn to pattern and adapt behaviour and ways of thinking and feeling to the standards considered appropriate in their respective cultures. Vygotsky's concept of the zone of proximal development stresses that cognitive development results from a dialogue. Children progress through that process at different rates and in different directions, depending on the amount and kind of coaching they receive by others. This concept makes it possible to explain why people in different cultural subgroups are socialized and enculturated in different ways.

10. Anthropologists have been critical of ideas of the individual self that assume it is a bounded, independent entity with a clear and non-contradictory sense of identity that persists through time. Early psychological anthropologists preferred to speak of individual personality, which always assumed that an individual's psychological processes were integrated within a socio-cultural matrix. More recently, anthropologists have shifted from a concern with relating personality to an individual's internal experiences and have paid more attention to attributions about individuals that emerge in social discourse about people's behaviour. Some anthropologists prefer to speak not of personality or self but of individual subjectivity, which focuses on internal experiences of individuals as they are shaped by their positions in a field of power relations.

11. Patterns of socialization and enculturation are sometimes overturned by experiences that intrude on predictable daily routines. Among the most powerful experiences are those occasioned by structural violence and social trauma, the investigation of which has become a significant topic for some contemporary psychological anthropologists.

Critical Thinking Questions

1. Developmental Systems Theory (DST) recognizes that a developing organism is subject to many environments, identifiable at different levels of analysis as it lives out its life cycle. What are some of the reciprocal influences important in the first year of life for the human child? How does DST 'fit' with a Vygotskian perspective?

2. Language is an open system and two of its interesting design features are *displacement* and *prevarication*. How can these concepts be used to better understand human psychology?

3. A standard IQ (Intelligence Quotient) test cannot be applied cross-culturally. Why do you suppose this is the case?

4. How is the anthropological perspective for understanding human cognition similar to the Giriama framework of associating different feelings with different parts of the body?

5. Distinguish between socialization and enculturation. Why are both needed to become 'human'?

Suggested Readings

Berlin, Brent, David G. Casagrande. 2000. 'Cognitive Prototypes in Tzeltal Maya Medicinal Plant Selection', available at: <http://gravlee.org/ang5091/proposals/casagrande_nsf.pdf>. *This article, an example of applied anthropology, discusses bridging the gap between traditional medicinal plant knowledge and Western biomedical knowledge. The objective of such research is to conserve biodiversity, continue to improve human health, and encourage the development of sustainable Indigenous livelihoods. For our purposes it also provides an excellent example of the concept of schema.*

Bock, Philip K. 1999. *Rethinking Psychological Anthropology: Continuity and Change in the Study of Human Action*, 2nd edn (Prospect Heights, IL: Waveland Press). *A thorough introduction to psychological anthropology, tracing developments from the early twentieth century to current directions in the field.*

Boellstorff, Tom, and Johan Lindquist. 2004. 'Bodies of Emotion: Rethinking Culture and Emotion through Southeast Asia', *Ethnos* 69, 4 (Dec.): 437–44, available at: <http://www.anthro. uci.edu/faculty_bios/boellstorff/Boellstorff-Emotion.pdf>. *This article, and the volume it comes from, attempts to develop analyses that treat emotion as cultural—and culturally specific—while recognizing the dogged persistence of the individual/social binarism (dualism). The task is to develop theoretical and methodological tools to prise open this binarism despite deeply held assumptions (and not just Western ones) about the relationship between embodied versus transpersonal modes of being.*

Cole, Michael, and Sylvia Scribner. 1974. *Culture and Thought: A Psychological Introduction* (New York: Wiley). *A clear, readable survey of the literature and case studies on the cultural shaping of cognition.*

Kenny, Michael G. 1999. 'A Place for Memory: The Interface between Individual and Collective History', *Comparative Studies in Society and History* 41, 3 (July): 420–37. *The 'tricks' of memory and how they are situated in a wider context than the self are discussed in this paper.*

Miller, Jonathan. 1983. *States of Mind* (New York: Pantheon). *A series of interviews in which Jonathan Miller (English actor, writer, physician, director) talks to several of the most interesting scholars on the mind, including George Mandler, Richard Gregory, and Clifford Geertz. This book is witty and enjoyable.*

Schwartz, Theodore, Geoffrey M. White, and Catherine A. Lutz, eds. 1992. *New Directions in Psychological Anthropology* (Cambridge: Cambridge University Press). *A survey of psychological anthropology with articles by experts in the fields of cognition, human development, bio-psychological studies, and psychiatric and psychoanalytic anthropology.*

Related Websites

British Journal of Psychiatry: http://bjp.rcpsych.org/cgi/content/full/185/5/361

Culture and Personality School: http://www.encyclopedia.com/doc/1O88-CultureandPersonalitySchl.html

Partners in Health: http://www.pih.org/who/vision.html

Prototype Theory: http://www.nationmaster.com/encyclopedia/Prototype-Theory

Student Guide to Cognitive Anthropology: http://www.as.ua.edu/ant/Faculty/murphy/436/coganth.htm

Chapter 6

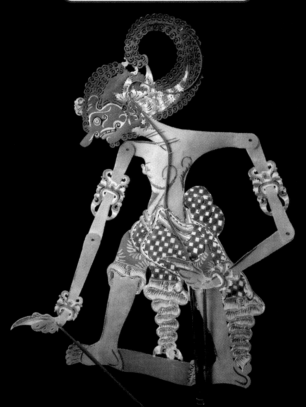

Play, Art, Myth, and Ritual

Chapter Outline

Learning Objectives

By the end of Chapter 6, you will be able to:

- perceive play as an open system that relates to cognition,
- consider the nature of metacommunication as framing and reflexivity,
- understand the effects of play,
- consider sport as play embedded in the prevailing social order,
- recognize sport as metaphor,
- appreciate art as 'play' producing transformation-representation,
- think about the nature of 'authenticity',
- distinguish the nature of the mythic as providing stories of truth and thus paramount reality,
- regard myths as a conceptual tool or charters for social action,
- perceive ritual as a culturally defined schema that brings *text* and *performance* together, and
- integrate play and ritual as complementary forms of metacommunication.

During her fieldwork in Botswana in the late 1970s, Roberta Robin Dods—one of the authors of this book—took time off from the work to drive over to a station called Red Shields. On one side of the road a group of children were gathered. The group was made up of three boys and eight girls about nine years of age. One boy was drawing shapes in the red, dusty earth with a long stick. A large circle was inscribed and inside this circle a number of smaller circles were drawn. The boy stood in the middle of the circle and pointed his stick at each girl saying 'You will be the mommy.' He concluded, 'I will be the daddy.' Each of the girls went to one of the smaller circles, and two of the boys retired to the remaining circle. And so the game of 'playing house' was inscribed in the dust and described by the children playing—what all children play—family.

This is a culture where polygyny, a man with more than one wife, is practised and where adult sons may live in separate quarters in a family compound. Children at play tell us so much about how play is culturally defined and defining. Childhood is a time when adult roles can be 'tried on' with little or no consequences. Think of the games you may have played as a child—let's pretend school, house, doctor, etc.—each works through specific aspects of potential adult roles. Play can be fun, but for the observer it is more than fun—it is a window into many aspects of cultural identity. Children's play can reflect the changing realities in which they live—the emerging new realities in a culture. Play is one of four elements (along with art, myth,

and ritual) in which the interplay of openness and creativity with rules and constraints enables people to produce powerful and moving phenomena.

However, as we study these sensitive aspects of culture, we are brought to what Riddington describes as shared 'ethnographic authority'. He notes:

> The reasons for sharing authority are more than political and aesthetic. An ethnography that places the ethnographer's monologue above the voices of people being represented risks sacrificing effective engagement with its subject. . . . its claim to objectivity may actually disguise the subjectivity of its singular isolated author. (1998: 344)

It is the 'voice' of those living in and through their engagement with play, art, myth, and ritual that resonate with meaning. Riddington cautions that theorizing occurs in the genre of Western academic expression and is not necessarily founded on the theoretical constructs of the peoples who provided the data (345). Although, he continues by noting:

> many of the anthropologists who studied people of the Subarctic also made contributions to anthropological theory that were significantly influenced by the theoretical constructs of the people they studied. A. Irving Hallowell [Ojibwa], for instance, wrote that 'a higher order of objectivity' may be obtained by 'adopting a perspective which includes an analysis of the outlook of the people themselves as a complementary procedure'. (1998)

Play

Openness is the ability to talk or think about the same thing in different ways and different things in the same way. When we expand openness to include all behaviour we can begin to define **play**. Many species play, but we believe that humans play the most and continue play throughout their lives.

Robert Fagen sees animal play as the product of natural selection that gives young animals (including young human beings) needed exercise, preparing them for the rigours of adulthood like fighting, hunting, or fleeing when pursued. Importantly, during a brief period of neural development, peak brain development associated with motor skills and peak periods of play occur at the same time. The development of cognitive and motor skills may be affected by play behaviour. Playful exploration of the environment aids learning and allows for the development of behavioural versatility (see Fagen 1981: 350–5). It also seems to have a connection with the repair of developmental damage caused either by injury or by trauma. All of these functions of play may have significant value for the survivability of individuals.

Fagen proposes an additional social function of play: the communication of the message 'all's well' (1992: 48–9). 'It seems likely that a frequent consequence and possible biological function of play is to convey information about short-term and long-term health, general well-being, and biological fitness to parents, littermates, or other social companions' (51).

Thinking about Play

Joking, which can be verbal or physical (practical jokes, pranks, horseplay), is a good example of how play operates in its cultural context. Anthropologist Andrew Miracle discusses joking behaviour among Aymara people in Bolivia (see Figure 6.1; see also EthnoProfile 6.1: Aymara). He notes that the Aymara do not laugh in the presence of strangers because it is considered disrespectful. They laugh and joke only within a circle of acquaintances and friends; this kind of joking reinforces existing social bonds (1991: 151).

Much of the joking Miracle observed took place on the crowded buses or trucks that transport rural people around the country. Ordinarily, Aymara personal space extends about one arm's length. Where there is any

EthnoProfile 6.1

Aymara

Region: South America

Nation: Bolivia, Peru, Chile

Language: There are over 2,000,000 speakers of Aymar aru in Bolivia, Peru, Chile, and western Argentina; it is one of the three official languages of Bolivia and Peru

Population: 2,000,000

Environment: The Andes and Altiplano lake basin regions with many living about Lake Titicaca

Livelihood: Peasant farmers

Political organization: Pre-conquest state societies conquered first by Inkas and later by Spanish; today, part of a modern nation-state

For more information: Miracle, Andrew. 1991. 'Aymara Joking Behaviour', *Play and Culture* 4, 2: 144–52

choice, people do not get any closer to one another. They also show respect and honour other people's privacy by not staring. Miracle notes that in everyday situations, 'when stared at, the Aymara may yell at the one staring and become quite rude' (146). On buses or trucks, however, the context changes, and people who are strangers to one another are forced into artificial intimacy. They must sit or stand very close to one another for long periods of time, frequently looking right at one another. Their response, Miracle writes, is often to joke and laugh, behaviour normally reserved for intimates. Put another way, they choose to do 'different things' (passing time with close friends and passing time with strangers in unusually close quarters) in the same way—by joking. This altered definition of

play A framing (or orienting context) that is (1) consciously adopted by the players; (2) somehow pleasurable; and (3) systemically related to what is non-play by alluding to the non-play world and by transforming the objects, roles, actions, and relations of ends and means characteristic of the non-play world.

Figure 6.1 An Aymara woman rowing near the Uros Islands in Peru.

context gives joking among strangers a new meaning, playfully changing strangers, if only for a short time, into friends and thus making a socially unpleasant situation more tolerable.

Moving from everyday reality to play reality requires a radical transformation of perspective. To an outside observer, the switch from everyday reality to play reality may go undetected. However, sometimes the switch can have serious consequences for other people and their activities. In this case, play and non-play must be signalled clearly so that one is not mistaken for the other.

According to Gregory Bateson (1972), this shift requires a level of communication called **meta-communication**, or communication about communication. It provides information about the relationship between those who are communicating. In play there are two kinds of metacommunication.

(1) **Framing**. It is a cognitive boundary that marks certain behaviours as 'play' or as 'ordinary life'. Dogs, for example, have a *play face*, a signal understood by other dogs indicating a willingness to play. If dogs agree to play, they bare their fangs and one animal attacks the other. But the bite is not consummated; it becomes a nip. Both dogs have agreed to enter the *play frame*, an imaginative world in which bites don't mean bites. To put it another way, a basic element of Western logic—that A = A—does not apply in play; the same thing is being treated in different ways. Human beings have many ways of marking the play frame: a smile, a particular tone of voice, a referee's whistle, or the words 'Let's play', 'Let's pretend', or 'You can be the king.' The marker says that 'everything from now until we end this activity is set apart from everyday life'.

(2) **Reflexivity**. Play offers us the opportunity to think about the social and cultural dimensions of the world in which we find ourselves. Because play suggests that ordinary life can be understood in more than one way, play can be a commentary on the nature of ordinary life (Handelman 1977: 186). It communicates about what *can be* rather than about what *should be* or what *is* (186). This is what we mean when we say that jokes keep us from taking ourselves too seriously. Through jokes, we see that there are alternative, even ridiculous, explanations for our experience.

Some Effects of Play

Some scholars see play as rehearsal for the 'real world' (Figure 6.2). Consider again the game of 'playing house'. Play can convey the 'rightness', if this is the appropriate word here, of the adult role the child is trying on—the 'rightness' of being Mommy or Daddy or the 'rightness' of changing adult roles in changing cultural circumstances. How do children frame their experiences when growing up with lesbian or gay parents or in single-parent homes? Will play have the space to mirror the homes of these children or will it be forced into the model of the supposed dominant cultural form? Consider that in Canada in 2006, 26 per cent of all families with children were single-parent families. This means that in excess of 2.1 million Canadian children live in single-parent families. Does 'playing house' have a different construct for these children? Does it reflect their realities and their expectations?

Some view children's play as an imitation of adult activities; others think it (especially make-believe play) increases children's creativity and originality by allowing them to overcome their limitations of age, experience, and maturity and by permitting a richer reproduction of adult life potential (Schwartzman 1978: 116).

Psychologist Brian Sutton-Smith finds this approach limiting, suggesting that play activities are important not because they provide a socializing force for society but because they allow for innovation (1992; summarized in Schwartzman 1978: 124ff.). Schwartzman has demonstrated how play, through satire and clowning, may allow children to comment on and criticize the world of adults (1978: 232–45). Some adult play forms, such as the pre-Lenten Carnival or Halloween, also act as a commentary on the 'real world'. They sanction insults and derision of authority figures, inversions of social status, clowning, parody, satire, stepping outside of everyday life, and the like (124).

Societies contain the threat posed by play by defining it as 'unserious', 'untrue', 'pretend', 'make-believe', 'unreal', and so forth (Handelman 1977: 189). Many political figures recognize that play can undermine the established political order. Repressive political regimes frequently attempt to censor humour critical of their rulers, with the result that such humour becomes an accepted mode of political resistance. Here joking can become satirical comment on the nature of what is and what can be.

While children can affirm their childhoods and try on various adult roles, they can also try on other ways of being through imagination. This has become evident in an emerging and growing children's literature with themes around these realities in North American society as well as themes on family formation by interracial adoption. Sometimes a children's book hits on several of these themes. This can be seen in *The White Swan Express* (2002) where four Chinese baby girls await adoption by four different North American families, including a lesbian couple and a single woman. The book is described as a 'joyfully touching story' that 'describes the international adoption process in terms that are meaningful to both children and adults' (Betts 2008). However, the book does not address the cultural conditions that made these four baby girls 'orphans'. This will be commented on later when we consider dimensions of inequality in the world today.

Figure 6.2 Play enables this girl in Guider, Cameroon, to incorporate her European doll into the world she knows.

framing A cognitive boundary that marks certain behaviours as 'play' or as 'ordinary life'.

metacommunication Communicating about the process of communication itself.

reflexivity Critically thinking about the way one thinks; reflecting on one's own experience.

Play and Alternative Views of Reality

We can easily see how humour shows an alternative view of reality, but what about non-joking play? What about adults who climb rocks? 'Is climbing a vertical face of rock at the risk of one's life play, or is it done in earnest?' (Csikszentmihalyi 1981: 16). Indeed, a rock climber risks serious injuries. Is rock climbing, then, not play? It fits a definition of play—it is consciously adopted by the player, it is somehow pleasurable, it transforms the relations of ends and means characteristic of the non-play world—and yet 'the climber is as immersed in reality as anyone can be in this world'. This suggests that one's perspective on reality can vary. Each person's view of reality 'is relative to the goals that cultures and individuals create' (17). Reality is defined in terms of the goals toward which each player directs their attention at any given time. In rock climbing, the goal is to find hand and toeholds in order to get to the top of the rock; it is to put one's body at risk rather than to *avoid* putting one's body at risk. In other words, people do not always submit to the rules of paramount reality (the everyday social order), which is their basic referential perspective.

Play allows us to recognize that *no referential perspective is absolute*. Play exists when there is an awareness of alternatives, 'of two sets of goals and rules, one operating here and now, one that applies outside the given activity' (19), a set of rules that are different from those of our paramount reality. Importantly, play creates the awareness of alternatives and demonstrates the openness in human experience and all its ambiguity.

Sport

Sport is

> a physically exertive activity that is aggressively competitive within constraints imposed by definitions and rules. A component of culture, it is ritually patterned, game-like, and of varying amounts of play, work, and leisure. In addition, sport can be viewed as having both athletic and non-athletic variations, *athletic* referring to those activities requiring the greater amount of physical exertion. (Blanchard and Cheska 1985: 60)

It is play embedded in the prevailing social order. Sports reflect the basic values of the cultural setting in which they are performed, and they are transformed when they are translated into a new cultural setting.

Beyond play, sport can be work for the players and an investment for the owners of professional teams. It is also a form of personal and social identification for fans, who are invited into a make-believe world in which they may playfully identify with their heroes, rage at the opponents, imagine coaching the team, suffer, and rejoice. It is framed as play, but conflict in games and sports is different from conflict in ordinary life although game metaphors may be used for serious conflicts such as war. Competitors agree 'to strive for an incompatible goal—only one opponent can win—within the constraints of understood rules' (Lever 1983: 3). As with all forms of play, the relationships of means and ends in sport are altered. Sport is struggle for the sake of struggle.

Sport can transform from one culture to another. Cricket in the Trobriand Islands (see EthnoProfile 9.1: Trobriand Islanders) offers us an excellent example of this. An English missionary introduced the sport of cricket to the Trobrianders in the early twentieth century. By the 1970s, in the more rural parts of the islands, it had become a different game. Played between two villages, it became a substitute for warfare and a way of establishing political alliances. If the hosts had 40 men ready to play and the visitors had 36, then there were 36 to a side instead of the 'correct' 11. The game was always won by the home team—but not by too many runs because that would shame the visitors. War magic was employed to aid batsmen and bowlers. Teams had dances and chants for taking the field, leaving it, and celebrating outs. These dances and chants were used to comment on current events and became fertile ground for additional competition beyond that of the sporting event itself. The bat was redesigned for greater accuracy, and the entire activity was associated with the ceremonial exchange of food and other goods. Cricket, the sport of empire, was radically transformed.

From the perspective of some Trobrianders, in fact, their version of cricket was a way of taking the English colonizers' favourite game—a game that was supposed to teach Trobrianders how to become 'civilized'—and using it to express their rejection of the colonial world. As one Trobriand leader says in the film *Trobriand Cricket* (1974), 'we rubbished the white man's game; now it's our game'. Here is the 'openness' of play as it functions as a statement of cultural transformation while making social commentary on the colonial experience.

Sport in the Nation-state

The full institutionalization of sport seems to have taken place in the nation-state fairly recently. The most important and universal feature of sport in the nation-state is that it helps complex modern societies cohere (Lever 1995: 3). In her study of soccer in Brazil (see Map 6.2), aptly titled *Soccer Madness*, Janet Lever argues that large-scale organized sport presents a mechanism for building political unity and allegiance to the nation (Figure 6.3). 'Sport's paradoxical ability to reinforce societal cleavages while transcending them makes soccer, Brazil's most popular sport, the perfect means of achieving a more perfect union between multiple groups . . . [by giving] dramatic expression to the strain between groups while affirming the solidarity of the whole' (5, 9).

In Brazil, there is at least one professional soccer team in every city. The larger cities have several teams representing different social groups. In Rio de Janeiro, for example, separate teams tend to be supported by the old rich, the modern middle class, the poor, the blacks, the Portuguese, and a number of neighbourhood communities. The teams come to represent these different groups in a concrete, visible fashion. Through these teams, separate groups maintain their identities. At the same time, the teams bring their opposing fans together through a shared enthusiasm for soccer. City and national championships similarly unify the socio-economically and geographically diverse groups of Brazil.

Figure 6.3 A Brazilian fan celebrates during a World Cup 2010 qualifying soccer match between Brazil and Uruguay in Sao Paulo.

For many Brazilians—indeed, for many people around the world—the experience of supporting a sports team may be their first and perhaps only experience of a loyalty beyond the local community. Unity is achieved by demonstrating that different teams, and the groups they represent, are in conflict only at one level. At a higher level, the fans of those teams are really united; for example, fans of all Rio teams support the team that goes on to represent Rio in the national championships. This process reaches a climax in international competition as the supporters of the many local teams back the national team. At this highest level of integration, soccer provides a way of affirming one's 'Brazilianness'.

There is one important exception to the global mass culture of sport: it regularly separates women from men. Soccer is incredibly important to Brazilian men and to many other men in the rest of the world, but it is much less important to women. The gender segregation of the sport has significant consequences for the experience of growing up male or female. It also affects relationships later in life between men and women who do not share the same experiences. There is a fundamental ambiguity in the relation of sports

Map 6.2 Brazil

sport 'A physically exertive activity that is aggressively competitive within constraints imposed by definitions and rules. A component of culture, it is ritually patterned, game-like, and of varying amounts of play, work, and leisure.'

and integration: as sports bring people together in one domain, they separate them in another. Sports can maintain and sharpen distinctions that are already significant in many other areas of a culture.

Sport as Metaphor

Why soccer? Why is it so important in Brazil and other parts of the world? French anthropologist Christian Bromberger (1995), writing about soccer based on field research in Marseille, France, and Naples and Turin in Italy, observes that soccer is fascinating because 'it lays bare the major symbolic horizon of our societies: the course of a match, of a competition, resembles the uncertain fate of people in the contemporary world. Further, the combination of rules that mould the genre give this uncertainty an *acceptable* feel' (197). It all becomes a metaphor for the fragility and the mobility of both individual and collective status. The complexity and sudden changes of a single game or a tournament offer what Bromberger calls 'a shortcut to the joys and dramas that make up a life' (197). A match or a championship season feature not only achievement on the basis of merit but also uncertainties introduced by strategy, luck, law, (in)justice in the form of the referee, trickery, and unfairness. It offers the fan the opportunity to compare players, to reflect, to plan, to strategize, and to be surprised. As one of Bromberger's informants put it, 'At bottom, what most fascinates me is when a player chooses a solution which I had not thought of . . . and it works!' As in life, the best team doesn't always win.

Art

When anthropologists talk about art in non-Western societies, they begin by focusing on activities or products that resemble art in the West. Whether non-Western peoples refer to such activities or products as 'art', the activities and products themselves are universal. They seem rooted in playful creativity, a birthright of all human beings. And yet, like sport, those activities defined as 'art' differ from free play because they are circumscribed by rules. Artistic rules direct particular attention to, and provide standards for evaluating, the *form* of the activities or objects that artists produce.

A Definition of Art

Anthropologist Alexander Alland defines **art** as 'play with form producing some aesthetically successful

transformation-representation' (1977: 39). 'Form' refers to the rules of the art game: the culturally appropriate restrictions on the way this kind of play may be organized in time and space, the culturally acceptable style and media. A style is a schema (a distinctive patterning of elements) that is recognized within a culture as appropriate to a given medium. The media in which art is created and executed are culturally recognized and characterized (Anderson 1990: 272–5). A painting is a form: it is two-dimensional; it is done with paint; it is intentionally made; it represents or symbolizes something in the world outside the canvas, paper, or wood on which it is created. There are different kinds of paintings as well. There is the painting form called *portrait*—a portrait depicts a person, it resembles the person in some appropriate way, it is done with paint, it can be displayed, and more.

By 'aesthetic', Alland means appreciative of, or responsive to, form in art or nature (xii). 'Aesthetically successful' means that the creator of the piece of art (and possibly its audience as well) experiences a positive or negative response. Indifference is the sign of something that is aesthetically unsuccessful. It is probably the case that the aesthetic response is a universal feature in all cultures and, as with play, may be part of the human condition.

Aesthetic response is holistic, involving all our faculties, including emotion, especially as these are shaped by our social and cultural experience. Voloshinov argued that aesthetic response to form in a work of art is based largely on a culturally shaped evaluation of the appropriateness of form to content. He observed that artistic form allows both creator and audience to exert agency: although 'the form in and of itself need not necessarily be pleasurable . . . what it must be is a *convincing evaluation* of the content . . .' (1987 [1926]: 108). Evaluations of appropriateness and of technical perfection involve a broad range of intellectual, emotional, and moral judgments on the part of the viewer.

Aesthetic value judgments guide the artist's choice of form and material; they also guide the observers' evaluations. This implies that art involves more than just objects. Voloshinov argues that art is a creative 'event of living communication' involving the work, the artist, and the artist's audience (107). Artists create their works with an audience in mind, and audiences respond to these works as if the works were addressed to them. Sometimes the response is enthusiastic;

sometimes it is highly critical. In either case, the aesthetic event does not leave its participants indifferent. In a sense it is not dissimilar to the experience of intersubjectivity in fieldwork.

Art also includes the *process* through which some product is made. In a practical way archaeologists can tell us about this from their insights gained through the study of material culture. They note there is an 'order' to making each 'thing'—essentially a pattern not unlike the syntax of a language. To achieve the desired result one must follow the *chaîne opératoire*, and, when followed, it produces a specific result, such as a Clovis Point (Figure 6.4). Art of course has a process but with artistic licence.

Transformation-representation

To understand the term **transformation-representation** in Alland's definition of art, we must recall that symbols represent something other than themselves. They are arbitrary in that they have no necessary connection with what they represent. This means that they can be cut away from the object or idea represented and appreciated for their own sake. They may also be used to represent a totally different meaning. When a Javanese leather puppet maker makes a puppet of the mythic hero Bhima, he is representing the traditional form of the hero in his work, but he is also *transforming* a three-dimensional human form into a two-dimensional flat puppet made of buffalo hide in which the colours, style, inclination of the head, and adornment stand for the internal state of the hero at a specific moment (Figure 6.5). At the same time, he is carrying out this work more or less skilfully and is embodying the meanings that Bhima has for the Javanese.

Because transformation and representation depend on each other, Alland (1977: 35) refers to them as *transformation-representations*; they are *metaphors*. A drawing, for example, is a metaphoric transformation of experience into visible marks on a two-dimensional

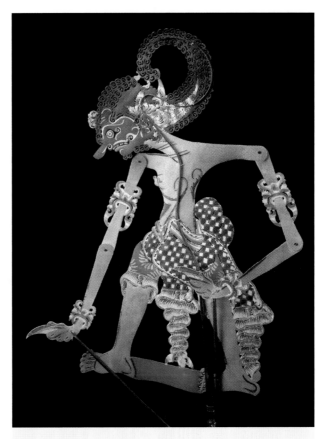

Figure 6.5 Bhima, the great mythic hero of Javanese wajang, is represented here.

surface. Similarly, a poem metaphorically transforms experience into concentrated and tightened language. This process is one place where the technical skill of the artist is involved.

'But Is It Art?'

Alland's definition of art attempts to capture something universal about human beings and their cultures. As Errington observes, all human cultures have '"symbolic forms": artifacts, activities, or even aspects of the landscape that humans view as densely meaningful' (1998: 84).

Figure 6.4 A Clovis Point.

> **art** 'Play with form producing some aesthetically successful transformation-representation'.
>
> **transformation-representation** The process in which experience is transformed as it is represented symbolically in a different medium.

In the Western prototype of art, there is a distinction between art and non-art. Some paintings, songs, stories, carvings, dances, and the like are considered art; some are not. People who accept this perspective might argue, for example, that the *Mona Lisa* is art but paintings of Elvis Presley on black velvet are not. Why? Part of the answer may have to do with how successfully the artist has captured something that he or she considers to be important about Elvis and the culture to which both the artist and Elvis belong—that is, how aesthetically successful is the transformation-representation? But part of the answer also involves the high degree of specialization in Western societies, which has led to the emergence of an 'art establishment' that includes critics, art historians, art teachers, journalists, schools, and museums—as well as professional artists. These people define what art is and what it is not, as well as the appropriate styles, media, and forms. They distinguish between art and craft. That a painter may in fact have created an image of Elvis that is important and meaningful to the many people who have purchased the paintings—that it speaks to them both in style and medium—does not change the art establishment's opinion that the paintings are not art.

Thus, to them Elvis on velvet is not art because it does not address problems in art theory, because it does not refer to the beautiful and the true, because it does not portray the artist's struggle to produce a new expressive style or, indeed, because the artist seems ignorant or disdainful of the stylistic experimentation that makes up Western art history.

Nevertheless, many people—anthropologists included—have resisted the notion that art is only what a group of Western experts define as art. To highlight the ethnocentrism of Western art experts, they stressed that the division of art and non-art is not universal. In many cultures, there is no category of art distinct from other human activities. On the other hand, convinced that all people were endowed with the same aesthetic capacities, anthropologists felt justified in speaking of art and of artists in non-Western societies. Their goal was to recognize a fully human capacity for art in all societies but to redefine art until it became broad enough to include, on an equal basis, aesthetic products and activities that Western art experts would qualify, at best, as 'primitive', 'ethnic', or 'folk' art.

For example, some anthropologists focused on the evaluative standards that artists use for their own work, and other work in the same form, and how these may differ from the standards used by non-artists. Forge, for example, notes that Abelam carvers in New Guinea discuss carvings in a language that is more incisive than that of non-carvers (1967). Other anthropologists pointed out that artists in traditional non-Western societies created objects or engaged in activities that presented and represented the central values of a culture. Thus their work helped maintain the social order, and they did not see themselves as (nor were they understood to be) alienated critics of society as they are in modern Western societies.

Recent work in the anthropology of art, however, has prompted many anthropologists to rethink this position. They have turned their attention to the way certain kinds of material objects made by tribal peoples flow into a global art market where they are transformed into 'primitive' or 'ethnic' art. Some anthropologists, like Shelly Errington, point out that even in the West most of the objects in fine arts museums today, no matter where they came from, were not intended by their makers to be 'art'. They were intended to be, for example, masks for ritual use; paintings for religious contemplation; reliquaries for holding the relics of saints, ancestor figures, furniture, jewelry boxes, architectural details, and so on. They are in fine arts museums today because at some point they were claimed to be art by someone with the authority to put them in the museum.

For these reasons, Errington distinguishes 'art by intention' from 'art by appropriation'. Art by intention includes objects that were made to be art, such as Impressionist paintings. Art by appropriation, however, consists of all the other objects that 'became art' because at a certain moment certain people, usually those in power situations in colonial settings, decided that they belonged to the category of art. Because museums, art dealers, and art collectors are found everywhere in the world, it is now the case that potentially any material object crafted by human hands can be appropriated by these institutions as 'art'. For an example of such conflicting ideas about the nature of specific pieces of 'art', we can consider the Haisla Nation's Mis'kusa G'psgolox totem pole (Figure 6.6). It was cut down in 1929 by Indian agent Iver Fougner and sold to Sweden's Museum of Ethnography. The debate within the Haisla Nation, beyond the issue of the struggle for the repatriation of the pole, focused on the original 'use' of the pole. In Western art tradition the pole was to be preserved, but

Figure 6.6 Members of the Haisla Nation and UBC Museum of Anthropology personnel move the Mis'kusa G'psgolox to its new home in Vancouver.

in Haisla Nation tradition such a pole was situated in a specific time and place, and its 'life' had a beginning and an end—essentially in its process of biodegradation, it moved into the realm of the ancestors.

To transform an object into art, Errington argues, it must have *exhibition value*—someone must be willing to display it. Objects that somehow fit into the Western definition of art will be selected for the art market. Looking at the collection of objects that have been defined as 'art' over the years, Errington sees that the vast majority show certain elements to be embedded rather deeply in the Western definition of art: the objects are 'portable (paintings preferred to murals), durable (bronze preferred to basketry), useless for practical purposes in the secular West (ancestral effigies and Byzantine icons preferred to hoes and grain grinders), representational (human and animal figures preferred to, say, heavily decorated ritual bowls)' (1998: 116–17). In other words, for Errington, art requires that someone *intend* that the objects be art but that someone does not have to be the object's creator. She notes that 'we humans are amazingly inventive, and we make and have always made things that we imbue with meaning, as befits creatures having both opposable thumbs and consciousness. Human artifacts are admirable. They are ingenious. They are dense with meaning. They are worthy of deep study' (103). But, she argues, they are not art until someone who carries around a particular definition of art says they are.

This is successful when the artifacts in question can be metaphorically transformed and represented as Western art objects. In their original contexts, most meaningful symbolic forms involve more than one sense: an audience hears drumming while looking at masked dancers and feeling the warm breeze carrying the smell of palm oil while hearing the shouts of children frightened by the dancers. But some of the sensory experiences that make richly symbolic performances do not last. As masks, audio recordings, and other objects are moved into the international art market, 'they slough off their . . . performance contexts, . . . retaining only the durable part that can be set aside in a frame or on a pedestal' (84) or can be burned onto a CD and sold in the World Music section of a music store.

It can be fruitful to talk about art as a kind of play. Like play, art presents its creators and participants with alternative realities, a separation of means from ends, and the possibility of commenting on and transforming the everyday world. In today's global art market, however, restrictions of an entirely different order also apply. Errington observes that the people who make 'primitive art' are no longer 'tribal' but have become

modern-day peasants or a new type of proletariat. . . . They live in rain forests and deserts and other such formerly out-of-the-way places on the peripheries . . . within national and increasingly global systems of buying and selling, of using natural and human resources, and of marketing images and notions about products. Some lucky few of them make high ethnic art, and sell it for good prices, and obtain a good portion of the proceeds. Others make objects classed as tourist or folk art, usually for much less money, and often through a middleperson. (268)

Others fulfill orders from elsewhere, 'producing either masses of "folk art" or expensive handmade items designed by people in touch with world taste and world markets' (269). Errington points out the bitter irony that international demand for 'exotic' objects is growing at the very moment when the makers of these objects are severely threatened by international economic policies and resource extraction projects that impoverish them and undermine the ways of life that give the objects they make their 'exotic' allure. And, it should also be noted that what counts as fashionable decoration this year—'world taste'—may be unfashionable next year, leaving the producers with very little to fall back on.

'She's Fake': The Problem of the Authentic

Michelle Bigenho is an anthropologist and violinist whose multi-sited ethnography examines music performance in Bolivia, in part through her experiences performing with *Música de Maestros* (Figure 6.7). This ensemble has chosen to perform the works of master Bolivian composers and also attempts to recreate accurate performances of contemporary cultural originals that they have studied in the countryside (Bigenho 2002: 4). The ensemble was made up of both classically trained and traditionally trained musicians as well as three foreigners: a Japanese who played the Andean flute, a Cuban who played violin, and Bigenho, from the United States, who also played violin. Along with a dance ensemble, the musicians were invited to represent Bolivia in a folklore festival in France. As the bands were lining up, a member of the Belgian delegation walked over to Bigenho and announced in French 'She's fake.' The Belgian woman then 'pointed to one of the Bolivian dancers dressed in her dancing costume with her long fake braids worked into her short brown hair. As she pointed, she said "She's real"' (88).

In this way, Bigenho raises the question of 'authenticity'. What is real when it comes to music, painting, sculpture, dance, or other 'folk' art forms? How do the images that people in dominant nations have of 'folk' or Indigenous peoples affect the production and circulation of art? And, finally, who gets to decide what is authentic? To address these issues, Bigenho distinguishes three different forms of authenticity: experiential, cultural–historical, and unique.

(1) *Experiential authenticity* refers to 'the entire sensory experience of music performances. . . . It is connected to a shared experience with others, a fleeting moment of the groove, a listener's great night at a concert' (17, 18).

(2) *Cultural–historical authenticity* is connected to how music is represented: it makes a claim to a connection with the origin of the music, either in a historical or mythical past. The ensemble with which Bigenho played explicitly sought to perform culturally and historically authentic renditions of Bolivian music. They performed music from the Chaco War (1932–5), as well as music from different regions and ethnic groups in Bolivia, and seemed to be quite successful in performing authentically in the different styles. (Similarly, Meisch [2002] notes that there is an ensemble in Italy that plays music from Otavalo, Ecuador, so authentically that Otavalos she knows refuse to believe that the musicians are not themselves Otavalos.) Bigenho points out that in terms of Indigenous art, the power of the cultural and historical authenticity derives from the Native's position in relation to the nation-state.

(3) *Unique authenticity* is a term that Bigenho uses to refer to the creative activity of composing musicians. It is, as she puts it, 'the founding myth of modern concepts of authorship and copyright' (20). Unique authenticity refers to the individual artist's new, innovative, and personal production. It raises the issue of who owns cultural products and whether it is possible to talk about collective creation and ownership of the music of a community, a people, or an ethnic group. This is a particularly significant issue at the moment as the politics and economics of culture raise questions about who owns experiences and representations.

Bigenho came face to face with this when she compiled a cassette of music from one of the villages in which she worked. She discussed with the villagers

Figure 6.7 *Música de Maestros* in costume performing in a folklore festival in France.

how to register the copyright on the cassette. While the villagers recognized that the music they played was composed by individuals, they felt strongly that ownership of the music was collective. In doing so, they moved from uniquely authentic individual compositions—intellectual property—to collective ownership of a 'culturally authentic representation'—cultural property (217). When Bigenho went to La Paz to register the copyright, however, she found that it was impossible to register the cassette under collective authorship or ownership. In fact *she*, as the compiler, could register the work but not the people who created the work, unless they were willing to be recognized as individuals. What she discovered was that according to Bolivian law, the music on the cassette was legally folklore,

> the set of literary and artistic works created in national territory by unknown authors or by authors who do not identify themselves and are presumed to be nationals of the country, or of its ethnic communities, and that are transmitted from generation to generation, constituting one of the fundamental elements of traditional cultural patrimony of the nation. (221)

As a result, the music was part of the 'National Patrimony' and belonged to the nation-state. But in the context of Bolivian cultural and ethnic politics, Bigenho observes, the villagers gained visibility and connections as a collective Indigenous entity, which they believed would provide them with possible economic advantages. Whether they were correct remains to be seen, but this example of the connections of art and authority is being repeated all over the world at present.

Sculpture and the Baule Gbagba Dance

The Baule of the Ivory Coast are renowned for their sculpture (see Figure 6.8). Susan Vogel (1997), who has been studying Baule sculpture for over 30 years, identifies four forms of Baule sculpture, which she refers to as:

(1) art that is watched (performances featuring carved masks),
(2) art that is seen without looking (sacred sculpture),
(3) art that is glimpsed (private sculptures of personal figures for hunting and sculpture for spirit spouses), and

(4) art that is visible to all (the profane; everyday objects that Baule see as beautiful trifles).

As we saw in Chapter 5, Baule visuality is distinctive; people learn to look in a way that is different from that of people in the West—'the more important a Baule sculpture is, the less it is displayed' (Vogel 1997: 108). The Western concept of 'art' in the sense that it is used in Western languages does not exist in Baule villages. Rather, 'to approach art from a Baule perspective entails speaking of experiences that are not primarily visual and of art objects that are animate presences, indistinguishable from persons, spirits, and certain prosaic things'. The Baule attribute great powers to their artwork—powers that Westerners would consider incredible. The meaning of most art objects, and the emotional responses that these objects have, derives from their ability to act. For the Baule, what Western museum-goers call *sculpture* contains enormous

Figure 6.8 The Baule of the Ivory Coast are renowned for their sculpture.

powers of life and death, and Baule people do not consider their sculpture apart from these powers (85).

We will consider one use of art objects in performance: the Gbagba dance, described by Vogel. While anthropologists have often studied dance as an independent art form (see below), we are looking here at the intersection of sculpture and dance. The Gbagba dance is an entertainment performance that lasts much of a day and may also be performed for the funeral of an important woman. The style of mask that is used in the performance is called *Mblo*, and in the past, a village may have had as many as a dozen or more such masks—some representations of animals, some portraits of people. Portrait masks are usually of a specific woman, and the subject of the portrait always dances alongside the male who dances the mask. Only the best dancers wear these masks, and they appear at the very end of the dance.

The Gbagba begins with skits that include unmasked performers, young dancers who are just getting started. The skits are supposed to be funny as they present scenes from everyday life from which a moral is drawn. They often feature masks of domestic animals—generally sheep and goats. These skits are followed by masks representing the large wild animals that the Baule hunt and always end with the successful 'killing' of the portrayed animal. Older, more skilled dancers are featured in these skits and there is more actual dancing. At the same time that the first masks appear so too does a costumed figure of the trickster Ambomon, who wears a cloth hood rather than a mask and who dances in a rapid and acrobatic way, including somersaults and tumbling. Ambomon is a completely ambiguous figure, even to the Baule who speculate as to whether or not he is a god. He has no respect for possessions, rank, and decent behaviour. While comical, he also takes things from people, sits on the ground, and gets things dirty. He never does any real damage, and people regard him as an amusing nuisance. He stands in direct contrast to the orderly vision of the world, as expressed by the masks; he is the sprit of disorder. Yet at the same time, Ambomon is the only figure in the dance that *must* appear—he can appear without any of the other masks, but the other masks cannot appear without him. When Gbagba is danced for a funeral, only Ambomon enters the courtyard to pay his respects to the deceased and to greet the mourners. Vogel suggests that the obligatory presence of Ambomon suggests to the Baule that the only certainty in life is the threat of disorder and death (167).

Vogel notes that Ambomon's style of dance is quite different from the ideal Baule dance style, which seems to minimize movement. She notes that a female solo dance moves forward very slowly in a curved line, with body and neck held upright, the hands in front, palms up. Sometimes the dancer carries something in her hand. The dancer's facial features are impassive, the eyes are downcast, and the main movement is in the neck, shoulders, and back, often marking two different rhythmic patterns in the polyrhythmic music. A male dancer may be a bit more vigorous, but

> Baule dancing in general can be characterized as symmetrically balanced and essentially vertical (the dancer's knees may be flexed but the head and torso are held upright). As in so many other Baule creations, the dancer's body is closed in outline. These qualities are also characteristic of Baule sculpture and must be recognized as expressing an aesthetic preference with moral connotations that is deeply embedded in Baule culture and is expressed in myriad ways. (156)

Gbagba includes singing, and two of the songs that are repeated throughout the day refer to death. They are sung both when Gbagba is danced for women's funerals and when it is danced for entertainment. Finally, at the end of the day, one or more portrait masks appear, one by one, each accompanied by its human 'double'. At that moment, the finest skills in the community are on display—the best dancers, the most beautiful masks, the best drummers and singers, and the distinguished women who are represented now take their places (Figure 6.9).

The term *double* is the term that the Baule themselves use for the portrait mask and its subject. The portrait mask is considered the person's true double; the mask never performs unless the person is there to dance. Vogel tells us that the 'relationships between individuals and their portrait masks are close, complex, and lifelong and become elements of their identities' (166). When the subject of a portrait mask dies or cannot dance any more, a relative becomes the new double or the mask is never danced again.

In sum, Vogel proposes that a Gbagba performance is a joyous occasion that brings everyone in the village, of all ages and persuasions, together in a happy celebration, the importance of which cannot be underestimated in a world with little entertainment or distractions.

> The performance teaches basic lessons about the Baule world—about hierarchies and mysteries. Each skit has a simple moral lesson, evident even to children: that humans, for example, with skill and supernatural aid, can dominate even the largest and most awesome wild animals, while the portrait masks present a model of human accomplishment and beauty. At the same time, the dance provides deeper insights about blurred boundaries—about the interpenetration of bush and village and the complexity of gender. The subject of a portrait, most often a woman, sees herself impersonated by a man dancing 'like a woman' and wearing a mask that is her double or namesake. A frequent theme of Baule art is opposite-sex doubling, meaning that two figures appear not as a pair of complementary beings but as manifestations of a single being having qualities of both sexes. The concept is too troubling to articulate openly in words, but in Gbagba it is available to wordless contemplation. (167–8)

Dance and Gender in Northern Greece

Jane Cowan has explored how dance may play a role in the social construction of gender in northern Greece. She considers three different kinds of dance events in the town of Sohos (see Map 6.3): the wedding dance, the formal evening dance, and the private dance at home. At each dance event, individuals present themselves publicly by eating, drinking, and talking, as well as dancing, and other people at the event evaluate them. Men and women, however, do not present themselves in the same way nor are they evaluated in the same way. They perform and experience themselves as gendered subjects—that is, males or females as these are defined in Sohos. 'In dance events associated with pleasure, sensual intensity, and public sociability, gender inequalities and other social hierarchies are constituted and even celebrated' (Cowan 1990: 4).

In contrast, culturally specific images of male and female sexuality in northern Greece are given a particular public form in the dance. From the perspective of women in northern Greece, dances are places where they can 'escape' and 'forget' their relatively restricted everyday lives. Everyone at the dance—men and women alike—encourages them to do this in order to be good, carefree celebrants. But dance presents problems for women: they are keenly aware that they are being watched, that they not only act but are also acted upon. So women know they must control themselves emotionally and physically. The limits of appropriate bodily expression are learned early in life and continue to be internalized throughout life. A woman's expression of 'letting go' may be at the boundaries of those limits but rarely overstep them in any fundamental way (228).

Dance provides a place where northern Greek women play with the boundaries of 'good' and 'bad' female sexuality. Should she take the first position in a

Figure 6.9 Portrait mask of Moya Yanso about to enter the Gbagba dance in the Baule village of Kami in 1972. The mask—an important object—is hidden by the cloths until the last moment when the mask, its dancer, and its subject will appear dramatically in the performance.

Map 6.3 Sohos

circle dance or is that too forward? How intense should her *tsifte teli* (belly dance) be? Should she move closer to her partner, lean toward him, and playfully shimmy her shoulders? When a man dances an intense *tsifte teli*, should she break plates at his feet, a conventional statement of deep understanding of, and empathy with, the dancer's inner state? 'In this dance space, ambivalent attitudes toward female sexuality are juxtaposed. Girls and women are not necessarily expected to mute or hide their sexuality. Flirtation, energy, the display of beauty, even subtle seduction, are acknowledged and valued aspects of female performance in these events' (228). But there is always a potential problem: a female who is thought to lack control in these displays can be censured.

> A female celebrant's experience of the dance, then, is rooted in her position in gender relations, but it is not only men who keep her 'in her place'. Women do as well. Only when she believes that everybody is truly 'all together' can the female celebrant really feel free to let go; for girls, everybody being 'all together' is both the precondition for, and the expression of, collective *kefi* [high spirits]. (229)

The Mass Media: A Television Serial in Egypt

In recent years, anthropologists have begun to pay more attention to the importance of the mass media as cultural productions. Given the ever-increasing importance of media such as film, comic books, radio, the Internet, and television, and their centrality in people's lives all over the world, this is not surprising. The anthropological study of mass media can go in several different directions, including studies of globalization (Chapter 13), but we want to highlight the creativity of producers and consumers of media in the interpretation and incorporation of these art forms. This is, perhaps, the most important thing anthropology can add to the study of media: the fine-grained ethnographic assessment of the effects and impact of popular media among the people who watch, listen, read, and interpret (cf. Herzfeld 2001: 298), and some of whom also create, those media.

In many nations in the world, soap operas or television serials are among the most popular mass entertainments, watched by millions. These programs are seen by their creators in some parts of the world not simply as entertainment but also as tools, useful for teaching certain people in their societies what they need to learn to be modern citizens. But what the intended audience gets from the program is not always the message the creators thought they were transmitting. Anthropologist Lila Abu-Lughod studied an Egyptian television serial called *Hilmiyya Nights* that was broadcast during Ramadan (the Islamic holy month) over five successful years. The serial followed the fortunes and relationships of a group of characters from the traditional Cairo neighbourhood of Hilmiyya, taking them from the late 1940s, when Egypt was under the rule of King Farouk and the British, up to the early 1990s, even incorporating Egyptian reaction to the first Gulf War.

The central action revolved around the rivalry, financial wheeling–dealing, and love interests of two wealthy men—in many ways it resembles an Egyptian version of the TV show *Dallas*. However, *Hilmiyya Nights* attempted to tie the lives of its characters to Egyptian national political events. Above all, it promoted the theme of national unity. With few exceptions, all the characters were shown to be basically good and patriotic.

Abu-Lughod studied two separate groups of Egyptians during the 1990s: poor working-class women in Cairo and villagers in Upper Egypt. When she asked poor women in Cairo what they liked about the show, they volunteered not the serious political or social messages but two female characters: the glamorous, aristocratic femme fatale and the arrogant belly dancer turned cabaret-owner. Although these two characters were hardly respectable, they were nevertheless favourites because they defied the moral system that kept good women quiet. Indeed, Abu-Lughod found that both the urban women and the villagers accepted the moral stances presented in the program only when they resonated with their own worlds and ignored those aspects of the serial that were not part of their experiences.

Most interestingly, she argues that television, especially for the villagers, created its own world, one that was a small part of their daily lives. 'What they experienced through television added to, but did not displace, whatever else already existed. They treated the television world not as a fantasy escape but as a sphere unto itself with its familiar time slots and specific attitudes' (Abu-Lughod 1995: 203–4). Moreover, the villagers did not compartmentalize the 'modernity' that television serials present in order to preserve a 'traditional' community untouched by the outside world. On the contrary, these villagers were deeply affected in a wide variety of ways by the outside world, whether through local government policies or transnationally through the effect of advertising by multinational corporations. 'Television is, in this village, one part of a complex jumble of life, and the dramatic experiences and visions it offers are surprisingly easily incorporated as discrete—not overwhelming—elements in the jumble' (205).

Television in Egypt, she notes, has had measurable social effects: for example, families prefer to stay home to watch television rather than visit among households in the evenings. Television may also have increased the number of 'experiences' shared across generation and gender as young and old, men and women, now spend time together watching television.

The intended impact of *Hilmiyya Nights* was not undermined because nobody was watching television: both urban poor and villagers had their sets on almost constantly. Rather, the positive messages that the creators of *Hilmiyya Nights* and similar serials intended were lost because they were only part of the complex flow of programming in Egypt, which included many other kinds of information: news, entertainment, advertising, and so on. More important, all these messages were evaluated in terms of the life experiences of the viewers and hence were often neutralized or contradicted by the powerful everyday realities within which poor urban women and Egyptian villagers move. Even soap operas are contested sites, open for multiple interpretations, not simply places for the transmission of messages from the elite to the masses. This is not unique to the Egyptian experience.

Myth

We have suggested that play lies at the heart of human creativity. However, because the openness of play is random and thus just as likely to undermine the social order as to enhance it, societies tend to circumscribe play with cultural rules, channelling it in directions that appear less destructive. Rules designed to limit artistic expression are one result of this channelling process. As we have seen, artists in various media are permitted a wide range of expression as long as they adhere to rules governing the form that expression takes. Societies differ in how loose or strict the rules of artistic form may be. Artists who challenge the rules, however, are often viewed negatively by those in power who believe they

have the right to restrict artistic expressions that question social, religious, or sexual precepts that ought not to be questioned.

In fact, all societies depend on the willingness of their members not to question certain assumptions about the way the world works. Because the regularity and predictability of social life might collapse all together if people were free to imagine, and act upon, alternatives to the local version of paramount reality, most societies find ways to persuade their members that the local version of paramount reality is the only reality—period. The most venerable way of doing this is through the use of myth. **Myths** are stories whose truths seem self-evident because they do such a good job of integrating personal experiences with a wider set of assumptions about the way society, or the world in general, must operate. As stories that involve a teller and an audience, myths are products of high verbal art (and increasingly of cinematic art). Frequently the official myth tellers are the ruling groups in society: the elders, the political leaders, the religious specialists. They may also be considered master storytellers. The content of myths usually concerns past events (usually at the beginning of time) or future events (usually at the end of time). Myths are socially important because if they are taken literally they tell people where they have come from, where they are going, and, thus, how they should live right now (Figure 6.10).

Societies differ in the degree to which they permit speculation about key myths. In complex Western societies like that of Canada, many different groups, each with its own mythic tradition, often live side by side. Because the Canadian government supports cultural diversity, or multiculturalism, it regularly prohibits one group from silencing an opposing group. Our myth is this multiculturalism myth and the assumption that it makes us more tolerant. Can this be supported by the actual experiences of those who do not 'belong' to the two founding nations—white Anglo or Franco?

Myths and related beliefs that are taken to be self-evident truths are sometimes codified in an explicit manner. When this codification is extreme and deviation

myths Stories whose truths seem self-evident because they do such a good job of integrating our personal experiences with a wider set of assumptions about the way society, or the world in general, must operate.

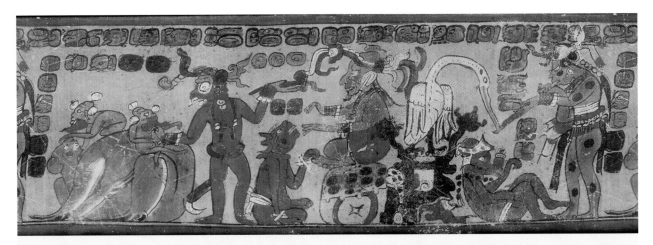

Figure 6.10 A vase painting illustrating part of the *Popul Vuh*, the Mayan creation story.

from the code is treated harshly, we sometimes speak of **orthodoxy** (or 'correct doctrine'). Societies differ in the degree to which they require members to adhere to orthodox interpretations of key myths. But even societies that place little emphasis on orthodoxy are likely to exert some control over the interpretation of key myths because myths have implications for action. They may justify past action, explain present action, or generate future action. To be persuasive, myths must offer plausible explanations for our experience of human nature, human society, and human history. The power of myths comes from their ability to make life meaningful for those who accept them.

The success of Western science has led many members of Western societies to dismiss non-scientific myths as flawed attempts at science or history. Only recently have some scientists come to recognize the similarities between scientific and non-scientific storytelling about events such as the origin of life on earth. Scientific stories about origin—*origin myths*—must be taken to the *natural* world to be matched against material evidence; the success of this match determines whether they are accepted or rejected. By contrast, non-scientific origin myths get their vitality from how well they match with the *social* world.

Myth as a Charter for Social Action

Early in the twentieth century, anthropologist Bronislaw Malinowski introduced a new approach to myth. He believed that to understand myths, we must understand the social context in which they are embedded. Malinowski argued that myths serve as 'charters' or 'justifications' for present-day social arrangements. Myths contain some 'self-evident' truth that explains why society is as it is and why it cannot be changed. If the social arrangements justified by the myth are challenged, the myth can be used as a weapon against the challengers.

Malinowski's famous example is of the origin myths of the Trobriand Islanders (1948 [1926]; see EthnoProfile 9.1: Trobriand Islanders). Members of every significant kinship group know, mark, and retell the history of the place from which their group's ancestress and her brother emerged from the depths of the earth. These origin myths are set in the time before history began. Each ancestress–brother pair brought a distinct set of characteristics that included special objects and knowledge, various skills, crafts, spells, and the like. On reaching the surface, the pair took possession of the land. That is why, today, the people on a given piece of land have rights to it. It is also why they possess a particular set of skills, crafts, and spells. Because the original sacred beings were a woman and her brother, the origin myth can also be used to endorse present-day social arrangements. Membership in a Trobriand clan depends on a person's ability to trace their kinship to that clan's original ancestress through matrilineage. A brother and a sister represent the prototypical members of a clan because they have both descended from the ancestress through

In Their Own Words

The Grizzly Gave Them the Song

Wendy Wickwire, in discussing the fieldwork of James Teit and Franz Boas, provides some insights into bear ritual in Aboriginal British Columbia. So many aspects of what are highlighted in this chapter can be seen in this article—myth, ritual, art (song), and learning adult roles through childhood interactions.

Teit's field notes by way of contrast (to those of Boas) present a much fuller picture of bear culture. Through the medium of songs and stories about direct encounters with bears, this source highlights the nurturing/protective role of the bear. Teit recorded 12 songs associated with bears along with contextual notes drawn from the commentary of seven singers (four men and three women). All seven focus on the close physical and spiritual bond between bears and humans. This source also highlights the prominent role of the female grizzly.

Six of the 12 songs, for example, are lullabies or cradle songs said to have been given to the Nlaka'pamux by female grizzlies. Such songs, according to Teit, were closely associated with women (CMC, cylinder collection VI.M.58). Kax.pítsa's song, catalogued by Teit as VI.M.125 'cradle song', is typical. A member of the Spences Bridge Band, Kax.pítsa told Teit that she had obtained this directly from the bear when she was a young woman.

> She had a vision in which she saw a female grizzly bear with four children under a tree. The children (or cubs) were all males and all of them were in birch bark carriers. The children were crying much and the mother was singing trying to stop them from crying. When the grizzly woman saw Kax.pítsa she called on her to come over and sing to the children. Kax.pítsa told her she did not know how to sing to them properly and the grizzly told her she would teach her. Kax.pítsa took up one after the other and sang to them as the grizzly directed and one after another they quit crying. When all were pacified (or asleep) the grizzly told Kax.pítsa, 'You will now have this song for a cradle song and by singing it to children when they cry,

you will have the power of quickly pacifying them.' Kax.pítsa claims to have this power but only for male children. (VI.M.125)

The song is similar to another in the collection sung by NsElkapéskEt, a young Spences Bridge man. Teit catalogued it as a 'lullaby song called the "Black Bear's Lullaby"' (CMC, cylinder collection VI.M.195) and noted that it

> Is said to be old and is said to have originated or been introduced by some person who had heard the black bear singing it. The person saw a black bear come over a hill carrying her baby. The latter was crying and as the mother came along travelling down the hill she sang this song to her baby thus quieting it. Since then the women of the Up.Ntlak (Thompson) have used the song when travelling to quiet their babies when they cried.

Chief TetlEnítsa of Spences Bridge also sang a 'cradle song' with close links to the female bear. He told Teit that he had received the song in a dream in which a 'dark woman and her baby' had appeared to him and led him to her den. Teit believed that this woman 'was likely simply a different manifestation of the black bear woman who became manitou of TetlEnítsa when he was a young man. She appears in different forms in his dreams . . . [She] often carries baby' (CMC, cylinder collection VI.M.49–50). Although TetlEnítsa claimed this as his own song, he explained that the women of his band liked it and so adopted it as their cradle song. These examples . . . underscore the importance of the *female* bear in the Nlaka'pamux world. Her songs and instructions were a key component of women's culture, especially motherhood.

Source: Wickwire, Wendy. 2001. 'The Grizzly Gave Them the Song: James Teit and Franz Boas Interpret Twin Ritual in Aboriginal British Columbia, 1897–1920', *American Indian Quarterly* 25, 3 (summer): 431–52.

female links. Should anyone question the wisdom of organizing society in this way, the myth can be cited as proof that this is indeed the correct way to live.

orthodoxy 'Correct doctrine'; the prohibition of deviation from approved mythic texts.

In Trobriand society, clans are ranked relative to one another in terms of prestige. In the Trobriand myth that explains rank, one clan's ancestor, the dog, emerged from the earth before another clan's ancestor, the pig, thus justifying ranking the dog clan highest in prestige. To believe in this myth, Malinowski asserted, is to accept a transcendent justification for the ranking of clans. He made it clear, however, that if social arrangements change, the myth changes too—in order to justify the new arrangements. At some point, the dog clan was replaced in prominence by the pig clan. This social change resulted in a change in the mythic narrative. The dog was said to have eaten food that was taboo. In doing so, the dog gave up its claim to higher rank. Thus, to understand a myth and its transformations, one must understand the social organization of the society that makes use of it.

Myth as a Conceptual Tool

Beginning in the mid-1950s, a series of books and articles by French anthropologist Claude Lévi-Strauss (1967 [1962]) transformed the study of myth. Lévi-Strauss argued that myths have meaningful structures that are worth studying in their own right, quite apart from the uses to which the myths may be put. He suggested that myths should be interpreted the same way we interpret musical scores. In a piece of music, the meaning emerges not just from the melody but also from the harmony. In other words the structure of the piece of music, the way in which each line contributes to the overall sound and is related to other lines, carries the meaning.

For Lévi-Strauss, myths are tools for overcoming logical contradictions that cannot otherwise be overcome. They are put together in an attempt to deal with the oppositions of particular concern to a particular society at a particular moment. Using a linguistic metaphor, Lévi-Strauss argued that myths are composed of smaller units—phrases, sentences, words, relationships—that are arranged in ways that give both narrative (or 'melodic') coherence and structural (or 'harmonic') coherence. These arrangements represent and comment upon aspects of social life that are thought to oppose each other. Examples include the opposition of men to women, opposing rules of residence after marriage (living with the groom's father or the bride's mother), the opposition of the natural

world to the cultural world, of life to death, of spirit to body, of high to low, and so on.

The complex syntax of myth works to relate those opposed pairs to one another in an attempt to overcome their contradictions. However, these contradictions can never be overcome; for example, the opposition of life to death is incapable of any earthly resolution. But myth can transform an insoluble problem into a more accessible, concrete form. Mythic narrative can then provide the concrete problem with a solution. For example, a culture hero may bridge the opposition between life and death by travelling from the land of the living to the land of the dead and back. Alternatively, a myth might propose that the beings who transcend death are so horrific that death is clearly preferable to eternal life. Perhaps a myth describes the journey of a bird that travels from the earth, the home of the living, to the sky, the home of the dead. This is similar to Christian thought, where the death and resurrection of Jesus may be understood to resolve the opposition between life and death by transcending death.

From this point of view, myths do not just talk about the world as it is, but they also describe the world as it might be. To paraphrase Lévi-Strauss, myths are good to think with; mythic thinking can propose other ways to live our lives. He insists, however, that the alternatives myths propose are ordinarily rejected as impossible. Thus, even though myths allow for play with self-evident truths, this play remains under strict control.

Is Lévi-Strauss correct? There has been a great deal of debate on this issue since the 1955 publication of his article 'The Structural Study of Myth' (1967 [1962]). But even those who are most critical of his analyses of particular myths agree that mythic structures are meaningful because they display the ability of human beings to play with possibilities as they attempt to deal with basic contradictions at the heart of human experience.

For Malinowski, Lévi-Strauss, and their followers, those who believe in myths are not conscious of how their myths are structured or of the functions their myths perform for them. More recent anthropological thinking takes a more reflexive approach. This research recognizes that ordinary members of a society *are* often aware of how their myths structure meaning, allowing them to manipulate the way myths are told or interpreted in order to make an effect, to prove a point, or to buttress a particular referential perspective on human nature, society, or history. Therefore myths are, to paraphrase Riddington, the poetics by which people create meaning through language. The stories of a people are metonyms—where parts can stand for wholes (more on this in Chapter 7), and 'each story is connected to every other and to a highly contextualized discourse that assumes familiarity with biography and shared experience' (1998: 346).

Ritual

Play allows unlimited consideration of alternative referential perspectives on reality. Art permits consideration of alternative perspectives but imposes certain limitations restricting the form and content. Myth aims to narrow radically the possible referential perspectives and often promotes a single, orthodox perspective presumed to be valid for everyone. It thus offers a kind of intellectual indoctrination. But because societies aim to shape action as well as thought to orient all human faculties in the approved direction, art, myth, and ritual are often closely associated with one another.

A Definition of Ritual

Our definition of **ritual** has four elements.

(1) Ritual is a repetitive social practice composed of a sequence of symbolic activities in the form of dance, song, speech, gestures, the manipulation of certain objects, and so forth.

(2) It is set off from the social routines of everyday life.

(3) Rituals in any culture adhere to a characteristic, culturally defined ritual schema. This means that members of a culture can tell that a certain sequence of activities is a ritual even if they have never seen that particular ritual before.

(4) Ritual action is closely connected to a specific set of ideas that are often encoded in myth. These ideas might concern the nature of evil, the relationship of human beings to the spirit world, how people ought to interact with one another, and so forth.

The purpose for which a ritual is performed guides how these ideas are selected and symbolically enacted. What gives rituals their power is that the people who perform them assert that the authorization for the ritual comes from outside themselves—from their state, society, God, ancestors, or 'tradition'. They have not made up the ritual themselves; rather, it connects them to a source of power that they do not control but that controls them.

The Western prototype of ritual includes the notion that it is 'religious'. However, in anthropological terms, ritual includes a much broader range of activities. According to the definition given in the preceding paragraph, a scientific experiment, a graduation ceremony, procedures in a court of law, and a child's birthday party are rituals just as much as weddings, bar mitzvahs, Hmong sacrifices to their ancestors, and Catholic Mass.

Consider a young child's birthday party in North America. Several children are formally invited to help celebrate the birthday. Each arrives bringing a wrapped gift, which is handed to the birthday child and then set aside. The children often put on birthday hats. They then play group games of some kind, some of which are now *only* played at birthday parties. The games culminate with the appearance of a birthday cake, illuminated by candles (one for each year of the child's life) and accompanied by the singing of 'Happy Birthday'. The birthday child makes a wish and blows out the candles. Following the cake and ice cream, the birthday child opens the presents. There is much commotion as the guests urge the birthday child to open theirs first. As the birthday child opens each gift, he or she examines it and thanks the guest (often with an adult's prompting). Shortly after the presents are opened, the guests' parents or guardians appear and the guests receive party favours and leave. The ritual order of these events matters. The central events of the party—the giving of gifts; the events associated with the cake, the candles, the singing of 'Happy Birthday',

ritual A repetitive social practice composed of a sequence of symbolic activities in the form of dance, song, speech, gestures, or the manipulation of objects, adhering to a culturally defined ritual schema and closely connected to a specific set of ideas that are often encoded in myth.

the wish; and the opening of the gifts—must occur in this order. Additionally, if you, the reader, come from a tradition in which birthday parties are celebrated, it is likely that you cannot remember *learning* how to celebrate a birthday party—it is something you have always known. It's what everyone does. It's just how it is. Its authority comes from 'tradition'.

In the birthday party ritual, children (both hosts and guests) learn to associate receiving gifts with important moments in life. They discover the importance of exchanging material objects in defining significant social relations. They learn to defer gratification (the presents cannot be opened immediately). They live out patterns of sociability and friendship (as anyone who has heard the ultimate preschool threat, 'I'm not inviting you to my birthday party', knows) while recognizing the centrality of the individual (there are few things worse than sharing your birthday party with someone else!). Finally, the children participate in patterns of sharing, of celebrating the self, and of recognizing relationships with friends and kin that are important in other areas of North American life.

Ritual as Action

A ritual has a particular sequential ordering of acts, utterances, and events: that is, ritual has a *text*. Because ritual is action, however, we must pay attention to the way the ritual text is performed. The *performance* of a ritual cannot be separated from its text; text and performance shape each other dialectically. Through ritual performance the ideas of a culture become concrete, take on a form and, as Bruce Kapferer (1983) puts it, give direction to the gaze of participants. At the same time, ritual performance can serve as a commentary on the text to the extent of transforming it. For example, Jewish synagogue ritual following the reading of the Torah (the Five Books of Moses, the Hebrew Bible) includes lifting the Torah scroll, showing it to the congregation, and then closing it and covering it. In some synagogues a man and a woman, often a couple, are called to lift and cover the Torah: the man lifts it and after he seats himself the woman rolls the scroll closed, places the tie around it, and covers it with the mantle that protects it. Robert Lavenda once observed a performance of this ritual in which the woman lifted the Torah and the man wrapped it; officially, the ritual text was carried out, but the performance became a commentary on the text—on the role of women in

Judaism, on the Torah as an appropriate subject of attention for women as well as for men, on the roles of men and women overall, and so on. The performance was noteworthy—indeed, many of the regular members of the congregation seemed quite surprised—precisely because it violated people's expectations and in doing so directed people's attention toward the role of men and women in religious ritual at the end of the twentieth century, as well as toward the Torah as the central symbol of the Jewish people.

Ritual performers are not robots but active individuals whose choices are guided by, but not rigidly dictated by, previous ritual texts (see, e.g., Drewal 1992). This is what we should expect if human behaviour is fundamentally open. Rituals highlight the fact that human understanding of the world is not just mental and not just physical but a holistic coming together of mind and body, thought and feeling. By performing our ideas, by feeling the implications of our myths, their truths become self-evident.

Rites of Passage

Let us examine this process by looking at one kind of ritual performance: the **rite of passage**. At the beginning of the twentieth century, Belgian anthropologist Arnold Van Gennep noted that certain kinds of rituals around the world had similar structures. These were rituals associated with the movement (or passage) of people from one position in the social structure to another. They included births, initiations, confirmations, weddings, funerals, and the like (Figure 6.11).

Van Gennep (1960) found that all these rituals began with a period of *separation* from the old position and from normal time. During this period, the ritual passenger left behind the symbols and practices of his or her previous position. For example, military recruits leave their families behind and are moved to a new place. They are forced to cut their hair and leave behind the clothing and activities that marked who they were in civilian life.

The second stage in rites of passage involves a period of *transition*, in which the ritual passenger is neither in the old life nor in the new one. This period is marked by rolelessness, ambiguity, and perceived danger. Often, the person involved is subjected to ordeal by those who have already passed through this stage. In the military service, this is the period of basic training, in which recruits (not yet soldiers but no longer

Figure 6.11 Certain kinds of rituals around the world have similar structures. A funeral procession in Kyoto, Japan.

civilians) are forced to dress and act alike. They are subjected to a grinding-down process, after which they are rebuilt into something new.

During the final stage—*re-aggregation*—the ritual passenger is reintroduced into society in his or her new position. In the military this involves the graduation from basic training and a visit home, but this time in uniform, on leave, and as a member of the armed forces, a new person. One familiar rite of passage in youth culture in North America is high-school graduation, which is understood as a movement from one social position to another.

The work of Victor Turner has greatly increased our understanding of rites of passage. Turner concentrated on the period of transition, which he saw as important both for the rite of passage and for social life in general. Van Gennep referred to this part of a rite of passage as the liminal period, from the Latin *limen* ('threshold'). During this period, the individual is on the threshold, betwixt and between, neither here nor there, neither in nor out. Turner notes that the symbolism accompanying the rite of passage often expresses this ambiguous state. **Liminality**, he tells us, 'is frequently likened to death, to being in the womb,

to invisibility, to darkness, to bisexuality, to the wilderness, and to an eclipse of the sun or moon' (1969: 95). We are familiar with this concept from the tales by the Brothers Grimm. Many of what we call *fairytales* were originally folktales and have rites of passage and liminality as part of the 'story'. Consider the original *Snow White*, *Sleeping Beauty*, and *Rapunsel*. People in the liminal state tend to develop an intense comradeship with each other in which their non-liminal distinctions disappear or become irrelevant. Turner calls this modality of social relationship **communitas**, which is best understood as an unstructured or minimally structured community of equal individuals.

communitas An unstructured or minimally structured community of equal individuals frequently found in rites of passage.

liminality The ambiguous transitional state in a rite of passage in which the person or persons undergoing the ritual are outside their ordinary social positions.

rite of passage A ritual that serves to mark the movement and transformation of an individual from one social position to another.

Turner contends that all societies need some kind of communitas as much as they need structure. Communitas gives 'recognition to an essential and generic human bond, without which there could be no society' (97). That bond is the common humanity that underlies all culture and society. However, periods of communitas (often in ritual context) are brief. Communitas is dangerous, not just because it threatens structure but because it threatens survival itself. Lost in a world of communitas, the things that structure ensures—production of food and physical and social reproduction of society—cannot be provided. Communitas gives way to structure, which in turn generates a need for the release of communitas. The feeling of oneness is also possible in play and art. Indeed, it may well be that for people in contemporary nation-states the experience of communitas comes through experiencing the climactic winning moments of a sports team, attendance at large-scale rock concerts, or participation in mass public events like Carabana in Toronto, Carnaval de Québec, or the Calgary Stampede (Figure 6.12).

Play and Ritual as Complementary

How does play differ from ritual? Play and ritual (like metaphorical and literal language) are complementary forms of metacommunication (Handelman 1977). Just as the movement from non-play to play is based on the premise of metaphor ('Let's make-believe'), the movement to ritual is based on the premise of literalness ('Let's believe'). From the perspective of paramount reality, the result of these contrasting premises is the 'inauthenticity' of play and the 'truth' of ritual.

Because of the connection of ritual with self-evident truth, the metacommunication of the ritual frame ('This is ritual') is associated with an additional metacommunication: 'All messages within this frame are true.' It is ritual that asserts *what should be* to play's *what can be*. The ritual frame is more rigid than the play frame. Consequently, ritual is the most stable liminal domain, whereas play is the most flexible. Players can move with relative ease into and out of play but such is not the case with ritual.

Finally, play usually has little effect on the social order of ordinary life. This permits play a wide range of commentary on the social order. Ritual is different: its role is explicitly to maintain the status quo, including

the prescribed ritual transformations. Societies differ in the extent to which ritual behaviour alternates with everyday, non-ritual behaviour. When nearly every act of everyday life is ritualized and other forms of behaviour are strongly proscribed, we sometimes speak of **orthopraxy** ('correct practice'). Traditionally, observant Jews and Muslims, for example, lead a highly ritualized daily life, attempting from the moment they awaken until the moment they fall asleep to carry out even the humblest of activities in a manner that is ritually correct. In their view, ritual correctness is the result of God's law, and it is their duty and joy to conform their every action to God's will.

Ritual may seem overwhelming and all-powerful. Yet individuals and groups within a society can sometimes manipulate ritual forms to achieve non-traditional ends. This can range from pushing against tradition as far as it can go without actually destroying the ritual (as when a bride and groom have an alternative wedding outdoors, write their own vows, and still have a member of the clergy officiating), to emphasizing the importance of one ritual and ignoring or downplaying another (as when Protestant Baptists downplayed the communion ritual and emphasized the baptism ritual as a way of articulating their challenge to Roman Catholicism), to exchanging one set of rituals for another (as when lone rural migrants

Figure 6.12 Many Canadians experience communitas through mass public events such as the Calgary Stampede.

of northern Cameroon converted to Islam shortly after their arrival, abandoning their traditional rituals together with the rural way of life into which they were born).

Drewal argues that, at least among the Yoruba, play and ritual overlap (see Map 6.4). Yoruba rituals combine spectacle, festival, play, sacrifice, and so on, and integrate diverse media—music, dance, poetry, theatre, sculpture (1992: 198). They are improvisatory events, spontaneous individual moves in which the mundane order is not only inverted and reversed but may also be subverted through power play and gender play. In Yoruba life, gender roles are rigidly structured. Yoruba rituals, however, allow some cross-dressing by both men and women, providing institutionalized opportunities for men and women to cross gender boundaries and to express the traits that Yoruba consider to be characteristic of the opposite sex, sometimes as parody but sometimes seriously and respectfully (190).

Combining Play, Art, Myth, and Ritual

As commented on earlier, play, art, myth, and ritual are often experienced together. To reiterate through example, consider Kapferer's study of demon exorcism in Sri Lanka (see Map 6.5). The demon exorcism ceremonies of the Sinhalese Buddhist working class and peasantry last an entire night and are designed

Map 6.5 Sinhalese

to cure disease. The performance combines in 'a marvelous spectacle' ritual, comedy, music, and dance. Its goal is 'to change the experiential condition of [the] patients and to bring patients back into a normal conception of the world' (1983: 177, 236). In other words, the entire performance is transformative. During the course of the ceremony, a demonic reality is created and then destroyed.

At the beginning of the exorcism, the patient and the audience are in different realities. The audience is in the paramount reality of everyday life; the patient is in the alternative reality of his or her illness. In that reality, demons are central and powerful actors. During the Evening Watch, through music, song, and eventually dance, the audience becomes increasingly engaged in this alternative reality. In this part of the ceremony, the demons are portrayed as figures of horror.

At midnight, the process is complete: the audience has joined the patient's reality. The demons, played by actors, appear. At this point, the Midnight Watch begins. This part of the ceremony is a comic drama that lasts until nearly 3 a.m. The eruption of comedy into what had been an intensely serious ceremony transforms the demons into figures of ridicule. Through the comedy, the demonic reality begins to fragment as the gods appear and reassert their

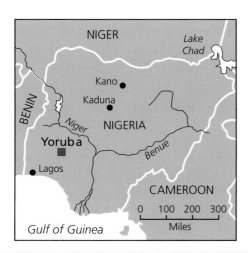

Map 6.4 Yoruba

orthopraxy 'Correct practice'; the prohibition of deviation from approved forms of ritual behaviour.

dominance. As this occurs, the sick person begins to see that the demons are really subordinate to the gods, not superior to them.

The last part of the exorcism is the Morning Watch, which continues until 6 a.m. During this period, the patient and audience become re-engaged in the reality of ordinary life. The final comic drama of the performance 'confirms the demonic absurdity and destroys the demonic as powerful and relevant to normal experience in daily life' (220). Having played on the mind, body, and emotions of the patient and the audience, the performance ends.

To understand the performance as a whole, the interactions of all aspects of the performance must be grasped. Kapferer calls this the ceremony's *aesthetics.*

He argues that the ceremony succeeds because it is composed of many different parts that fit together in a way that is satisfying to the Sinhalese. Only in the aesthetic realm are ideas, symbolic objects, and actions brought into the relationship from which their meaning comes.

Play, art, myth, and ritual are different facets of the holistic human capacity to view the world from a variety of perspectives. The human capacity to play is channelled in different directions in different cultures, but it is always present. When the products of this containment process come together in key cultural productions, such as the Sinhalese curing ceremony, they display both the opportunities and dangers that result from open human creativity.

Key Terms

art 134

communitas 149

framing 130

liminality 149

metacommunication 130

myths 143

orthodoxy 144

orthopraxy 150

play 129

reflexivity 130

rite of passage 148

ritual 147

sport 132

transformation-representation 135

Chapter Summary

1. Play is a generalized form of behavioural openness: the ability to think about, speak about, and do different things in the same way or the same thing in different ways. Play can be thought of as a way of organizing activities, not merely a set of activities. We put a frame that consists of the message 'this is play' around certain activities, thereby transforming them into play. Play also permits reflexive consideration of alternative realities by setting up a separate reality and suggesting that the perspective of ordinary life is only one way to make sense of experience.

2. The functions of play include exercise, practise for the real world, increased creativity in children, and commentary on the real world.

3. The fate of national sports teams can come to represent the nation itself, and the devotion of sports fans becomes a way of affirming patriotism. When sports are translated from one culture to another, they are frequently transformed to fit the patterns appropriate to the new culture.

4. Art is a kind of play that is subject to certain culturally appropriate restrictions on form and content. It aims to evoke a holistic, aesthetic response from the artist and the observer. It succeeds when the form is culturally appropriate for the content and is technically perfect in its realization. Aesthetic evaluations are culturally shaped value judgments. We recognize art in other cultures because of its family resemblance to what we call *art* in our own culture.

Although people with other cultural understandings may not have produced art by intention, we can often successfully appreciate what they have created as art by appropriation. These issues are addressed in ethnographic studies that call into question received ideas about what counts as 'authentic' art.

5. Myths are stories whose truths seem self-evident because they do such a good job of integrating personal experiences with a wider set of assumptions about the way the world works. As stories, myths are the products of high verbal art. A full understanding of myth requires ethnographic background information.

6. Ritual is a repetitive social practice composed of sequences of symbolic activities such as speech, singing, dancing, gestures, and the manipulation of certain objects. In studying ritual, we pay attention not just to the symbols but also to how the ritual is performed. Cultural ideas are made concrete through ritual action.

7. Rites of passage are rituals in which members of a culture move from one position in the social structure to another. These rites are marked by periods of separation, transition, and re-aggregation. During the period of transition, individuals occupy a liminal position. All those in this position frequently develop an intense comradeship and a feeling of oneness, or communitas.

8. Ritual and play are complementary. Play is based on the premise 'Let's make-believe', while ritual is based on the premise 'Let's believe'. As a result, the ritual frame is far more rigid than the play frame. Although ritual may seem overwhelming and all-powerful, individuals and groups can sometimes manipulate ritual forms to achieve non-traditional ends.

Critical Thinking Questions

1. How would you contrast framing with reflexivity as two forms of metacommunication?

2. Can play be culturally framed or is play cross-culturally understood?

3. Janet Lever argues, 'Sport's paradoxical ability to reinforce societal cleavages while transcending them makes soccer, Brazil's most popular sport, the perfect means of achieving a more perfect union between multiple groups . . . [by giving] dramatic expression to the strain between groups while affirming the solidarity of the whole'. Does this pertain for Hockey Night in Canada?

4. How are art and play alike in presenting alternative realities?

5. Consider the three different forms of authenticity from Michelle Bigenho. How would you consider these forms from your own cultural perspective? Indeed, what would you consider authentic in your cultural context?

6. How do you remember learning adult roles through childhood play?

Suggested Readings

Alland, Alexander. 1977. *The Artistic Animal* (New York: Doubleday Anchor). *An introductory look at the bio-cultural bases for art. This work is very well written, very clear, and fascinating.*

Archetti, Eduardo P. n.d. 'Anthropology of Sport', available at: <http://www.forskningsradet.no/servlet/Satellite?blobcol= urlvedleggfil&blobheader=application%2Fpdf&blobkey=id& blobtable=Vedlegg&blobwhere=1143099791066&cachecontrol= 5%3A0%3A0+*%2F*%2F*&ssbinary=true>. *Considers sport as a field of analysis for understanding rituals, complex processes of identity construction, rites de passage, and bodily performances.*

Blanchard, Kendall. 1995. *The Anthropology of Sport*, rev. edn (Westport, CT: Bergin & Garvey). *An excellent introduction to the field.*

Errington, Shelly. 1998. *The Death of Authentic Primitive Art and Other Tales of Progress* (Berkeley: University of California Press). *A sharp and witty book about the production, distribution, interpretation, and sale of 'primitive art'.*

Fagen, Robert. 1981. *Animal Play Behaviour* (New York: Oxford University Press). *The definitive work.*

Halliday-Scher, Kathy, Kathryn A. Urberg, Melissa Kaplan-Estrin. 1995. 'Learning to Pretend: Preschoolers' Use of Meta-communication in Socio-dramatic Play', *International Journal of Behavioural Development* 18, 3: 451–61, available at: <http://jbd.sagepub.com/cgi/content/abstract/18/3/451>. *Explores how children's ability to structure socio-dramatic play may depend on their ability to communicate pretense transformations effectively.*

Hallowell, A. Irving. 1960. 'Ojibwa Ontology, Behavior, and World View', in *Culture and History: Essays of Paul Radin*, ed. Stanley Diamond (New York: Columbia University Press), 19–52. *This work focuses on Anishinabe organization of various knowledge domains—what we describe as schemas and prototypes in the context of this text.*

Kapferer, Bruce. 1989. *A Celebration of Demons*, 2nd edn (Washington, DC: Smithsonian Institution Press). *An advanced text that is well worth reading.*

King, Thomas. 1993. *Green Grass, Running Water* (Toronto: HarperCollins). *Like the work of Gabriel Garcia Márquez, in a style called* magic realism *(One Hundred Years of Solitude being an excellent example), this story, an exploration of contemporary Native American culture and North American literature and literary theory, juxtaposes the real and the magical with the magical giving essential meaning to the real. It is an example of both metacommunication and transformation-representation.*

Lever, Janet. 1995. *Soccer Madness* (Prospect Heights, IL: Waverland Press). *A fascinating study of soccer in Brazil.*

Riddington, Robin. 1998. 'Coyote's Cannon: Sharing Stories with Thomas King', *American Indian Quarterly* 22, 3 (summer): 343–62. *The counterpoint of Coyote is King as he presents a Native American perspective on the American literary and cultural canon.*

Schwartzman, Helen. 1978. *Transformations: The Anthropology of Children's Play* (New York: Plenum). *A superlative work that considers how anthropologists have studied children's play with some insightful suggestions about how they might do this in the future.*

Steiner, Christopher. 1994. *African Art in Transit* (Cambridge: Cambridge University Press). *Traces the social life of objects made in rural West African villages from their creation to their resting places in galleries, museums, tourist shops, or private Western art collections, highlighting the role of African merchants who make this transit possible.*

Turner, Victor. 1969. *The Ritual Process* (Chicago: Aldine). *An important work in the anthropological study of ritual, this text is an eloquent analysis of rites of passage.*

Vogel, Susan. 1997. *Baule: African Art/Western Eyes* (New Haven: Yale University Press). *A book of extraordinary photographs and beautifully clear text, this work explores both Baule and Western views of Baule expressive culture.*

Wickwire, Wendy. 2001. 'The Grizzly Gave Then the Song: James Teit and Franz Boas Interpret Twin Ritual in Aboriginal British Columbia, 1897–1920', *American Indian Quarterly* 25, 3 (summer): 431–52. *Compares and contrasts the ethnographic information collected and interpreted by two researchers in British Columbia. The focus of this comparison is the songs of the Bear.*

Related Websites

The Antiquity of Man: http://www.antiquityofman.com/Solomon_myth_ritual.html

Canadian Art: http://www.canadianart.ca

Illinois State Museum: http://www.museum.state.il.us/muslink/nat_amer/post/htmls/il_am.html

Turtle Island Native Network: http://www.turtleisland.org/culture/culture-haisla.htm

Chapter 7

World View

What is it that we attempt to do to give life meaning? How do we devise cultural forms through which we can make sense of our being and belonging? How do we frame our physical and metaphysical contexts? In this chapter we attempt to answer these very complex questions. (Note Peter Gose, *In Their Own Words.*)

The Role of Metaphor, Metonymy, and Symbol

Metaphor

One way to grasp the pattern that may be found in a particular **world view**, an encompassing picture of reality created by members of a society, is to 'follow the metaphor'. This strategy was adopted by Emily Martin, who followed the metaphor of 'flexibility in American culture and was able to reveal the outlines of an emergent world view in the United States at the end of the twentieth century. Following metaphors successfully, however, requires understanding how metaphors work.

Metaphor asserts the existence of a meaningful link between two expressions from different semantic domains. For example, metaphorical statements such as 'Arnold is a turkey' create an ambiguity that can only be resolved in context. If we know Arnold is characteristically inept, ignorant, and annoying, and that turkeys are prototypically stupid and clumsy, our metaphor becomes intelligible and apt. But why resort to metaphor to represent our opinion of Arnold? Why not simply say 'Arnold is inept, ignorant, and annoying'? When we choose to use metaphoric language instead of literal language, it is usually because literal

language is not equal to the task of expressing the depth of meaning we intend. Our experience of Arnold may be complex and difficult to pin down in literal language. That is, there is something about the image of a turkey that encompasses more of what we think about Arnold than can ever be represented by a list of adjectives. We therefore select a figurative image whose features are more familiar and use it as a tool to help us express what kind of person Arnold is. The metaphor does not demonstrate unequivocally that Arnold *is* a turkey. Rather, using a particular metaphor simply asserts that a particular link exists and invites those who know both Arnold and turkeys to decide (and perhaps to debate) the extent to which the metaphor is apt. Similarly, the metaphor 'The Lord is my shepherd' links a subject we have trouble describing ('The Lord') to an image ('my shepherd') that is familiar and well understood in Christian societies. This metaphorical statement is an invitation to ponder what it means to be a shepherd, what it means to be my shepherd, and then to apply this knowledge to one's understanding of the Lord.

World views aim to encompass the widest possible understanding of how the world works. In constructing world views, people tend to examine what they already know for clues that might help them make sense of what puzzles them. Metaphor is a powerful tool for constructing world views because it clarifies areas of human experience that are vague or poorly understood. The first part of a metaphor, the **metaphorical subject**, represents the domain of experience that needs to be clarified ('The Lord'). The second part of a metaphor, the **metaphorical predicate**, suggests the

In Their Own Words

House Re-thatching in an Andean Annual Cycle

Canadian social anthropologist Peter Gose illustrates that Andean roofing can be very complex and, at the same time, provide meaningful insights into many areas of life.

By Andean standards, house re-thatching is only a moderately ritualized labour process. Its imagery varies considerably from locality to locality, and. . . . [it] is best understood through its position in the annual cycle of agrarian labour and ritual. . . . [T]he relatively modest ritual imagery of house re-thatching means little if anything in itself and cannot stand on its own as symbolism. Rather, it is motivated and given most of its significance by the practices that surround and support it in the annual cycle. House re-thatching in the Andes takes place as the dry season is giving way to the growing season. This seasonal shift involves a corresponding change in social relations from an emphasis on private appropriation by individual households during the harvest to an extensive and institutionalized inter-household co-operation that will prevail throughout the growing season. . . . [T]hese seasonally opposed moralities overlap in the house re-thatching and each lay claim to its content. . . . [C]ontradiction animates the imagery of this act and makes it signify in a way that we would miss if we considered it in abstraction from its grounding in the annual cycle. . . . [I]t is only when the imagery of the performance is subsumed by the annual cycle that it acquires the directedness necessary to 'reflect and refract' another part of reality, that is, to become properly symbolic. . . . The . . . images do not function as self-contained 'semantic values' that just happen to crop up around the house re-thatching but as metaphorical vehicles that intervene in and organize the very nature of the act. Put differently, this imagery does not exist for itself, in isolation from the instrumentality of the house re-thatching as a labour process, but in order to give that labour process a cultural form. And in turn, the seasonal position of the house re-thatching gives this imagery direction and entry into a real context within which it can truly signify. An example of this sort of interaction can be found in the transportation of hay down the mountain on the first day, which at first appears entirely unremarkable but, on further consideration, is seen to be embroiled in the entire 'domestication' complex, including the origins of agriculture in descent. If this theme of 'domestication' were not so thoroughly developed by other aspects of the rite, there would be no justification for this interpretation of the downward movement of hay. But once such a theme is established, it becomes equally hard to deny that the apparently technical act of transporting hay contributes to it. In sum, this rite teaches not only a negative lesson, that it is impossible to separate meaning from practice, but also a positive one, that the two taken together as praxis form a whole that is greater than its parts. Yet the praxis of commoners within the annual cycle is characterized not by a vapid holism but rather by a contradictory interpenetration of opposed moralities of private appropriation and collective production. This contradiction is most evident in the seasonal position of the rite, but it also works through its spatial and sequential organization and can even be identified in each of its individual symbols. Because the source of these contradictions lies beyond the act itself, house re-thatching must be understood as a moment in a larger seasonal process, not as a self-contained 'text'.

Source: Gose, Peter. 1991. 'House Re-thatching in an Andean Annual Cycle: Practice, Meaning, and Contradiction', *American Ethnologist* 18, 1: 38, 57.

domain of experience that is familiar (shepherding) and may help us understand what the Lord is all about (Figure 7.1).

To understand the metaphor, we have to list every conceivable attribute of shepherds and then decide which ones describe the Lord. These attributes of

metaphor A form of thought and language that asserts a meaningful link between two expressions from different semantic domains.

metaphorical predicate The second part of a metaphor, which suggests the familiar domain of experience that may clarify the metaphorical subject.

metaphorical subject The first part of a metaphor, which indicates the domain of experience that needs to be clarified.

world view An encompassing picture of reality created by members of a society.

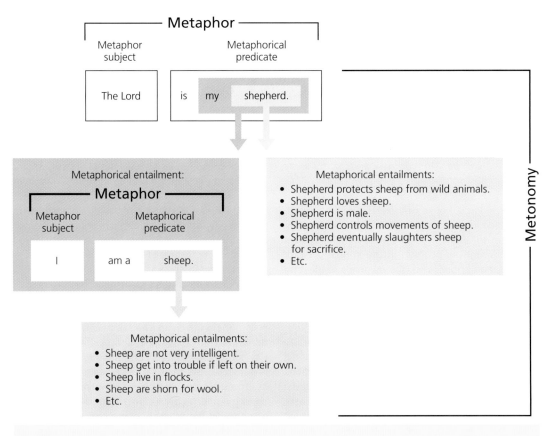

Figure 7.1 An analysis of the metaphor 'The Lord is my shepherd', illustrating the links of metaphor and metonymy.

shepherds and sheep are called **metaphorical entailments** (Lakoff and Johnson 1980). They suggest what follows from, or is entailed by, calling the Lord a *shepherd*. If we were to assert that 'The Lord is my friend', an entirely different set of metaphorical entailments would follow.

Metonymy

Metonymy is the relationship that links the parts of a semantic domain to one another. In the metaphor 'The Lord is my shepherd', the link between the metaphorical predicate *shepherd* and its metaphorical entailments is a link of metonymy. The word *shepherd* can stand for any and all attributes connected to the semantic domain defined by shepherding. At the same time, any of these attributes (such as protecting sheep from wild animals) may entail the word *shepherd*. Because semantic domains are culturally defined, the meaningful elements that are linked by metonymy within any

semantic domain are also culturally defined. Shepherding occurs in many societies, and yet the range of meanings associated with it may vary: compare a society in which shepherds are women, sheep graze freely, and mutton is primarily for family consumption with a different society in which shepherds are men, sheep graze in enclosed fields, and most animals are sold on the market for cash. Of course, members of the first society may think that theirs is the only sensible way to herd sheep and vice versa. Put another way, in any society, semantic domains defined by links of metonymy are viewed as 'natural' or 'true' associations.

The links of metonymy we discover within a particular semantic domain may help us make sense of experiences that seem chaotic and meaningless. Consider what happens in the case of what some people call *religious conversion*. An individual who is troubled and confused may see his personal situation suddenly come into focus when he starts thinking of himself as a lost sheep. Further, he may reason that a lost sheep must have been lost by someone—the shepherd to whom it belonged. This reflection, in turn, may lead him to ask who his shepherd might be. If he learns that some people believe that the Lord is their shepherd, he may be attracted to them and want to learn more. Thus, his exploration of the links of metonymy within a particular semantic domain in the context of his own life may lead him to conclude that the metaphor 'The Lord is my shepherd' resonates with the power of divine revelation. Such reflections play an important role in religious conversion, but they are equally important in science, for example, when a new theory is adopted because it makes sense of otherwise puzzling data (see Kuhn 1970; Poewe 1989).

Symbol

As people increase their understanding of themselves and the wider world by creating apt metaphors, they devise symbols to remind themselves of their significant insights and the connections between them. As noted in Chapter 1, a symbol is something that stands for something else—be it a word, image, or action. Symbols signal the presence and importance of given domains of experience. They are special cases of metonymy. Some symbols—what Sherry Ortner (1973) calls *summarizing symbols*—represent a whole semantic domain and invite us to consider the various elements within it. Others—what Ortner calls *elaborating symbols*—represent only one element of a domain and invite us to place that element in its wider semantic context.

Key Metaphors for Constructing World Views

Differences in world views ultimately derive from differences in experience, which people try to explain to themselves by means of metaphor. World views are attempts to answer the following question: What must the world be like for my experiences to be what they are? Over the ages, thoughtful people in all cultural traditions have suggested various answers to this question. Those suggestions that have become entrenched in any particular tradition are based on especially apt metaphors whose power to make sense of experience in a variety of circumstances and historical periods has been

demonstrated repeatedly. But that power is limited. New metaphors that are appropriate for changed circumstances can provide insight when the old metaphors fail and can also form the basis for new world views.

Anthropologist Robin Horton suggests that people who construct a world view are 'concerned above all to show order, regularity, and predictability where primary theory [i.e., commonsense experience] has failed to show them'. As they search for key metaphors, therefore, they look at those areas of everyday experience that are most associated with order, regularity, and predictability (1982: 237). **Key metaphors** that have served as the foundation of world views in different societies include societal, organic, and technological metaphors.

Societal Metaphors

In many societies, human social relations provide great order, regularity, and predictability. In such societies, the model for the world is the social order. For example, geneticist Richard Lewontin and his colleagues point out that biologists studying cells have used a **societal metaphor** almost from the very beginning. They liken cells to a factory assembling the biochemical products needed to support the body's economy. This metaphor recurs in the twentieth-century work of Francis Crick, one of the discoverers of the structure of DNA (deoxyribonucleic acid). Lewontin and colleagues suggest: 'Read any introductory textbook to the new molecular biology and you will find these metaphors as a central part of the cellular description. Even the drawings of the protein synthesis sequence are often deliberately laid out in "assembly-line" style' (Lewontin, Rose, and Kamin 1984: 59) (Figure 7.2).

Similarly, contemporary sociobiologists have borrowed certain concepts from modern economic thought and used them to describe the behaviour of

---

key metaphors Metaphors that serve as the foundation of a world view.

metaphorical entailments All the attributes of a metaphorical predicate that relate it to the culturally defined domain of experience to which it belongs.

metonymy The culturally defined relationship of the parts of a semantic domain to the domain as a whole and of the whole to its parts.

societal metaphor A world view metaphor whose model for the world is the social order.

genes or of living organisms. Sociobiologists describe the nurturing behaviour of parents toward their offspring as 'parental investment'. They talk about the cost–benefit analyses that people make before deciding whether or not to sacrifice themselves for others and even describe genes as 'selfish'. To some sociobiologists, the natural world is just the capitalist market on a larger scale. Indeed, anthropologist Marshall Sahlins (1976a) and others have argued that, from its inception, modern biology took its key metaphors from the social world familiar to the biologists. That world, at its beginning in the late eighteenth century, was the world of early capitalism.

Organic Metaphors

An **organic metaphor** applies the image of a living body to something. Indeed, this metaphor is responsible for the social-scientific theoretical perspective called *structural-functionalism*, which conceives of society as an organism. The body of a living organism can be divided into different systems (digestive, reproductive, respiratory, and so on), each carrying out a specialized task. When all these systems are functioning in harmony with one another, the organism is said to be healthy. If we compare society to a living organism, we look for

the subsystems into which society can be divided, identify the tasks each is supposed to perform, and describe a healthy society as one in which all the subsystems are functioning harmoniously. Alternatively, we can use this metaphor to analyze the life course of a society or civilization in terms of its birth, youth, maturity, old age, and death.

Personification (attributing human characteristics to non-human entities) is another organic metaphor. The belief that the vending machine in your office has a malevolent and greedy personality or that you can persuade your car to start on a cold morning by speaking gentle and encouraging words to it both involve personification.

Technological Metaphors

A **technological metaphor** uses objects made by human beings as metaphorical predicates. Technological metaphors that use machines as metaphorical predicates have been prominent in the world view(s) of Western society since the rise of science. As Western science and technology have grown in importance, machine metaphors have also become more widespread.

In the twentieth century, a major revolution in cognitive psychology was brought about by a shift in key technological metaphors. Psychologists rejected the steam engine metaphor of nineteenth-century industrial technology in favour of the **computer metaphor** of twentieth-century cybernetic technology. Computer jargon has become popular among scientists investigating the functions of the brain, the nervous system, and even the whole human body. It seems impossible to avoid such language given the many suggestive insights into human mental functioning that the computer metaphor makes possible.

Using a computer as a model for the mind can produce varying interpretations. Everything depends on the kind of computer you choose as the metaphorical predicate or the aspects of computer operations you emphasize. For example, biological determinists might prefer to think of the mind as a 'dedicated' computer whose functions are fully specified and wired into the hardware, allowing little flexibility. But if we think of the mind as a sophisticated general-purpose computer, we cannot predict the specific tasks it performs simply by knowing the design of its hardware. Rather, by loading different software programs, we direct the computer's hardware to perform particular tasks. Thus, the

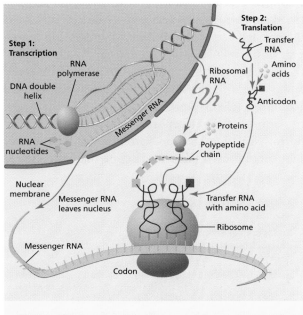

Figure 7.2 An example of a protein synthesis diagram laid out in 'assembly-line' style.

'functional processes [of the brain] cannot be guessed at from its design. . . . Although we may have biological origins, these may not be much more relevant than, say, soil for flowers. . . . Soil chemistry tells us remarkably little about orchids' (Gregory 1981: 566).

Were we to pursue this kind of computer metaphor, we could argue that the co-evolution of brain and culture could be described as the process by which a program hungry for system memory makes demands on hardware design. Random alterations that result in new central processing unit (CPU) chips and hardware design (mutations) allow more applications to be developed. At a certain point, however, the capacity of the CPU chip to access memory is reached. An external 'swap file' to handle the users' ever-increasing memory demands must be created in some sort of external storage system—flash memory or hard disks. The human cultural equivalent of this swap file would be oral tradition and later forms of symbolic inscription, such as writing.

Religion

For many readers of this text, the most familiar form of world view is probably **religion**. The anthropological concept of religion, like many analytic terms, began as a description of a certain domain of Western culture. As a result, it has been very difficult for anthropologists to settle on a definition of religion that is applicable in all human societies. Scholars have often argued that religion differs from other kinds of world views because it assumes the existence of a supernatural domain: an invisible world populated by one or more beings who are more powerful than human beings and are able to influence events in the 'natural' human world. The problem is that the distinction between 'natural' and 'supernatural' was originally made by non-religious Western observers, where 'real' was equated to the 'natural' world that was separate from their defined 'imaginary' or 'supernatural' world. However, 'humans do not have a world that is fixed for their kind; instead, there is a vital experience of space. . . . The vital functions of a body subject are carried out within a vital space, which is not given as such but is shaped by that being's actions' (Von Maltzahn 1994: 67). These actions are based on belief systems, and the sentient world may be interpreted through a set of mythological constructs that give meaning to the 'animate beings in

motion against the backdrop of a terrain that . . . [is] . . . itself continually in process . . .' (Riddington 1982: 473). Thus many anthropologists who study different religious traditions believe that it is less distorting to begin with their informants' statements about what exists and what does not. In this way, they are in a better position to understand the range of forces, visible and invisible, that religious believers perceive as active in their world.

Therefore the inquiry needs to begin with broad objectives that can move to increasing specificity as the details of a particular religious tradition are revealed by the informant(s). Bowen defines religion as 'ideas and practices that postulate reality beyond that which is immediately available to the senses' (2002: 5). These ideas and practices are not individual; they are *social*: they are shared among a group of people and shape their interactions with one another and with the universe in a variety of ways that can be observed and studied (Figure 7.3). In individual societies, this may take the shape of beliefs in spirits and gods, in impersonal forces that affect the world, in the correct practice of ritual, or in the awareness that the ancestors continue to be active in the world of the living. It is important to note that this definition of religion encompasses both practices and ideas; religions involve actions as well as beliefs. Indeed, anthropologist A.F.C. Wallace proposed a set of 'minimal categories of religious behaviour' that describe many of the practices usually associated with religions (1966). Several of the most salient are:

(1) *Prayer.* Where there are personified cosmic forces, there is a customary way of addressing them, usually by speaking or chanting out loud. Often people pray in public, at a sacred location and with special apparatuses: incense, smoke, objects (such as rosary beads or a prayer wheel), and so on.

---

computer metaphor A technological metaphor that employs computers as metaphorical predicates.

organic metaphor A world view metaphor that applies the image of the body to social structures and institutions.

religion 'Ideas and practices that postulate reality beyond that which is immediately available to the senses'.

technological metaphor A world view metaphor that employs objects made by human beings as metaphorical predicates.

(2) *Physiological exercise.* Many religious systems have methods for physically manipulating psychological states to induce an ecstatic spiritual state. Wallace suggests four major kinds of manipulation: (a) drugs; (b) sensory deprivation; (c) mortification of the flesh by pain, sleeplessness, and fatigue; and (d) deprivation of food, water, or air. In many societies, the experience of ecstasy, euphoria, dissociation, or hallucination seems to be a goal of religious effort.

(3) *Exhortation.* In all religious systems, certain people are believed to have closer relationships with the invisible powers than others, and they are expected to use those relationships in the spiritual interests of others. They give orders, heal, threaten, comfort, and interpret.

(4) *Mana.* Mana refers to an impersonal superhuman power that is sometimes believed to be transferable; for example, by laying their hands on a sick person, the power of a healer enters the person's body to remove or destroy an illness. In Guider, Cameroon, some people believe that the ink used to copy passages from the Quran has power. Washing the ink off the board on which the words are written, and drinking the ink, transfers the power of the words into the body of the drinker. The principle here is that sacred things are to be touched so that power may be transferred.

(5) *Taboo.* Objects or people that may not be touched are taboo. Some people believe that the cosmic power in such objects or people may 'drain away' if touched or may injure the toucher. Many religious systems have taboo objects. Traditionally, Catholics were not to touch the Host during communion; Jews may not touch the handwritten text of the biblical scrolls. In ancient Polynesia, commoners could not touch the chief's body; even an accidental touch resulted in the death of the commoner. Food may also be taboo; many societies have elaborate rules concerning the foods that may or may not be eaten at different times or by different kinds of people.

(6) *Feasts.* Eating and drinking in a religious context is very common. The Holy Communion of Catholics and Protestants is a meal set apart

by its religious context. The Passover Seder for Jews is another religious feast. For the Huichol of Mexico, the consumption of peyote is set apart by its religious context. Even everyday meals may be seen to have a religious quality if they begin or end with prayer.

(7) *Sacrifice.* Giving something of value to the invisible forces or their agents is a feature of many religious systems. This may be an offering of money, goods, or services. It may also be the immolation of animals or, very rarely, human beings. Sacrifices may be made in thanks to the cosmic forces in hopes of influencing them to act in a certain way or simply to gain general religious merit.

Religion and Communication

Those who are committed to religious world views are convinced of the existence and active involvement of beings or forces in their lives that are ordinarily invisible. Indeed, some of the most highly valued religious practices, such as religious ecstasy or trance,

Figure 7.3 A Hindu devotee making the painful pilgrimage to Batu Caves, Kuala Lumpur.

produce outer symptoms that may be perceived by others, but their most powerful effects can be experienced only by the individual who undergoes them personally. What if you wanted to know what it felt like to experience religious ecstasy? What if you were someone who had such an experience and wanted to tell others about it? What if you were convinced that the supreme power in the universe had revealed itself to you and you wanted to share this revelation with others? How would you proceed?

You might well begin by searching for metaphors based on experiences already well known to your audience. One Hindu Tamil worshipper in Kuala Lumpur who successfully went into trance during the festival of Thaipusam (Figure 7.4) described his experience as 'floating in the air, followed by the wind' (*Floating in the Air* 1973). And the Hebrew poet who wrote the Twenty-third Psalm tried to express his experience of the power and love of his God by comparing God to his shepherd and himself to a sheep. Many contemporary theologians argue that the language human beings use to talk about omnipresent and omniscient supernatural beings is full of metaphors (see, e.g., Gillman 1992). Even those who claim to have had personal experience of this reality, such as the People of the Book (Jews, Christians, and Muslims who call to Elohim, God, or Allah), will probably still find themselves forced to resort to poetic, metaphorical language if they want to explain that experience to other people—and perhaps even to themselves.

When societal metaphors are used, members of the tradition are likely to conceive of the force(s) at work in the universe as personified beings with many of the attributes of human agents at work in the society they know well. As societies differ from one another, so too does the way they characterize the universe. Thus societies organized in strong groups based on kinship usually conceive of a universe peopled with the spirits of powerful ancestral figures who take an interest in the lives of their living descendants. However, members of societies run by vast and complex bureaucracies, as was the Roman Empire, are apt to picture the universe as being run by an army of hierarchically ordered gods and spirits, all of which may be supervised by a chief god. It is not likely that 'The Lord is my shepherd' would be an apt description of cosmic reality by people living in a society that lacks class distinctions and has no experience of shepherding.

Figure 7.4 People gathered at the Hindu festival of Thaipusam in Kuala Lumpur.

Organic metaphors may also figure in the construction of religious understanding. Anthropologist James Fernandez reports that organic metaphors are common in the Bwiti religion of the Fang (see Map 7.1). The human heart, for example, is an apt metaphor for Bwiti devotees because '(1) it is the heart which is the most alive of the bloody organs, (2) it is traditionally conceived by the Fang to be the organ of thought, and (3) in its bloodiness it is associated with the female principle. . . . Many meanings are at work in this metaphor, for that bloody organ, the heart, has a congeries of useful associations' (1977: 112).

The popularity of technological metaphors in the Western world accompanied the rise of science and the invention of machines that began to transform the world in unprecedented ways, stimulating peoples' imaginations in new ways. The increasing complexity of machines, coupled with their builders' intimate knowledge of how they were put together, made them

Map 7.1 Fang

highly suggestive as metaphorical predicates; they gave rise to a set of metaphorical entailments that were very different from the entailments of societal and organic metaphors. For example, in the seventeenth century, philosopher René Descartes popularized the notion that the human body was a machine, albeit one inhabited by an immortal soul. Subsequently, Julien La Mettrie carried this metaphor to its radical conclusion in *L'homme-machine* ('man-machine'), where he argued that the concept of the human soul was superfluous because machines do not have souls.

Today when we say that we are only cogs in a machine, or talk about social status and roles as interchangeable parts, we are using machine metaphors. What if people should conclude that the structure of the universe is the same as the structure of a machine—say, a clock or a computer? To view the cosmos as complex, orderly, predictable, and knowable, such that effective intervention into cosmic processes is possible, would certainly qualify as a world view even if the cosmos was deaf to human prayer and indifferent to human affairs. Would the resulting world view still be a religion?

Religious Organization

In the societal metaphor the forces in the universe are personalized and people seeking to influence those forces must handle them as they would handle powerful human beings. Thus communication is the central feature. When we address each other we expect a response.

The same is true when we address personalized cosmic forces, and this can become a tremendously complex undertaking. It is not surprising, therefore, that some societies have developed complex social practices to ensure that it is done properly. In other words, religion becomes institutionalized and social positions are created for specialists who supervise or embody correct religious practice.

Anthropologists have identified two broad categories of religious specialists: shamans and priests. A **shaman** is a part-time religious practitioner who is believed to have the power to contact invisible powers directly on behalf of individuals or groups. Shamans are often thought to be able to travel to the cosmic realm to communicate with the beings or forces that dwell there. They often plead with those beings or forces to act in favour of their people and may return with messages for them. In many societies, the training that a shaman receives is long and demanding and may involve the use of powerful psychotropic substances, producing altered states of consciousness to access cosmic beings. This can embody dangerous ambiguities: someone who can contact such beings for positive benefits may also be able to contact them to produce negative outcomes like disease or death.

However, Barbara Tedlock (2005) expands on the concept of healing practices and shamanism, claiming it was originally the domain of women. From extensive cross-cultural investigations and information from past investigations, she observes that this was the world's oldest form of religion and medicine and that it remains a force for healing in today's world. Thus we can see an intimate link between traditional religious practices and traditional medicine. Kunitz (1983) gives insight into the incorporation of traditional medicine and what has been termed *shamanistic practices* into institutions of Western medicine with his discussion of the Navajo experience (see Map 7.2).

A **priest**, by contrast, is skilled in the practice of religious rituals, which are carried out for the benefit of the group. Priests do not necessarily have direct contact with cosmic forces. Often their major role is to mediate such contact by ensuring that the required ritual activity has been properly performed. Priests are found in hierarchical societies. Status differences separating rulers and subjects in such societies are reflected in the unequal relationship between priest and laity.

Map 7.2 Navajo

Figure 7.5 A Huichol shaman's violin and arrows, together with a basket of freshly gathered peyote.

World Views in Operation: Two Case Studies

Anthropologists often say that people of different cultures live in different worlds. This itself is a metaphorical statement. It asserts that our understanding of reality depends on the particular point of view embodied in our culture. Of course, every culture contains subcultures that may draw pictures of reality that conflict with each other. The experience of juggling multiple points of view in our own society helps us to cope with unfamiliar perspectives in different societies.

We have been discussing how world views are constructed, but most of us encounter them fully formed, both in our own society and in other societies. We face a rich tapestry of symbols and rituals and everyday practices linked to one another in what often appears to be a seamless web. Where do we begin to sort things out?

Mind, Body, and Emotion in Huichol Religious Practice

Barbara Myerhoff (1974) discusses the peyote hunt of the Huichol (Figure 7.5). This ritual pilgrimage is a religious experience in which mind, body, and emotion all come together.

The Huichol are corn farmers who live in the Sierra Madre Occidental of northern Mexico (see Map 7.3). Annually, they travel to a desert about 600 kilometres from their homes to hunt peyote. Because peyote is

sacred to the Huichol, this journey is also sacred, representing a pilgrimage to Wirikuta, the original Huichol homeland where the First People, both deities and ancestors, once lived. The journey is hard and dangerous, both physically and spiritually. The pilgrims seek to restore and experience the original state of unity that existed at the beginning of the world.

This state of unity is symbolized by deer, maize, and peyote. The deer symbolizes the masculine, hunting past and thus connects the Huichol with their ancestors. In Huichol thought, the deer gave them peyote and appears every year in the hunt in Wirikuta. Blood from a sacrificed deer makes the maize grow and makes it nourishing. The deer is more powerful than human beings but not as remote as the gods. It symbolizes independence, adventure, and freedom.

Although the Huichol have only recently begun to grow maize, it is central to their present-day life. A life

priest A religious practitioner skilled in the practice of religious rituals, which he or she carries out for the benefit of the group.

shaman A part-time religious practitioner who is believed to have the power to travel to or contact supernatural forces directly on behalf of individuals or groups.

Map 7.3 Huichol

based on maize is tedious and precarious: the Huichol have to stay home to watch the crops, and even if they are careful, the maize may not grow. Maize symbolizes the labour of the present: food, domesticity, sharing between the sexes, routine, and persistent diligence. It also provides the Huichol with the language of beauty. 'Maize', the Huichol say, 'is our life.'

Peyote, when gathered in the land of its origins, is sacred. It is used to induce private visions, which are not shared with others. It is also used ritually, in which case so little is eaten that no visions are produced. It seems that the purpose of ritual consumption is to reach communion with the deities. The Huichol think of peyote as plant and animal at once; at the climactic moments of the peyote hunt, it is hunted like the deer. 'Peyote is neither mundane, like maize, nor exotic and exciting, like deer. It is that solitary, ahistorical, asocial, asexual, non-rational domain without which [human beings] are not complete, without which life is a lesser affair' (Myerhoff 1974: 227). In Huichol religious thought, deer, maize, and peyote fit together: maize cannot grow without deer blood, the deer cannot be sacrificed until after the peyote hunt, the ceremony that brings the rain cannot be held without peyote, and the peyote cannot be hunted until the maize has been cleaned and sanctified.

The Peyote Hunt

In 1966, Barbara Myerhoff and Peter Furst accompanied Huichol pilgrims on the peyote hunt. Each pilgrim was given the name of a Huichol god for the duration

of the pilgrimage. The pilgrims, under the guidance of a shaman, all followed strict rules about sexual continence and other behaviours, separating themselves from their everyday routine. Once the pilgrims entered Wirikuta, many ways of speaking and acting were reversed. 'Stand up' meant 'sit down'; 'go away' meant 'come here'. The van in which they travelled became a 'burro' that would stop 'if he ran out of tequila'. The shaman who led the pilgrimage told Myerhoff that 'on the peyote hunt, we change the names of things because when we cross over there, into Wirikuta, things are so sacred that all is reversed' (148).

> In the sacred land, the pilgrims became hunters, searching for peyote. Once the first peyote cactus was found, it was trapped by two arrows. The pilgrims then encircled it and presented their offerings. The shaman cut it out of the ground, sliced sections, and put one section in each pilgrim's mouth. The little group was sharply etched against the desert in the late afternoon sun—motionless, soundless, the once-bright colours of their costumes now muted under layers of dust—chewing, chewing the bitter plant. So Sahagún described the ancient Indians who wept in the desert over the plant they esteemed so greatly. The success of the undertaking was unquestionable and the faces changed from quiet wonder to rapture to exaltation, all without words, all at the same moment. . . . Their camaraderie, the completeness of their communion with one another was self-evident. The companions were radiant. Their love for life and for one another was palpable. Though they did not speak and barely moved, no one seeing them there could call the experience anything less than collective ecstasy. (155–7)

Following this moment of communitas, the pilgrims collected as much peyote as they would need for their community and hastened to depart. The reversals and other requirements remained in effect until they reached home.

The unification of deer, maize, and peyote gives the peyote hunt its power. As Myerhoff puts it, 'In the climactic moments of the rituals in Wirikuta, these symbols provide the Huichol's with a formulation of the large questions dealt with by religion, the questions of ultimate meaning and purpose' (1974).

She suggests that the way the Huichol's religious system answers these questions is distinctive. Some religions explain present-day moral incoherence by asserting that an original paradise was lost following an ancient sin. Other systems assert that there is an afterlife in which all the suffering of the world will be set right, but the Huichol refuse to let go of their past.

> Their most precious religious heritage—their beginnings—is idealized and recovered. Even if only for a little while, by means of the peyote hunt, Paradise may be regained. Through the deer–maize–peyote complex, the deer and a life dedicated to hunting the deer is still a fact of present-day life rather than a fading, shabby memory, chewed over by old men at the end of the day. (1974: 262)

In the terms we have been using so far, the deer–maize–peyote complex and the peyote hunt represent the union of mind, body, and emotion. Through a holistic ritual experience that is profoundly meaningful, deeply moving, and thoroughly physical, the Huichol re-experience the correctness of their way of life.

Witchcraft, Oracles, and Magic among the Azande

Anthropologist E.E. Evans-Pritchard, in his classic work *Witchcraft, Oracles, and Magic among the Azande* (1976 [1937]), shows how Azande beliefs and practices concerning witchcraft, oracles, and magic are related to one another (see EthnoProfile 7.1: Azande). He describes how Azande use witchcraft beliefs to explain unfortunate things that happen to them and how they employ oracles and magic to exert a measure of control over the actions of other people. Evans-Pritchard was impressed by the intelligence, sophistication, and skepticism of his Azande informants. For this reason, he was all the more struck by their ability to hold a set of beliefs that many Europeans would regard as superstitious.

Azande Witchcraft Beliefs

The Azande believe that *mangu* (translated by Evans-Pritchard as **witchcraft**) is a substance in the body of witches, generally located under the sternum.* Being part of the body, the witchcraft substance grows as the body grows; therefore, the older the witch, the more potent

---

* Beliefs and practices similar to those associated with Azande *mangu* have been found in many other societies, and it has become traditional in anthropology to refer to them as 'witchcraft'. This technical usage must not be confused with everyday uses of the word in contemporary Western societies, still less with the practices of followers of movements like Wicca, which are very different.

EthnoProfile 7.1

Azande

Region: Central Africa

Nations: Northeast Democratic Republic of the Congo (Zaire), southwest Sudan, and southeast Central African Republic

Language: The Azande speak Zande (Pazande), an Adamawa-Ubangi language of the Niger-Congo group

Population: Estimated to be 1,000,000–4,000,000

Environment: Sparsely wooded savannah

Livelihood: Agriculture with maize, rice, and groundnuts (peanuts); cassava and sweet potatoes as main crops; hunting, fishing, and chicken raising

Political organization: Traditionally, highly organized, tribal kingdoms; today, part of modern nation-states

For more information: Evans-Pritchard, E.E. 1976 [1937]. *Witchcraft, Oracles, and Magic among the Azande*, abr. edn (Oxford: Oxford University Press)

his or her witchcraft. The Azande believe that children inherit witchcraft from their parents. Men and women may both be witches. Men practise witchcraft against other men, women against other women. Witchcraft works when its 'soul' removes the soul of a certain organ in the victim's body, usually at night, causing a slow, wasting disease. Suffering such a disease is therefore an indication that an individual has been bewitched.

Witchcraft is a basic concept for the Azande, one that shapes their experience of adversity. All deaths are due to witchcraft and must be avenged by **magic**. Other misfortunes are also commonly attributed to witchcraft unless the victim has broken a taboo, has failed to observe a moral rule, or is believed to be responsible for his own problems. Suppose I am an incompetent

magic A set of beliefs and practices designed to control the visible or invisible world for specific purposes.

witchcraft The performance of evil by human beings believed to possess an innate, non-human power to do evil whether or not it is intentional or self-aware.

potter and my pots break while I am firing them. I may claim that witchcraft caused them to break, but everyone will laugh at me because they know I lack skill. Witchcraft is believed to be so common that the Azande are neither surprised nor awestruck when they encounter it. Their usual response is anger.

To the Azande, witchcraft is a completely natural explanation for events. Consider the classic case of the collapsing granary. Azandeland is hot, and people seeking shade often sit under traditional raised granaries, which rest on logs. Termites are common in Azandeland, and sometimes they destroy the supporting logs, causing a granary to collapse. Occasionally, when a granary collapses, people sitting under it are killed. Why does this happen? The Azande are well aware that the termites chew up the wood until the supports give way but to them that explanation is not enough. Why, after all, should that particular granary have collapsed at that particular moment? To skeptical observers, the only connection is coincidence in time and space. Western science does not provide any explanation for why these two chains of causation intersect. But the Azande do: witchcraft causes the termites to finish chewing up the wood at just that moment and that witchcraft must be avenged.

Dealing with Witches

How to expose the witch? For this task, the Azande employ **oracles** (invisible forces to which people address questions and whose responses they believe to be truthful). Pre-eminent among these is the poison oracle. The poison is a strychnine-like substance imported to Azandeland. The oracle 'speaks' through the effect the poison has on chickens. When witchcraft is suspected, a relative of the afflicted person will take some chickens into the bush along with a specialist in administering the poison oracle. This person will feed poison to one chicken, name a suspect, and ask the oracle to kill the chicken if this person is the witch. If the chicken dies, a second chicken will be fed poison, and the oracle will be asked to spare the chicken if the suspect just named is indeed the witch. Thus, the Azande double-check the oracle carefully; a witchcraft accusation is not made lightly.

People do not consult the oracle with a long list of names. They need only consider those who might wish them or their families ill: people who have quarrelled with them, who are unpleasant, anti-social, and whose

behaviour is somehow out of line. Indeed, witches are always neighbours because neighbours are the only people who know you well enough to wish you and your family ill.

Once the oracle has identified the witch, the Azande removes the wing of the chicken and has it taken by messenger to the compound of the accused person. The messenger presents the accused witch with the chicken wing and says that he has been sent concerning the illness of so-and-so's relative. 'Almost invariably the witch replies courteously that he is unconscious of injuring anyone, that if it is true that he has injured the man in question he is very sorry, and that if it is he alone who is troubling him then he will surely recover because from the bottom of his heart he wishes him health and happiness' (Evans-Pritchard 1976 [1937]: 42). The accused then calls for a gourd of water, takes some in his mouth, and sprays it out over the wing. He says aloud, so the messenger can hear and repeat what he says, that if he is a witch he is not aware of it and that he is not intentionally causing the sick man to be ill. He addresses the witchcraft in him, asking it to become cool, and concludes by saying that he makes this appeal from his heart, not just from his lips (42).

People accused of witchcraft are usually astounded; no Azande thinks of himself or herself as a witch. However, the Azande strongly believe in witchcraft and in the oracles, and if the oracle says someone is a witch, then that person must be one. The accused witch is grateful to the family of the sick person for letting this be known. Otherwise, if the accused had been allowed to murder the victim, all the while unaware of it, the witch would surely be killed by vengeance magic. The witchcraft accusation carries a further message: the behaviour of the accused is sufficiently outside the bounds of acceptable Azande behaviour to have marked him or her as a potential witch. The accused witch, then, is being told to change his or her behaviour.

Patterns of Witchcraft Accusation

Compared with the stereotypes of Euro-American witchcraft—old hags dressed in black, riding on broomsticks, casting spells, causing milk to sour, or people to sicken—Azande witchcraft seems quite tame. People whose impression of witchcraft comes from Western European images may believe that witchcraft and witch-hunting tear at the very fabric of society. Yet anthropological accounts like Evans-Pritchard's suggest that practices such as witchcraft accusation can sometimes keep societies together.

Anthropologist Mary Douglas looked at the range of witchcraft accusations worldwide and discovered that they fall into two basic types (1970: xxvi–xxvii): in some cases, the witch is an evil outsider; in others, the witch is an internal enemy, either the member of a rival faction or a dangerous deviant. These different patterns of accusation perform different functions in a society. If the witch is an outsider, witchcraft accusations can strengthen in-group ties. If the witch is an internal enemy, accusations of witchcraft can weaken in-group ties; factions may have to regroup, communities may split, and the entire social hierarchy may be reordered. If the witch is a dangerous deviant, the accusation of witchcraft can be seen as an attempt to control the deviant in defence of the wider values of the community. Douglas concludes that how people understand witchcraft is based on the social relations of their society.

Maintaining and Changing a World View

What makes a world view stable? Why is a world view rejected? These questions are related to general questions about persistence and change in human social life. Anthropologists recognize that culture change is a complex phenomenon, and they admit that they do not have all the answers.

Changes in world view must, first of all, be related to the practical everyday experiences of people in a particular society. Stable, repetitive experiences reinforce the acceptability of any traditional world view that has successfully accounted for such experiences in the past. When experiences become unpredictable, however, thinking people in any society may become painfully aware that past experiences can no longer be trusted as guides for the future, and traditional world views may be undermined (see Horton 1982: 252).

Coping with Change

Drastic changes in experience lead people to create new interpretations that will help them cope with the changes. Sometimes the change is an outcome of local or regional struggles. The Protestant Reformation, for

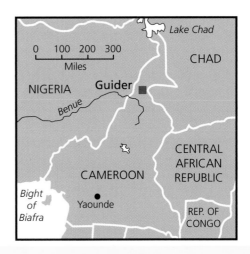

Map 7.5 Guider

example, adapted the Christian tradition to changing social circumstances in northern Europe during the Renaissance by breaking ties to the Pope, turning church lands over to secular authorities, allowing clergy to marry, and so forth. Protestants continued to identify themselves as Christians even though many of their religious practices had changed.

In Guider (see Map 7.5), lone rural migrants frequently abandoned old religious practices and took on urban customs and a new identity through conversion to Islam. However, the conflict between new and old need not necessarily lead to conversion. Sometimes the result is a creative synthesis of old religious practices and new ones, a process called **syncretism**. Under the pressure of Christian missionizing, Indigenous people of Central America identified some of their own pre-Christian, personalized superhuman beings with particular Catholic saints. Similarly, Africans brought to Brazil identified Catholic saints with African gods to produce the syncretistic religion Candomblé.

Anthropologists have debated the nature of syncretistic practices, noting that while some may be viewed as a way of resisting new ideas imposed from above, others may be introduced from above by powerful

oracles Invisible forces to which people address questions and whose responses they believe to be truthful.

syncretism The synthesis of old religious practices (or an old way of life) with new religious practices (or a new way of life) introduced from outside, often by force.

In Their Own Words

The Iroquois and the World's Rim

George Hammel speculates on colour, culture, and contact among the Iroquois.

Contact between the peoples of the New World and of the Old World had ideational consequences for both. The event of Contact, and more importantly the process of Contact, initiated the reciprocal redefinition of the mythical realities which for centuries, if not millennia, had structured New World and Old World thoughts and behaviours about the other world. Neither the event nor the process of Contact are over. For the Iroquois, dwelling beneath the Great Tree at the centre of Earth-Island, indirect knowledge of Contact at the eastern World's Rim and the indirect receipt of exotic trade goods emanating there, appear to have reified and reinvigorated the traditional ritual meanings and functions of light, bright (reflective), and white things. Not least among these were white marine shell and red, upper Great Lakes native copper, into whose meanings and functions were incorporated and assimilated analogous European trade goods of glazed ceramic, glass, and metal. This seemingly innocuous exchange of European baubles, bangles, and beads along the mid-Atlantic Coast of northeastern North America during the sixteenth century catalyzed profound changes in the ideational, socio-political, and economic subsystems of coastal and interior Native populations.

The lure of exotic and of, literally and figuratively, precious substances brought the mythical reality of the *Old* World into tangential relations with the *New* World. What were among these substances, so precious in the Old World, that lured men in small boats to the ends of the world, as known? Gold, silver, diamonds, and pearls, which had long been and still are traditional Western European material metaphors of value, not only of *economic* value but of *ideational* value as well (cf. Gombrich 1963: 12–29). Before bank books, stocks and bonds, and paper currencies, that is, paper symbols of wealth, these substances comprised tangible and conspicuous metaphors of cultural value, encoded and manifested linguistically and synesthetically within figures of speech, in clothing and adornment, and in works of art and architecture. Invested within these substances and the artifacts made from them was a millennia-old fusion of aesthetic and ideational interest and value.

Like most biological organisms, humans are photo-tropic: they grow toward the light. As sentient biological organisms, humans tend toward the light, whether it be the Sun or *the Son*. As sentient biological organisms, humans understand that light is life and that light is the prerequisite to animacy and sentience. This is a fundamental and, I dare say, universal cultural axiom that has generated parallel dependent corollaries manifested cross-culturally in human thought and behaviour, linguistic and physical. Light (sources), bright (reflective), and white things are tangible metaphors for abstractions of greatest cultural value: for life itself, and for positive states of physical, social, and spiritual well-being. We should remind ourselves that the great value that Western culture places upon the Golden Rule, or upon a gem or pearl of wisdom, lies not with their economic worth but with their reflective virtues.

For millennia, in the Old World, such substances and artifacts fashioned from them have represented wealth as weal- or well-being. The Iroquois and other Northeastern Woodland Indian peoples would agree with this characterization of wealth as well-being. Among them, however, wealth as well-being is more generally appreciated as medicine: the insurance and assurance of physical, social, and spiritual well-being, individually or collectively invoked in ritual. Within ritual contexts, these concepts of well-being have traditionally constelled about white shell, and more recently about another, bright, light-reflective, white substance: a 'white metal', silver.

In the interior mid-Atlantic region at Contact, the 'diamonds of the country' were the relatively scarce and small cylindrical or barrel shaped beads of white marine shell, which were to become recorded in contemporary documents as *sewant* (Dutch), *porcelaine* (French), and *wampumpeague*, shortened to *wampum* (English). It was Jacques Cartier in 1535, who speaking of the St Lawrence Iroquoians, established the convention of making the comparison between the Northeastern Woodland Indians' interest and desire for these seemingly inconsequential, small white (marine) shell beads and that of Western Europeans for gold, silver, diamonds, and pearls.

Among the Northern Iroquoians and the Northeastern Woodland Indians, generally, colour is a semantically organizing principle of ritual states-of-being and of ritual material culture. Three colours predominate: white, black, and red. These colours organize ritual states-of-being into three contrastive and complementary sets: social states-of-being, asocial states-of-being, and anti-social states-of-being, respectively. Ritual is the means to maintain a desired state-of-being or to transform one state-of-being into an at least temporarily more desirable state-of-being. Within ritual contexts, material culture functions to synesthetically manifest through its attribute of colour the present state-of-being of its participants and to synesthetically manifest through colour the desired state-of-being to be ritually effected. This may be the status quo or one of the other two contrastive states-of-being.

The colours white, black, and red potentially organize ritual states-of-being and ritual material culture into either triadic or dyadic contrastive–complementary sets. White social states-of-being, black asocial states-of-being, and red anti-social states-of-being form the one contrastive–complementary, triadic set; white *and* red social states-of-being in contrast to black asocial states-of-being form one dyadic opposition; and white social states-of-being in contrast to black and red anti-social states-of-being form the other. Within these ritual states-of-being, the colours white, black, and red also individually manifest varying valencies (+, 0, or -) of potency, evaluation, and activity (cf. Adams 1973; Osgood, May, and Miron 1975) depending upon the state-of-being being ritually foregrounded and the state-of-being with which it is being contrasted. For example white(ness), the colour of (day)light and thus of life itself, is the most potent colour and the most highly evaluated colour if that potency is consecrated to socially constructive purposes. However, white *and* red are both *potent* colours since they are generally identified with the sentient aspect and the animate aspect (i.e., blood) of life, respectively.

White and red are also positively evaluated colours to the extent that their (life) potency is ritually consecrated to socially constructive functions. However, since red is the most *active* or animate of the three colours, it is also bivalent: if its animacy is consecrated to socially destructive functions, it manifests anti-social states-of-being in contrast to white social states-of-(physical, social, and spiritual)being; if its animacy is consecrated to socially constructive functions, it manifests social states-of-(physical well-)being. When conjoined, white and red manifest the sentient and animate aspects of social states-of-being, respectively, and are most frequently

contrasted to black states-of-being, characterized by the absence of sentience and animacy, as in states of mourning. Concepts of greatest (life) potency, and consequently of greatest positive cultural evaluation—which are semantically identified with whiteness—are the common ideational denominators underlying the ritual functions of white shell throughout the Northeastern Woodlands. Within social states-of-being, white shell, whether freshwater or marine in origin, and regardless of its natural or manufactured form, functions as a metaphor for light and thus for life itself, particularly in its sentient aspect. White shell is a material metaphor for the biological continuity of life in general and for the biological and social continuity of human life in particular (Hamell 1986). This function and meaning of white shell underwrote the intense interest in white marine shell 'ornaments', particularly, in those small cylindrical beads called *sewant*, *porcelaine*, and *wampum*, which became after Contact the medium and the message of social exchanges between Native and Native, and Native and newcomer. Red(-painted) and/or purple ('black') wampum beads, bead strings, and bead belts were the media of socially contrastive messages.

Light, bright, and white were and still are good to think with among the Iroquois and other Northeastern Woodland Indians. This ritual function and meaning of light, bright, and white material culture, shellwork in particular, may with confidence be projected far back into prehistory, as can the contrastive–complementary functions and meanings of black and red material culture. This proposed semantics of colour, ritual, and material culture most probably accounts for the differential and deferential disposal in mortuary contexts during the Terminal Archaic and during the Early and Middle Woodland periods of white (marine) shell, white freshwater pearls, white (= transparent) rock crystal, white chalcedony, white (muscovite) mica, white free-state metals (silver, galena); red cedar, red ocher (hematite), red chalcedony, red jasper, red pipestone (catilinite), red native copper; and black charcoal, black obsidian, black chalcedony (and chert), black (biotite) mica, and black meteoric iron. I suggest that in the reporting of archaeologically recovered ritual material culture, a presentation organized by colour may be as meaningful, and perhaps more so, than its reportage by the traditional analytical categories of raw material and function.

Source: Hammel, George R. 1992. 'The Iroquois and the World's Rim: Speculations on Colour, Culture, and Contact', *American Indian Quarterly* 16, 4: 451, 455–8.

outsiders deliberately making room for local beliefs within their own supralocal world view. The Romans, for example, made room for local deities within their imperial pantheon, and post-Vatican II Catholicism explicitly urges non-European Catholics to worship using local cultural forms (Stewart and Shaw 1994).

When groups defend or refashion their own way of life in the face of outside encroachments, anthropologists sometimes describe their activities as **revitalization**—a deliberate, organized attempt by some members of a society to create a more satisfying culture (Wallace 1972: 75). Revitalization arises in times of crisis, most often among groups who are facing oppression and radical transformation, usually at the hands of outsiders (such as colonizing powers). Revitalization movements engage in a 'politics of religious synthesis' that produces a range of outcomes (Stewart and Shaw 1994). Sometimes syncretism is embraced; other times it is rejected in favour of nativism, a return to the old ways. Some nativistic movements expect a messiah or prophet who will bring back a lost golden age of peace, prosperity, and harmony, a process often called *revivalism, millenarianism,* or *messianism.*

A classic New World example of a millenarian movement was the Ghost Dance movement among Indigenous peoples on the Great Plains of the United States in the 1890s. When the buffalo were exterminated, Indigenous Plains dwellers lost their independence and were herded onto reservations by numerically superior and better-armed Euro-Americans. Out of this final crisis emerged Wovoka, a prophet who taught that the existing world would soon be destroyed and that a new crust would form on the earth. All settlers and Indigenous people who followed the settlers' ways would become buried. Those Indigenous people who abandoned the settlers' ways, led pure lives, and danced the Ghost Dance would be saved. As the new crust formed, the buffalo would return, as would all the ancestors of the believers. Together, all would lead lives of virtue and joy.

Because the world was going to change by itself, violence against the oppressors was not a necessary part of the Ghost Dance. Nevertheless, the movement frightened settlers and the US Army, who suspected an armed uprising. Those fears and suspicions led to the massacre at Wounded Knee, in which the cavalry troopers killed all the members of a Lakota (Sioux)

band, principally women and children, whom they encountered off the reservation.

A revitalization movement that has enjoyed greater longevity is the syncretistic Bwiti religion of the Fang in Central Africa (Figure 7.6). In the last century, the Fang have faced three important challenges to their world view. First, the reality of 'the far away' represented by French colonialism came to challenge the reality of 'the near' and familiar. Second, the protective traditional powers of 'the below' were challenged by Christian missionaries' messages of divinity in 'the above'. Third, the pluralism of colonial life is a double standard in which the colonized were treated differently from the colonizers (Fernandez 1982: 571). Bwiti allows its members to cope with the first challenge by using the drug *eboga* to go out to the far and convert it into the near. In the second case, the Christian god of 'the above' and the traditional gods of 'the below' are both incorporated into the Bwiti pantheon. For the third, Bwiti ritual promotes among members the communal feeling of 'one-heartedness'.

Bwiti has created a world view that allows many Fang to cope with the strains of exploitation. Within Bwiti, some old metaphors (the forest, the body social, the kinship system) have been reanimated, some new

Figure 7.6 Fang women perform the Belebele dance during a Bwiti ceremony.

ones (red and white uniforms, a path of birth and death, the world as a globe or a ball) have been created, and all have been fitted together in a satisfying way. This world has, however, closed itself off from the wider society of the Gabon Republic. Bwiti represents a kind of escape from the pressures of the outside world (566).

Nativistic movements, however, may represent resistance to, rather than escape from, the outside world, actively removing or avoiding any cultural practices associated with those who seek to dominate them. One such 'anti-syncretistic' group is the Kwaio, living on the island of Malaita in the Solomon Islands (see Map 7.6). Almost all their neighbours have converted to Christianity, and the nation of which they are a part is militantly Christian. Members of other groups wear clothing, work on plantations or in tourist hotels, attend schools, and live in cities. The Kwaio have refused all this: 'Young men carry bows and arrows; girls and women, nude except for customary ornaments, dig taro in forest gardens; valuables made of strung shell beads are exchanged at mortuary feasts; and priests sacrifice pigs to the ancestral spirits on whom prosperity and life itself depend' (Keesing 1982: 1).

Roger Keesing (1992) admits that he does not know exactly why the Kwaio responded to colonial influence in this way. He suspects that pre-colonial social and political differences between the Kwaio and their coastal neighbours influenced later developments. The colonial encounter was certainly relevant. In 1927, some Kwaio attacked a British patrol, killing the district officer and 13 Solomon Islands troops. The subsequent massacre of many Kwaio by a police force of other Malaitans, and their marginalization and persecution by the colonial government, contributed to Kwaio resistance.

It is important to emphasize that the Kwaio maintain their old ways deliberately, in the face of alternatives; their traditional way of life is therefore lived in a modern context. 'In the course of anti-colonial struggle, *kastomu* (custom) and commitment to ancestral ways have become symbols of identity and autonomy' (Keesing 1982: 240). In the eyes of the Kwaio, the many Solomon Islanders who became Christianized and acculturated lost their cultural ties and thereby their ties to the land and to their past, becoming outsiders in their own homeland. Thus, maintaining tradition is a form of

Map 7.6 Kwaio

political protest. From this perspective, many contemporary anti-syncretistic movements in the world, from various religious fundamentalisms to movements for national identity and cultural autonomy, can be understood as having aims very similar to those of the Kwaio, sparked by many of the same forces.

World Views as Instruments of Power

We have discussed the process that people use to build their world views and have noted how world views vary enormously from culture to culture. But within any particular cultural tradition, there are probably always different world views.

How does a particular picture of reality become the 'official' world view for a given culture? And once that position is achieved, how is it maintained? To be in the running for the official picture of reality, a world view must be able, however minimally, to make sense of some people's personal and social experiences. Sometimes, however, it may seem to some members of society that barely credible views of reality have

revitalization A conscious, deliberate, and organized attempt by some members of a society to create a more satisfying culture in a time of crisis.

In Their Own Words

Custom and Confrontation

In the following passage, the late Roger Keesing recorded the words of one of his Kwaio informants, Dangeabe'u, who defends Kwaio custom.

The government has brought the ways of business, the ways of money. The people at the coast believe that's what's important and tell us we should join in. Now the government is controlling the whole world. The side of the Bible is withering away. When that's finished, the government will rule, unchallenged. It will hold all the land. All the money will go to the government to feed its power. Once everything—our lands, too—are in their hands, that will be it.

I've seen the people from other islands who have all become Christians. They knew nothing about their land. The white people have gotten their hands on their lands.

The whites led them to forget all the knowledge of their land, separated them from it. And when the people knew nothing about their land, the whites bought it from them and made their enterprises. . . .

That's close upon us too. If we all follow the side of the Bible, the government will become powerful here, too, and will take control of our land. We won't be attached to our land, as we are now, holding our connections to our past. If the government had control of our land, then if we wanted to do anything on it, we'd have to pay them. If we wanted to start a business—a store, say—we'd have to pay the government. We reject all that. We want to keep hold of our land, in the ways passed down to us.

Source: Keesing, Roger. 1992. *Custom and Confrontation: The Kwaio Struggle for Cultural Autonomy* (Chicago: University of Chicago Press), 184.

triumphed over alternatives that seem far more plausible. Thus, something more than persuasive ability alone must be involved and that something is power. As Lakoff and Johnson put it, 'People in power get to impose their metaphors' (1980: 157). Powerless people may be unable to dislodge the official world view of their society. They can, however, refuse to accept the imposition of someone else's world view and develop an unofficial world view based on metaphors that reflect their own condition of powerlessness (Scott 1990). Such unofficial world views may even suggest appropriate action for transforming that condition.

How can metaphors, or the symbols that represent them, be used as instruments of power and control? First, a symbol can be used to refer to a self-evident truth when people in power seek to eliminate or impose certain forms of conduct. Thus, a deceased parent, whose memory must be respected, may be invoked to block some actions or to stimulate others. Holy books, like the Quran, may also be used in this way. For example, a legal record from Guider indicates that a son once brought suit against his father for refusing to repay him a certain amount of money.

The father claimed that he had paid. Both father and son got into an increasingly heated argument in which neither would give ground. Finally, the judge in the case asked the father to take a copy of the Quran in his hand and swear that he was telling the truth. This he did. The son, however, refused to swear on the Quran and finally admitted that he had been lying. In this case, the status of the Quran as the unquestioned word of God, which implied the power of God to punish liars, controlled the son's behaviour.

Second, a symbol may be under the direct control of a person wishing to affect the behaviour of others. Consider the role of official interpreters of religious or political ideology, such as priests or kings. Their pronouncements define the bounds of permissible behaviour. As Keesing points out:

> Senior men, in Melanesia as elsewhere in the tribal world, have depended heavily on control of *sacred knowledge* to maintain their control of earthly politics. By keeping in their hands relations with ancestors and other spirits, by commanding magical knowledge, senior men could maintain a control mediated by the supernatural. Such religious ideologies served

too, by defining rules in terms of ancient spirits and by defining the nature of men and women in supernatural terms, to reinforce and maintain the roles of the sexes—and again to hide their nature. (1982: 219)

Keesing's observations remind us that knowledge, like power, is not evenly distributed throughout a society. Just as some people speak or write or carve better than others, so too do some people possess knowledge and control symbols to which others are denied access. Furthermore, this distribution of knowledge is not random: different kinds of people know different things. In some societies, what men know about their religious system is different from what women know, and what older men know may be different from what younger men know. Such discrepancies can have important consequences. Keesing suggested that men's control over women and older men's control over younger men are based on differential access to knowledge (14). It is not just that these different kinds of people know different things; rather, the different things they know (and don't know) enable them (or force them) to remain in the positions they hold in the society.

Religion and Secularism

The European Enlightenment gave birth to a new world view that has come to be called **secularism**, and the spread of this world view has had repercussions across the globe. The development of secular ideas and practices profoundly transformed the religious and political institutions that had dominated European society in the Middle Ages. Earlier generations of anthropologists took secularism for granted as the expected outcome of cultural evolution. More recently, however, anthropologists have been led to reconsider the nature of both the Enlightenment and secularism, prompted most sharply by resistance to the secular institutions of Western nation-states, both by some immigrant groups living within those states and by groups in non-Western nation-states who insist that citizenship and religious identity belong together. Perhaps the most difficult have been the struggles of some Muslim groups to adjust to life in Western secular states.

What happens when individuals and groups whose religious and political roots lay outside this European history come to live in modern, secular Europe? The distinction between what the liberal democratic state expects and what some Muslims want has recently been explored by anthropologist Talal Asad. His efforts to develop an 'anthropology of secularism' highlights the ways in which notions of the secular were shaped in the course of European history, particularly by the Protestant Reformation of Christianity, the subsequent wars of religion in the sixteenth and early seventeenth centuries and by the Enlightenment and French Revolution of the eighteenth century. Secularism is usually defined as the separation of religion and state, and is commonly understood as the Enlightenment solution to the bloody and irresolvable wars of religion that followed the Reformation. But Asad's account shows that European secularism presupposed a specific post-Reformation concept of 'religion' and a very specific post-Enlightenment concept of 'the state', as well as a notion of secular citizenship that owes much to the notion of individual agency developed in Protestant theology. 'The secular', he argues, 'is a concept that brings together certain behaviours, knowledges, and sensibilities in modern life' (2003: 25).

The particularities of modern secularism may be clarified if we return to the distinction made in Chapter 6 between orthodoxy and orthopraxy. Religious disputes in the Reformation and the wars of religion concerned questions of doctrinal *orthodoxy*—that is, correct religious beliefs. In European secularism, thus, *religion* is defined primarily in terms of the beliefs to which its adherents are committed. Similarly, the secular *state* is always understood to be the modern nation-state within a capitalist economy. It is from these understandings of *religion* and *state* that the Enlightenment concept of *citizenship* develops. Secular citizenship, Asad explains, is supposed to 'transcend the different identities built on class, gender, and religion, replacing conflicting perspectives by unifying experience. In a sense, this transcendent mediation *is* secularism' (5). Secular citizens are first and foremost individuals unencumbered by ties to other social groups who possess *within themselves* the motivation to formulate goals, the resources to initiate action to pursue those goals, and who are responsible for the

secularism The separation of religion and state, including a notion of secular citizenship that owes much to the notion of individual agency developed in Protestant theology.

consequences of their actions. This concept of agency, absolutely crucial to the successful functioning of democratic government and the capitalist market, was itself the product of Protestant theology. In the religious context, independent, self-motivating individuals were responsible before God; in their role as citizens of a liberal secular state, they are individually responsible before the law.

Thus, secularism as a political doctrine clearly developed as a response to specific religious, political, and economic developments in early modern Europe. Secularism depends, for example, on the notion that a 'worldly' domain of social life exists that is distinct from a realm in which religion holds sway. In Christian Europe, this domain was recognized when proponents of what would become 'science', such as Francis Bacon and Robert Boyle, successfully argued that the 'supernatural', spiritual realm of God was separate and distinct from the 'natural', material world of lifeless, inert matter (Keller 1997). This distinction between supernatural and natural worlds 'signals the construction of a secular space that begins to emerge in early modernity' (Asad 2003: 27). That secular space would be the ground to which the modern nation-state would lay claim. Religion and state remained entangled after the wars of religion, however, since 'religious freedom' was left in the hands of the states themselves. That is, citizens were to profess the faith of their princes, and if their princes changed allegiance, the allegiance of citizens was to follow. But in every state, this arrangement created religious minorities of 'dissenters' whose rights as citizens were regularly curtailed. Protest against these inequalities fuelled the secular democratic political theory of the Enlightenment, embodied in the 'Declaration of the Rights of Man and the Citizen' and secured by the French Revolution. Now religious affiliation was a matter of individual conscience and could not be imposed by the state. But at the time, as Asad notes, 'the decisive movements that helped to break the allegiance of church and state seem to have been religious . . . aimed at securing the freedom of Christ's church from the constraints of earthly power' (174). One consequence of this change 'was the eventual emergence of "minority rights". But this consequence contained a paradox. Religious minorities in a secular state were at once equal to other citizens [and] . . . unequal to the majority, requiring special protection' (174).

Secularism is 'not a simple matter of absence of "religion" in the public life of the modern nation-state. For even in modern secular countries the place of religion varies' (5–6), as we will see in Chapter 14. But Asad's analysis suggests that adaptation to life in a liberal secular state is likely to be difficult and painful for those whose religious commitments are rooted primarily in forms of religious *orthopraxy*—correct practice. 'Many traditions', he writes,

> attribute to the living human body the potential to be shaped (the power to shape itself) for good or ill. . . . The living body's materiality is regarded as an essential means for cultivating what such traditions define as virtuous conduct and for discouraging what they consider as vice. The role of fear and hope, of felicity and pain, is central to such practices . . . the more one exercises a virtue the easier it becomes . . . the more one gives into vice, the harder it is to act virtuously. (89–90)

Islamic religious traditions are rooted in such orthopraxy, and cultivation of correct practice depends upon one's embeddedness within a community of like-minded practitioners. When successful, such orthopraxy is understood to produce 'the virtue of faithfulness, [which is] an unquestioning habit of obedience'. Faithfulness is 'a disposition that has to be cultivated like any other and that links one to others who are faithful, through mutual trust and responsibility' (90). Religious orthopraxy of this kind can only be sustained by faithful practitioners whose entire way of life is informed by, and acts to reinforce, these unquestioning habits of obedience. If this is the case, then such forms of orthopraxy would appear to be incompatible with secularism.

> For many Muslim minorities (though by no means all) being Muslim is more than simply belonging to an individual faith whose private integrity needs to be publicly respected by the force of law and being able to participate in the public domain as equal citizens. It is more than the cultural identity recognized by the liberal democratic state. It is being able to live as autonomous individuals in a collective life that extends beyond national borders. (180)

World views represent comprehensive ideas about the structure of the world and the place of one's own group, or one's own self, within that world.

The ethnographic record offers a broad array of different world views, each testifying to the imaginative, meaning-making cultural capacity of humans. These models of the world, moreover, do not exist apart from everyday social practices; on the contrary, they are heavily implicated in our interactions with others. And when those interactions lead to crisis, humans respond by seeking ways to make the crisis appear meaningful and therefore manageable. We are meaning-making, meaning-using, meaning-dependent organisms, and nowhere is this clearer than when a meaningful way of life is under assault.

Key Terms

computer metaphor 160
key metaphors 159
magic 167
metaphor 156
metaphorical entailments 158
metaphorical predicate 156
metaphorical subject 156
metonymy 158
oracles 168
organic metaphor 160

priest 164
religion 161
revitalization 172
secularism 175
shaman 164
societal metaphor 159
syncretism 169
technological metaphor 160
witchcraft 167
world view 156

Chapter Summary

1. People attempting to account for their experiences make use of shared cultural assumptions about how the world works. The encompassing pictures of reality that result are called *world views*. Metaphors are valuable tools for constructing world views by directing attention to certain aspects of experience and downplaying or ignoring others.

2. The distinction between metonymy and metaphor may be said to correspond to the distinction between semantic linkages viewed as literal or true and semantic linkages viewed as hypothetical or false. If the relationships asserted in metaphors fit the rest of our experience, they may be converted into accepted relationships of metonymy.

3. As people create apt metaphors that are transformed into metonymic structures of their world view, they mark the resulting semantic domains by symbols. Symbols that sum up an entire semantic domain are called *summarizing symbols. Elaborat-*

ing symbols, by contrast, are analytic and allow people to sort out complex and undifferentiated feelings and ideas.

4. Differences in world views derive from differences in experience that people try to explain by means of metaphor. People use at least three kinds of metaphors as foundations for particular world views: societal metaphors, organic metaphors, and technological metaphors.

5. A single society may have members who subscribe to different world views. Knowledge, like power, is not evenly distributed throughout a society. More powerful individuals and groups often impose their preferred key metaphors on the rest of society. Those without power can resist this imposition by creating their own contrasting metaphors and constructing alternative world views.

6. Anthropological studies of religion tend to focus on the social institutions and meaningful processes with which it is associated. Followers of religions

can address personalized forces symbolically and expect them to respond. Maintaining contact with cosmic forces is very complex, and societies have complex social practices designed to ensure that this is done properly. Two important kinds of religious specialists are shamans and priests.

7. Many anthropologists have attempted to display the rich, coherent tapestries of symbols, rituals, and everyday practices that make up particular world views, and to demonstrate the high degree to which world views vary from one another. They have also studied the ways in which drastic changes in peoples' experiences lead them to create new meanings to explain the changes and to cope with them. This can be accomplished through the elaboration of the old system to fit changing times, conversion to a new world view, syncretism, revitalization, or resistance.

8. Some anthropologists have begun to study the relationship between religion and secularism as these developed following the European Enlightenment. Earlier generations of anthropologists took secularism for granted as the expected outcome of cultural evolution. Contemporary resistance to secular institutions by religious groups in Western and non-Western nation-states, however, has prompted a reconsideration of secularism. An important issue is the extent to which life in a liberal secular state is likely to be difficult and painful for those whose religious practices do not recognize any domain of life in which religious considerations do not hold sway.

Critical Thinking Questions

1. How do *summarizing symbols* and *elaborating symbols* differ? Can you find examples from a Canadian context?

2. Key metaphors that have served as the foundation of world views in different societies include societal, organic, and technological metaphors. Using a specific example of each type of key metaphor, what are their individual metaphorical entailments?

3. Can we define a distinctly Canadian metaphor? If we 'follow the metaphor' what will we find as the Canadian world view? And is this Canadian world view markedly different from the American world view? Elaborate.

4. Drastic changes in experience lead people to create new interpretations that will help them cope with the changes. How can metaphors, or the symbols that represent them, be used as instruments of power and control in such times?

5. How do the pronouncements of official interpreters of religious or political ideologies define the bounds of permissible behaviour?

6. Keesing observes that some people possess knowledge and control symbols to which others are denied access and different kinds of people know different things. How can such non-random distribution of knowledge affect key metaphors in a society?

Suggested Readings

Bowen, John. 2002. *Religions in Practice: An Approach to the Anthropology of Religion*, 2nd edn (Needham Heights, MA: Allyn & Bacon). *An up-to-date introduction of the anthropology of religion focusing on religious practice and interpretation, with a very wide range of case studies.*

Evans-Pritchard, E.E. 1976 [1937]. *Witchcraft, Oracles, and Magic among the Azande*, abr. edn (Oxford: Oxford University Press). *An immensely influential and very readable anthropological classic.*

Fernandez, James. 1982. *Bwiti: An Ethnography of the Religious Imagination in Africa* (Princeton: Princeton University Press). *A book that is tremendously rewarding and demanding. A major study of a religious movement and its associated rituals in context.*

Frazer, James George. 2006 [1922]. *The Golden Bough* (NuVision Publications, LLC), available at: <http://books.google.ca/books?hl=en&id=SmSqmPSFzw8C&dq=the+golden+bough&printsec=frontcover&source=web&ots=fGIz9BVTLv&sig=NOpWHLw0hXzwmNACejPKFQkqV2w&sa=X&oi=book_result&resnum=3&ct=result>. *An example of the 'armchair' anthropology of the nineteenth century, this book, nonetheless, developed the theoretical background used for the anthropological analysis of religion.*

Keesing, Roger. 1992. *Custom and Confrontation: The Kwaio Struggle for Cultural Autonomy* (New York: Columbia University Press). *Based on 30 years of research, Keesing's final book provides a clear, readable, and committed discussion of Kwaio resistance.*

Klass, Morton. 1995. *Ordered Universes: Approaches to the Anthropology of Religion* (Boulder, CO: Westview Press). *A brief introduction to the issues involved in the anthropological study of religion, with an emphasis on an operational definition of religion.*

Lambek, Michael. 2002. *A Reader in the Anthropology of Religion* (Malden, MA: Blackwell). *An excellent collection of classic and contemporary readings in the anthropology of religion.*

Malinowski, Bronislaw. 1948 [1926]. *Magic, Science, and Religion, and other Essays* (New York: Doubleday Anchor), excerpt available at: <http://www.adolphus.nl/xcrpts/xcmalinow. html>. *The essays in this book cover many aspects of Malinowski's fieldwork in the Trobriand Islands and subsequently in Africa. His lifelong interest in the ideational life of the people he worked with is evident in this book.*

Myerhoff, Barbara. 1974. *Peyote Hunt* (Ithaca, NY: Cornell University Press). *A remarkable account of the world view and sacred journey of the Huichol Indians of Mexico, a journey in which the author participated. This work is accessible, very well written, and theoretically sophisticated.*

Related Websites

Association for Computing Machinery (ACM): http://www.acm.org/ubiquity/interviews/v4i26_kelty.html

CBC Digital Archives: http://archives.cbc.ca/politics/rights_freedoms/clips/3302/

Human Rights Watch: http://www.hrw.org/en/news/2004/02/26/france-headscarf-ban-violates-religious-freedom

National Gallery of Canada: http://www.gallery.ca/exhibitions/exhibitions/Norval_Morrisseau/english/index.html

The Navajo Nation: http://www.navajo.org/

Semiotics for Beginners: http://www.aber.ac.uk/media/Documents/S4B/sem07.html

Shamans: http://www.angelfire.com/electronic/awakening101/not_shamans.html

Winnipeg Art Gallery: http://www.wag.mb.ca/htmlfiles/EXHIBITIONS/CURRENT_/angakkuq.asp

Wounded Knee Museum: http://www.woundedkneemuseum.org/main_menu.html

Part Three

The Organization of Material Life

Although the human capacity for culture permits us to imagine worlds of pure possibility, we remain material beings whose lives are firmly located within the material world. This world is organized from the familial to the local, and now, to the global. In Part Three we will see how various levels of organization impart meaning, change, and accommodation in a world where the local is more and more informed by the global. In the following chapters on social organization, economics, kinship, and various forms of alliances, we come to consider how we live in and give meaning to the material world. However, the significant feature is how these areas of material world 'management' are interlinked yet rooted in our individual and group identities, our world views of who we are as individuals and as a people. In considering these linkages and integrations, we come to a deeper appreciation of the anthropological concept of *holism*. For although we may study the 'bits and pieces' of a culture, in actuality we cannot make sense of these minutiae on their own. They become meaningful when situated within the wider context of a culture as a whole.

Chapter 8

Organization and Power

Learning Objectives

By the end of Chapter 8, you will be able to:

- consider that social organization refers to the patterning of human interdependence,
- question why the complexities of human social relations can never be reduced to a single cause,
- understand power as an independent entity that is exercised by both coercive and persuasive means,
- distinguish coercive domination from hegemony,

- appreciate the power of the imagination for investing the world with meaning,
- recognize how people bargain for reality,
- see how history can be a prototype for action, and
- think about the power of negotiating the meaning of history and tradition.

In 1992, following 12 years of civil war and two years of intensive negotiation, representatives of the government of El Salvador and of the Salvadoran guerrilla movement known as the Farabundo Martí National Liberation Front (FMLN) signed a peace accord brokered by the United Nations. The civil war had cost over 75,000 lives and had turned a million Salvadorans into refugees.

In late 1989, both the government and the guerrillas had realized that neither side was close to victory. How could so many years of fierce fighting end at the negotiator's table? The civil war in El Salvador was one of the bloodiest insurrections in twentieth-century Latin America. The roots of the conflict go back to the nineteenth century, when a tiny elite of Salvadoran landowners managed to monopolize 60 per cent of the land in order to raise coffee for export. The result was one of the most highly polarized class structures in all of Latin America. Ninety-eight per cent of the citizens were forced to survive on plots too small to support them, to live as tenant farmers or labourers on land they did not own, or to become landless migrants. When the coffee market crashed during the depression of the 1930s, the majority on the bottom rebelled against their exploitation, and the Salvadoran army crushed them in a brutal massacre known as *la matanza*, meaning 'the massacre'. (Ironically the name of a town in Cuba, Matanza is where the last of the Indigenous peoples of the island were killed by the colonists.)

During the Cold War between the United States and the Soviet Union that began in the late 1940s, even comparatively mild efforts to reform the system were repressed. After 1958, Washington interpreted challenges to the Salvadoran government as signs that El Salvador might be vulnerable to a Cuban-style communist revolution and viewed Salvadoran repression of reformers and rebels as a fight against the spread of communism, an explanation the Salvadoran government willingly endorsed. By the late 1970s, convinced that peaceful social change would never occur, political moderates in El Salvador swelled the ranks of five guerrilla groups that united to form the FMLN. The government response in the 1980s was as brutal as it had been in the 1930s and included a new *matanza* in the peasant village of El Mozote in which over 200 men, women, and children were massacred for their supposed collaboration with the guerrillas (Danner 1994).

By 1990, Salvadoran society was still polarized, but the prospect of endless war caused Salvadorans on both sides to rethink their positions. Members of the National Republican Alliance party (ARENA) had won national elections and seemed less hostile to democracy, whereas their elite supporters had become convinced that continued fighting would only hurt their business interests. The United States, which supported the government, was also tiring of the war and could no longer ignore highly publicized human rights violations committed by the Salvadoran government. Furthermore, the notion that supporting the Salvadoran government was stemming the spread of communism lost its force following the collapse of communism in eastern Europe. At the same time, Salvadoran guerrillas concluded that military victory offered no permanent guarantees when the Sandinistas in neighbouring Nicaragua, who had won their revolution a decade earlier, were voted out of office. Led by guerrilla leaders like Rubén Zamora, who had long favoured a negotiated settlement, the FMLN eventually agreed to meet their enemies at the peace table.

What drives people to take up arms against powerful, well-armed government forces? What convinces battle-hardened fighters, who believe that their cause is just, to lay down their arms and negotiate? It is not as though the outcome of either decision can be predicted with any certainty. Historian Peter Winn observes that the 1992 UN-brokered accord in El Salvador 'was a political compromise that allowed both sides to claim victory while leaving the future in doubt' (1992: 535). Not all Salvadorans supported the negotiated settlement, and sporadic violence directed against some guerrillas-turned-politicians after 1992 threatened the fragile peace it brought about. In May of 1994, however, the first national elections held since the signing of the peace accord were peaceful. The ARENA presidential candidate, Armando Calderon Sol, won two-thirds of the vote against the left coalition whose candidate, Rubén Zamora, won one-third of the vote. By late 1996, the FMLN was reflecting on the experiences of its first legislative session and planning on making alliances with other parties for future elections.

To be sure, the absence of violence at one moment of political crisis does not mean that violence will not be used later. The UN accord did not end economic and political inequality in El Salvador. And the damage caused by Hurricane Mitch in 1998 and a series of powerful earthquakes in 2001 have only added to these continuing woes. But the political settlement of 1992 has held (Figure 8.1), and the mere fact that violence is not automatic suggests that even the most thoroughgoing systems of political oppression have points of vulnerability and that the exercise of power, even in a highly stratified society, is more complicated than it may appear.

There are always choices to be made about how a society is to be organized or how that organization may be changed. Who has the power to make and enforce these choices? Where does that power come from? What is power? To answer these questions, this chapter focuses on social organization and the power that human beings have to produce, reproduce, or change that organization.

Figure 8.1 Supporters for the Farabundo Martí Liberation Front (FMLN), now a political party, attend a campaign rally in 2006.

Varieties of Social Organization

We have already described the variety of forms of human society in Chapter 3 and looked at some attempts by anthropologists to analyze that variation. Lewis Henry Morgan urged anthropologists to pay close attention to what he called the *arts of subsistence*. But he ran into difficulties when he observed significant differences in ways of life that were *not* connected with significant differences in ways of making a living. In Morgan's scheme, for example, both barbarians and civilized peoples relied on farming and herding, and in many cases their technologies were quite similar. What did distinguish them were differences in who did what, how it was done, and for whom. That is, they differed from one another in terms of social organization. **Social organization** refers to the patterning of human interdependence in a given society through the actions and decisions of its members.

The Search for the Laws of Social Organization

Even before the birth of the social sciences, Western thinkers searched for the inflexible laws of society that would explain differences in social organization in a non-arbitrary way. Biological determinists look for processes operating deeply within human beings forcing them to act in some ways and forbidding them to act in other ways. Other thinkers explain similarities and differences in social organization as adaptations to particular ecological conditions. Unilineal evolutionists like Lewis Henry Morgan and Karl Marx, in the nineteenth century, believed that the laws of society are rooted in the dynamics of history and work themselves out over time for each human group. Although Marxist analysis still has its adherents, the use of the unilineal evolutionary approach is now seen as somewhat counterproductive to understanding the diversity of historical realities manifest in all cultures.

The Arbitrariness of Social Organization

Perhaps the most important and controversial contribution of anthropology to the debate about laws of social organization is the argument that social relations in any society are ultimately arbitrary. This does not mean that societies are free to do or be whatever they like; rather, there is no way to reduce the complexities of human societies to a single underlying cause.

For example, the demonstrated adaptive flexibility of the human brain and body would be impossible if our behaviour were under rigid genetic control. Environmental determinism is implausible because, historically speaking, no society has ever been left on its own long enough for so-called environmental pressures to exert their forces without outside human interference. European colonial conquest vividly demonstrates how the most delicately balanced societal adaptation to a given environment can be totally disrupted, if not destroyed, when outsiders arrive with plans of their own and the power to enforce them. Yet even if societies could be isolated from one another and left to work out their own destinies in their own environments, it is unlikely that identical societies would develop in identical environments or in identical step-by-step sequences as Morgan argued. I.M. Lewis points out, for example, that the northern Somalis and the Boran Galla live next to each other in semi-arid scrubland (see Map 8.1) and even herd the same animals (1967: 166ff.). Despite these similarities, the Somalis and the Boran are quite different in social structure: the Boran engage in much less fighting and feuding than the Somalis; Boran families split up to take care of the animals, whereas the Somalis do not; and lineage organization is less significant among the Boran.

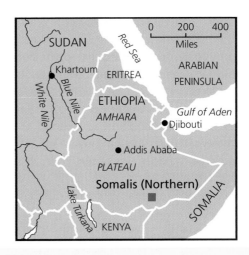

Map 8.1 Somalis (Northern)

The Power to Act

Human beings actively work to reshape the environments in which they live to suit themselves. Because the resources available in any environment can be used to sustain more than one way of life, however, human beings must choose which aspects of the material world to depend on. Human choice is equally important in the domain of social organization.

Some archaeologists suggest, for example, that population growth is a constant aspect of the human condition that determines forms of social organization. Marshall Sahlins (1976b: 13) reminds us, however, that population pressure determines nothing more than the number of people that can be supported when the environment is used in a particular way. Members of a society can respond to that pressure in various ways: they can try to get along on less, intensify food production by inventing new technology, reduce their numbers by inventing new social practices (infanticide or other forms of birth control), or migrate.

Indeed, the manner in which a group might choose to implement any of these options is equally undetermined by population pressure. Which members of the group will have to do with less? Which members

social organization The patterning of human interdependence in a given society through the actions and decisions of its members.

will control technological innovation? Who will be expected to migrate? And will the ultimate decision be imposed by force or voluntarily adopted? Population pressure alone cannot determine the answer to any of these questions.

The ability to choose implies the ability to transform a given situation. Thus, the ability to choose implies **power**, which may be understood broadly as 'transformative capacity' (Giddens 1979: 88). When the choice affects an entire social group, we speak of *social power*. Eric Wolf describes three different modes of social power:

(1) *interpersonal power* involves the ability of one individual to impose his or her will on another individual,

(2) *organizational power* highlights how individuals or social units can limit the actions of other individuals in particular social settings, and

(3) *structural power* organizes social settings themselves and controls the allocation of social labour (1994).

Uncovering the patterns of structural power requires paying attention to the large-scale and increasingly global division of labour among regions and social groups, the unequal relations between these regions and groups, and the way these relations are maintained or modified over time. The way in which clothing is manufactured now—in factories in Indonesia, El Salvador, Romania, or China for markets in Europe, the United States, and Japan—is an example of structural power. People are hired to work long hours for low wages in unpleasant conditions to make clothing that they cannot afford to buy, even if it were available for sale in the communities where they live.

The study of social power in human society is the domain of **political anthropology**. In a recent overview, Joan Vincent has argued that political anthropology continues to be vital because it involves a complex interplay between ethnographic fieldwork, political theory, and critical reflection on political theory (2002: 1). Vincent divides the history of political anthropology into three phases. The first phase, from 1851 to 1939, she considers the 'formative' era in which basic orientations and some of the earliest anthropological commentaries on political matters were produced. The second phase, from 1942 to about 1971, is the 'classic'

era in the field. It is most closely associated with the flourishing of British social anthropology rooted in structural-functionalist theory, and produced well-known works by such eminent figures as E.E. Evans-Pritchard, Max Gluckman, Fredrik Barth, and Edmund Leach. This period developed under conditions of the post-World War II British Empire through the period of decolonization in the 1950s and 1960s. Topics of investigation during this period were also the 'classic' topics of political anthropology: classifying pre-industrial political systems and attempting to reconstruct their evolution, displaying the characteristic features of different kinds of pre-industrial political systems and demonstrating how these functioned to produce political order, and studying local processes of political strategizing by individuals in non-Western societies (see, e.g., Lewellen 1983). Decolonization drew attention to emerging national level politics in new states and the effects of 'modernization' on the 'traditional' political structures that had formerly been the focus of anthropological investigation. But the turbulent politics of the 1960s and early 1970s called into question not only received social forms but also received forms of anthropological scholarship. Beginning in the 1960s, political anthropologists developed new ways of thinking about political issues and new theoretical orientations to guide them, inaugurating in the 1970s and 1980s a third phase in which political anthropology posed broader questions about power and inequality (Vincent 2002: 3). Under conditions of globalization, anthropologists interested in studying power have joined forces with scholars in other disciplines who share their concerns and have adopted ideas from influential political thinkers, such as Antonio Gramsci and Michel Foucault, to help them explain how power shapes the lives of those they describe in their ethnographies.

The cross-cultural study of social power reveals the paradox of the human condition. On one hand, open cultural creativity allows humans to imagine worlds of pure possibility; on the other hand, we all live in material circumstances that make many of those possibilities profoundly unrealistic. We can imagine many different ways to organize ourselves into groups, but, as Marx claims, the past weighs like a nightmare on the brain of the living—and the opportunity to remake social organization is ordinarily quite limited. Therefore, we will look closely at the ways in which the material circumstances of everyday life generate fields of power that channel and inhibit agency and cultural creativity—and how human beings can sometimes creatively exercise power and agency in order to evade or subvert those restrictions.

The Role of the State in Political Anthropology

In the beginning, political anthropologists were strongly influenced by other Western thinkers who had investigated the same topics. Many of these earlier thinkers had assumed that the state was the prototype of 'civilized' social power. The absence of a state, therefore, had to represent anarchy and disorder—what English philosopher Thomas Hobbes (1588–1679) called the 'war of all against all'. Although the state often perpetrated injustice or exploitation as a side effect of its monopoly of force, this could be viewed as a necessary price for social order.

Early anthropologists such as Lewis Henry Morgan, however, showed that kinship institutions organized social life in societies without states. A later generation of political anthropologists showed how different kinship institutions distribute power among their members and how non-kin institutions, such as secret societies, sometimes carry out important political roles. They were able to show repeatedly that societies without states can reach and carry out decisions affecting the entire social group by means of orderly traditional processes. This is reinforced by the analytical tool of a network–corporate/hierarchical–egalitarian matrix as discussed by Feinman et al. (2000). (Note Gary M. Feinman et al., *In Their Own Words*.) However, in Table 8.1 and Figure 8.2 we present how two ways of looking at power organization and application can be useful in avoiding unilineal approaches by moving into an analysis that applies to all societies regardless of their complexity. Thus this

expands on traditional evolutionary models through the recognition that an unequal distribution and ostentatious display of wealth does not always correlate tightly with the concentration of power or proscribed inheritance rules. It also recognizes a wide range of power-wielding strategies, which in themselves have marked organizational and integrative implications. (2000: 453)

Coercion: With and without Traditional State Institutions

The traditional Western prototype of power in human social relations is based on physical coercion. A typical 'natural' manifestation might be a fist fight. This prototype is an exceedingly pessimistic, even cynical, view of human nature. It suggests that co-operative social living is not natural for humans. Innate instincts lead us to pursue our own self-interest and to challenge one another for dominance. This is the power of **free agency** where political activity is competition between individual free agents over political control. When free agents make decisions, no larger groups, no historical obligations, and no collective beliefs can or ought to stand in their way. In this view, cultural evolution took a giant leap forward when our ancestors first realized that sticks and stones could be used as weapons, not only against non-human predators but especially against human enemies. In this view, human history is a chronicle of the production of better and better weapons. Thus the civilizations we are so proud of have been born and sustained in violence.

In the global systems of today, the consequences of power-seeking for territory and resources means that the violence of power-seeking states now impinges on the lives of those who traditionally lived in what were essentially stateless societies. (Note John Wagner, *In Their Own Words*.) It has been argued that in stateless societies control was sustained by the ability to punish those who deviated through other institutions. Such societies did not fear the king or the police but rather the ancestors, witchcraft, or the lineage elders. Power was still physical coercion, with co-operation resulting largely from the fear of punishment. However, when state and stateless coercion come into play in an atmosphere of ethnic, racial, religious, and economic power struggles, the Darfurs of the world emerge. Nothing can focus our understanding of this more than the

free agency The freedom of self-contained individuals to pursue their own interests above everything else and to challenge one another for dominance.

political anthropology The study of social power in human society.

power Transformative capacity; the ability to transform a given situation.

In Their Own Words

Political Hierarchies and Organizational Strategies in the Puebloan Southwest

Gary Feinman and his colleagues have been working on alternative ways to explain organization within societies. And although this example comes from researchers working in ancient Puebloan societies, it is informed by ethnography of the peoples of southwest US. Thus in attempting to find explanations for the past, they have given us insight for today.

The network strategy of political action is associated with heavily personalized or centralized forms of leadership. Wealth is concentrated in the hands of a few, who use their network of personal connections to enhance and expand their individualized power and authority. The network strategy broadly corresponds to descriptions of accumulators (Hayden 1990), aggrandizers (Clarke

and Blake 1994), strivers (Maschner 1995), and entrepreneurial elites (Hayden 1995), which are well entrenched in Western leader-centric ideas about power and individualism. In contrast, the corporate strategy bears certain similarities to Johnson's sequential hierarchies and Saitta's communal mode and adheres closely to descriptions of Renfrew's (1974) group-oriented chiefdoms and Lehman's (1969) concept of systemic power. In corporate organizations, economic resources are more dispersed, leadership is less personalized, and ostentatious displays and individual aggrandizement are less apt to be found. Instead, communal ritual, public construction, large co-operative labour tasks, shared power, social segments that are woven together through broad integrative ritual and ideological means, and suppressed economic differentiation are emphasized. . . . Corporate–network strategies of political action represent a continuous comparative dimension. We stress that these strategies are

Table 8.1 Tendencies of Network/Corporate Modes

Network	Corporate
Concentrated wealth	More even wealth distribution
Individual power	Shared power arrangements
Ostentatious consumption	More balanced accumulation
Prestige goods	Control of knowledge, cognitive codes
Patron/client factions	Corporate labour systems
Attached specialization	Emphasis on food production
Wealth finance	Staple finance
Princely burials	Monumental ritual spaces
Lineal kinship systems	Segmental organization
Power inherited through personal glorification	Power embedded in group association/affiliation
Ostentatious elite adornment	Symbols of office
Personal glorification	Broad concerns with fertility, rain

not an explicit substitute for the familiar dimensions of hierarchical complexity. Instead, corporate–network strategies are an orthogonal comparative dimension to that of hierarchies [see Figure 8.2]. In other words, corporate–network tendencies may be found in political organizations with little hierarchical development or in those characterized by complex bureaucracies with multiple levels of decision-making. . . . As a consequence, we propose that there are at least two important comparative dimensions (corporate–network and hierarchical complexity) relevant to explaining long-term change and variation.

Source: Feinman, Gary M., et al. 2000. 'Political Hierarchies and Organizational Strategies in the Puebloan Southwest', *American Antiquity* 65, 3 (July): 453–4, Table 1.

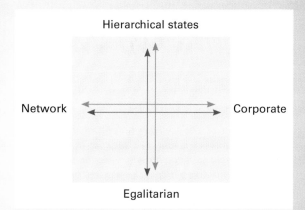

Figure 8.2 Two comparative dimensions for the examination of social organization.

personal accounts of those who have lived through such violence (see, e.g., Bashir 2008).

Domination and Hegemony

There is an ambiguity about power in human affairs. Do we submit to institutionalized power because we have been coerced and fear punishment? Or do we submit because we believe that the power structures in our society are legitimate given our understandings about the way the world works? So what leads people to accept coercion by others as legitimate (Figure 8.5)? A world view that justifies the social arrangements under which people live is sometimes called an **ideology**. Karl Marx argued that rulers consolidate their power by successfully persuading their subjects to accept a ruling-class ideology that portrays their domination as legitimate: that is, dominated groups suffer from *false consciousness*. However, the concept of false consciousness is problematic since it views people as passive and incapable of withstanding ideological indoctrination.

More promising was the approach taken by Antonio Gramsci (1971). Writing in the 1930s, Gramsci pointed out that coercive rule—what he called **domination**—is expensive and unstable. Rulers do better if they can persuade the dominated to accept their rule as legitimate, both by providing some genuine material benefits to their subjects and by using schools and other cultural institutions to disseminate an ideology justifying their rule. If they achieve all this—while also ensuring that none of these concessions seriously undermine their privileged position—they have established what Gramsci called **hegemony**. Hegemony is never absolute but always vulnerable to challenges: struggles may develop between rulers trying to justify their domination and subordinate groups who exercise agency by challenging 'official' ideologies and practices that devalue or exclude them. Hegemony may be threatened if subordinate groups maintain or develop alternative, or *counter-hegemonic*, cultural practices. Successful hegemony, by contrast, involves linking the understandings of dominant and subordinate groups into what appears to be mutual accommodation.

The concept of hegemony is attractive because it draws attention to the central role of cultural beliefs

domination Coercive rule.

hegemony Persuading subordinates to accept the ideology of the dominant group by mutual accommodations that nevertheless preserve the rulers' privileged position.

ideology A world view that justifies the social arrangements under which people live.

In Their Own Words

Water as Commodity in the Okanagan Valley of British Columbia

John Wagner of The University of British Columbia Okanagan works in PNG and the Okanagan in Canada. His research interest could be broadly described as environmental, but, more specifically, he focuses on water and the consequences of its commodification.

Conflict is a normal and inevitable part of life in all societies but wars involving the loss of thousands or even millions of human lives are not. Why do human beings go to war? Many recent and ongoing civil wars such as those in Rwanda, Sudan, or the former Yugoslavia are described in the media as either *ethnic* or *religious* in nature. In fact, the causes of war are always more complex than these simplistic explanations indicate and *competition over resources* is almost always a significant, if not a determining, factor. An increasing number of resource conflicts today are also global in scale, an outcome of the increasingly integrated nature of the world economy. Many analysts including Michael T. Klare (2001), author of *Resource Wars: The New Landscape of Global Conflict*, have proposed that water may well replace oil as the chief source of armed conflict in the twenty-first century.

The economic, military, and technological control of water has, in fact, been essential to the emergence of state-level human societies since they first occurred several thousands of years ago in Mesopotamia, Egypt, China, India, and the Americas. These *hydraulic societies*, as they are often called, typically acquired their economic strength through construction of large irrigation systems that facilitated greater agricultural productivity, food surpluses, and thus the capacity to maintain professional armies and bureaucracies.

As human demands on freshwater resources grow, and clean water in particular becomes an increasingly scarce resource, armed conflicts and other less immediately destructive forms of conflict are likely to become more frequent. Intensive commoditization of water under these conditions can worsen the divide between rich and poor, leaving the poor of many countries without sufficient access to clean water for even their most basic needs. Over the past few decades bottled water has become a billion dollar/year industry, water utility services are being privatized in both affluent and less developed nations, and bulk water transfers are occurring on a massive scale.

The Okanagan Valley of British Columbia illustrates another way in which water is being commoditized within today's global marketplace. Home originally to the *Syilx*, an Indigenous hunting/gathering society, this arid and mountainous region was settled by Europeans in the late nineteenth and early twentieth centuries. Irrigation systems were constructed by land development companies to carry water from upland reservoirs to subdivided lots on the valley bottom. Once irrigated, those lands were ideally suited to the intensive cultivation of tree fruits. A family-farm orchard industry thus emerged and became a dominant feature of Okanagan culture and landscape [Figure 8.3]. That economy is being displaced today, however, by an economy based on the region's growing popularity as a resort destination and retirement centre. Water as a commodity lies at the heart of this new form of development but in a very different sense than previously. Despite low levels of rainfall in the region, a series of large lakes stretch along the valley bottom, remnants of a glacier that covered the area 10,000 years ago. The lakes are valued for recreational purposes: for boating, scuba diving, and swimming; and waterfront and lakeview properties fetch a high premium in today's booming real estate market [Figure 8.4]. The orchard oases that surround the lakes at lower elevations enhance the aesthetic and economic value of lakeview properties, but, ironically, the orchard industry is in decline precisely because of this new form of commoditization. As a commodity, water has much higher value in the recreational tourism and housing industries than it does in the agricultural industry. As a consequence, land prices have escalated beyond the level at which they are affordable for agricultural purposes. In the Okanagan Valley, as elsewhere in Canada, conflict over water is not likely to result in armed conflict, but it is likely to result in long-term social and economic change and a sharper divide between water haves and have-nots.

Source: Wagner, John. 2009. 'Water as Commodity in the Okanagan Valley of British Columbia', guest editorial.

Figure 8.3 Historic apple box image from the Okanagan Valley.

Figure 8.4 In today's booming real estate market, the conversion of family-farm agricultural land in the Okanagan Valley to waterfront and lakeview properties for affluent hobby-farmers fetches a high premium.

and symbols in struggles to consolidate social organization and political control. Gramsci's contrast between domination (rule by coercive force) and hegemony (rule by persuasion) was central to his own analysis of the exercise of power (Crehan 2002: 153), and it has been helpful to anthropologists who study the exercise of power in societies with and without traditional state institutions. In analyses of non-state settings, anthropologists are able to avoid some of the tortuous and implausible accounts of power that depend on fear of punishment or false consciousness. In their place attention can be drawn to the verbal skills and personal charisma of leaders with limited coercive force at their disposal who can nonetheless persuade others to follow them by skilfully aligning shared meanings, values, and goals with a particular interpretation of events or proposed courses of action.

Consider, for example, witchcraft. The Azande believe that people use witchcraft only against those they envy. This seems highly plausible to people who experience daily friction with their neighbours. However, this belief makes it impossible to accuse Azande chiefs of using witchcraft against

Figure 8.5 Prior to colonial conquest by outsiders, Muslim emirs from northern Cameroon had coercive power.

commoners—because, as the Azande themselves ask, 'Why would chiefs envy their subjects?' In this way, hegemonic ideology deflects challenges that might be made against those in power.

Hegemonic ideology may justify social action in some individuals that would be condemned in others. Consider the example of the Beng of Ivory Coast (see Map 8.2) and the connection between witchcraft and kingship. There are two Beng regions, each ruled by a king and a queen, who come from a specific matrilineal clan. The king is said to be the owner of the Earth, which is the primary focus for worship. Violations of taboos concerning the Earth are believed to endanger the entire region and therefore must be dealt with by the king of the region who is said to have the power to foresee those natural calamities that are punishment for sins committed. In general, 'the king is responsible not only for the legal but also the moral and spiritual well-being of the people living in this region' (Gottlieb 1989: 249).

The legitimate power of the king is in direct contrast to the power of witches, who are considered to be utterly immoral. Using illegitimate power, working in secret, they kill and 'consume' their close matrilineal kin. Nevertheless, when a man becomes king, he has one year to bewitch three close relatives in his matriline. If he fails to do so, he will die. Rather than destroying his power, this exercise of illegitimate power legitimates his rule. By killing three close matrilineal relatives, the king shows his commitment to the greater public 'good'. He is demonstrating his control over, and independence from, the narrow interests of his own

kinship group. Operating on a plane beyond that of common morality the king, a man who has sacrificed part of himself, will rule the kingdom fairly. From the point of view of the Beng, including members of his own matrilineal clan, the king's actions are not only legitimate but also make it possible for him to rule.

As well, Gramsci was interested in how hegemony is (or is not) successfully established in state societies. In a post-colonial and globalizing world, where all people are presumed to be citizens of one nation-state or another, understanding the effects of decisions and actions of state authorities becomes crucial for making sense of many events on a local level. Anthropologists have often focused on the processes by which ruling groups in former colonies attempt to build national identities. For example, the British colony of Ceylon became independent in 1948, later changing its name to Sri Lanka. The residents of Ceylon belonged to two major populations: the Tamils, concentrated in the

EthnoProfile 8.1

Tamils

Region: South Asia

Nation: Northeast Sri Lanka although southeast India is populated as well

Language: The Tamils speak Tamil, one of the many (73) Dravidian languages

Population: 3,500,000 (several hundred thousand have fled the country) in Sri Lanka with a population in India in excess of 60 million

Environment: Low plains; tropical monsoon climate

Livelihood: Planation agriculture; clothing manufacture

Political organization: Modern nation-state; long-term armed dispute between the government and Tamil separatists

For more information: Trawick, Margaret. 2002. 'Reasons for Violence: A Preliminary Ethnographic Account of the LTTE', in *Conflict and Community in Contemporary Sri Lanka*, eds Siri Gamage and I.B. Watson (Thousand Oaks, CA: Sage); Indrapala, K. 2007. *The Evolution of Ethnic Identity: The Tamils of Sri Lanka* (Colombo: Vijitha Yapa)

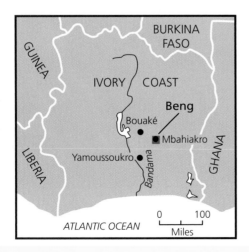

Map 8.2 Beng

northern part of the island, and the larger population of Sinhalese, who lived elsewhere (see Figure 8.6; see also EthnoProfile 8.1: Tamils). After independence, however, new Sinhalese rulers worked to forge a national identity rooted in their version of local history, which excluded the Tamils. In 1956, Sinhala was made the only official language; in the 1960s and 1970s, the Tamils' access to education was restricted and they were barred from the civil service and the army (Daniel 1997: 316). In 1979, when some Tamils began to agitate for a separate state of their own, the Sri Lankan government responded with severe and violent repression, sending many of the Tamils into exile and simulating the growth of the nationalist Liberation Tigers of Tamil Eelam (LTTE), which grew 'into one of the most dreaded militant organizations in the world' (323). Since the 1980s, thousands have died in ethnic violence although peace negotiations begun in 2001 suggest some hope for a conclusion to hostilities.

The exclusion of the Tamil residents from the Sri Lankan state has thus been pursued by means of violent coercion. But violence has also been used by the government against Sinhalese citizens who objected to state policies. Between 1987 and 1990, Indian troops were brought into Sri Lanka to supervise a peace agreement between Tamils and Sinhalese. These troops found themselves fighting the LTTE in the north, but they were also resisted violently in Sinhalese areas:

the rest of the country was convulsed by a wave of terror as young members of a group called the JVP (Janata Vimukti Peramuna, or People's Liberation Front) attacked the government not only for betraying the nation by allowing the Indian presence but also for its own unjust political and economic policies. . . . The government responded with a wave of terror, directed at young males in particular, which reached its climax with the capture and murder of the JVP leadership in late 1989. As far as we can tell, the government won the day by concentrated terror—killing so many young people, whether JVP activists or not, that the opposition ran out of resources and leadership. (Spencer 2000: 124–5)

Figure 8.6 Two Tamil women working in a Sri Lankan tea plantation.

After 1990, violence directed by the state against Sinhalese lessened, and in 1994, a new government promised to settle the ethnic conflict by peaceful means. But even before then, Sri Lankan government efforts at nation-building had not rested entirely on violence. Leaders also tried to exercise persuasive power to convince Sinhalese citizens that the state had their welfare in mind and was prepared to take steps to improve their lives. For example, anthropologist Michael Woost (1993) has described how the government of Sri Lanka has used a wide range of cultural media (television, radio, newspapers, the school system, public rituals, and even a lottery) to link the national identity to development. National development strategies are presented as attempts to restore Sinhalese village society to its former glory under the pre-colonial rule of Sinhalese kings. The ideal village, in this view, is engaged in rice-paddy cultivation carried out according to harmonious principles of Sinhala Buddhist doctrine. The villagers Woost knew could hardly escape this nationalist development discourse, but they did not resist it as an unwelcome imposition from the outside. On the contrary, all of them had incorporated development goals into their own values and had accepted that state-sponsored development would improve their lives. This might suggest that the state's attempt to establish hegemony had succeeded. But collaboration with the state was undermined as three different village factions selectively manipulated development discourse in their struggle to gain access to government resources. For example, nationalistic rhetoric connected development with 'improvement of the land'. One village faction claimed it had 'improved the land' first by building houses or planting tree crops. A second faction claimed it had 'improved the land' first by introducing paddy cultivation in the village. A third faction claimed it had 'improved the land' first since its members had intermarried with early settlers who had planted a large mango tree, a sign of permanent residence. Each faction made what the other factions interpreted as unjust claims, and each blamed the lack of village unity on the un-Buddhist greed of its opponents. These disagreements eventually led the state to withdraw its offer of resources, ultimately preventing the implementation of a village development scheme that all factions wanted!

Woost argues that the outcome of this political wrangling demonstrates the contradictory and fragile nature of the hegemonic process: paradoxically, the villagers' active appropriation of nationalist ideology undermined efforts to establish the very social order it was supposed to create. Gramsci himself was well aware that establishing successful hegemony in a nation-state was a difficult process whose outcome was not assured; indeed, it was the very inability of Italians to achieve this goal that stimulated many of his reflections on domination and hegemony. Gramsci's own description of a *colonial* state, emphasized by Indian historian Ranajit Guha as dominance *without* hegemony (Crehan 2002: 125), comes to mind when we consider the Sri Lankan state's repeated resort to violent coercion (e.g., the accusation that it withheld international aid to the Tamil region after the 2004 tsunami).

Bio-power and Governmentality

Is there a set of skills that would bring into existence—and sustain—a peaceful, prosperous nation-state in places like Sri Lanka? This question was addressed by French philosopher Michel Foucault, who looked at the way European thinkers from the end of the Middle Ages onward had posed (and attempted to answer) similar questions. Together with colleagues, he identified the emergence of a new form of power in the nineteenth century. He called this form of power *bio-power* or *bio-politics*, and it was preoccupied with bodies—both the bodies of citizens but also the social body itself (Hacking 1991: 183). As Gordon summarizes, bio-power refers to 'forms of power exercised over persons specifically insofar as they are thought of as living beings; a politics concerned with subjects as members of a *population* in which issues of individual sexual and reproductive conduct interconnect with issues of national policy and power' (1991: 4–5).

According to Foucault, a state based on bio-politics is very different from states in the Middle Ages based on the rule of law or administrative states of the fifteenth and sixteenth centuries based on regulation and discipline. A major concern in those states, especially, was making sure that the ruler maintained control of the state. Machiavelli's famous treatise *The Prince* is the best known of a series of handbooks explaining what an absolute ruler needed to do to maintain power. But by the seventeenth century, this approach to state rule was proving increasingly inadequate. Machiavelli's critics began to speak instead about *governing* a state, likening such government to the practices that preserved and perpetuated other social institutions, 'a household, souls, children, a province, a convent, a religious order, a family' (Foucault 1991: 90). The example of household management, at that time called *economy*, was a preferred model of government and debate concerned how to incorporate 'the correct manner of managing individuals, goods, and wealth within the family . . . into the management of the state' (92). Thus the concept of *political economy* was born (see also Chapter 9). But running the state in terms of political economy—managing citizens and their relations with goods and resources, with the territory, with customs, and coping with misfortunes such as famines, epidemics, and death—could not be undertaken effectively until rulers possessed adequate knowledge about such things. In the eighteenth century, such knowledge was produced by state bureaucracies that began to count and measure people and things subject to state control, giving birth to the discipline of *statistics*. Statistics suggested that populations had unique attributes, and rulers concluded that management of the population through the use of statistics was the proper task of government.

The art of governing appropriate to bio-politics—what Foucault calls **governmentality**—relies on tactics of measuring and intervening to prevent such calamities or to blunt their effects by using statistics to identify a series of possible and probable events, calculate their cost, and prescribe a form of intervention that would render such events tolerable, such that they would not undermine the security of the state. For example, such interventions include forms of insurance that protect economic activities in the event of a catastrophe that would otherwise curtail or destroy them (Gordon 1991: 18–20).

To an extent, governmentality is a form of power at work in the contemporary world and institutions that rely on it will be counting and measuring their members in a variety of ways (Figure 8.7). Although, as Ian Hacking insists, not all bureaucratic applications of such statistical knowledge are evil (1991: 183), the fact remains that providing the government (or any bureaucratic institution) with detailed vital statistics can be very threatening, especially in cases where people are concerned that the state does not have their best interests at heart. After all, states want to tax citizens, vaccinate and educate their children, restrict their activities to those that benefit the state, control their movements beyond (and sometimes within) state

Figure 8.7 Censuses are one way in which a state collects information in order to govern effectively.

borders, and otherwise manage what citizens do. In a globalizing world full of nation-states, anthropologists are increasingly likely to encounter both the pressures of governmentality and attempts to evade or manipulate governmentality in their fieldwork.

The Ambiguity of Power

The contrast between domination and hegemony and Foucault's explorations of the machinery of governmentality demonstrate that the exercise of power cannot be equated with physical violence alone. Moreover, the occasional violent outburst of one member of a foraging society against another is not the same thing as the organized violence of one army against another in a conflict between modern nation-states. No one

governmentality The art of governing appropriate to promoting the welfare of populations within a state.

can deny that human beings can be violent with one another. But is this the whole story?

'It is useful to accept the proposition that while men have in some sense always been equal (i.e., in that each always has some independent power), they have in another sense never been equal (in that some always have more power than others)' (Adams 1979: 409). Some political anthropologists who think of power as coercion have traditionally emphasized the universality of human inequality. Some have concentrated on power in societies without states, whereas others have taken a more Gramscian approach and reconsidered the nature of independent power available to individuals living in societies with states. The first focus involves looking at power as an independent entity. The second looks at the power of the human imagination to define the nature of social interactions and to persuade other actors to accept these definitions of the situation.

Power as an Independent Entity

In some of the traditionally stateless societies of Native North and South America, power is understood to be an entity existing in the universe independent of human beings. As such, it cannot be produced and accumulated through the interactions of human beings. Strictly speaking, power does not belong to human beings at all. At most, people can hope to *gain access* to power, usually through ritual means. From this point of view, 'control over resources is evidence of power rather than the source of power' (Colson 1977: 382). If people assume that power is part of the natural order of things yet independent of direct human control, certain consequences seem to follow.

- They may be able to tap into some of that power if they can discover how. Societies that see power as an independent entity usually know, through tradition, how to tap into it.
- Societies that see power as an independent force usually embed this understanding within a larger world view in which the universe consists of a balance of different forces. Individuals may seek to manipulate those natural forces to their own ends but only if they can do so without upsetting the universal balance.
- As a consequence, coercive means of tapping power sources are ruled out in such societies.

Violence threatens to undo the universal balance. Thus, in many Native North and South American societies, gentler measures were required. One approached power through prayer and supplication. The Native American vision quest (as among the Lakota) is a good example of such an approach: through fasting and self-induced suffering, individuals hoped to move the source of power to pity so that the source might then freely bestow on them the power they sought in the form of a vision or a song or a set of ritual formulas. Power freely bestowed would not disrupt the balance of the universe.

- In such a world view, violence and access to power are mutually contradictory. As our discussion of world view leads us to expect, cultures that conceive of cosmic power in this way also tend to view individual human beings as independent entities who cannot be coerced but must be supplicated. Individuals in such societies are not free agents in the Western sense—free of social ties and responsibilities—but they are free in the sense that they can refuse to be forced against their will to conform to someone else's wishes. They exercise the power of **resistance**. The power of individuals to resist affects how stateless societies arrive at decisions.
- The consequence of viewing power as an independent entity is an emphasis on **consensus** as the appropriate means to decide issues affecting the group. In seeking consensus, proponents of a particular course of action must use **persuasion** rather than coercion to get other members of the group to support their cause. They resort to verbal argument, not physical intimidation. As a result, the most respected members of stateless societies, those sometimes given the title 'chief' by outsiders, are persuasive speakers, great orators. Indeed, as Pierre Clastres (1977) points out, such respected individuals are often referred to by other members of their society as 'those who speak for us'. The shamans (or *mara'akate*) of the Huichol Indians of northern Mexico serve this function. By virtue of their verbal ability, they see themselves (and are seen by their

fellows) as especially well suited to negotiate for all the Huichol with outsiders, especially representatives of the Mexican state.

Clastres suggests that stateless forms of social organization are strongly resistant to the emergence of hierarchy (1977: 35). Indeed, he argues that members of stateless societies struggle to prevent such authority from emerging. They sense that the rise of state power spells the end of individual autonomy and disrupts beyond repair the harmonious balance between human beings and the forces of the wider world. Richard Lee agrees, arguing that band societies, and some farmers and herders, have found ways to limit

> the accumulation of wealth and power. Such societies operate within the confines of a metaphorical ceiling and floor: a ceiling above which one may not accumulate wealth and a floor below which one may not sink. These limits . . . are maintained by powerful social mechanisms known as levelling devices. . . . Such societies therefore have social and political resources of their own and are not just sitting ducks waiting to adopt the first hierarchical model that comes along. (1992a: 39–40)

Levelling devices, such as institutionalized sharing, are discussed in Chapter 9.

The Power of the Imagination

Gramsci's discussion of the interplay between coercion and persuasion and Foucault's discussions of governmentality and bio-politics offer more nuanced understandings of the different levels on which social power can operate. Many anthropologists feel that a discussion of social power is incomplete if it does not also pay attention to the way individuals make sense of and use the constraints and opportunities for action open to them, however limited they may be.

All people have the power to interpret their experiences, regardless of the complexity of a social system and whether or not the power of coercion is monopolized by a central authority. People retain this power even under totalitarian dictatorship. It is notoriously difficult to erase the sense of self from human consciousness, even in the face of degradation and imminent death as can be seen in the art and writings of inmates of the concentration camps of Nazi Germany.

Alverson argues that 'a belief in one's power to invest the world with meaning (the "will to believe") and a belief in the adequacy of one's knowledge for understanding and acting on personal experience are essential features of all human self-identity' (1978: 7). This is the power to resist outside influences, to reject alternative choices that others want to impose. This does not mean that individuals work out the meanings of their experiences in isolation. All human activities, including the growth and development of self-identity, take place in a social, cultural, and historical context. Still each individual retains the power to interpret that context from his or her unique vantage point, in terms of his or her unique experiences. Cynics might argue that the power of the imagination must, in the real world, be restricted to private opinions; the mind can resist, but the body must conform. From this perspective, for example, the actions of a miner who labours underground daily for a meagre wage are clear-cut and unmistakable: he works for money to buy food for his family. However, ethnographic data suggest that this may not be the whole story.

The prototype of the downtrodden and exploited human being was the industrial labourer, the sufferer of the dislocations of the Industrial Revolution. Social scientists in the early twentieth century attempted to describe these changes. Emile Durkheim coined the term **anomie** to refer to the pervasive feelings of rootlessness and normlessness that people were experiencing. Karl Marx used the term **alienation** to describe the deep separation workers seemed to experience between their innermost sense of identity and the labour they were forced to do in order to earn enough money to live.

Do industrial workers in what used to be called the Third World similarly suffer from anomie and alienation? The issue has been hotly debated. Some argue

---

alienation A term used by Karl Marx to describe the deep separation that workers seemed to experience between their innermost sense of identity and the labour they were forced to perform in order to earn enough money to live.

anomie A pervasive sense of rootlessness and normlessness in a society.

consensus An agreement to which all parties collectively give their assent.

persuasion Power based on verbal argument.

resistance The power to refuse being forced against one's will to conform to someone else's wishes.

that their condition should be far worse than that of Western workers because the context of non-Western industrialization is much more backward. This has been called the *scars of bondage* thesis. This thesis predicts that the more complete the political domination and exploitation of a people, the more deeply they will be scarred, brutalized, and dehumanized by the experience. For people suffering the twin exploitations of colonialism and industrialism, the outcome could only be the most bitter, unrelieved tragedy.

June Nash (1979), working among Bolivian tin miners (see Map 8.4), has made interesting observations about the power of human imagination to transform experiences by investing them with meaning (Figure 8.8). The labour force in Bolivian mines has been drawn from local Indigenous populations who have been effectively separated from their involvement in traditional Indigenous communities. Nonetheless, the tin miners of Bolivia have been able to combine elements of the dominant industrial culture with elements drawn from Indigenous traditions. Bolivian miners have created new, cohesive cultural patterns; far from being dissonant and alienating, the miners' culture provides an intact sense of self and belonging and an ability to celebrate life because it is viewed as meaningful.

How can we explain, in the lives of Bolivian miners, the combination of what appears to be both genuine suffering and genuine celebration? Exploitation certainly leaves its mark on its victims: poor health,

Figure 8.8 The offerings of cigarettes and coca leaves placed in front of a statue of 'El Diablo', a guardian of a government-run Bolivian tin mine complex, is an example of how the Bolivian miners have created new, cohesive cultural patterns. The roots of this custom dates from much earlier Inca times.

high infant mortality, intra-familial abuse, shattered hopes. Yet many Bolivian miners have not been irrevocably brutalized by these experiences. Their powers to invest their experiences with meaning remain intact, despite crushing conditions of exploitation. Nash notes, 'My experience living in mining communities taught me more than anything else, how a people totally involved in the most exploitative, dehumanizing form of industrialization managed to resist alienation' (1979: 319–20). She argues that the events people experience are less important than how they interpret those events. Nash concludes that the ethnocentrism of Western observers has kept them from recognizing the creative, revolutionary potential embodied in hybrid cultures like that of the Bolivian tin miners.

Bargaining for Reality

The power that people have to invest their experiences with meanings of their own choosing suggests that a ruler's power of coercion is limited, which was Gramsci's key insight. Thought alone may be unable to alter the material circumstances of coercion, yet it has the power to transform the meaning of those material circumstances.

Any hegemonic establishment runs the risk that the dominated may create new, plausible accounts of their experiences of domination. Political scientist

Map 8.4 Bolivian Tin Miners

James Scott (1990) refers to these unofficial accounts as 'hidden transcripts'. Occasionally, those who are dominated may be able to organize themselves socially in order to transform their hidden transcripts into a counter-hegemonic discourse aimed at discrediting the political establishment. Those who are dominated may be able to persuade some or all of those around them that their counter-hegemonic interpretation of social experience is better or truer than the hegemonic discourse of the current rulers. Such challenges to incumbent political power are frequently too strong to be ignored and too widespread to be simply obliterated by force. When coercion no longer works, what remains is a struggle between alternative accounts of experience.

Anthropologist Lawrence Rosen worked in the Moroccan city of Sefrou (see Map 8.5). As he listened to his informants discussing and defining their relationships with each other, he realized that none of the traditional concepts they used could be said to have a fixed meaning. Any definition offered by one person would be verbally challenged by another. Rosen concluded that political and social life in Sefrou could not be understood unless one accepted that, for his informants, negotiation was the norm. Rosen (1984) calls this socio-political negotiation *bargaining for reality*.

The reality bargained for is not an impersonal, unchangeable set of truths about the world. Moroccans aim to persuade one another to accept alternative ways of understanding a particular situation. Persuasive accounts must be *coherent*: they must explain events and processes central to the experiences of those to whom they are addressed, they must be expressed in language that other members of society can understand, and they must hang together in a way that is not blatantly contradictory.

The power relationship between men and women in Sefrou illustrates this process. Men view women as less intelligent, less self-controlled, and less altruistic, and they expect women to obey them. Although women often assent to the male account of this relationship, they do not accept it in all circumstances. Women have developed an alternative account that explains elements in their lives that the male account either overlooks or interprets differently.

Women in Sefrou depend on men—first their fathers, later their husbands, and perhaps eventually their sons—for material support. But marriages are fragile,

Map 8.5 Sefrou

and women often have to rely on males of their patriline when their husbands divorce them (a wife cannot legally divorce her husband). Consequently, security for women depends on strengthening their positions within their families. In particular, women attempt to influence marriage negotiations because marriage automatically rearranges social relationships within the family. Women are eager to protect themselves and their daughters from oppressive demands by a husband and his kin. They view their actions as sensible and compassionate, not as misplaced interference. Nor do they accept the view that men are intellectually and morally superior to women. Indeed, they often view men as self-centred and childish.

In effect, Moroccan men and women live side by side in different worlds. They share experiences but interpret those experiences differently. Because neither gender has much direct contact with the other during everyday life, these different interpretations of experience do not constantly come into conflict. But marriage negotiations inevitably bring these different perspectives into contention. The outcome is reality bargaining, as several different actors attempt to make their definitions of the situation prevail.

Rosen describes one marriage negotiation that he encountered in Sefrou (1984: 40–7). A girl refused to marry the suitor her family chose, and her continued resistance had disrupted the harmony of her father's household. Rosen visited the household in the company of a respected male informant who was an old friend of the family. During their visit, the family friend and the girl's mother discussed the betrothal and the girl's refusal to consent to it. Both parties interpreted the girl's refusal differently. The family friend described the girl's behaviour as a typical case of female selfishness and immorality. What other reason could there be for her refusal to obey her father, as dutiful daughters should? He spoke harshly of her and repeatedly asserted that when her father returned they would force her to come to her senses and make the marriage. Her mother never openly contradicted these assertions. All the while, however, she quietly and insistently continued to make counter-assertions of her own. She reported her daughter's reason for rejecting the match: her intended husband came from a distant city. If she married him she would have to leave her family behind and go live among strangers. It was not that she objected to an arranged marriage; rather, she did not want to marry this particular man because to do so would take her so far away from home. From a woman's perspective, the daughter's anxieties were entirely rational given the powerlessness and isolation that she would endure as a result of the marriage.

As it turned out, after a year and a half of successful resistance, the young girl was eventually persuaded to marry the suitor. She only changed her mind when she became convinced that consenting to the marriage was an economically sound move, not a submission to patriarchal authority. So women may agree with the male position in general terms and yet successfully

Map 8.6 Sedaka Village

dispute its relevance in a particular situation. Men may get women to comply with their wishes, and yet the women's reasons for doing so may have nothing to do with the reasons men offer to justify their demands.

James Scott carried out two years of ethnographic research among peasant rice farmers in a Malaysian village called Sedaka (a pseudonym) (see Map 8.6). Poor Malaysian peasants are at the bottom of a social hierarchy, dominated locally by rich farmers and nationally by a powerful state apparatus. These peasants are not kept in line by some form of state-sponsored terrorism; rather, the context of their lives is shaped by what Scott calls *routine repression*: 'occasional arrests, warnings, diligent police work, legal restrictions, and an Internal Security Act that allows for indefinite preventive detention and proscribes much political activity' (1985: 274).

Scott wanted to find out how this highly restrictive environment affected political relations between members of dominant and subordinate classes in the village. He quickly realized that the poor peasants of Sedaka were not about to rise up against their oppressors. But this was not because they accepted their poverty and low status as natural and proper. One reason was that organized overt defence of their interests would have been difficult given the conflicting loyalties generated by local economic, political, and kinship ties. Another reason was that the peasants knew that overt political action in the context of routine repression would be foolhardy. And they had to feed their families. Their solution was to engage in what Scott calls *everyday forms of peasant resistance*: this included 'foot dragging, dissimulation, desertion, false compliance, pilfering, feigned ignorance, slander, arson, sabotage, and so forth' (xvi). These actions may have done little to alter the peasants' situation in the short run; however, Scott argues, in the long run they may have been more effective than overt rebellion in undercutting state repression.

What we find in everyday forms of peasant resistance are indirect attempts to challenge local hegemony. Scott says: 'The struggle between rich and poor in Sedaka is not merely a struggle over work, property rights, grain, and cash. It is also a struggle over the appropriation of symbols, a struggle over how the past and present shall be understood and labelled, a struggle to identify causes and assess blame' (xvii).

When peasants criticize rich landowners or rich landowners find fault with peasants, the parties involved are not just venting emotion. According to Scott, each side is simultaneously constructing a world view. Rich and poor alike are offering 'a critique of things as they are as well as a vision of things as they should be. . . . [They are writing] a kind of social text on the subject of human decency' (23).

Scott describes the dynamics of this struggle during the introduction of mechanized rice harvesting in Sedaka (Figure 8.9). Traditionally, rice harvesting was manual labour. In the late 1970s, however, the introduction of combine harvesters eliminated the rich farmers' need for hired labour, a loss that dealt poor families a severe economic blow. When the rich and poor talked about the harvesters, each side offered a different account of their effect on economic life in the village.

Scott tells us that both sides agreed that using the machines hurt the poor and helped the rich. When each side was asked whether the benefits of the machines outweighed their costs, however, consensus evaporated. The poor offered practical reasons against the use of combine harvesters: they claimed that the heavy machines were inefficient and that their operation destroyed rice paddies. They also offered moral reasons: they accused the rich of being 'stingy', of ignoring the traditional obligation of rich people to help the poor by providing them with work and charity. The rich denied both the practical and the moral objections of the poor. They insisted that using harvesters increased their yield. They accused the poor people of bad faith. They claimed that the poor suffered because they were bad farmers or lazy, and they attributed their own success to hard work and prudent farm management.

Rich rice farmers would never have been able to begin using combine harvesters without the outside assistance of both the national government and the business groups who rented the machines to them at harvest time. Poor peasants were aware of this, yet they directed their critique at the local farmers and

Figure 8.9 Until recently, rice harvesting in rural Malaysia was manual labour that regularly allowed poor peasants to earn cash and receive grain from their employers as a traditional form of charitable gift.

In Their Own Words

Canaries in the Mines of Citizenship: Indian Women in Canada

Joyce Green, a political scientist from The University of Regina, discusses the issues of citizenship and membership for First Nations women in Canada.

So what is an excluded Indian woman to do? The standard responses to citizen dissatisfaction with an aspect of the political regime include legal challenge, political activism, partisan activity, and building new social consensus. Indian women concerned about citizenship and membership issues have tried all of these but have not yet found the political leverage to have their concerns ranked high by predominantly white or Aboriginal male politicians, mainstream political parties, and colonial courts.

Law, democratic mainstream politics, and Indigenous politics seem unable or unwilling to contend with the issues raised by this problematic minority. Denied band membership, meaningful exercise of Aboriginal and treaty rights, and, perhaps most importantly, denied the right to practise identity by living and raising children in their own communities, the affected women and their children are exiled to the dominant society where, thanks to racism, they are seen forever as 'Indian'.

Nor will the state apply its emerging view of rights in a way that works to the advantage of these women. Rather, the federal government retreats behind its self-serving rhetoric of respect for 'self' government, washing its hands of any responsibility to guarantee these women's rights. Meanwhile, Indian Act band governments claim to be governments of First Nations, practising a constitutionally recognized Aboriginal and treaty right which includes control of membership or citizenship.

The *Sawridge* pleadings suggest some of these invoke colonial sexist practices as constitutionally protected 'tradition'. In sum, neither the state nor band governments defended these women with rights discourse, though both use it when it suits them. Neither has affirmed their value as human resources to society. Neither guarantees equality of citizenship by taking the steps needed to permit these women to live in a way that honours their identity and values their participation.

Democracy fails these women. Premised on majority rule, and on the theoretical cultural-neutral and gender-neutral citizen and politician, it is unable to ensure their representation in a political system implicitly premised on their sex and ethnic inferiority. Privileging mythical notions of undifferentiated equality, the ideology grounding Canadian democracy is inherently hostile to affirming rights-bearing specificity, especially where Aboriginal rights may result in constitutional and public policy measures that benefit Aboriginal people in ways not available to non-Aboriginal Canadians; that is, where differing kinds of citizenship result. This hostility has been evident in non-Aboriginal opposition to treaty fishing rights and to land and governance rights sustained by the Supreme Court of Canada.

To date, Canadian law has failed these women, even with rights discourse foregrounded. The *Lavell* case of 1974, eight years prior to the entrenchment of the Canadian Charter of Rights and Freedoms, is infamous for dignifying sex discrimination as non-discrimination in law. The *Sawridge* case 21 years later sought to define Indian women's sexual equality rights out of existence. Lawmakers fail to see that any law affirming these women's rights must affirm them in their specificity as Indigenous women, part of colonized societies, to whom the state is historically an oppressor and only potentially an ally. While the Charter protections from discrimination on the basis of gender have motivated the federal government to eliminate the most egregious forms of legislative discrimination against Indian women, the measures are inadequate and stem from incomplete analyses that ignore the centrality to these women of their Aboriginal identities and rights, and their right to be fully acknowledged as part of their communities.

Yet citizenship may have the capacity to transcend the contradictions and pitfalls of decolonization in conditions defined by liberal and neo-liberal ideology and by the *realpolitik* of contemporary Canada. Even though Aboriginal rights constitute a different kind of right belonging only to members of Aboriginal nations, in addition to other citizenship rights enjoyed by all citizens of Canada, in the final analysis, people are not so incommensurable as to not share fundamental and inalienable human rights. All governments are impositions of authority upon those they govern, no matter how democratic or culturally authentic their processes. Authority must be held accountable for protecting the conditions fundamental to our humanity. In addition to human rights, which may be expressed and practised in different culturally specific fashions, Aboriginal rights must also be protected for all Aboriginal women and men.

Source: Green, Joyce. 2001. 'Canaries in the Mines of Citizenship: Indian Women in Canada', *Canadian Journal of Political Science* 34, 4: 736–8.

not at the government or outside business organizations. After all, the rich farmers 'are a part of the community and therefore *ought* not to be indifferent to the consequences of their acts for their neighbours' (161). The stinginess of the rich did not just bring economic loss. It also attacked the social identity of the poor, who vigorously resisted being turned into non-persons. The poor insisted on being accorded the 'minimal cultural decencies in this small community' (xviii). The only weapon they controlled in this struggle was their ability, by word and deed, to undercut the prestige and reputation of the rich.

This strategy worked in Sedaka because rich local farmers were not ready to abandon the traditional morality that had regulated relations between rich and poor. They had not yet become so Westernized that they no longer cared what other villagers thought of them. A shrewd campaign of character assassination may have caused at least some of the rich to hesitate before ignoring their traditional obligations. The improvement might have been minor, strictly in economic terms, but it would have been major in terms of the ability of the poor to defend their claims to citizenship in the local community. In addition, the wider political arena could always change in the future. Scott was convinced that many of the poor peasants he knew might well engage in open, active rebellion if routine repression disappeared.

When disputes are settled in this manner, experience is transformed. As Scott observes:

> The key symbols animating class relations in Sedaka—generosity, stinginess, arrogance, humility, help, assistance, wealth, and poverty—do not constitute a set of given rules or principles that actors simply follow. They are instead the normative raw material that is created, maintained, changed, and above all manipulated by daily human activity. (309)

In a similar way, Rosen refers to central Moroccan values such as intelligence, self-control, and generosity as **essentially negotiable concepts**: 'There is an element of uncertainty inherent in these terms such that their application to any situation by one person can be contested by another' (1984: 43). Bargaining for reality involves just this sort of manoeuvre: 'What is negotiable, then, is less one's view of reality as such than its scope, its impact, and its differential importance' (47).

World views articulated in language by different social subgroups aim 'not just to convince but to control; better stated, they aim to control by convincing' (Scott 1985: 23).

The issues arising from the post-colonial environment also extend into basic definitions and negotiations of rights of citizenship and who controls these definitions and negotiations. This is of concern to anthropologists. However, perhaps the best analysis can be found in the work of scholars other than anthropologists. (Note Joyce Green, *In Their Own Words*.) The rights of those designated by a society as *the least amongst us* are essentially the only rights existing under law for all. What can be granted by authorities to the 'least' can become the reality for the 'most' in any regime of subjugation. This moves beyond contested world views to contested human rights.

History as a Prototype of and for Political Action

When individual actors within a particular cultural and situational context attempt to impose their definition of the situation on those with whom they interact, they draw on elements of a shared tradition of values and beliefs. This shared tradition, however, does not consist of values and beliefs divorced from experience and history. To some degree, people in all cultures continue to reshape—to bargain over—not merely which part of an agreed-on tradition is relevant in a particular situation but also which version of the tradition ought to be agreed on. The combinations they come up with are sometimes surprising.

Consider the development of rural justice groups called *rondas campesinas* ('peasants who make the rounds') in the northern Peruvian highlands (see Map 8.7) in the mid-1970s. Rondas consist of armed groups of peasants who walk the paths around their hamlets at night keeping an eye out for animal rustlers (Figure 8.10). The rondas began in one small hamlet in the northern Peruvian department of Cajamarca in 1976. During the 1980s, they spread hundreds of

essentially negotiable concepts Culturally recognized concepts that evoke a wide range of meanings and whose relevance in any particular context must be negotiated.

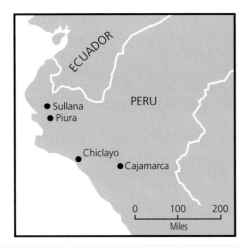

Map 8.7 Northern Peruvian Highlands

miles within Cajamarca and surrounding departments. At the same time, their functions were radically expanded: they became an alternative justice system with open peasant assemblies to resolve problems ranging from wife-beating to land disputes. By the early 1990s, rondas operated in 3,400 hamlets in the northern Peruvian Andes.

Olin Starn (1992) notes that at least five forces spurred campesinas to establish their alternative justice system.

Figure 8.10 *Rondas campesinas* have become an alternative justice system in highland Peru. Here, a group of ronderos pose with a stolen donkey recovered from rustlers in 1986.

(1) The theft of animals shot up dramatically with the onset of the Peruvian economic crisis of the mid-1970s. The rise in theft was extremely serious for the poor farmers of the northern Andes, most of whom had small flocks and earned less than $2,000 per year.

(2) Peasants got no relief from the official justice system. As the economy worsened, many government authorities tried to enlarge their shrinking salaries through bribery, kickbacks, and extortion, and poorer peasants were increasingly unable to pay.

(3) The government had only a weak presence in the mountains, providing an opportunity for peasants to develop a new form of community organization.

(4) Country people in northern Peru value toughness and bravery in the face of violence and were able to channel their aggressiveness into the service of order and discipline in the rondas.

(5) Local organizers had outside supporters. In the province where the rondas began, these were activists from the Maoist Red Homeland party. In a neighbouring province, peasant catechists trained in liberation theology became early ronda leaders and were defended by priests and nuns as well as the local bishop.

During the 1980s, rondas were transformed from vigilante groups to dispute-resolution groups. Compared to the expensive, time-consuming, humiliating, and ineffective official justice system, the ronda was inexpensive, efficient, effective, and local. By the late 1980s, rustling was virtually eliminated and rondas in some communities were adjudicating over 100 cases a month. The rondas also involve the elaboration of political identity and culture. Songs and poems celebrate the rondas and festivals commemorate their anniversaries.

To create the rondas, peasants drew on national and local cultural patterns. Peasants had served on patrols to stop thieves on haciendas before the haciendas were broken up in the late 1960s. Men in the hamlets who had served in the Peruvian military incorporated military strategies and forms into the rondas. The peasants also employed local patterns, keeping the ronda patrols under the collective authority of the community.

Likewise, when the rondas took on adjudication roles, they adopted some forms from the state bureaucracy, using a table like a judge's bench, rubber stamps, a recording secretary with notarized minutes, and so on. But the openness of the ronda system is very different from the state bureaucracy, for the final decision rests on the ronda president's evaluation of the response of the people attending. Assemblies of the ronda are often held outside, where the event occurred, such as a farmyard. All attending have detailed knowledge of some kind that may be brought into play, and everyone jumps in to attempt to settle the dispute.

But the rondas, for all their effective innovation, are sometimes still enmeshed in old practices.

- They are connected with political parties in Peru, and squabbles involving the parties have weakened the ronda movement.
- Although they have challenged the government's monopoly on the administration of justice, they are not working to overthrow the state; rather, they see themselves as the genuine upholders of the law and the Peruvian constitution.
- Although constant rotation in many communities discourages permanent leaders, in some rondas the leaders stay on for many years, hoard power, and begin to show favouritism.
- The rondas perpetuate the problems of patriarchy. Many peasant women march in ronda protests, and in some rondas the women oversee the patrol scheduling. The rondas have given women a place to censure wife-beating, and a number of offenders have received a stern warning or whipping. Nevertheless, only men patrol; female participation in assemblies is limited and mostly passive, and women are never ronda officers.
- There is the problem of violence. The ronderos have learned some of the techniques of the Peruvian police, including whipping with barbed wire or hanging accused rustlers by their arms. But it is important to note that the rondas began as a means of creating peace and order in a violent environment. As rustling has been brought under control, cases of harsh physical treatment have diminished. The leaders of rondas have worked within their communities to prevent the use of excessive force.

Starn concludes that, on the whole, the rondas have given Peruvian peasants the vision of an alternative modernity and have renewed among them a powerful sense of independent identity.

Negotiating the Meaning of History

The meanings of the central symbols of any cultural tradition are essentially negotiable. That is, each symbol evokes a wide range of meanings among those who accept it. But what that symbol means in any particular situation, as well as the appropriateness of applying that symbol to the situation, is never obvious. Such matters are cultural dilemmas that people struggle to resolve. Consider the Moroccan and Peruvian examples and the power to invest experience with one's own meanings. This is a very real power. And yet many anthropologists are divided about the effectiveness of resistance as a solution to the problems of those at the very bottom of society. While there is much ethnographic evidence documenting the ability of some individuals and groups to assert themselves and their view of the world in the face of tremendous oppression, there is also much evidence that other individuals and groups have been destroyed by such oppression. Political anthropologist John Gledhill observes that it would be 'dangerous to be over-optimistic. "Counter-hegemonic" movements exist but much of the world's population is not participating in them' (1994: 198). He is particularly skeptical about the power of everyday forms of peasant resistance: the ability of such practices to undermine the local elite, he warns, may 'merely provide the scenario for the replacement of one elite by another, more effective, dominant group' (92). At the beginning of the twenty-first century, with no utopian solutions in sight, the most that anthropologists may be able to do is agree with historian A.R. Tawney, who wrote about the agrarian disturbances in sixteenth-century England: 'Such movements are a proof of blood and sinew and of a high and gallant spirit. . . . Happy the nation whose people has not forgotten how to rebel' (quoted in Wallerstein 1974: 357).

Key Terms

alienation 197
anomie 197
consensus 196
domination 189
essentially negotiable concepts 202
free agency 187
governmentality 195

hegemony 189
ideology 189
persuasion 196
political anthropology 186
power 186
resistance 196
social organization 184

Chapter Summary

1. Social organization refers to the patterning of human interdependence in a given society through the actions and decisions of its members. The power that human beings have to reproduce or to change their social organization is an important focus of anthropological study.

2. Biological determinists, environmental determinists, and unilineal evolutionists all assume that a single material force uniquely determines forms of social organization. They reject the anthropological argument that the complexities of human social relations can never be reduced to a single cause.

3. The ability to act implies power. The study of social power in human society is the domain of political anthropology. In most societies, at most times, power can never be reduced to physical force, although this is the Western prototype of power. Power in society operates according to principles that are cultural creations. As such, those principles are basically arbitrary, are affected by history, and may differ from one society to another.

4. Western thinkers traditionally assumed that without a state, social life would be chaotic, if not impossible. They believed that people were free agents who would not co-operate unless forced to do so. Anthropologists have demonstrated that power is exercised both by coercive and by persuasive means. People may submit to institutionalized power because they fear punishment, but they

may also submit because they believe it is the right thing to do.

5. Anthropologists interested in how power is exercised in states have been influenced in recent years by the works of Antonio Gramsci and Michel Foucault. Gramsci argued that coercion alone is rarely sufficient for social control. He distinguished coercive domination from hegemony. Successful hegemonic practice deflects challenges to the coercive power of the ruling group, but hegemony is always the outcome of struggle, and success is never guaranteed. Foucault's concept of governmentality addresses practices developed in Western nation-states in the nineteenth century that aimed to create and sustain peaceful and prosperous social life by exercising power over persons who could be counted, whose physical attributes could be measured statistically, and whose sexual and reproductive behaviours could be shaped by the exercise of state power.

6. Anthropological research in societies without states has shown how social obligations can restrict individuals from pursuing their own self-interest to the detriment of the group. In those societies, power is usually seen to be an independent entity to which one may gain access by supplication, not coercion. Likewise, individuals cannot be coerced but must be persuaded to co-operate. They are not free agents, but they are empowered to resist conforming to another's wishes.

7. All human beings possess the 'power to invest the world with meaning'. Many anthropologists feel that a discussion of social power is incomplete if it does not also pay attention to the ways individuals make sense of and use the constraints and opportunities for action open to them, however limited they may be. Rulers always face the risk that those they dominate may create new, persuasive accounts of their experience of being dominated, organize themselves to defend and disseminate their account, acquire a following, and unseat their rulers.

8. When people bargain for reality, they draw on elements of a shared culture and shared history in order to persuade others of the validity of their position. But they must often bargain over not merely which part of an agreed-on tradition is relevant but also which version of the tradition ought to be agreed on. Much political debate concerns which lessons from the past are relevant to the present. When disputes are settled in this manner, experience is transformed.

Critical Thinking Questions

1. Why would the anthropological contention that social relations in any society are ultimately arbitrary be a controversial idea?
2. What was the initial bureaucratic role of statistics and why were (are) they considered important?
3. What are the similarities and differences between domination and hegemony?
4. If power is part of the natural order of things yet independent of direct human control, what are the consequences that follow?
5. How would you describe the 'scars of bondage' thesis in the context of the exploitations of colonialism in Canada?

Suggested Readings

Alverson, Hoyt. 1978. *Mind in the Heart of Darkness* (New Haven: Yale University Press). *Difficult in places, but important and gripping: A study of how Tswana miners in South Africa maintain a sense of who they are under the most hellish circumstances.*

Arens, W., and Ivan Karp, eds. 1989. *Creativity of Power: Cosmology and Action in African Societies* (Washington, DC: Smithsonian Institution Press). *Contains 13 essays exploring the relationship among power, action, and human agency in African social systems and cosmologies.*

Bashir, Halima. 2008. *Tears of the Desert: A Memoir of Survival in Darfur* (New York: One World). *One woman's description of her survival of torture and gang-rape, inflicted for speaking out about an attack on primary school children. Dr Bashir continues in the work of defending others.*

Fogelson, Raymond, and Richard N. Adams, eds. 1977. *The Anthropology of Power* (New York: Academic Press). *A collection of 28 ethnographic essays on power all over the world.*

Keesing, Roger. 1983. *'Elota's Story* (New York: Holt, Rinehart & Winston). *The autobiography of a Kwaio Big Man with interpretative material by Keesing. First-rate, very readable, and involving. We come to know 'Elota by the end of the book.*

Vincent, Joan, ed. 2002. *The Anthropology of Politics: A Reader in Ethnography, Theory, and Critique* (Malden, MA: Blackwell Publishers). *A bit challenging for beginning students but an excellent collection of key texts in political anthropology ranging from the eighteenth-century Enlightenment to twenty-first century critique.*

Related Websites

The Andean World: http://www.mundoandino.com/Peru/ Ronda-Campesina
Council on Hemispheric Affairs (COHA): http://www.coha. org/2008/10/a-new-face-to-salvadoran-politics/
Farabundo Martí National Liberation Front (FMLN): http://www. fmln.ca/

Liberation Tigers of Tamil Eelam (LTTE): http://www.ltteps.org/
Sawridge Band v. *Canada*: http://www.parl.gc.ca/information/ library/PRBpubs/bp410-e.htm#csawridgetx

Chapter 9

Making a Living

Learning Objectives

By the end of Chapter 9, you will be able to:

- recognize how human beings have devised a variety of subsistence strategies,
- understand the relationship between production, distribution, and consumption,
- detail the various forms of economic theory,
- identify various forms of exchange,
- compare and contrast internal (needs) and external (resources) explanations of consumption patterns,

- consider the cultural and symbolic nature of consumption in the dialectic between the meaningful and the material, and
- appreciate distribution and exchange at local and global levels.

The morning after ethnographer Richard Lee arrived in the Dobe Ju/'hoansi area in the central Kalahari Desert of southern Africa in 1963 (see Ethno-Profile 10.1: Ju/'hoansi [!Kung]), his neighbours, including a man named N!eishi, asked him to give them a ride in his Land Rover to get some food. They said there was little left in their area—mostly bitter roots and berries. They wanted to collect mongongo nuts—a staple of their diet and a great favourite—in a nearby grove (Figure 9.1). Lee agreed to take them. 'The travel was anything but high-speed, and our destination was anything but near. We ground along for hours in four-wheel drive at a walking pace where no truck had ever been before, swerving to avoid ant bear holes and circumventing fallen trees' (1992b: 39).

By the time they stopped, Lee figured they were about 10 miles north of Dobe. He was amazed by how fast the Ju/'hoansi, both men and women, were able to gather the nuts. After two hours, they left the grove. He later weighed the food collected in that short time: the women had gathered loads weighing 30 to 50 pounds each; the men, 15 to 25 pounds each. Lee continued:

> That worked out to about 23,000 calories for food for each woman collector, and 12,000 for each man. Each woman had gathered enough to feed a person for 10 days and each man enough for five days. Not at all a bad haul for two hours' work!
>
> My first full day of fieldwork had already taught me to question one popular view of hunter–gatherer subsistence: that life among these people was precarious, a constant struggle for existence. My later studies were to show that the Ju/'hoansi in fact enjoyed a

rather good diet and that they didn't have to work very hard to get it. . . . only 20 hours a week in subsistence. But what about the fact that N!eishi had come to me that morning saying that they were hungry and that there was no food nearby? Strictly speaking, N!eishi spoke the truth. October is one of the harder months of the year, at the end of the dry season, and the more desirable foods had been eaten out close to Dobe. What N!eishi did not say was that a little farther away food *was* available, and, if not plentiful, there was enough to see them through until the rains came. When N!eishi came to me with his proposition, he was making an intelligent use of his resources, social and otherwise. Why hike in the hot sun for a small meal when the bearded white man might take you in his truck for 10 large ones? (40–1)

Figure 9.1 Anthropologist Richard Lee and Ju/'hoansi informants gathering mongongo nuts.

It is a stereotype of Western culture that human beings who forage for a living lead lives that, in Thomas Hobbes's famous phrase in *Leviathan*, are 'nasty, brutish, and short'. Only recently have anthropologists lived closely enough with foraging peoples to discover the inaccuracy of the Hobbesian position. Lee's Ju/'hoansi informants were well nourished, with balanced diets. What is more, they were choosy about what they ate, unwilling to settle for food they disliked. Such behaviour is entirely familiar to us. Much has changed in the Dobe area since the 1960s, and the Ju/'hoansi no longer forage as they once did. Until recently, however, the cultural, indeed traditional, knowledge of the Ju/'hoansi enabled them to live rather well in what some see as a marginal environment.

Culture and Livelihood

Our cultures suggest a range of options for making a living as well as furnishing the tools to pursue those options. Anthropologist Richard Wilk has defined economic anthropology as 'the part of the discipline that debates issues of *human nature* that relate directly to the decisions of daily life and making a living' (1996: xv).

In ordinary conversation, when we speak of making a living we usually mean doing what is necessary to obtain the material things—food, clothing, shelter—that sustain human life, seldom distinguishing needs from wants. Making a living thus encompasses what is generally considered economic activity. However, anthropologists and other social scientists disagree about what the term *economy* ought to represent. The rise of the capitalist market led to one view of what economy might mean: buying cheap and selling dear. That is, economy means maximizing utility—obtaining the greatest possible satisfaction for the smallest possible cost. This view is based on the assumption of **scarcity**. Many economists and economic anthropologists believe that people's resources (e.g., money) are not, and never will be, great enough for them to obtain all the goods they want. This view of economy also assumes that economic analyses should focus on *individuals* who must maximize their utility under conditions of scarcity. An economizing individual sets priorities and allocates resources rationally according to those priorities. Economic anthropology should therefore investigate the different priorities set by different societies and study how those priorities affect the maximizing decisions of individuals.

Other economic anthropologists regard this way of thinking about economic life as ethnocentric. They present evidence to show that different societies use different principles to organize economic life, and they argue that the job of economic anthropology should be to describe and explain these cultural variations. This view of economy focuses on **institutions**: stable and enduring cultural practices that organize social life. From an institutional point of view, a society's **economy** consists of the culturally specific processes its members use to provide themselves with material resources. Therefore, economic processes cannot be considered apart from the cultural institutions in which they are embedded (Halperin 1994). Thus, culturally, decisions that seem to be based on 'wants' may actually be based on 'needs'.

Subsistence Strategies

Subsistence is the term often used to refer to the satisfaction of the most basic material survival needs: food, clothing, and shelter. The different ways that people in different societies go about meeting these needs are called **subsistence strategies**. Subsistence strategies are the intricate ways of actualizing relationships in specific physical environments. Anthropologists have devised a typology of subsistence strategies that has gained wide acceptance (Figure 9.2). The basic division is between **food collectors** (those who gather, fish, or hunt) and **food producers** (those who depend on domesticated plants or animals, or both).

The strategies followed by food collectors depend on the richness of the environments in which they live circumscribed by the patchiness, seasonality, and mobility of the resources available. Small-scale food collectors, like the Ju/'hoansi throughout the 1960s, live in environments poorly endowed with resources and are likely to change residence often in search of them. By contrast, complex food collectors live in environments richly endowed with dependable food sources and may even, like the Indigenous peoples of the northwest coast of North America, build settlements with permanent architecture. Archaeological evidence shows, moreover, that some of the first food producers in the world continued food collection for

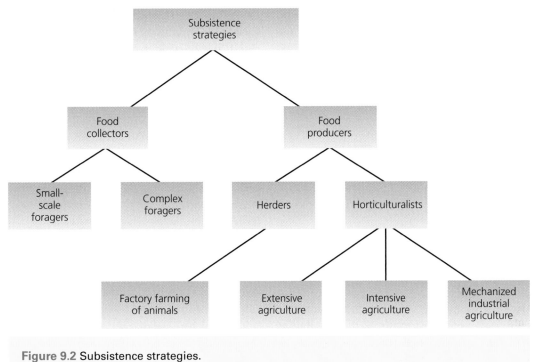

Figure 9.2 Subsistence strategies.

many generations, raising a few crops on the side and occasionally abandoning food production to return to full-time foraging.

Food producers may farm or herd, or both. Among those who farm, there are three major distinctions.

(1) Some farmers depend primarily on human muscle power plus a few simple tools such as digging sticks, hoes, or machetes. They clear plots of uncultivated land, burn the brush, and plant their crops in the ash-enriched soil that remains. This is called *slash-and-burn* or *swidden*. Because this technique eventually exhausts the soil, the plot must then lie fallow as a new plot is cleared and the process repeated. (This cycle may range from two years, as in Yucatán, Mexico, to 20–30 years, as with the Iroquoian peoples at the time of European contact.) This form of cultivation is called **extensive agriculture**, emphasizing the extensive use of land as farm plots are moved every few years, or in some instances *temporal*, in recognition of the fact that they rely on rainwater for their crops.

(2) Other farmers use plows, draft animals, irrigation, fertilizer, and the like. Their method of farming—known as **intensive agriculture**—brings much more land under cultivation at one time.

economy The material-means provisioning process in cultural systems.

extensive agriculture A form of cultivation based on the technique of clearing uncultivated land, burning the brush, and planting the crops in the ash-enriched soil, which requires moving farm plots every few years as the soil becomes exhausted.

food collectors Those who gather, fish, or hunt for food.

food producers Those who depend on domesticated plants or animals for food.

institutions Stable and enduring cultural practices that organize social life.

intensive agriculture A form of cultivation that employs plows, draft animals, irrigation, fertilizer, and such, to bring much more land under cultivation at one time.

scarcity The assumption that resources (e.g., money) will never be plentiful enough for people to obtain all the goods they desire.

subsistence strategies The patterns of production, distribution, and consumption that members of a society employ to ensure the satisfaction of their basic material survival needs.

(3) **Mechanized industrial agriculture** is found in societies in which farming or animal husbandry has become organized along industrial lines. Agribusiness 'factories in the field' or animal feedlots transform food production into a large-scale, technology-dependent industry of its own.

Phases of Economic Activity

Economic activity is usefully subdivided into three distinct phases:

(1) **production**, transforming nature's raw materials into products useful to human beings;
(2) **distribution**, getting products to people; and
(3) **consumption**, using up the products—for example, by eating food or wearing clothing.

Anthropologists merely differ in the importance they attach to each phase. For example, the distributive process known as *exchange* is central to the functioning of capitalist-free enterprise. Some anthropologists have assumed that exchange is equally central to the functioning of all economies and have tried to explain the economic life of non-Western societies in terms of exchange. Anthropologists of a Marxian bent, however, have argued that exchange cannot be understood properly without first studying the nature of production. They point out that production shapes the context in which exchange can occur, determining which parties have how much of what kind of goods to exchange. Other anthropologists have suggested that neither production nor exchange patterns make any sense without first specifying the consumption priorities of the people who are producing and exchanging. Consumption priorities, they argue, are designed to satisfy material needs. But the recognition of needs, and appropriate ways to satisfy them, is shaped by arbitrary cultural patterns. Still others argue that patterns of production, exchange, and consumption are all seriously affected by the kind of *storage* used in a particular society (Figure 9.3).

Distribution and Exchange

Neo-classical Economic Theory and the Rise of Capitalism

In the early years of the rise of capitalist enterprises in western Europe, thinkers such as Adam Smith and his disciples struggled to devise theories to explain the profound changes in European economic and social life. Their work became the foundation for **neo-classical economic theory**, a formal attempt to explain the workings of capitalism.

Capitalism differed in many ways from the preceding feudal economic system, particularly in distribution. Feudal economic relations allotted goods and services to different social groups and individuals on the basis of a person's position in society, or their *status*. Because lords had high status and many obligations, they had a right to more goods and services. Peasants, with low status and few rights, were allowed far less. This distribution of goods was time-honoured and not open to modification. The new capitalist economic relations, by contrast, were considered 'free' precisely because they swept away all such traditional restrictions. Distribution under capitalism was negotiated between buyers and sellers in the market.

In Smith's ideal market, everyone has something to sell (if only his or her willingness to work), and everyone is also a potential buyer of the goods (or services) brought to the market. There is economic exchange. Ideally, because there are many buyers, many sellers, and no traditional restrictions governing who should get how much of what, prices can fluctuate depending on levels of supply and demand. Distribution is carried out in line with the preferences of individuals (needs/wants = desired goods). High demand by individuals for certain items raises the price for those items, as many buyers bargain to obtain few goods. This high demand, in turn, entices more people to produce those goods to take advantage of their higher prices. As competition between suppliers increases, however, prices go down, as each supplier attempts to obtain a greater share of the market. Ideally, prices stabilize as suppliers begin offering 'desired' goods at a cost sufficiently high to allow a profit but sufficiently low for buyers to afford.

Capitalist market exchange of goods and services (labour) for other goods and services (labour) for labour for cash was an important development in Western economic history. It is not surprising, therefore, that Western economic theory was preoccupied with explaining how the capitalist market worked. Markets clearly had a new, decisive importance in capitalist society, which they had not possessed in feudal times. Western neo-classical economics is based on the assumption that market forces are the central forces

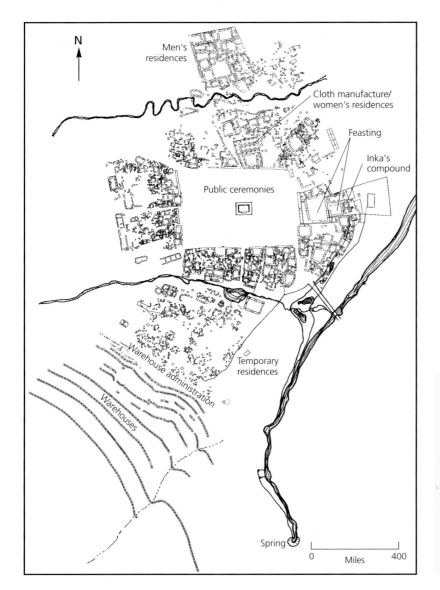

Figure 9.3 A seventeenth-century drawing of storage warehouses built at the height of the Inka Empire (above). At left, the plan of Huánuco Pampa shows the location of these storage warehouses. Some anthropologists argue that food storage practices buffer a population from ecological fluctuations, making considerable cultural manipulation of the economic relations of consumption possible.

determining levels of both production and consumption in society. Therefore, neo-classical economic analysis focuses on markets, scarcity hypotheses, and 'laws' of supply and demand. In such a system everything has a price.

Modes of Exchange

Some anthropologists argued, however, that to take self-interested, materialistic decision-making in the capitalist market as the prototype of human rationality was both reductionistic and ethnocentric. Further, such analyses frequently encourage the use of unilineal evolutionary and neo-evolutionary models of organization and interaction in the discussion of cultures defined as 'other'. Thus, Morgan's ethnical stages

of savagery, barbarism, and civilization (discussed in Chapter 3) become embedded, overtly or covertly, in the categories used in such discussions. More on this

consumption Using up material goods necessary for human survival.

distribution The allocation of goods and services.

mechanized industrial agriculture Large-scale farming and animal husbandry that is highly dependent on industrial methods of technology and production.

neo-classical economic theory A formal attempt to explain the workings of capitalist enterprise, with particular attention to distribution.

production The transformation of nature's raw materials into a form suitable for human use.

later as we consider alternative approaches to understanding political economies.

In this context, we must remember that the capitalist market and neo-classical economic theory are relatively recent cultural inventions specific to societies with certain basic values, institutions, and assumptions about the human condition. In other words, it is specific to peoples with a certain shared world view on the nature of the political economies in which they live. Non-Western, non-capitalist societies have also devised modes of exchange that distribute material goods in ways that are in accord with their basic values, institutions, and assumptions about the human condition—their world view.

Characteristic of the Western-focused analysis of non-Western cultures, and illustrating the embedded nature of the unilineal evolutionary approach, is the work of French anthropologist Marcel Mauss (2000 [1950]). Mauss contrasted non-capitalist *gift* exchanges with impersonal *commodity* exchanges typical of the capitalist market. Gift exchange is deeply embedded in social relations of kinship, partnerships, and acquaintanceships, always requiring a return 'gift'. Commodity exchange only links the participants by cash—the cost of and payment for an item. However, cultures are not compartmentalized into one of these forms of economic activity but may well engage in various permutations of both. Similarly, the work of Marshall Sahlins (1972) has this ancient–modern directional tone. He drew on the writings of economic historian Karl Polanyi to propose that three **modes of exchange** could be identified historically and cross-culturally: reciprocity, redistribution, and market exchange.

Reciprocity

The most ancient mode of exchange, **reciprocity** is characteristic of egalitarian societies, as the Ju/'hoansi once were. Sahlins identified three kinds of reciprocity.

(1) *Generalized reciprocity* is found when those who exchange do so without expecting an immediate return and without specifying the value of the return. Everyone assumes that the exchanges will eventually balance out.

(2) *Balanced reciprocity* is found when those who exchange expect a *return* of equal value within a specified time limit. Lee noted that the Ju/'hoansi distinguish between barter, which requires an immediate return of an equivalent value, and *hxaro*, which is a kind of generalized reciprocity that encourages social obligations to be extended into the future (1992b: 103).

(3) *Negative reciprocity* is an exchange of goods and services in which at least one party attempts to get something for nothing without suffering any penalties. These attempts can range from haggling over prices to outright seizure.

Redistribution

The second mode of exchange, **redistribution**, requires some form of centralized social organization. Those who occupy the central position receive economic contributions from all members of the group. It is then their responsibility to redistribute the goods they receive in a way that provides for every member of the group. The Canada Revenue Agency is probably the institution of redistribution that Canadians come to know best.

The potlatch (Ýaqʷ qʷa) or gift-giving ceremony of First Nations peoples of the Canadian west coast has frequently been used erroneously to illustrate this form of exchange (Figure 9.4). However much 'redistribution' has some level of charm, it does not do justice to the complexity of the social interactions represented by the potlatch and the *Pəssa* systems: payment to witness specific socially significant events and institutional management of credit and debt. Redistribution did occur but in a complex exchange that engaged (and still engages) people in political processes, ritual commitments, and ceremonies of historical importance and documentation in what was originally an oral-tradition milieu. (Note Daisy Sewid-Smith, *In Their Own Words*.) Further, Tollefson (1995: 71) notes that politics plays a very large part in what has been termed *economic* because

certain clan goals could only be fulfilled through potlatching. These include (1) installation of clan leaders, (2) evaluation and verification of clan titles to resources, (3) bestowal of clan titles, (4) resolution of inter-clan disputes, (5) establishing or reaffirming clan alliances, (6) investment and diversification of clan wealth, (7) social removal of shame, and (8) maintenance of regional stability.

This is reinforced, below, in the discussion of network/corporate analysis and the Pueblo peoples (introduced

Figure 9.4 A classic anthropological case study of redistribution involves the potlatch of the Kwakiutl of the Canadian west coast, once banned by the Canadian government.

in Chapter 8). Thus we see that the analysis of such 'exchanges' in all their ramifications illustrates the anthropological concept of holism perhaps more effectively than any one specific analysis. (Also note Naomi McPherson, *In Their Own Words*, in Chapter 10.)

Market Exchange

Invented in capitalist society, **market exchange** is the most recent mode of exchange, according to Polanyi (Figure 9.5). Capitalism involves an exchange of goods (*trade*) calculated in terms of a multi-purpose medium of exchange and standard of value (*money*) and carried on by means of a 'supply–demand–price mechanism' (the *market*). Polanyi was well aware that trade, money, and market institutions had developed independently of one another, historically. He also knew that they could be found in societies outside the West. The uniqueness of capitalism was how all three institutions were linked to one another in the societies of early modern Europe.

But Polanyi was quite right when he noted that different modes of exchange often coexist within a single society. Indeed, this becomes evident if we consider looking at economic relationships through network and corporate theory, introduced in Chapter 8. Further, consider that network and corporate arrangements have the potential to bind the chapters in this section on the organization of material life.

market exchange The exchange of goods (trade) calculated in terms of a multi-purpose medium of exchange and standard of value (money) and carried on by means of a 'supply–demand–price mechanism' (the market).

modes of exchange Patterns according to which distribution takes place: reciprocity, redistribution, and market exchange.

reciprocity The exchange of goods and services of equal value. Anthropologists distinguish three forms of reciprocity: generalized, in which neither the time nor the value of the return are specified; balanced, in which a return of equal value is expected within a specified time limit; and negative, in which parties to the exchange hope to get something for nothing.

redistribution A mode of exchange that requires some form of centralized social organization to receive economic contributions from all members of the group and to redistribute them in a way that provides for every member of the group.

In Their Own Words

The Continuing Reshaping of Our Ritual World by Academic Adjuncts

Daisy Sewid-Smith, a daughter of the late Chief James Sewid, is a member of the Mamaliliq la tribe of Village Island, British Columbia. She is the head of the First Nations Education Department of School District No. 72 in Campbell River, an advisory council member for the Centre for Studies in Religion and Society at the University of Victoria, and author of Prosecution or Persecution *(Kwagiulth Museum, Cape Mudge, Quadra Island, British Columbia, 1979).*

My great-uncle joined with the other nobility to lament the loss of the great economic institutions of the past when he stated to Dr Wolcott, 'It's no use giving a potlatch any more. The old people don't do it; so nobody pays you back, and the young people don't even understand what it's all about.' He was referring to the grossly misunderstood economic system we called *Pǝssa*. This was the investing institution of the Kʷakʷakǝwakaʷ and Liǧʷidaxʷ League of Nations. This institution charged interest, called in debts, gave credit, and kept records of all transactions for future generations. Both my father and my great-uncle held hereditary positions in this complex system. It was to this institution that my great-uncle was referring when he spoke of the young not understanding and the investment not being repaid.

Most of our people today have only seen what was known as Y̓aqʷ qʷa, meaning *gift-giving*. That is the reason why the term *potlatch*, a Chinook word meaning *to give*, was assigned to this system by the Chinook speakers of our old trade world. The Y̓aqʷ qʷa, or potlatch, was a system that paid witnesses to validate such events as marriages, memorials, and the succession of ancestral names. The Y̓aqʷ qʷa, or potlatch system, did not have the same principles, purpose, laws, or membership as the *Pǝssa*.

Unfortunately, my great-uncle understood too well the changing landscape of his ritual world. He and the nobility he came from had struggled so hard to keep the culture alive despite the institutionalized oppression of our beliefs by the state and by religious zealots; the loss of their sacred land and resources by the encroachment and laws of the newcomers; the loss of life due to disease, social breakdown, and the very personal identity struggles of the younger generation; and the diminished use of our precious language that holds the keys to our past, our values, and our religion. Today, our struggle is not just of legal or religious prosecution. Today our struggle is sadly the reshaping of our ritual world by academic interpretations.

The academic world must, in its need to publish accounts of my Nation, begin to subscribe to rules that are consistent with our ritual structure. They must begin to identify the trained specialists who are working within our culture and use the same rules we have of validation and authority to ensure an accurate view of our ritual world. It is not enough to read and cite from previous misinterpretations to make a theory right. When a house is built on a foundation of sand, its structure is weak and unstable. So is it for our ritual world within academic rendering. We have sorrily witnessed the reshaping of the foundations of our old institutions, the validation of those within our Nation unschooled in our complexes, and the loss of our precious rights and privileges so embedded in our history.

The last words belong to one of our chiefs addressing the first academic to come among us, Franz Boas, when he said in 1894, 'It is a strict law that bids us dance. It is a strict law that bids us distribute our property among our friends and neighbours. It is a good law. Let the white man observe his law, we shall observe ours.'

Source: Sewid-Smith, Daisy. 1997. 'The Continuing Reshaping of Our Ritual World by Academic Adjuncts', *Anthropology & Education Quarterly* 28, 4 (Dec.): 594–602.

Network/Corporate Organizational Styles

How do power and politics tie to economic activity? On the basis of the ethnographic work of Benedict (1934), Dozier (1960; 1970), Eggan (1950), and Parsons (1939), Feinman and his colleagues offer one

suggestion in this example of Pueblo groups in the southwest United States. In these groups

> economic resources are dispersed (on family, clan, or sodality basis) rather than centralized, leadership is not personalized, and ostentatious displays

Figure 9.5 Shirts for sale at the market in Guider, Cameroon. Markets can be found in many societies, but capitalism links markets to trade and money in a unique way.

discouraged or even punished. Instead community ritual dominates the ceremonial cycle, and social segments are woven together through broad integrative ritual and ideological means. Importantly, ceremonial redistribution suppresses formal economic differentiation. Thus the tendencies to network strategies are dampened. (2000: 454)

They go on to note that network organizational strategies can emerge and create a hierarchical society but that for the Pueblos 'Power was not centralized in a single ruler. Nor was trade or production monopolized . . .' (455). The authors continue to note that this cannot be interpreted as evidence of an egalitarian society (456). Such analytical tools could also be used in the example of the potlatch discussed above. One of the important upshots of this approach is that Elman Service's ordering of society as bands, tribes, chiefdoms (non-state organization), and states (1975) is challenged, and the definition of chiefdoms does not apply in the Pueblo example. However, that is all to the good of moving away from unilineal evolutionary approaches even if they only infer such directionality.

Production

Some economic anthropologists see production as the driving force behind economic activity. Production creates supplies of goods to which demand must accommodate, and it determines levels of consumption as well. Anthropologists who stress the centrality of production borrow their perspective on economic activity, as well as many key concepts, from the works of Karl Marx. They argue that this perspective is far more insightful than the one taken by neo-classical theorists of market exchange.

Labour

Labour is perhaps the most central Marxian concept these anthropologists have adopted. **Labour** is the activity linking human social groups to the material world around them; human labour is therefore always

labour The activity linking human social groups to the material world around them; from the point of view of Karl Marx, labour is therefore always social labour.

social labour. Human beings must actively struggle together to transform natural substances into forms they can use. This is most clear in the case of food production but includes the production of clothing, shelter, and tools. Marx emphasized the importance of human physical labour in the material world, but he also recognized the importance of mental or cognitive labour. Human intelligence allows us to reflect on and organize productive activities. Mentally and physically, human social groups struggle together to ensure their material survival. In struggling, they reproduce patterns of social organization, production, and thought.

Modes of Production

Marx attempted to classify the ways different human groups carry out production. Each way is called a **mode of production**. Anthropologist Eric Wolf defined a mode of production as 'a specific, historically occurring set of social relations through which labour is deployed to wrest energy from nature by means of tools, skills, organization, and knowledge' (1982: 75). Tools, skills, organization, and knowledge constitute what Marx called the **means of production**. The social relations linking human beings who use a given means of production within a particular mode of production are called the **relations of production**. That is, different productive tasks (clearing the bush, planting, harvesting, and so on) are assigned to different social groups, all of which must work together for production to be successful.

The concept of mode of production is holistic, highlighting recurring patterns of human activity in which certain forms of social organization, production practices, and cultural knowledge co-determine one another. Wolf notes that Marx speaks of at least eight different modes of production in his own writings, although he focused mainly on the capitalist mode. Wolf finds the concept of mode of production useful. But like most anthropologists inspired by Marx's work, he does not feel bound to accept Marx's conclusions as a matter of course. He suggests that three modes of production have been particularly important in human history:

(1) a *kin-ordered mode* in which social labour is deployed on the basis of kinship relations (e.g., husbands/fathers clear the fields, the whole family plants, mothers/wives weed, children keep animals out of the field);

(2) a *tributary mode* 'in which the primary producer, whether cultivator or herdsman, is allowed access to the means of production while tribute is exacted from him by political or military means' (79); and

(3) the *capitalist mode*.

The capitalist mode has three main features:

(a) the means of production are property owned by the capitalists,

(b) workers are denied access to such ownership and must sell their labour to the capitalists in order to survive, and

(c) this labour for capitalists produces surpluses of wealth that capitalists may retain or plow back into production to increase output and generate further surpluses.

An overlap exists between this classification of modes of production and the traditional anthropological classification of subsistence strategies. The kin-ordered mode of production is found among foragers and those farmers and herders whose political organization does not involve domination by one group. The tributary mode is found among farmers or herders living in a social system that is divided into classes of rulers and subjects. Subjects produce both for themselves and for their rulers, who take a certain proportion of their subjects' product as tribute. The capitalist mode, the most recent to develop, can be found in the industrial societies of North America and western Europe beginning in the seventeenth and eighteenth centuries.

Thus, in some ways the mode-of-production concept simply recognizes the same variation in the arts of subsistence that Lewis Henry Morgan recognized in the nineteenth century. Yet the concept of mode of production also highlights certain attributes of subsistence strategies that the Morgan approach tended to downplay. For example, modes of production have as much to do with forms of social and political organization as with material productive activities. That is, the kin-ordered mode of production is distinctive as much for its use of the kinship system to allocate labour to production as for the kind of production undertaken, such as farming. In a kin-ordered mode of production, the *relations of kinship* serve as the *relations of production* that enable a particular *mode of production* to be carried out.

The Role of Conflict in Material Life

Traditionally anthropologists have emphasized the important links between a society's social organization (kinship groups, chiefdom, state) and the way that society meets its subsistence needs, either to demonstrate the stages of cultural evolution or to display the functional interrelationships between parts of a particular society. In both cases, however, the emphasis of the analysis was on the harmonious fashion in which societies either changed or stayed the same. This implied that social stability should not be tampered with. Social change was possible, but it would take place in an equally orderly fashion, in the fullness of time, according to laws of development beyond the control of individual members of society.

Many anthropologists have not been persuaded that social change is orderly or that social organization by nature is harmonious. They find the Marxian approach useful precisely because it treats conflict as a natural part of the human condition. The concept of mode of production makes a major contribution to economic anthropology precisely because of the very different interpretation it gives to conflict, imbalance, and disharmony in social life.

Marx pointed out, for example, that the capitalist mode of production incorporates the workers and the owners in different and contradictory ways. These groups, which he called *classes*, have different interests, and what is good for one class may not be good for all classes. The workers' desires (higher wages to purchase more goods) are inevitably opposed to the owners' desires (lower wages to increase their profits or to reinvest in tools and raw materials).

This does not mean that warfare is constant between the different classes engaged in a particular mode of production; however, it does mean that the potential for conflict is built into the mode of production. The more complex and unequal the involvement of different classes in a mode of production, the more intense the struggle between them is likely to be. Such struggle may not always lead to outright rebellion for sound political reasons, but we should not be surprised to find the 'everyday forms of peasant resistance' that Scott discussed in his analysis of life in Sedaka Village. When viewed from a Marxian perspective, such struggles are clearly not just 'healthy competition'. Marx was one of the first social analysts, and certainly one of the most eloquent, to document the high level of human suffering generated by certain modes of production, particularly the capitalist mode.

Wolf's three modes of production (kin-ordered, tributary, and capitalist) describe not only a society's subsistence strategy but also that society's social organization. As a result, they accent the lines of cleavage along which tension and conflict may develop—or may have developed historically—between different segments of the society: between, say, parents and children or husbands and wives in the kin-ordered mode; between lords and peasants in the tributary mode; and between capitalists and workers in the capitalist mode.

Applying Production Theory to Social and Cultural Life

Economic anthropologists who focus on production as the prime causal force in material life tend to apply the metaphor of production to other areas of social life as well. They see production as involving far more than short-term satisfaction of material survival needs. If a given *mode* of production is to persist over time, the *means* and *relations* of production must also persist.

For example, farmers produce grain and leave behind harvested fields. They exchange some grain with cattle herders for milk and meat, and they permit the herders' cattle to graze in the harvested fields in exchange for manure they need to fertilize their fields. Consequently, farmers and herders alike end up with a mix of foodstuffs to sustain human life (i.e., to reproduce the producers). In addition, each group has what it needs in the coming season to renew its means of production. Both groups will want to ensure that similar exchanges are carried out by their children; that is, they must find a way to ensure that the next generation will consist of farmers and cattle herders producing the same goods and willing to exchange them. Therefore, not only must the means of production perpetuate

means of production The tools, skills, organization, and knowledge used to extract energy from nature.

mode of production 'A specific, historically occurring set of social relations through which labour is deployed to wrest energy from nature by means of tools, skills, organization, and knowledge'.

relations of production The social relations linking the people who use a given means of production within a particular mode of production.

but so must the relations of production. The result, then, is the reproduction of society from generation to generation.

People also produce and reproduce *interpretations* of the productive process and their roles in that process. *Marx* used the term **ideology** to refer to the cultural products of conscious reflection such as morality, religion, or metaphysics. As used in Marxian analysis, ideology refers in particular to those beliefs that explain and justify the relations of production to those who engage in them. For Marx, ideology was not independent of the productive process itself. On the contrary, 'men, developing their material production and their material intercourse, alter, along with this their real existence, their thinking and the products of their thinking. Life is not determined by consciousness, but consciousness by life' (Marx 1977 [1932]: 164). As a result, Marxian economic anthropologists investigate the kinds of ideas, beliefs, and values that are produced and reproduced in societies with different modes of production. The class in power usually holds to an ideology that justifies their domination, as we saw in Scott's discussion of Sedaka in Chapter 8. Those who are dominated may assent publicly to the ideology of the rulers, but in private they are likely to be highly critical and to offer alternative interpretations.

The use of the production metaphor in the analysis of social and cultural life has yielded some important results in anthropology.

- It highlights certain processes and relationships that the exchange metaphor tends to downplay or ignore. For example, exchange theorists are less likely to care why the different parties to an exchange have different quantities of resources with which to bargain. Production theorists, by contrast, aim to show that access to resources is determined *before* exchange by the relations of production, which decide who is entitled to how much of what. In particular, they reject the assumption that access to valued resources is open to anyone with gumption and the spirit of enterprise. Different modes of production stack the deck in favour of some classes and against others. This is most clear in the capitalist mode, where owners have disproportionate access to wealth, power, and prestige and where workers' access to these goods is sharply restricted. Thus, the classes who fare poorly do so not because of any inherent inferiority, laziness, or improvidence; they fail to get ahead because the rules of the game (i.e., of the mode of production) were set up in a way that keeps them from winning.

- A production metaphor provides an especially dynamic perspective on cultural persistence and cultural change. Production theory relates peoples' preferences for different goods to the interests and opportunities of the different classes to which they belong. People buy and sell as they do, not out of idiosyncratic whimsy but because the choices open to them are shaped by the relations of production. From this perspective, poor people do not purchase cheap goods because they have poor taste and cannot recognize quality when they see it; rather, their deprived position within the mode of production provides them with very limited income, and they must make do with the only goods they can afford.

- Production theory focuses on people as much as or more than it focuses on the goods they produce. It views human beings as social agents involved in the construction and reconstruction of human society on all levels in every generation. Traditions persist but only because people labour to reproduce them from one day to the next. Linking production (and reproduction), social relations, and ideologies highlights the contingent nature of social life, even as it suggests how traditions are carried on.

Consumption

Consumption usually refers to using up material goods necessary for human survival. These goods include—at a minimum—food, drink, clothing, and shelter; they can and often do include much more. The study of consumption by economists and others was, until recently, much neglected. To some extent, this is because many observers assumed that there were no interesting questions to ask about consumption. That is, it seemed clear that people either consume goods for obvious reasons, such as survival, or consume goods as a result of idiosyncratic personal preferences.

Anthropologists who make cross-cultural comparisons, however, have always noticed striking differences in consumption patterns in different societies that seemed hard to reconcile with accepted economic explanations. Historically, they have taken three basic approaches to account for these patterns:

(1) the internal explanation,
(2) the external explanation, and
(3) the cultural explanation.

The Internal Explanation

The internal explanation for human consumption patterns comes from the work of Malinowski. His version of functionalist anthropology explains social practices by relating them to the basic human needs that can be biological or psychological. Whatever their origin, if they go unmet, the society might not survive. Malinowski proposed a list of basic human needs, which includes nourishment, reproduction, bodily comforts, safety, movement, growth, and health. Every culture responds in its own way to these needs with some form of the corresponding institutions: food-collecting techniques, kinship, shelter, protection, activities, training, and hygiene (Malinowski 1944: 91).

Malinowski's approach had the virtue of emphasizing human beings' dependency on the physical world in order to survive. Further, Malinowski was able to show that many customs that appear bizarre to uninitiated Western observers are in fact 'rational' because they help people satisfy their basic human needs. Nonetheless, this approach fell short of explaining why all societies do not share the same consumption patterns. A later generation of anthropologists was influenced by evolutionary and ecological studies. They tried to answer this question with an external explanation for the diversity of human consumption patterns.

The External Explanation

The study of how living species relate to one another and their physical environment is called **ecology**. That environment is divided into different **eco-zones** (Figure 9.6) formed of the mixture of plant and animal species living there. A species adapts to an eco-zone by constructing an **eco-niche**—plants and animals on which it can depend for survival. *Socio-ecologists* investigate the features of eco-zones to explain why a

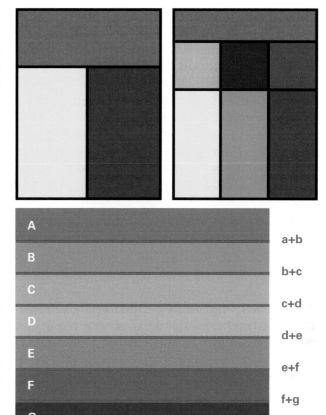

Figure 9.6 Eco-zones and eco-tones. The effective use of eco-toning for food acquisition can be seen in many cultures. In the top diagrams, the brown square has the most potential as it has resources from all three eco-zones (red, blue, yellow). In the bottom diagram, we can see the toning effect on a coastline from the deep forest or mountain side to the deep ocean side.

particular animal population—a troop of baboons, for example—organizes itself the way it does in a particular environment.

ecology The study of the ways in which living species relate to one another and to their natural environment.

eco-niche The plants and animals in an eco-zone on which a species relies for survival; essentially a place in the natural world where a species is at 'home'.

eco-zones The particular mixture of plant and animal species occupying any particular region of the earth.

ideology According to Marx, those products of consciousness—such as morality, religion, and metaphysics—that purport to explain to people who they are and to justify the kinds of lives they lead.

Cultural Ecology

Cultural ecology is an anthropological attempt to apply socio-ecology to human beings and their societies. For cultural ecologists, patterns of human consumption (production and distribution) derive from features of the eco-zones in which groups live. Every human group must learn to make use of the resources available in its eco-zone if it is to survive. Thus consumption patterns found in a particular society do not just depend on the obvious, internal hunger drive. Rather, they depend on the particular external resources present in the eco-zone to which they must adapt.

Why do people X raise peanuts and sorghum? The internal, Malinowskian explanation would be: to meet their basic human need for food. The external, socio-ecological explanation would be: because peanuts and sorghum are the only food crops available in their eco-zone that, when cultivated, will meet their subsistence needs. Both these answers are suggestive, but they remain incomplete. We might ask whether the local food sources that people X choose to exploit are the *only* local food sources available to them. Ethnographic data show that no society exploits every locally available food source to meet its consumption needs. Quite the contrary, consumption needs are selective; in other words, they are culturally shaped.

Economic anthropologist Rhoda Halperin (1994) has examined the relationship between ecological anthropology and economic anthropology. Borrowing concepts from Polanyi, she argued that every economic system can be analyzed in terms of two kinds of movements: *locational movements*, or 'changes of place'; and *appropriational movements*, or 'changes of hands'. In her view, ecological relationships that affect the economy are properly understood as changes of place, as when people must move into the grasslands, gather mongongo nuts, and transport them back to camp. Economic relationships, by contrast, are more properly understood as changes of hands, as when mongongo nuts are distributed to all members of the camp, whether or not they helped to gather them. Thus, ecological (locational) movements involve transfers of energy; economic (appropriational) movements, by contrast, involve transfers of rights (Halperin 1994: 59). Analyzed in this way, people's rights to consume mongongo nuts cannot be derived from the labour they expended to gather them.

Another way of seeing the difference between ecological and economic arrangements is to pay attention to the connection between food storage and food sharing. A socio-ecologist might argue that those who gather mongongo nuts are obliged to share them and consume them immediately because they have no way to store them. Ecological anthropologist Tim Ingold (1983) agrees that the obligation to share makes storage unnecessary, but he also points out that sharing with others today ordinarily obligates them to share with you tomorrow (reciprocity). Put another way, sharing food can be seen not only as a way of avoiding spoilage but also as a way of storing IOUs for the future!

Once societies develop ways to preserve and store food and other material goods, however, new possibilities open up. Archaeological evidence indicates that the more food there is to store, the more people invest in storage facilities (such as pits or pottery vessels), and the more quickly they become sedentary. Large-scale food storage techniques involve a series of 'changes of place' that buffer a population from ecological fluctuations for long periods of time. But techniques of food storage alone predict nothing about the 'changes of hands' that food will undergo once it has been stored. Food storage techniques have been associated with all subsistence strategies, including that of complex food collectors. This suggests that economic relations of consumption, involving the transfer of rights in stored food, have long been open to considerable cultural elaboration and manipulation (Halperin 1994: 178).

Both ecological and economic transfers are important in any economy. However, economic transfers of rights to material resources cannot be separated from wider political forces that impinge on those rights. According to anthropologist Elliot Fratkin, 'a shift in theoretical understanding from *cultural* ecology to *political* ecology' (1997: 236; italics in original) is necessary. For example, the current adaptations of eastern African pastoralists and their herds to the semi-arid environment is strongly affected by political pressures coming from the nation-states of eastern Africa. As a result, Fratkin says, contemporary anthropological studies of pastoralists explain human–livestock interactions 'less in terms of "carrying capacity" or "desertification" and more in terms of loss of common property rights, increased economic differentiation and social stratification, and incorporation and domination of tribal pastoral groups by larger state systems' (236).

The Cultural Explanation

A major shortcoming of both internal and external explanations for human consumption patterns is that they ignore or deny the possibility of *agency*. Malinowski, and many cultural ecologists, assumed that patterns of consumption were dictated by an iron environmental necessity that did not allow for alternatives. From such a perspective, choice of diet is a luxury that most non-Western societies cannot afford. Yet to rob non-Western peoples of choice is to dehumanize them.

Sahlins urged anthropologists to pay close attention to consumption because consumption choices reveal what it means to be a human being. Human beings are *human*, he tells us,

> precisely when they experience the world as a concept (symbolically). It is not essentially a question of priority but of the unique quality of human experience as meaningful experience. Nor is it an issue of the reality of the world; it concerns *which worldly dimension becomes pertinent*, and in what way, to a given human group. (1976a: 142; emphasis added)

The Original Affluent Society

Many Westerners believed that foraging peoples led the most miserable existence, spending all their waking hours on a food quest that yielded barely enough to keep them alive. Some researchers have argued that contemporary foragers are all dispossessed herders who were forced into this 'despised and despicable' way of life as a result of European colonial oppression (see, e.g., Wilmsen 1989; 1991). While dispossession and exploitation has been the lot of many of the original foraging and hunting peoples of southern Africa (see, e.g., Gordon 1992), Lee and other ethnographers have been able to show that the Ju/'hoansi were able, until very recently, to find refuge beyond the reach of these forces (Lee 1992a; 1992b; Solway and Lee 1990). They have also argued powerfully that, for people like the Ju/'hoansi, full-time foraging was anything but a 'despised and despicable' way of life. Although full-time foraging has been impossible in the Dobe area since the 1980s, and the Ju/'hoansi have had to make some difficult adjustments, Lee documented a way of life that contrasts vividly with their current settled existence.

The results of Lee's research on subsistence in the 1960s were surprising. The Ju/'hoansi provided themselves with a varied and well-balanced diet based on a *selection* from the food sources available in their environment. Although they classified more than 100 species of plants as edible, only 14 were primary or major sources (Lee 1992b: 45ff.). Some 70 per cent of this diet consisted of vegetable foods; 30 per cent was meat. Mongongo nuts alone made up more than one-quarter of the diet. Women provided about 55 per cent of the diet and men provided 45 per cent, including the meat. The Ju/'hoansi spent an average of 2.4 working days—or about 20 hours—per person per week in food-collecting activities. Ju/'hoansi bands periodically suffered from shortages of their preferred foods and were forced to resort to less desired items. Most of the time, however, their diet was balanced and adequate and consisted of foods of preference (56ff.).

Sahlins coined the expression 'the original affluent society' (1972) to refer to the Ju/'hoansi and other foragers like them, thus challenging the traditional Western assumption that the life of foragers is characterized by scarcity and near-starvation. **Affluence**, he argued, is having more than enough of whatever is required to satisfy consumption needs. There are two ways to create affluence:

(1) to *produce much* (the path taken by Western capitalist society) and
(2) to *desire little* (the option, Sahlins argues, that foragers have taken).

Their wants are few, but they are abundantly supplied by nature. Moreover, foragers do not suppress their natural greed; rather, their society simply does not institutionalize greed or reward the greedy. As a result, foragers cannot be considered poor, even though their material standard of living is low by Western standards. Poverty is not an absolute condition nor is it a relationship between means and ends;

affluence The condition of having more than enough of whatever is required to satisfy consumption needs.

it is a relationship between people and a cultural definition of needs and wants.

The Cultural Construction of Needs

The original affluent society of the Ju/'hoansi reinforces the observation that 'needs' is a vague concept. Hunger can be satisfied by beans and rice or steak and lobster. Thirst can be quenched by water or beer or soda pop. In effect, culture defines needs and provides for their satisfaction according to its own logic. And cultural logic is irreducible to biology, psychology, or ecological pressure.

By adopting this cultural approach to consumption, the distinctions between needs and wants or necessities and luxuries disappear. Mary Douglas and Baron Isherwood deplore

> the widespread and misleading distinction between goods that sustain life and health and others that service the mind and heart—spiritual goods. . . . The counter-argument proposed here is that all goods carry meaning, but none by itself. . . . The meaning is in the relations between all the goods, just as music is in the relations marked out by the sounds and not in any one note. (1979: 72–3)

For instance, a good's meaning may have to do with its edibility, but edibility is always culturally determined.

Furthermore, the meaning of any individual item of food cannot be explained in isolation. That meaning only becomes clear when the item is compared with other consumption items that are also marked by the culture as edible or inedible.

The Abominations of Leviticus

Consider the prohibition against eating pork. For Jews and Muslims, pork is inedible, culturally speaking. According to Mary Douglas (1966), this has nothing to do with ecological problems associated with pig raising in southwestern Asia nor with defects in the digestive systems of Jews or Muslims. Douglas analyzed the Jewish dietary prohibitions detailed in the biblical Book of Leviticus. She argued that certain animals were prohibited as food because something about them violated the prototypes for edibility recognized in ancient Hebrew culture (Table 9.1). Prototypically 'clean' land animals were supposed to have four legs and cloven hooves and to chew the cud; pigs were an 'abomination' because they were four-legged, cloven-hoofed beasts that did not chew the cud. 'Clean' beasts of the air were supposed to have feathers and to fly with wings; therefore, hopping insects were 'unclean' because they had six legs, neither walked nor flew, and lacked feathers. 'Clean' water animals were supposed to have fins and scales;

Table 9.1 Jewish Dietary Prohibitions

	Class prototype	Clean examples	Unclean examples	Reason prohibited
Earth	Four-legged animals that hop, jump, or walk (i.e., cloven-hoofed, cud-chewing ungulates)	Cattle, camels, sheep, goats	Hare, hyrax Pig Weasel, mouse, crocodile, shrew, chameleon, mole	Cud-chewing but not cloven-hoofed Cloven-hoofed but not cud-chewing Two legs, two hands, but go about on all fours
Air	Two-legged fowl that fly with wings	Chicken	Grasshoppers	Six legs, cannot walk or fly, and lack feathers
Water	Scaly fish that swim with fins	Carp, whitefish	Shrimp, clams	Possess neither fins nor scales but still live in water

Source: Adapted from Douglas 1966: 41–57.

shrimp were forbidden because, although they lived in the sea, they lacked fins and scales.

By itself, Douglas argued, a prohibition against eating pork is meaningless and appears irrational. However, when the prohibition against pork is taken together with other dietary prohibitions in Leviticus, and when these are compared with the foods that were permitted, a pattern emerges. Douglas and Isherwood write, 'Goods assembled together in ownership make physical, visible statements about the hierarchy of values to which their chooser subscribes' (1979: 5). Thus, Jews who consume only 'clean' foods that meet the ritual requirements laid down by their tradition are doing more than procuring the means to satisfy their hunger; they are also making a social declaration of solidarity with their religious community, and the care with which they adhere to the dietary laws is a measure of their commitment. Their need for food is being met, but selectively, and the selection they make carries a social message.

Dietary laws deal with food and drink and so might still be explained in biological or ecological terms. Such explanations are more difficult to construct, however, when we consider the role of banana leaves in the Trobriand Islands.

Banana Leaves in the Trobriand Islands

Anthropologist Annette Weiner travelled to the Trobriand Islands more than half a century after Malinowski carried out his classic research there (see Figure 9.7; see also EthnoProfile 9.1: Trobriand Islanders). To her surprise, she discovered a venerable local tradition involving the accumulation and exchange of banana leaves, or women's wealth. Malinowski had never described this tradition, even though there is evidence from photographs and writing that it was in force at the time of his fieldwork. There are probably two reasons why Malinowski overlooked these transactions:

(1) they are carried out by women, and Malinowski did not view women as important actors in the economy; and

(2) banana leaves would be an unlikely item of consumption because Malinowski only labelled activities that satisfied biological survival needs as 'economic', and you can't eat banana leaves.

EthnoProfile 9.1

Trobriand Islanders

Region: Oceania

Nation: Milne Bay Province of Papua New Guinea

Language: Trobriand Islanders speak Kilivila of the Kilivila-Louisiades language family

Population: 12,000

Environment: Tropical rainforest on main islands of Kiriwina, Kailevna, Vakuta, and Kitava

Livelihood: Subsistence horticulturalists (yams as main crop)

Political organization: Traditionally, chiefs and others of rank in matriclans; today, part of a modern nation-state

For more information: Malinowski, Bronislaw. 1984 [1922]. *Argonauts of the Western Pacific* (Waveland Press); Weiner, Annette. 1988. *The Trobrianders of Papua New Guinea* (New York: Holt, Rinehart & Winston)

Figure 9.7 Yams are the main source of subsistence for Trobriand Islanders. Pictured here are Trobriander yam houses and Trobriander lodgings.

However, explaining transactions involving women's wealth turns out to be crucial for understanding Trobriand kinship obligations.

Banana leaves might be said to have a 'practical' use in that women make skirts out of them. These skirts are highly valued, but the transactions involving women's wealth more often involve the bundles of leaves themselves. Why bother to exchange great amounts of money or other goods to obtain bundles of banana leaves? This would seem to be a classic example of irrational consumption. And yet, as Weiner demonstrates, banana bundles play exactly the role Douglas and Isherwood have suggested that consumption goods play in society: 'As an economic, political, and social force, women's wealth exists as the representation of the most fundamental relationships in the social system' (Weiner 1980: 289).

Trobrianders are matrilineal, and men traditionally prepare yam gardens for their sisters. After the harvest, yams from these gardens are distributed by a woman's brother to her husband. Weiner's research suggests that what Malinowski took to be the *redistribution* of yams, from a wife's kin to her husband, could be better understood as a *reciprocal exchange* of yams for women's wealth. The parties central to this exchange are a woman, her brother, and her husband. The woman is the person through whom yams are passed from her own kin to her husband and also the person through whom women's wealth is passed from her husband to her own kin.

Transactions involving women's wealth occur when someone in the woman's kinship group dies. Surviving relatives must 'buy back', metaphorically speaking, all the yams or other goods that the deceased person gave to others during his or her lifetime. Each payment marks a social link between the deceased and the recipient, and the size of the payment marks the importance of their relationship. All the payments must be made in women's wealth.

The dead person's status, as well as the status of her or his family, depends on the size and number of the payments made, and the people who must be paid can number into the hundreds. Women make women's wealth themselves and exchange market-bought trade goods to obtain it from other women, but when someone in their matrilineage dies, they collect it from their husbands. Indeed, a woman's value is measured by

the amount of women's wealth her husband provides. Furthermore,

> if a man does not work hard enough for his wife in accumulating wealth for her, then her brother will not increase his labour in the yam garden. . . . The production in yams and women's wealth is always being evaluated and calculated in terms of effort and energy expended on both sides of production. The value of a husband is read by a woman's kin as the value of his productive support in securing women's wealth for his wife. (Weiner 1980: 282)

Weiner argues that women's wealth upholds the kinship arrangements of Trobriand society. It balances out exchange relationships between lineages linked by marriage, reinforces the pivotal role of women and matriliny, and publicly proclaims, during every funeral, the social relationships that make up the fabric of Trobriand society. The system has been stable for generations, but Weiner suggests that it could collapse if cash ever became widely substitutable for yams. Under such conditions, men might buy food and other items on the market; they would no longer be dependent on yams from their wives' kin, and they could therefore refuse to supply their wives' kin with women's wealth. This had not yet happened at the time of Weiner's research, but she saw it as a possible future development.

The Cultural Construction of Utility

Just as culture shapes needs, so too does it offer standardized ways of satisfying them. No social exchange can occur unless all parties are able to assess the value of the items to be exchanged. Because of the openness of culture and the ambiguity inherent in many social situations, values and exchange rates may well be bargained over. Such exchanges ultimately rest on cultural principles for assessing value and fairness.

Once consumption is defined as the use of goods and services to communicate cultural values, a new understanding of wealth and poverty is possible. We have noted Sahlins's comment that foragers with simple needs and ample means of satisfying those needs are affluent—rich, not poor. Douglas and Isherwood also refuse to use the sheer amount of material possessions as a universal measure of wealth or poverty. They write:

Many of the countries that anthropologists study are poor on such material criteria—no wall-to-wall carpets, no air conditioning—but they do not regard themselves as poor. The Nuer of the Sudan in the 1930s would not trade with the Arabs because the only things they had to sell were their herds of cattle, and the only things they could possibly want from trade were more cattle. (1979: 17–18)

For the Nuer, to have few or no cattle constituted poverty because cattle mattered as much for their use as markers of social relations as for their use as food. 'To be rich means to be well integrated in a rich community. . . . To be poor is to be isolated' (160).

Institutionalized Sharing

Capitalist societies have passed laws and created social institutions that reward individuals for accumulating wealth. The economic practices of some non-capitalist societies, by contrast, prevent individual accumulation; the goal is to spread any wealth that exists throughout the community. This pattern is called *institutionalized sharing.*

People accustomed to capitalist practices are often either incredulous or cynical when it is suggested that institutionalized sharing can be the backbone of economic life. They assume that such widespread 'generosity' can only be expected of saintly altruists, not of ordinary human beings. Nevertheless, people in societies with institutionalized sharing are not saints who never experience greed any more than people in capitalist societies are devils who never experience compassion. Both societies, however, make it difficult to get away with practices that undercut established social arrangements.

Institutionalized sharing can be found among the Plains Cree of North America (see Map 9.2), studied by Niels Braroe (1975: 143ff.). In the past, the Cree were bison hunters living in bands. Each band had a leader who provided his followers with the materials necessary for hunting. This leader was the focus of a redistributive mode of exchange, and generosity in redistribution qualified him to be the band leader. At the time of Braroe's fieldwork, the Cree no longer hunted bison, but they still practised the institutionalized sharing of consumption items such as food, clothing, beer, or cigarettes. For example, Braroe tells us that 'it is not considered improper, as it is among whites, to ask for someone's last cigarette; to refuse a request, however, is frowned upon' (145). Generosity is further reinforced in ceremonies known as *giveaway dances*. The central event in these ceremonies is dancing around the room and giving away material goods, such as clothing, to other guests. Dancers aim to give away more than they receive. It is an insult to shower someone with gifts in the course of such an event.

The Cree ideal is that generosity should be spontaneous and contempt for material goods genuine. Nevertheless, Braroe's informants sometimes possessed consumption goods or money that they clearly wanted to keep for themselves. Individuals could enjoy such goods in private but only if their existence were kept a secret. Men sometimes hid beer to avoid having to share it with others. A woman informant once asked Braroe's wife to keep a sizable amount of cash for her so others would not know she had it and demand some. The rule seemed to be that 'any visible resource may legitimately be requested by another' (146), and Braroe reported that direct refusals of such requests were rare.

For the Cree, institutionalized sharing is supposed to ensure that consumption goods are not hoarded but spread out and enjoyed by all in the band. This consumption pattern clashes with that of the capitalist, who views accumulation and consumption by individuals in a positive light. Some individual Cree earned money off the reserve and tried to save it in order to

Map 9.2 Cree (Short Grass Reserve)

get ahead—by capitalist standards. Those people were considered stingy by other Cree and were resented; they could not hope to gain a position of leadership in the band.

Consumption Studies Today

The foregoing examples focus attention on distinctive consumption practices in different societies, and remind us forcefully not to take the Western market as the measure of all things. These studies also encourage respect for alternative consumption practices that, in different times and places, have worked as well or better than capitalist markets to define needs and provide goods to satisfy those needs. They have also often drawn attention to the way in which the arrival of capitalism, usually in the context of colonialism, has regularly undermined such alternatives, attempting to replace them with new needs and goods defined by the market. This helps explain why, as Daniel Miller summarizes, 'much of the early literature on consumption is replete with moral purpose', emphasizing the ways in which vulnerable groups have resisted commodities or have developed ritual means of 'taming' them, based on an awareness at some level of their capacity to destroy (1995: 144–5). In an era of globalization, however, the consumption of market commodities now occurs everywhere in the world. Moreover, the evidence is mounting that not only are Western commodities sometimes embraced by those whom we might have expected to reject them (e.g., video technology by Indigenous peoples of the Amazon), but this embrace frequently involves making use of these commodities for local purposes to defend or to enrich local culture rather than to replace it (e.g., the increasing popularity of sushi in North America).

Miller, a pioneer in this kind of consumption study, has therefore urged anthropologists to recognize that these new circumstances require that they move beyond a narrow focus on the destructive potential of mass-produced commodities to broader recognition of the role commodities play in a globalizing world. 'Desire for goods is not assumed to be natural nor goods per se as either positive or negative. Poverty is regarded as a relative lack of resources rather than the preservation of authenticity' (143). But this shift does not mean that concern about the negative consequences of capitalist practices disappears. In a global world in which everyone everywhere increasingly relies on commodities provided by a capitalist market, Miller believes that critical attention needs to refocus on 'inequalities of access and the deleterious impact of contemporary economic institutions on much of the world's population' (143).

A Dialectic between the Meaningful and the Material

Material goods carry culturally defined meanings, and what is viewed as meaningful (as stipulated by culture) can have material consequences. It is out of this dialectic between the meaningful and the material that the modes of livelihood followed by human beings everywhere emerge.

Key Terms

affluence 223
consumption 212
distribution 212
ecology 221
eco-niche 221
economy 210

eco-zones 221
extensive agriculture 211
food collectors 210
food producers 210
ideology 220
institutions 210

Chapter Summary

1. Our cultures suggest a range of options for making a living as well as furnishing the tools to pursue those options. Human beings have devised a variety of subsistence strategies to satisfy their material survival needs.

2. Human economic activity is usefully divided into three phases: production, distribution, and consumption. Some anthropologists argue that storage practices affect production, distribution, and consumption. In capitalist societies, market exchange is the dominant mode of distribution, yet many non-Western societies have traditionally carried out distribution without money or markets.

3. Formal neo-classical economic theory developed in an attempt to explain how capitalism works. Building on the emphasis which this theory gives to market exchange, economic anthropologists showed that non-capitalist societies regularly relied on non-market modes of exchange, such as reciprocity and redistribution, which still play restricted roles in societies dominated by the capitalist market.

4. Marxian economic anthropologists view production as more important than exchange in determining the patterns of economic life in a society. They argue that societies can be classified in terms of their modes of production. Each mode of production contains within it the potential for conflict between classes of people who receive differential benefits and losses from the productive process.

5. The internal explanation for consumption patterns argues that people produce material goods to satisfy basic human needs. The external explanation argues that consumption patterns depend on the particular external resources available within the eco-zone to which a particular society must adapt. Ethnographic evidence demonstrates that both internal and external explanations for consumption patterns are inadequate because they ignore how culture defines our needs and provides for their satisfaction according to its own logic—a logic that is irreducible to biology, psychology, or ecological pressure.

6. Particular consumption preferences that may seem irrational make sense when considered in the context of other consumption preferences and prohibitions in the same culture. Examples include Jewish dietary prohibitions, the role of banana leaves in the Trobriand Islands, and institutionalized sharing of consumption goods among the Plains Cree.

7. In an era of globalization, the consumption of Western market commodities is often embraced by those whom we might have expected to reject them. Moreover, this embrace frequently involves making use of market commodities for local purposes to defend or enrich local culture rather than to replace it. In a global world in which everyone everywhere increasingly relies on commodities provided by a capitalist market, critical attention needs to refocus on inequalities of access and the negative impact of contemporary economic institutions on most of the world's population.

Critical Thinking Questions

1. A basic division has been made between *food collectors* (those who gather, fish, or hunt) and *food producers* (those who depend on domesticated plants or animals, or both). How does this hearken back to the ethnical stages proposed by Lewis Henry Morgan in the nineteenth century?

2. Is reciprocity in all its forms an efficient way of distributing material goods for consumption? Support your answer with examples.

3. How does the discussion of network and corporate arrangements have the potential to bind the chapters in Part Three on the organization of material life?

4. Compare and contrast Wolf's *kin-ordered, tributary,* and *capitalist* modes of production. Is there an overlap between this classification of modes of production and the traditional anthropological classification of subsistence strategies?

5. Rhoda Halperin has argued that every economic system can be analyzed in terms of *locational movements,* or 'changes of place', and *appropriational movements,* or 'changes of hands'. How would you distinguish these two forms of 'movements'? Discuss their relevance in an economic analysis.

Suggested Readings

Douglas, Mary, and Baron Isherwood. 1996. *The World of Goods: Towards an Anthropology of Consumption,* rev. edn (New York: Routledge). *A discussion of consumption, economic theories about consumption, and what anthropologists can contribute to the study of consumption.*

Fagen, Brian M. 1996. 'Intellectual History of Archaeology', in *The Oxford Companion to Archaeology* (Oxford: Oxford University Press), 280–5; also available at: <http://www.ruf.rice.edu/~anth/people/faculty/docs/rmcintosh/paper3-rmcintosh.pdf>. *Roderick J. McIntosh of Rice University in Houston, Texas, writes on African and Old World comparative prehistory, intellectual history of prehistoric archaeology. Here he discusses how we consider the act of 'knowing' in the Western tradition and how we have wrestled with this problem of what we can never come to know.*

Lee, Richard. 2002. *The Dobe Ju/'hoansi,* 3rd edn (Belmont, CA: Wadsworth). *This highly readable ethnography contains important discussions about foraging as a way of making a living.*

Miller, Daniel, ed. 1995. *Acknowledging Consumption: A Review of New Studies* (New York: Routledge). *Groundbreaking essays that reconfigured the study of consumption anthropology.*

Plattner, Stuart, ed. 1989. *Economic Anthropology* (Palo Alto, CA: Stanford University Press). *A readable collection of articles by economic anthropologists. Displaying the achievements of formalist-inspired research, it also reconciles with substantivism and recognizes the contribution of Marxian analyses.*

Sahlins, Marshall. 1972. *Stone Age Economics* (Chicago: Aldine). *A series of classic essays on economic life, written from a substantivist position. Includes 'The Original Affluent Society'.*

Service, Elman R. 1975. *Origins of the State and Civilization: The Process of Cultural Evolution* (New York: Norton). *A discussion of the social organization in state and non-state societies.*

Wilk, Richard. 1996. *Economies and Cultures* (Boulder, CO: Westview). *A current, accessible 'theoretical guidebook' to the conflicting views of human nature that underlie disputes in economic anthropology.*

Related Websites

Cattle and War—The Nuer of Sudan: http://www.sudan101.com/nur.htm

Kwakiutl Indians: http://www.kwakiutl.bc.ca/

Mongongo Nuts: http://www.naturalhub.com/natural_food_guide_nuts_uncommon_Ricinodendron_rautanenii.htm

Morgan's Ethnical Stages: http://www.sociologyguide.com/thinkers/lh-morgan.php

Pictures of Nuer Culture: http://www.dlib.indiana.edu/collections/nuer/slides/

Potlatch: http://www.peabody.harvard.edu/POTLATCH/PAGE2.HTML

Pueblo Indians: http://www.puebloindian.com/

Part Four

Alliances for Living: Relationships

Human life starts with the individual but only succeeds as group life. In Part Four we examine some of the social relations that inventive human beings draw on as cultural resources in the struggle against the material conditions of life. The following two chapters explore how people bind themselves to one another by creating cultural relationships of kinship, marriage, and family, as well as other forms of community that reach beyond the bounds of these institutions, to create larger and more complex groupings that will inform their social, economic, and political lives.

Chapter 10

Systems of Relatedness and Relating

Chapter Outline

Learning Objectives

By the end of Chapter 10, you will be able to:

- understand the various ways humans organize their interdependence,
- detail the ways relatedness and group membership are determined,
- reflect on kinship terminology as a statement of rights and obligations,
- consider sex and gender and how this is marked in kinship,

- recognize patterns of descent in kinship,
- realize the importance of extended kin in cultures where this has significance,
- compare and contrast kin-based versus non-kin-based societies, and
- appreciate the nuances of the dimensions of group life.

Elisabeth Tooker, in her article on Lewis Henry Morgan and his contemporaries, observed that *Systems of Consanguinity and Affinity of the Human Family* (Lewis 1871) 'established the most esoteric of all anthropological studies: kinship . . .' (1992: 357). Indeed, although the anthropological study of kinship dates to the nineteenth century, it remains relevant. Michael G. Peletz (1995) commented that kinship as a study is alive and well and vital to anthropology. This is particularly so in the study of social relations. Kinship is the place to begin. For modern analysis to proceed, anthropological (and other) social historians require an understanding of socio-cultural transformation and the ethnographic context in which such transactions were first recorded. Here kinship is a central issue. As well, the twentieth century has witnessed profound far-reaching changes in relations between expansive political economies on the one hand and domains of household, kinship, and marriage on the other. The spread of capitalism and the attendant global transformations continue in this century. The nexus of kinship, gender, and social inequality is a problem relevant to pre-industrial, pre-modern societies and to their modern and postmodern counterparts. Indeed, analyzing gender, social inequality, social history and the entailments of capitalist transformation, modernity, and postmodernity begins with understanding relationships, and this has its foundation in kinship analysis (1995: 366–7).

Systems of Relatedness: Ways of Organizing Human Interdependence

The science fiction novel *Slapstick, or Lonesome No More!* by the late Kurt Vonnegut Jr (at that time Sr was still alive—kinship!) (1976) gives us Dr Wilbur Daffodil-11 Swain's plan to end loneliness by developing a new system of interrelatedness for Americans where everyone will be given new middle names composed of an item from nature and a number, thus Swain's Daffodil-11. Everyone with the same name (e.g., Daffodil) would be cousins and everyone with the same name and number would be siblings. A side effect was the development of clubs based on shared numbers (e.g., the 13 Club). Regardless, this send-up of American, indeed North American, feelings of loneliness illustrates that kinship relatedness is more or less a concern of all humans. We all want to belong. What this amounts to is the fact that although kinship is not a major organizational feature for many people who live in industrial societies such as ours, it does remain a concern to some extent.

In many contemporary societies (as well as most societies of the past), kinship is such a fundamental way of defining who people are and how they connect with others that outsiders, even anthropologists in their fieldwork situations, are made part of the system. Kinship enmeshes people in a web of relatives; it creates belonging. Each person in the web is aware of his or her rights and obligations; the position of each in relation to all others is made clear. Life together becomes organized, and organization was just what Dr Wilbur Daffodil-11 Swain wanted to regain for a disintegrating, lonely America.

Even after the dependency of infancy and childhood, human survival is immeasurably enhanced when people organize in groups. How we choose to organize ourselves is open to creative variation. Our traditional practices make survival possible but also constrain the forms our relationships may take.

This chapter focuses specifically on how human experiences such as sexuality, conception, birth, and nurturance are selectively interpreted and culturally shaped into the deeply layered practices that anthropologists call *relatedness, gender, marriage, family,* and *kinship*. It is important to remember that these relationships are always embedded in, and shaped by, politics, economics, and world views.

Determining Relatedness and Group Membership

People in all societies recognize that they are connected to some people in a variety of ways and that they are not connected to other people at all. Some anthropologists refer to these connections as **relatedness** (Carsten 2000). There are many forms of relatedness—relations based on friendship, marriage, adoption, parenthood, procreation, descent from a common ancestor, common labour, and so on.

One of the key forms of relatedness that anthropologists have studied for more than a century have been those forms of relatedness believed to come from shared substance and its transmission (Holy 1996: 171). That substance is either bodily substance (e.g., blood, genetic material, or mother's milk) or spiritual substance (e.g., soul, rebirth, the spirit world, nurturance, or love), or both. In the West, as well as in many other cultures in the world, this substance and its transmission are often seen as resulting from the process of sexual reproduction. The system of social relations based on prototypical procreative relationships is called **kinship** and was assumed to be a human universal based on biology, specifically the biology of procreation. This implied that Western beliefs about which people counted as one's 'real' relatives were universally

valid, leading anthropologists to conclude that all societies, especially the kinds of societies that anthropologists traditionally studied, would be organized in terms of genealogical relationships: mother, father, sister, brother, son, daughter, and so on.

Anthropologists saw their job as comparative and formal. Their goal was to compare kinship data from different societies in order to discover the universe of genealogical relatives. They tried to specify the formal 'rules' that would be characteristic of, for example, all patrilineal societies. This work did bring some important patterns to light. However, ethnographic evidence began to mount, indicating that the principles of relatedness that any group of people used to organize themselves were sometimes at odds with genealogical principles. Indeed, in some cases, relatedness based on birth was only one of several ways in which people created strong and enduring ties with one another.

Anthropologists call relationships based on mating **marriage** and those based on birth **descent**. Although nurturance is ordinarily seen to be closely connected with mating and birth, it need not be, and all societies have ways of acknowledging a relationship based on nurturance alone. We call this relationship **adoption**.

Although marriage is based on mating, descent on birth, and adoption on nurturance, marriage is not the same thing as mating, descent is not the same thing as birth, and adoption is not the same thing as nurturance. Different societies choose to highlight some features of those experiences while downplaying or even ignoring others. Europeans and North Americans know that in their societies mating is not the same as marriage, although a valid marriage encourages mating between the married partners. Similarly, all births do not constitute valid links of descent: children whose parents have not been married according to accepted legal or religious specifications do not fit the cultural logic of descent, and many societies offer no positions that they can properly fill. Finally, not all acts of nurturance are recognized as adoption: consider, for example, foster parents in Canada, whose custody of foster children is officially temporary.

Marriage, descent, and adoption are thus selective. One society may emphasize women as the bearers of children and base its kinship system on this fact, paying little formal attention to the male's role in conception. Another society may trace connections through men, emphasizing the paternal role in conception and reducing the maternal role. A third society may encourage its members to adopt not only children but also adult siblings, blurring the link between biological reproduction and family creation. Even though they contradict one another, all three understandings can be justified with reference to the pan-human experiences of mating, birth, and nurturance.

Consider the North American kinship term *aunt*. This term seems to refer to a woman who occupies a unique position in one of four different ways: as a father's sister, a mother's sister, a father's brother's wife, or a mother's brother's wife. All those women have something in common, placed as they are into a single kinship category. Prototypically, they are one generation older than you and are sisters or sisters-in-law of your parents. However, in North America, we may also refer to our mother's best friend as an *aunt*, thereby making her *fictive kin*. By doing so, we recognize the strengths of this system of classification. By way of contrast, in Chile, *tía*, the Spanish term that translates as 'aunt', is regularly used by children to refer to female friends of their parents. Indeed, well into early adulthood, people continue to use the term to refer to women who take on the role of 'mother' but with whom they are not as intimate as they would be with their own mothers.

Thus, kinship is the idiom of a selective interpretation of the common human experiences of mating, birth, and nurture resulting in a set of coherent principles allowing people to assign one another group membership. These principles normally cover several significant issues: how to carry out the reproduction of legitimate group members (marriage or adoption), where group members should live after marriage (residence rules), how to establish links between generations (descent), and how to pass on positions in society (succession) or material goods (inheritance). Thus people are located within social groups in relation to one another both in space and over time.

Sex, Gender, and Kinship

Kinship is based on, but irreducible to, biology. It is a cultural interpretation of the 'facts' of human reproduction, and a most basic 'fact', recognized in some form in all societies, is that two different kinds of human beings, males and females, must co-operate sexually to produce offspring (although what they believe to be

the contribution of each party to the outcome varies from society to society). Anthropologists use the term **sex** to refer to the observable physical characteristics that distinguish females and males. People everywhere pay attention to *morphological sex* (the appearance of external genitalia and observable secondary sex characteristics such as enlarged breasts in females). Scientists also consider *gonadal sex* (ovaries in females; testes in males) and *chromosomal sex* (♀, two X chromosomes; ♂, one X chromosome and one Y chromosome).

Cross-cultural research demonstrates that physical sex differences do not allow us to predict the roles that we will play in any particular society. Consequently, anthropologists distinguish sex from **gender**—the cultural construction of beliefs and behaviours considered appropriate for each sex.

Outward physical features used to distinguish females from males may not always be obvious. Sometimes genetic or hormonal factors produce ambiguous external genitalia, a phenomenon called *hermaphroditism*. Steroid 5-alpha reductase deficiency (5ARD), a rare hormonal defect in males, is one example. At puberty, increased testosterone levels cause changes typical of males: a deepening voice, muscle development, growth of the penis, and descent of the testicles. Gilbert Herdt (1994) investigated cases of individuals with 5ARD in the Dominican Republic and

adoption Kinship relationships based on nurturance, often in the absence of other connections based on mating or birth.

descent The principle based on culturally recognized parent–child connections that define the social categories to which people belong.

gender The cultural construction of beliefs and behaviours considered appropriate for each sex.

kinship Social relationships that are prototypically derived from the universal human experiences of mating, birth, and nurturance.

marriage An institution that prototypically involves a man and a woman, transforms the status of the participants, carries implications about sexual access, gives offspring a position in society, and establishes connections between the kin of a husband and the kin of a wife.

relatedness The socially recognized ties that connect people in a variety of ways.

sex Observable physical characteristics that distinguish two kinds of humans, females and males, needed for biological reproduction.

in New Guinea. In both places, the sexually anomalous individuals had been assigned to a locally recognized third sex called *guevedoche* ('testicles at twelve') in the Dominican Republic and *kwolu-aatmwol* ('changing into a male thing') among the Sambia of New Guinea.

The existence of *supernumerary* (i.e., more than the standard two) sexes in cultures where the presence of ambiguous genitalia at birth seem to play no obvious role has been documented. In the Byzantine civilization of late antiquity, phenotypic differences were deliberately created in the case of eunuchs, whose testicles were removed or destroyed, often before puberty (Ringrose 1994). In the case of the hijras of Gujarat, India, adult males deliberately cut off both penis and testicles in order to dedicate themselves to the Mother Goddess Bahuchara Mata (Nanda 1994; Figure 10.1). In both cases, third gender roles distinct from traditional feminine and masculine gender roles are believed appropriate for third-sexed individuals.

Perhaps the most famous example of supernumerary without morphological sex anomalies is that of the so-called berdache. Will Roscoe points out that

> the key features of male and female berdache roles were, in order of importance, *productive specialization* (crafts and domestic work for male berdaches; and warfare, hunting, and leadership roles in the case of female berdaches), *supernatural sanction* (in the form of an authorization and/or bestowal of powers from extra-societal sources), and *gender variation* (in relation to normative cultural expectations for male and female genders)

commonly, but not always, marked by cross-dressing (1994: 332). Berdaches were accepted and respected members of their communities, and their economic and religious pursuits were culturally more significant than their sexual practices.

Early French explorers in the Americas used *berdache* to mean 'male prostitute'. For this reason, many gay and lesbian anthropologists refuse to use the term, as do those members of contemporary Indigenous societies who want to reclaim this alternative gender role for themselves. No single term, however, has yet reached universal acceptance. Perhaps no single term is adequate; after all, male berdaches have been described in almost 150 Indigenous North American societies and female berdaches in perhaps half that number. For a deeper discussion, see the work of Jean-

Figure 10.1 In hijra communities, third gender roles—distinct from traditional masculine and feminine gender roles—are considered appropriate for third-sexed individuals. Above, a hijra onlooker watches another hijra apply make-up.

Guy A. Goulet (1996). Goulet, in discussing personhood and gender, argues that 'anthropologists have conceptualized gender variance among Native North Americans without paying attention to the ways in which Indigenous practices "construct members of a community 'as' woman or 'as' man (or member of other gender category)"' (1996: 683).

For many people, the 'natural' existence of only two sexes, each with its own gender role, seems too obvious to question. Nevertheless, Thomas Laqueur (1990) has shown that the 'two-sex model', which most contemporary Westerners accept as transparently obvious, only took root after the Renaissance. Prior to that, the bodies of all human beings were evaluated in terms of a 'one-sex model' based on the Platonic notion that there was one ideal human form, which all actual human beings embodied to greater or lesser degrees. Moreover, as Roscoe points out, 'the presence of multiple genders does not require belief in the existence of three or more physical sexes but, minimally, a view of physical differences as unfixed, or insufficient on their own to establish gender, or simply less important than individual and social factors' (1994: 342). These observations sustain the key assertion of Collier and Yanagisako: 'there are no "facts", biological or material, that have social consequences and cultural meanings in and of themselves' (1987: 39).

Interestingly, supernumerary sexes and genders can coexist alongside strongly marked male–female duality, as among the Sambia, perhaps serving to temper the absolutism of that duality. That male–female duality should be an issue for the Sambia reminds us that no human society is unconcerned about biological and social reproduction. However kinship institutions, which build on gender duality, do more than provide for reproduction. Kinship not only classifies people, but it also establishes and enforces the conventions by which different classes of people interact with one another. In this way, societies are able to maintain social order without central government.

Understanding Different Kinship Systems

Kinship practices, rather than written statutes, clarify for people what rights and obligations they owe one another. But the first Westerners who encountered different kinship practices found some of them highly unusual. Western explorers discovered, for example, that some non-Western people only distinguished among their relatives on the basis of generation and sex. To refer to people one generation older than the speaker required only two terms: one applying to men and one applying to women. The explorers mistakenly concluded that these people were unable to tell the difference between their fathers and their uncles because they used the same kin term, *father*, for both. They assumed that terms like *father* and *uncle* were universally recognized kinship categories. However, by referring to all these men by the same kin term, they were no more deluded than English speakers are when they assert that their father's sister and mother's brother's wife are equally their *aunts*.

The categories of feeling these people associated with different kin were as real as, but different from, the emotions Westerners associate with kin. 'Just as the word *father* in English means a great deal more than lineal male ancestor of the first ascending generation, *aita* in Basque has many local connotations irreducible to *father*, as we understand the term' (Greenwood and Stini 1977: 333). Because the world of kin is a world of expectations and obligations, it is fundamentally a moral world charged with feeling. In some societies, a man's principal authority figure is his mother's brother, and his father is a figure of affection and unwavering support. A phrase like 'God the Father' would not mean the same thing in those societies as it does in a society in which the father has life-and-death control over his children and a mother's brothers are without significant authority.

Patterns of Descent in Kinship

A central aspect of kinship is descent—the principle that defines social categories through culturally recognized parent–child connections. Descent groups are defined by ancestry and so exist in time. Descent involves the transmission of membership through parent–child links and the incorporation of these people into groups. In some societies, descent group membership controls how people mobilize for social action.

Two major strategies are employed in establishing patterns of descent.

(1) In **bilateral descent** (or *cognatic descent*), the descent group is formed by people who believe they are related to each other by connections made through their mothers and fathers *equally*. Two kinds of bilateral kinship groups have been identified by anthropologists. One relatively rare form is made up of people who claim to be related to one another through ties either from the mother's side or from the father's side to a common ancestor. The other kind, called a *bilateral kindred*, is much more common and consists of the relatives of one person or group of siblings.

(2) **Unilineal descent**, the most common form, is based on the assumption that the most significant kin relationships must be traced through *either* the mother *or* the father. Unilineal descent groups with links traced through a father are called *patrilineal*; those traced through a mother are called *matrilineal*.

Bilateral Kindreds

Europeans and North Americans are most familiar with the **bilateral kindred** kinship group, which forms around a particular individual. It includes all the people linked to that individual through kin of

bilateral descent The principle that a descent group is formed by people who believe they are related to each other by connections made through their mothers and fathers equally (sometimes called *cognatic descent*).

bilateral kindred A kinship group that consists of the relatives of one person or group of siblings.

unilineal descent The principle that a descent group is formed by people who believe they are related to each other by links made through a father or mother only.

both sexes—people conventionally called *relatives* in English (Figure 10.2). These people form a group only because of their connection to the central person or persons, known in the terminology of kinship as *Ego*. In North American society, bilateral kindreds assemble when Ego is baptized, confirmed, bar or bat mitzvahed, graduated from university, married, or buried. Each person within Ego's bilateral kindred has his or her own separate kindred. For example, Ego's father's sister's daughter has a kindred that includes people related to her through her father and his siblings—people to whom Ego is not related. The major strength and major weakness of bilateral kindreds is that they are widely extended and can form broad networks, but they do not endure beyond the lifetime of an individual Ego.

A classic bilateral kindred is found among the Ju/'hoansi (!Kung) of the Kalahari Desert in southern Africa (see Figure 10.3; see also EthnoProfile 10.1: Ju/'hoansi [!Kung]). Canadian anthropologist Richard Lee points out that for the Ju/'hoansi, every individual in the society can be linked to every other individual by a kinship term, either through males or through females.

In essence, a Ju/'hoan camp consists of relatives, friends, and in-laws who have found that they can live and work well together. Under this flexible principle, brothers may be united or divided; fathers and sons may live together or apart. Further, during his or her lifetime a Ju/'hoan may live at many water holes with many different groups. (1992b: 62)

A wide range of kinspeople make this flexibility possible. When someone wanted to move, he or she had kin at many different water holes and could choose to activate any of several appropriate kin ties.

Bilateral kindred provides social flexibility although these can become problematic in at least four kinds of social circumstances:

(1) where clear-cut membership in a particular social group must be determined,
(2) where social action requires the formation of groups that are larger than individual families,
(3) where conflicting claims to land and labour must be resolved, and
(4) where people are concerned to perpetuate a particular social order over time.

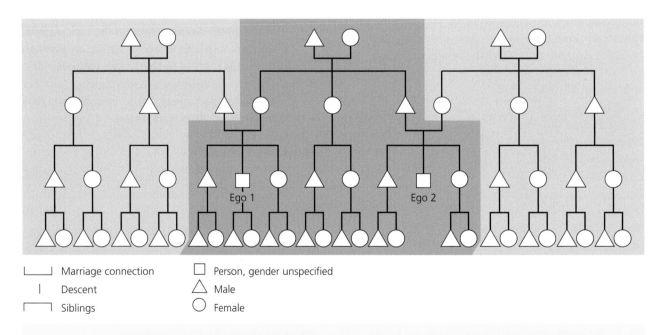

Marriage connection	Person, gender unspecified
Descent	Male
Siblings	Female

Figure 10.2 A bilateral kindred includes all recognized relatives on Ego's father's and mother's sides. The dark area in the centre indicates where the kindreds of Ego 1 and Ego 2 overlap.

EthnoProfile 10.1

Ju/'hoansí (!Kung)

Region: Southern Africa

Nations: Botswana and Namibia

Language: The Ju/'hoansi are speakers of Ju/'hoan of the Ju language family

Population: 45,000

Environment: Desert

Livelihood: Hunting and gathering

Political organization: Traditionally, egalitarian bands; today, part of modern nation-states

For more information: Lee, Richard B. 1992b. *The Dobe Ju/'hoansi,* 2nd edn (New York: Holt, Rinehart & Winston); Solway, Jacqueline, ed. 2006. *The Politics of Egalitarianism: Theory and Practice* (New York: Berghahn Books)

In societies that face these dilemmas, unilineal descent groups are usually formed.

Unilineal Descent Groups

Unilineal descent groups are found all over the world and are based on the principle that certain kinds of parent–child relationships are more important than others. In patrilineal systems, an individual belongs to a group formed through male sex links, the lineage of his or her father. In matrilineal systems, an individual belongs to a group formed through female sex links, the lineage of his or her mother. In a patrilineal society, women and men belong to a **patrilineage** formed by father–child links (Figure 10.4); similarly, in a matrilineal society, men and women belong to a **matrilineage** formed by mother–child connections (Figure 10.5). In other words, membership in the group is, on the face of it, unambiguous. An individual belongs to only one lineage. This is in contrast to a bilateral kindred. However, as Segalen observes, a pattern of unilineal descent itself is 'no more than a kind of external framework', which can support a wide range of cultural variations (1986: 51–2).

Figure 10.3 A classic bilateral kindred, a kinship group that consists of the relatives of one person or group of siblings, is found among the Ju'hoansi. A !Kung bushman grandmother holds her grandchild.

Lineages

The *-lineal* in patrilineal and matrilineal refers to the nature of the social group formed, and they vary in size, ranging from 20 or 30 members to several hundred. Before 1949, some Chinese lineages were composed of more than 1,000 members. **Lineages** can endure over time and in a sense have an independent existence. As long as people can remember from whom they descended, lineages can endure. Most lineages have a time depth of about five generations: grandparents, parents, Ego, children, and grandchildren. When members of a group believe that they can no longer accurately specify the genealogical links that connect them, but believe that they are in some way connected, we find what anthropologists call *clans*. A **clan** is usually made up of lineages that the society's members believe to be related to each other through links that go back into mythic times. Sometimes the common ancestor of

clan A descent group formed by members who believe they have a common (sometimes mythical) ancestor, even if they cannot specify the genealogical links.

lineages The *consanguineal* members, or blood relatives, of descent groups who believe they can trace their descent from known ancestors.

matrilineage A social group formed by people connected by mother–child links.

patrilineage A social group formed by people connected by father–child links.

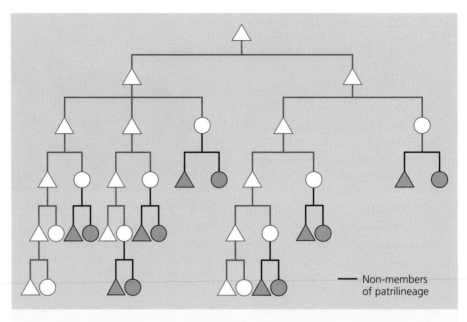

Figure 10.4 Patrilineal descent: all those who trace descent through males to a common male ancestor are indicated in white.

each clan is said to be an animal that lived at the beginning of time.

The memories people have of their ancestry are often transmitted in the form of myth or legend. Rather than accurate historical records, they are better understood in Malinowskian terms as mythical charters, justifications from the invisible world for the visible arrangements of the society (see the discussion of myth in Chapter 6). While lineages might look solid and unchanging, they are often more flexible than they appear.

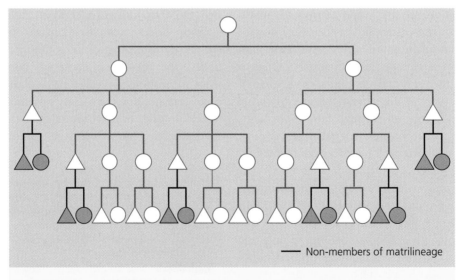

Figure 10.5 Matrilineal descent: all those who trace descent through females to a common female ancestor are indicated in white.

The most important feature of lineages is that they are *corporate* in organization—that is, a lineage has a single legal personality. As the Ashanti put it, a lineage is 'one person' (Fortes 1953). To outsiders, all members of a lineage are equal *in law* to all others. Lineages are also corporate in that they control property, especially land, as a unit. Such groups are found in societies where rights to use land are crucial and must be monitored over time.

Lineages are also the main political associations in the societies that have them. Individuals have no political or legal status in such societies except through lineage membership. They have relatives outside the lineage, but their own political and legal status comes through the lineage.

Patrilineages

By far the most common form of lineage organization is the patrilineage. The prototypical kernel of a patrilineage is the father–son pair. Although women normally leave these lineages when they marry, they do not relinquish their interest in them, and they may play an active role in the affairs of their own patrilineages for many years.

An assumption of hierarchy exists in patrilineal societies: men believe they are superior to women, and many women seem to agree. However, there is a puzzle at the heart of these societies. Women with little power, who are strangers to the lineage, nevertheless marry its members and produce the children who perpetuate the lineage. Ironically, the future of the patrilineage depends on people who do not belong to it! A second irony is that women must leave their own lineages to reproduce the next generation of somebody else's lineage. Women in patrilineal societies are often torn between conflicting interests and loyalties (see Karp 1986). Should they support their own children or their fathers and brothers?

A classic patrilineal system was found among the Nuer of the Sudan and Ethiopia (see Map 10.2). At the time of his fieldwork in the 1930s, English anthropologist E.E. Evans-Pritchard noted that the Nuer were divided into at least 20 clans defined as the largest groups of people who

- trace their descent patrilineally from a common ancestor,

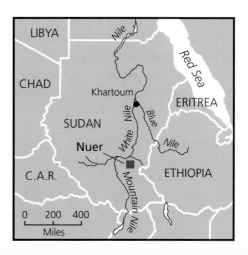

Map 10.2 Nuer

- cannot marry each other, and
- consider sexual relations within the group to be incestuous.

The 20 clans each consisted of lineages linked to each other by presumed ties of patrilineal descent. The most basic is what Evans-Pritchard called a *minimal lineage*, consisting of three to five generations.

For example, members of lineages A and B might consider themselves related because they believed that the founder of lineage A had been the older brother of the founder of lineage B. These two minimal lineages formed a *minor lineage*—all those descended from a common father, believed to be the father of the two founders of A and B. Minor lineages connect to other minor lineages, by yet another presumed common ancestor, forming *major lineages*. These major lineages are also believed to share a common ancestor and thus form a *maximal lineage*. The members of two maximal lineages believed their founders had been the sons of the clan ancestor; thus, all members of the clan are believed to be patrilineally related.

Disputes among the Nuer emerged along lineage lines. Suppose a quarrel erupted between two men whose minimal lineages were in different minor lineages. Each would be joined by men who belonged to his minor lineage, even if they were not in his minimal lineage. The dispute would be resolved when the quarrelling minor lineages recognized that they were all part of the same major lineage. Similarly, the minor lineages to one major lineage would ally if a dispute with an opposed major lineage broke out. This process of groups coming together and opposing one another, called **segmentary opposition**, is expressed in kinship terms but represents a very common social process.

Evans-Pritchard noted that lineages were important to the Nuer for political purposes. Members of the same lineage in the same village were conscious of being in a social group with common ancestors and symbols, corporate rights in territory, and common interests in cattle. When a son in the lineage married, these people helped provide the **bridewealth** cattle. If the son were killed, they—indeed, all members of his patrilineage regardless of where they lived—would avenge him and would hold the funeral ceremony for him. Nevertheless, relationships among the members of a patrilineage were not necessarily harmonious:

> A Nuer is bound to his paternal kin from whom he derives aid, security, and status, but in return for these benefits he has many obligations and commitments. [However,] duties and rights easily conflict. Moreover, the privileges of [patrilineal] kinship cannot be divorced from authority, discipline, and a strong sense of moral obligation, all of which are irksome to Nuer. They do not deny them, but they kick against them when their personal interests run counter to them. (1951: 162)*

Matrilineages

In matrilineages, descent is traced through women rather than through men. In a patrilineage, a woman's children are not in her lineage; in a matrilineage, a man's children are not in his lineage. However, certain features of matrilineages make them more than just mirror images of patrilineages.

- The prototypical kernel of a matrilineage is the sister–brother pair; a matrilineage may be thought of as a group of brothers and sisters connected through links made by women. Brothers marry out and often live with the family of their wives, but they maintain an active interest in the affairs of their lineage.

- The most important man in a boy's life is not his father (who is not in his lineage) but his mother's brother, from whom he will receive his lineage inheritance.

- A matrilineage is not the same thing as a *matriarchy* (a society in which women rule); brothers often retain what appears to be a controlling interest in the lineage. Indeed, some anthropologists claim that the male members of a matrilineage are supposed to run the lineage even though there is more autonomy for women in matrilineal societies than in patrilineal societies. However, trying to say something about matrilineal societies in general is difficult. The ethnographic evidence suggests that matrilineages must be examined on a case-by-case basis.

With the matrilineal Navajo, the basic unit of social organization is the subsistence residential unit composed of a head mother, her husband, and some of their children with their spouses and children (Witherspoon 1975: 82; Figure 10.6). The leader of the unit is normally a man, usually the husband of the head mother. He directs livestock and agricultural operations and is the one who deals with the outside world: 'He speaks for the unit at community meetings, negotiates with the traders and car salesmen, arranges marriages and ceremonies, talks to visiting strangers, and so on.' He seems to be in charge. But it is the head mother around whom the unit is organized as she

> is identified with the land, the herd, and the agricultural fields. All residence rights can be traced back to her, and her opinions and wishes are always given the greatest consideration and usually prevail. In a sense, however, she delegates much of her role and prestige to the leader of the unit. If we think of the unit as a corporation, and the leader as its president, the head mother will be the chairman of the board. . . . Because the power and importance of the head mother offer a deceptive appearance to the observer, many students of the Navajo have failed to see the importance of her role. But if one has lived a long time in one of these units, one soon becomes aware of who ultimately has the cards and directs the game. When there is a divorce between the leader and the head, it is always the leader who leaves and the head mother who returns, even if the land originally belonged to the mother of the leader. (82–3)

---

*Readers interested in what has happened to Nuer kinship and relatedness as a consequence of the seemingly unending civil war in the Sudan should look at Hutchinson 1996 or 2002.

Figure 10.6 The head mother of a Navajo subsistence residence unit 'is identified with the land, the herd, and the agricultural fields'.

Overall, evidence from matrilineal societies reveals some domains of experience in which men and women are equal, some in which men are in control, and some in which women are in control. Observers and participants may disagree about which of these domains of experience is more or less central to Navajo life.

Matrilineal societies can have contradictions, and this is especially clear in societies that are strongly matrilineal and encourage residence with the wife's matrilineage. Among the Bemba of Zambia, for example, a man is a stranger in his wife's house, where he goes when he marries. A man may feel great affection for his father, but he will not be his father's heir. He will inherit from his mother's brother, who lives elsewhere. And although a father may wish to have his son inherit from him, he must give to his sister's son (Richards 1954).

Traditionally, the classic case comes from the Trobriand Islands. Malinowski interpreted it in the way just described (see EthnoProfile 9.1: Trobriand Islanders). But more recently, Annette Weiner called Malinowski's interpretation into question. Weiner argues that to understand matrilineal kinship in the Trobriand Islands, one must begin by seeing the sister–brother pair as an integral unit:

> [The sister–brother pair] makes complementary contributions both to a woman's brother's children and to a woman's own children. . . . In the former instance, a man and his sister (father and father's sister to a child) contribute their own [lineage] resources to the man's

children, thus building up these children with resources that they may use but may not subsequently pass on to their own children. . . . In the latter case, a woman and her brother (mother and mother's brother) contribute to the regeneration of [the matrilineage]—the woman through the process of conception and the man through the control and transmission of [matrilineage] property such as land and palm trees. (1980: 286–7)

The result is that both a man and his sister 'give' to the man's children, and his children return things to them later in life.

Kinship Terminologies

People everywhere use special terms to refer to people they recognize as relatives. Anthropologists have identified six major patterns of kinship terminology, based on how people categorize their cousins, that reflect common solutions to structural problems faced by societies organized in terms of kinship. They provide clues concerning how the vast and undifferentiated world of potential kin may be divided. Kinship terminologies suggest both the external boundaries and internal divisions of the kinship groups, and they outline the structure of <u>rights and obligations</u> assigned to different members of the society.

In recent years, however, anthropologists have questioned the value of these idealized models, mostly because they are highly formalized and do not capture the full range of people's actual practices. Perhaps the main value to come from formal kinship studies is the fact that anthropologists took the ways other people classified their relatives seriously, and they were able to show the logic that informed such classifications and direct our attention to the important categories in a society.

---

bridewealth The transfer of certain symbolically important goods from the family of the groom to the family of the bride on the occasion of their marriage. It represents compensation to the wife's lineage for the loss of her labour and for child-bearing capacities.

segmentary opposition A mode of hierarchical social organization in which groups beyond the most basic emerge only in opposition to other groups on the same hierarchical level.

Criteria for Distinctions

Anthropologists have identified several criteria that people use to indicate how people are related to one another. From the most common to the least common, these criteria include the following:

- *Generation.* Kin terms distinguish relatives according to the generation to which the relatives belong. In English, the term *cousin* conventionally refers to someone of the same generation as Ego.
- *Gender.* The gender of an individual is used to differentiate kin. In Spanish, *primo* refers to a male cousin and *prima* to a female cousin. In English, cousins are not distinguished on the basis of gender, but *uncle* and *aunt* are distinguished on the basis of both generation and gender.
- *Affinity.* A distinction is made on the basis of a connection through marriage. This criterion is used in Spanish when *suegra* (Ego's spouse's mother) is distinguished from *madre* (Ego's mother). In matrilineal societies, Ego's mother's sister and father's sister are distinguished from one another on the basis of affinity. The mother's sister is a direct, lineal relative; the father's sister is an affine; and they are called by different terms.
- *Collaterality.* A distinction is made between kin who are believed to be in a direct line and those who are 'off to one side', linked to Ego through a lineal relative. In English, the distinction of **collaterality** is exemplified by the distinction between *mother* and *aunt* or *father* and *uncle*.
- *Bifurcation.* The distinction of **bifurcation** is employed when kinship terms referring to the mother's side of the family differ from those referring to the father's side.
- *Relative age.* Relatives of the same category may be distinguished on the basis of whether they are older or younger than Ego. Among the Ju/'hoansi, for example, speakers must separate 'older brother' (*!ko*) from 'younger brother' (*tsin*).
- *Gender of linking relative.* This criterion is related to collaterality. It distinguishes *cross-*

relatives (usually cousins) from *parallel relatives* (also usually cousins). Parallel relatives are linked through two brothers or two sisters. **Parallel cousins**, for example, are Ego's father's brother's children or mother's sister's children. Cross-relatives are linked through a brother–sister pair. Thus, **cross-cousins** are Ego's mother's brother's children or father's sister's children. The gender of either Ego or the cousins does not matter; rather, the important factor is the gender of the linking relative (Figure 10.7).

Kinship and Alliance

Societies based on kinship attempt to resolve the difficulties of intergroup relations by connecting kinship with marriage. By promoting or *prescribing* certain kinds of marriage, reproduction of their own memberships and long-term alliances with other groups are ensured.

Anthropologists find two major types of prescriptive marriage patterns in patrilineal societies.

(1) *Father's sister's daughter marriage system* sets up a pattern called *direct exchange marriage.* In this pattern, a line that has received a wife from another line in one generation gives a wife back in the next generation. This is called a *father's sister's daughter marriage system* because, from a man's point of view, that woman is the prototypical spouse. However, any woman of the appropriate line is an eligible marriage partner for him. Before the marriage occurs, the men and women of the groom's line negotiate with those of the bride's line to determine the appropriate match.

(2) *Mother's brother's daughter marriage system*, which is more common, sets up a pattern of *asymmetrical exchange marriage.* Unlike direct exchange systems, this marriage pattern does not balance out over the generations. Women always marry into the line their father's sisters married into, and men always find wives in the line their mothers came from. This pattern provides a permanent alliance among the lines involved. The prototypical wife for a man is his mother's brother's daughter.

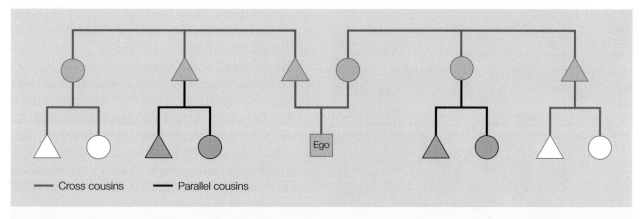

Figure 10.7 Cross-cousins and parallel cousins: Ego's cross-cousins are the children of Ego's father's sister and mother's brother. Ego's parallel cousins are the children of Ego's father's brother and mother's sister.

People recognize certain classes of kin as potential marriage partners, and their kinship terminologies reflect this fact. Hence, if Ego's mother's brother doesn't have a daughter, all is not lost. Ego may not be looking for a literal mother's brother's daughter. Women whom anthropologists refer to as 'mother's brother's daughters' are any women of Ego's generation who are members of his mother's patrilineage.

Birth order can also be significant in lineage and family dynamics and illustrate alliances. For example, Canadian anthropologist Naomi McPherson (2007) discusses trade networks and trade-friendships in Northwest New Britain, Papua New Guinea. In an excerpt of her work (note Naomi McPherson, *In Their Own Words*) we see the link between economics, trade networks, friendships (trade partners), and kinship affiliation (being first-born). Such integrated analysis gives us deeper insight into the 'workings' of a society and, further, generally reinforces our dedication to holism in anthropology. Interesting features McPherson discusses are the ceremonies that maintain trade-friendships. The ceremonial dress for the first-born becomes a display of trade items, both raw materials (a geographic speciality) such as red ochre and obsidian as well as traded 'craft' materials such as the '*poipoi sara* woven armband [which] is only manufactured by the Lolo from a black vine that grows in their particular environment' (2007). In effect, the items used in the ceremonial dress of the first-born advertise the extent of the trade-friendship and the family's access to the network (Figure 10.8).

First-borns are exemplars of parental achievement and facilitate the trade partnerships and networks for their younger siblings.

Adoption

Kinship systems may appear to be fairly rigid sets of rules that use the accident of birth to thrust people into social positions laden with rights and obligations they cannot escape. Social positions that people are assigned at birth are sometimes called **ascribed statuses**, and positions within a kinship system have long been viewed as the prototypical ascribed statuses in any society. Ascribed statuses are often contrasted with

ascribed statuses Social positions people are assigned at birth.

bifurcation A criterion employed in the analysis of kinship terminologies in which kinship terms referring to the mother's side of the family are distinguished from those referring to the father's side.

collaterality A criterion employed in the analysis of kinship terminologies in which a distinction is made between kin who are believed to be in a direct line and those who are 'off to one side', linked to the speaker by a lineal relative.

cross-cousins The children of a person's parents' opposite-gender siblings (a father's sister's children or a mother's brother's children).

parallel cousins The children of a person's parents' same-gender siblings (a father's brother's children or a mother's sister's children).

Figure 10.8 In West New Britain, a Bariai boy is decorated by his clansmen for one of the numerous firstborn (*lautave*) ceremonies held in his name (top). Bariai men display and distribute shell money (*vula*) at the naming ceremony of a first-born child (bottom).

achieved statuses, those social positions that people may attain later in life, often as the result of their own (or other people's) effort, such as becoming a spouse or university graduate. All societies have ways of incorporating outsiders into their kinship groups, however, which they achieve by converting supposedly ascribed kinship statuses into achieved ones, thus undermining the distinction between them. We will use the term

adoption to refer to these practices, which allow people to transform relationships based on nurturance into relations of kinship.

Nurturance is the central theme in Barbara Bodenhorn's (2000) discussion of adoption with the Iñupiat, whalers on the North Slope of northern Alaska. Adoption, which is very common in the polar region, highlights how the practice of parenting overrides 'begetting and bearing'. Bodenhorn estimates that most adults have themselves been adopted or have lived in a household in which children have been adopted. People who adopt usually know each other but do not have to be close kin. The most common reasons that people gave Bodenhorn for adopting was that they 'wanted to', that they had too many boys and wanted a girl (or vice versa), that 'all my other brothers and sisters have adopted', that 'we kind of exchanged', or that 'we had too many kids'. Often adoption occurred because the child wanted to be adopted. In many cases, the shift was to everyone's satisfaction, but even when it was not, the question of where the child should end up was never based on the argument that he or she belonged with his or her biological parents. After adoption, the degree to which a relationship is maintained between the birth parents and the child is up to the child and ranges from no contact to regular shared activities. The point here is that recognition of the biological relationship becomes a matter of choice— there is no social stigma involved if a child ignores his or her biological parents, but people do disapprove if the child does not act like a son or daughter to his or her adoptive parents.

From the Iñupiaq perspective, the people who do the parenting are the parents—biology does not create parents but action does. Thus, many kinds of people may play the role of parents. People do not deny biological kinship, but their primary relationships are with the people who brought them up. There seems to be little that is permanent about Iñupiaq relatedness, for people move in and out of relatedness with others. From another perspective, however, it is the possibility of reactivating 'additions' at any time that endures. But to reactivate 'additions' people have to act, and act intentionally. This is kinship based on agency: 'What is real is acted on and mutually recognized' (143). Keeping such ties active is not easy. Because relatedness is not permanent, the maintenance of connections requires constant reciprocal activity: 'shared tools, food, labour, political alliance, ceremonial participation, and simply company. . . . It is *this* labour—the work of being related—rather than the labour of giving birth or the 'fact' of shared substance that marks out the kinship sphere from the potentially infinite universe of relatives who may or may not belong' (143).

Kinship Extended: Cultures of Relatedness

Negotiation of Kin Ties among the Ju/'hoansi

Michael Peletz observes that many contemporary kinship studies in anthropology 'tend to devote considerable analytic attention to themes of contradiction, paradox, and ambivalence' (1995: 343). This is true of Richard Lee's analysis of kinship among the Ju/'hoansi. Lee learned that for the Ju/'hoansi 'the principles of kinship constitute, not an invariant code of laws written in stone but instead a whole series of codes consistent enough to provide structure but open enough to be flexible'. He adds, 'I found the best way to look at [Ju/'hoansi] kinship is as a game, full of ambiguity and nuance' (1992b: 62).

The Ju/'hoansi have what seems to be a straightforward bilateral kindred with alternating generations. Outside the nuclear core of the system, the same terms are used by Ego for kin of his or her generation, his or her grandparents' generation, and his or her grandchildren's generation. Likewise, the same terms are used for Ego's parents' generation and children's generation. These terms have behavioural correlates, which Lee calls *joking* and *avoidance*. Anyone in Ego's own generation (except opposite-gender siblings) and in the grandparents' generation or the grandchildren's generation is joking kin. Anyone in Ego's parents' generation or children's generation is avoidance kin, as are Ego's same-gender siblings. Relatives in a joking relationship can be relaxed and affectionate and can speak using familiar forms. In an avoidance relationship, however, respect and reserve are required, and formal language must be used. Many of these relationships may be warm and friendly if the proper respect is shown in public; however, people in an avoidance relationship may not marry one another.

The 'game', as Lee puts it, in the Ju/'hoansi system begins when a child is named. The Ju/'hoansi have very few names: 36 for men and 32 for women. Every child must be named for someone: a first-born son should get his father's father's name and a first-born daughter her father's mother's name. Second-born children are supposed to be named after the mother's father and mother. Later children are named after the father's brothers and sisters and the mother's brothers and sisters. It is no wonder that the Ju/'hoansi invent a host of nicknames to distinguish among people who have the same name. Ju/'hoansi naming practices impinge upon the kinship system because all people with the same name will claim to be related. A man older than you with your name is called *!kun!a* ('old name'), which is the same term used for *grandfather*. A man younger than you with your name is called *!kuna* ('young name'), the same term used for *grandson*. It does not matter how people are 'really' related to others with the same name or even if they are related at all according to formal kinship terminology; the name relationship takes precedence.

But the complications do not end here. By metaphorical extension, anyone with your father's name you call *father*, anyone with your wife's name you call *wife*, and so on. Worse, 'a woman may not marry a man with her father's or brother's name, and a man may not marry a woman with his mother's or sister's name' (Lee 1992b: 74). Sometimes a man can marry a woman, but if his name is the same as her father's she can't marry him! Further, you may not marry anyone with the name of one of your avoidance kin. As a result, parents who do not want their children to marry can almost always find a kinship-related reason to block the marriage. Once again, it does not matter what the exact genealogical relationships are.

The name relationship ties Ju/'hoansi society closer together by making close relatives out of distant ones. At the same time, it makes nonsense of the formal kinship system. How is this dilemma resolved? The Ju/'hoansi have a third component to their kinship system, the principle of *wi*, which operates as follows: relative age is one of the few ways the Ju/'hoansi have of marking distinctions. Thus, in any relationship that can be described by more than one kin relationship, the older party chooses the kin term to be used.

achieved statuses Social positions people may attain later in life, often as the result of their own (or other people's) effort.

For example, a man may get married only to discover that his wife's aunt's husband has the same name he has. What will he and his wife's aunt call each other? According to the principle of *wi*, the aunt decides because she is older. If she calls him *nephew* (rather than *husband*), he knows to call her *aunt*.

The principle of *wi* means that a person's involvement with the kinship system is continually changing over the course of his or her lifetime. For the first half of people's lives, they must accept the kin terms their elders choose, whether they understand why or not. After midlife, however, they begin to impose *wi* on their juniors. For the Ju/'hoansi, kinship connections are open to manipulation and negotiation rather than being rigidly imposed from the outside.

Compadrazgo in Latin America

An important set of kinship practices in Roman Catholic Latin America is **compadrazgo**, or ritual co-parenthood. The baptism of a child requires the presence of a godmother and a godfather as sponsors. By participating in this ritual, the sponsors become the ritual co-parents of the child. In Latin America, godparents are expected to take an active interest in their godchildren and to help them wherever possible. However, the more important relationship is between the godparents and the parents. They become *compadres* ('co-parents'), and they are expected to behave toward each other in new ways.

Sometimes the godparents are already kin; in recent years, for example, Nicaraguans have been choosing relatives living in the US as compadres (Lancaster 1992: 66). A couple often chooses godparents whose social standing is higher than their own: the owners of the land they farm, for example, or of the factory where they work. Participating together in the baptism changes these unequal strangers into ritual kin whose relationship, although still unequal, is now personalized, friendlier, more open. The parents will support the godparents when that support is needed (e.g., politically), and the godparents will do favours for the parents. They even call each other *compadre* rather than, say, 'Señor López' or 'José'.

Catherine Allen notes that the bonds of *compadrazgo*, in combination with marriage alliances and kinship,

> form constellations of mutual obligation and dependence that shift with time as new *compadrazgo*

relationships are formed, young relatives come of age, and old bonds fall into disuse through death or quarrelling. Like kin ties, bonds of *compadrazgo* can become as much a burden as an asset, and like kin ties they can be ignored or honoured in the breach. (1988: 90)

Euro-American Kinship and New Reproductive Technologies

Western medicine has developed new reproductive technologies such as in vitro fertilization, sperm banks, and surrogate motherhood that are creating challenges in ethics and law. And for Western concepts of kinship (Figure 10.9), Marilyn Strathern (1992) observed that in the Euro-American world, kinship is understood as the social construction of natural facts, a logic that both combines and separates the social and natural worlds—meaning the recognition of kin related by blood and kin related by marriage. They also believe that the process—procreation—that brings kin into existence is part of nature. Ties of kinship are supposed to stand for what is unalterable in a person's social world in contrast to what is open to change. Yet the new reproductive technologies make clear that nothing is unalterable: even the world of natural facts is subject to social intervention.

As Janet Dolgin (1995) reported, contemporary ambiguities surrounding kinship in the United States and Canada have put pressure on the courts to decide

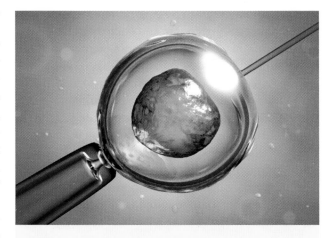

Figure 10.9 In vitro fertilization (IVF), one of the new reproductive technologies, is already having an effect on what it means to be a 'natural' parent.

what constitutes biological parenthood and how it is related to legal parenthood.

Surrogacy cases demonstrate directly the complications that can result from new reproductive technologies. The 'Baby M' situation was a traditional surrogacy arrangement in which the surrogate, Mary Beth Whitehead, was impregnated with the sperm of the husband in the couple who intended to become the legal parents of the child she bore. Whitehead was supposed to terminate all parental rights when the child was born, but she refused to do so. The court faced a dilemma. Existing law backed Whitehead's maternal rights, but the court was also concerned that the surrogacy agreement looked too much like baby-selling or womb-rental. The American court's opinion focused on Whitehead's attempt to break the surrogacy contract to justify terminating her legal rights, although she was awarded visitation rights.

More complicated than traditional surrogacy, *gestational surrogacy* deconstructs the role of genetrix into two roles that can be performed by two different women. In another key American case, the Calverts, a childless married couple, provided egg and sperm that were used in a laboratory to create an embryo, which was then implanted in Anna Johnson's uterus. But when Johnson gave birth to the baby, she refused to give it up. As Dolgin points out, this case 'provided a context in which to measure the generality of the assumption that the gestational role both produces and constitutes maternity' (1995: 58). Several other court cases emphasized the role of gestation in forming an indissoluble bond between mother and child; in this case, however, the court referred to Anna Johnson 'as a "gestational carrier", a "genetic hereditary stranger" to the child, who acted like a "foster parent"' (59). The court declared the Calverts and the child a family unit on genetic grounds and ruled that the Calverts were the baby's 'natural' and legal parents.

Dolgin notes that in these cases, the courts awarded legal custody to those parties whose living arrangements most closely approximated the traditional middle-class, North American two-parent family. 'Biological facts were called into judicial play only . . . when they justified the preservation of traditional families' (63). Biological facts that might have undermined such families were systematically overlooked. Perhaps the clear-cut biological basis of North American kinship is not so clear-cut after all.

Kinship and Practice

Kinship systems are not straitjackets; as we have seen, they offer a flexible series of opportunities for people to choose how to deal with others. They also provide multiple social vectors along which relations of alliance, association, mutual support, opposition, and hatred may develop.

In his work on the Iteso of Kenya (see Map 10.3), Ivan Karp discusses the options for action that a kinship system can provide (principally Karp 1978). Karp notes that among the Iteso, **affinal** (kin through marriage, or **affinity**) and **consanguineal** kin have very different and even contradictory rights and obligations. Two people who share links both through marriage and through patrilineal descent must choose which tie to emphasize; it is often the affinal tie rather than the consanguineal tie. However, they may be ambivalent about the choice. Close members of a patrilineage often quarrel and may be ritually dangerous to one another, but they will—indeed, must—help one another in ritual and conflict situations. By contrast, affinal relatives are amiable and helpful but cannot be counted on in times of crisis.

Karp recounts a story that serves as an example. An Iteso man who was widowed and had remarried moved away from his lineage and was living with his maternal kin. His daughters by his first marriage were living with their mother's brother. One daughter was bitten by a snake and died. Karp was asked to help bring the body back to her father's house for burial. The father went to all his neighbours—his maternal kin—for help in burying her but none would help. Only at the last moment did some members of his patrilineage arrive to help with the burial. This story illustrates the drawbacks associated with living apart from one's close lineage mates. The father had left himself open to a lack of support in a crisis by cutting himself off from his lineage and choosing to live with his maternal kin. Moreover, the Iteso kinship system provides no rule for

affinal (or affinity) Kinship connections through marriage.
compadrazgo Ritual co-parenthood in Latin America and Spain, established through the Roman Catholic practice of having godparents for children.
consanguineal Kinship connections based on descent.

Map 10.3 Iteso

resolving conflicting loyalties to maternal and paternal kin. Indeed, the system almost ensures the creation of overlapping loyalties that are difficult to resolve.

Indeed, the everyday lived experiences of people provide them with the opportunity to create cultures of relatedness that are meaningful, that enable them to get on with life, and that allow them to evade the attempts of others who would impose orderly systems of organization, control, or analysis upon them.

Kinship may seem awesomely complete and utterly basic to the life of some societies, but, as the preceding discussion makes clear, kinship varies in importance between societies and even between subgroups within the same society. Kinship is 'a variety of social idiom, a way of talking about and understanding, and thus of shaping, some aspects of social life' (Geertz and Geertz 1975: 169). There is more to life than kinship, but kinship provides one holistic framework for interpreting life. Furthermore, it is only one way of thinking about how people 'relate' to one another. They also provide multiple social vectors along which relations of alliance, association, mutual support, opposition, and hatred may develop.

Beyond Kinship: Another Framework for Interpreting Life

Jasper Friendly Bear, Gracie Heavy Hand, and Tom King of *The Dead Dog Café Comedy Hour*, a social commentary radio serial (CBC) on First Nations realities written by Tom King, have taught us about the struggle

to find and keep friendships while seeking a safe place in hostile environments. Sardonically, at each sign-off we are told to 'stay calm; be brave; wait for the signs'. And one of the signs of friendship, more than merely buddy-buddy casual relationships, can be seen in the work of the National Association of Friendship Centres (NAFC). They focus their efforts on strengthening the ability of 117 Friendship Centres across Canada to respond to the problems of isolation and alienation experienced by First Nations peoples in urban settings. Here we see the quintessential example of the importance of alliances for survival.

If human beings are social by nature, then no individual can be self-sufficient and autonomous. For many human societies, for most of our history, kinship or other intimate forms of relatedness organized human interdependence within a fairly restricted local arena. Still, every society would risk going bust if its members had no way of establishing links with non-kin. Thus we examine some of the ways non-kin loyalties are created and nurtured.

Kin-based versus Non-kin-based Societies

When anthropologists began to compare Western societies with non-Western societies over a century ago, they were struck by the way in which an elaborate kinship system could regulate social life and organize behavioural patterns. In the Western world, however, kinship has long been reduced to the realm of personal and family relations. In the nineteenth century, scholars of classical antiquity recognized that kinship groups had played roles in ancient European societies comparable to the role they played in many contemporary non-Western societies. Somehow, over time, those kin-ordered forms of social life had been displaced by the large-scale, impersonal, bureaucratically ordered forms of social life typical of a modern nation-state. What was responsible for this transformation?

Sir Henry Maine, an English jurist who studied the roots of Roman law, described the shift as one from status to contract. Ancient societies organized people's relationships by the particular position, or **status**, that each held within the group. Each status carried with it a bundle of rights and obligations, which modern social scientists call a **role**. Statuses and their roles complemented one another: holders of each status were responsible for particular tasks and could rely on other members of the system to perform different tasks. Ideally these fit together like pieces of a puzzle, ensuring that all tasks needed for group survival were carried out.

Societies organized on the basis of kinship were the prototype of status-based societies. For Maine, the crucial feature was that people were not free to choose their own statuses, nor could they modify the rights and responsibilities associated with those statuses. Status and role were *ascribed*. Status-based societies contrasted in four major ways with societies organized on the basis of contract, such as modern nation-states:

(1) ideally, the parties to contractual relationships enter into them freely;

(2) the contracting parties are equally free to specify the rights and obligations between them for the duration of the contract (consider here the prenuptial agreement or marriage contract);

(3) the range of possible statuses and roles is limitless, bound only by the imagination and interests of the contracting parties; and

(4) once the terms of the contract are met, the parties may choose to terminate their relationship with one another.

Emile Durkheim described the shift in terms of the social bonds that held societies together. For Durkheim, 'primitive' societies (ancient and contemporary) were held together on the basis of **mechanical solidarity**. In this view, 'primitive' societies assigned the same social tasks to everybody who occupied the same kinship status. Tasks were based on age and sex with each kinship group containing the full range of roles necessary to carry out all subsistence—the full range of tasks needed for survival. Keeping kin groups together as parts of a larger whole was problematic as nothing bound these groups together except 'mechanical' similarities in language, mode of livelihood, and so on. Mechanical solidarity, therefore, was brittle. Groups could split and go their own way without seriously affecting their ability to survive.

For Durkheim, 'modern' societies were held together by **organic solidarity**. Although still composed of groups, each group specialized in a particular task needed for the survival of the larger whole. That is, organic solidarity depended on a highly developed **division of labour** by group rather than the kinship roles within each group. With organic solidarity the division of labour became more elaborate, with some people specializing in food production and others in trade, government, and so on. Full-time specialization meant that each group had to depend on other groups to provide it with things it could not provide for itself, and if any one specialized group were to disappear, the society as a whole would suffer.

Both Maine and Durkheim, like Hobbes, were asking: What is the social glue that ensures social co-operation? Anthropologist David Schneider (1968) argued that the social glue created by kinship was the feeling of 'enduring diffuse solidarity'. However, in many cases human beings seek to establish enduring diffuse solidarity with a wide range of other people who are not formally recognized as kin. Sociologist Zygmunt Bauman argues, in fact, that 'All supra-individual groupings are first and foremost processes of collectivization of friends and enemies. . . . More exactly, individuals sharing a common group or category of enemies treat each other as friends' (1990: 152).

Thus people in all societies have developed patterned social relationships that aim to bind them for the long term, and some of these reach beyond, and even cut across, ties forged in terms of everyday relatedness. Earlier, we discussed *compadrazgo*. What is the status of the people linked through such arrangements? They are not formal kin because they do not fit the prototypes of the formal kinship system, yet they treat one another according to roles associated with the formal kinship system, so they are not non-kin either. The concept of relatedness helps explain how the boundaries of formal kinship systems can be breached

division of labour Work specialization within a society based on membership in a given group. The most basic human divisions of labour are based on age and sex.

mechanical solidarity According to Durkheim, the sense of fellow feeling and interdependence in so-called primitive societies, based on similarities such as language and mode of livelihood.

organic solidarity According to Durkheim, the sense of fellow feeling and interdependence in so-called modern societies, based on specializations of different social groups; contributions from each group are necessary for the survival of the society.

role The rights and obligations associated with a status.

status A particular social position in a group.

and even why, in some societies, they are relatively unimportant. So it is not surprising that ritual co-parents use a kinship idiom to refer to each other—*compadres*—and to the expectations each has concerning the other's behaviour. Similarly, members of Catholic monastic orders refer to one another as *brother, sister, father,* and *mother* and take as the prototype the formal role obligations of family members. Such religious orders are large international institutions fitting into the overall global hierarchy of the Catholic Church. Thus the kinds of connections established among members reach far beyond the contexts of everyday, face-to-face relatedness.

The connections recognized in formal kinship systems may or may not be recognized in formal kinship studies and are often supplemented by connections to people who are not formally kin. Such organizational openness makes the elaboration and extension of ties of relatedness possible.

Supra-local forms and supra-individual communities are essentially 'imagined communities'. Anderson notes that 'all communities larger than primordial villages of face-to-face contact (and perhaps even these) are imagined' (1983: 6) because the ties that bind such communities have not existed for all time but are rather social constructions from historical circumstances. They are the outcome not only of shared habitual practices but also of symbolic images of common identity conveyed by group members hoping to make their imagined identity endure.

Class, caste, race, ethnicity, and nationalism are all important areas of interest in contemporary cultural anthropology, as we will see in Chapter 12, and play a part in the 'imagined community' identity. And so we reach beyond kinship into other realms of relatedness.

Friendship

Institutions such as *compadrazgo* are, in effect, cases of *institutionalized friendship*. The definition of *friend* is 'one joined to another in intimacy and mutual benevolence independent of sexual or family love' (Brain 1976: 15). Brain points out that the Western belief that

friendship and kinship are separate phenomena often breaks down in practice. For example:

- some husbands and wives in Western societies consider each other 'best friends', and
- we may become friends with some of our relatives while treating others the same way we treat non-relatives.

Sandra Bell and Simon Coleman suggest that typical 'markers' for **friendship** are the relatively 'unofficial' bonds that people construct with one another—bonds that are personal, affective, and—to a varying extent from society to society—a matter of choice (Figure 10.10). The line between friendship and kinship is often a very fuzzy one; thus it has been difficult for some anthropologists to study since, in the past, they have concentrated on trying to find regular, long-term patterns of social organization in societies with non-centralized forms of political organization (Bell and Coleman 1999: 4). With globalization the importance of friendship seems to be increasing: 'In many shifting social contexts, ties of kinship tend to be transformed and often weakened [while] new forms of friendship are emerging' (5). In Rio de Janeiro, Claudia Barcellos Rezende (1999) observed the ways in which middle-class women and their maids could come to refer to each other as 'friends' in 'friendships' consisting of affection, care, and consideration that both sets of women valued in their work relationship, thus

Figure 10.10 Friendships are based on the 'unofficial' bonds that people create with one another, which vary from society to society. These two young men in Cameroon are the best of friends.

friendship The relatively 'unofficial' bonds that people construct with one another that tend to be personal, affective, and, often, a matter of choice.

In Their Own Words

Myth Primogeniture and Long Distance Trade-friends in Northwest New Britain, Papua New Guinea

Trade-friendships form important 'official' bonds, as seen in the trade-friendships of the Bariai of Northwest New Britain, Papua New Guinea. Naomi McPherson examines how trade-friendships, kinship, and economics are intimately intertwined, and she emphasizes how human existence is spiritually and materially enriched by the interlinkage of all aspects of existence.

Bariai trade-friendships are, in fact, relations between individual women and men (and their spouses) rather than kin groups or communities. Although couched in an idiom of kinship, trade-friendships entail different, albeit parallel, sets of rights, obligations, and motivations from those operating among consanguineal and affinal exchange partners. . . .

Rules for conduct between trade-friends in the Vitiaz Strait include offering one another hospitality and protection and both parties are under obligation to proffer, to accept, and to reciprocate pre-stations of all sorts. One ought not to lure away the trade-friends of others and, as a trade-friend host, one should act as intermediary for any exchanges between community members and one's trade-friend visitor (Harding 1967: 166–7). Harding characterizes the trade-friend relationship as 'an expression of the social ethic of kinship' (166), an ethic that entails 'generosity and mutual aid' (182). Rather than being the substrate out of which trade-friendships develop, 'kin-like bonds develop partly as a consequence of [these] socially conducive relations' (176). The difference is that a trade-friendship depends on the two parties meeting their obligations; that is, they have a special performance of duty (Harding 1967). Kinship relations, on the other hand, are composed of a variety of acquired obligations and interests, and default in trade specifically does not sever the acquired ties. One can take advantage of kinspeople and get away with it. 'Trading with relatives, therefore, may be burdensome for either side. . . . It is good to have kinsmen in faraway places, but it is better to have good trade-friends' (153). . . .

The analytical conflation of kinship and trade-friendship (prevalent in alliance theories of kinship) has made it difficult to fully appreciate trade-friendships as something other than kinship relations. For example, the idiom of kinship characterizes the Bariai concept of the trade-friend as an affine—indeed, some trade-friends are affinal kin based on contemporary intermarriages—and the trade-friend relationship is also subject to the rights and moral obligations that inform human relations in kinship-based societies. However, the majority of Bariai adults are hard pressed to trace definitive kinship connections with their trade-friends. Rather, a first-born formally inherits his or her mother's and father's trade-friendships within the context of the *mata pau* first-born ceremony. None of the first-born's subsequent siblings is the focus of a *mata pau*, but, as head of the sibling set, the first-born is expected to oversee and facilitate younger siblings' access to inherited trade-friendships. This provides a means for younger siblings to participate in the established trade-friendships while presenting them an opportunity to develop their own trade-friendships through these connections. Not unlike a system of descent reckoning, trade-friendships remain intact over generations while the origin of the relationship, which is of little immediate concern relative to the continuity, substance, and meaning of the relationship itself, is lost in the mists of antiquity. That trade-friendships resemble kinship relations should come as no surprise in societies where human relationships generally are founded on the moral obligations inherent in kinship relations. For the Bariai, trade-friendships can be distinguished from kinship in three important ways. First, the Bariai use the unique, non-kin term *sobo* to encompass the trade-friend relationship. Second, participation in trade-friendships is a household, rather than a descent group or lineage activity (cf. Harding 1967: 182). Within the framework of day-to-day household activities, it is the spousal partners who, working as a team, produce or procure items of trade and who undertake the transactions involved in trade-friend activities, and it is their first-born who inherits the fruits and friendships of their joint labours. Finally, as noted above, the trade-friendship can be curtailed whereas the kinship relationship cannot. Bariai can and do bring pressure to bear on trade-friends and may even sever a relationship if it is exploitative, an outcome that is next to impossible in the entangled world of affinal and consanguineal relations of kinship. . . .

Exchange relationships with kin and trade-friendships depend upon an ability to manipulate competently the complicated system of debits and credits of the prestige economy and an ability to balance one's own self-interests and the interests of others according to the principles of morality which structure human relations. The locus of trade (and renown) is the wife/husband team. Transactions between spouses and their kin/affines and between spouses and their trade-friends occur constantly and rather inconspicuously within the context of the household. Similarly, first-born ceremonies are not group efforts but are carried out individually by parents and their *baulo* for their first-born child, when and as they have the wherewithal to do so. These public events effectively deflect individual endeavours onto the person of the first-born who exemplifies parental abilities in forging and maintaining bonds beyond the household. Without a first-born and performance of first-born ceremonies no one can hope to achieve a reputation for renown.

The Bariai distinguish between first-born ceremonies that require 'small work' (K: *ololo kaukau*) and those that require 'big work' (*ololo kapei*). The difference between the two types is one of relative scale. 'Small work', or minor ceremonies, usually do not require the exchange of pigs, pork, or shell money, and there is no large assembly of witnesses/kin from other villages. Minor ceremonies are contingent upon circumstances and available resources, and none of the key participants (mother and child) is dressed in ceremonial finery. Minor ceremonies celebrate 'firsts' in two senses: they mark the first occasion that others receive a particular food or consumable in the name of the child, and some minor ceremonies confirm phases in the child's physical development (first tooth, first haircut, first fish, first clothing). For these ceremonies, young, inexperienced, first-time parents depend on the resources provided for them by their parents and grandparents who, for example, planned for their descendants by planting stands of sago, coconut, and areca (betel nut) palms for them. Accomplishing certain of the minor ceremonials also serves to release the parents from various taboos on food, mobility, personal hygiene, and appearance that were imposed upon them when their child was

born. Ideally, the minor ceremonies are accomplished by the time the child is four to six years of age. (I have calculated that, in an ideal world, it can take a married couple 15 to 20 years to complete the 17 first-born ceremonies; some parents never do complete them all.)

While the expenditure of energy and wealth required for the performance of minor ceremonials is anything but small, it is only a fraction of that required for major ceremonials. For their proper performance, these ceremonies require vast quantities of one or more of the following: raw/cooked foods (especially taro, sago flour, and coconuts); pigs and/or pork; shell money; and other forms of material wealth such as clay pots, carved bowls, mats, and more. In contrast to the minor ceremonials where the wealth distributed in the child's name was acquired in large part from the child's grandparents and ancestors, the wealth in the major ceremonies is produced and acquired by the child's parents. Parents use their 'strength' to produce more and larger gardens, to acquire and husband numerous pigs, and to access other wealth items by actively developing and engaging in an ever-widening network of social obligations, especially trade networks. Some of the major ceremonies are also concerned with 'firsts', such as the child's first trip to the reef or first wearing of clothes, first excursion to another village. Others focus on a particular item of decorative finery (such as sago fringe, armbands, red and yellow paint), items that parents and first-born are forbidden to display as personal adornment until the appropriate ceremony is complete. Many of these objects of value are only obtainable through trade; thus, when the first-born is elaborately decorated and paraded through the village to display the item of wealth, the child publicly demonstrates parental ability to forge and maintain relations of trade and exchange.

Source: McPherson, Naomi. 2007. 'Myth Primogeniture and Long Distance Trade-friends in Northwest New Britain, Papua New Guinea', *Oceania* 77, 2 (July): 129–57.

establishing trust: an 'affinity that brings these people together as parts of the same social world' (1999: 93).

Kinship in Non-kin Relationships

In many societies kin are not trusted, and friends must be sought outside the kinship group. Non-kin patterns

of social relations do not follow the rules of recruitment or enforce the traditional status distinctions and role obligations that are at the heart of kinship. And yet those involved in such non-kin social relations often use a kinship idiom to refer to each other and to evaluate each other's behaviour. Ritual co-parents refer to themselves as co-parents (compadres). They also take, as the prototype for these interpersonal relationships, the formal role obligations of family members.

David Schneider (1968) argued that the prototypical emotion of North American kinship is the

sodalities Non-kin forms of social organization; special-purpose groupings that may be organized on the basis of age, sex, economic role, and personal interest.

feeling of 'enduring diffuse solidarity'. This definition might just as well apply to friendship. Perhaps enduring diffuse solidarity is something that human beings regularly seek to establish in their relations with other people—kin or not.

Sodalities

Sodalities are 'special-purpose groupings' that may be organized on the basis of age, sex, economic role, and personal interest.

> [Sodalities] serve very different functions—among them police, military, medical, initiation, religious, economic, and recreation [Figure 10.11]. Some sodalities conduct their business in secret, others in public. Membership may be ascribed or it may be obtained via inheritance, purchase, attainment, performance, or contract. Men's sodalities are more numerous and highly organized than women's and, generally, are also more secretive and seclusive in their activities. (Hunter and Whitten 1976: 362)

Sodalities create enduring diffuse solidarity among members of a large society, in part because they draw their personnel from a number of 'primary' forms of social organization, such as lineages. An example of this in industrial North American and European societies is the union—an affiliation of workers who seek certain economic and workplace conditions from employers. Sometimes such negotiations highlight issues of human rights, such as pay parity and harassment in the workplace. The place of union protection in a world where so much is outsourced to non-union sectors (significantly Third World nations) has raised the issue of how our consumer society is sustained— where and how the goods we crave are manufactured. For example, we may ask: Are they made in sweatshops? Are they made by children?

Age Sets

All societies recognize in some way that people pass through stages as they grow from infancy to maturity to old age. Generational differences are marked in every kinship system. But some groups emphasize generational distinctions to an unusual degree and use them as the basis for forming sodalities. In eastern Africa a number of societies assign men from different kinship groups to sodalities defined in terms of relative age.

Figure 10.11 Men of the devil sodality prepare for Carnival parade in Oruro, Bolivia.

Age sets are composed of young men born within a specific time span (e.g., five years). Each age set is 'one unit in a sequence of similar units' that succeed each other in time as their members pass through youth, maturity, and old age. 'Sets are part of the formal social order blessed by tradition, and membership is usually ascribed, and is always obligatory' (Baxter and Almagor 1978: 4). Age-set systems for women are not found in these societies. Baxter and Almagor suggest that this may be because women are involved in domestic matters from an early age and marry shortly after puberty (11).

Like kinship systems, age-set systems assign people membership in groups on the basis of generation and age. But they are built on two additional assumptions:

(1) that the generations of fathers and sons will succeed one another regularly, and
(2) that the succession will follow a uniform timetable.

Unfortunately, experience belies both assumptions. Members of age-set systems must continually work to reconcile age, generation, and the passage of time. 'Age systems which are based on measured units of time are unsuccessful attempts to tame time by chopping it up into manageable slices' (5).

The classic study of eastern African age sets was by Monica Wilson (1951), who examined their role among the Nyakyusa (see Map 10.4). At the time of Wilson's

Map 10.4 Nyakyusa

fieldwork, the Nyakyusa were patrilineal and patrilocal. Their society was divided into many independent chiefdoms. Nyakyusa age sets initially included a group of boys from about 10 to 15 years of age. When the members of this junior set were about 33 to 35 years old, an elaborate series of rituals was held to mark their 'coming out'. At that time, the reigning senior generation 'handed the country over to them'. At any point in time, there were three strata in the Nyakyusa age system:

(1) retired elders,
(2) active senior men who carried political and military responsibilities for the entire society, and
(3) immature juniors.

In pre-colonial times, each set had distinctive dress and titles and exhibited flamboyant behaviour. According to Baxter and Almagor, however, it was unusual for junior age sets to take on political or military roles, even though they are most often found in societies with no central authority. Baxter and Almagor argued that the colourful activities of junior sets should not distract observers from recognizing that the seniors run things. If junior sets act, they usually act as agents of seniors. Indeed, the wildness of junior sets is conventional in many societies with age systems. Although this custom allows juniors to enjoy themselves, it also publicly reinforces traditional wisdom that places power and property in the hands of elders. These observations are interesting in the context of the age categories found in North American societies.

Age-set systems foster a sense of enduring diffuse solidarity among their members, especially if membership in a set comes after a rigorous initiation ritual. That age-mates are supposed to be the best of friends is illustrated by the widespread rule that forbids age-mates to accuse one another of adultery and demand compensation. This means, in practice, that a married man cannot prevent sexual relationships that might develop between his wife and his age-mates. Here, the refusal to recognize adultery is institutionalized. It emphasizes that nothing, especially not sexual jealousy, must come between age-mates. The rule appears most onerous for the first members of junior sets who marry. Members of senior sets usually all have wives of their own (Baxter and Almagor 1978: 17).

Nyakyusa age sets were able to cultivate an unusual degree of solidarity among their members because each set was required to live in its own village. Indeed, the Nyakyusa believed that the main purpose of *age villages* was to allow set members to enjoy *ukwangala*, 'good company'—the company of friends and equals. Wilson wrote that to attain *ukwangala*,

> men must build not only in villages, rather than in scattered homesteads, but also with contemporaries rather than with kin, since there can be no free and easy intercourse and sharing of food and beer between fathers and sons. *Ukwangala* implies eating and drinking together frequently and cannot be fully enjoyed by people who do not live close to one another. (1951: 163)

Wilson also suggested that age villages helped control sexual behaviour. He noted that the Nyakyusa argued that young men had to live apart from their fathers to prevent incest between the son's wife and his father. The same arrangement also prevented sexual involvements between a son and his father's wives. Such involvement was a real risk because a son traditionally inherited his father's wives (excluding his own mother) when his father died.

Age-set systems may play an important cognitive role in the societies where they are found. Baxter argues that the *gada* age-set system of the Boran of Kenya and Ethiopia (see Map 10.5) provides the idiom the Boran use to describe and debate social and political life. The complex *gada* system recognizes five generation sets that succeed one another over a 40-year period. Every eight years, a new generation set is formed and the oldest set retires. The retirement of the most senior set is marked by an elaborate culmination ceremony called the *gaadamoji*. 'The set organization is said to be there to ensure that these ceremonies are held. From another point of view the organization generates a set of men every eight years who, for their own ritual needs require the opportunity, as they enter the condition of *gaadamoji*, to undergo the culmination ceremony' (Baxter 1978: 160). *Gada* is a conceptual system that guides the society in political and social matters according to the Boran. However, in a classic emic/etic juxtaposition, Baxter rejects the suggestion that the *gada* system ever played a political role in Boran society, stating:

Map 10.5 Boran

> *Gada* exists primarily . . . in the folk view as well as in mine, to ensure the well-being of the Boran and to regulate the ritual growth and development of individuals and to do so in such a way as to permit all men who survive life's full span to achieve responsible and joyful sanctity. It is this last, joyful aspect of *gada* as an institution which performs rituals that has struck intelligent non-professional observers . . . and not its political ones. (156)

Secret Societies in Western Africa

Several neighbouring peoples in western Africa use **secret societies** as a way of drawing members of different kinship groups into crosscutting associations. The most famous secret societies are the Poro and Sande, which are found among the Mende, Sherbro, Kpelle, and other neighbouring peoples of Sierra Leone, Ivory Coast, Liberia, and Guinea.

Poro is secret society for men, responsible for initiating young men into social manhood; Sande, a secret society for women, initiates young women into

age sets Non-kin forms of social organization composed of young men born within a specified time span, which are part of a sequence of age sets that proceeds through youth, maturity, and old age.

secret societies Non-kin forms of social organization that initiate young men or women into social adulthood. The secrecy concerns certain knowledge that is only known to initiated members.

social womanhood. These sodalities are secret in the sense that members of each have certain knowledge that can only be revealed to initiated members. Both sodalities are hierarchically organized. The higher a person's status within the sodality, the greater the secret knowledge revealed.

Poro and Sande are responsible for supervising and regulating the sexual, social, and political conduct of all members of the wider society. To carry out this responsibility, high-status sodality members impersonate important supernatural figures by donning masks and performing in public. One secret kept from the uninitiated is that these masked figures are not the spirits themselves.

Membership is automatic on initiation, and all men and women are ordinarily initiated. 'Until he has been initiated in the society, no Mende man is considered mature enough to have sexual intercourse or to marry' (Little 1967: 245). Each community has its own local Poro and Sande congregations, and a person initiated in one community is eligible to participate in the congregations of other communities. Initiates must pay a fee for initiation, and if they wish to receive advanced training and progress to higher levels within the sodality, they must pay additional fees. In any community where Poro and Sande are strong, authority in society is divided between a sodality of mature women and one of mature men. Together, they work to keep society on the correct path. Indeed, the relationship between men and women in societies with Poro and Sande tends to be highly egalitarian.

Anthropologist Beryl Bellman (1984) was initiated into a Poro chapter among the Kpelle of Liberia. He describes initiation as a ritual process that takes place about every 16 to 18 years, about once each generation. One of the Poro's forest spirits, or 'devils', metaphorically captures and eats the novices—only for them to be metaphorically reborn from the womb of the devil's 'wife' later. Marks incised on the necks, chests, and backs of initiates represent the 'devil's teeth marks'. After this scarification, initiates spend a year living apart from women in a special village constructed for them in the forest. During this period, they carry out various activities under the strict supervision of senior Poro members. Female Sande initiates undergo a similar experience during their year of initiation, which

normally takes place several years after the Poro initiation has been completed.

In Kpelle society, the relationship between a mother's brother (*ngala*) and a sister's son (*maling*) describes the formal relationship between kin. There is also a metaphoric aspect to this connection that is used to describe relationships between patrilineages, sections of a town, and towns themselves. 'Besides the serious or formal rights and obligations between *ngala* and *maling*, other aspects of the relationship are expressed as joking behaviour between kinsmen. . . . The *ngala–maling* relationship is also the basis of labour recruitment, financial assistance, and a general support network' (Bellman 1984: 22–3). This kinship idiom is used within the Poro society to describe the relationships between certain members. For example, two important Poro officials involved in initiation are the *Zo* and the *kwelebah*. The *Zo* directs the ritual, and the *kwelebah* announces both the ritual death and the ritual rebirth of the initiates to the community at large. The *Zo* is said to be the *ngala* of the *kwelebah*, and the *kwelebah* is said to be the *maling* of the *Zo*.

MacCormack (1980) studied secret societies among the Sherbro (see Map 10.6). The Sherbro have a third secret society called *Thoma*, which initiates both men and women. Members of one society cannot be initiated into the others, and families with several children usually try to initiate at least one child into each.

MacCormack writes:

> With Poro and Sande, the contrastive gender categories are split apart and the uniqueness of each gender is emphasized, but always with the final view that the complementarity of the two constitutes human society, the full cultural unity. *Thoma* is a microcosm of the whole. Its local congregations or chapters are headed by a man and a woman, co-equal leaders who are 'husband and wife' in a ritual context but are not married in mundane life. (1980: 97)

The Sherbro are concerned with the reproduction of their society. *Reproduction* here means not just production of children but also continuation of the division of labour between men and women. The Sherbro say that the ritual function of the *Thoma* sodality is to 'wash the bush'—that is, 'to cleanse the land and

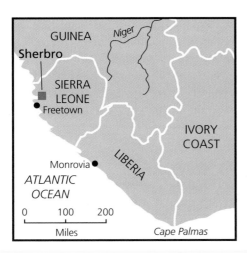

Map 10.6 Sherbro

the village from evil and restore its fertility and well-being' (MacCormack 1980: 98).

The purpose of *Thoma* initiation is to transform uninitiated, proto-social beings into initiated, fully social adult human beings. The *Thoma* society has four masks representing two pairs of spirits: an animal pair and a humanoid pair. The masks, which are considered very powerful, appear when initiates are nearing the end of their ritual seclusion in the forest. They 'symbolize that "wild", unsocialized children are being transformed into cultured adults but will retain the fertile vigour of the animal world' (MacCormack 1980: 100). The humanoid masks represent male and female ancestral spirits who appear when the initiates are about to be reborn into their new adult status. 'Human beings must abide by ancestral rules of conduct if they are to be healthy and fertile. Indeed, they wish to be as healthy and strong as forest animals which give birth in litters. Only by becoming fully "cultural", vowing to live by ancestral laws, may they hope to avoid illness and barrenness' (116).

The Meaning of Secrecy

Bellman was interested in the secrecy that surrounded membership in Poro and other similar sodalities. He argued that Poro (and Sande) initiation rituals are primarily concerned with teaching initiates how to keep a secret. Discretion—knowing when, how, and even whether to speak about various topics—is a prized

virtue among the Kpelle and is required of all mature members of their society. So learning how to 'practise secrecy' is a central lesson of initiation. 'It was always crucial for members to be certain whether they have the right to talk as well as the right to know. The two are not necessarily related. Non-members very often know some of the secrets of membership; yet they must maintain a description of the event comparable to that of non-members' (1984: 51).

Based on this interpretation of 'secrecy' in the secret society he knew, Bellman analyzed what the secret societies meant to outsiders. What do the uninitiated actually believe about these societies? In the case of the Poro, the women speak of devils killing and eating novices as though they believe this to be literally true. Bellman and his informants believe that the women know perfectly well what is 'really' happening when Poro novices are taken away into the forest. But women are not allowed to talk about what they know except in the language of ritual metaphor. In the context of the initiation ritual, participation of the 'audience' of women and other non-initiates is as important as the participation of the Poro elders and the initiates themselves. In playing their appropriate ritual role, women show respect for traditional understandings concerning which members of society have the right to speak about which topics in which manner and under which circumstances. 'The enactment of Poro rituals serves to establish the ways in which that concealed information is communicated. . . . It offers methods for mentioning the unmentionable' (141).

The Dimensions of Group Life

In a deep historical context, many of the social forms we have described developed in societies whose component groups were roughly equal to one another in terms of wealth, power, and prestige—**egalitarian societies**. Many anthropologists would argue, however, that a broad threshold is crossed once social organization becomes hierarchical and social inequality becomes

egalitarian societies Societies in which no great differences in wealth, power, or prestige divide members from one another.

permanent. As we shall see, social organization based on class or caste marks a change not just in a degree of complexity but also in a kind of complexity—in the contract of rights and obligations. But complex forms of social organization do not develop in a vacuum. Many of the complexities of the contemporary world, including hierarchies based on race, ethnicity, and nationality, took shape during the 500 years of European imperial expansion. Moreover, at the beginning of the twenty-first century, the group life of all societies is everywhere affected by forces that originate elsewhere in the world, as we will see in Chapter 12.

Key Terms

achieved statuses 246
adoption 234
affinal (or affinity) 249
age sets 256
ascribed statuses 245
bifurcation 244
bilateral descent 237
bilateral kindred 237
bridewealth 242
clan 239
collaterality 244
compadrazgo 248
consanguineal 249
cross-cousins 244
descent 234
division of labour 251
egalitarian societies 259
friendship 252

gender 235
kinship 234
lineages 239
marriage 234
matrilineage 239
mechanical solidarity 251
organic solidarity 251
parallel cousins 244
patrilineage 239
relatedness 234
role 250
secret societies 257
segmentary opposition 242
sex 235
sodalities 255
status 250
unilineal descent 237

Chapter Summary

1. Human life is group life; we depend upon one another to survive. The idiom of kinship is one way all societies organize this interdependence. Although relationships between kin reveal complexities that require special study, it is important to remember that these relationships are always embedded in, and shaped by, politics, economics, and world views.

2. People in all societies recognize that they are connected to some people in a variety of ways and that they are not connected to other people at all. One of the key forms of relatedness studied by anthropologists focuses on ideas about shared substance and its transmission, often thought to take place in the process of sexual reproduction. The system of social relations based on prototypical procreative relationships is called *kinship*. For many years, anthropologists engaged in the formal analysis of kinship patterns, but they came to realize that the principles of relatedness that people use to organize themselves are sometimes at odds with the genealogical principles of kinship.

3. Kinship principles are based on, but irreducible to, the universal experiences of mating, birth, and

nurturance. Kinship systems help societies maintain social order without central government. Although female–male duality is basic to kinship, many societies have developed supernumerary sexes or genders.

4. Descent links members of different generations with one another. Bilateral descent results in the formation of groups called *kindreds* that include all relatives from both parents' families. Unilineal descent results in the formation of groups called *lineages* that trace descent through either the mother or the father. Unlike kindreds, lineages are corporate groups. Lineages control important property, such as land, that collectively belongs to their members. The language of lineage is the idiom of political discussion, and lineage relationships are of political significance.

5. Patterns of descent in kinship systems are selective. Matrilineal societies emphasize that women bear children and trace descent through women. Patrilineal societies emphasize that men impregnate women and trace descent through men.

6. Anthropologists recognize six basic systems of kinship terminology, based on how people classify their cousins. In recent years, however, anthropologists have become quite skeptical of the value of these idealized models because they are highly formalized and do not capture the full range of people's actual practices.

7. Kinship terminologies pay attention to certain attributes of people that are then used to define different classes of kin. The attributes most often recognized include, from most common to least common, generation, gender, affinity, collaterality, bifurcation, relative age, and gender of linking relative.

8. By prescribing certain kinds of marriage, lineages establish long-term alliances with one another. Two major types of prescriptive marriage patterns in unilineal societies are a father's sister's daughter marriage system (which sets up a pattern of direct exchange marriage) and a mother's brother's daughter marriage system (which sets up a pattern of asymmetrical exchange marriage).

9. Achieved kinship statuses can be converted into ascribed kinship statuses by means of adoption. Adoption pays attention to relationships based on nurturance, whether or not they are also based on mating and birth.

10. The complexities of Ju/'hoansi kinship negotiations, as well as the unique features of *compadrazgo* in Latin America and the dilemmas created in North America and Europe by new reproductive technologies, demonstrate some of the varied ways in which kinship is a cultural construction that cannot be reduced to biology.

11. Early social scientists described and explained the differences they saw between 'primitive' and 'modern' human societies. They thought of 'primitive' society as organized in terms of kinship and therefore characterized by personalized, face-to-face relationships, ascribed statuses, and mechanical solidarity. 'Modern' society, by contrast, was characterized by impersonal relationships, achieved statuses, and organic solidarity. In 'modern' society, kinship played a reduced role, and most of the people with whom an individual dealt with were non-kin.

12. Every society provides ways of establishing links with non-kin. It is sometimes difficult to draw a neat line between kinship and non-kin relationships because kinship terms may be used between 'friends' or kinship roles may be the prototypes for the roles expected of friends, or both. In any case, the relationships cultivate a sentiment of enduring diffuse solidarity.

13. The larger a society is the more complex its division of labour will be. The more specialized the division of labour is, the more likely institutionalized relationships will exist between non-kin. Such institutions are minimally developed in most band societies but become increasingly important in tribal societies, in the form of sodalities.

14. Eastern African age sets and western African secret societies are examples of pan-tribal sodalities. These institutions tend to be found in non-hierarchical societies. Members of the sodalities, drawn from the various kinship groups, ordinarily take on responsibility for various public functions of a governmental or ritual nature. Membership in such sodalities is often a mark of adulthood and may be connected with initiation rituals.

Critical Thinking Questions

1. What would be the advantage to adopting adult siblings?

2. In what way is kinship an idiom? As such, can it be discussed in the context of symbols as outlined earlier in this book?

3. Emile Durkheim used the term *mechanical solidarity*. In what context did he use this term and what meaning did he give it?

4. What are the criteria that people use to indicate relatedness?

5. What are some of the organizational differences between kin-based and non-kin-based societies?

Suggested Readings

Chute, Janet E. 1999. 'Frank G. Speck's Contributions to the Understanding of Mi'kmaq Land Use, Leadership, and Land Management', *Ethnohistory* 46, 3 (summer): 481–540. *An interesting article on an early Canadian ethnographer's work with an Algonquian group.*

Ginsburg, Faye D. 1998. *Contested Lives: The Abortion Debate in an American Community*, rev. edn (Berkeley: University of California Press). *A study of gender and procreation in the context of the abortion debate in Fargo, North Dakota, in the 1980s.*

———, and Rayna Rapp, eds. 1995. *Conceiving the New World Order: The Global Politics of Reproduction* (Berkeley: University of California Press). *An important collection of articles by anthropologists who address the ways human reproduction is structured across social and cultural boundaries.*

Hallowell, A. Irving. 1932. 'Kinship Terms and Cross-cousin Marriage of the Montagnais-Naskapi and the Cree', *American Anthropologist* 34, 2 (Apr.): 171–99. *An early ethnographic work on kinship in a First Nations setting.*

Jarvenpa, Robert. 2004. 'Silot'ine: An Insurance Perspective on Northern Dene Kinship Networks in Recent History', *Journal of Anthropological Research* 60, 2 (summer): 153–78. *Current work from a historical perspective on kinship's importance in an Athabaskan group.*

Kahn, Susan Martha. 2000. *Reproducing Jews: A Cultural Account of Assisted Conception in Israel* (Durham, NC: Duke University Press). *An exceptionally interesting ethnographic study of the effects of new reproductive technologies on kinship in Israel.*

Michelson, Truman. 1916. 'Terms of Relationship and Social Organization', *Proceedings of the National Academy of Sciences of the United States of America* 2, 5 (May): 297–300. *An early work and an important reference for all interested in kinship studies.*

PBS. 2001. 'Sex: Unknown' (30 Oct.), available at: <http://www.pbs.org/wgbh/nova/transcripts/2813gender.html>. *This site discusses the Reimer twins, Bruce and Brian, of Winnipeg and the subsequent outcomes for one of the boys after his circumcision went horribly wrong.*

Smith, Mary F. 1981 [1954]. *Baba of Karo* (New Haven: Yale University Press). *A remarkable document: the autobiography of a Hausa woman born in 1877. A master storyteller, Baba provides much information about Hausa patterns of friendship, clientage, adoption, kinship, and marriage.*

Speck, Frank G. 1918. 'Kinship Terms and the Family Band among the Northeastern Algonkian', *American Anthropologist* 20, 2 (Apr.): 143–61. *The original article that is the basis for Chute 1999, listed above.*

Stone, Linda. 2000. *Kinship and Gender*, 2nd edn (Boulder, CO: Westview). *A recent discussion of human reproduction and the social and cultural implications of male and female reproductive roles.*

———, ed. 2001. *New Directions in Anthropological Kinship* (Lanham, MD: Rowman & Littlefield Publishers, Inc.). *An excellent collection of recent articles on kinship.*

Tooker, Elisabeth. 1992. 'Lewis H. Morgan and His Contemporaries', *American Anthropologist* 94, 2 (June): 357–75. *An excellent review article on the early development of kinship studies in anthropology.*

Related Websites

Kinship and Social Organization: http://www.umanitoba.ca/faculties/arts/anthropology/tutor/kinmenu.html

National Association of Friendship Centres (NAFC): http://www.nafc-aboriginal.com/

NOVA: http://www.pbs.org/wgbh/nova/gender/

Chapter 11

Marriage and Family

Chapter Outline

Learning Objectives

By the end of Chapter 11, you will be able to:

- understand the process of attempting to define 'marriage' in a cross-cultural perspective,
- appreciate marriage as a social process,
- consider marriage in the context of economic exchange,
- through cross-cultural perspective, come to appreciate the interconnections of brothers and sisters,
- identify variations in family structure,
- place families in historical and transformative contexts,

- recognize the transformations families face in situations of international migration,
- appreciate adaptability and the flexibility of marriage,
- consider sexual practices and relationship construction, and
- realize aspects of sexuality and power.

In the summer of 1980, funeral ceremonies were conducted for a young woman in the Egyptian village of Maskuta, near Ismailia. She had been the first young woman of the village to attend teacher's college, and she had married a young man from a prominent Ismailia family. Her education was a matter of pride and her marriage was a matter of serious social and economic consideration. In the context of her community, her marriage was *exogamous* (a marriage without certain social boundaries; in this case her socio-economic position and extended patriline). This was important to this small, rather poor, farming community on the banks of the Wadi Tumilat (Figure 11.1). The contacts her marriage alliance afforded her extended family into a wider social and economic community, and how these contacts could benefit the community as a whole, were important in a cultural setting where marriage and friendship ties are central to so many interactions. Her death in a car accident was seen not only as a familial tragedy but as a communal tragedy. This example illustrates that marriage extends beyond the individuals, regardless of whether the alliance is through arrangement or love, to the extended family and the larger community in many, if not all, cultures. Indeed, it is a relationship between a husband and a wife, but it can also be a symbol, and actuality, of important alliances. Her death was mourned not only for the loss of a beloved and valued daughter but also for the now severed lines of alliance that may have offered access

Figure 11.1 Children near the water pump in the Egyptian village of Maskuta, near Ismailia, in the early 1980s. For many homes in the village at that time this was the main source of drinking water.

into a wider, more prosperous, more influential sector of Egyptian society.

Toward a Definition of Marriage?

Marriage and *family* are two concepts anthropologists use to describe how mating and its consequences are understood and organized in different societies. Each culture has its own definition of marriage, yet nowhere is *marriage* synonymous with *mating*. Marriage involves a change in the social position of two people and affects the social position of their offspring. For Canadians, this reality has changed considerably. In July 2005, Bill C-38 was passed, altering the traditional definition of marriage. Legislation opened civil marriage to same-sex couples and brought the Civil Marriage Act into line with the Canadian Charter of Rights and Freedoms (1985).

Criteria for defining marriage are common in most societies. In the past, the traditional definition of the prototypical marriage would suffice. It would consist of the following list:

- it transforms the status of a man and a woman;
- it stipulates the degree of sexual access the married partners may have to each other, ranging from exclusive to preferential;
- it establishes the legitimacy of children born to the wife; and
- it creates relationships between the kin of the wife and the kin of the husband.

Certainly, this still pertains in many cultures. To this, though, we must add what is now prototypical in societies such as Canada. The list would now look something like this:

- it transforms the status of two *people* entering into the marriage;
- it *infers* sexual access the married partners may have to each other, ranging from exclusive to preferential;
- it *potentially* creates a legal placement for any children added to the family unit; and
- it creates relationships between the kin of the *partners*.

In the context of marriage patterns in many cultures around the world, these changes are not that drastic for Canadians. On considering the traditional definition of the prototypical marriage involving a man and a woman, however, there are cases that offer alternative ways of understanding the combination of features that define appropriate unions in a particular society.

Woman Marriage and Ghost Marriage among the Nuer

Among the Nuer, as E.E. Evans-Pritchard observed during his 1930s, a woman could marry another woman and become the 'father' of the children the wife bore. This practice, which also appears in some other parts of Africa, involves a distinction between *pater* and *genitor*. The female husband (the *pater*) had to have some cattle of her own to use for bridewealth payments to the wife's lineage. Once the bridewealth had been paid, the marriage was established. The female husband then got a male kinsman, friend, or neighbour (the *genitor*) to impregnate the wife and to help with certain tasks around the homestead that the Nuer believed could be done only by men.

A female husband was unable to have children herself 'and for this reason counts in some respects as a man' (Evans-Pritchard 1951). Indeed, she played the social role of a man. She could marry several women if she was wealthy. She could demand damage payment if those wives engaged in sexual activity without her consent. She was the *pater* of her wives' children. On the marriage of her daughters, she received the portion of the bridewealth that traditionally went to the father, and her brothers and sisters received the portions appropriate to the father's side. Her children were named after her, as though she was a man, and they addressed her as *father*. She administered her compound and her herds as a male head of household would, and she was treated by her wives and children with the same deference shown to a male husband and father.

More common in Nuer social life was what Evans-Pritchard called *ghost marriage*. The Nuer believed that a man who died without male heirs left an unhappy and angry spirit who might trouble his living kin. The spirit was angry because a basic obligation of Nuer kinship was for a man to be remembered through and by his sons: his name had to be continued in his lineage. To appease the angry spirit, a kinsman of the dead man—a brother or a brother's son—would often marry a woman 'to his name'. Bridewealth cattle were paid in the name of the dead man to the patrilineage of the woman. She was then married to the 'ghost' but lived with one of his surviving kinsmen. In the marriage ceremonies, and afterwards, this kinsman acted as though he were the true husband. The children of the union were referred to as though they were the kinsman's—but officially they were not. That is, the ghost husband was their *pater* and his kinsman their *genitor*. As the children got older, the name of their ghost father became increasingly important to them. The ghost father's name, not his stand-in's name, would be remembered in the history of the lineage. The social union between the ghost and the woman took precedence over the sexual union between the ghost's surrogate and the woman.

Ghost marriage serves to perpetuate social patterns. Although it was common for a man to marry a woman 'to his kinsman's name' before he himself married, it became difficult, if not impossible, for him to marry later in his own right. His relatives would tell him he was 'already married' and that he should allow his younger brothers to use cattle from the family herd

Figure 11.2 Muslim brides wait for their turn during a mass wedding ceremony in Hyderabad, India. The state government organized this mass wedding for financially poor Muslims.

so they could marry. Even if he eventually accumulated enough cattle to afford to marry, he would feel that those cattle should provide the bridewealth for the sons he had raised for his dead kinsman. When he died, he died childless because the children he had raised were legally the children of the ghost. He was then an angry spirit, and someone else (in fact, one of the sons he had raised for the ghost) had to marry a woman to *his* name. Thus the pattern continued, as, indeed, it does in the present day.

To this we may also add the practice of **levirate** (conversely **sororate**). This is familiar to us from the Old Testament of the Bible: 'When brethren dwell together, and one of them dieth without children, the wife of the deceased shall not <u>marry</u> to another: but his brother shall take her, and raise up seed for his brother: and the first son he shall have of her he shall call by his <u>name</u>, that his <u>name</u> be not abolished out of <u>Israel</u>' (Deuteronomy 25: 1–5).

Marriage as a Social Process

Thinking of marriage as a social process allows us to describe all forms of marriage, even those that do not fit the traditional definition (Figure 11.2). Marriages set up new relationships between the kin of the partners. These are called *affinal* relationships (based on *affinity*—relationships created via marriage) and contrast with *consanguineal* relationships (or 'blood' relationships based on descent). Affinity and consanguinity are centrally associated with the definition of marriage and the formation of social groups. Mating (sex) alone does not create in-laws, nor does it set up a way of locating the offspring in space and time as members of a particular social group. Marriage does both.

Not only is marriage a social process, but it is in process in many countries, Canada included. The Vanier Institute of the Family reports on marriage trends, as does Statistics Canada. One trend that is obvious is the increase in common-law relationships as seen in Figure 11.3 and Table 11.1. The 2006 census also showed that, for Quebec, this trend is quite significant with 35 per cent of couples choosing common-law arrangements compared to 30 per cent in 2001. 'In the other provinces, the proportion of common-law couples was closer to 13 per cent. Canada's national average of 18 per cent is well below Sweden and Finland, . . . but no other

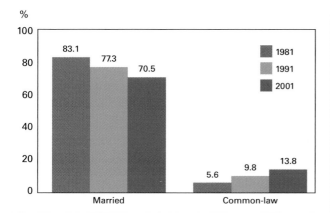

Figure 11.3 Proportion of common-law families grows while it declines for married families, Canada. **Source:** <http://www12.statcan.ca/english/census01/products/analytic/companion/fam/marriedclu.cfm>.

Table 11.1 **Proportion of Couples which Cohabit**

Country	Year	As % of all couples
Sweden	2000	30.0
Norway	2000	24.5
Finland	2000	18.5
Mexico	2000	18.7
New Zealand	2001	18.3
France	1999	17.5
Canada	2001	16.0
Quebec	2001	29.8
Other provinces	2001	11.7
United States	2000	8.2

Source: Statistics Canada. 2002. '2001 Census: Marital Status, Common-law Status, Families, Dwellings and Households', *The Daily* (22 Oct.), available at: <http://www.vifamily.ca/library/cft/cohabitation.html>.

jurisdiction in the world outpaces Quebec when it comes to unmarried unions' (*The Star*, 12 Sept. 2007).

Socially, marriage has four characteristics:

(1) it transforms the status of the participants;
(2) it alters the relationships among the kin of each party;
(3) it perpetuates social patterns through the production of or adoption of offspring, who also have certain kinds of rights and obligations (see Karp 1986); and
(4) it is always symbolically marked in some way.

Marriage marks a major transformation of social position: two individuals become one married couple. In an important way, the third party to any wedding—the rest of the community—must acknowledge the legitimacy of the new union.

Every society has ways of matching the rights and obligations of the bride and the groom. Sometimes these rights have to be redefined as societal concepts are redefined. Let us consider the civil rights of women in Quebec before 1964. A woman who entered marriage without a legal marriage contract before this date essentially lost her status as an independent adult. For example, among other things, she was not allowed to inherit property, open a bank account, or sign her children into a hospital for treatment. These 'rights' were reserved for her husband. This was an artifact of the pre-Napoleonic civil code in place in Quebec.

Emancipation of married women came about from the work of Marie-Claire Kirkland-Casgrain, and this part of the civil code was changed with the passing of Bill 16. Also consider the passing of Bill C-31 in Ottawa in 1985. With the Charter of Rights and Freedoms, First Nations women were able to challenge the Indian Act where it denied them their rights if they married non-Native men. The 1985 amendment to the Indian Act reinstated 16,000 women and 46,000 first-generation dependants. The great Mohawk woman activist Mary Two-axe Earley (Figure 11.4) from Kahnawake, Quebec, who was the symbolic representative of all these women at the ceremony in Toronto on 5 July 1985, observed: 'Now I'll have legal rights again. After all these years, I'll be legally entitled to live on the reserve, to own property, die and be buried with my own people' (*The Gazette*, 5 July 1985).

levirate Marriage practice where a widow marries the brother of her deceased husband.
sororate Marriage practice where a widower marries a sister or specific cousin of his deceased wife.

Figure 11.4 Mohawk activist Mary Two-axe Earley was a catalyst for the establishment of Bill C-31, which led to the reinstatement of treaty status for First Nations women married to non-Native men.

Sometimes marriages must be contracted within a particular social group, a pattern called **endogamy**. In other cases, marriage partners must be found outside a particular group, a pattern called **exogamy**. In Nuer society, for example, a person has to marry outside his or her lineage. Even in North American society, we are told to marry 'our own kind', which usually means our own ethnic or racial group, religious, or social class. This was certainly true for Canadian First Nations women before Bill C-31, when the legal ramifications of exogamy were quite profound. In all societies, some close kin are off limits as spouses or as sexual partners. This exogamous pattern is known as the *incest taboo*.

Patterns of Residence after Marriage

Once married, a couple must live somewhere. There are four major patterns of post-marital residence. Most familiar to North Americans is **neolocal** residence, in which the new couple sets up an independent household at a place of their own choosing. Neolocal residence tends to be found in societies that are more or less individualistic in their social organization.

When the married couple lives with (or near) the husband's father's family, it is called **patrilocal** residence, which is observed by more societies in the contemporary world than any other residence pattern. It produces a characteristic social grouping of related men: a man, his brothers, and their sons, along with their wives, all live and work together. This pattern is common in both herding and farming societies; some anthropologists argue that survival in such societies depends on activities that are best carried out by groups of men who have worked together all their lives.

When the married couple lives with (or near) the family in which the wife was raised, it is called **matrilocal** residence, which is usually found in association with matrilineal kinship systems. Here, the core of the social group consists of a woman, her sisters, and their daughters, together with their husbands. This pattern is most common among horticultural groups.

Less common, but also found in matrilineal societies, is the pattern known as **avunculocal** residence. Here, the married couple lives with (or near) the husband's mother's brother. The most significant man in a boy's matrilineage is his mother's brother, from whom he will inherit. Avunculocal residence emphasizes this relationship.

There are other, even less common patterns of residence. In *ambilocal* residence, the couple shifts residence, living first with the family of one spouse and later with the family of the other. At some point, the couple usually has to choose which family they want to affiliate with permanently. *Duolocal* residence is found where lineage membership is so important that husbands and wives continue to live with their own lineages even after they are married. The Ashanti of Ghana (see EthnoProfile 11.1: Ashanti) observe duolocal residence. We will see later how this residence pattern affects other aspects of Ashanti social and cultural life.

Single and Plural Spouses

The number of spouses a person may have varies cross-culturally. Anthropologists distinguish forms of marriage in terms of how many spouses a person may have. **Monogamy** is a marriage form in which a person may only have one spouse at a time, whereas **polygamy** is a marriage system that allows a person to have more than one spouse. Within the category of polygamy are two subcategories: **polygyny**, or multiple wives, and

In Their Own Words

The Bourgeois Family, Aboriginal Women, and Colonial Governance in Canada

Julia V. Emberley writes on colonialism, family, and Aboriginal women in Canada.

The best-known example of the exclusion of Aboriginal women from political governance is to be found in the Canadian Indian Act (1876) and its subsequent amendments up to 1951. The Indian Act is, perhaps, the most notorious document of the nineteenth century to exercise the authority of the nation-state to secure political power for the colonial bourgeoisie. The history of sexual abuse in the church-run residential school systems, the removal of children from their families and communities and their placement in non-Native foster homes, and the regulation of status for Indian women who married non-status Indians or non-Indians are but a few examples of strategies used to affirm bourgeois colonial power through the subjugation of Indigenous children and female bodies. From early on, colonial policies were implemented to regulate the bodies of Indigenous women by controlling their sexual, reproductive, and kinship relations, as were patriarchal measures to help to secure colonial relations

of governance. What these policies tell us is that for First Nations women, the reproductive body represented a central bio-political obstruction to colonial governance that had to be regulated and controlled for colonial rule to secure hegemony. This bio-politics of control over the species body became the justification for the exclusion of Indigenous women as proper Christian, white, and middle-class women from public arenas of political decision-making and newly formed political institutions. The potential failure of the Aboriginal family to model itself on the bourgeois nation-building family resulted in a divide-and-rule approach to Indigenous gender relations, confirming enlightenment candidacy only on Aboriginal men who could manage, regulate, and govern Aboriginal women and children. Feminist critics in colonial cultural studies might well ask, then, by what mechanisms of bio-power (to borrow from Michel Foucault) did existing and emergent colonial governing bodies seek to secure and maintain their ruling status in the Canadian context?

Source: Emberley, Julia V. 2001. 'The Bourgeois Family, Aboriginal Women, and Colonial Governance in Canada: A Study in Feminist Historical and Cultural Materialism', *Signs* 27, 1: 71–2.

polyandry, or multiple husbands. Most societies in the world permit polygyny.

Monogamy

The form of marriage most celebrated in Canada, according to the relevant provincial marriage act, is monogamy. There are variations in the number of times a monogamous person can be married. Before the twentieth century, people in western European societies generally only married once unless death intervened. Today, some observers suggest that we practise *serial monogamy*; we may be married to several different people but only one at a time.

Polygyny

Polygynous societies vary in the number of wives a man may have. Islam permits a man to have as many as four wives but only on the condition that he can support them equally. Some Muslim authorities today

avunculocal A post-marital residence pattern in which a married couple lives with (or near) the husband's mother's brother (from *avuncular*, 'of uncles').

endogamy Marriage within a defined social group.

exogamy Marriage outside a defined social group.

matrilocal A post-marital residence pattern in which a married couple lives with (or near) the wife's mother.

monogamy A marriage pattern in which a person may be married to only one person at a time.

neolocal A post-marital residence pattern in which a married couple sets up an independent household at a place of their own choosing.

patrilocal A post-marital residence pattern in which a married couple lives with (or near) the husband's father.

polyandry A marriage pattern in which a woman may be married to more than one man at a time.

polygamy A marriage pattern in which a person may be married to more than one person at a time.

polygyny A marriage pattern in which a man may be married to more than one woman at a time.

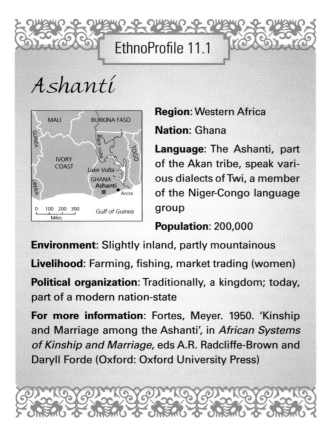

EthnoProfile 11.1

Ashanti

Region: Western Africa

Nation: Ghana

Language: The Ashanti, part of the Akan tribe, speak various dialects of Twi, a member of the Niger-Congo language group

Population: 200,000

Environment: Slightly inland, partly mountainous

Livelihood: Farming, fishing, market trading (women)

Political organization: Traditionally, a kingdom; today, part of a modern nation-state

For more information: Fortes, Meyer. 1950. 'Kinship and Marriage among the Ashanti', in *African Systems of Kinship and Marriage*, eds A.R. Radcliffe-Brown and Daryll Forde (Oxford: Oxford University Press)

argue, however, that equal support must be emotional and affective, not just financial. Convinced that no man can feel the same toward each of his wives, they have concluded that monogamy must be the rule. Other polygynous societies have no limit on the number of women a man may marry. Nevertheless, not every man can be polygynous. There is a clear demographic problem: for every man with two wives, there is one man without a wife. Men can wait until they are older to marry and women can marry very young, but this imbalance cannot be eliminated. Polygyny is also expensive, for a husband must support all his wives as well as their children (Figure 11.5).

Polyandry

Polyandry is the rarest of the three marriage forms. In some polyandrous societies, a woman may marry several brothers; in others, she may marry men who are not related to each other and who will all live together in a single household. Sometimes a woman is allowed to marry several men who are not related, but she will only live with the one she most recently married.

Recent studies of polyandry have shed new light on the dynamics of monogamy and polygyny.

Polyandry, Sexuality, and the Reproductive Capacity of Women

Different marriage patterns reflect significant variation in the social definition of male and female sexuality. Monogamy and polygyny are in some ways similar because both are concerned with controlling women's sexuality while giving men freer rein. Even in monogamous societies, men (but not women) are often expected to have extramarital sexual adventures. Polyandry is worth a closer look; it differs from monogamy or polygyny in instructive ways.

Polyandry is found in three major regions of the world: Tibet and Nepal, southern India and Sri Lanka, and northern Nigeria and northern Cameroon. The forms of polyandry in these areas are different, but all involve women with several husbands.

Fraternal Polyandry

The traditional anthropological prototype of polyandry has been found among some groups in Nepal and Tibet, where a group of brothers marry one woman. This is known as *fraternal polyandry*. During one wedding, one brother, usually the oldest, serves as the groom. All brothers (including those yet to be born to the husbands' parents) are married by this wedding, which establishes public recognition of the marriage. The wife and her husbands live together, usually patrilocally. All brothers have equal sexual access to the wife, and all act as fathers to the children. In some cases—notably among the Nyinba of Nepal (Levine 1980; 1988; see Map 11.2)—each child is recognized as having one particular *genitor*, who may be a different brother than the *genitor* of his or her siblings. In other cases, all the brothers are considered jointly as the father, without distinguishing the identity of the *genitor*.

There appears to be little sexual jealousy among the men, and the brothers have a strong sense of solidarity with one another. Levine (1988) emphasized this point for the Nyinba. If the wife proves sterile, the brothers may marry another woman in hopes that she may be fertile. All brothers also have equal sexual access to the new wife and are treated as fathers by her children. In societies that practise fraternal polyandry, marrying sisters (or *sororal polygyny*) may be preferred

Figure 11.5 The wives and children of a polygynous family.

or permitted. In this system, a group of brothers could marry a group of sisters.

According to Levine, Nyinba polyandry is reinforced by a variety of cultural beliefs and practices (1988: 158ff.).

- It has a special cultural value. Nyinba myth provides a social charter for the practice because Nyinba legendary ancestors are polyandrous, and they are praised for the harmony of their family life.
- The solidarity of brothers is a central kinship ideal.
- The corporate, landholding household, central to Nyinba life, presupposes polyandry.
- The closed corporate structure of Nyinba villages is based on a limited number of households, and polyandry is highly effective in checking the proliferation of households.
- A household's political position and economic viability increase when its resources are concentrated.

Associated Polyandry

A second form of polyandry, known as *associated polyandry*, refers to any system in which polyandry is open to men who are not necessarily brothers (Levine and

Sangree 1980). There is some evidence that associated polyandry was an acceptable marriage variant in parts of the Pacific and among some Indigenous peoples of North and South America. The best-described form of associated polyandry, however, is from Sri Lanka. Among the Sinhalese, a woman may marry two men but rarely more than two. Unlike fraternal polyandry, which begins as a joint venture, Sinhalese-associated polyandry begins monogamously. The second husband is brought into the union later. Also, unlike fraternal

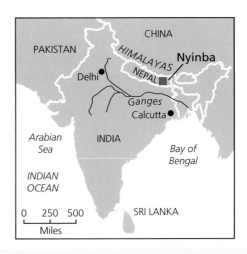

Map 11.2 Nyinba

polyandry, the first husband is the principal husband in terms of authority. A woman and her husbands live and work together, although economic resources are held independently. Both husbands are considered fathers to any children the wife bears.

This system allows many individual choices. For example, two husbands and their wife may decide to take another woman into the marriage—often the sister of the wife. Thus, their household becomes simultaneously polygynous and polyandrous, a marriage pattern called *polygynandry*. Thus, depending on relative wealth and the availability of economic opportunity, a Sinhalese household may be monogamous, polyandrous, or polygynandrous.

As we mentioned at the beginning of the chapter, one important aspect of marriage is the creation of ties between the bride's and the groom's families. The two forms of polyandry just discussed sharply curtail the potential network of ties created by marriage. This is particularly true where fraternal polyandry occurs with preferred or permitted sororal polygyny. For example, in a Tibetan household of four brothers married to one woman, the entire household is tied affinally only to the family of the wife. If these same brothers take another wife by marrying a sister of their first wife, they would be giving up the possibility of establishing ties with other households in favour of fortifying the relationship already established by the first marriage. Nancy Levine and Walter Sangree call this *alliance intensifying* (1980).

Secondary Marriage

The final form of polyandry, sometimes referred to as *secondary marriage*, is found only in northern Nigeria and northern Cameroon. In secondary marriage, a woman marries one or more secondary men while staying married to all her previous husbands (Levine and Sangree 1980: 400). The woman lives with only one husband at a time, but she retains the right to return to a previous husband and to have legitimate children by him at a later date. No divorce is permitted in the societies that practise secondary marriage; marriage is for life.

In this system, men are polygynous and women polyandrous. A man marries a series of women and lives with one or more of them at his homestead. At the same time, the women independently pursue their own marital careers. Secondary marriage is really neither polyandry nor polygyny but rather a

combination of the two, resulting from the overlap of men seeking several wives and women seeking several husbands. Secondary marriage is the opposite of Tibetan fraternal polyandry. It is *alliance proliferative*, serving to connect rather than to concentrate groups as people build extensive networks of marriage-based ties throughout a region.

The Distinction between Sexuality and Reproductive Capacity

Polyandry demonstrates how a woman's sexuality can be distinguished from her reproductive capacity. This distinction is absent in monogamous or purely polygynous systems, in which polyandry is not permitted; such societies resist perceiving women's sexual and reproductive capacities as separable (except, perhaps, in prostitution), yet they usually accept such separation for men without question. 'It may well be a fundamental feature of the [world view] of polyandrous peoples that they recognize such a distinction for *both* men and women' (Levine and Sangree 1980: 388). In the better-known polyandrous groups, a woman's sexuality can be shared among an unlimited number of men, but her child-bearing capacities cannot. Indeed, among the Nyinba (Levine 1980), a woman's child-bearing capacities are carefully controlled and limited to one husband at a time. But she is free to engage in sexual activity outside her marriage to the brothers as long as she is not likely to get pregnant.

Marriage and Economic Exchange

In many societies, marriage is accompanied by the transfer of certain symbolically important goods. Anthropologists have identified two major categories of marriage payments, usually called *bridewealth* and *dowry*.

Bridewealth is most common in patrilineal societies that combine agriculture, pastoralism, and patrilocal marriage although it is found in other types of societies as well. When it occurs among matrilineal peoples, a post-marital residence rule (e.g., avunculocal) usually takes the woman away from her matrilineage.

The goods exchanged have significant symbolic value to the people concerned. They may include shell ornaments, ivory tusks, brass gongs, bird feathers, cotton cloth, and animals. Bridewealth in animals is prevalent in eastern and southern Africa, where cattle have the most profound symbolic and economic value. In these societies, a man's father, and often his entire patrilineage, give a specified number of cattle (often in installments) to the patrilineage of the man's bride. Anthropologists view bridewealth as a way of compensating the bride's relatives for the loss of her labour and child-bearing capacities. When the bride leaves her home, she goes to live with her husband and his lineage. She will be working and producing children for his people, not her own.

Bridewealth transactions create affinal relations between the relatives of the wife and those of the husband. The wife's relatives, in turn, use the bridewealth they receive for her to find a bride for her brother in yet another kinship group. In many societies in eastern and southern Africa, a woman gains power and influence over her brother because her marriage brings the cattle that allow him to marry and continue their lineage. This is why Goody describes bridewealth as 'a societal fund, a circulating pool of resources, the movement of which corresponds to the movement of rights over spouses, usually women' (Goody and Tambiah 1973: 17). Or, as the Southern Bantu put it, 'cattle beget children' (Kuper 1982: 3).

Dowry, by contrast, is typically a transfer of family wealth, usually from parents to their daughter at the time of her marriage (Figure 11.6). It is found primarily

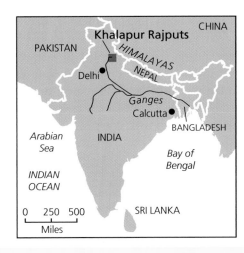

Map 11.3 Khalapur Rajputs

in the agricultural societies of Europe and Asia but has been brought to some parts of Africa with the arrival of religions like Islam that support the practice. In societies where both women and men are seen as heirs to family wealth, dowry is sometimes regarded as the way women receive their inheritance. Dowries are often considered the wife's contribution to the establishment of a new household, to which the husband may bring other forms of wealth. In stratified societies, the size of a woman's dowry often ensures that when she marries she will continue to enjoy her accustomed lifestyle. The goods included in dowries vary in different societies and may or may not include land (Goody and Tambiah 1973).

Leigh Minturn (1993) worked among the Khalapur Rajputs of northern India (see Map 11.3) and studied how dowries fit into their marriage system. To begin with, all land is held and inherited by men, who live together in a patrilocal *joint family* centring on a group of brothers with their wives and children. Rajput marriages are not only village exogamous but also *hypergamous*: that is, women normally marry into lineages of higher status than the ones into which they were born. This means that women must leave their home villages to live in another village as low-ranking

Figure 11.6 A large dowry display in Khalapur, India, from 1955.

dowry The transfer of wealth, usually from parents to their daughter at the time of her marriage.

outsiders in the households of their husbands. How well they marry and how well they are treated by their in-laws depend on the size of their dowries. Rajputs told Minturn that 'It is best to have two sons and one daughter, because then you will receive two dowries, but give only one' (1993: 130). Poor people whose sons cannot attract women with dowries often engage in a practice called *buying a wife*, in which the husband's family gives money to the bride's family to purchase her dowry goods. Rajput dowries consisted exclusively of transportable items such as money, jewelry, clothing, and household decorations.

In the 1950s, when Minturn first visited Khalapur, new Rajput wives were under the strict control of their

In Their Own Words

Law, Custom, and Crimes against Women

John van Willigen and V.C. Channa describe the social and cultural practices surrounding dowry payments that appear to be responsible for violence against women in some parts of India.

A 25-year-old woman was allegedly burnt to death by her husband and mother-in-law at their East Delhi home yesterday. The housewife, Mrs Sunita, stated before her death at the Jaya Prakash Narayana Hospital that members of her husband's family had been harassing her for bringing inadequate dowry.

The woman told the Shahdara subdivisional magistrate that during a quarrel over dowry at their Pratap Park house yesterday, her husband gripped her from behind while the mother-in-law poured kerosene over her clothes.

Her clothes were then set ablaze. The police have registered a case against the victim's husband, Suraj Prakash, and his mother.

— *Times of India*, 19 Feb. 1988

This routinely reported news story describes what in India is termed a *bride-burning* or *dowry death*. Such incidents are frequently reported in the newspapers of Delhi and other Indian cities. In addition, there are cases in which the evidence may be ambiguous, so that deaths of women by fire may be recorded as kitchen accidents, suicides, or murders. Dowry violence takes a characteristic form. Following marriage and the requisite giving of dowry, the family of the groom makes additional demands for the payment of more cash or the provision of more goods. These demands are expressed in unremitting harassment of the bride, who is living in the household of her husband's parents, culminating in the murder of the woman by members of her husband's family or by her suicide. The woman is typically burned to death with kerosene, a fuel used in pressurized cook stoves, hence the use of the term *bride-burning* in public discourse.

Dowry death statistics appear frequently in the press and parliamentary debates. Parliamentary sources report the following figures for married women 16 to 30 years of age in Delhi: 452 deaths by burning for 1985; 478 for 1986, and 300 for the first six months of 1987. There were 1,319 cases reported nationally in 1986 (*Times of India*, 10 Jan. 1988). Police records do not match hospital records for third-degree burn cases among younger married women; far more violence occurs than the crime reports indicate.

There is other violence against women related both directly and indirectly to the institution of dowry. For example, there are unmarried women who commit suicide so as to relieve their families of the burden of providing a dowry. A recent case that received national attention in the Indian press involved the triple suicide of three sisters in the industrial city of Kanpur. A photograph was widely published showing the three young women hanging from ceiling fans by their scarves. Their father, who earned about 4000 Rs [rupees] per month, was not able to negotiate marriage for his oldest daughter. The grooms were requesting approximately 100,000 Rs. Also linked to the dowry problem is selective female abortion made possible by amniocentesis. This issue was brought to national attention with a startling statistic reported out of a seminar held in Delhi in 1985. Of 3,000 abortions carried out after sex determination through amniocentesis, only one involved a male fetus. As a result of these developments, the government of the state of Maharashtra banned sex determination tests except those carried out in government hospitals.

Source: van Willigen, John, and V.C. Channa. 1991. 'Law, Custom, and Crimes against Women', *Human Organization* 50, 4: 369–70.

mothers-in-law, who assigned them tasks, limited their contact with their husbands, and controlled their dowries. Every time a wife visited her parents, moreover, she was expected to return with more gifts for her husband's family. In 1961, the government of India passed a law prohibiting dowries, but it has proven impossible to enforce. Nevertheless, by 1975, attitudes and practices regarding dowries had changed, especially among educated Rajputs. Many believed that dowries were a woman's rightful inheritance from her parents, and educated brides refused to relinquish control of their dowries to their mothers-in-law. Indeed, following the passage of a law in 1956 that permitted daughters, widows, and mothers to inherit land, the size of dowries in Khalapur increased in order to discourage daughters from claiming family land. Much was at stake, and Minturn knew of wives who had been killed to keep them from withdrawing their husband's portion of the land from traditional joint holdings.

Violence within families does not have to fall within the interfamilial area of dowry to be found within specific societies. Issues of violence can be situated and discussed within the context of social and/ or individual maladjustment. Regardless, the toll on families is significant. Consider a *Daily* report from Statistics Canada and the observation that women are more likely to experience more serious forms of spousal violence than men:

> Nearly one-quarter (23 per cent) of female victims reported that the most serious form of violence experienced was being beaten, choked, or threatened by having a gun or knife used against them. This was the case for 15 per cent of male victims.
>
> About 44 per cent of female victims of spousal violence indicated that they suffered injury because of the violence, more than twice the proportion of 19 per cent among male victims. In addition, 13 per cent of female victims sought medical attention, compared with only 2 per cent of male victims.
>
> Over one-third of women victims said that the violence was reported to the police, compared to 17 per cent of men victims. In addition, 38 per cent of women who reported to the police also sought a restraining order, more than twice the proportion of men. . . .
>
> About three-quarters of victims of homicide–suicides were killed by a family member, while the remainder involved an acquaintance or a stranger. Over one-half (57 per cent) of family homicide–suicides involved spouses, and of these incidents,

virtually all (97 per cent) involved female victims killed by a male spouse.

> Since 1991, when data became available to distinguish between the various types of spousal relationships, victims of spousal homicide–suicide were killed by a legally married (42 per cent), separated (30 per cent), common-law (23 per cent), or a divorced husband (3 per cent). About 2 per cent of spousal homicide–suicide victims were male spouses killed by a female spouse.
>
> One-quarter of the homicide–suicides, which occurred between 1961 and 2003, involved children and youth aged 18 and under. The vast majority of these were family related. The accused involved in family related homicide–suicides against a child or youth was most often a parent of the victim. In 66 per cent of cases, the accused was the father, in 27 per cent the mother, and in 2 per cent a stepfather.
>
> Parent–child homicide–suicides often involved multiple victims. About 35 per cent of cases involved two victims, while 36 per cent involved three to five victims, and 28 per cent of incidents involved one victim. (Statistics Canada 2005a)

The numbers reveal that, as a society, we are not removed from issues of violence within familial situations.

Brothers and Sisters in Cross-cultural Perspective

The brother–sister relationship and its link to marriage deserves special attention. In North American society, we tend to interpret all relationships between men and women in terms of the prototypical relationship between husbands and wives. Such an interpretation is unnecessarily limiting and overlooks significant variations in how people view relationships (see Sacks 1979). In some cultures, the most important relationships a man and a woman have are those with their opposite-sex siblings. This is perhaps clearest in matrilineal societies, where, for example, a man's closest ties to the next generation are with his sister's children.

Brothers and Sisters in a Matrilineal Society

A classic illustration comes from the Ashanti of Ghana, as described by Meyer Fortes in the late 1940s. The central legal relationship in Ashanti society is the tie between brother and sister. A brother has power over his sister's children because he is their closest male relative and because Ashanti legal power is vested in males (Fortes 1950). A sister has claims on her brother because she is his closest female relative and represents the only source of the continuity of his lineage. In patrilineal societies like that of the Nuer, a man is centrally concerned with his own ability to produce children. Among the Ashanti, a man is centrally concerned with his *sister's* ability to produce children (Figure 11.7). 'Men find it difficult to decide which is more important to them, to have children or for their sisters to have children. But after discussion most men conclude that sad as it may be to die childless, a good citizen's first anxiety is for his lineage to survive' (1950: 274–5).

More than this, the Ashanti brother and sister are supposed to be close confidants:

> Quoting their own experiences, men say that it is to his sister that a man entrusts weighty matters, never to his wife. He will discuss confidential matters, such as those that concern property, money, public office, legal suits, and even the future of his children or his matrimonial difficulties, with his sister, secure in the knowledge that she will tell nobody else. He will give his valuables into her care, not his wife's. He will use her as go-between with a secret lover, knowing that she will never betray him to his wife. His sister is the appropriate person to fetch a man's bride home to him, and so a sister is the best watch-dog of a wife's fidelity. Women, again, agree that in a crisis they will side with their brothers against their husbands. There is often jealousy between a man's sister and his wife because each is thinking of what he can be made to do for her children. That is why they cannot easily live in the same house. Divorce after many years of marriage is common and is said to be due very often to the conflict between loyalties toward spouse and toward sibling. (275)

Because Ashanti women may be sisters and wives simultaneously, they often experience conflict between these two roles. In North America, the relationship of the spousal pair ordinarily takes precedence over the brother–sister relationship, which is attenuated at marriage. But for the Ashanti, the lineage comes first. In part, the closeness of brothers and sisters is reinforced by the Ashanti residence pattern: people live in their matrilineages' neighbourhoods, and, often, husbands and wives do not live together.

Since the late 1940s, the status of women within Ashanti matrilineages has eroded, according to Gracia Clark, who did fieldwork in Kumasi, Ghana, in the 1980s (Clark 1994). The market women she knew

Figure 11.7 The men living in the Ashanti's matrilineal society were more likely to trust their sisters with important information than their wives.

could still turn to their matrilineages for support against the risks of divorce, illness, or bankruptcy. At the same time, support beyond the subsistence level is not automatic and must be negotiated between a woman and her kin. Clark concludes that Ashanti girls and women 'unfortunately seem to be increasingly marginalized within their lineages, in leadership, residence, and inheritance' (1994: 335).

Brothers and Sisters in a Patrilineal Society

The relationship of brother and sister is important in patrilineal societies, too, and even in some contemporary urban nation-states. Thomas Belmonte noted that in the slums of Naples, Italy, a brother still maintains a moral control over his sister that her husband does not have (1978: 193). In patrilineal societies, the strength of the relationship depends on how the kinship group is organized. Where sisters do not move too far from home upon marriage, and where they are not incorporated into their husbands' lineages, a group of brothers and sisters may control the lineage and its economic, political, social, and religious aspects. The senior members of the lineage—males and females alike—exercise control over the junior members. Although the brothers generally have more control than the sisters (in part because they are the ones who stay in place while the sisters move when they marry), sisters still have influence.

In the Mount Hagen area of the New Guinea highlands (see Map 11.4), for example, women marry into many different sub-tribes, usually within a two-hour walk from home. However, they retain rights to the wealth of their own lineages and to its disposal. A clan sister married outside the clan is believed to remain under the control of her clan ghosts. At her death, in association with them, she is able to influence the affairs of her own lineage. Nevertheless, over the course of time, a woman becomes more interested and involved in the affairs of her husband's clan. As this happens, it is believed that she comes increasingly under the control of her husband's clan ghosts. After her death, in addition to her influence on her own clan as a ghostly sister, she is believed to have influence on her husband's clan as a ghostly mother (Strathern 1972: 124).

Family Structure

The process by which a woman becomes gradually involved in her husband's clan or lineage was recorded by Evans-Pritchard during his fieldwork among the Nuer. Affinal ties gradually become kinship ties: *ruagh* (in-law relationships) became *mar* (kinship) (Evans-Pritchard 1951: 96). The birth of a child gave the wife kinship with her husband's relatives, and it gave the husband kinship with his wife's relatives. In many patrilineal societies, a woman begins to identify with and become more interested in the affairs of her husband's lineage, partly because she has been living there for many years and comes to be more intimate with the details of the lineage. More significantly, however, what had been her *husband's* lineage becomes her *children's* lineage. The children create a link to the lineage that is independent of her husband. This is one example of how family relationships inevitably transform over time.

What is a family? A minimal definition of a **family** would be that it consists of a woman and her dependent children. While some anthropological definitions require the presence of an adult male, related either by marriage or descent (e.g., husband or brother), recent feminist and primatological scholarship has called this requirement into question. As a result, some anthropologists prefer to distinguish the **conjugal family**, which is a family based on marriage—at its minimum, a spousal pair and their children—from the **non-conjugal family**, which consists of a woman and her children. In a non-conjugal family, the husband/father may be occasionally present or completely absent. Non-conjugal families are never the only form of family

Map 11.4 Mount Hagen

organization in a society and, in fact, cross-culturally are usually rather infrequent. In some large-scale industrial societies including Canada, however, non-conjugal families have become increasingly common. In most societies, the conjugal family is co-resident—that is, spouses live in the same dwelling, along with their children—but there are some matrilineal societies in which the husband lives with his matrilineage, the wife and children live with theirs, and the husband visits his wife and children.

The Nuclear Family

The structure and dynamics of neolocal monogamous families are familiar to North Americans. They are called *nuclear families*, and it is often assumed that most North Americans live in them (although in 2000, only about one-quarter of North Americans did). For anthropologists, a **nuclear family** is made up of two generations: parents and their unmarried children.

conjugal family A family based on marriage; at a minimum, a spousal pair and their children.

family Minimally, a woman/man and her/his dependent children.

non-conjugal family A woman and her children; the husband/father may occasionally be present or completely absent. Here we should add a man and his children; the wife/mother may occasionally be present or completely absent.

nuclear family A family made up of two generations: parents and their unmarried children.

Figure 11.8 Co-wives in polygynous households frequently co-operate in daily tasks like food preparation.

Each member of a nuclear family has a series of evolving relationships with every other member: spousal pair, parents and children, and children with each other. These are the lines along which jealousy, competition, controversy, and affection develop in neolocal monogamous families; sibling rivalry, for example, is a form of competition characteristic of nuclear families that is shaped by the relationships between siblings and between siblings and their parents.

The Polygynous Family

Polygynous families are significantly different in their dynamics. Each wife has a relationship with her co-wives as individuals and as a group (Figure 11.8). Co-wives, in turn, individually and collectively, interact with the husband. These relationships change over time, as Emily Schultz and Robert Lavenda were once informed during their fieldwork in Guider, Cameroon. The nine-year-old daughter of their landlord announced one day that she was going to become Lavenda's second wife. 'Madame [Schultz]', she said, 'will be angry at first, because that's how first wives are when their husbands take a second wife. But after a while, she will stop being angry and will get to know me and we will become friends. That's what always happens.'

The differences in internal dynamics in polygynous families are not confined to the relationships of husband and wives. An important distinction is made between children with the same mother and children with a different mother. In Guider, people ordinarily refer to all their siblings (half and full) as brothers or sisters. When they want to emphasize the close connection with a particular brother or sister, however, they say that he or she is 'same father, same mother'. This terminology conveys a relationship of special intimacy and significance. Children, logically, also have different kinds of relationships with their own mothers and their fathers' other wives—and with their fathers as well.

Where there is a significant inheritance, these relationships serve as the channels for jealousy and conflict. The children of the same mother, and especially the children of different mothers, compete with one another for their father's favour. Each mother tries to protect the interests of her own children, sometimes at the expense of her co-wives' children.

Competition in the Polygynous Family

Although the relationships among wives in a polygynous society may be very close, among the Mende of Sierra Leone (see Map 11.5), co-wives eventually compete with each other. Caroline Bledsoe (1993) explains that this competition is often focused on children: how many each wife has and how likely it is that each child will obtain things of value, especially education. Husbands in polygynous Mende households should avoid overt signs of favouritism, but wives differ from one another in status. First, wives are ranked by order of marriage. The senior wife is the first wife in the household, and she has authority over junior wives. Marriage-order ranking structures the household but also lays the groundwork for rivalries. Second, wives are also ranked in terms of the status of the families from which they came. Serious problems arise if the husband shows favouritism toward a wife from a high-

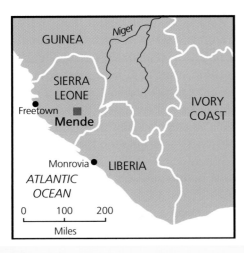

Map 11.5 Mende

status family by educating her children ahead of older children of other wives or children of wives higher in the marriage-order ranking.

The level of her children's education matters intensely to a Mende woman because her principal claim to her husband's land or cash, and her expectations of future support after he dies, comes through her children. She depends not only on the income that a child may earn to support her but also on the rights her children have to inherit property and positions of leadership. Nevertheless, education requires a significant cash outlay in school fees, uniforms, books, and so on. A man may only be able to send one child to school, or he may be able to send one child to a prestigious private school only if he sends another to a trade apprenticeship. These economic realities make sense to husbands but can lead to bitter feuds—and even divorce—among co-wives who blame the husband for disparities in the accomplishments of their children. In extreme cases, co-wives are said to use witchcraft to make their rivals' children fail their exams. To avoid these problems, children are frequently sent to live with relatives who will send them to school. Such competition is missing in monogamous households unless they include adopted children or spouses who already have children from a previous marriage.

Extended and Joint Families

Within any society, certain patterns of family organization are considered proper. In North American nuclear families, two generations live together. In some societies, three generations—parents, married children, and grandchildren—are expected to live together in a vertical **extended family**. Still, in other societies the extension is horizontal: brothers and their wives (or sisters and their husbands) live together in a **joint family**. These are ideal patterns, which all families may not be able or willing to emulate.

Individual families also change in their basic structures over time. In a polygynous society with extended families, consider a recently married husband and wife who set up housekeeping by themselves. They are monogamous. After a while, a child is born, and they become a monogamous nuclear family. Some time later, elderly parents come to live with them, and they become an extended family. Later the husband takes another wife, and the family becomes polygynous. Then the elderly parents die, and the family is no longer extended. After a time, the husband's younger brother and his wife and children move in, creating a joint household. One wife leaves, and the husband is monogamous again. His brother and his wife and children leave, the husband takes another wife, and the family is polygynous again. The eldest son marries and brings his wife to live in the household, and the household is once again an extended family. One wife dies, and the children all move away, and there is now a monogamous couple living in the household. Finally, with the death of the husband, there is a solitary widow who is supported by her eldest son but lives alone. In this example, each household structure is different in its dynamic. These are not several nuclear families that overlap. Extended and joint families are fundamentally different with regard to the relationships they engender.

Transformations in Families over Time

Families change over time. They have a life cycle and a lifespan. The same family takes on different forms and provides different opportunities for the interaction

---

extended family A family pattern made up of three generations living together: parents, married children, and grandchildren.

joint family A family pattern made up of brothers and their wives or sisters and their husbands (along with their children) living together.

of family members at different points in its development. New households are formed and old households change through divorce, remarriage, the departure of children, and the break-up of extended families.

Divorce and Remarriage

Most human societies make it possible for married couples to separate. In some societies, the process is long, drawn-out, and difficult, especially when bridewealth must be returned. A man who divorces a wife in such societies, or whose wife leaves him, expects some of the bridewealth back. But for the wife's family to give the bridewealth back, a whole chain of marriages may have to be broken up. Brothers of the divorced wife may have to divorce to get back enough bridewealth from their in-laws. Sometimes a new husband will repay the bridewealth to the former husband's line, thus letting the bride's relatives off the hook.

Divorce in Guider

In other societies, divorce is easier. Marriages in Guider, for example, are easily broken up. The Fulbe of Guider prefer that a man marry his father's brother's daughter. In many cases, such marriages are contracted simply to oblige the families involved; after a few months, the couple splits up. In other cases, a young girl (12 or 13 years old) is married to a man considerably her senior, despite any interest she may have had in men closer to her own age. Here, too, the marriage may not last long. In general, there is enough dissatisfaction with marriage in Guider to make household transformation through divorce quite common.

Among Muslims in Guider, divorce is controlled by men; women are not legally allowed to initiate divorces. A man wanting a divorce need only follow the simple procedure laid down in the Quran and sanctioned by long practice in Guider: he appears before two witnesses and pronounces the formula 'I divorce you' three times. He is then divorced, and his wife must leave his household. She may take an infant with her, but any children at the toddler stage or older stay with the father. If she takes an infant, she must return the child to the father's household by the time the child is six to eight years old. In case she was pregnant at the time of the divorce, a woman must wait three months after she is divorced before she can remarry. After this time, the vast majority of women remarry.

Do women in Guider, then, have no power to escape from marriages that are unsatisfactory? Legally, perhaps not. But several conventionally recognized practices allow a woman to communicate her desire for a divorce. She can ask her husband for a divorce, and in some cases he will comply. If he does not, or if she is unwilling to confront him directly, she can neglect household duties—burn his food, stop cooking for him entirely, or refuse to sleep with him. She can also leave, going to live in the compound of her father or brother.

Grounds for Divorce

Depending on the society, nagging, quarrelling, cruelty, stinginess, or adultery may be cited as causes for divorce. In almost all societies, childlessness is grounds for divorce as well. For the Ju/'hoansi of the Kalahari Desert, most divorces are initiated by women, mainly because they do not like their husbands or do not want to be married (Lee 1992b; Shostak 1981; see Ethno-Profile 10.1: Ju/'hoansi [!Kung]). After what is often a considerable debate, a couple that decides to break up merely separates. There is no bridewealth to return, no legal contract to be renegotiated. Mutual consent is all that is necessary. The children go with the mother. Ju/'hoansi divorces are cordial, Richard Lee (1992b) tells us, at least compared with the Western norm. Ex-spouses may continue to joke with each other and even live next to each other with their new spouses.

There are very few societies in which divorce is not recognized. In ancient Rome, for example, divorce was impossible. This followed from legal consequences of the marriage ritual. When she married, a woman was cut off from the patrilineage into which she was born and incorporated into her husband's patrilineage. Were she to leave her husband, she would have no place to go and no lineage to protect her.

Separation among Inuit

Among the northwestern Inuit, the traditional view is that all kin relationships, including marital ones, are permanent (Burch 1970). Thus, although it is possible to deactivate a marriage by separating, a marriage can never be permanently dissolved. (Conversely, re-establishing the residence tie is all that is needed to reactivate the relationship.) A husband and wife who stop living together and stop having sexual relations with each other are considered to be separated and ready for another marriage. If each member of a separated couple remarried, the two husbands of the wife would become co-husbands; the two wives of the husband co-wives; and the children of the first and second marriages co-siblings. In effect, a 'divorce' among the Inuit results in more, not fewer, connections. (The consequences of this approach, as well as some additional details, are found in Chapter 10 in the discussion of relatedness among the Iñupiat, also in northwestern Alaska.)

Blended Families

In recent years in North America, anthropologists have observed the emergence of a new family type: the **blended family**. A blended family is created when previously divorced or widowed people marry, bringing with them children from their previous marriages. The internal dynamics of the new family—which can come to include his children, her children, and their children—may resemble the dynamics of polygynous families, as the relations among the children and their relations to each parent may be complex and negotiated over time.

Breaking up Complex Households

The formation of new households following the break-up of extended families is best illustrated in joint families. In a joint family, the pressures that build up among co-resident brothers or sisters often increase dramatically on the death of the father. In theory, the eldest son inherits the position of head of the household from his father, but his younger brothers may not accept his authority as readily as they did their father's. Some younger brothers may decide to establish their own households, and gradually the joint family splits. Each brother whose household splits off from the joint stem usually hopes to start his own joint family; eventually, his sons will bring their wives into the household, and a new joint family emerges out of the ashes of an old one.

Something similar happens among the Nyinba, the polyandrous people of Nepal discussed earlier. In a family with many brothers widely separated in age, the corporation of brothers may take a second wife. At first, all brothers have equal sexual access to her, but in time the brothers will tend to form groups around each wife, with some preferring the first and others preferring the second. At this point, the time is ripe for

Map 11.6 Los Pinos

splitting the household in two. The Nyinba recognize that bringing a second fertile wife into the house sets in motion the transformation of the family into two polyandrous households and the division of land ownership. Hence, family systems contain the seeds of their own transformation.

International Migration and the Family

Migration to find work in another country has become increasingly common worldwide and has important effects on families. Anthropologist Eugenia Georges (1990) examined these effects on people who migrated to the United States from Los Pinos, a small town in the Dominican Republic (see Map 11.6). Migration divided these families, with some members moving to New York and some remaining in Los Pinos. Some parents stayed in the Dominican Republic while their children went to the United States. A more common pattern was for spouses to separate, with the husband migrating and the wife staying home. Consequently, many households in Los Pinos were headed by women. In most cases, however, the spouse in the United States worked to bring the spouse and children in Los Pinos to the US.

blended family A family created when previously divorced or widowed people marry, bringing with them children from their previous families.

This sometimes took several years because it involved completing paperwork for the visa and saving money beyond the amount regularly sent to Los Pinos. Children of the couple who were close to working age also came to the United States, frequently with their mother, and younger children were sent for as they approached working age. Finally, after several years in the United States, the couple who started the migration

In Their Own Words

Why Migrant Women Feed Their Husbands Tamales

Brett Williams suggests that the reasons why Mexican migrant women feed their husbands tamales may not be the stereotypical reasons that outside observers often assume.

Because migrant women are so involved in family life and so seemingly submissive to their husbands, they have been described often as martyred purveyors of rural Mexican and Christian custom, tyrannized by excessively masculine, crudely domineering, rude and petty bullies in marriage, and blind to any world outside the family because they are suffocated by the concerns of kin. Most disconcerting to outside observers is that migrant women seem to embrace such stereotypes: they argue that they should monopolize their foodways and that they should not question the authority of their husbands. If men want tamales, men should have them. But easy stereotypes can mislead; in exploring the lives of the poor, researchers must revise their own notions of family life, and this paper argues that foodways can provide crucial clues about how to do so.

The paradox is this: among migrant workers, both women and men are equally productive wage earners, and husbands readily acknowledge that without their wives' work their families cannot earn enough to survive. For migrants the division of labour between earning a living outside the home and managing household affairs is unknown; and the dilemma facing middle-class wives who may wish to work to supplement the family's income simply does not exist. Anthropologists exploring women's status cross-culturally argue that women are most influential when they share in the production of food and have some control over its distribution. If such perspectives bear at all on migrant women, one might be led to question their seemingly unfathomable obsequiousness in marriage.

Anthropologists further argue that women's influence is even greater when they are not isolated from their

kinswomen, when women can co-operate in production and join, for example, agricultural work with domestic duties and child care. Most migrant women spend their lives within large, closely knit circles of kin and their work days with their kinswomen. Marriage does not uproot or isolate a woman from her family but rather doubles the relatives each partner can depend on and widens in turn the networks of everyone involved. The lasting power of marriage is reflected in statistics which show a divorce rate of 1 per cent for migrant farm workers from Texas, demonstrating the strength of a union bolstered by large numbers of relatives concerned that it go well. Crucial to this concern is that neither partner is an economic drain on the family, and the Tejano pattern of early and lifelong marriages establishes some limit on the whimsy with which men can abuse and misuse their wives.

While anthropology traditionally rests on an appreciation of other cultures in their own contexts and on their own terms, it is very difficult to avoid class bias in viewing the lives of those who share partly in one's own culture, especially when the issue is something so close to home as food and who cooks it. Part of the problem may lie in appreciating what families are and what they do. For the poor, public and private domains are blurred in confusing ways, family affairs may be closely tied to economics, and women's work at gathering and obligating or binding relatives is neither trivial nor merely a matter of sentiment. Another problem may lie in focusing on the marital relationship as indicative of a woman's authority in the family. We, too, often forget that women are sisters, grandmothers, and aunts to men as well as wives. Foodways can help us rethink both of these problematic areas and understand how women elaborate domestic roles to knit families together, to obligate both male and female kin, and to nurture and bind their husbands as well.

Source: Williams, Brett. 1984. 'Why Migrant Women Feed Their Husbands Tamales: Foodways as a Basis for a Revisionist View of Tejano Family Life', in *Ethnic and Regional Foodways in the United States*, eds Linda Keller Brown and Kay Mussell (Knoxville: University of Tennessee Press).

cycle would often take their savings and return to the Dominican Republic. Their children stayed in the United States and continued to send money home. Return migrants tended not to give up their residence visas and therefore had to return to the United States annually. Often, they stayed for a month or more to work. This also provided them with the opportunity to buy clothing and household goods at a more reasonable cost, as well as other items—clothing, cosmetics, and the like—to sell to neighbours, friends, and kin in the Dominican Republic.

Georges observes that the absent family member maintained an active role in family life despite the heavy psychological burden of separation. Although he might be working in a hotel in New York, for example, the husband was still the breadwinner and the main decision-maker in the household. He communicated by visits, letters, and occasional telephone calls. Despite the strains of migration, moreover, the divorce rate was actually slightly lower in migrant families. In part, this was because the exchange of information between Los Pinos and New York was both dense and frequent but also because strong ties of affection connected many couples. Finally, 'the goal of the overwhelming majority of the migrants [from Los Pinos] I spoke with was permanent return to the Dominican Republic. Achievement of this goal was hastened by sponsoring the migration of dependents, both wives and children, so that they could work and save as part of the reconstituted household in the United States' (Georges 1990: 201). This pressure also helped keep families together.

In recent years, the Internet has come to play an increasingly important role in the lives of families that are separated by migration, education, work, and so on. Daniel Miller and Don Slater (2000) studied Internet use in Trinidad, finding that e-mail and instant messaging have considerably strengthened both the nuclear and extended families, allowing closer relations between distant parents and children, among siblings, and among other relatives as well. They remark on the experiences of a widow they knew who, depressed after her husband's death, was convinced by relatives to learn to use e-mail to contact a beloved grandchild who had gone abroad. This experience was so valuable to her that she began to contact other relatives abroad and in Trinidad, and younger members of her family 'swear it has given "new lease of life"' (Miller and Slater 2000:

61). Overall, the use of the Internet offers anthropologists the opportunity to observe how family separation can be moderated and offers people around the world opportunities for relaxed, expansive, and everyday forms of communication that seem to have important effects on family life.

Families by Choice

In spite of the range of variation in family forms that we have surveyed, some readers may still be convinced that family ties depend on blood and that blood is thicker than water. It is therefore instructive to consider the results of research carried out by Kath Weston (1991) on family forms among gays and lesbians in the San Francisco Bay area during the 1980s. A lesbian herself, Weston knew that a turning point in the lives of most gays and lesbians was the decision to announce their sexual orientation to their parents and siblings. If blood truly was thicker than water, this announcement should not destroy family bonds, and many parents have indeed been supportive of their children after the announcement. Often enough, however, shocked parents have turned away, declaring that this person is no longer their son or daughter. Living through—or even contemplating—such an experience has been enough to force gays and lesbians to think seriously about the sources of family ties.

By the 1980s, some North American gays and lesbians had reached two conclusions:

(1) that blood ties *cannot* guarantee the 'enduring diffuse solidarity' supposedly at the core of North American kinship (Schneider 1968), and
(2) that new kin ties *can* be created over time as friends and lovers demonstrate their genuine commitment to one another by creating families of choice.

'Like their heterosexual counterparts, most gay men and lesbians insisted that family members are people who are "there for you", people you can count on emotionally and materially' (Weston 1991: 113). Some gay kinship ideologies now argue that 'whatever endures is real' as a way of claiming legitimacy for chosen families that were not the product of heterosexual marriages (Figure 11.9). Such a definition of family is compatible with understandings of kinship based on nurturance

Figure 11.9 Lesbian mothers, one an immigrant from Greece, another from Israel, watch their five-year-old son play. They have been together for 21 years.

described in Chapter 10. Gay and lesbian activists have used this similarity as a resource in their struggles to obtain—for long-standing families by choice—some of the same legal rights enjoyed by traditional hetero-sexual families, such as hospital visiting privileges, joint adoption, and property rights (Weston 1995: 99).

The Flexibility of Marriage

It is easy to get the impression that marriage rules compel people to do things they really do not want to do. Younger people, for example, seem forced by elders to marry complete strangers of a certain kin category belonging to particular social groups; or women appear to be pawns in men's games of prestige and power. Marriage rules, however, are always subject to some negotiation.

Sometimes the contrast between the formal rules of marriage and the actual performance of marriage rituals can be revealing. Ivan Karp (1978) asked why Iteso women laugh at marriage ceremonies. During his fieldwork, Karp was struck by a paradox. The marriage ritual is taken very seriously by the patrilineal Iteso; it is the moment of creation for a new household, and it paves the way for the physical and social reproduction of Iteso patrilineages. But the ritual is carried out entirely by women who are not consanguineal members of the patrilineage! Despite the seriousness of the occasion, and although they are carrying out the ritual for the benefit of a lineage to which they do not belong, Iteso women seem to find the ceremony enormously funny.

To explain this apparently anomalous behaviour, Karp suggests that the meaning of the marriage ritual needs to be analyzed from two different perspectives: that of the men and that of the women. The men's perspective constitutes the official (or hegemonic) ideology of Iteso marriage. It emphasizes how marriage brings the bride's sexuality under the control of her husband's lineage. It distinguishes between women of the mother-in-law's generation and women of the wife's generation. It stresses the woman's role as an agent of reproduction who is equivalent, in a reproductive sense, to the bridewealth cattle.

The women's perspective constitutes an unofficial (or counter-hegemonic) ideology. For the men and women of a given lineage to succeed in perpetuating that lineage, they must control women's bodies. But the bodies they must control belong to female outsiders who marry lineage men. These same female outsiders direct the two ritual events crucial to lineage reproduction: marriage and birth. And men of the lineage are not allowed to attend either of these rituals. In sum, female outsiders control the continued existence of a patrilineage whose male members are supposed to control them!

Iteso women, Karp says, can see the irony in this: they are at once controlled and controlling. In the marriage ritual itself, they comment on this paradox through their laughter. In doing so, they reveal two things:

(1) they show that they know the men are dependent on them; and
(2) even as the men assert their control over women's bodies, the women's ritual actions escape the men's control.

The official ideology of male control is subverted, at least momentarily, by the women's laughter. Even as they ensure that lineages will continue, they are able to comment on the paradoxical relation of women to men. It should be remembered, however, that all the women could do was comment on those relations; they did not have the power to change them.

Sexual Practices

Some anthropologists seem to regard marriage as an abstract formal system, having little, if anything, to do with human sexuality. As a result, their discussions tend to ignore its carnal aspects. But sexual intercourse is part of almost all marriages. And because in many societies marriage is the formal prerequisite for becoming sexually active (at least for females), a desire for sex is a strong motivation for getting married (Spiro 1977: 212).

Ranges of Heterosexual Practices

The range of sexual practice in the world is vast. In many Oceanian societies—Tikopia, for example (see Map 11.7)—the young are expected to have a great deal of sexual experience before marriage. Young men and young women begin having sexual relations at an early age, and having several lovers is considered normal for the young. Getting married, as in many societies, is considered the final step (or the beginning of the final step) in becoming an adult. Distinguished British anthropologist Sir Raymond Firth notes that for the Tikopia, marriage represents a great change for both partners in this regard. The woman must abandon sexual freedom, but she replaces it with what Firth calls 'a safe and legalized sexual cohabitation' (1984 [1936]: 434). The man is theoretically free to continue to have affairs, but in practice he will 'settle down'. This pattern is seen in many cultures; 'settling down' and 'safety' do not seem to be the case in Canada where 38.3 per cent of marriages end in divorce by the couple's thirtieth wedding anniversary (Statistics Canada 2005b).

The Ju/'hoansi also begin sexual activity at an early age. As a result, the social and sexual constraints of marriage represent quite a shock at first, especially for young women. Some Ju/'hoansi are strictly faithful to one another, but a significant minority take lovers. The Ju/'hoansi have no double standard; both men and women are free to take lovers, and women are sometimes eloquent about the time they spend with lovers. However, discretion is necessary when taking a lover because both husbands and wives can become very jealous and start fights. Sexual satisfaction is important to the Ju/'hoansi; female orgasm is known, and women expect both husbands and lovers to satisfy them sexually.

Not all societies have the same attitude. Robert Murphy and Yolanda Murphy (1974) noted that for the Mundurucu, a group of about 1,250 gardening and hunting people in the Brazilian Amazon, female orgasm is more accidental than expected. Many societies require a woman's virginity at marriage; in some Arab societies, bloodstained sheets must be produced the morning after the consummation of a marriage to demonstrate that the bride was a virgin.

Particularly interesting in this regard is Karl Heider's research (1979) among the Dani, a people of highland New Guinea (see Map 11.8). Heider discovered that the Dani have extraordinarily little interest in sex. For five years after the birth of a child, the parents do not have sexual intercourse with each other. This practice, called a *postpartum sex taboo*, is found in all cultures, but in most societies it lasts for a few weeks or months. (In North America, we say that the mother needs time to heal; other societies have other

Map 11.7 Tikopia

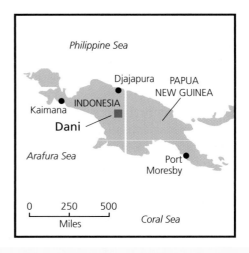

Map 11.8 Dani

justifications.) In a few cases, the postpartum sex taboo is two years long, which is considered a very long time. Five years is hard to believe. What could explain it?

Heider points out that Westerners assume that the sex drive is perhaps the most powerful biological drive of all, and that if this drive is not satisfied directly in sexual activity, then some other outlet will be found. In fact, some suggest that the Dani's high levels of out-group aggression may be connected with their low level of sexual intercourse. The Dani are not celibate, and they certainly have sexual intercourse often enough to reproduce biologically, yet they do not seem very interested in sex (1979: 78–81). Heider cannot explain why the Dani have such a low level of sexuality, but the implications of this pattern for understanding the range of human sexual behaviour are significant. The Dani, who are not abnormal physically or mentally, represent an extreme in the cultural construction of sexuality.

Other Sexual Practices

The traditional anthropological focus on what Euro-Americans call *heterosexual relationships* is understandable. People in every society are concerned about perpetuating themselves, and most have developed complex ideological and ritual structures to ensure that this occurs. The fact that such elaborate cultural constructions seem necessary to encourage heterosexual practices, however, suggests that human sexual expression would resist such confinement if it were not under strict control. As we saw in the previous chapter, anthropological information about supernumerary sexes and genders undermines the 'two-sex model' that is hegemonic in Euro-American cultures. In their own work dealing with the cultural shaping of female desires, for example, anthropologists Evelyn Blackwood and Saskia Wieringa have concluded that focusing on the ways that female bodies are assigned cultural meanings in different historical and ethnographic settings, and on how those meanings affect the way females constitute their relations with other females, reveals a wide range of 'varied and rich cultural identities and same-sex practices between those with female bodies' (1999: ix). This sort of research does not assume that having a male body or a female body necessarily determines any individual's traits, feelings, or experiences (x). As a result, it provides a vital comparative context which can

illuminate our understanding of sexual practices that Euro-Americans call *homosexuality* and *bisexuality*.

Female Sexual Practices in Mombasa

Anthropologist Gill Shepherd shows that traditional patterns of male–female interaction among Swahili Muslims in Mombasa, Kenya (see Map 11.9; Figure 11.10), make male and female homosexual relationships perfectly intelligible (1987). For one thing, men and women in Muslim Mombasa live in very different subcultures. For women, the most enduring relationship is between mothers and daughters, mirrored in the relationship between an older married sister and a younger unmarried sister. By contrast, relationships between mothers and sons and between brothers and sisters are more distant. Except in the case of young, modern, educated couples, the relationship between husband and wife is often emotionally distant as well. Because the worlds of men and women overlap so little, therefore, relationships between the sexes tend to be one-dimensional. Men and women join a variety of sex-segregated groups for leisure-time activities such as dancing or religious study. Within these same-sex groups, individuals compete for social rank.

Of the some 50,000 Swahili in Mombasa, about 5,000 could be called *homosexual*. The number is misleading, however, because men and women shift between what Euro-Americans call *homosexuality* and *heterosexuality* throughout their lives. Women

Map 11.9 Mombasa Swahilis

are allowed to choose other women as sexual partners only after they have been married. Therefore, all such women in Mombasa are married, widowed, or divorced. Both men and women are open about their same-sex relationships, and 'nobody would dream of suggesting that their sexual choices had any effect on their work capabilities, reliability, or religious piety' (Shepherd 1987: 241).

Because women in many all-female households do not have sexual relationships with one another, Shepherd uses the term *lesbian* to imply an overt sexual relationship between two women. Lesbian couples in Mombasa are far more likely to live together than

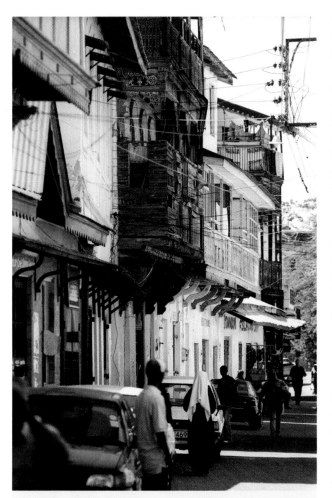

Figure 11.10 In Mombasa, Kenya, traditional patterns of male–female interaction make male and female homosexual relationships perfectly intelligible.

are male homosexual couples. In addition to having private, sexual relationships with other women, they also form club-like groups that regularly meet in one another's houses. Each group is composed of an inner circle of relatively wealthy older women who are friends. The rule is that younger, lower-status women visit older, higher-status women. Wealthy lesbian women hold court in the afternoons, when Swahili women have the chance to go visiting. Women in the inner circle compete for status by, for example, trying to outdo one another by dressing their lovers as opulently as possible.

Many women were quite clear about the practical reasons that had led them into sexual relationships with other women. Women with little money are unlikely to marry men who cannot offer them jewelry, shoes, new dresses, status, or financial security, but a wealthy lesbian lover can offer them all these things. Also, a poor young woman in an unhappy marriage may have no way to support herself if she leaves her husband unless she has a lesbian lover. Occasionally a wealthy lesbian woman will help a girl who has remained single after all her peers have married. Adult status and freedoms only come with marriage, but a woman who is well-educated, or from a high-status family, may still be unmarried in her late twenties or early thirties due to her parents' intimidation of potential suitors. A wealthy lesbian who wants to help such a woman finds a man willing to make a marriage of convenience and finances his marriage to the woman. The couple is divorced shortly thereafter, and the girl goes to live with her lesbian benefactress.

According to Islamic law, a wealthy, high-ranking Muslim woman can only marry a man who is her equal or superior. A marriage of this kind brings a great deal of seclusion, and her wealth is administered by her husband. The wealthy partner in a lesbian relationship, however, is freed from these constraints. 'Thus if she wishes to use her wealth as she likes and has a taste for power, entry into a lesbian relationship or living alone as a divorced or widowed woman are virtually her only options' (Shepherd 1987: 257). Financial independence for a woman offers the chance to convert wealth to power. If she pays for the marriages of other people or provides financial support in exchange for loyalty, a woman can create a circle of dependents.

Shepherd points out that a few women, some lesbians, have achieved real political power in Mombasa in this way (257).

Still, it is not necessary to be a lesbian to build a circle of dependents. Why do some women follow this route? The answer, Shepherd tells us, is complicated. It is not entirely respectable for a woman under 45 or 50 to be unmarried. Some women can maintain autonomy by making a marriage of convenience to a man, who already lives with a wife, and then living apart from him. Many women, however, find this arrangement both lonely and sexually unsatisfying. Living as a lesbian is less respectable than being a second, non-resident wife, but it is more respectable than not being married at all. The lesbian sexual relationship does not reduce the autonomy of the wealthy partner 'and indeed takes place in the highly positive context of the fond and supportive relationships women establish among themselves anyway' (258).

Shepherd suggested that the reason sexual relationships between men or between women are generally not heavily stigmatized in Mombasa is because social rank takes precedence over all other measures of status. Rank is a combination of wealth, the ability to claim Arab ancestry, and the degree of Muslim learning and piety. Rank determines marriage partners, as well as relations of loyalty and subservience, and both men and women expect to rise in rank over a lifetime. Although lesbian couples may violate the prototype for sexual relations, they do not violate relations of rank. Shepherd suggests that a marriage between a poor husband and a rich wife might be more shocking than a lesbian relationship between a dominant rich woman and a dependent poor one. It is less important that a woman's lover be a male than it is for her to be a good Arab, a good Muslim, and a person of wealth and influence.

Anthropologists working in Africa have described a range of relations between females, such as woman marriage, that have been likened to European or North American models of lesbian relationships, but disputes have arisen about whether such relationships included an erotic involvement between the female partners. In a survey of this evidence, Blackwood and Wieringa note that woman marriage can take many forms, some of which are more likely than others to have included sexuality between the female partners. Among those where such sexual relations appear more likely are cases like that described by Shepherd, 'in which a woman of some means, either married (to a man) or unmarried, pays bride-price for a wife and establishes her own compound' (Blackwood and Wieringa 1999: 5). Such evidence is not merely of academic interest. In the contemporary world of intensified global communication and exchange, Western and non-Western same-sex practices are becoming increasingly entangled with one another, leading to the emergence of local movements for 'lesbian' and 'gay' rights in Africa and elsewhere. In this context, the presidents of Zimbabwe, Kenya, and Namibia recently declared that homosexuality is 'un-African'. Based on the ethnographic evidence, however, Blackwood and Wieringa side with those arguing that, on the contrary, it is homophobia that is 'un-African': 'President Mandela from South Africa is a striking exception to the homophobia of his colleagues. The South African constitution specifically condemns discrimination on the basis of sexual orientation' (1999: 27).

Male Sexual Practices in Nicaragua

In the 1980s, anthropologist Roger Lancaster spent many months studying the effects of the Sandinista Revolution on the lives of working people in Managua, Nicaragua. While he was there, he learned about *cochones*. *Cochón* could be translated into English as *homosexual*, but this would be highly misleading. As Lancaster discovered, working-class Nicaraguans interpret sexual relations between men differently than North Americans, and their interpretation is central to the traditional Nicaraguan ideas about masculinity that have been called *machismo*.

To begin with, a 'real man' (or *macho*) is widely admired as someone who is active, violent, and dominant. In sexual terms, this means that the penis is seen as a weapon used violently to dominate one's sexual partner, who is thereby rendered passive, abused, and subordinate. North Americans typically think of machismo as involving the domination of women by men, but as Lancaster shows, the system is equally defined by the domination of men over other men. Indeed, a 'manly man' in working-class Nicaragua is defined as one who is the active, dominant, penetrating sexual partner in encounters with women *and* men. A 'passive' male who allows a 'manly man' to have sexual intercourse with him in this way is called a *cochón*.

A gay man himself, Lancaster found that Nicaraguan views of male–male sexual encounters differ considerably from contemporary North American ideas about male homosexuality. In Nicaragua, for example, the people Lancaster knew assumed that men 'would naturally be aroused by the idea of anally penetrating another male' (1992: 241). Only the 'passive' *cochón* is stigmatized, whereas males who take the 'active' role in sexual intercourse with other males and with females are seen as 'normal'. Nicaraguans, moreover, find hate crimes such as gay-bashing inconceivable: *cochones* may be made fun of, but they are also admired performers during Carnival. In North America, by contrast, the active–passive distinction does not exist, and anal intercourse is not the only form that male homosexual expression may take. Both partners in same-sex encounters are considered homosexual and equally stigmatized, and gay-bashing is sometimes a deadly reality, probably because it is *not* assumed that 'normal' males will naturally be aroused by the idea of sex with another man.

In Nicaragua, public challenges for dominance are a constant of male–male interaction, even when sexual intercourse is not involved. The term *cochón* may be used as an epithet not only for a man who yields publicly to another man but also for cats that don't catch mice or indeed anything that somehow fails to perform its proper function. In Lancaster's view, *cochones* are made, not born: 'Those who consistently lose out in the competition for male status . . . discover pleasure in the passive sexual role or its social status: these men are made into *cochones*. And those who master the rules of conventional masculinity . . . are made into *machistas*' (1992: 249).

These ideas about gender and sexuality created an unanticipated roadblock for Sandinistas who wanted to improve the lives of Nicaraguan women and children. The Sandinista government passed a series of New Family Laws, which were designed to encourage men to support their families economically and to discourage irresponsible sex, irresponsible parenting, and familial dislocation. When Lancaster interviewed Nicaraguan men to see what they thought of these laws, however, he repeatedly got the following response: 'First the interrogative: "What do the Sandinistas want from us? That we should all become *cochones*?" And then the tautological: "A man has to be a man." That is, a man is defined by what he is not—a *cochón*' (1992: 274).

Sexuality and Power

The physical activity that we call *sexual intercourse* is not just doing what comes naturally. Like many things in human life, sex does not speak for itself nor does it have only one meaning. Sexual practices can be used to give concrete form to more abstract notions we have about the place of men and women in the world. They may serve as a metaphor for expressing differential power within a society. This is particularly clear in the sexual practices that embody Nicaraguan machismo or North American date rape and family violence. That is, sexual practices can be used to enact, in unmistakable physical terms, the reality of differential power. This is equally clear in the arguments over 'gay marriage' in the United States, since marriage in a nation-state has legal consequences and protections, as well as embodying the legitimacy of the couple's commitment to each other. Although same-sex marriage is now covered under federal legislation in Canada, it is still a matter of debate in certain circles and frequently used as a cynical 'chip' in the game of politics. This reminds us that marriages, families, and sexual practices never occur in a vacuum but are embedded in other social practices such as food production, political organization, legal protection, and kinship.

Key Terms

avunculocal 268

blended family 281

conjugal family 277

dowry 273

endogamy 268

exogamy 268

extended family 279

family 277

joint family 279

levirate 266

matrilocal 268

monogamy 268

neolocal 268

non-conjugal family 277

nuclear family 277

patrilocal 268

polyandry 269

polygamy 268

polygyny 268

sororate 266

Chapter Summary

1. Marriage is a social process that transforms the status of the participants, stipulates the degree of sexual access the married partners may have to each other, positions children, and creates relationships between the kin of the partners.

2. Woman marriage and ghost marriage highlight several defining features of marriage and also demonstrate that the roles of husband and father may not be dependent on the gender of the person who fills it.

3. In some instances same-sex marriages are recognized. Canada is an example of such a society.

4. There are four major patterns of post-marital residence: neolocal, patrilocal, matrilocal, and avunculocal.

5. A person may be married to only one person at a time (monogamy) or to several people at a time (polygamy). Polygamy can be further subdivided into polygyny, in which a man is married to two or more women, and polyandry, in which a woman is married to two or more men.

6. There are three main forms of polyandry: fraternal polyandry, associated polyandry, and secondary marriage. The study of polyandry reveals the separation of a woman's sexuality and her reproductive capacity, something not found in monogamous or polygynous societies.

7. Bridewealth is a payment of symbolically important goods by the husband's lineage to the wife's lineage. Anthropologists see this as compensation to the wife's family for the loss of her productive and reproductive capacities. A woman's bridewealth payment may enable her brother to pay bridewealth to get a wife.

8. Dowry is typically a transfer of family wealth from parents to their daughter at the time of her marriage. Dowries are often considered the wife's contribution to the establishment of a new household.

9. In some cultures, the most important relationships a man and a woman have are those with their opposite-sex siblings. Adult brothers and sisters may see one another often and jointly control lineage affairs.

10. Different family structures produce different internal patterns and tensions. There are three basic family types: nuclear, extended, and joint. Families may change from one type to another over time and with the birth, growth, and marriage of children.

11. Most human societies permit divorce, although it is not always easy. Sometimes nagging, quarrelling, cruelty, stinginess, and adultery are causes for divorce. In most societies, childlessness is grounds for divorce. In some societies, only men may initiate a divorce. In very few societies is divorce impossible.

12. Families have developed ingenious ways of keeping together even when some members live abroad for extended periods. Gays and lesbians in North America have created families by choice, based on nurturance, which they believe are as enduring as families based on marriage and birth.

13. Marriage rules are subject to negotiation, even when they appear rigid. This is illustrated by Iteso marriage. The Iteso depend upon women from the outside to perpetuate their patrilineages, and the women express their ironic awareness of this fact through ritualized laughter at marriage.

14. Sexual practices vary greatly worldwide, from the puritanical and fearful to the casual and pleasurable. In some societies, young men and women begin having sexual relations from an early age. Sexual practices that North Americans call *homosexuality* or *bisexuality* may be understood very differently in different societies. In the contemporary globalizing world, Western and non-Western same-sex practices are becoming increasingly entangled with one another, leading to the emergence of local movements for 'lesbian' and 'gay' rights on many continents.

Critical Thinking Questions

1. What is the 'prototypical' marriage? How has this changed in various contexts?

2. Distinguish between *pater* and *genitor*. Are they always the same person?

3. How have the lives of First Nations women in Canada been affected by the patriarchal constructs of the political system?

4. How are joint, extended, and blended families different from nuclear families?

5. Considering gay kinship ideologies and the development of families in gay and lesbian relationships and marriages, what are the challenges such families face?

Suggested Readings

Bohannan, Paul, and John Middleton. 1968. *Marriage, Family, and Residence* (New York: Natural History Press). *A classic collection with important and readable articles.*

Carter, S. 1997. *Capturing Women: The Manipulation of Cultural Imagery in Canada's Prairie West* (Montreal and Kingston: McGill-Queen's University Press). *An interesting analysis of historical documents that reveal the invention of the dangerous 'red' man stereotype for the political ends of the dominant sector of Canadian society.*

Foucault, M. 1978. *The History of Sexuality, Vol. I: An Introduction*, trans. Robert Hurley (New York: Pantheon). *An overview of human sexuality that is cross-cultural and diachronic.*

Jamieson, Kathleen. 1986. 'Sex Discrimination and the Indian Act', in *Arduous Journey: Canadian Indians and Decolonization*, ed. J. Rick Ponting (Toronto: McClelland & Stewart), 112–36. *A discussion of the discrimination toward First Nations women found in the Indian Act and government policies associated with this Act.*

Kirby, Peter. 1985. 'Marrying Out and Loss of Status: The Charter and the New Indian Act Legislation', *Journal of Law and Social Policy* 1 (fall): 77–95. *Discusses the consequences of exogamy in light of the Indian Act of Canada.*

Lancaster, Roger. 1992. *Life is Hard* (Berkeley: University of California Press). *A stunning analysis of machismo in Nicaragua in which sexual practices North Americans consider homosexual are interpreted very differently.*

Sacks, Karen. 1979. *Sisters and Wives* (Urbana: University of Illinois Press). *A Marxian analysis of the notion of sexual equality. This book includes very important data and analysis on sister–brother relations.*

Shostak, Marjorie. 1981. *Nisa: The Life and Words of a !Kung Woman* (New York: Vintage). *A wonderful book. The story of a Ju/'hoansi (!Kung) woman's life in her own words. Shostak provides background for each chapter. There is much here on marriage and everyday life.*

Status of Women Canada. *Polygamy in Canada: Legal and Social Implications for Women and Children—A Collection of Policy Research Reports*, available at: <http://www.swc-cfc.gc.ca/pubs/pubspr/0662420683/200511_0662420683-3_2_e.html>. *A discussion of polygamy in a Canadian context. What we see here is a consideration of polygamy in the context of existing laws and concepts of rights and freedoms in response to the influx of migrants from societies where such marriage patterns are not only legal but usual.*

Suggs, David, and Andrew Miracle, eds. 1993. *Culture and Human Sexuality* (Pacific Grove, CA: Brooks/Cole). *A collection of important articles from a variety of theoretical perspectives on the nature and culture of human sexuality.*

Related Websites

The Civil Marriage Act: http://www.parl.gc.ca/common/bills_ls.asp?Parl=38&Ses=1&ls=c38

Library and Archives Canada: http://www.collectionscanada.gc.ca/women/002026-846-e.html

National Clearinghouse on Family Violence: http://www.phac-aspc.gc.ca/ncfv-cnivf/familyviolence/

Vanier Institute of the Family: http://www.vifamily.ca/

Part Five

From Local to Global

Human beings have used their cultural creativity, together with political and economic resources, to create imagined communities that now encompass the entire world. These communities have complex hierarchical forms of social organization. We look at some of the most significant ways in which social inequality has been institutionalized, and we turn to the rise of global forms of inequality, particularly as they are associated with European colonial empires and their aftermath. Finally, we examine the work of those anthropologists who have tried to do more than record and analyze contemporary social change and who have taken on the task of applying anthropological information to the solution of contemporary human social problems.

Chapter 12

Dimensions of Inequality in the Contemporary World: Class, Caste, Race, Ethnicity, and Nationalism

Chapter Outline

Learning Objectives

By the end of Chapter 12, you will be able to:

- identify aspects of social stratification resulting in class structures,
- distinguish the stratification created by caste-based societies,

- consider and challenge the concept of race,
- appreciate the forms ethnicity may take, and
- understand aspects of nation-building and nationalism.

Earlier we described some of the distinctive forms of social organization that were relatively egalitarian in political organization. But anthropologists have also been interested in documenting the various forms of hierarchies in **stratified societies**, societies made up of permanently ranked subgroups. In stratified societies higher-ranking groups have a disproportionate access to wealth, power, and prestige. In those societies that anthropologists call *chiefdoms*, stratification is minimal, frequently with only the office of chief as a permanently superior status. Meanwhile social and economic relations among non-chief members may remain relatively egalitarian. More elaborate social stratification is found in societies classified as *states*, which are not only much larger than chiefdoms but also employ a variety of mechanisms to bind different subgroups together into a hierarchy that regulates each group's access to wealth, power, and prestige.

All people in the world today, even refugees, must deal with the authority of one nation-state or another, and all nation-states are socially stratified. But inequality within nation-states may be constructed out of multiple categories arranged in different, and sometimes contradictory, hierarchies of stratification. We can refer you to the earlier discussion of gender and then consider the problems of sexism, the discrimination that results from sexual orientation, and the need to consider ageism; however, we shall confine our discussion in this chapter to five categories of inequality:

(1) class,
(2) caste,
(3) race,
(4) ethnicity, and
(5) nationality.

It is important to understand that *every one of these categories is a cultural invention* designed to create boundaries around one imagined community or another. *None* of these categories maps onto permanent biological subdivisions within the human species although members of societies that employ these categories often will invoke 'nature' to shore up their legitimacy.

Some of these patterns (i.e., class, caste) reach back thousands of years. Others (i.e., race, ethnicity, and nationality) appear to be far more recent in origin and are closely associated with changes that began in Europe some 500 years ago and continued with the spread of capitalism and colonialism. New forms of stratification were introduced to formerly independent, egalitarian societies while forms of stratification that predated European contact were reshaped. Anthropologists and other social scientists have argued with one another about how these categories should be defined and whether or not they can be usefully applied cross-culturally, and we will look at some of their arguments.

Class

In general, **classes** are hierarchically arranged social groups defined on economic grounds. That is, higher-ranked social classes have disproportionate access to sources of wealth in the society, whereas members of low-ranked classes have much more limited access to wealth (Figure 12.1).

classes Ranked groups within a hierarchically stratified society whose membership is defined primarily in terms of wealth, occupation, or other economic criteria.

stratified societies Societies in which there is a permanent hierarchy that accords some members privileged access to wealth, power, and prestige.

The concept of class has a double heritage in modern anthropology, one stemming from Europe, the other from the United States. European social scientists lived in states with a long history of social class divisions reaching back to the Middle Ages and beyond. In their experience, entrenched social classes are relatively closed groups. The Industrial Revolution and the French Revolution promised to end the oppressive privileges of the ruling class and to equalize everyone's access to wealth. However, class divisions did not wither away in Europe during the nineteenth century; they just changed their contours. Followers of Marx judged that, at best, an old ruling class had been displaced by a new one: feudal aristocrats by bourgeois capitalists. The lowest level in European societies—rural peasants—were partially displaced as well with the appearance of the urban working class. But the barriers separating those at the top of the class hierarchy from those at the bottom seemed just as rigid as ever.

Significantly, Marx defines classes in terms of their members' different relations to the means of production. This means that as long as a particular set of unequal productive relations flourishes in a society, the classes defined by these unequal roles in the division of labour will also persist. The French Revolution had triggered the displacement of aristocrats and peasants who had played the key roles in European feudalism only to replace them with new key classes—industrial entrepreneurs and the industrial working class linked together within the capitalist mode of production. In time, Marx predicted, these industrial workers would become the new 'leading class', rising up to oust capitalists when the socialist revolution came.

As Marx was well aware, all those who are linked to the means of production in the same way (e.g., as workers) do not often recognize what they have in common and may therefore fail to develop the kind of solidarity—the 'class consciousness'—that could, in Marx's view, lead to revolution. Indeed, the possibility of peasant- or working-class solidarity in many of the stratified societies studied by anthropologists is actively undercut by institutions of **clientage**. According to anthropologist M.G. Smith, clientage 'designates a variety of relationships, which all have inequality of status of the associated persons as a common characteristic' (1981 [1954]: 31). Clientage is a relationship between individuals rather than groups. The party of superior status is the **patron**, and the party of inferior status is the **client**. Stratified societies united by links of clientage can be very stable. Low-status clients believe their security depends on finding a high-status individual who can protect them. For example, clientage is characteristic of *compadrazgo* relationships, especially when the ritual parents are of higher social status than the biological parents. In fact, the Latin American societies in which *compadrazgo* flourishes are class societies, and parents who are peasants or workers often seek landowners or factory owners as compadres.

Marx's view of class is clearly different from the view of class hegemony in North America. For generations the 'American Dream' has been that, in the United States, individuals may pursue wealth, power, and prestige unhampered by the unyielding class barriers characteristic of 'Old World' societies. Interestingly, the close relationship we have had as the Canadian

Figure 12.1 Social classes often live within easy sight of one another. Here, luxury apartments and squatter settlements rub shoulders in Caracas, Venezuela.

neighbours of the United States has meant that this 'dream' of equal opportunity for upward class mobility has had some currency here. What we need to question is how this 'dream' has been realized in the Canadian context. How do we differ, or do we differ at all, from our neighbours to the south? Thus the analysis that follows contains meaning for Canadians as well. As a result, many social scientists trained in North America have tended to define social classes primarily in terms of income level and to argue that such social classes are open, porous, and permeable rather than rigid and exclusionary. Upward class mobility is supposed to be, in principle, attainable by all people, regardless of how low their social origins are. Even poor boys like Abraham Lincoln, born in a log cabin on the frontier, can grow up to be president.

But the promise of the American Dream of equal opportunity for upward class mobility has not been realized. In the early twentieth century, both black and white social scientists concluded that an unyielding 'colour bar' prevented upward class mobility. First argued for citizens with African ancestry, the analysis could also be extended to Indigenous peoples. One participant in these studies, an anthropologist named W. Lloyd Warner, argued in 1936 that the colour bar looked more like the rigid barrier reported to exist between castes in India than the supposedly permeable boundary separating social classes. That is to say, membership in a **caste** is ascribed at birth and each ranked caste is closed such that individuals are not allowed to move from one caste into another. Membership in social classes is also ascribed at birth, according to Warner, but unlike castes, classes are not closed and individual social mobility from one class into another is possible (Harrison 1995; 1998; Sharma 1999: 15; Warner 1936). Warner's distinction between caste and class became standard for decades in North American cultural anthropology.

Is this a plausible contrast? The aspect of caste that impressed Warner was the reported rigidity of the barrier between castes, which seemed much like the barrier separating blacks and whites in the United States. But in 1948, an African American sociologist named Oliver Cromwell Cox rejected an equation between caste and race. Cox pointed out that many authorities on caste in India claimed that Hindu castes were harmoniously integrated within a *caste system* shaped by Hindu religious beliefs about purity and pollution. Most importantly, it appeared that members of low-

ranked 'impure' castes did not challenge the caste system even though it oppressed them. If this were true, Cox concluded, caste relations were *unlike* race relations in the United States, and by extension Canada, because whites had imposed the colour bar by force, and only by force had they been able to repress black resistance to the injustice of the system. Ursula Sharma (1999) points out, however, that both Warner and Cox were relying on an understanding of Hindu castes that, today, is considered highly misleading.

Caste

The word *caste* comes from the Portuguese word *casta*, meaning 'chaste'. Portuguese explorers applied it to the stratification systems they encountered in South Asia in the fifteenth century. They understood that these societies were divided into a hierarchy of ranked subgroups, each of which was 'chaste' in the sense that sexual and marital links across group boundaries were forbidden (endogamy was practised). Most Western scholars have taken the stratification system of India as the prototype of caste stratification, and some insist that caste cannot properly be said to exist outside India. Others, however, do find value in applying the term to forms of social stratification, developed elsewhere, that bear a family resemblance to the South Asian pattern.

Caste in India

The term *caste*, as most Western observers use it, collapses two different South Asian concepts:

(1) **varna** refers to the widespread notion that Indian society is ideally divided into four functional subdivisions analogous to the estates of medieval and early modern Europe—priests, warriors, farmers, and merchants (Guneratne 2002; Sharma 1999); and

> **caste** A ranked group within a hierarchically stratified society that is closed, prohibiting individuals to move from one caste into another.
>
> **client** The party of inferior status in a clientage.
>
> **clientage** The institution linking individuals from upper and lower levels in a stratified society.
>
> **patron** The party of superior status in a clientage.
>
> **varna** A caste that refers to the widespread notion that Indian society is divided into four functional subdivisions: priests, warriors, farmers, and merchants.

(2) **jati** refers to localized, named, endogamous groups. Although jati names are frequently the names of occupations (e.g., farmer, saltmaker), there is no conventional way to group the many local jatis within one of the four varnas, which is why jati members can disagree with others about where their own jati ought to belong.

In any case, varna divisions are more theoretical in nature, whereas *jati* is the more significant term in most of the local village settings where anthropologists have traditionally conducted fieldwork.

Villagers in the southern Indian town of Gopalpur defined a jati for anthropologist Alan Beals (see Map 12.1). They said it was 'a category of men thought to be related, to occupy a particular position within a hierarchy of jatis, to marry among themselves, and to follow particular practices and occupations' (Beals 1962: 25). Beals's informants compared the relationship between jatis of different rank to the relationship between brothers. Ideally, they said, members of low-ranking jatis respect and obey members of high-ranking jatis, just as younger brothers respect and obey older brothers.

Villagers in Gopalpur were aware of at least 50 different jatis, although not all were represented in the village. Because jatis have different occupational specialties that they alone can perform, villagers were sometimes dependent on the services of outsiders. For example, there was no member of the Washerman jati in Gopalpur. As a result, a member of that jati from another village had to be employed when people in Gopalpur wanted their clothes cleaned ritually or required clean cloth for ceremonies.

Jatis are distinguished in terms of the foods they eat as well as their traditional occupations. These features have a ritual significance that affects interactions between members of different jatis. In Hindu belief, certain foods and occupations are classed as pure and others as polluting. In theory, all jatis are ranked on a scale from purest to most polluted (Figure 12.2). Ranked highest of all are the vegetarian Brahmins, who are pure enough to approach the gods. Carpenters and Blacksmiths, who also eat a vegetarian diet, are also assigned a high rank. Below the vegetarians are those who eat 'clean', or 'pure', meat. In Gopalpur, this group of jatis included Saltmakers, Farmers, and Shepherds, who eat sheep, goats, chicken, and fish but not pork or beef. The lowest-ranking jatis are 'unclean' meat-eaters, who include Stoneworkers and Basketweavers (who eat pork) and Leatherworkers (who eat pork and beef). Occupations that involve slaughtering animals or touching polluted things are themselves polluting. Jatis that traditionally carry out such activities as butchering and washing dirty clothing are ranked below jatis whose traditional work does not involve polluting activities.

Map 12.1 Gopalpur

Figure 12.2 Gautam Ganu Jadhao, a city worker, removes a cart full of sewage waste from a Bombay neighbourhood in July 2005. People like him, whose occupations are characterized as polluting, are ranked at the bottom of Hindu caste society.

Hindu dietary rules deal not only with the kinds of food that may be eaten by different jatis but also with the circumstances in which members of one jati may accept food prepared by members of another. Members of a lower-ranking jati may accept any food prepared by members of a higher-ranking jati. Members of a higher-ranking jati may only accept certain foods prepared by a lower-ranking jati. In addition, members of different jatis should not eat together.

In practice, these rules are not as confining as they appear. In Gopalpur, '"food" referred to particular kinds of food, principally rice. "Eating together" means eating from the same dish or sitting on the same line. . . . Members of quite different jatis may eat together if they eat out of separate bowls and if they are facing each other or turned slightly away from each other' (Beals 1962: 41). Members of jatis that are close in rank and neither at the top nor at the bottom of the scale often share food and eat together on a daily basis. Strict observance of the rules is saved for ceremonial occasions.

The way in which non-Hindus were incorporated into the jati system in Gopalpur illuminates the logic of the system. For example, Muslims have long ruled the region surrounding Gopalpur; thus, political power has been a salient attribute of Muslim identity. In addition, Muslims do not eat pork or the meat of animals that have not been ritually slaughtered. These attributes, taken together, led the villagers in Gopalpur to rank Muslims above the Stoneworkers and Basketweavers, who eat pork. All three groups were considered to be eaters of unclean meat because Muslims do eat beef.

There is no direct correlation between the status of a jati on the scale of purity and pollution and the class status of members of that jati. Beals noted, for example, that the high status of Brahmins meant that 'there are a relatively large number of ways in which a poor Brahmin may become wealthy' (1962: 37). Similarly, members of low-status jatis may find their attempts to amass wealth curtailed by the opposition of their status superiors. In Gopalpur, a group of Farmers and Shepherds attacked a group of Stoneworkers who had purchased good rice land in the village. Those Stoneworkers were eventually forced to buy inferior land elsewhere in the village. In general, however, regardless of jati, a person who wishes to advance economically 'must be prepared to defend his gains against jealous neighbours. Anyone who buys land is limiting his neighbour's opportunities

to buy land. Most people safeguard themselves by tying themselves through indebtedness to a powerful landlord who will give them support when difficulties are encountered' (39).

Although the interdependence of jatis is explained in theory by their occupational specialties, the social reality is a bit different. For example, Saltmakers in Gopalpur are farmers and actually produce little salt, which can be bought in shops by those who need it. It is primarily in the context of ritual that jati interdependence is given full play. Recall that Gopalpur villagers required the services of a Washerman when they needed *ritually* clean garments or cloth; otherwise, most villagers washed their own clothing.

> To arrange a marriage, to set up the doorway of a new house, to stage a drama, or to hold an entertainment, the householder must call on a wide range of jatis. The entertainment of even a modest number of guests requires the presence of the Singer. The Potter must provide new pots in which to cook the food; the Boin from the Farmer jati must carry the pot; the Shepherd must sacrifice the goat; the Crier, a Saltmaker, must invite the guests. To survive, one requires the co-operation of only a few jatis; to enjoy life and do things in the proper manner requires the co-operation of many. (Beals 1962: 41)

Beals's study of Gopalpur documented three dimensions of caste relations in India that have become increasingly significant over time. First, Beals describes a rural village in which jati membership mattered most on ritual occasions. In the last 30 years, cultural practices associated with caste in village India have become even more attenuated or have disappeared as increasingly large numbers of Indians have moved to large cities where they are surrounded by strangers whose caste membership they do not know (Sharma 1999: 37). They still use the idiom of purity and pollution to debate the status of particular castes, but otherwise their understanding of caste usually has nothing to do with ritual status.

Second, Beals describes members of middle-ranking jatis in Gopalpur who treated one another as

jati A caste that refers to localized, named, endogamous groups.

equals outside of ritual contexts. Mitra points out that 'By the 1960s, electoral mobilization had led to a new phenomenon called *horizontal mobilization* whereby people situated at comparable levels within the local caste hierarchy came together in caste associations', many of which formed new political parties to support their own interests (1994: 61). Moreover, increased involvement of Indians in capitalist market practices has led to 'a proliferation of modern associations that use traditional ties of jati and varna to promote collective economic well-being' (65). For example, a housing trust set up for Brahmins in the Indian state of Karnataka recruits Brahmins from throughout the Karnataka region in an effort to overcome 'jati-based division into quarrelling sects of Brahmins' (66). The interests that draw jatis into coalitions of this kind 'often turn out to be class interests. . . . This does not mean that caste and class are the same, since commentators note caste as blurring class divisions as often as they express them. Rather it tells us that class and caste are not "inimical" or antithetical' (Sharma 1999: 68).

Third, Beals showed that middle-ranking jatis in Gopalpur in the 1960s were willing to use violence to block the upward economic mobility of members of a low-ranking jati. Similar behaviour was reported in the work of other anthropologists like Gerald Berreman, who did fieldwork in the peasant village of Sirkanda in the lower Himalayas of North India in the late 1950s. Berreman observes that low-caste people in Sirkanda 'do not share, or are not heavily committed to, the "common official values" which high-caste people affect before outsiders. . . . Low-caste people resent their inferior position and the disadvantages which inhere in it' while 'high castes rely heavily on threats of economic and physical sanctions to keep their subordinates in line' such that when low-caste people publicly endorse 'common official values' they do so only out of fear of these sanctions (1962: 15–16).

In recent years, a number of low-caste groups in urban India have undertaken collective efforts to lift themselves off the bottom of society, either by imitating the ritual practices of higher castes (a process called *Sanskritization*) or by converting to a non-Hindu religion (such as Buddhism or Christianity) in which caste plays no role. Typically, however, these moves have had no effect in changing the negative stereotypes of so-called untouchables held by the so-called clean castes. However, the constitution of India prohibits the practice

of untouchability, and the national government has acted to improve the lot of the low castes by regularly passing legislation designed to improve their economic and educational opportunities. In some cases, these measures seem to have succeeded, but violent reprisals have been common. In rural areas many disputes continue to be over land, as in Gopalpur. However, even worse violence has been seen in urban India, as in 1990 when unrest was triggered by the publication of a report recommending increases in the numbers of government jobs and university enrolment quotas for members of low castes. At the end of the twentieth century, relations between low-caste and high-caste Hindus were described as 'conflictual rather than competitive in some localities' with 'caste violence . . . recognized as a serious problem in contemporary India' (Sharma 1999: 67).

The concept of caste has been applied by anthropologist Jacques Maquet (1970) to describe the closed, endogamous ranked strata Tutsi, Hutu, and Twa in the central African kingdom of Rwanda prior to 1959. Pierre van den Berghe (1970) documents the history of caste-like relationships dating from the beginnings of white settlement in southern Africa that culminated in the twentieth-century 'colour caste' system, distinguishing Whites, Asians, Coloureds, and Bantu that was enforced in apartheid South Africa. De Vos and Wagatsuma (1966) used the term *caste* to describe the *burakumin* of Japan, low-ranking endogamous groups, traditionally associated with polluting occupations, who have been subject to dehumanizing stereotypes and residential segregation from other

Figure 12.3 De Vos and Wagatsuma argue that the term *caste* is an accurate term to apply to the burakumin, low-ranking endogamous groups traditionally associated with polluting occupations.

Japanese (Figure 12.3). Sharma suggests that the concept of caste might be fruitfully used to characterize the relations between the Rom (or Gypsies) of Europe and their non-Rom neighbours, who for centuries have subjected the Rom to stigmatization, social segregation, and economic exclusion (1999: 85–6).

A key element recognized by all anthropologists who use the concept of caste is the endogamy that is enforced, at least in theory, on the members of each ranked group. As van den Berghe put it, membership in such groups is 'determined by birth and for life' (1970: 351). Sharma notes the significance of this link between descent and caste, observing that 'in societies where descent is regarded as a crucial and persistent principle (however reckoned, and whatever ideological value it is given), almost any social cleavage can become stabilized in a caste-like form' (1999: 85). She suggests the term *castification* to describe a political process by which ethnic or other groups become part of a rank order of some kind, probably orchestrated from the top but which need not result in the construction of a caste system (92–3).

But the principle of descent has also played a central role in the identification and persistence of race, ethnicity, and nation. As noted above, these three categories are all closely bound with historical developments over the past 500 years that built the modern world. Indeed, these categories are particularly significant in nation-states, and many contemporary nation-states are of very recent, post-colonial origin. Clearly, to make sense

In Their Own Words

The Slave Narrative in Life History and Myth, and Problems of Ethnographic Representation of the Tuareg Cultural Predicament

Susan J. Rasmussen speaks to us on the slave 'story' and identity.

Anthropologists and narrators may become mutually implicated with one another in a variety of ways. As a researcher among the Tuareg, I stood in a relationship of friendship, but also of marginality, to the community. In effect, I became a sign facilitating the storytellers in making their points. The act of constructing a life narrative can expand historical and ethnographic consciousness by compelling the author to move from accounts of discrete experiences to an account of why and how his or her life took the shape it did, at a given time, and why this was revealed from a particular viewpoint. The Personal Narratives Group (1989: 4–5) observes that the dynamics of gender emerge more clearly in personal narratives of women than in those of men. Likewise, it would seem to follow that the dynamics of social differentiation, inequality and domination, negotiation and resistance, would also emerge more clearly in slave narratives than in non-slave narratives. Or do they? Former slave and noble both used the experience of marginality and interdependence as a device by which to express their sense of how they have been treated in the post-colonial era. The tales of Tama the noble woman, as a discourse on servitude, in effect complement the narrative of the former slave man although they are not mirror images of each other. Gender and age were shown to be significant in both of them, in historical memory as well as social practice. Women and former slaves were also revealed as united in certain contexts, rather than always competing or opposed.

Discourse about past servitude offers an expressive vocabulary that provides not only reflection about social stratification and gender but also meaning for suffering from any basis of declared social difference. Additionally, these slave narratives—both in life history and myth—empower, each in their own manner. They enable an inversion of deprivation and effect a recasting of roles and relationships in a way that does not merely recreate social difference or redirect oppression but that reconciles the interests of all the parties to the narratives. There emerges from them an expanded consciousness, on the part of local residents of diverse origins and outside anthropologists in the audiences. The personal slave narrative/life history and the mythology about slavery constitute a counterpoint through which Atakor and other Tuareg remember, but also recast, their social and political history.

Source: Rasmussen, Susan J. 1999. 'The Slave Narrative in Life History and Myth, and Problems of Ethnographic Representation of the Tuareg Cultural Predicament', *Ethnohistory* 46, 1 (winter): 67–108.

of contemporary post-colonial forms of social strati-fication, we will also need some understanding of the categories of race, ethnicity, and nation.

Race

The concept of **race** developed in the context of European exploration and conquest beginning in the fifteenth century. Europeans conquered Indigenous peoples in the Americas and established colonial political economies that soon depended on the labour of Africans imported as slaves. By the end of the nineteenth century, light-skinned Europeans had established colonial rule over large territories inhabited by darker-skinned peoples, marking the beginnings of a global racial order (see Harrison 1995; Köhler 1978; Smedley 1993; 1998; Sanjek 1994; Trouillot 1994). Both as a way of explaining the existence of the human diversity they had encountered, and as a way of justifying the domination of Indigenous peoples and the enslavement of Africans, European intellectuals argued that the human species was subdivided into 'natural kinds' of human beings called *races* that could be sharply distinguished from one another on the basis of outward physical (or *phenotypic*) appearance. All individuals assigned to the same race were assumed to share many other common features, of which phenotype was only the outward index.

Belief in the existence of biologically distinct races (sometimes called **racialism**) was then joined to an ancient Western notion called the Great Chain of Being, which proposed that all 'natural kinds' could be ranked in a hierarchy. In the latter half of the nineteenth century, European thinkers, including many anthropologists, devised schemes for ranking the 'races of mankind' from lowest to highest. Not surprisingly, the 'white' northern Europeans at the apex of imperial power were placed at the top of this global hierarchy. Darker-skinned peoples like the Indigenous inhabitants of the Americas or of Asia, were ranked somewhere in the middle. But Africans, whom Europeans had bought and sold as slaves, and whose homelands in Africa were later conquered and incorporated into European empires, ranked lowest of all. In this way, the identification of races was transformed into **racism**: the systematic oppression of one or more socially defined 'races' by another socially defined 'race' that is justified in terms of the supposedly inherent biological

superiority of the rulers and the supposed inherent biological inferiority of those they rule.

It is important to emphasize once again that all the so-called races of human beings are *imagined communities*. The racial boundaries that nineteenth-century European observers thought they had discovered *do not correspond to major biological discontinuities* within the human species. Although our species as a whole does exhibit variation in phenotypic attributes such as skin colour, hair texture, or stature, these variations do *not* naturally clump into separate populations with stable boundaries that can be sharply distinguished from one another. Put another way, *the traditional concept of race in Western society is biologically and genetically meaningless.*

But even though the concept of race is biologically meaningless, racial thinking persists in the twenty-first century. Anthropologists have long argued that race is a culturally constructed social category whose members are identified on the basis of certain selected phenotypic features (such as skin colour) that all of them are said to share. The end result is a highly distorted but more or less seemingly coherent set of criteria that members of a society can use to assign people they see to one culturally defined racial category or another. Once this happens, members of society can treat racial categories *as if* they reflect biological reality, using them to build institutions that include or exclude particular culturally defined races. In this way, race can become 'real' in its consequences, even if it has no reality in biology.

The social category of race is a relatively recent invention. Audrey Smedley reminds us that in the worlds of European classical antiquity, and through the Middle Ages, 'no structuring of equality . . . was associated with people *because of their skin colour*' (1998: 693; emphasis in original), and Faye Harrison points out that 'phenotype prejudice was not institutionalized before the sixteenth century' (1995: 51). By the nineteenth century, European thinkers were attempting to classify all humans in the world into a few, mutually exclusive racial categories. Significantly, from that time until this, as Harrison emphasizes, 'blackness has come to symbolize the social bottom' (1998: 612; see also Smedley 1998: 694–5).

White domination of Euro-American and Canadian racial hierarchies has been a constant. However, some anthropologists who study the cultural construction of whiteness point out that, even in North America, 'whiteness' is not monolithic and that the cultural attributes supposedly shared by 'white people' have varied in different times and places. Some members of white ruling groups in the southern United States, for example, have traditionally distanced themselves from lower-class whites, whom they call *white trash*; and the meaning of whiteness in South Africa has been complicated by differences of class and culture separating British South Africans from Afrikaners (Hartigan 1997). Moreover, the sharp 'caste-like' racial divide between blacks and whites in North America is currently complicated by new immigrants identified with so-called brown/Latin American/Hispanic (or Indian/ Pakistani) and yellow/Asian racial categories. Harrison and others recognize that racial categorization and repression take different forms in different places. As we shall see, anthropologists working in Latin America describe racial practices that do not match those characteristic of the United States and Canada.

Race in Colonial Oaxaca

Anthropologist John Chance studied the development of ideas about race and class in the city of Oaxaca, Mexico (see Figure 12.4; see also EthnoProfile 12.1: Colonial Oaxaca [1521–1812]). Oaxaca (known as

Figure 12.4 Colonial buildings in Oaxaca, Mexico.

Antequera during the period of Spanish colonial domination) is a highland city founded in an area that was densely populated, prior to the Spanish conquest, by Indigenous people who participated in Mexican high civilization. Chance (1978) examined how social stratification changed from the period of Spanish conquest, in 1521, to the early years of the Mexican war of independence, in 1812. He used an anthropological perspective to interpret census records, wills, and other archival materials preserved in Mexico and Spain. As a result, he was able to show that changes occurred both in the categories used to describe social groups and in the meanings attached to those categories, with associated changes in the dynamics of social stratification itself.

When the Spanish arrived in Mexico in 1521, they found a number of Indigenous societies organized into states. The Aztecs, for example, were divided into an upper ruling stratum of nobles and a lower, commoner stratum. The Spanish conquerors also came from a society stratified into a system of *estates*, which were legally recognized social categories entitled to a voice in

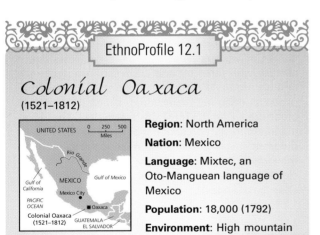

EthnoProfile 12.1

Colonial Oaxaca
(1521–1812)

UNITED STATES

0   250   500
Miles

Rio Grande

Gulf of California

MEXICO

Gulf of Mexico

PACIFIC OCEAN

Mexico City

Oaxaca

Colonial Oaxaca (1521–1812)

GUATEMALA-EL SALVADOR

Region: North America

Nation: Mexico

Language: Mixtec, an Oto-Manguean language of Mexico

Population: 18,000 (1792)

Environment: High mountain river basin; temperate

Livelihood: Administrative centre, clothing and textile industries

Political organization: Colony of Spain

For more information: Chance, John. 1978. *Race and Class in Colonial Oaxaca* (Stanford: Stanford University Press)

race A human population category whose boundaries allegedly correspond to distinct sets of biological attributes.

racialism Belief in the existence of biologically distinct races.

racism The systematic oppression of one or more socially defined 'races' by another socially defined 'race' that is justified in terms of the supposedly inherent biological superiority of the rulers and the supposed inherent biological inferiority of those they rule.

government. European estates prototypically included the nobility, the clergy, and the common people. By 1529, African slaves had been brought to New Spain. The colonizers in colonial Oaxaca reworked the European notion of estates to accommodate these new cleavages by assigning people membership into one or another estate on the basis of their outward phenotypes, the key criterion used to define *race*.

In theory, the clergy and nobility were reserved for the 'white' Spanish; all 'non-white' Indigenous groups were merged together to form the common people, and 'black' African slaves formed a final layer at the bottom of the colonial hierarchy. There were exceptions to this system, however. Indigenous nobles were given special status in post-conquest society and were used by the colonial administration to control their own people. Moreover, the conquistadors, who brought no Spanish women with them, soon established sexual relationships with local Indigenous women. In the early years, if these unions involved marriage, the offspring were usually considered Spanish, but if they were casual or clandestine, the offspring were more likely to be considered Indigenous. Europeans, Indigenous peoples, and Africans interbred, and a population of mixed descent was created.

According to the system of estates, people of mixed ancestry were not supposed to exist. By the mid-sixteenth century, however, their numbers and their economic importance made them impossible to ignore. As a result, the rulers of New Spain developed the *sistema de castas* to classify all people of mixed racial heritage (Figure 12.5). The first castas recognized were *mestizos* (people of mixed Spanish and Indigenous descent) and *mulatos* (people who showed evidence of African ancestry).

As soon as there were enough mestizos and mulattos to attract attention, the colonial government tried to limit their social mobility by legal means. Yet their status was ambiguous. Mestizos were ranked above mulattos because they had no African ancestry but were ranked below the Spanish because of their 'illegitimacy'. In cases where Indigenous and Spanish people were legally married, their children were called *españoles* (creoles). They were distinguished from *españoles europeos* (Spaniards born in Spain). In later years, the term *creole* (*criollo*) was also used to refer to people of presumably 'pure' European ancestry who were born in America. Some

Figure 12.5 By the late eighteenth century, the number of castas recognized in Mexico had proliferated. This contemporary painting displays 16 different outcomes of various cross-casta matings. Note that a castizo (with three español [Spanish] grandparents) and an española (with four Spanish grandchildren) produce offspring considered español (seven of eight great-grandparents are españoles). The painting attempts to represent not only the phenotypes of different castas but also the relative social statuses their members might occupy, as suggested by the clothing they wear (note especially the presence or absence of shoes).

mestizos managed to obtain elite privileges, such as the right to carry arms. Most mulattos were classed with Africans and could be enslaved. Yet free mulattos could also apply for the right to carry arms, which shows that even their status was ambiguous.

During the seventeenth century, the castas were acknowledged as legitimate strata in the system of colonial stratification. A number of new castas were recognized: *castizo* (a person of mixed Spanish and mestizo descent), *mulato libre* ('free mulatto'), *mulato esclavo* ('mulatto slave'), *negro libre* ('free black'), and *negro esclavo* ('black slave'). Perhaps most striking is the castizo category. This seems to have been designed by the colonial elite to stem the tide of ever 'whiter' mestizos who might be mistaken for genuine Spaniards. Chance points out that racial mixing was primarily an urban phenomenon and that the castas perceived themselves, and were perceived by the elite, as belonging to Hispanic rather than Indigenous society (1978: 126). It is perhaps not surprising that lighter-skinned castas became increasingly indistinguishable from middle-class and lower-class creoles. In fact, census records in Oaxaca list creoles as the largest segment of the city's population throughout the entire colonial period.

Other Stratification Systems

As if the *sistema de castas* were not enough, colonial society recognized three additional systems of classification that cut across the castas. One distinguished groups required to pay tribute to the Spanish crown (Indigenous groups, Africans, and mulattos) from everyone else. The second distinguished *gente de razon* ('rational people', who practised the Hispanic culture of the city) from *indios* (the rural, culturally distinct Indigenous population). And a third distinguished *gente decente* ('respectable people') from *la plebe* (the 'common people'). Chance suggests that the last distinction, which made most sense in the urban setting, represented an embryonic division into socioeconomic classes (1978: 127).

Mobility in the Casta System

Throughout the colonial period, the boundaries of the stratification system in Oaxaca were most rigid for those of 'unmixed' Indigenous, African, and European descent. Paradoxically, those of mixed background had the most ambiguous status—and the greatest opportunity to improve it. For example, when a couple married, the priest decided the casta membership of the bride and groom. The strategy for upward mobility called for choosing a marriage partner who was light-skinned enough for the priest to decide that both spouses belonged in a high-ranking casta. Over time, such manoeuvring swelled the ranks of the creoles.

The growth of the casta population coincided with the transformation of the colonial economy from one based on tribute and mining to one based on commercial capitalism. The prosperity this transformation brought to Oaxaca was greatest in the eighteenth century, when the city became the centre of an important textile and dye-manufacturing industry. Many castas were able to accumulate wealth, which together with light skin and adoption of the urban culture made it possible for them to achieve the status of creole.

Chance argued that during the late colonial period, racial status had become an achieved, rather than an ascribed, status. By that time, the increasing rate of legitimacy in all castas meant that descent lost its importance as a criterion of group membership. Creole status could be claimed by anyone who was able to show that his or her ancestors had not paid tribute. At the same time, in a dialectical fashion, people's image of what high-status people looked like had changed. As people with Indigenous and African ancestry moved up the social scale, their phenotypes widened the range of phenotypes considered prototypical for creoles.

Chance concludes that the *sistema de castas* is best understood as 'a cognitive and legal system of ranked socio-racial statuses' (1978: viii). Anthropologists have used the term **social race** to describe the system of ranking to which it eventually gave birth. The stratification system in Oaxaca was a hybrid, beginning with closed, caste-like racial categories whose 'purity' could not be maintained and ending up with open, class-like categories with racial labels.

Colourism in Nicaragua

Some observers might expect that once race becomes an achieved status, racism has disappeared. But the situation is not so simple. Let us compare the case of Oaxaca, Mexico, with that of Managua, Nicaragua. Roger Lancaster argues that, in Nicaragua, racism exists but that it is 'not as absolute and encompassing a racism as that which one encounters in the United States' even though it remains, in his opinion, 'a significant social problem' (1992: 215). One dimension of Nicaraguan racism contrasts the Spanish-speaking mestizo majority of the highlands with the Indigenous Miskitos and

social race An achieved status with a racial label in a system of stratification that is composed of open, class-like categories to which racial labels are assigned.

African Caribbeans along the Atlantic coast. Highland mestizos whom Lancaster knew tended to regard these coastal groups as backward, inferior, and dangerous—notions overlain with political suspicions deriving from the fact that some Miskito factions had fought with the contras against the Sandinistas.

But Lancaster came to see racism toward the coastal peoples as an extension of the pattern of race relations internal to highland mestizo culture that he calls **colourism**: a system of colour identities negotiated situationally along a continuum between white and black. In colourism, no fixed race boundaries exist. Instead, individuals negotiate their colour identity anew in every social situation they enter, with the result that the colour they might claim or be accorded changes from situation to situation.

Lancaster's informants used three different systems of colour classification. The first, or *phenotypic* system, has three categories—*blanco* (white), *moreno* (brown), and *negro* (black)—that people use to describe the various skin tones that can be seen among Nicaraguan mestizos:

> Nicaraguan national culture is mestizo; people's physical characteristics are primarily Indigenous; and in the terms of this phenotypic system, most people are *moreno*. In this system, *negro* can denote either persons of African ancestry or sometimes persons of purely Indigenous appearance, whether they are culturally classified as Indio or mestizo. (1992: 217)

Lancaster calls the second system the *polite* system, in which all the colours in the phenotypic system are 'inflated'. That is, Europeans are called *chele* (a Mayan word meaning 'blue', referring to the stereotype that people of European ancestry have blue eyes), *morenos* are called *blanco*, and *negroes* are called *moreno*. Polite terms are used in the presence of the person about whom one is speaking, and Lancaster was told that it was 'a grave and violent offence to refer to a black-skinned person as *negro*' (217). In rural areas, for similar reasons, Indians are called *mestizos* rather than *Indios*.

Lancaster calls the third system of colour terms the *pejorative and/or affectionate* system. This system has only two terms, *chele* (fairer skin, lighter hair) and *negro* (darker skin, darker hair). When the less powerful person in an interaction feels he is being imposed upon by the more powerful person, the former might express his displeasure by addressing the latter as *chele* or *negro*,

both of which would be heard as insulting. Paradoxically, members of families call one another *negro* or *negrito mio* as affectionate and intimate terms of address, perhaps precisely because these terms are 'informal' and violate the rules of polite discourse (218).

Lancaster discovered that 'Whiteness is a desired quality, and polite discourse inflates its descriptions of people' (219). People compete in different settings to claim whiteness. In some settings, individuals may be addressed as *blanco* if everyone else has darker skin; in other settings, they may be addressed as *moreno* if someone else has lighter skin than theirs.

Because it allows people some freedom of manoeuvre in claiming higher-status colour for themselves, Nicaraguan colourism may seem less repressive than the rigid black–white racial dichotomy traditional in North America. Lancaster points out, however, that all three systems of colourist usage presuppose white superiority and black inferiority. 'Africanos, Indios, and lower-class mestizos have been lumped together under a single term—*negro*—that signifies defeat' (223). Of course, the achieved social races of Oaxaca also oscillated along a continuum with whites on the top and blacks on the bottom. Lancaster is not optimistic about the possibilities of successfully overturning this system in Nicaragua any time soon. Similarly, Harrison argues that racial solidarity and rebellion are hard to achieve or sustain in societies where social race is present, and she is not optimistic that adoption of a similar system in the United States would improve race relations. On the contrary, she fears that a 'more multi-shaded discourse' would be more likely to contribute to 'an enduring stigmatization of blackness' than to 'democratization and the dismantling of race' (1998: 618–19).

Ethnicity

For anthropologists, **ethnic groups** are social groups whose members distinguish themselves (and/or are distinguished by others) in terms of **ethnicity**—that is, in terms of distinctive cultural features such as language, religion, or dress. Ethnicity, like race, is a culturally constructed concept. Many anthropologists today would agree with John Comaroff and Jean Comaroff that ethnicity is created by historical processes that incorporate distinct social groups into a single political structure under conditions of inequality (1992:

In Their Own Words

The Emergence of a New Political Paradigm

John Matthiasson first went to Baffin Island, in the Canadian Arctic, to do fieldwork among the Inuit in 1963. He returned a decade later to carry out additional fieldwork and has kept up with events in the Canadian Arctic since then. Here, he writes about a people's name.

The names by which we refer to ourselves or others can also be used to manipulate our identity and to align with or isolate ourselves from others, as well as to rationalize our treatment of others. When I lived with the Aullativikmiut in the 1960s they referred to themselves as Eskimos, as did all of the Tununermiut. By the 1970s many of them had ceased to use the term, which was now considered pejorative. (Its etymological origins have always been murky, although many sources claim that it means 'eaters of raw meat'.) It was, of course, replaced in both singular and plural by Inuk and Inuit, for 'a person' and 'the people'. The change in terminology of self-reference had, I am convinced, enormous political significance.

Not everyone accepted the change readily, and in some instances it was never adopted. One elderly man who had lived virtually all of his life in the camps told me in 1973, 'I was born an Eskimo and I will die an Eskimo.' However, his was to become a minority position. Others—even of his generation—soon saw the political significance of rejecting the term, and certainly that man's children and grandchildren did. This change, which was so important in the construction of new individual and group identities, was the work of The Inuit Tapirisat of Canada (ITC), or Inuit Brotherhood, a new organization that sought to create a pan-Inuit consciousness. The ITC was external to the Tununermiut, but when it offered them a new political agenda, they responded and, in the process, took further steps toward a renewed sense of self-determination.

Source: Matthiasson, John S. 1992. 'The Emergence of a New Political Paradigm', in *Living on the Land: Northern Baffin Inuit Respond to Change* (Peterborough, ON: Broadview Press), 161–2.

55–7; see also Williams 1989; Alonso 1994). Comaroff and Comaroff point out that ethnic consciousness existed in pre-colonial and pre-capitalist societies; however, they and most contemporary anthropologists have been more interested in forms of ethnic consciousness that were generated under capitalist colonial domination.

Ethnicity develops as members of different groups try to make sense of the material constraints they experience within the single political structure that confines them. This is sometimes described as a struggle between *self-ascription* (i.e., insiders' efforts to define their own identity) and *other-ascription* (i.e., outsiders' efforts to define the identities of other groups). In Comaroff and Comaroff's view, furthermore, the ruling group turns both itself and the subordinated groups into *classes* because all subordinated social groupings lose independent control 'over the means of production and/or reproduction' (1992: 56).

One outcome of this struggle is the appearance of new ethnic groups and identities that are not continuous

with any single earlier cultural group (Comaroff and Comaroff 1992: 56). In northern Cameroon, for example, successive German, French, and British colonial officials relied on local Muslim chiefs to identify significant local social divisions for them, and they adopted the Muslim practice of lumping together all the myriad non-Muslim peoples of the hills and plains and calling them *Haabe* or *Kirdi*—that is, 'Pagans'. To the extent, therefore, that Guidar, Daba, Fali, Ndjegn, or Guiziga were treated the same by colonial authorities

colourism A system of social identities negotiated situationally along a continuum of skin colours between white and black.

ethnic groups Social groups that are distinguished from one another on the basis of ethnicity.

ethnicity A principle of social classification used to create groups based on selected cultural features such as language, religion, or dress. Ethnicity emerges from historical processes that incorporate distinct social groups into a single political structure under conditions of inequality.

In Their Own Words

Indigenous Medicine and Identity in Nicaragua

Hugo De Burgos is an Associate Professor of Anthropology at the University of British Columbia Okanagan.

> Rescuing our Indigenous medicine is to recover our Indigenous identity and culture. Using our traditional medicine is expressing our Indigenous identity.
> —Antonio Guzmán,
> Nicaraguan Indigenous leader

Medical systems are more than social schemes for healing. They are also systems of ecological adaptation, explanatory models for physical and social suffering, and mechanisms for social control. The practical and symbolic functions of a medical system are not restricted to medical concerns. Their multiple implications pervade non-medical spheres of social life, shaping in this way their initial medical purpose. Medical beliefs and practices constitute cultural configurations that inform, shape, and mediate human experience in ways that go beyond purely medical functions.

The people of Veracruz del Zapotal, or Veracruceños, are a Spanish-speaking Indigenous community of Nahua descent from Nicaragua. Currently figuring approximately 3,800, they inhabit the Veracruz del Zapotal valley and the mountain region between the rivers of *El Camarón*, *Guachipilín*, and *Rio Grande* in the department of Rivas, in southern Nicaragua. In their struggle to remain culturally distinct, Veracruceños have been able

to direct their medical behaviour, articulate their medical ideas, and organize their medical resources for non-medical—and political—purposes. Since the early 1990s they have used their Indigenous medicine as a strategy to claim and assert their precariously kept ethnic identity. In the past, these people made use of medical knowledge according to tradition but not in a political manner. With the introduction of the 'revival of Indigenous medicine', a new disposition toward their Indigenous medicine emerged.

Claiming ethnic identity through the use of medicine is informed by an elaborate discourse on how traditional medicine *is* Indigenous identity and on how Indigenous identity is conversely embedded in traditional medicine. Through the use of Indigenous medicine as both *material medica* and a symbolic system, Veracruceños promote community practices that enhance an Indigenous world view. Indigenous medicine is for Veracruceños, as W.H.R. Rivers noted so long ago, a symbolic system; and all symbolic systems are valuable sites for meaning-making, at the level of the individual as well as the community. Indigenous medicine is seen by Veracruceños as a cultural trait, a part of the repertoire of practices and knowledge that makes Veracruceños culturally distinct. This sharply contrasts with the construction of scientific biomedicine, which is, categorically, non-specific to any particular people or culture.

Source: De Burgos, Hugo. 2009. 'Indigenous Medicine and Identity in Nicaragua', guest editorial.

and came to share a common situation and set of interests, they developed a new, more inclusive level of ethnic identity. This new, post-colonial identity, like many others, cannot be linked to any single pre-colonial cultural reality but has been constructed out of cultural materials borrowed from a variety of non-Muslim Indigenous groups who were incorporated as 'Pagans' within the colonial political order.

Comaroff and Comaroff argue that, a particular structure of nesting, opposed identities was quite common throughout European colonies in Africa. The lowest and least inclusive consisted of local groups, often

called *tribes*, who struggled to dominate one another within separate colonial states. The middle levels consisted of a variety of entities that crossed local boundaries, sometimes called *supertribes* or *nations*. For example, the British administered the settler colony of Southern Rhodesia (later to become Zimbabwe) according to the policy of 'indirect rule', which used Indigenous 'tribal' authorities to maintain order on the local level. The effect of indirect rule was thus both to reinforce 'tribal' identities where they existed and to create them where they had been absent in pre-colonial times. Two such tribal identities, those of the Shona and Ndebele, became pre-eminent, and each gave rise to its own '(supratribal) nationalist movement'.

Both movements joined together in a 'patriotic front' to win a war of independence fought against white settlers. This confrontation took place at the highest level of the ethnic hierarchy, which Comaroff and Comaroff call *race*. At this level, 'Europeans' and 'Africans' opposed one another, and each group developed its own encompassing ethnic identity. For example, Africans regularly dealing with Europeans began to conceive of such a thing as 'African culture' (as opposed to European culture) and 'pan-African solidarity' (to counter the hegemony of the European colonizers). Conversely, in the British settler colonies of southern and eastern Africa, European immigrants defined themselves in opposition to Africans by developing their own 'settler–colonial order' based on a caricature of aristocratic Victorian English society (1992: 58).

Because ethnic groups are incorporated into the colony on unequal terms (and, if we follow Comaroff and Comaroff, in different class positions), it is not surprising to discover that many individuals in colonies attempted to achieve upward mobility by manipulating ethnicity. Anthropological studies of such attempts at ethnic mobility constitute, as Comaroff and Comaroff put it, 'the very stuff of the ethnography of urban Africa' (1992: 63).

Emily Schultz investigated ethnic mobility in Guider, Cameroon (Figure 12.6). Guider began as a small settlement of non-Muslim Guidar. In 1830 it was brought into the Muslim Fulbe empire of Yola and remained a Fulbe stronghold under subsequent colonial rule. The Fulbe remained numerically dominant in town until after World War II; by 1958, individuals from over a dozen non-Fulbe groups had migrated to town, primarily from the neighbouring countryside. By 1976, 83 per cent of household heads in town were recent migrants, and 74 per cent did not claim Fulbe origins.

In Comaroff and Comaroff's terms, all these groups, including the Fulbe, had lost political and economic independence with the coming of colonial rule and, under conditions of inequality, were incorporated as ethnic groups into, first, the German and, later, the French colony of Cameroon. The colonizers uniformly admired the political, cultural, and religious accomplishments of the Muslim Fulbe. In their own version of indirect rule, they allowed Fulbe chiefs to administer territories they had controlled prior to colonization and, in some cases, handed over additional territories, whose residents had successfully resisted Fulbe domination in pre-colonial times.

In 1976, the local ethnic hierarchy in Guider placed Fulbe at the top and recent non-Muslim, non-Fulfulde-speaking migrants from rural areas at the bottom. But in the middle were numerous individuals and families of Fulfulde-speaking Muslims who could claim, and in some cases be accorded, recognition as Fulbe by others in the town. For example, two young men Emily Schultz hired as field assistants first described themselves as '100 per cent Fulbe'. As she got to know them better, however, she learned that the family of one was Ndjegn, and the family of the other was Fali. Neither young man saw anything

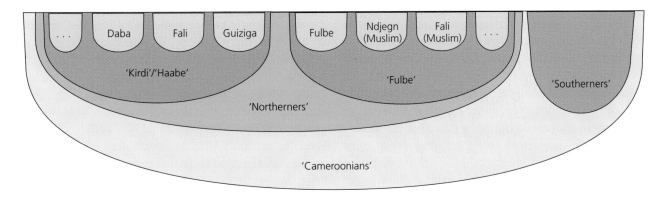

Figure 12.6 Nesting identities in northern Cameroon in 1976.

contradictory about being both Fulbe and Ndjegn, or Fulbe and Fali. And in fact, each ethnic identity was emphasized in different situations. Ndjegn and Fali ethnicity mattered to them in the domain of family and kinship; these ethnic identities nested within the broader Fulbe ethnicity that mattered in urban public settings, especially high-status ones associated with education and cash salaries.

Indeed, by 1976, Fulbe identity had become an achieved status; it was the ethnicity claimed by the upwardly mobile in Guider. People born outside the dominant Fulbe ethnic group could achieve Fulbe status in their lifetimes (Schultz 1984). To do this, they had to be successful in three tasks: they had to adopt the Fulbe language (Fulfulde), the Fulbe religion (Islam), and the Fulbe 'way of life', which was identified with urban customs and the traditional high culture of the western Sudan. Many Fulbe claimed that descent from one Fulbe lineage or another was needed in order to claim Fulbe identity. Nevertheless, they seemed willing to accept 'Fulbeized Pagans' as Fulbe (e.g., by giving their daughters to them as brides) because those people were committed defenders of the urban Fulbe way of life. Those who were 'Fulbeizing', however, came from societies in which descent had never been an important criterion of group membership. For those people, ethnic identity depended on territorial affiliation of the group to which they were currently committed. In becoming Fulbe, they had simply chosen to commit themselves to Fulfulde, Islam, and life in 'Fulbe territory'—the town.

This example illustrates some of the key attributes often associated with ethnicity: it is fluid, malleable, and something that can be voluntarily embraced or successfully ignored in different situations. Ambitious individuals and groups in an ethnically stratified society can manipulate ethnicity as a resource in order to pursue their interests. When nesting identities are present, people may regularly alternate between different identities in different contexts. Ethnic Fulbeization in northern Cameroon might be described as the formation of a 'supertribe'. Like the formation of caste alliances in India, it involves the expansion of group boundaries, allowing for the creation of stronger solidarity linkages among more people of different backgrounds. When such expanded alliances actually achieve increased success in political, economic, and social struggles, they may affect the very structures that gave rise to them (as the Shona–Ndebele alliance did in Zimbabwe) (Comaroff and Comaroff 1992: 61).

For dominant groups, however, defence of ethnic identity can be a way of defending privilege. They may be threatened rather than flattered by subordinate groups who master elite cultural practices. Members of the dominant ethnic group may stress their cultural superiority and question the eligibility (and even the humanity) of subordinate groups who challenge them. It is at this point that anthropologists like Faye Harrison would argue that ethnicity becomes *racialized*. In her view, race differs from ethnicity precisely because it is used to 'mark and stigmatize certain peoples as essentially and irreconcilably different, while treating the privileges of others as normative. This quality of difference, whether constructed through a bio-determinist or culturalist idiom, is what constitutes the social category and material phenomenon of "race"' (Harrison 1998: 613). Racialization in Western societies would thus bear a family resemblance to castification in South Asian societies.

Harrison argues that by the middle of the nineteenth century white northern Europeans, connecting their growing colonial power with their whiteness, began to racialize ethnic, religious, or class stereotypes associated with other Europeans (e.g., Irish, Jews, Italians, Poles, Slavs), viewing them as less human or, at any rate, differently human from themselves and attributing this difference to biologically inherited factors (1995: 52). Conversely, some racialized ethnic groups, such as the Irish, were able to reverse this process once they moved to the United States, shedding their stigma and *ethnicizing* into just another American ethnic group. Some social scientists might argue, or at any rate hope, that all racialized groups should be able to ethnicize sooner or later. But such a perspective risks ignoring the plight of racialized groups whose status never seems to change. Historians argue, for example, that the Irish were able to ethnicize precisely because they accepted the racialization of black Americans (Allen 1994–97). Indeed, operating under material conditions that presuppose white privilege, non-white races in the United States 'historically have defined layers of the social bottom vis-à-vis several successive waves of immigrants' (Harrison 1995: 49; see also Smedley 1998: 690).

For these reasons, Harrison argues that attempts to interpret race relations in the United States as ethnic relations 'euphemized if not denied race' by failing to address the social, political, and economic factors responsible for keeping groups like African Americans excluded and stigmatized at the bottom of society (1995: 48). Harrison agrees that African Americans do engage in 'ethnicizing practices emphasizing cultural heritage', but in her view such practices have never been able to overcome the 'caste-like assumptions of the most systematically oppressive racial orders' like that of the United States (1998: 613; 1995: 54; see also Sharma 1999: 91).

As we have seen, anthropologists have argued about which technical terms ought to be used to describe which forms of identity under which circumstances. We would agree with Sharma that social scientists should use a particular term only if it highlights a dimension of social relationships that would otherwise go unnoticed (1999: 93). Thus, ethnicity probably needs to be supplemented by the notion of race in order to distinguish the dehumanizing confinement of certain social groups to the bottom layers of society, and caste's emphasis on endogamy and hierarchical ranking highlights features of social organization that elude the usual scope of race, class, or ethnicity. Anthropologist Pnina Werbner (1997) further builds on these distinctions when she argues that in order to make progress in analyzing ethnic violence as a social force, practices of 'everyday' ethnic identification need to be distinguished from racism.

Based on her research on multicultural social relations in Britain, Werbner distinguishes two different social processes: **objectification** and **reification**. Objectification simply refers to the intentional construction of a collective public identity; it is the process that produces 'everyday' or 'normal' ethnicity. Ethnic identities are distinguished by the fact that they are 'evoked situationally . . . highlighted pragmatically, and objectified relationally and contingently' and by the fact that they focus on two key issues: 'a demand for ethnic rights, including religious rights, and a demand for protection against racism' (1997: 241). Social relations between objectified ethnic groups are based on a 'rightful performance' of multiple, shifting, highly valued forms of collective identification based on religion, dress, food, language,

and politics. Interaction between groups that differentiate themselves along such lines ordinarily do not lead to violent confrontations (229). Reification, by contrast, is a form of negative racial or ethnic absolutism that encourages the violent elimination of targeted groups and is central to the practice of racism. Reification 'distorts and silences'; it is 'essentialist in the pernicious sense' (229). It is violence that differentiates racism from everyday ethnicity, and if ethnic confrontation becomes violent, then it turns into a form of racism (234–5). For Werbner, making this distinction is crucial in multi-ethnic situations because when people fail to distinguish non-violent forms of everyday ethnicity from racism, they are, in effect, criminalizing valid ethnic sentiments and letting racists off the hook (233).

Nation and Nationalism

As we saw earlier, state societies are not new social forms. Nation-states, however, are a far more recent invention. Prior to the French Revolution, European states were ruled by kings and emperors whose access to the throne was officially believed to have been ordained by God. After the French Revolution in 1789, which thoroughly discredited the divine right of kings, rulers needed to find a new basis on which to found legitimate state authority. The solution that was eventually adopted rooted political authority in **nations**: groups of people believed to share the same history, culture, language, and even the same physical substance. Nations were associated with territories, as were states, and a **nation-state** came to be viewed as an ideal political unit in which national identity and political territory coincided.

---

nations Groups of people believed to share the same history, culture, language, and even the same physical substance.

nation-state An ideal political unit in which national identity and political territory coincide.

objectification The intentional construction of a collective public identity; it is the process that produces 'everyday' or 'normal' ethnicity.

reification A form of negative racial or ethnic absolutism that encourages the violent elimination of targeted groups and is central to the practice of racism.

The building of the first nation-states is closely associated with the rise and spread of capitalism and its related cultural institutions during the nineteenth century. Following the demise of European colonial empires and the end of the Cold War, the final decades of the twentieth century witnessed a scramble in which former colonies or newly independent states struggled to turn themselves into nation-states capable of competing successfully in what anthropologist Liisa Malkki has called a 'transnational culture of nationalism' (Malkki 1992).

On the one hand, the ideology of the nation-state implies that every nation is entitled to its own state. (Here we could consider the aspirations of the Kurds.) On the other hand, it also suggests that a state containing heterogeneous populations *might be made into a nation* if all peoples within its borders could somehow be made to adopt a common **nationality**: a sense of identification with and loyalty to the nation-state. The attempt made by government officials and state institutions to instill this sense of nationality into the citizens of a state has been called **nation-building**, or **nationalism**.

As we learned in our discussion of ethnicity, states are the very political structures that generate ethnic identities among the various cultural groupings unequally incorporated within them. Thus, anthropologists studying state formation often find themselves studying ethnicity as well as nationalism (Alonso 1994). However, groups with different forms of identity that continue to persist within the boundaries of the nation-state are often viewed as obstacles to nationalism. If such groups successfully resist assimilation into the nationality that the state is supposed to represent, their very existence calls into question the legitimacy of the state. Indeed, if their numbers are sufficient, they might well claim that they are a separate nation, entitled to a state of their own!

To head off this possibility, nationalist ideologies typically include some cultural features of subordinate cultural groups. Thus, although nationalist traditions are invented, they are not created out of thin air. The prototype of national identity is usually based on attributes of the dominant group, into which specially chosen elements of the cultural practices of other, subordinated groups are integrated. That is, those who control the nation-state will try to define nationality in ways that 'identify and ensure loyalty among citizens

... the goal is to create criteria of inclusion and exclusion to control and delimit the group' (Williams 1989: 407). The hope seems to be that if at least some aspects of their ways of life are acknowledged as essential to national identity, subordinated groups will identify with and be loyal to the nation. Following Gramsci, Williams calls this process a **transformist hegemony** in which nationalist ideologues are attempting to 'create purity out of impurity' (1989: 429, 435).

National leaders will measure the trustworthiness and loyalty of citizens by how closely they copy (or refuse to copy) the cultural practices that define national identity (Williams 1989: 407). Unfortunately, the practices of subordinated groups that do not get incorporated into nationalist ideology are regularly marginalized and devalued, and continued adherence to such practices may be viewed as subversive. Some groups, moreover, may be totally ignored. Alonso points out, for example, that Mexican nationalism is 'mestizo nationalism' rooted in the official doctrine that the Mexican people are a hybrid of European whites and the Indigenous people they conquered. As we saw in colonial Oaxaca, African slaves were also a part of early colonial Mexican society. Nationalist ideology, however, erases their presence entirely (1994: 396).

Australian Nationalism

Australia began its existence as a settler colony of Great Britain. Over the past 200 years, the prototype of Australian national identity was based on the racial and cultural features of the settler population. The phenotypically distinct Indigenous people, called Aborigines by the settlers, were completely excluded from citizenship. Settlers' claims to land and other resources rested on the doctrine of *terra nullius*: the idea that before their arrival, the land had been owned by nobody. In European capitalist terms, 'ownership' meant permanent settlement and 'improvement' of the land by clearing it and planting crops or grazing animals. Since the Aboriginal peoples living on the continent of Australia were foraging peoples who did not depend on domesticated plants or animals, European settlers felt justified in displacing them and 'improving' the land as they saw fit. Aborigines were viewed as a 'dying race', and white settler domination was taken as a foregone conclusion.

But times change and, currently, Australians are seriously rethinking the nature of Australian national identity. Indeed, according to Robert Tonkinson (1998), two kinds of nation-building are going on at the same time. First, an intense national debate has developed in recent years that favours creating a new Australian Republic whose constitution would affirm the existence and rights of the country's Indigenous peoples. For that to happen, however, 'the nation as a whole must re-imagine itself via a myth-making process, in which the search for distinctively Australian national symbols may well include elements drawn from Indigenous cultures' (Tonkinson 1998: 287–8).

And this will not be easy because such a myth-making process (or transformist hegemony) immediately runs up against a second, alternative myth-making process generated by Australia's Indigenous minorities who have, for decades, struggled to construct a sense of 'pan-Aboriginal' identity. Since the 1970s, a central theme in this struggle has been the demand for land rights, which was given an enormous boost by the decision handed down by the High Court of Australia in 1992 in the case of *Eddie Mabo and Others* v. *The State of Queensland*. The so-called *Mabo* decision rejected the doctrine of *terra nullius*, proclaiming that the Native title of Australia's Indigenous people was part of Australian common law.

The symbolic significance of the *Mabo* decision has been enormous. For those Australians who want to remake Australian nationalism, *Mabo* clears ground for constructing a multicultural national identity. The Australian federal government has therefore made reconciliation with Indigenous minorities a major policy goal, well aware that 'unless Australia achieves a formal and lasting reconciliation with its Indigenous people, its self-image as a fair and just land will continue to be mocked by the history of its oppression of them' (Tonkinson 1998: 291). Many white Australians and the national government are seeking ways of incorporating Aboriginality into Australian national identity. A measure of success is indicated by increasing interest on the national level in the artistic, literary, and athletic accomplishments of Aboriginal people. As a popular reconciliation slogan puts it, 'White Australia Has a Black History' (Figure 12.7).

While all this might augur favourably for a reconstructed Australian national identity that includes Aboriginal people, many problems remain. Some come from white Australians who reject a multicultural national identity or who see their economic

Figure 12.7 Australian Aboriginal people marching in protest over the Australian Bicentennial celebrations, which, they argued, did not pay appropriate attention to them.

interests threatened by the *Mabo* decision. But even Aboriginal people, whom it is supposed to help, criticize the *Mabo* decision because of its limitations and unresolved complexities. For example, the only lands eligible for Indigenous claims turn out to be those that have demonstrable historical connection to contemporary Aboriginal groups who continue to practise 'traditional' Aboriginal customs. This not only exempts most of Australia from Indigenous land claims, but it also means that most of Australia's quarter of a million Aboriginal people will be barred from making land claims because they live in Australia's large towns and cities and have, for generations, been separated from the lands of their ancestors.

Since the *Mabo* decision, however, expressions of Aboriginality seem to be moving toward 'a more culture-centred—and to non-Aboriginal Australians more easily accommodated—emphasis on Aboriginal commonalities, continuity, and survival' (Tonkinson 1998: 289). The *Mabo* decision has ratified the legitimacy and revival not only of Aboriginal land rights

nationality A sense of identification with and loyalty to a nation-state.

nation-building, or nationalism The attempt made by government officials to instill a sense of nationality into the citizens of a state.

transformist hegemony A nationalist program to define nationality in a way that preserves the cultural domination of the ruling group while including enough cultural features from subordinated groups to ensure their loyalty.

but also of Aboriginal customs. This has stimulated the explosion of Aboriginal cultural expression that white Australians have come to appreciate, as well as numerous programs that have brought urban Aboriginals into remote areas to work, to learn about rural Aboriginal traditions, and to contribute to the growth of biculturalism among rural Aboriginal people. Even in a multicultural Australia, however, many Aboriginal people would insist that they must not be lumped together with other 'ethnic minorities', given their special status as descendants of the original inhabitants and victims of centuries of exploitation. Tonkinson concludes that, at the end of the twentieth century, 'despite the limitations of *Mabo* . . . its symbolic force is such that it may provide the basis for reconciliation between Indigenous and other Australians' (300).

Naturalizing Discourses

We have emphasized that all the social categories under discussion—class, caste, race, ethnicity, and nation—are culturally created and cannot be justified with reference to biology or nature. At the same time, many members of the societies anthropologists study argue just the opposite, employing what some anthropologists call **naturalizing discourses**. That is, they regularly represent particular identities as if they were rooted in biology or nature, rather than in history or culture, thereby making them appear eternal and unchanging.

Naturalizing discourses rely on the imaginary reduction, or *conflation*, of identities to achieve persuasive power (Williams 1989). For example, every one of the forms of identity we have discussed in this chapter has been described or justified by someone, at some time, in terms of *shared bodily substance*. Thus, living within the same borders is conflated with having the same ancestors and inheriting the same culture, which is conflated with sharing the same blood or the same genes. Culture is reduced to blood, and 'the magic of forgetfulness and selectivity, both deliberate and inadvertent, allows the once recognizably arbitrary classifications of one generation to become the given inherent properties of reality several generations later' (Williams 1989: 431).

Nation-states frequently use trees as national symbols, rooting the nation in the soil of its territory (Figure 12.8). Sometimes they use kinship imagery, referring to the nation-state as a 'motherland' or 'fatherland'; sometimes the territory of a nation-state itself can be a unifying image, especially when portrayed on a map (Alonso 1994). The case of Australia shows, however, that doctrines like *terra nullius* enable newcomers to deny the 'natural' links to the land of Indigenous inhabitants while specifying how newcomers may proceed to establish their own 'natural' links to the land through 'improvement'.

The Paradox of Essentialized Identities

The struggle of Aboriginal people to defend themselves and claim their rights after centuries of exploitation and neglect has been extraordinarily important in making the *Mabo* decision possible. In response to dominant groups that attempted to conflate their humanity with a narrow, unflattering stereotype, they chose to accept the racial designation but to view it as a positive *essence*, an 'inner something or distinctive "spirituality" possessed by everyone who is Aboriginal' (Tonkinson 1998: 294–5). Similar kinds of essentialist rhetoric have helped many stigmatized groups build a positive self-image and unite politically.

Figure 12.8 The tree-like symbol at the centre of the Mexican national seal (the cactus on which an eagle perches holding a snake in its beak) is a pre-Conquest Aztec symbol. The image is encircled by the Spanish words *Estados Unidos Mexicanos* (United Mexican States). These combined elements stand for the officially mixed—'mestizo'—Mexican people the state is supposed to represent—the offspring of Spanish conquerors and the Indigenous people they conquered.

Many anthropologists and other observers would argue that the essentialist rhetoric of Aboriginal activists does not, in fact, reflect their beliefs about Aboriginality at all. They would describe what the activists are promoting as *strategic essentialism*: that is, essentialist rhetoric is being used as a conscious political strategy. Most activists are perfectly aware that essentialized racial or ethnic identities have no scientific validity. Nevertheless, they press their claims, hoping that by stressing their difference they may be able to extract concessions that the national government cannot refuse without violating its own laws and sense of justice. The concessions may be substantial, as in the case of the *Mabo* decision. At the same time, strategic essentialism is troubling to many observers and participants in these struggles, for those who promote it as a political strategy risk 'reproducing the same logic that once oppressed them' (Hale 1997: 547) and, rather than bringing about a more just society, may simply 'serve to perpetuate an ethnically ordered world' (Comaroff and Comaroff 1992: 62).

Nation-building in a Post-colonial World: The Example of Fiji

While the citizens of nation-states need to construct a shared public identity, they also need to establish concrete legal mechanisms for taking group action to influence the state. That is, as John Kelly and Martha Kaplan (2001) argue, nation-states are more than imagined communities; they are also *represented* communities. For this reason, nation-building involves more than constructing an image of national unity; it also requires institutions of political representation that channel the efforts of citizens into effective state support. But what happens when citizens of a nation-state do not exactly agree about what nation they are building or what kinds of legal and political structures are necessary to bring it about? One answer to these questions can be seen in the South Pacific island nation of Fiji, which became independent from Britain in 1970 and has experienced four political coups in the last 20 years, the most recent being the coup d'état of December 2006.

At independence, the image of the Fijian nation was that of a 'three-legged stool'; each 'leg' was a separate category of voters: 'general electors' (a minority

of the population including Europeans), 'Fijians' (ethnic Fijians, descended from the original inhabitants of the island), and 'Indians' (or Indo-Fijians, descendents of indentured labourers brought to Fiji by the British from Bombay and Calcutta in the nineteenth century). Kelly and Kaplan show that these three categories have deep roots in the colonial period, where they were said to correspond to separate 'races'. In the British Empire, race was an accepted way to categorize subordinated peoples, even though in many cases—as in the case of the Indo-Fijians—the people so labelled had shared no common identity prior to their arrival in Fiji.

These racial distinctions were concretized in colonial law, and the legal status of the ethnic Fijians was different from the legal status of Indo-Fijians. The status of ethnic Fijians was determined by the Deed of Cession, a document signed by some Fijian chiefs with the British in 1874, which linked ethnic Fijians to the colonial government through their hierarchy of chiefs. The status of Indo-Fijians, by contrast, was determined by the contracts of indenture (*girmit*) which each individual labourer had signed in order to come to Fiji. Thus, ethnic Fijians were accorded a hierarchical, collective legal identity, whereas the Indo-Fijians had the status of legal individuals, with no legally recognized ties to any collectivity.

Inspired by the Freedom Movement in India in the early twentieth century, Indo-Fijians began to resist racial oppression and struggle for equal rights in Fiji, but their efforts were repeatedly quashed by the British. When it became possible for them to vote after 1929, for example, Indo-Fijians lobbied for equal citizenship and the abolition of separate racial voting rolls, and they lost: the voting rolls were divided by race in order to limit representation for Indo-Fijians in government. At the time of World War II, Indo-Fijians agreed to serve in the armed forces, but only if they were treated as equals with white soldiers, and their efforts were resisted: they spent the war serving in a labour battalion for very low wages, while ethnic Fijians joined

naturalizing discourses The deliberate representation of particular identities (e.g., caste, class, race, ethnicity, and nation) as if they were a result of biology or nature, rather than history or culture, making them appear eternal and unchanging.

a Fijian Defence Force. It was primarily Indo-Fijians who pushed for independence in the late 1960s, and once again they engaged in difficult negotiations for equal citizenship and a common voting roll but finally consented to separate race-based voting rolls in 1969 in order to obtain independence.

> Thus, when Fiji's independence became real in 1970, the constitution insisted that races still existed in Fiji and had to vote separately. Since then parties have generally and increasingly followed racial lines, and the army has remained an enclave of Indigenous Fijians. When political parties backed mostly by Indo-Fijian voters won Fiji's 1987 election, this army took over the country after only a month. The constitution that was then installed in 1990 returned to even more naked discrimination against Indo-Fijians in regard to voting rights. (Kelly and Kaplan 2001: 77)

The constitution was revised yet again, in a manner that favoured ethnic Fijian chiefly interests and seemed guaranteed to prevent parties backed by Indo-Fijian voters from winning control of the government in the 1999 election. To everyone's surprise, parties backing ethnic Fijians lost again. A second coup came on 19 May 2000 (Figure 12.9). Finally, after new elections in 2001, ethnic Fijians won control of the government. The military coup d'état of 2006 was a direct result of the continuing consequences of the coup of 2000. It focused primarily on the Reconciliation Tolerance and Unity Bill that proposed amnesty legislation for those involved in the 2000 coup. The coup of 2006 resulted in the military effectively taking control of the country. In October 2008, the Fiji High Court ruled that the resulting government was the legal government.

What lessons does this history suggest about nation-building in post-colonial states? The issues are many and complex. But one key factor emphasized by Kelly and Kaplan is that the image of a united Fijian nation projected at independence was severely undermined by legal mechanisms of political representation carried over from the colonial period, particularly the race-based voting rolls. What became apparent in the years after independence was the fact that Indo-Fijians and ethnic Fijians had imagined very different national communities. Indo-Fijians had supported the image of a Fijian nation in which all citizens, Indo-Fijian or

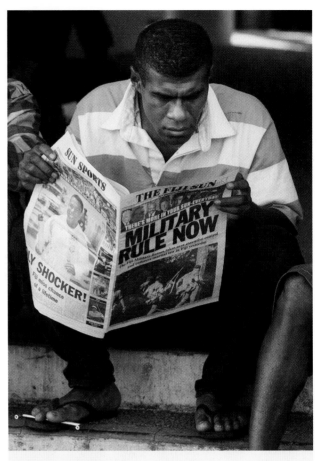

Figure 12.9 A Fijian citizen reads a newspaper on the day of the military coup in May 2000.

ethnic Fijian or 'general elector', would have equal status, voting on a single roll, working together to build a constitutional democracy. However, 'few among the ethnic Fijians have yet come to see themselves as partners with immigrants' (2001: 41). Ever since independence, and particularly after each coup, ethnic Fijians worked to construct an image of the Fijian nation based solely on chiefly traditions in which Indo-Fijians had no meaningful place. Thus, Kelly and Kaplan conclude, in Fiji (and in many other parts of the world) '"the nation" is a contested idea, not an experienced reality' (142).

Nationalism and Its Dangers

The most horrifying consequence of nation-building movements in the twentieth century has been the discovery of just how far the ruling groups of some nation-states are willing to go in order to enforce their version of national identity.

After World War II, the world was shocked to learn about Nazi programs to 'liquidate' Jews, Gypsies, and other groups that failed to conform to Nazi ideals of Aryan purity (Linke 1997). Many people hoped that the Nazi Holocaust was exceptional, but subsequent developments suggest that it may have been the most dramatic example of an exterminationist temptation that accompanies all drives to nationalism. Sociologist Zygmunt Bauman argued in his book *Modernity and the Holocaust* (1989) that modern nation-states with rationalized bureaucracies and industrial technology were the first societies in history to make efficient mass extermination of deviants technically possible. In a transnational culture of nationalism, not to belong to a nation-state made up of loyal, ambitious, like-minded citizens is a severe, possibly fatal, handicap. Using violence against all citizens who undermine claims of national homogeneity and common purpose may thus be a peculiarly modern way for insecure rulers of embattled nation-states to try to bring about solidarity and stability. In the late twentieth century, warring nationalities in the former Yugoslavia deployed selective assassinations and forced migration to rid their fledgling nation-states of unwanted others, a policy known as *ethnic cleansing* (Figure 12.10). Thus, rather than relics of a barbarian past, ethnic cleansing, *ethnocide* (the destruction of a culture) and *genocide* (the extermination of an entire people), may constitute a series of related practices that are all signs of things to come. All are measures of the high stakes for which rulers of these nation-states see themselves competing.

Inevitably, such policies create populations of immigrants and refugees whose social status is anomalous and ambiguous in a world of nation-states and whose presence as new pockets of heterogeneity in a different nation-state sets the stage for new rounds of social struggle that may lead to violence. As we will see in the next chapter, the economic, political, and cultural processes that made this possible have undergone important shifts in the last few years.

Figure 12.10 Relatives of 8,000 Muslim men and boys slaughtered in the 1995 Srebrenica massacre walk between rows of coffins next to freshly dug graves, looking for those belonging to their relatives, in a field in the town on 31 March 2003.

Key Terms

caste 297
classes 295
client 296
clientage 296
colourism 306
ethnic groups 306
ethnicity 306
jati 298
nationality 312
nation-building, or nationalism 312
nations 311
nation-state 311

naturalizing discourses 314
objectification 311
patron 296
race 302
racialism 302
racism 302
reification 311
social race 305
stratified societies 295
transformist hegemony 312
varna 297

Chapter Summary

1. All people in the world today, even refugees, must deal with the authority of one nation-state or another, each of which contains multiple, and sometimes contradictory, hierarchies of stratification. Every one of these hierarchies is a cultural invention designed to create boundaries around different kinds of imagined communities. Some patterns of stratification may reach back thousands of years, but others are closely associated with the rise of European capitalism and colonialism.

2. The concept of class in anthropology has a double heritage: Europeans tended to view class boundaries as closed and rigid, whereas North Americans tended to view them as open and permeable. Class solidarity may be undercut by clientage relations that bind individuals to one another across class boundaries.

3. The stratification system of India has been taken as the prototype of caste stratification although anthropologists also have applied the concept to social hierarchies encountered elsewhere in the world. Local caste divisions in village India adhere to rules of purity and pollution defined in terms of the occupations their members perform and the foods they eat and which govern whom they may marry. Members of jatis of similar rank do not observe such distinctions with one another,

especially in urban settings. Caste associations in large cities of India use jati ties to promote their members' economic well-being. The use of violence by higher-ranking jatis to block the advance of lower-ranking jatis has also increased in recent years. Contemporary anthropologists reject views of caste in India that portray it as internally harmonious and uncontested by those at the bottom of the caste hierarchy, pointing to the rise in caste violence in recent years.

4. The contemporary concept of race developed in the context of European exploration and conquest beginning in the fifteenth century, as light-skinned Europeans came to rule over darker-skinned peoples in different parts of the world. The so-called races whose boundaries were forged during the nineteenth century are imagined communities; human biological variation does not naturally clump into separate populations with stable boundaries. Despite variations in opinions and practices regarding race over the centuries, a global hierarchy persists in which whiteness symbolizes high status and blackness symbolizes the social bottom.

5. Although ethnic consciousness existed in pre-colonial and pre-capitalist societies, contemporary anthropologists have been most interested in forms

of ethnicity that were generated under capitalist colonial domination, when different groups were subordinated within a single political structure under conditions of inequality. This process can produce ethnic groups not continuous with any single earlier group and is often characterized by nesting, opposed identities that individuals often manipulate in order to achieve upward mobility. When dominant ethnic groups feel threatened, they may attempt to stigmatize subordinate groups by 'racializing' them.

6. Nation-states were invented in nineteenth-century Europe, but they have spread throughout the world along with capitalism, colonialism, and political decolonization. Nationalist thinking aims to create a political unit in which national identity and political territory coincide, and this has led to various practices designed to force subordinate social groups to adopt a national identity defined primarily in terms of the culture of the dominant group. When subordinate groups resist, they may become the victims of genocide or ethnic cleansing.

Alternatively, the dominant group may try to recast its understanding of national identity in a way that acknowledges and incorporates cultural elements belonging to subordinate groups. If the creation of such an imagined hybrid identity is not accompanied by legal and political changes that support it, however, the end result may be political turmoil, as shown in the recent history of Fiji.

7. Because membership in social categories such as class, caste, race, ethnicity, and nation can determine enormous differences in peoples' life chances, much is at stake in defending these categories and all may be described as if they were rooted in biology or nature, rather than history or culture. Conceptualizing these forms of identity as essences is one way of stereotyping and excluding, but it has also been used by many stigmatized groups to build a positive self-image and as a strategic concept in struggles with dominant groups. Although strategic essentialism may be successful in such struggles, it also risks repeating the same logic that justifies oppression.

Critical Thinking Questions

1. Which aspects of social stratification would you consider to be associated with capitalism?
2. Discuss open and closed stratification systems. Beyond their permeable or non-permeable boundaries, what would you consider to be their main differences?
3. How and why do dominant ethnic groups stigmatize subordinate groups by 'racializing' them?
4. Nationalist thinking aims to create a political unit in which national identity and political territory coincide. How would you consider this statement as it applies to Quebec?
5. What are naturalizing discourses? Give some examples and include explanatory comments.

Suggested Readings

Anderson, Benedict. 1991. *Imagined Communities*, rev. edn (London: Verso). *The classic discussion of the cultural processes that create community ties between people—such as citizens of a nation-state—who have never seen one another, producing the personal and cultural feeling of belonging to a nation.*

Dusenbery, Verne A. 1997. 'The Poetics and Politics of Recognition: Diasporan Sikhs in Pluralist Polities' *American Ethnologist* 24, 4 (Nov.): 738–62. *A discussion of political identity in Sikh overseas communities, cogent to the analysis of the Air India bombing.*

McAlpine, Lynn, Alice Eriks-Brophy, and Martha Crago. 1996. 'Teaching Beliefs in Mohawk Classrooms: Issues of Language and Culture', *Anthropology & Education Quarterly* 27, 3 (Sept.): 390–413. *Here, the importance of teaching language is examined in the context of culture retention for a First Nations community.*

Magat, Ilan N. 1999. 'Israeli and Japanese Immigrants to Canada: Home, Belonging, and the Territorialization of Identity', *Ethos* 27, 2 (June): 119–44. *Israel and Japan both have a strong sense of uniqueness central to their national discourse. This frames this article that investigates identity formation, management, and change, and the interrelationship of the personal, the cultural, and the national for immigrants to Canada from Israel and Japan.*

Malkki, Liisa. 1995. *Purity and Exile: Memory and National Cosmology among Hutu Refugees in Tanzania* (Chicago: University of Chicago Press). *This ethnography chronicles a recent example in Africa of the bloody consequences of nationalist politics and explores the connections between the conditions of refugee resettlement and the development of refugee identities.*

Nash, Manning. 1989. *The Cauldron of Ethnicity in the Modern World* (Chicago: University of Chicago Press). *Nash looks at ethnicity in the post-colonial world and sees more of a seething cauldron than a melting pot. He examines the relations between Ladinos and Maya in Guatemala, Chinese and Malays in Malaysia, and Jews and non-Jews in the United States.*

Razack, Sherene. 2000. 'From the "Clean Snows of Petawawa": The Violence of Canadian Peacekeepers in Somalia', *Cultural Anthropology* 15, 1 (Feb.): 127–63. *Discusses the violence of Canadian peacekeepers in the context of gender roles and racist responses.*

Robidoux, Michael A. 2002. 'Imagining a Canadian Identity through Sport: A Historical Interpretation of Lacrosse and Hockey', *The Journal of American Folklore* 15, 456 (spring): 209–25. *Do we have a key metaphor as a country based on the game of hockey? Here, we can examine this in a historical perspective.*

Schryer, Frans J. 2001. 'Multiple Hierarchies and the Duplex Nature of Groups', *The Journal of the Royal Anthropological Institute* 7, 4 (Dec.): 705–21. *Examines the links between multiple hierarchies and broad-based groups to create a theoretical framework for integrating group phenomena, social identities, and political mobilization.*

Sharma, Ursula. 1999. *Caste* (Philadelphia: Open University Press). *A brief, up-to-date survey of recent anthropological scholarship dealing with caste in South Asia.*

Smedley, Audrey. 1998. *Race in North America: Origin and Evolution of a World View*, 2nd edn (Boulder, CO: Westview Press). *This book offers a comprehensive historical overview of the development of the concept of race in North America, beginning in the late eighteenth century. The second edition includes additional coverage of developments in the nineteenth and twentieth centuries. Smedley shows how the concept of race is a cultural construct that over time has been used in different ways, for different purposes.*

Related Websites

French Canadian Nationalism: http://www.thecanadianencyclopedia.com/index.cfm?PgNm=TCE&Params=A1ARTA0003061

History of Racism in Canada: http://www.hopesite.ca/remember/history/racism_canada_1.html

The Immigration and Refugee Board of Canada: http://www.irb-cisr.gc.ca/en/about/orgchart/index_e.htm

The Inuit Tapirisat of Canada: http://www.itk.ca/

The Politics of Racism: http://www.japanesecanadianhistory.ca/

Chapter 13

A Global World

Chapter Outline

Learning Objectives

By the end of Chapter 13, you will be able to:

- understand the history of the development of political economies,
- appreciate cultural process as the global world emerged,
- consider globalization and the pressures on the nation-state,

- recognize the challenges of human rights in a 'globalized world', and
- compare and contrast cultural imperialism, cultural hybridization, and cosmopolitanism.

Orlando, Claudio, and Leonardo Villas Bôas were middle-class Brazilians who took part in an expedition that explored central Brazil in the early 1940s. Their experiences led them to dedicate their lives to protecting Brazil's Indigenous peoples from the ravages of contact with Western society. They were instrumental in persuading the government to create Xingu National Park, in 1952, a large area in the state of Mato Grosso where Indigenous groups could live undisturbed by outsiders. Since that time, they have worked to contact threatened Indigenous groups and to persuade them to move to Xingu.

One such group was the Kréen-Akaróre, now known as the Panará, whose existence was menaced by a highway being built through their traditional territory. In February 1973, after years of avoiding outsiders, the Panará finally made contact with Claudio Villas Bôas, who had been following them in hopes of finding them before the highway builders did. Shortly after this, Orlando Villas Bôas gave a press conference in which he forcefully urged that a reserve be created for the Panará by the Brazilian government. The reserve was not located in traditional Panará territory, however, and it was bounded by the Santarém-Cuiabá Highway. Within months, the 300 remaining Panará who settled there had abandoned their gardens; sick and in despair, they were begging for food from truck drivers. Finally, in October 1974, the Villas Bôas brothers were able to fly the 135 surviving Panará to Xingu National Park (Davis 1977: 69–73). Within a year, there were only 79 left.

Disease, devastation, and misery have been all too common for Indigenous peoples who have encountered Western expansion. Many observers, including anthropologists, have long feared that Indigenous Amazonian peoples were destined for extinction. After all, of a population of 5 million in 1500, only 280,000 remain today, and some groups have already died out (Gomes 1996). Recent history, however, suggests a reversal of fortune. During the last 30 to 40 years, the 220 surviving Indigenous groups have seen their populations grow. Although some still strive to keep free of outside entanglements, others have been educated and live in cities; one has even been elected to the Brazilian National Congress (Gomes 1996). Even the Panará population has rebounded to over 160 people, and they recently received title to a 1.2 million acre tract of the land they had originally inhabited, as well as a legal settlement for damages resulting from unsupervised contact with outside society. This was the first time that the Brazilian state has had to pay an Indigenous people for pain and suffering (Schwartzman 1998; Rainforest Foundation 2003).

This remarkable and heartening turn of events is illustrated by more recent events involving the Kayapó (see Figure 13.1; see also EthnoProfile 13.1: Kayapó). In March 1989, the *Anthropology Newsletter* published a report from anthropologist Terence Turner describing how Indigenous Amazonians had organized themselves to resist outside encroachment on their traditional lands. They were the people most directly affected by continued destruction of the Amazonian rain forest, but no one could have imagined that they might be leaders in defence of the environment, working successfully with national and international allies. Yet they brought some 28 Indigenous nations together in a huge inter-tribal village built in the path of a proposed hydroelectric dam complex at Altamira, on the Xingu River. The Kayapó leader Payakan combined traditional Indigenous political skills with a knowledge of Portuguese and a keen understanding of the international media. He and other Kayapó chiefs, such as Raoni, toured Europe and appeared publicly with well-known celebrities, such as rock musician Sting, who supported their cause. The Brazilian government, moreover, has still not built its dam. As Turner observes, 'The boldness and global vision of this project are breathtaking; nothing like such a concerted action by even a few, let alone 28 unrelated Indian societies has ever taken place in the Amazon. The Indians are trying to tell us something important; we should listen' (1989: 21–2).

By 1992, the Kayapó had established legal and physical control of 28.4 million acres of their traditional land, but some Kayapó had been illegally selling very valuable mahogany trees, in part to buy boats and radios to protect their borders. In that year, one Kayapó village began working with Conservation International

Figure 13.1 The Kayapó were effective in organizing themselves to resist outside encroachment on their traditional lands.

to create a sustainable and income-generating research station to replace cutting trees. By 2002, all 15 Kayapó villages had signed agreements with Conservation International for conservation-based development projects, and Conservation International was also helping to develop a system for effective border surveillance (Conservation International 2003).

Peoples like the Panará and the Kayapó have struggled with the effects of European contact for over 500 years, but rather than disappear forever, they have now moved out of the forest and into the thick of Brazilian national life. Indeed, they and other Indigenous people elsewhere in the world have been able to create global alliances by making use of contemporary Internet technology (Ribeiro 1998). Anthropological research on Amazonian peoples has also changed. Today, Gomes observes, 'one's living objects of research are easy to find, not more than a few hours away by plane, at the most a few days away by boat. They are on the outskirts of cities, in hospitals and medical centres, and even in the corridors of the National Congress. . . . They will also be available in the future' (1996: 19).

In this chapter, we take up the story of how the Western world and the societies where anthropologists work are interrelated, how those interrelationships have changed over the last 50 years, and with what consequences. We look at ourselves as much as we look at the traditional subjects of anthropological research. Through this reflexive exercise, we try to establish a context for contemplating the common fate of humankind.

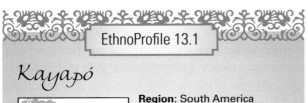

EthnoProfile 13.1

Kayapó

Region: South America

Nation: Brazil

Language: The Kayapó are speakers of Kayapó of the Gê family. 'The language most nearly related to Kayapó is Apinayé, with barely a 20 per cent difference in their vocabulary. . . . There are, however, slight dialectal differences between the various groups' (Advameg Inc. 2008)

Population: 7,096 (2003)

Environment: Rain forest and savannah; wet and dry seasons

Livelihood: Extensive agriculture and hunting and gathering

Political organization: Headmen with no formal power; age grades

For more information: Rabben, Linda. 1999. *Unnatural Selection: The Yanomami, the Kayapó and the Onslaught of Civilization* (London: Pluto Press); http://www.ethnologue.com/14/show_family.asp?subid=2136; http://www.nationmaster.com/encyclopedia/Kayapo-people

Views of the Political Economy

It has become evident as we have moved through the chapters of this book that anthropologists have made use of a variety of theoretical perspectives over the years to explain the relationship between the West and the rest of the world. In the last 50 years, two important phases of anthropological theorizing can be distinguished. The first phase corresponded to the period of the Cold War—from the end of World War II to the break-up of the Soviet Union in 1989—which was also the period in which European colonial empires were dismantled. The struggle between the First World (the Western capitalist 'free world') and the Second World (the Soviet 'communist world', which sometimes included communist China as well) focused on the Third World (or 'non-aligned world'), which included the new nation-states being formed out of former European colonies. The larger political struggle between First and Second worlds affected anthropologists working in what was now the Third World, and the major debates were between proponents of modernization theory and proponents of dependency theory and its various offshoots. The second period began in 1989, with the end of the Cold War and the dismantling of economic and political barriers that had separated the First, Second, and Third worlds from each other, events which unleashed new patterns of movement and exchange that have come to be called *globalization.* Issues connected to globalization now dominate anthropological discussions related to matters of political economy. However, the three-world analysis structure still has some currency although the Second World is no longer strictly represented by the USSR's successor states. But there are still nation-states such as China and North Korea more or less in the 'communist' mold, and perhaps here we could now place those states in conflict with First World 'development' and 'democratization' aspirations. Thus included could be ideologically based opposition as found with radical Islamic societies. This would fit with the original First/Second World construct because it was based on an ideological framework as well. Then again we can question if the First World is not represented by a new ideology as well, an ideology of elites—the ideology of globalization. This ideological conflict is not merely characterized as economic but as the conflict between tribalism and globalization. Benjamin R.

Barber (1995), Whitman professor of Political Science and director of the Whitman Center at Rutgers University, sees both of these ideologies as dangerous to the survival of democracy.

More importantly, there has been an expansion of the analytical framework to include a Fourth World—the world of Indigenous peoples living in neo-colonial/ex-colonial areas of the world—including the First Nations peoples of Canada. The range of analytical expansion in this Fourth World domain of concern challenges all of us. Thus the analysis of alignments is evolving.

Nonetheless, in order to understand the anthropological discussion of globalization, it is necessary to review briefly the preceding perspectives on global relationships.

Modernization versus Dependency: The Colonial Legacy

The meaning of colonialism and, consequently, alternative understandings of the significance of decolonization were reframed with First World leaders supporting **modernization theory**. Colonial empires were reframed as newly independent states. It was postulated they would become prosperous, self-sustaining countries similar to Britain or the US so long as they imitated the policies and practices believed to have been responsible for the original successes of those countries. In this model, colonization was viewed as a positive process because it had taught backward peoples the (capitalist) skills and Western-style institutions they needed to move forward. By adopting those skills and institutions they would eventually become 'modern' and prosperous independent nation-states.

Former colonies were viewed as 'young' nation-states in need of paternal guidance from 'mature' modern states such as the US, which emerged from World War II as the richest and most powerful capitalist country in the world. Paternalistic supervision seemed particularly necessary after the successful communist revolution in Cuba in 1959, and modernization theory became the foundation of US foreign aid policy in the 1960s. It was presented as a road map that promised to guide newly decolonized nations to self-sustaining prosperity, but only if they avoided revolution. There were no shortcuts to the future.

Many observers, particularly those living in former colonies, rejected such a view as they saw that the prosperity of Western nations had *depended on* the exploitation of cheap raw materials, cheap labour, and the captive markets that colonies provided. **Dependency theory** was developed in the 1960s by Latin American economists and social scientists who wanted to explain why, after more than a century of independence from colonial domination, their countries were still poor and weak. They challenged the assumption that nations are naturally autonomous and independently responsible for their own success or failure at modernizing. If colonies and other peoples' resources are necessary for a nation to become modern, then countries without colonies, whose own resources were long ago removed by others, can never hope to become modern. On this account, the nation-states of North America differed from European colonial powers only in that their expansion had been able to incorporate the lands and resources of Indigenous peoples living within their expanding borders. In both cases, the West would never have prospered if colonial powers had not expropriated the wealth of other people to fuel their own development. The success of a few has required the failure of many. Indeed, the prophetic view was that the capitalist nations of the world would remain prosperous only as long as others were dependent on them for economic direction. And of course the dénouement is the recent (2008) meltdown of the market economy of the Western nation-states.

If modernization theory rests on the metaphor of individual growth, many dependency accounts are based on the *metaphor of sexual violation*. European colonialism was seen as a violent rape of the colonies. Dependency theory drew attention to the way that dependent colonies or nations endure the reshaping of their economic structures to meet demands generated outside their borders. For example, land that could be used to raise food crops for local consumption is used to grow export goods such as flowers, bananas, or coffee; thus, local needs are pushed into the background. Thus the international capitalist economic order was directly responsible for distorting the economies of these nations. (This is a theme in documentaries such as *Man Made Famine* (1987) or in novels such as *One Hundred Years of Solitude* by 1982 Noble Prize winner for literature, Garcia Marquez, where the foreign-owned banana company plays a role in the police massacre of plantation workers.) Such an analysis suggested that 'underdevelopment' would persist until dependent countries took

control of their own destinies and restructured their economies and societies to meet local needs. Thus the 1960s, 1970s, and 1980s were notable for the attempts of anti-capitalist revolutionary movements in various Third World countries, as in the Cuban example.

Wallerstein's functionalist **world-system theory**, based on the *metaphor of society as a living organism, compared the shared patterns of domination and dependency found in Third World countries*. In *The Modern World System* (1974), he set forth a global framework for understanding problems of development and underdevelopment, rejecting modernization theory. He argued that exploitative relations between First World and Third World countries took shape and were fine-tuned during the colonial era, embedding these developments within a broader and deeper historical narrative. Beginning in the late fifteenth and early sixteenth centuries, emerging European capitalism began incorporating other regions and peoples into a world economy based on the capitalist mode of production. We might think of the Hudson's Bay Company as a Canadian example of this process. Wallerstein deliberately chose to speak of a world *economy* rather than a world empire or other political entity because a world economy

> precisely encompasses within its bounds empires, city-states, and the emerging 'nation-states'. It is a 'world' system, not because it encompasses the whole world but because it is larger than any juridically defined political unit. And it is a 'world *economy*' because the basic linkage between the parts of the system is economic. (1974: 15)

dependency theory A theory that argues that the success of 'independent' capitalist nations has required the failure of 'dependent' colonies or nations whose economies have been distorted to serve the needs of dominant capitalist outsiders.

modernization theory A theory that argues that the social change occurring in non-Western societies under colonial rule was a necessary and inevitable prelude to higher levels of social development that had been reached by the more 'modern' nations.

world-system theory A theory that argues that, from the late fifteenth and early sixteenth centuries, European capitalism began to incorporate other regions and peoples into a world system whose parts were linked economically but not politically.

At the time, the European world economy was not the only world economy in existence. Perhaps its most important competitor centred on China. Nevertheless, the European world economy was able to surpass these other world economies because of capitalism. 'The secret of capitalism was in the establishment of the division of labour within the framework of a world economy that was *not* an empire' (1974: 127). Banking, finance, and highly skilled industrial production became the specialty, or the **core**, of the world economy of western European nations. The core exploited the **periphery**, draining off its wealth to support highly skilled 'free' labour and a high standard of living. The periphery, by contrast, practised various forms of coerced labour to produce goods to support core industries, and the standard of living for coerced workers was generally low. In this model, there was also a **semi-periphery** consisting of states like Mexico and Brazil that played peripheral roles in the past but that seemed to have accumulated sufficient industrial capacity and other resources to possibly achieve core status in the future.

The main critique of this model is that it only offers two possibilities for change:

(1) units within the system may change roles (a semi-peripheral state may move to the core, or vice versa), or
(2) the system as a whole may be transformed into something else as the result of a system-wide socialist revolution.

These rather grim scenarios were criticized mostly because in their abstraction they missed the actual vibrancy of local activity.

Globalization: Post-Cold War Debates

No part of the world after the Cold War was unaffected, to some extent, by capitalist economic practices. For some, this period of uncertainty seemed to present an opportunity to challenge the previously unquestioned truths about development and underdevelopment. Such challenges were seen in what were called *new social movements*. From vigilante movements (such as the *rondas campesinas* of Peru) to squatter movements in cities, to movements defending the rights of women and homosexuals to movements defending the rain forests, people were attempting to construct cultural institutions that met their needs in ways that often bypassed national

governments or development agencies (Figure 13.2). Anthropologist Arturo Escobar (1992) argued that such social movements in Latin America were struggles over meanings as well as material conditions.

Further, Escobar and anthropologists like James Ferguson attacked the notion of 'development' supported and promoted by Western governments and international aid agencies. They argued that the source of the problems in 'underdeveloped' countries was misidentified. 'By uncompromisingly reducing poverty to a technical problem, and by promising technical solutions to the sufferings of powerless and oppressed people, the hegemonic problematic of "development" is the principal means through which the question of poverty is de-politicized in the world today' as well as being 'a machine for reinforcing and expanding the exercise of bureaucratic state power, which incidentally takes "poverty" as its point of entry' (Ferguson 2002: 407).

Yet while the critique of Western efforts at modernization via development continued, the world toward which such arguments were aimed was already disappearing. The apparent triumph of capitalism reanimated the defenders of modernization theory, now repackaged as *neo-liberalism*, while the Marxian analysis was called into question. Now, states would be encouraged by international institutions like the World Bank and the International Monetary Fund to accept that prosperity depended on their finding a niche in the growing global capitalism market. Market discipline would force state bureaucrats, first, to support economic enterprises that would earn them income in the market and, second, to eliminate the role of state institutions and subsidies that had provided a safety net for the poor. Western leaders enthusiastically embraced the beckoning opportunity to bring the entire world within the compass of the capitalist economy. Less enthusiastic observers began to suspect that forces unleashed were remaking the global political economy in unprecedented ways, with outcomes that no one could predict or control.

Cultural Processes in a Global World

The theories discussed above presuppose a world of relatively clear-cut geographic and cultural boundaries. However, the cybernetics revolution led to

Figure 13.2 Following the Cold War, a number of 'new social movements' developed around the world, including Wangari Maathai's Green Belt Movement, a tree-planting project in Kenya, run mostly by women.

advances in manufacturing, transportation, and communications technology that removed the seemingly insuperable barriers to communication and contact that characterized much of the period of capitalist development. We live with a phenomenon called 'space–time compression' (Harvey 1990) where changes are easier, cheaper, and faster than ever before. It is now possible to stretch social relationships of all kinds over huge distances that previously would have been unbridgeable (Giddens 1990). No part of the globe escaped the effects of these changes—changes called **globalization**. The local is reshaped by powerful global forces on an ever-intensifying scale, 'the intensification of global interconnectedness, suggesting a world full of movement and mixture, contacts and linkages, and persistent cultural interaction and exchange' (Inda and Rosaldo 2002: 2).

Globalization is not only local it is personal—experienced in unique ways by individuals and cultures. Therefore the effects of globalization are *uneven*: 'There are large expanses of the planet only tangentially tied to the webs of interconnection that encompass the globe' (Inda and Rosaldo 2002: 4). As a result, global processes are interpreted and experienced in contradictory ways by different groups and actors. Anthropologists Faye Ginsburg and Rayna Rapp, for example, describe the global process of *stratified reproduction*, in which some

categories of people are empowered to nurture and reproduce, while others are not: 'Low-income African American mothers, for example, often are stereotyped as undisciplined "breeders" who sap the resources of the state through incessant demands on welfare. But historically and in the present, they were "good enough" nurturers to work as child care providers for other, more privileged class and ethnic groups' (1995: 3). Globalization has created new opportunities for some groups, like the Kayapó and other Indigenous peoples, to build worldwide organizations to defend their interests (Kearney 1995: 560). At the same time, global forces can also reinforce old constraints. Evaluating the record of new social movements in Latin America, for example, Gledhill writes that 'to date the challenge that popular forces have been able to mount to the remorseless

core In world-system theory, the nations specializing in banking, finance, and highly skilled industrial production.

globalization Reshaping of local conditions by powerful global forces on an ever-intensifying scale.

periphery In world-system theory, those exploited former colonies of the core that supply the core with cheap food and raw materials.

semi-periphery In world-system theory, states that have played peripheral roles in the past but that now have sufficient industrial capacity and other resources to possibly achieve core status in the future.

progress of the neo-liberal, neo-modernization agenda, has remained limited' (1994: 198).

It would be difficult to find any research project by contemporary cultural anthropologists that does not in some way acknowledge the ways in which global forces affect the local societies in which they work. For them it is a truism that *the global articulates with the local.* Therefore 'globalizing processes exist in the context of, and must come to terms with, the realities of particular societies' (Inda and Rosaldo 2002: 4). So 'while everyone might continue to live local lives, their phenomenal worlds have to some extent become global' (9).

Globalization is seen in the growth of transnational corporations that relocate their manufacturing operations from core to periphery or that appropriate local cultural forms and turn them into images and commodities to be marketed throughout the world (Figure 13.3). It is seen in tourism, which has grown into the world's largest industry, and in migration from periphery to the core on such a massive scale that observers now speak of the 'de-territorialization' of peoples and cultures that, in the past, were presumed to be firmly attached to specific geographical locations. Not only that: de-territorialized people always 're-territorialize' in a new location. Such re-territorialization regularly sparks social conflicts and generates new forms of cultural identity, as nation-states try to retain control over citizens living beyond their borders and as relocated populations struggle both for recognition in their new homes and for influence in their places of origin. Globalization has drawn the attention of many anthropologists to regions such as the borderland between northern Mexico and the southwestern US, where struggles with contradictory social practices and ambiguous identities have long been the rule, rather than the exception. Such contexts exhibit a 'diffusion of culture traits gone wild, far beyond that imagined by the Boasians' (Kearney 1995: 557). Since borderland conditions are now becoming worldwide, they undermine views of culture that depend upon settled peoples with distinct cultural attributes.

Where does Wallerstein's portrayal of the global processes as part of a world *system* fit now? Anthropologist Arjun Appadurai points out that ever-intensifying global flows of people, technology, wealth, images, and ideologies are highly contradictory, generating global processes that are fundamentally disorganized and unpredictable (1990). Meanwhile Friedman argues that the disorder may be real but it is also a predictable consequence of the breakdown of Western global hegemony (1994). In his view, these developments exemplify a pattern of commercial expansion and contraction that began at least 5,000 years ago with the rise of the first commercial civilizations—world systems in Wallerstein's sense—each of which was characterized by its own form of 'modernity'. Thus, the capitalist world system of the West 'tends, as in previous mercantile civilizations, to become decentralized and more competitive. Weakened and crisis-ridden, the centre is likely to decline and lose its hegemonic power to new rising centres of imperialist accumulation' (1994: 2–3). As a result, 'modernity in this sense is just another tradition, labile and fragile, that has emerged, however partially, and disappeared numerous times on the stage of human history'; for example, in ancient Greece, Rome, China, India, and the Arab Middle Ages (229–30). Awareness of this oscillating pattern reveals that 'the variety of social structures documented in the anthropological literature can be understood as transformations of one or two basic types of organization in changing conditions of marginality in larger systems' based on whether they occur as a new commercial civilization begins to spread or as that civilization begins to decline (40). Recognition of this pattern makes Friedman even more pessimistic than Wallerstein about possibilities for the future. He sees current changes in the

Figure 13.3 One dimension of globalization involves the appropriation of local cultural forms and their use on a variety of widely sold commodities. For example, the image of 'Kokopelli', taken from ancient rock art of the southwestern US, has been reproduced on many items with no connection to its region or culture of origin, including this doormat, purchased from a mail-order catalogue.

capitalist world system as simply the latest example of 'a more cyclically sinister history of civilizational systems' that have risen and fallen repeatedly throughout history (99; cf. Abu-Lughod 1991). Friedman remains unmoved by those who suggest that anything new or hopeful might emerge from the current state of the world: 'The capacity to even conceive of consciously changing the world for the better lies, perhaps, in changing the system as a whole, a system whose more general properties have eluded the storms of innumerable revolutions and cataclysm' (1994: 41). Not all anthropologists accept Friedman's conclusions as they cannot account for the 'local structures' and 'autonomous cultural schemes' that appear at any point in the cycle. It is this historically specific local detail—what Inda and Rosaldo (2002: 27) call 'the conjunctural and situated character of globalization'—that anthropologists aim to document and analyze.

In Their Own Words

Cofan: Story of the Forest People and the Outsiders

Randy Borman is president of the Centro Cofan Zabalo. He was born to missionary parents and grew up in Cofan culture in the Ecuadorian Amazon. Borman briefly attended school in North America and then returned to Ecuador to become a leader in the Cofan fight for economic and cultural survival. He has written in Cultural Survival Quarterly *about the development of ecotourism in the Cofan area of Ecuador. The results of tourism elsewhere in the world are not always as positive as they have been for the Cofan people, in part because tourism is often imposed from the outside.*

I had the fortune to grow up as a forest person, enjoying the clean rivers and unlimited forests, learning the arts and skills of living comfortably in a wonderland of the marvelous, beautiful, and deadly. I experienced first-hand both the good and the bad of a world, which will never again be possible, at least in the foreseeable future. And I also experienced the crushing physical, psychological, and spiritual impact of the invasion of the outside that erased our world.

In 1955, the Cofan people were the sole inhabitants of more than 1,000,000 hectares of pristine forest in northeastern Ecuador. By 1965, oil exploration and exploitation had begun. And by 1975, the forest was fast disappearing before a massive mestizo colonization, which was brought in by roads created to access vast quantities of oil. The rivers were fouled with chemicals and raw crude; the animals disappeared; boom towns sprung up all over; and the Cofan struggled to survive on less than 15,000 hectares of badly degraded forest. The old life was gone forever, and my companions and I faced the numbing prospect of discarding our culture and way of life, and becoming peasant farmers like so many others, trying to eke out a living from crops and animals which were never meant to grow in this environment. We had been powerless to maintain our forests in the face of outsider pressures to make every given piece of land profitable. If we were to save anything from the wreckage we needed alternatives, and quickly. . . .

[As the only member of his community with an outsider education, Borman worked with the community in trying to develop strategies for community survival, including those associated with marketing forest products. These strategies did not work.]

As we were wrestling with these possible alternatives, we were also acting as boatmen for the slowly increasing economy on the river. Several of us had managed to buy outboard motors with carefully saved returns from corn fields, animal skins, and short stints as trail makers with the oil companies. We had a long tradition of carving dugouts, and soon our canoes were travelling up and down the rivers with loads of lumber, corn, and coffee; occasional trips carrying cattle provided excitement and variety. This was not an alternative for the entire community, and it was only viable until roads were built, but it worked as a stop-gap measure for some of us. And unexpectedly, it led us directly into the alternative, which we have adopted as our own in the years since.

Travellers were coming to our region. The roads made it easier than at any previous time, and people from First World countries—the US, Canada, England, Germany, Israel, Italy—began to come, searching for the vanishing rain forest. Most of them were primarily interested in seeing wildlife. This fit with our view of the situation precisely. We had our motorboats. There was still a lot of good forest out there, but it was hard to access with regular paddling and poling expeditions. So when these travellers arrived and wanted to go to 'wild jungle', we were delighted to take them. They paid the transportation cost, and we took our shotguns and spears along to go hunting. Our attitude was that if the traveller wanted to go along with us, and didn't mind that we were hunting, why, we were happy to have them along to help carry the game home! From such a pragmatic beginning, we slowly developed our concept of tourism.

There were changes. We soon learned that the traveller had a lot more fun if we modified our normal hunting pattern a bit, and we even got paid extra for it. We found out that the average tourist didn't mind if we shot birds that looked like chickens, even if they were rare. But if we shot a toucan they were outraged, despite the fact that toucans are very common. Tourists preferred a board to a stick as a seat in the canoe, and a pad made them even happier. Tourists' food needed to be somewhat recognizable, such as rice, rather than the lumpy, thick manioc beer we normally eat and drink. But the community as a whole decided early that our role would be that of guides and service providers for tourists interested in the forest. We would not dress up and do dances, or stage fake festivals, or in any way try to sell our traditions and dress. We would not accept becoming the objects of tourism—rather, we would provide the skills and knowledge for the tourist to understand our environment. We would sell our education at a price that was in line with the importance to the outsiders who wanted to buy it, such as lawyers, biologists, doctors, teachers, and other professionals the world over do.

Being guides for the tourism experience, not the objects of it, has provided both a very real economic alternative and a very solid incentive for the younger generation to learn the vast body of traditional knowledge, which lies at the heart of our culture. A deep conservation ethic—the roots of which lie at the hearts of most cultures who maintain a viable relation with their environments—has helped the Cofan community to create a number of projects which combine outsider science with our traditional knowledge. Interestingly enough, this has also turned out to be an economic success, as many of our projects began to receive funding in recognition of their innovation and replicability in other communities throughout Amazonia.

At present, the Cofan community most involved in both tourism and conservation is my community, Zabalo. Located in what is now part of the Cuyabeno Wildlife Reserve near the northern border of Ecuador with Peru, this community owns and manages over 100,000 hectares of forest in coordination with the Ecuadorean national parks system. With four community-operated cabins, an interpretation centre, and a series of trails and camps both in deep forest and on the black water streams of the area, Zabalo plays host in varying scale to over 3,000 visitors annually. Most of these visitors come via an Ecuadorean tourism agency, Metropolitan Touring, which operates a floating hotel in the region (appropriately the Flotel), and spend only a few hours at the interpretation centre and market. However, perhaps 200 visitors per year spend up to 10 days enjoying the village's programs—trekking, canoeing, birding, wildlife watching; learning to know the forest intimately in the company of Cofan guides, cooks, and administrators. Both the cabins and the interpretation centre generate income for the community. Working as crew and as guides for the groups provides individual income. And the sale of crafts both directly to tourists and to retailers elsewhere in the country is a steady and important source of cash for the families of the community. . . .

Tourism is not for everyone. Some of our experiences have been negative. One of our biggest and most constant headaches is effective commercialization. To operate a community-based tourism business while maintaining our cultural heritage is not possible using the outsider formula of a tour operator. The implied hierarchy of manager, finance department, buyers, transport specialists, etc., all working eight hours a day, five days a week, with an office and a fax machine is clearly not applicable. Instead, we rely on teams, which rotate in their work, leaving time for farms, family duties, crafts, fishing, hunting, and the garden. But the lack of a full-time office makes it difficult to commercialize effectively, and we walk the precarious line between too much tourism (no time left over to live a normal life, and possible loss of our cultural way of life) and too little (not enough jobs, not enough income, lack of attraction for a forest-based life and education for our young people). If we commercialize effectively, we run the risk of the operation snowballing, with more and more tourists arriving, and eventually we are all wealthy in outsider goods and income but without our culture's wealth of time and interpersonal relationships that we all value so much now. If we don't commercialize effectively, we will wake up tomorrow back at the beginning, with the need to destroy our forest for short-term survival.

But in the overall scheme of things, our experiment with tourism has been overwhelmingly positive. Contact with people who wish to know what we can teach, who value our forests and are willing to pay to help us maintain them has been very important. Our increased awareness of the conservation imperatives facing us has led to many changes in our way of life, all aimed at preserving core values for future generations.

Source: Borman, Randy. 1999. 'Cofan: Story of the Forest People and the Outsiders', *Cultural Survival Quarterly* 23, 2: 48–50.

Globalization and the Nation-state

Are Global Flows Undermining Nation-states?

In the recent past, one of the fundamental suppositions about global social organization was that it consisted of an international order of independent nation-states. This is an assumption rooted in the nineteenth-century nationalist struggles in Europe although it came fully into its own after World War II as former colonies achieved independence. The United Nations presupposed a world of nation-states. Modernization theorists and dependency theorists alike assumed that the world was a mosaic of nations who were entitled to self-determination and a state of their own (Figure 13.4). The flows of people, technology, wealth, images, and ideologies unleashed by globalization, however, has undermined the ability of nation-states to police their boundaries effectively and has seemed to suggest that the conventional ideas about nation-states require revision. Further, many nation-states are actually composed of disparate ethnic groups with diverging self-interests. National governments are virtually powerless to control what their citizens read or watch in the media: satellite services and telecommunications and the Internet elude the censor. Nation-states allow migrants or students or tourists to cross their borders because they need their labour or tuition or vacation dollars, but in doing so states must contend with the political values or religious commitments or families that these outsiders bring with them. Is the weakening of boundaries between states a good thing?

Massive global displacements of people have characterized Western modernity, starting with the slave trade and the movement of indentured labour to the colonies. In the nineteenth century, as developing capitalist markets pushed and pulled waves of European and Asian emigrants out of their homelands and installed them in different parts of the globe, colonial authorities revived the institution of indentured labour to rearrange populations within their dominions. For example, consider that over 100,000 'home children' were shipped from Great Britain to Canada between 1869 and 1930. When volumes of immigration were lower and moved at a slower pace, and jobs were plentiful, the possibilities of assimilation into the society of re-territorialization were often possible. But globalization has changed all that. Today, desperate economic and

Figure 13.4 Queen Elizabeth II at Nigerian Independence ceremonies, 1956.

political situations in migrants' home territories, plus ease of transportation, have increased the volume and speed of migration, while market crises in the countries where they have settled have sharply reduced the economic opportunities available to them. Migrants often find themselves caught between the potential for better opportunities for economic survival and political security and local economic crises. Their visibility in enclaves of settlement, often in the poorer areas of cities, and the hostility, sometimes with violence, directed against them by locals, promotes the sense that the possibility or that hopes of assimilation are unrealistic. In such an atmosphere it is difficult to break off ties to the homeland.

Migration, Transborder Identities, and Long-distance Nationalism

The term *diaspora* is commonly used to refer to migrant populations with a shared identity who live in a variety of different locales around the world, but Nina Glick Schiller and Georges Fouron point out that not all such populations see themselves in the same way. They describe different types of *transborder identities* that can characterize different groups of migrants. They prefer to use the term **diaspora** to identify a form of transborder

diaspora Migrant populations with a shared identity who live in a variety of different locales around the world; a form of transborder identity that does not focus on nation-building.

identity that does not focus on nation-building. Should members of a diaspora begin to organize in support of nationalist struggles in their homeland, or to agitate for a state of their own, they become **long-distance nationalists** (2002: 360–1). *Long-distance nationalism* is a term coined by political scientist Benedict Anderson to describe the efforts of émigrés to offer moral, economic, and political support to the nationalist struggles of their countries of origin. In his original discussion, Anderson emphasized the dangerous irresponsibility of the 'citizenshipless participation' of long-distance nationalists: 'while technically a citizen of the state in which he comfortably lives, but to which he may feel little attachment, he finds it tempting to play identity politics by participating (via propaganda, money, weapons, any way but voting) in the conflicts of his imagined *Heimat* [homeland]' (2002 [1992]: 269–70). Schiller and Fouron argue, however, that the conditions of globalization have led to new forms of long-distance nationalism that do not correspond to Anderson's original description. They point to the emergence of the **transborder state**: a form of state 'claiming that its emigrants and their descendants remain an integral and intimate part of their ancestral homeland, even if they are legal citizens of another state' (2002: 357).

In today's global world, political leaders of many states sending emigrants not only accept the likelihood that those emigrants will permanently settle elsewhere but also insist that such permanently settled émigrés will retain full membership in the nation-state from which they came. This form of long-distance nationalism creates what Schiller and Fouron call a **transborder citizenry**: 'Citizens residing within the territorial homeland and new emigrants and their descendants are part of the nation, whatever legal citizenship the émigrés may have' (2002: 358).

Transborder states and transborder citizenries are more than symbolic identities: they have become concretized in law. Canadians can hold dual citizenship; and several Latin American countries, including Mexico, Colombia, the Dominican Republic, Ecuador, and Brazil, permit emigrants who have become naturalized citizens in countries such as the US to retain dual nationality and even voting rights in their country of origin. They may go so far as to set up special government ministries to address the needs of citizens living abroad. This is very different from Anderson's notion of 'citizenshipless participation'. Schiller and Fouron

stress that transborder states and citizenries 'cannot be seen as top-down fostering of elite beliefs' but that they spring instead 'from the life experiences of migrants of different classes' and are 'rooted in the day-to-day efforts of people in the homeland to live lives of dignity and self-respect that compel them to include those who have migrated' (2002: 359).

But some transborder citizenries face difficulties.

- First, their efforts at nation-building are sometimes blocked by political forces in the homeland who do not welcome their contributions. This has been the case for Haitians living abroad while Haiti was ruled by the Duvalier dictatorship or for Cubans living abroad whose efforts are blocked by Castro's revolutionary government.
- Second, the states in which immigrants have settled may not welcome the continued involvement of transborder citizens in the affairs of another state. Such involvement has often been seen as even more threatening since terrorists destroyed the World Trade Center and attacked the Pentagon on 11 September 2001.

Yet in an era of globalization, attempts to control migration threaten to block the global flows of people that keep the global economy going. Moreover, the vulnerability of transborder citizens in these circumstances often increases the appeal of long-distance nationalism (Schiller and Fouron 2002: 359–60).

The globalizing forces that produce long-distance nationalism and transborder states and citizens have undermined previous understandings of what a world made up of nation-states should look like. In addition, unacknowledged contradictions and weaknesses of actual nation-states are revealed. For example, the existence and strength of transborder states and citizenries show that some nation-states—especially those sending migrants—are actually what Schiller and Fouron call *apparent states*: they have all the outward attributes of nation-states (government bureaucracies, armies, a seat in the UN), but in fact they are unable to meet the needs of their people (2002: 363). The strength of long-distance nationalism and transborder citizenries also exposes inconsistencies and paradoxes in the meaning of citizenship in the nation-states where migrants settle.

Schiller and Fouron contrast legal citizenship with what they call *substantive citizenship*, and point out that, for transborder citizens, the two do not often coincide. **Legal citizenship** is accorded by state laws and can be difficult for migrants to obtain. But even those transborder citizens who obtain legal citizenship often experience a gap between what the legal citizenship promises and the way they are treated by the state. For example, people of colour and women who are US citizens are not treated by the state the same way white male citizens are treated. By contrast, **substantive citizenship** is defined by the actions people take, regardless of their legal citizenship status, to assert their membership in a state and to bring about political changes that will improve their lives. Some transborder citizenries call for the establishment of fully fledged **transnational nation-states**. That is, 'they challenge the notion that relationships between citizens and their state are confined within that territory' and work for the recognition of a new political form that contradicts the understandings of political theory, but which reflects the realities of their experiences of national identity (Schiller and Fouron 2002: 359). The contrast between formal and substantive citizenship suggests that conventional notions of citizenship that previously seemed straightforward begin to break down in the context of globalization. Anthropologist Aihwa Ong suggests these contradictions and ambiguities speak to **flexible citizenship**: 'the strategies and effects of mobile managers, technocrats, and professionals seeking both to circumvent *and* benefit from different nation-state regimes by selecting different sites for investment, work, and family relocation' (2002: 174).

Ong's research concerns diaspora communities of elite Chinese families who have played key roles in the economic successes of the Pacific Rim in recent years. Although their success is often attributed by outsiders to 'Chinese culture', Ong's research calls this simplistic explanation into question. She documents the ways in which Chinese families have responded creatively to opportunities and challenges they have encountered since the end of the nineteenth century, when Chinese merchants first became involved in overseas commercial capitalism in the economic centres of European colonial empires in East and Southeast Asia. Their success has come because they were able to cultivate values and practices that allow them to evade or exploit the governmentality of three different kinds of institutions: Chinese kinship and family, the nation-state, and the marketplace.

The break from mainland Chinese ideas of kinship and Confucian filial piety came when Chinese first moved into the capitalist commercial circuits of European empires. Money could be made in these settings, but success required Chinese merchant families to cut themselves off from ties to mainland China and to reinforce bonds among family members and business partners in terms of *guanxi* ('relationships of social connections built primarily upon shared identities such as native place, kinship, or attending the same school' [Smart 1999: 120]). Shaped primarily by the pressures of intense economic competition and tight state restrictions on permissible economic and political activity, diaspora Chinese merchant and industrial families developed a set of values and practices that centred on the well-being of the family.

> An individual's sense of moral worth is based on endurance and diligence in income-making activities, compliance with parental wishes, and the making of sacrifices and deferral of gratification, especially on the part of women and children. . . . Children, especially sons, are expected to collect symbolic capital in the form of educational certificates and well-paying jobs that help raise the family class position and prestige. (Ong 2002: 178)

flexible citizenship The strategies and effects employed by managers, technocrats, and professionals who regularly move across state boundaries who seek both to circumvent and benefit from different nation-state regimes.

legal citizenship The rights and obligations of citizenship accorded by the laws of a state.

long-distance nationalists Members of a diaspora begin to organize in support of nationalist struggles in their homeland or to agitate for a state of their own.

substantive citizenship The actions people take, regardless of their legal citizenship status, to assert their membership in a state and to bring about political changes that will improve their lives.

transborder citizenry A group made up of citizens of a country who continue to live in the homeland plus the people who have emigrated from the country and their descendents, regardless of their current citizenship.

transborder state A form of state in which it is claimed that those people who left the country and their descendents remain part of their ancestral state, even if they are citizens of another state.

transnational nation-states Nation-states in which the relationships between citizens and their states extend to wherever citizens reside.

Having managed to evade the discipline of mainland Chinese kinship and family practices, the family discipline of overseas Chinese enabled them to become wealthy and provided the resources to subvert the governmentality of the nation-state. The orientation of these wealthy families toward national identity and citizenship, Ong explains, is 'market-driven'. In Hong Kong, for example, in the years leading up to its return to mainland China in 1997, many wealthy Chinese thought of citizenship 'not as the right to demand full democratic representation but as the right to promote familial interests apart from the well-being of society' (178). None of the overseas Chinese she knew expressed any commitment to nationalism, either local or long-distance. This understanding of citizenship could not be more different from the committed transborder citizenship of long-distance nationalists described by Schiller and Fouron.

Quite the contrary. Relying on family discipline and loyalty, and buttressed by considerable wealth and strong interpersonal ties, they actively worked to evade the governmentality of nation-states. For example, Chinese from Hong Kong who wanted to migrate to Britain in the 1960s were able to evade racial barriers that blocked other 'coloured' immigrants because of their experience with capitalism and their reputation for peaceful acquiescence to British rule. When the British decided to award citizenship to some Hong Kong residents in the 1990s, they used a point system that favoured applicants with education, fluency in English, and training in professions of value to the economy, such as accountancy and law. These attributes fit the criteria for citizenship valued under the government of Margaret Thatcher, while other applicants for citizenship who lacked such attributes were excluded. Citizenship, or at least a passport, could be purchased by those who had the money: 'well-off families accumulated passports not only from Canada, Australia, Singapore, and the US but also from revenue poor Fiji, the Philippines, Panama, and Tonga (which required in return for a passport a down payment of US $200,000 and an equal amount in installments' (Ong 2002: 183) (Figure 13.5).

Wealthy overseas Chinese families had thus managed to evade or subvert both the governmentality of Chinese kinship and family and the governmentality of nation-states. But they remained vulnerable to the discipline of the market. To be sure, market discipline

Figure 13.5 Overseas Chinese are to be found in many parts of the world, as here in Toronto. They are not always millionaire businesspeople but are shopkeepers and small-business owners as well.

under globalization was very different from the market discipline typical in the 1950s and 1960s, before the development of the transportation, communication, and manufacturing technologies that enabled people to move money and factories with ease around a world no longer divided by the Cold War. Making money in the context of globalization required the flexibility to take advantage of economic opportunities wherever and whenever they appeared; accordingly, overseas Chinese took steps to position family members in different settings. Ong describes one family in which the eldest son remained in Hong Kong to run part of the family hotel chain located in the Pacific region while his brother lived in San Francisco and managed the hotels located in North America and Europe. Children can be separated from their parents when they are, for example, installed in one country to be educated while their parents manage businesses in other countries on different continents. These flexible business arrangements are not without costs. 'Familial regimes of dispersal and localization . . . discipline family members to make do with very little emotional support; disrupted parental responsibility, strained marital relations, and abandoned children are such common circumstances that they have special terms.' At the same time, individual family members truly do seem to live comfortably as citizens of the world. A Chinese banker in San Francisco told Ong: 'I can live anywhere in the world, but it must be near an airport' (2002: 190).

The values and practices to which overseas Chinese adhere, and which seem responsible for their tremendous achievements in a globalized capitalist economy, suggest to Ong that, for these elite Chinese, the concept of nationalism has lost its meaning. Instead, she says, they seem to subscribe to a **post-national ethos** in which they submit to the governmentality of the capitalist market while trying to evade the governmentality of nation-states, ultimately because their only true loyalty is to the family business (2002: 190). Ong notes, however, that flexible citizenship informed by a post-national ethos is not an option for non-elite migrants: 'whereas for bankers, boundaries are always flexible, for migrant workers, boat people, persecuted intellectuals and artists, and other kinds of less well-heeled refugees, this . . . is a harder act to follow' (190).

She also points out that, on the way to their success, contemporary Chinese merchants 'have also revived pre-modern forms of child, gender, and class oppression, as well as strengthened authoritarianist regimes in Asia' (190). Yet neither the positives nor the negatives should, she insists, be attributed to any 'Chinese' essence; instead, she thinks these strategies are better understood as 'the expressions of a habitus that is finely tuned to the turbulence of late capitalism' (191).

Human Rights and Globalization
Human Rights Discourse as the Global Language of Social Justice

The original UN Declaration on Human Rights in 1948 followed by numerous subsequent declarations accompanied by the intensification of processes of globalization have created conditions for growing discussions of **human rights**. The challenge has been the emerging, different understandings about what it means to be human, or what kinds of rights people may be entitled to under radically changed conditions of everyday life. The context within which human rights discourse becomes relevant is often described as **multiculturalism**: living permanently in settings surrounded by people with cultural backgrounds different from your own and struggling to define the degree to which the cultural beliefs and practices of different groups should or should not be accorded respect and recognition by the wider society. It is precisely in multicultural

settings—found everywhere in today's globalized world but of particular interest to Canadians—that questions of rights become salient, and different cultural understandings of what it means to be human, and what rights humans are entitled to, become the focus of contention and resolution.

Human rights discourses now extend into areas of gender politics. For example, in 1992, the Committee for the Elimination of Discrimination against Women (CEDAW) declared that violence against women was a form of gender discrimination that violated the human rights of women. This declaration was adopted by the UN General Assembly in 1993 and became part of the rights platform at the Fourth World Conference on Women in Beijing, China, in 1995. Anthropologist Sally Merry observes that this declaration 'dramatically demonstrates the creation of new rights—rights which depend on the state's failure to protect women rather than its active violation of rights' and that 'the emergence of violence against women as a distinct human rights violation depends on redefining the family so that it is no longer shielded from legal scrutiny' (2001: 36–7). Although CEDAW has proved particularly contentious, other human rights documents have been signed without controversy by many national governments. Signing on to a human rights declaration ostensibly binds governments to take official action to implement changes in local practices that might be seen to violate the rights asserted in the declarations. Human rights discourses are common currency in all societies, at all levels. As Jane Cowan, Marie-Bénédicte Dembour, and Richard Wilson write, it is 'no use imagining a "primitive" tribe which has not yet heard of human rights . . . what it means to be "Indigenous" is itself transformed through interaction with human rights discourses and institutions' (2001: 5).

---

human rights A set of rights that should be accorded to all human beings everywhere in the world.

multiculturalism Living permanently in settings surrounded by people with cultural backgrounds different from your own and struggling to define the degree to which the cultural beliefs and practices of different groups should or should not be accorded respect and recognition by the wider society.

post-national ethos An attitude toward the world in which people submit to the governmentality of the capitalist market while trying to evade the governmentality of nation-states.

Because of the wide adoption of human rights discourses throughout the world, some people have come to speak of an emerging 'culture of human rights' which has now become 'the pre-eminent global language of social justice' (Merry 2001: 38). These developments mean that anthropologists need to take note of the important influence this human rights discourse is having in the various settings where they do their research. What counts as 'human rights' has changed over time, due not only to the action of international bodies like the UN but also to the efforts of an increasing number of non-governmental organizations (NGOs) that have become involved in various countries of the world, many of them deeply committed to projects designed to improve people's lives and protect their rights. As Merry says, these developments 'have created a new legal order' that has given birth to new possibilities throughout the world for the elaboration and discussion of what human rights are all about (2001: 35). In addition, because the 'culture of human rights' is increasingly regarded, in one way or another, as the 'culture of globalization', it would seem to be a topic well-suited to anthropological analysis. This is because, as we shall see, human rights discourse is not as straightforward as it seems. On the face of things, defending human rights for all people would seem unproblematic. Few people who are aware of the devastation wrought by colonial exploitation, for example, would want to suggest that the victims of that exploitation did not have rights that needed to be protected at all costs. And yet, when we look closely at particular disputes about human rights, the concept no longer seems so simple.

Jane Cowan and her colleagues have noted that there are two major arguments that have developed for talking about the way human rights and culture are related:

(1) that *human rights are opposed to culture* and that the two cannot be reconciled, and
(2) that a key universal human right is precisely one's *right to culture.*

We will consider each in turn.

Rights versus Culture

Arguments that pit human rights against culture depend on the assumption that 'cultures' are homogeneous, bounded, and unchanging sets of ideas and practices and that each society has only one culture, which its members are obligated to follow. As we saw in Chapter 1, this view of culture has been severely criticized by cultural anthropologists. But it is a view of culture that is very much alive in many human rights disputes. For if people have no choice but to follow the rules of the culture into which they were born, international interference with customs said to violate human rights would seem itself to constitute a human rights violation: disrupting a supposedly harmonious way of life and preventing those who are committed to such a way of life from observing their own culturally specific understandings about rights. Thus, cultures should be allowed to enjoy absolute, inviolable protection from interference by outsiders. This has been the position adopted, for example, by some national governments that have refused to sign the CEDAW declaration that violence against women violates women's human rights. As of 2 March 2006, 182 (90 per cent) UN member countries are party to CEDAW although some countries, such as the US, have yet to ratify, thus not moving as a nation to full implementation. The US remains the only industrialized nation to be in this position of non-ratification.

Sometimes the reasons for defending culture against rights discourses is explicitly linked to the nineteenth-century struggle between defenders and opponents of the European Enlightenment. Thus, representatives of non-Western nation-states may feel free to dismiss rights talk as an unwelcome colonial imposition of ideas that, far from being universal, reflect ethnocentric European preoccupations. But such dismissal of human rights discourse needs to be closely examined. In the case of the right of women to protection from violence, for example, Merry points out that although some forms of violence against women may be culturally sanctioned in some societies, there are many forms that violence against women can take even in those societies, and not all of these are accorded the same amount of cultural support. Even practices like wife-beating or female genital cutting (Figure 13.6), that in the past could be justified in some circumstances as appropriate cultural actions, are now being questioned and even outlawed in the societies where they were practised. This suggests 'culture values' cannot be held responsible for everything that people do in any society and that members of the same society can

(2) their own struggles with the concept of culture allow them to mount a critique of some of the ways that this concept has been mobilized in the discussion of human rights.

Rights as Culture

The ways that anthropologists have developed to study cultural patterns in other contexts seem well suited as tools for investigation to the extent to which a 'culture of human rights' can be said to have emerged in recent years. As in the cultures traditionally studied by anthropologists, the culture of human rights is based on certain ideas about human beings and their needs and their ability to exercise agency, as well as the kinds of social connections between human beings that are considered legitimate and illegitimate. The entire question of 'legitimacy' in human rights discourse points to the central role played by *law*, both as a way of articulating specific human rights and as a tool for defending those rights. Cowan, Dembour, and Wilson have drawn on earlier anthropological work in which systems of law were analyzed as cultural systems.

One important source has been the 'law and culture' framework developed by anthropologists Clifford Geertz, Laura Nader, and Lawrence Rosen and non-anthropologists like Boaventura de Sousa Santos. In this framework, 'law is conceived as a world view or structuring discourse . . . "facts" . . . are socially constructed through rules of evidence, legal conventions, and the rhetoric of legal actors' (Cowan et al. 2001: 11). Analysts who talk about a 'culture of human rights' as the new culture of a globalizing world point out that the key features of the human rights world view clearly indicate its origins in Western secular discourse: it focuses on the rights of individuals; it proposes to relieve human suffering through technical rather than ethical solutions, and it emphasizes rights over duties or needs (11). To the extent that this is the case, human rights culture is well designed to function as, what anthropologist James Ferguson has called, an 'anti-politics' machine: 'by uncompromisingly reducing poverty to a technical problem, and by promising technical solutions to the sufferings of powerless and oppressed people . . . the question of poverty is de-politicized in the world today' with the consequence that politics is suspended 'from even the most sensitive political operations' (2002: 407).

Earlier, Ferguson had a negative view of technical solutions to political problems. They not only failed to solve the problems of poverty, they also reinforced the power of the state to interfere in and control the lives of their poor citizens. In the early twenty-first century where state structures are under stress and the dynamics of transnational and multicultural living sometimes provoke violent and bloody political confrontations, a human rights discourse—or discourses—capable of 'de-politicizing' such confrontations might have an important role to play. The development of such discourses is seen by some anthropologists as a vital need and key challenge in a globalized world, as we discuss below.

In the meantime, to the extent that human rights discourse is conceived to be a 'culture', most anthropologists would probably agree that this culture concept would be more illuminating if it reflected current anthropological understandings of culture (Cowan et al. 2001: 13). An understanding of culture as open, heterogeneous, and supple can become an effective analytic tool to help us understand how human rights processes work.

Culture as a Way of Thinking about Rights

To use the culture concept as a tool for analyzing human rights processes means looking for 'patterns and relationships of meaning and practice between different domains of social life' that are characteristic of the culture of human rights (Cowan et al. 2001: 13). Since human rights are articulated in legal documents and litigated in courts, one of the most important patterns that becomes visible in the culture of human rights is the way they are shaped to accommodate the law. Groups and individuals who assert that their human rights have been violated regularly take their cases to courts of law. But this means that in order to get the courts to take them seriously, they need to understand how the law operates. A key feature of this understanding involves a realistic awareness of the kinds of claims that the law pays attention to and the kinds of claims that will be dismissed. Looking at human rights law as culture reveals that only certain kinds of claims are admissible. As we saw above, the culture of human rights as currently constituted is best suited to redress the grievances of individuals, not groups; to provide technical, not ethical, remedies; and it emphasizes rights over duties or needs. Plaintiffs are therefore likely to have a difficult time if they want to claim that their group rights have been violated, that they want the violator exposed and punished, or that the state itself has failed to fulfill its responsibilities toward them. Part of the human rights process therefore involves learning how to craft cases that will fit the laws, and this can be tricky if the categories and identities recognized in human rights law do not correspond to categories and identities that are meaningful to the plaintiffs.

Many social groups among whom anthropologists work have engaged in political struggles with national governments in which they argue for protection of their rights to practise their culture freely. This portrayal of a group's culture in these kinds of political struggles regularly includes claims about protecting its distinct and unchanging values and practices from state policies. As we saw in Chapter 12, these kinds of arguments for a right to culture are often cases of 'strategic essentialism' in which the unity and unchanging homogeneity of a particular 'culture' is deliberately constructed in order to build group solidarity and to engage the state in a focused and disciplined way. But the 'essentialism' that often comes to dominate discussions of group rights is not due entirely to the strategies of activists. Once they choose to make their case in a court of law, they become subject to the 'essentializing proclivities of the law' (Cowan et al. 2001: 11). Because human rights law only recognizes certain kinds of rights violations, groups with grievances must tailor those grievances to fit the violations that human rights law recognizes. According to Merry, for example, groups like the Hawaiian Sovereignty Movement have successfully achieved some of their political goals by making claims based on the requirements of their 'traditional culture'. But this is because they live in a society that is 'willing to recognize claims on the basis of cultural authenticity and tradition but not reparations based on acts of conquest and violation' (2001: 42–3). Outside the courtroom, many members of Indigenous groups think of their culture the way contemporary anthropologists think about culture: there are some common patterns but culture is basically unbounded, heterogeneous, and open to change. But human rights law is ordinarily written in such a way that claims for cultural rights will only be considered if the culture in question is presented as bounded, homogenous, and unchanging. As a result, Indigenous peoples are often forced to portray themselves and their cultures in ways that are very different from their own everyday understandings of who they are. While doing so may enable them to win legal judgments in their favour, it can also reshape their ideas about what their culture is. Groups that enter into the human rights process, thus, are entering into ethically ambiguous territory that is 'both enabling and constraining' (Cowan et al. 2001: 11).

Human Rights in Thailand: Child Prostitution

Reaching successful accommodations between human rights discourse and local cultural practices is not always easy. A particularly difficult set of issues must be confronted when attempting to enforce the rights of children. Anthropologist Heather Montgomery did field research in a slum settlement in Thailand that was located near a prosperous seaside resort catering to foreign tourists (2001) (see Map 13.2). Those who lived in this settlement had broken all ties to other kin and other places from which they had migrated, which meant, Montgomery tells us, that the bonds linking parents and children in the settlement had become especially strong. Of overriding importance among these families was the duty of children to work to help support their families. Children did their best to fulfill this duty as soon as they were able, trying many different jobs, including begging. But none of these options earned very much. And so, sooner or later, children began working as prostitutes for wealthy foreign tourists who visited the resort. At the time of her research, 65 children in the community were working as prostitutes.

Children could earn five times as much money working as prostitutes as they could get from begging; plus they were able to visit fancy hotels and were well fed. Many of the clients, moreover, developed long-term relationships with the families of the child prostitutes, often lending them large sums of money—in one case, enough to rebuild the family home of one girl. It was friends and neighbours of the children, not their mothers, who recruited them into prostitution. When faced with the reality of the nature of their children's employment, mothers were able to claim that they had not found out until it was too late, and

In Their Own Words

AFN Praises Sharon McIvor on 6 October, First Nations Women's Day

AFN National Chief Phil Fontaine and AFN Women's Council Chair, Kathleen McHugh are calling on women across Canada to celebrate First Nations Women's Day by making donations to support 'one of the longest standing and important human rights cases in Canadian history'.

McIvor's case, which will be heard by the BC Court of Appeal on 14 October 2008, could restore the right to Indian Status to more than 30,000 First Nations women and children. Thousands of First Nations women and their children do not have the legal right to vote in band elections or to own or inherit property on reserves because of a clause in the Indian Act that continues to discriminate against First Nations women by removing their ability to pass Indian Status on to their children. The clause has existed in varying forms in the Indian Act since 1869.

Sharon McIvor, a descendant of the Lower Nicola Valley Band, first launched her case in 1989, hoping to win Indian Status for her own children. Shortly before her case reached the courts in 2006, the federal government agreed to restore status to McIvor's children.

'Sharon could have dropped the case at that point, once her own children were granted their rights. Instead she pushed forward on behalf of all First Nations women and children', says AFN Women's Council Chair, Kathleen McHugh. 'She is a true champion and heroine.'

McIvor has had trouble funding the case since October 2006, when the federal government cancelled the Court Challenges program. The government's decision came just after McIvor won her preliminary case in the BC Supreme Court, and just before the government decided to appeal her victory. The AFN Women's Council has led several fundraising events among chiefs to support McIvor's case.

'This is not only a First Nations issue, and it is not only a woman's issue. It's an issue of fairness and human rights that I believe all Canadians care about. Our preference always is to negotiate rather than litigate to achieve resolution. However, by choosing litigation the federal government denies our peoples the full expression of our fundamental human rights', said AFN National Chief Phil Fontaine.

Source: Assembly of First Nations. 2008. 'AFN Praises Sharon McIvor on 6 October, First Nations Women's Day', available at: <http://www.afn.ca/article.asp?id=4244>.

---

they interpreted the children's acts as evidence of their strong sense of filial duty in fulfilling obligations to help support the family. 'Both adult and child were aware of the child's duties, but there was a degree of unease about how far a child had to go to fulfill them' (Montgomery 2001: 90). The children claimed not to hate the men whom they worked for, especially those who kept in touch even when not in Thailand and who continued to send money to the children. Because of the financial generosity and long-term involvement of these men with their children, mothers said they felt the men were trustworthy. The actual sexual acts for which the children are paid take place outside the settlement and are never publicly discussed, and the obvious physical consequences for the children are, to a point, studiously ignored. On the basis of estimates

Map 13.2 Thailand

from UNICEF, between 60,000 and 200,000 Thai children are prostitutes, and HIV/AIDS is a serious and continuing issue.

Commercial sex and even child prostitution are not new in Thailand, but in recent years many Thais working in the media and for NGOs have denounced child sex tourism and have tried to force the national government to put a stop to it. Human rights discourse—particularly discourse about the rights of the child—have played a prominent role in this campaign (Figure 13.7). Montgomery points out that, since 1924, international bodies have issued nine separate documents dealing with human rights and the rights of the child. Children's rights, like human rights in general, are based on Western middle-class ideas about what constitutes an acceptable human childhood and on Western ideas of when childhood begins and ends. For example, the 1989 Convention on the Rights of the Child defines a child as anyone under 18 years of age, and Anti-slavery International has claimed that child-marriage is a form of slavery and therefore violates human rights. But as Montgomery observes, 'it does not take an anthropologist to recognize that a child marrying at 15 in full accordance with traditional norms and local custom in India is very different from a child marrying at 15 in the UK' (2001: 82). In common with other forms of human rights discourse, declarations on the rights of the child normally emphasize the importance of rights over duties, although this is not universal. But this is the issue that needs to be emphasized, Montgomery argues, in order to talk meaningfully about the rights of the children working as prostitutes in the Baan Nua slum.

The model of ideal Western childhood contained in the UN Convention on the Rights of the Child includes the idea that, as Montgomery puts it, 'every child has a right to a childhood that is free from the responsibilities of work, money, and sex' (83). The problem with this standard is that it fits so poorly with understandings of childhood in which, for example, children are expected (or needed) to work for money to support the family, and it seems unable to imagine situations in which the entire support of a family depends on a child's earnings from prostitution. Yet that is an accurate description for many families and children in Baan Nua.

Local Thai activists have been particularly interested in enforcing Article 34 of the Convention, which aims to protect children 'from all forms of sexual exploitation and sexual abuse' (Montgomery 2001:

Figure 13.7 Doctors without Borders runs a rehabilitation centre for child prostitutes in Thailand.

86). But the Convention also recognizes many other children's rights, including the notion that the child's best interests must always be kept uppermost and that they have a right to live with their families. The problem is that 'the assurance of one right often occurs at the expense of others. How these rights are prioritized is not culturally neutral' (85). 'Too often . . . Article 34 is quoted in isolation, decontextualizing sexual abuse and presenting it as the paramount difficulty that poor children face without linking it to global issues of poverty, cultural background, and discrimination' (86–7). The child's best interests are certainly compromised through prostitution, but they are also compromised when children are removed from their families and communities or when they have nothing to eat. This is particularly poignant in the case of the children of Baan Nua, many of whom claimed that they were not exploited, and all of whom were strongly motivated to engage in prostitution based on the cultural belief that children are obliged to support their parents. Montgomery concludes:

> By ensuring that their families could stay together and have a sustainable income, it would be possible to eradicate child prostitution without enforcing punitive measures against their parents. . . . Thailand's positions in globalized political and economic relations are as important as cultural specificities in perpetuating that sexual exploitation. . . . Article 34 would be redundant if the other rights enshrined in the convention . . . could be reliably enforced. (97–8)

The lesson of these and other examples suggest two important conclusions:

(1) it is possible to find ways of accommodating the universal discourse of human rights to the particularities of local conditions, and
(2) no single model of the relationship between rights and culture will fit all cases.

Moreover, as the culture of human rights becomes better established, it increasingly becomes enmeshed in political and legal institutions that go beyond the local level. As activists become more experienced operating in globalized circumstances, they are likely to become more sophisticated about making use of these different settings as they plan their human rights strategies

(Cowan et al. 2001: 21). Struggles over human rights are hardly likely to go away; indeed, along with struggles over global citizenship, they can be seen as the prime struggles of our time (Mignolo 2002). Anthropologists are well positioned to help make sense of these complex developments as they unfold.

Cultural Imperialism, Cultural Hybridization, and Cosmopolitanism

Cultural Imperialism or Cultural Hybridization?

The *impact* of the global spread of people, technology, wealth, images, and ideologies in local social settings has clearly been profound, as illustrated by the preceding examples. But how should anthropologists characterize the processes by which these changes have come about? One explanation, formulated during the Cold War debates about modernization and dependency, was in the concept of **cultural imperialism**. Cultural imperialism is based on two notions.

(1) The idea that some cultures dominate other cultures. In recent history, it is the culture(s) of Europe, or the US, or 'the West' that are seen to have come to dominate all other cultures of the world, due to the spread of colonialism and capitalism.
(2) The idea that cultural domination by one culture leads inevitably to the destruction of subordinated cultures and their replacement by the culture of those in power. Thus, Western cultural imperialism is seen as responsible for destroying, for example, local music, technology, dress, and food traditions and replacing them with rock and roll, radios, flashlights, cellphones, T-shirts, blue jeans, McDonald's hamburgers, and Coca-Cola.

cultural imperialism The idea that some cultures dominate other cultures and that cultural domination by one culture leads inevitably to the destruction of subordinated cultures and their replacement by the culture of those in power.

The inevitable outcome of Western cultural imperialism is seen to be 'the cultural homogenization of the world', with the unwelcome consequence of 'dooming the world to uniformity' (Inda and Rosaldo 2002: 13, 14).

The discourse of cultural imperialism developed primarily outside anthropology, but anthropologists could not ignore it because it purported to describe what was happening to the people they studied.

Anthropologists, too, were aware that Western music, fashion, food, and technology had spread among those they worked with. But cultural imperialism did not seem to be a satisfactory explanation for this spread for at least three reasons (Inda and Rosaldo 2002: 22–4).

(1) Cultural imperialism denies *agency* to non-Western peoples who make use of Western cultural forms. It assumes that they are passive

In Their Own Words

Past Wars, Present Dangers, Future Anthropologies

With the War on Terrorism, what of Native and minority populations and their aspirations for political justice? David Price questions the position of the Canadian government on the issues of who is defined as a terrorist.

It is imperative that anthropologists critically evaluate and speak out about the dangers the War on Terrorism will present to Native and minority populations around the world if the governments managing them and their lands are given a new international legitimacy to repress them as 'terrorists'. The United Nations' support for new anti-terrorist policies is helping to establish new forms of co-operation among member nations, yet these arrangements proceed with explicit agreement that terrorism shall remain strategically undefined. International human rights groups and even the German Foreign Ministry have raised concerns that these policies will usher in renewed state terrorism against minority populations. But for the most part these objections have been suppressed in the interest of the Western world's new unity of purpose.

There are signs that the US Secretary of State, Powell-the-coalition-builder, is purchasing the co-operation and approval of the world leaders by adopting policies whereby the United States will not protest or intervene when these states suppress or attack their own ethnic minority populations. As the United States signals President Putin that it can learn to see Russia's bloody war in Chechnya as part of the global War on Terrorism, this signal is welcomed by other world leaders hoping for a free hand to deal with domestic Indigenous troubles.

Anthropologists know that most of the world's nation-states are in internal conflict with one or more domestic groups contesting power relations; and these conflicts are frequently marked by violence and counter-violence. The idiom of power dictates that the violence of the state is legitimized as peace-keeping, while that of the dispossessed becomes terrorism. It is this hypocrisy that prevents the formation of a coherent behavioural definition of terrorism—and without such a definition the War on Terrorism must be viewed with informed skepticism.

Anthropologists also know that colonial powers and nation-states have long designated a wide range of cultural practices as terrorist threats. Historically, activities categorized as 'terrorism' have not been limited to acts of violence. The historical range of non-violent practices defined as terrorism includes certain forms of speech, teaching Native languages, and a wide range of religious or cultural ceremonies. North American examples of this include outlawed cultural and religious practices associated with resistance or non-assimilation such as the Ghost Dance, potlatch, peyote rituals, and lodge ceremonies. As terrorism remains undefined we are left to wonder if world leaders will be freely allowed to oppress their own minority populations for engaging in similar non-violent acts of rebellion.

There is a present danger of the wholesale categorization of people who resist domination as 'terrorists'—thereby sidestepping all issues that an in-depth cultural and historical analysis would raise. Whether it is the Basques in Spain, the Irish Catholics in Northern Ireland, the Tamils in Sri Lanka, Zapatistas in Mexico, Chechens in Russia, post-colonial wars of Africa smouldering along ethnic lines, or struggles of other excluded groups, there are contentious battles for power that will rapidly become even more lopsided if the currently ill-defined anti-terrorism campaign continues. . . .

Source: Price, David. 2002. 'Past Wars, Present Dangers, Future Anthropologies', *Anthropology Today* 18, 1 (Feb.): 3–5.

and without the resources to resist anything of Western origin that is marketed to them.

(2) Cultural imperialism assumes that non-Western cultural forms never move 'from the rest to the West'. But this is clearly false. Non-Western music and food and material culture have large and eager followings in western Europe and the US.

(3) Cultural imperialism ignores the fact that cultural forms and practices sometimes move from one part of the non-Western world to other parts of the non-Western world, bypassing the West entirely. Movies made in India have been popular for decades in northern Nigeria (Larkin 2002), Mexican soap operas have large followings in the Philippines, and karaoke is popular all over the world.

Cultural Hybridization

Dissatisfied with the discourse of cultural imperialism, anthropologists began to search for alternative ways of understanding global cultural flows. From the days of Boas and his students, anthropologists had not only recognized the significance of cultural borrowing but had emphasized that borrowing cultural forms or practices from elsewhere always involves *borrowing-with-modification*; that is, people never adopt blindly but always adapt what they borrow for local purposes. Put another way, people rarely accepted ideas or practices or objects from elsewhere without *domesticating* or *indigenizing* them—finding a way of reconciling them with local practices in order to serve local purposes. In the 1980s, for example, weavers in Otavalo, Ecuador, who were making a lot of money selling textiles to tourists, organized small production firms and purchased television sets to entertain their employees while they worked at their looms. In addition, some men had so much business that they encouraged their wives to take up weaving, even though women were not traditionally weavers. In order to spend more time weaving, women started to use indoor cookstoves, which relieved them from the time-consuming labour of traditional meal preparation over an open fire (Colloredo-Mansfeld 1999). From the perspective of anthropologist Rudi Colloredo-Mansfeld, these adoptions of items of Western technology could not be understood as the consequences of Western cultural imperialism because they clearly had nothing to do with trying to imitate a

Figure 13.8 Musical performance has become an important part of the Otavalo Indian economy, as musicians from Otavalo travel throughout the world performing and selling woven goods. They have domesticated CD production as well and have been quite successful in selling CDs of their music to tourists in Otavalo and to listeners abroad.

Western lifestyle. It made more sense to interpret these changes as Otavalan *domestication* or *indigenization* of televisions and cookstoves, since these items from elsewhere were adopted precisely in order to promote Indigenous Otavalan weaving. Put yet another way, borrowing-with-modification always involves *customizing* that which is borrowed to meet the purposes of the borrowers, which may be quite remote from the purposes of those among whom the form or practice originated (Inda and Rosaldo 2002: 16). This form of cultural change is very different from having something from elsewhere forced upon you against your will (Figure 13.8).

At the same time, it also is necessary to recognize that the consequences of borrowing-with-modification can never be fully controlled. Thus, Otavalan weavers may start watching television because local reruns of old American television series relieve the tedium of weaving, but once television-watching becomes a habitual practice, it also exposes them to advertising and news broadcasts, which may stimulate other local changes that nobody can predict. The domestication or indigenization of cultural forms from elsewhere makes it possible *both* to do old things in new ways *and* to do new things as well. Put another way, cultural borrowing is double-edged; borrowed cultural practices are both amenable to domestication and yet able to escape it. No wonder that cultural borrowing is often viewed with ambivalence. The challenges are particularly acute in globalizing conditions, colonial or postcolonial, where borrowed ideas, objects, or practices remain entangled in relationships with donors even as they are made to serve new goals by recipients (Thomas 1991). It is not surprising, therefore, that people in multicultural settings who must deal with tempting cultural alternatives emanating from more powerful groups regularly struggle to control processes of cultural borrowing and to contain domesticated cultural practices within certain contexts or in the hands of certain people.

Many social scientists have borrowed a metaphor from biology to describe this complex process of globalized cultural exchange and speak of *cultural hybridization* or *hybridity*. For example, sociologist Jan Nederveen Pieterse writes that 'Dependency theory may be read as a theory of structural hybridization in which dependent capitalism is a mélange category. . . . The contested notion of semi-periphery may also be viewed as a hybrid formation' (1995: 50–1). Anthropologist Ulf Hannerz, by contrast, objects to the 'biologistic' overtones of hybridity metaphors and prefers to borrow the concept of *creolization* from linguistics (see Chapter 4). 'Creolist concepts suggest that cultural mixture is not necessarily deviant, second-rate, unworthy of attention, matter out of place. . . . What is at the core of the concept of creole culture, I think, is a combination of diversity, interconnectedness, and innovation in the context of global centre-periphery relations' (1996: 66–7). Both cultural hybridization and creolization were meant to highlight forms of cultural borrowing that produced something new that could not be collapsed or subsumed, either within the culture of the donor or within the culture of the recipient. In addition, both terms stressed the positive side

of cultural mixing: rather than indicating a regrettable loss of original purity, hybridity and creolization draw attention to positive processes of cultural creativity.

The move from talk of dependency and cultural imperialism to talk about globalization and cultural hybridization is widely seen as a move from *modernist* discourse to *postmodernist* discourse. Modernist discourse embodies Enlightenment assumptions about rationality, science, progress, capitalism, and democracy. Postmodernist discourse calls all these Enlightenment assumptions into question. The 'writing against culture' movement in anthropology was a postmodernist critique of modernist social science assumptions that portrayed 'authentic' non-Western societies and cultures as bounded, orderly, and unchanging. Postmodernists argued, on the contrary, that all social and cultural borders were porous, and thus open to people, ideas, and practices from elsewhere. This postmodern position is not confined to academic contexts, but has had important implications regarding everyday cultural choices. For example, if hybridity is a normal part of all human social experience, then the idea that 'authentic' traditions never change can legitimately be challenged. For members of a social group who wish to revise or discard cultural practices that they find outmoded or oppressive, hybridity talk is liberating. Choosing to revise or discard, borrow or invent, *on terms of one's own choosing* also means that one possesses agency, the capacity to exercise at least some control over one's life. And exercising agency calls into question charges that one is succumbing to cultural imperialism or losing one's cultural 'authenticity'.

However, as anthropologist Nicholas Thomas puts it, 'hybridity is almost a good idea, but not quite' (1996: 9). Close examination of talk about cultural hybridization or creolization reveals at least three problems. First, it is not clear that either concept actually frees anthropologists from the modernist commitment to the existence of bounded, homogeneous, unchanging 'cultures'. That is, the idea of cultural **hybridity** is based on the notion of cultural mixing. But what is it that is mixed? Two or more non-hybridized, original, 'pure' cultures! But such 'pure' homogeneous, bounded, unchanging cultures are not supposed to exist. Thus we are caught in a paradox. For this reason Jonathan Friedman, among others, is highly critical of discussions of cultural hybridity; in his view, cultures have *always* been hybrid and it is the existence of *boundaries*, not cultural borrowing, that anthropologists need to explain. Besides, hybrid cultural mixtures often get transformed into new, unitary cultural identities. This process can be seen, he argues, in the way in which the 'mixed race' category in the US has been transformed into a 'new, unitary group of mixtures for those who feel 'disenfranchised' by the current single-race categories' (1997: 83). Friedman also points out that hybrid identities are not liberating when they are thrust upon people rather than being adopted freely. He draws attention to cases in Latin America where the 'mestizo' identity has been used 'as a middle-/upper-class tool' against Indigenous groups by '"creolizing" them from above': that is, criticizing their claims to a common Indian identity in order to undermine their sense of solidarity as members of a single group. 'We are all part-Indian, say members of the elite who have much to lose in the face of minority claims' (1997: 81–2).

These examples highlight a second difficulty with hybridity talk: those who celebrate cultural hybridization often ignore the fact that its effects are experienced differently by those with power and those without power. As Friedman says, 'the question of class becomes crucial' (1997: 81). The complexity of this issue is seen in many popular discussions of 'multiculturalism' that celebrate cultural hybridization and that, in the context of globalizing capitalism, turn hybridity into a marketable commodity. The commodification of hybridity is problematic because it smooths over differences in the experience of cultural hybridization, offering multiculturalism as an array of tempting consumables for outsiders. 'Multiculturalism is aimed at nourishing and perpetuating the kind of differences which do not [threaten]', writes Nira Yuval-Davis (1997: 197). International Folk Festivals, Festivals of Nations, and the like—events that emphasize costume, cuisine, music, and dance—spring to mind. But the troubling fact is that cultural hybridity is experienced as both non-threatening and very threatening, depending on the terms on which it is available. Because of power differences among groups challenged by cultural hybridization, any globalized 'multicultural' setting reveals active processes of cultural hybridization *together with* the defence of discrete cultural identities that seem to *resist* hybridization (Werbner 1997: 3). Cultural hybridization is

unobjectionable when actors perceive it to be under their own control, but cultural hybridization is resisted when it is 'perceived by actors themselves to be potentially threatening to their sense of moral integrity' (Werbner 1997: 12). The threat is greatest for those with the least power who feel unable to control forms of cultural hybridization that threaten to undermine the fragile survival structures on which they depend in an unwelcoming multicultural setting.

And this leads to a third problem with the concept of cultural hybridization. Fashionable hybridity talk hides the differences between elite and non-elite experiences of multiculturalism. Anthropologist John Hutnyk, for example, deplores the way 'world music' is marketed to middle-class consumers because such sales strategies divert attention 'from the urgency of anti-racist politics' (1997: 122). When cultural hybridization becomes fashionable, it easily turns the experiences of hybridized elites into a hegemonic standard, suggesting that class exploitation and racial oppression are easily overcome or no longer exist. But to dismiss or ignore continuing non-elite struggles with cultural hybridization can spark dangerous confrontations that can quickly spiral out of control.

Anthropologist Peter van der Veer argues that such a dynamic ignited the furor in Britain that followed the publication of Salmon Rushdie's novel *The Satanic Verses*. Rushdie is an elite, highly educated South Asian migrant to Britain who experienced cultural hybridity as a form of emancipation from oppressive religious and cultural restrictions. His novel contained passages describing Islam and the Prophet Muhammad that, from his elite point of view, embodied 'transgression' that was liberating. But migrants from South Asia in Britain are not all members of the elite. Most South Asian Muslim immigrants in Britain are workers, and they saw *The Satanic Verses* not as a work of artistic liberation but as a deliberate attempt to mock their beliefs and practices. 'These immigrants, who are already socially and culturally marginalized, are thus double marginalized in the name of an attack on "purity" and Islamic "fundamentalism"' (van der Veer 1997: 101–2). Even more important, however, may be the way popular interpretations of their objections in the press and among Western intellectuals ignored these immigrants'

hybridity Cultural mixing.

own, very different but very real, *non-elite* experiences of cultural hybridization. Van der Veer stresses that British Muslims who objected to the novel were

> not necessarily fundamentalists at all; their religious ideas are just as hybrid and syncretic as those of the author. They, too, are migrants, but the sources of their identity are authenticated not by profane literary texts but by what are to them sacred religious traditions. It is ironic, therefore, to find that migrants who are at the vanguard of political resistance to the assimilationist tendencies of the nation-state, who have their own cultural project for living hybrid cultural lives in a non-Islamic nation expressed, for example, in demand for state-funded Muslims schools or the extension of the blasphemy laws—are condemned, while the postmodernist hybrid novelist is celebrated by liberals and the state, extolled for his struggle against that very oppositional resistance, against the supposed 'backwardness' of the 'fundamentalist' British Muslim community. (1997: 102)

Put simply, elites experience cultural hybridization in ways that are often very different from the way non-elites experience cultural hybridization. We all ignore this fact at our peril.

From Cultural Hybridity to Cosmopolitanism

The era of globalization in which we live is an era of uncertainty and insecurity. Possibilities for emancipatory new ways of living are undercut by sharpening economic and political differences and the looming threat of violence. Is it possible, in the midst of all this confusion and conflict, to devise ways of coping with our circumstances that would provide guidance in the confusion or moderation to the conflict? No one expects such efforts to be easy. But anthropologists and other concerned scholars are currently struggling to come up with concepts and practices that might be helpful. Our era is not the first to have faced such challenges. Walter Mignolo argues that multiculturalism was born in the sixteenth century when Iberian conquest in the New World first raised troubling issues among Western thinkers about the kinds of relationships that were possible and desirable between the conquerors and the Indigenous peoples whom they had conquered. During the ensuing centuries, the challenges posed by a multicultural world did not disappear. In the context of eighteenth-century Enlightenment promises of

human emancipation based on the Rights of Man and the Citizen, philosopher Emmanuel Kant concluded that the achievements of the Enlightenment offered individuals new opportunities for developing ways of being at home in the world wherever they were.

To identify this orientation, he revived a concept that was first coined by the Stoic philosophers of ancient Rome: **cosmopolitanism** (Mignolo 2002). Kant's cosmopolitanism was firmly embedded within the values and practices of Enlightenment civilization, which meant, in the terms of our preceding discussion, that it was embedded in Western elite forms of cultural hybridization. That is, Kantian cosmopolitanism 'by and large meant being versed in Western ways, and the vision of "one world" culture was only a sometimes unconscious, sometimes unconscionable, euphemism for "First World" culture' (Abbas 2002: 210). To the extent that discussions of cosmopolitanism continue to focus on Western elites only, they would seem to offer little to anthropologists and others who are interested in finding a place for non-elite and non-Western experiences of cultural hybridization. Perhaps it is for this reason that Jonathan Friedman has written that those who celebrate their own cultural hybridity are simply 'all those who can afford a cosmopolitan identity' (1997: 81).

But is it possible to rework our understandings of cultural hybridity to stretch the notion of cosmopolitanism beyond its traditional association with privileged Western elites? Many anthropologists have become comfortable talking about 'alternative' or 'minority modernities' that depart from the western European norm. In a similar fashion, any new anthropological understanding of cosmopolitanism would have to be plural, not singular, and it would have to include non-elite experiences of cultural hybridization—'minoritarian' or 'discrepant' cosmopolitanisms—that reflect the experiences of those who have been the victims of modernity (Abu-Lughod 1991: 134; Breckenridge et al. 2002: 6, 8). The goal would be to develop new concepts and new skills enabling one to handle difficult cultural situations with grace 'by juggling with multiple perspectives' (Abbas 2002: 223), new ways of thinking 'beyond the local' or 'ways of living at home abroad or abroad at home—ways of inhabiting multiple places at once, of being different beings simultaneously, of seeing the larger picture stereoscopically with the smaller' (Breckenridge et al. 2002: 1, 10–11; see Figure 13.9).

Does anthropological talk about a world of 'cosmopolitanisms' offer any advantage over earlier anthropological talk about a world of 'cultures'? It might, if anthropologists can find a way to think about cultural hybridization (and resistance to hybridization) that moves beyond the current stalemate. Pnina Werbner suggests that this might be possible if we can think about cultural hybridization as a *process* rather than as a series of momentary, shocking 'transgressive' challenges that periodically disrupt the ongoing, tense stand-off among defenders of different cultural positions. Rather than assuming that all hybridity (or all resistance to hybridity) is the same—either all 'good' or all 'bad'—Werbner's approach would make it possible to distinguish *different processes* of cultural hybridization and cultural resistance. To illustrate, Werbner insists on distinguishing between cultural processes that lead to ethnicity and cultural processes that lead to racism (see Chapter 12). A processual theory of cultural hybridization 'must differentiate . . . between a politics that proceeds from the legitimacy of difference [ethnicity] and a politics that rests on coercive unity [racism]' and it 'must explain how and why cultural hybrids are still able to disturb and "shock" . . . in a postmodern world that celebrates difference' (Werbner 1997: 21). Previous anthropological work can suggest how such a processual analysis might proceed. For example, Victor Turner's analysis of rites of passage (see Chapter 6) demonstrated that 'liminality is itself structured processually . . . categories are exaggerated and caricatured *in order to be worked upon and reconfigured*. . . . By analogy we need to think . . . of the way discourses interact to create bridges or precipitate polarizing processes' (Werbner 1997: 21; emphasis added).

Werbner's approach to cultural hybridization as a process has much in common with what Walter Mignolo calls *border thinking*. That is, in a globalized world, concepts like 'democracy' and 'justice' can no longer be defined within a single Western logic—or, for that matter, from the perspective of the political left or the political right. Border thinking involves detaching these concepts from their hegemonic 'Western' meanings and practices, and using them as 'connectors', tools for imagining and negotiating new, cosmopolitan forms of democracy or justice informed by the ethical and political judgments of non-elites (Mignolo 2002: 179, 181). Finally, in re-imagining what cosmopolitanism might mean, it is important not only to go beyond

Figure 13.9 Cosmopolitanism is no longer only for Western elites. Otavalo Indian tourist José María Cotachaci, visiting the San Francisco Bay area, November 2000. Otavalos have created their own form of modernity.

Kantian limitations but also to go beyond standard anthropological orientations to other ways of life. An understanding of cosmopolitanism that is limited to being open to other cultures or to being inclusive—the traditional orientation of cultural relativism—is insufficient to cope with the challenges presented by a globalizing world. For one thing, 'Otherness has lost its innocence as a result of the colonial experience' (Abbas 2002: 226). For another, 'silenced and marginalized voices are bringing themselves into the conversation of cosmopolitan projects rather than waiting to be included' (Mignolo 2002: 174).

The hope is that border thinking can produce a *critical cosmopolitanism* capable of negotiating new understandings of human rights and global citizenship in ways that can dismantle barriers of gender and race that are the historical legacies of colonialism (Mignolo 2002: 161, 180). In many cases this may require seriously revising Western modernist ideas and practices, if that is the only honourable way of overcoming power differentials and threats to moral integrity experienced by non-elites. But because cosmopolitanism involves border thinking, this means that ideals and practices with Enlightenment credentials may also turn out to be valuable counterweights

cosmopolitanism Being at ease in more than one cultural setting.

to extremism and violence. This is apparent in the stance taken by those citizens of Bombay (Mumbai), India, who resist attempts by radical Hindus to banish Muslims from the city and to turn India into a Hindu state. Relationships between Hindus and Muslims in India took a severe turn for the worse after Hindu vandals destroyed a mosque in the city of Ayodhya in 1992. Appadurai, who has followed these developments closely, notes that the brutal Hindutva movement pushing to turn India into a Hindu state 'violates the ideals of secularism and inter-religious harmony enshrined in the constitution' (2002: 73–4). Appadurai writes of Indians from many walks of life, rich and poor, Muslim and Hindu, who have shown 'extraordinary displays of courage and critical imagination in Mumbai', who have 'held up powerful images of a cosmopolitan, secular, multicultural Bombay'. Their 'radical moderation' in resisting violent religious polarization is, he argues, neither naïve nor nostalgic: 'These utopian visions and critical practices are resolutely modernist in their visions of equity, justice, and cultural cosmopolitanism' (79). Secularism, as we saw in Chapter 7, is a notion with

impeccable Enlightenment credentials that arrived in India with British colonialism. And yet it is this 'situated secularism'—indigenized, customized, domesticated, *Indian* secularism, opposed to *Indian* inter-religious violence—that Appadurai and many other Indian citizens see as a key element of a form of local Indian cosmopolitanism that have been effective in preventing religious strife in the past and may be able to do so again.

Many of the cases in this chapter demonstrate the human ability to cope creatively with changed life circumstances. They remind us that human beings are not passive in the face of the new, that they actively and resiliently respond to life's challenges. Nevertheless, the example of the Panará reminds us that successful outcomes are never ensured. Modes of livelihood that may benefit some human groups can overwhelm and destroy others. Western capitalism and modern technology have exploded into a vortex of global forces that resist control. A critical cosmopolitanism involving concerted practical action to lessen violence and exploitation may be all that can prevent these forces from destroying us all.

Key Terms

core 326
cosmopolitanism 348
cultural imperialism 343
dependency theory 325
diaspora 331
flexible citizenship 333
globalization 327
human rights 335
hybridity 346
legal citizenship 333
long-distance nationalists 332

modernization theory 324
multiculturalism 335
periphery 326
post-national ethos 335
semi-periphery 326
substantive citizenship 333
transborder citizenry 332
transborder state 332
transnational nation-states 333
world-system theory 325

Chapter Summary

1. Anthropologists have made use of a variety of theoretical perspectives to explain the relationship between the West and the rest of the world. During the Cold War, anthropologists debated the relative merits of modernization theory and dependency theory. Later, they were influenced by world system theory, which divided the territories controlled by capitalism into core, periphery, and

semi-periphery and argued that the relationships between these regions had been established during the years when capitalism was first introduced outside Europe.

2. The end of the Cold War and the fall of communism led to a crisis in Marxian thought, and many of the tenets of modernization theory were revived in neo-liberal economic theory, which promised to bring prosperity to any nation-state to find its niche in the globalizing capitalist market.

3. Globalization is understood and evaluated differently by different observers, but most anthropologists agree that the effects of globalization are uneven. In a globalizing world, people, technology, wealth, images, and ideologies are de-territorialized. Some groups in some parts of the world benefit from global flows, contacts, and exchanges, whereas others are bypassed entirely.

4. Anthropologists and others disagree about whether these global processes are systemic or not or whether they are only the latest in a series of expansions and contractions that can be traced back to the rise of the first commercial civilizations several thousand years ago. But none of these overall schemas can, by itself, account for the historically specific local details of the effects of global forces in local settings, which is what most anthropologists aim to document and analyze.

5. The flows unleashed by globalization have undermined the ability of nation-states to police their boundaries effectively, suggesting that conventional ideas about nation-states require revision. Contemporary migrants across national borders have developed a variety of transborder identities. Some become involved in long-distance nationalism that leads to the emergence of transborder states claiming emigrants as transborder citizens of their ancestral homelands, even if they are legal citizens of another state. Some transborder citizenries call for the establishment of fully fledged transnational nation-states.

6. The contrasts between formal and substantive citizenship suggest that conventional notions of citizenship are breaking down in the context of globalization. Diaspora communities of elite Chinese families have developed a strategy of flexible citizenship that allows them to both circumvent and benefit from different nation-state regimes by investing, working, and settling their families in different sites. For these elite Chinese, the concept of nationalism has lost its meaning, and they seem to subscribe instead to a post-national ethos in which their only true loyalty is to the family business.

7. Discussions of human rights have intensified as global flows juxtapose and, at least implicitly, challenge different understandings of what it means to be human or what kinds of rights people may be entitled to under radically changed conditions of everyday life. But different participants in this discourse have different ideas about the relationship that human rights and culture have with one another. As talk about human rights becomes incorporated into local cultural discussions, the notion is transformed to make sense in local contexts. Sometimes, 'culture' may be used as a scapegoat for a government unwilling to extend certain rights to its citizens.

8. Some arguments about human rights include the right to one's culture. One of the key issues involved concerns the kinds of legal mechanisms needed to ensure such protection. But most international human rights documents only protect individual human rights, not group rights. And even those who seek to protect their individual rights are supposed to appeal to the governments of their own nation-states to enforce rights defended in international documents. Many activists, and others, view this factor as a serious contradiction in human rights discourse that undermines its effectiveness.

9. Some anthropologists argue that a 'culture of human rights' has emerged in recent years that is based on certain ideas about human beings, their needs, and their abilities that originated in the West. Some consider this culture of human rights to be the culture of a globalizing world that emphasizes individual rights over duties or needs and that proposes only technical rather than ethical solutions to human suffering. Anthropologists disagree about the value of such a culture of human rights in contemporary circumstances.

10. Groups and individuals who assert that their human rights have been violated regularly take their cases to courts of law. But because human rights

law only recognizes certain kinds of rights violations, groups with grievances must tailor those
grievances to fit the violations that human rights
law recognizes. Groups that enter into the human
rights process are entering into ethically ambiguous
territory that is both enabling and constraining.

11. Debates about children's rights in Thailand show
both that it is possible to accommodate the universal discourse of human rights to local conditions and that no single model of the relationship
between rights and culture will fit all cases.
Struggles over human rights, along with struggles
over global citizenship, can be seen as the prime
struggles of our time.

12. The discourse of cultural imperialism, which developed primarily outside anthropology, tried to
explain the spread of Western cultural forms outside the West. But anthropologists reject cultural
imperialism as an explanation because it denies
agency to non-Western peoples, because it assumes
that cultural forms never move 'from the rest to
the West', and because it ignores flows of cultural
forms that bypass the West entirely.

13. Anthropologists have developed alternatives to
the discourse of cultural imperialism. They speak
about borrowing-with-modification, domestication, indigenization, or customization of practices

or objects imported from elsewhere. Many anthropologists describe these processes as examples
of cultural hybridization or hybridity.

14. Talk of cultural hybridization has been criticized
because the very attempt to talk about cultural
mixtures assumes that 'pure' cultures existed prior
to mixing. Others object to discussions of cultural
hybridization that fail to recognize that its effects
are experienced differently by those with power
and those without power. Cultural hybridization
is unobjectionable when actors perceive it to be
under their own control but is resisted when they
see it threatening their moral integrity.

15. Some anthropologists are working to devise ways
of coping with the uncertainties and insecurities
of globalization. Some would like to revive the
notion of cosmopolitanism originally associated
with Western elite forms of cultural hybridization
and rework it in order to be able to speak about
alternative or discrepant cosmopolitanisms that
reflect the experiences of those who have been the
victims of modernity. The ideal end result would
be a critical cosmopolitanism capable of negotiating new understandings of human rights and
global citizenship in ways that can dismantle barriers of gender and race that are the historical legacies of colonialism.

Critical Thinking Questions

1. Are national boundaries being challenged by the
ubiquitous and non-censorable nature of the
Internet? How and to what possible ends?

2. What are some of the ways elites and non-elites
experience cultural hybridization in different
ways? Why do you suppose there are differences?

3. What do you consider some of the key factors in the
local variations on the acceptance of globalization?

4. How would you compare and contrast formal and
substantive citizenship?

5. What would you consider the main factor(s) in the
emergence of globalization?

Suggested Readings

Barber, Benjamin R. 1995. *Jihad versus McWorld: How Globalism
and Tribalism Are Reshaping the World* (New York: Times
Books). *This book examines the basis for the misunderstanding
between the Muslim world and the capitalist Western world.*

Dyck, Noel, and James B. Waldram. 1993. *Anthropology, Public
Policy, and Native Peoples in Canada* (Montreal and Kingston:
McGill-Queen's University Press). *A comprehensive review of
governmental policy issues and the present conditions experienced
by First Nations peoples.*

Fischer, Michael M.J. 1999. 'Emergent Forms of Life: Anthropologies of Late or Postmodernities', *Annual Review of Anthropology*
28: 455–78. *Three key overlapping arenas of attention are the centrality of science and technology; decolonization, post-colonialism,
and the reconstruction of societies after social trauma; and the
role of the new electronic and visual media. In this context, how
do we write various genres of anthropology?*

Hobart, Mark, ed. 1993. *An Anthropological Critique of Development* (London: Routledge). *Anthropologists from Britain, Holland,*

and Germany challenge the notion that Western approaches to development have been successful. They use ethnographic case studies to demonstrate how Western experts who disregard Indigenous knowledge contribute to the growth of ignorance.

Inda, Jonathan Xavier, and Renato Rosaldo, eds. 2002. *The Anthropology of Globalization: A Reader* (Malden, MA: Blackwell). *A recent, comprehensive collection of articles by anthropologists who address the process of globalization from varied points of view and different ethnographic situations.*

Jenkins, Janis H. 1998. 'The Medical Anthropology of Political Violence: A Cultural and Feminist Agenda', *Medical Anthropology Quarterly* 12, 1 (Mar.): 122–31. *The examination of political violence and warfare has become important in the theoretical and empirical exchanges in medical anthropology. This article explores these issues.*

Márquez, Gabriel García. 1998. *One Hundred Years of Solitude* (New York: HarperCollins). *Noble Prize winning author Márquez chronicles the history of a family and their fictional town of Macondo. The story spans one hundred years, more or less, but its style of magic realism created a time that emphasizes the fact that in the life of humans, time has a nebulous quality—it lapses, repeats, speeds up, and can even stop altogether.*

Merry, Sally Engle. 1992. 'Anthropology, Law, and Transnational Processes', *Annual Review of Anthropology* 21: 357–79. *In the context of globalization, colonialism, and post-colonialism, power disparities are formed that require interpretation through transnational legal processes. This paper discusses anthropology's place in the process.*

Murray, David A.B. 2000. 'Between a Rock and a Hard Place: The Power and Powerlessness of Transnational Narratives among Gay Martinican Men', *American Anthropologist* 102, 2 (June): 261–70. *Murray argues that Quebec is signified as utopic in specific gay narratives in terms that are antithetical and therefore profoundly connected to impressions of social life in France and Martinique.*

No'eau Warner, Sam L. 1999. '"Kuleana": The Right, Responsibility, and Authority of Indigenous Peoples to Speak and Make Decisions for Themselves in Language and Cultural Revitalization', *Anthropology & Education Quarterly* 30, 1 (Mar.): 68–93. *This paper addresses the issue of Hawaiian language revitalization becoming highly politicized by non-Indigenous Hawaiian language educators. This is characterized as colonization of the field in an attempt to control specific resources.*

Rigney, Lester-Irabinna. 1999. 'Internationalization of an Indigenous Anti-colonial Cultural Critique of Research Methodologies: A Guide to Indigenist Research Methodology and Its Principles', *Wicazo Sa Review* 14, 2, (fall): 109–21. *The author states: 'Indigenous peoples' interests, knowledge, and experiences must be at the centre of research methodologies and construction of knowledge about Indigenous peoples'.*

Shand, Peter. 2000. 'Can Copyright Be Reconciled with First Nations' Interests in Visual Arts?', paper presented at Protecting Knowledge: Traditional Resource Rights in the New Millennium, organized by the Union of BC Indian Chiefs, Feb., University of British Columbia, Vancouver. *This paper looks at the interaction and cross-influences of Indigenous peoples' rights, the visual arts, intellectual property, and concepts of cultural authenticity.*

Wallerstein, Immanuel. 1974. *The Modern World System* (New York: Academic Press). *A difficult but tremendously influential work that started the world-system approach to understanding and explaining patterns of social change in recent world history.*

Wolf, Eric. 1999 [1969]. *Peasant Wars of the Twentieth Century* (Norman: University of Oklahoma Press). *An important, readable study of the commonalities of last century's major wars of revolution.*

Related Websites

AIDS Portal: http://www.aidsportal.org/overlay_details. aspx?nex=91&gclid=CI_FydmqqpgCFShRagodbD3oYw

Arjun Appadurai: http://www.appadurai.com/homebio.htm

Conservation International: http://www.conservation.org/Pages/default.aspx

Cultural Appropriation: http://copycamp.ca/self-organized-sessions-appropriation-of-aboriginal-culture-and-traditional-knowledge

Did You Know: http://www.youtube.com/watch?v=jpEnfwiqdx8&feature=related

Division for the Advancement of Women (DAW): http://www.un.org/womenwatch/daw/daw/index.html

Doctor's without Borders: http://www.doctorswithoutborders.org/

International Bureau for Children's Rights: http://www.ibcr.org/Publications/CRC/Draft_CP_Asia/ThailandPDF.pdf

International Women's Right Project (IWRP): http://www.iwrp.org/cedaw.htm

Native Planet: http://www.nativeplanet.org/indigenous/ethnicdiversity/latinamerica/brazil/indigenous_data_brazil_kayapo.shtml

SIL International: http://www.sil.org/americas/brasil/langpage/englkppg.htm

UNAIDS: http://www.unaids.org/en/KnowledgeCentre/HIVData/EpiUpdate/EpiUpdArchive/2007/default.asp

UNICEF: http://www.unicef.org/infobycountry/Thailand.html

Women Activities & Social Services Association: http://www.counterpart-afg.org/wassa.html

Chapter 14

Applying Anthropology in Everyday Life

Chapter Outline

- Learning Objectives
- Anthropology beyond the University
- Anthropology and the Challenges of Global Citizenship
- Awareness and Uncertainty

- Freedom and Constraint
- Chapter Summary
- Critical Thinking Questions
- Suggested Readings
- Related Websites

Learning Objectives

By the end of Chapter 14, you will be able to:

- understand that anthropology is not all about the academy,
- appreciate anthropology as a portal to effective global citizenship,

- consider the world of uncertainty and the awareness needed to confront it (reflexivity), and
- challenge views on freedom and constraint.

How do the narratives of men and women of diverse cultures inform us in today's world? How do these stories find a place in the practice of anthropology? The answers are found in relatively recent developments in cultural anthropology—applied anthropology and medical anthropology (very much an applied form itself). In this chapter, we examine some of the ramifications of seeing anthropology as an 'action' social science in the examination of modern issues in a 'global' world made up of a multitude of local traditions. And as students of anthropology, regardless of the depth of our involvement in the study, we can find personal answers to our place as global citizens.

Anthropology beyond the University

Why study anthropology? The appropriate response usually comes in three parts. The first part addresses the practical concern.

Do anthropologists do anything other than teach at universities? The answer is 'yes'. Today, anthropologists can be found in all sorts of areas, many in the area now called *applied anthropology*. A few are psychotherapists, employing the insights of anthropologist Gregory Bateson and others on family systems and family therapy. Others are cross-cultural social workers. Still others are actively involved in international development, sometimes working with various development agencies. Such work can include projects dealing with issues such as appropriate technology, fuelwood shortages, potable water sources, agricultural and micro-credit (that began with the work of Nobel

Peace Prize winner Professor Muhammad Yunus and his Grameen Bank), new lands development, feasibility studies for dams and other projects, bilingual education, livestock improvement and range management, and the like (for more examples, see Partridge 1984; van Willigen 1991).

Other anthropologists are in medical anthropology, a growing field of research and applied results. Investigations of traditional medical practices are defining traditional identities. (Note Hugo De Burgos, *In Their Own Words*, in Chapter 12.) Discussions of medical ethics are seen in the work of researchers such as Margaret Lock; for example, in her discussion of medicalization and resistance (2001), she considers *moral economy* and biomedical 'cultures':

Recognition of moral economies permits us to pose questions about scientific knowledge, its production and application, and its methods of relegating other methodologies, including ethnography, to the sidelines. Ethnography makes it possible to examine the way in which scientific knowledge is selectively deployed in different global contexts by drawing on morals and value systems that are historically, politically, and culturally informed. . . . By researching boundary objects, hybrids of nature and culture, and techno-human complexes, insights about scientific 'work' that is needed to sustain beliefs in neutrality, objectivity, and progress become apparent. Here medical anthropologists join forces with historians and sociologists of science to tackle some of the most pressing questions of our day involving moral conundrums requiring debate. . . . For several years now, anthropology has been going through the culture wars, with opponents arguing for and against the worth of culture as a concept. I find culture (used reflexively and in conjunction with a political/economy framework) a necessary concept for most research projects, especially when culture is explicitly made to do work by the particular people or institutions that one is studying. (488)

Of particular interest here are the health and well-being of women and children in a world where pre-natal care, general nutrition, access to clean water and immunization programs are patchy while diseases like malaria and HIV are rampant (Figure 14.1). A number of anthropologists are involved in issues of aging and gerontology, designing programs for the elderly and doing research on aging in different cultures. Others work in public or community health, medical education, nursing, or hospital planning. Another important area of work is in medical care delivery to distinct ethnic groups. This is related to applied anthropological work in international health, which includes demographics, epidemiology, planning and development of health programs, family planning, environmental health, and the like. Many applied anthropologists are also working on AIDS-related projects. Consider Holly Wardlow's work on HIV infections in rural Papua New Guinea. It provides an excellent example of such research involvement where her site-specific observations have wider implications. She notes that 'married women are at risk for HIV primarily because of their husbands'

extramarital sexual liaisons, and wives have little control over this risk, which is not lessened by their own fidelity . . . the dynamics of marital HIV transmission (are embedded in) economic, social, and cultural factors that propel and structure men's extramarital sexuality' (2007: 1006). Thus the local is global!

Some anthropologists have gone into public policy and planning as interpreters, mediators, civil servants, or urban planners. Others have begun to work with Indigenous peoples' organizations or with human rights organizations such as Survival International and Cultural Survival. We examine three cases below in greater detail.

Sorghum and Millet in Honduras and the Sudan

Applied anthropologists carry out much work in international development, often in agricultural programs. The US Agency for International Development (USAID) is the principal instrument of US foreign development assistance. One new direction taken by USAID in the mid-1970s was to create multidisciplinary research programs to improve food crops in developing countries. An early research program dealt with sorghum and millet, important grains in some of the poorest countries in the world (Figure 14.2). This was the International Sorghum/Millet Research Project (INTSORMIL). Selected American universities investigated one of six areas: plant breeding, agronomy, plant pathology, plant physiology, food chemistry, and socio-economic studies.

Anthropologists from the University of Kentucky, selected for the socio-economic study, used ethnographic field research techniques to gain first-hand knowledge of the socio-economic constraints on the production, distribution, and consumption of sorghum and millet among limited-resource agricultural producers in the western Sudan and in Honduras. They intended to make their findings available to INTSORMIL as well as to scientists and government officials in the host countries. They believed sharing such knowledge could lead to more effective research and development. This task also required ethnographic research and anthropological skill.

The principal investigators from the University of Kentucky were Edward Reeves, Bill DeWalt, and Katherine DeWalt. They took a holistic and comparative approach, called Farming Systems Research (FSR).

Figure 14.1 Medical anthropologist Andrea Wiley (left) in the Himalayas of Ladakh (India) where she studied maternal and child health.

In Their Own Words

What Can You Learn from an Anthropology Major?

The Career Development Center at SUNY *Plattsburgh developed a document that highlights what students typically learn from a major in anthropology.*

1. Social agility

In an unfamiliar social or career-related setting, you learn to quickly size up the rules of the game. You can become accepted more quickly than you could without this anthropological skill.

2. Observation

You must often learn about a culture from within it, so you learn how to interview and observe as a participant.

3. Analysis and planning

You learn how to find patterns in the behaviour of a cultural group. This awareness of patterns allows you to generalize about the group's behaviour and predict what they might do in a given situation.

4. Social sensitivity

Although other people's ways of doing things may be different from your own, you learn the importance of events and conditions that have contributed to this difference. You also recognize that other cultures view your ways as strange. You learn the value of behaving toward others with appropriate preparation, care, and understanding.

5. Accuracy in interpreting behaviour

You become familiar with the range of behaviour in different cultures. You learn how to look at cultural causes of behaviour before assigning causes yourself.

6. Ability to appropriately challenge conclusions

You learn that analyses of human behaviour are open to challenge. You learn how to use new knowledge to test past conclusions.

7. Insightful interpretation of information

You learn how to use data collected by others, reorganizing or interpreting the data to reach original conclusions.

8. Simplification of information

Because anthropology is conducted among publics as well as about them, you learn how to simplify technical information for communication to non-technical people.

9. Contextualization

Although attention to details is a trait of anthropology, you learn that any given detail might not be as important as its context and can even be misleading when the context is ignored.

10. Problem solving

Because you often function within a cultural group or act on culturally sensitive issues, you learn to approach problems with care. Before acting, you identify the problem, set your goals, decide on the actions you will take, and calculate possible effects on other people.

11. Persuasive writing

Anthropologists strive to represent the behaviour of one group to another group and continually need to engage in interpretation. You learn the value of bringing someone else to share—or at least understand—your view through written argument.

12. Assumption of a social perspective

You learn how to perceive the acts of individuals and local groups as both shaping and being shaped by larger socio-cultural systems. The perception enables you to 'act locally and think globally'.

Source: Omohundro, John. 2000. 'What Can You Learn from an Anthropology Major?', in *Careers in Anthropology* (New York: McGraw-Hill).

This approach attempts to determine the techniques used by farmers with limited resources to cope with the social, economic, and ecological conditions under which they live. FSR is holistic because it examines how the different crops and livestock are integrated and managed as a system. It also relates farm productivity to household consumption and off-farm sources of family income (Reeves, DeWalt, and DeWalt 1987: 74). This is very different from the traditional methods of agricultural research, which grow and test one crop at a time in an experiment station. The scientists at INTSORMIL are generally acknowledged among the best sorghum and millet researchers in the world, but their expertise comes from traditional agricultural research methods.

Figure 14.2 INTSORMIL has been involved in the improvement of the cultivation of sorghum, shown here, and millet.

They have spent little time working on the problems of limited-resource farmers in Third World countries.

The anthropologists saw their job as facilitating 'a constant dialogue between the farmer, who can tell what works best given the circumstances, and agricultural scientists, who produce potentially useful new solutions to old problems' (Reeves, DeWalt, and DeWalt 1987: 74–5). However, this was easier said than done in the sorghum/millet project. The perspectives of farmers and scientists were very different from one another. The anthropologists found themselves having to learn the languages and the conceptual systems of both the farmers and the scientists for the two groups to be able to communicate. The FSR anthropologists had four research goals:

(1) to discover what was holding back the increased production of sorghum and millet so that they could identify areas that needed attention from the agricultural researchers;

(2) to discover which aspects of new technology the farmers thought might benefit them the most;

(3) to suggest how new crop 'varieties and/or technologies might most easily and beneficially be introduced into communities and regions'; and

(4) '[t]o suggest the long-term implications that changing production, distribution, and consumption patterns might have on these communities' (1987: 74).

The anthropologists began research in June 1981 in western Sudan and in southern Honduras. They were in the field for 14 months of participant-observation and in-depth interviewing, as well as survey interviewing of limited-resource farmers, merchants, and middlemen. They discovered that the most significant constraints the farmers faced were uncertain rainfall, low soil fertility, and inadequate labour and financial resources (Reeves, DeWalt, and DeWalt 1987: 80). Equally important were the social and cultural systems within which the farmers were embedded. Farmers based their farming decisions on their understanding of who they were and what farming meant in their own cultures.

As a result of the FSR group's research, it became increasingly clear that 'real progress in addressing the needs of small farmers in the Third World called for promising innovations to be tested at village sites and on farmers' fields under conditions that closely approximated those which the farmers experience' (Reeves, DeWalt, and DeWalt 1987: 77). Convincing the scientists and bureaucrats of this required the anthropologists to become advocates for the limited-resource farmers. Bill DeWalt and Edward Reeves ended up negotiating INTSORMIL's contracts with the Honduran and Sudanese governments and succeeded in representing the farmers. They had to learn enough about the bureaucracies and the agricultural scientists so they could put the farmers' interests in terms the others could understand.

As a result of the applied anthropologists' work, INTSORMIL scientists learned to understand how small farmers in two countries made agricultural decisions. They also learned that not all limited-resource farmers are alike. The poorest third of the Sudanese farmers, for example, have to decide during the cropping season whether to weed their own gardens or someone else's for a wage. If they choose the former, they realize a long-term gain but they and their families go hungry. The latter choice enables them to buy food in the short run but lowers their own harvests later. The decisions farmers make, and the needs they have, are context-sensitive.

Together with INTSORMIL, the Honduran and Sudanese governments have increased funding for projects aimed at limited-resource farmers. Staff have been assigned to work with INTSORMIL, new programs have begun, and the research results of the anthropologists are guiding the breeding of sorghum.

Reeves, DeWalt, and DeWalt warn that it is too early to demonstrate gains in sorghum or millet production and use in either country.

> Nevertheless, INTSORMIL scientists are clearly coming to accept the farming systems research goals and the value of anthropological fieldwork. The FSR group has argued that on-site research is both desirable and necessary for the problems of farmers to be correctly identified and that eventually on-farm testing of new plant varieties and technologies will be essential to ensure that farmers are going to accept them. (1987: 79)

The INTSORMIL staff was so impressed by the anthropologists' work that it has begun funding long-term research directed at relieving the constraints that limited-resource farmers face. Rather than trying to develop and then introduce hybrids, INTSORMIL research is now aimed at modifying existing varieties of sorghum. The goal is better-yielding local varieties that can be grown together with other crops.

In summary, Reeves, DeWalt, and DeWalt point out that without the anthropological research, fewer development funds would have been allocated to research in Sudan and Honduras. More important, the nature of the development aid would have been different.

Doing Business in Japan

Anthropologist Richard Reeves-Ellington (1993) designed and implemented a cross-cultural training program for a North American company doing business in Japan (see Map 14.1). He found that many of the traditional methods of anthropology—cultural

understanding, ethnographic data, and participant-observation—helped managers conduct business in Japan. Reeves-Ellington began the training program by having employees first gather general cultural information artifacts ('How are things classified? What are the artifacts of an agreed classification system?'), social knowledge ('What are proper principles for behaviour? What are the values that drive the categories and artifacts?'), and cultural logic. Social knowledge or values are based on an underlying, taken-for-granted cultural logic. Coming to understand Japanese cultural logic is of great importance to foreigners wishing to live and work in Japan.

The managers at the company decided to learn how to carry out introductions, meetings, leave-taking, dinner, and drinking in Japan. Each practice was analyzed according to the framework of artifacts, social knowledge, and cultural logic and was taught by a combination of methods that included the general observations that the managers collected while visiting Japanese museums, theatres, shrines, baseball games, and business meetings. The managers analyzed these observations and discussed stories that show how badly things can go when cultural knowledge is not sufficient. For example, one thing Reeves-Ellington's students needed to learn about introductions involved the presentation of the business card (*meishi*). The proper presentation and use of the *meishi* is the central element in the practice of making introductions at business meetings. Reeves-Ellington explained that,

Map 14.1 Japan

to a Japanese business person, the *meishi* is an extension of the self. Damage to the card is damage to the individual. Therefore, mistreatment of a *meishi* will ruin a relationship. Reeves-Ellington notes that his colleagues did not fully appreciate the consequences of these beliefs until he told them a story:

> A major US company was having problems with one of its distributors, and the parties seemed unable to resolve their differences. The president of the US company decided to visit Japan, meet with his counterpart in the wholesaler organization, and attempt to resolve their differences. The two had not met previously and, upon meeting, each followed proper *meishi* ritual. The American, however, did not put the Japanese counterpart's *meishi* on the table; instead he held on to it. As the conversation became heated, the American rolled up the *meishi* in his hand. Horror was recorded on the face of the Japanese businessman. The American then tore the *meishi* into bits. This was more than the Japanese could stand; he excused himself from the meeting. Shortly afterward the two companies stopped doing business with each other. (1993: 209)

Table 14.1 shows the information regarding introductions and the use of the *meishi* that Reeves-Ellington's students derived from their work based on their analytic framework of artifacts, social knowledge, and cultural logic.

On three critical measures—effective working relationships with Japanese executives, shortened project times, and improved financial returns—the anthropologically based training program that Reeves-Ellington designed was a success. Both employees and their Japanese counterparts felt more comfortable working with each other. Prior to the program, joint projects required an average of 15 months to complete; projects run by executives applying the methodologies of the program cut completion time to an average of eight months. Financial returns based on contracts negotiated by personnel who had not participated in the program averaged gross income of 6 per cent of sales, whereas those negotiated by personnel applying the anthropological techniques averaged gross income equal to 18 per cent of sales.

Urban Social Planning and Restructuring in Canada

Alexander Ervin is an anthropologist in Saskatoon, Saskatchewan, in Canada, who has had considerable experience in collaborative, community-based research in social service and health agencies (Figure 14.3; see also EthnoProfile 14.1: Saskatoon). In his view, anthropologists seem to be particularly well-suited for this kind of applied work since they 'have been trained conceptually and methodologically to seek linkages among

Table 14.1 Introductions at Business Meetings

Artifacts	Social knowledge	Cultural logic
Technology • Business cards. • *Meishi*. Visual behaviour • Presentation of *meishi* by presenting card, facing recipient. • Senior people present *meishi* first. • Guest presents first, giving name, company affiliation, and bowing. • Host presents *meishi* in same sequence. • Upon sitting at conference table, all *meishi* are placed in front of recipient to assure name use.	• Once given a card is kept—not discarded. • *Meishi* are not exchanged a second time unless there is a position change. • Before the next meeting between parties, the *meishi* are reviewed for familiarization with the people attending the meeting. • The *meishi* provides status for the owner.	Human relations • *Meishi* provide understanding of appropriate relations between parties. • *Meishi* take uncertainty out of relationships. Environment • *Meishi* help establish insider/outsider environment. • *Meishi* help establish possible obligations to environment. Human activity • *Meishi* help to establish human activities.

Source: Reeves-Ellington, Richard H. 1993. 'Using Cultural Skills for Co-operative Advantage in Japan', *Human Organization* 52, 2: 203–16.

behaviours, institutions, and values, and to attempt to construct integrated overviews of whatever is the phenomenon under investigation' (1996: 324). As government policy-makers move to cut costs by downsizing, few policy disciplines are able to provide information about how the different social service providers and their services fit together, nor are they able to listen effectively to grassroots perceptions of issues, needs, and solutions. Anthropologists, however, are trained to do precisely these things.

To illustrate, Ervin discusses his work with the Saskatoon Social Planning Council. The council was established in 1992 with a push from activists from the approximately 200 human service delivery organizations in Saskatoon. In Canada, social planning councils focus attention on local social issues. They are involved with an extremely wide range of policies and issues and carry out policy research, including needs assessment, program evaluations, and problem-focused investigations. Ervin's main task has been to design a plan for an annual investigation of a specific policy domain or issue to be carried out by the council. The goal of the

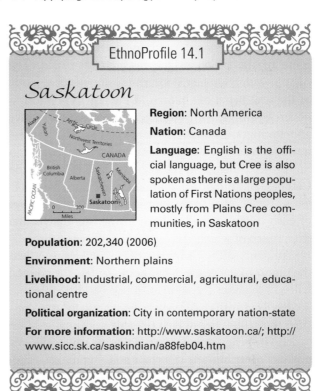

EthnoProfile 14.1

Saskatoon

Region: North America

Nation: Canada

Language: English is the official language, but Cree is also spoken as there is a large population of First Nations peoples, mostly from Plains Cree communities, in Saskatoon

Population: 202,340 (2006)

Environment: Northern plains

Livelihood: Industrial, commercial, agricultural, educational centre

Political organization: City in contemporary nation-state

For more information: http://www.saskatoon.ca/; http://www.sicc.sk.ca/saskindian/a88feb04.htm

Figure 14.3 Saskatoon's University Bridge, also called the 25th Street Bridge, provides access to the University of Saskatchewan. The 'Bridge City' is also home to numerous colleges and research institutes affiliated with the University and the Saskatchewan Institute of Applied Science and Technology.

research would be to provide the data that the human service organizations could use to solve effectively some of the problems the research identified. The pilot investigation has been a multi-dimensional study of the well-being of children in the city in relation to poverty, hunger, recreation, education, family, Native and immigrant issues, substance abuse, and general health concerns. Several organizations collaborated in the project, including the regional health board, the Catholic and public school boards, and the social services district office. A working group of representatives of each organization has been formed to analyze the data, much of which was collected by three anthropology students at the University of Saskatchewan. When the report of the research has been written, the council will call together those organizations and people that are involved with children's issues in Saskatoon to consider the results and discuss possible solutions.

Ervin believes that anthropologists can make important contributions in urban policy contexts, especially in needs assessment, 'the process of identifying and seeking solutions to problems of particular populations, irrespective of whether programs have already been designed to address them' (330). Anthropologists seem particularly well placed for these projects, given their commitment to participatory research and holism. Indeed, from his point of view, the major need in the kinds of urban policy research that he has been engaged in is for flexible generalists—anthropologists who can move from one policy domain to another and construct integrated overviews of the phenomenon under investigation.

Anthropology and Policy

In all this work—and there is much more—the anthropological perspective illustrated throughout this text has been employed. Applied anthropologists do their work using holism, comparison, relativism, and a concern for particular cases.

Nevertheless, anthropologists are hesitant to make detailed policy recommendations that other professional disciplines make. This may be because anthropologists are particularly aware of the problems in applied work, the problems in trying to make people, or systems, change. Anthropologists are trained to analyze social and cultural systems, but when they are asked how to change them, they begin to ask questions.

These questions are based on an awareness of the enormous complexity of human life when it is viewed from ground level. Anthropologists have developed a keen awareness that not everyone makes the same basic assumptions about the world that planners and officials make. They know that sometimes technical experts providing help in other cultures know less than the people they are advising or give advice that is culturally inappropriate. Anthropologists realize that no change benefits everyone equally and that some gain as others lose. They also understand that even if they get involved in planning a program, implementation depends on external factors over which they have no control: cash flow problems to government agencies, fear over a legislator's response, political issues, elections, budget reductions, lack of interest, and so on.

Anthropologists believe they have much to contribute in helping build a better world, yet they are also highly sensitive to the kinds of issues that arise when dealing with the complex human systems we have discussed throughout this text. Applied anthropologists are well aware of the ambiguities of the human experience.

Anthropology and the Challenges of Global Citizenship

Not everyone who studies anthropology, of course, goes on to work as an anthropologist. One of the challenges faced by people everywhere in the world at the beginning of the twenty-first century is that of citizenship in a complex, diverse, and difficult world. Can anthropologists provide ways for people to understand the issues involved?

Anthropology and Democracy

As we saw in the previous chapter, the end of the Cold War appears to have marked a turning point in the world system. The capitalist market has spread into all parts of the globe, and many observers have assumed that other Western institutions are bound to follow. The fall of dictatorial political regimes in a number of Latin American and central European countries, for example, was viewed as an opportunity to introduce Western political practices, including political parties and formal elections. Many members of the Western political and economic elite eagerly proclaimed the arrival of democracy as soon as the first elections were held and have often been very suspicious of political movements—such as some of the new social movements we described in the previous chapter—that challenge formal electoral institutions in the name of democracy.

But anthropologists and other social scientists working in these same countries are often able to present a different perspective on the 'transition' to democracy. Fieldwork brings them into close, regular contact with citizens who have their own ideas about what kinds of social institutions do or do not operate in a democratic fashion. Taking these observations seriously has drawn anthropologists into a growing debate about what democracy has been and can be. In particular, their work has helped to show that formal Western electoral politics may produce less democratic outcomes than other, traditional institutions.

For example, anthropologist Serge Tcherkézoff (1998) has followed debates about the shape democracy ought to take in the independent nation of Samoa (see EthnoProfile 4.1: Samoa). Traditionally, Samoa has been a land of villages, each of which was governed by a council of *matai*, or 'sacred chiefs'. This system had survived Christian missionaries, German colonization, and the effects of 42 years as a protectorate of New Zealand. A referendum sponsored by the UN in 1962 led to independence, and the people of what was called Western Samoa, until 1997, then voted to set up a parliamentary system of national government (Figure 14.4). However, their constitution specified that only *matai* could vote and run for office. In 1990, the law was changed to allow all citizens to vote, but *matai* were still the only ones allowed to run for office.

Does this hybrid of Western parliamentary system and the Samoan *faamatai*, or 'chief-system', represent an undemocratic attempt by chiefly 'aristocrats' to maintain power within formally democratic political institutions? In Tcherkézoff's opinion, the question is deeply misleading because it rests on a fundamental misunderstanding of how the Samoan chief-system functions. He points out that if outsiders insist on thinking of *matai* as aristocrats then there are no families in Samoa who are not aristocratic. This is because each *matai* is actually the head of an extended family. Each extended family is held together by kinship connections, joint ownership of land, and joint participation

Figure 14.4 The parliament building in Samoa. Today, Samoans are taking part in a debate that involves a variety of ideas about what democracy means and what kinds of institutional arrangements are most likely to ensure it.

in rituals directed to their founding ancestor. *Matai*, in fact, means 'the one who bears the family name', and members of each extended family choose the person who will be ritually invested with this title. It is the job of each *matai* to serve his family and his *matai* name by leading worship directed to the ancestor and engaging in other activities designed to elevate the reputation of his extended family. If a *matai* fails to live up to these expectations, his extended family can strip him of his title and give it to someone else. Every family has a *matai*, which is why Tcherkézoff says that there are no families that are not chiefly families; and *matais* serve at the will of the kin who choose them, which is why, he tells us, 'when Samoans heard about "democracy", they said that they "already have it"' (1998: 423).

So why are Samoans arguing about the connection between the *matai* system and democracy? As Tcherkézoff explains, this debate involves a variety of different ideas about what democracy means and which kinds of institutional arrangements are most likely to ensure it. Those who want universal suffrage favour a view of democracy in which the emphasis is on individual freedom: anyone can run for office and anyone can vote. They point out, for example, that traditionally nobody becomes a *matai* until he has served his family for many years and his predecessor has died, which limits the field of possible parliamentary candidates to one (relatively) old man per extended family. How can it be democratic to restrict the opportunities of younger people to run for office? These sorts of arguments fit well with traditional Western arguments that speak of democracy in connection with individual freedom from arbitrary restrictions.

But those Samoans who want the *matai* system to continue stress that it is more democratic than universal suffrage because it creates representatives who can never forget that they are responsible to those who elected them—the other members of their extended family. In thinking about democracy in this way, these Samoans are refusing to reduce democratic citizenship to the right to vote. Rather, they take the view that democracy involves not just being treated as an equal by others but also the obligation of those who make political decisions for others to remain accountable and accessible to those whom they represent (O'Donnell and Schmitter 1986; Rubin 1997). Thus, the *matai* system can be viewed as more democratic than universal

suffrage because it ensures that every extended family will be represented in some form in the electoral process and that any *matais* elected to parliament will not be able to ignore the wishes of those who put them in office.

Politics in Samoa also has a regional dimension. Tcherkézoff points out that until recently, Samoa was primarily a nation of villages but that the capital city has been growing in size in recent years. Many of those who live in the growing urban area depend more on wage labour and less on agriculture and fishing, the activities central to village life where *matais* traditionally exercised their authority. Thus, those who want to preserve the *matai* system also defend it as a way of maintaining equality between those who live in the city and those who still live in rural areas. They fear that if parliamentary elections were to operate in terms of universal suffrage, Samoa would be fractured into two societies: an urban sector with a Western political system, and no way to hold their parliamentary representatives accountable, and a rural sector in which *matais* still exist but would be powerless guardians of local folklore. Should this happen, 'then some Samoans say that "democracy" will not be achieved and will even go backwards' (Tcherkézoff 1998: 427).

As Tcherkézoff makes clear, the debate about democracy in Samoa is complex and subtle: Samoans have a sophisticated understanding of the advantages and drawbacks of different democratic political forms, some of which are indigenous to Samoa and some of which came from elsewhere.

> The problem is that Samoa has the chance to build its future on ideas and experiences that come both from the *faamatai* tradition and from the Western tradition of democracy and to maybe create a new synthesis where the advent of democracy will not just be the replacement of hierarchy (in the *faamatai*) by inequality (in the Western-style politics). There lies the real question of the future of the country. (430)

Anthropology and Multicultural Politics in the New Europe

One of the more interesting things about the early twenty-first century is that Europe, the continent that gave birth to the Enlightenment and colonial empires and to anthropology itself (along with North American contributions) has now become a key setting for the anthropological study of social and cultural changes. During the last half of the twentieth century, the countries of Europe, including Italy, were the target of large waves of migration from all over the world. Europeans are struggling with the concept of multiculturalism in ways we in Canada can recognize. Indeed, we are the people with the Canadian Multiculturalism Act, passed in Parliament in 1988, which recognizes 'the diversity of Canadians as regards race, national or ethnic origin, colour, and religion as a fundamental characteristic of Canadian society . . . while working to achieve the equality of all Canadians in the economic, social, cultural, and political life of Canada' (Preamble). How is Europe dealing with the influx of people they consider non-European?

Visitors to Rome regularly make stops at the ancient ruins in the centre of the city. One venerable working-class Roman neighbourhood, only a short walk from the Coliseum, is Rione Monti (see Map 14.3), which has a fascinating history of its own. In 1999, anthropologist Michael Herzfeld moved into Rione Monti to do fieldwork exploring social change in the uses of the past (2003). Long-time residents of Monti share a common local culture, which includes use of the *romanesco* dialect rather than standard Italian and a strong sense of local identity that distinguishes them from 'foreigners', including diplomats and non-Roman Italians. Their identity survived Mussolini's demolition of part of the neighbourhood in the early twentieth century. They successfully dealt with a local criminal underworld by mastering a refined urbane code of politeness. The underworld had faded away by the 1970s, but beginning in the 1980s, residents began to face two new challenges to their community.

(1) Historic Roman neighbourhoods became fashionable, and well-to-do Italians began to move into Rione Monti, pushing many workers into cheaper housing elsewhere.

(2) In the 1990s, another group of newcomers arrived: immigrants from eastern Europe.

Italy is one of the more recent destinations of immigration into Europe, reversing the country's historical experience as a source, rather than a target, of immigration. However, after Germany, France, and Britain passed laws curtailing immigration in the

Map 14.3 Rione Monti

1970s, Italy became an increasingly popular destination for immigrants from Africa, Asia, Latin America, and, after the Cold War, the European Union, including eastern Europe. Until recently, laws regulating immigration were few, and the country appeared welcoming. But this is changing. 'Italy has not historically been a racist country, but intolerant attitudes toward immigrants have increased. To a large extent, this seems to be the result of a long-standing underestimation of the magnitude of the changes and thus poor policy implementation for a lengthy period, in spite of the best intentions officially proclaimed' (Melotti 1997: 91).

Umberto Melotti contrasts the distinctive ways in which immigration is understood by the governments of France, Britain, and Germany. According to him, the French project is *ethnocentric assimilationism*: since the early nineteenth century, when French society experienced a falling birth rate, immigration was encouraged and immigrants were promised all the rights and privileges of native-born citizens as long as they adopted French culture completely, dropping other ethnic or cultural attachments and assimilated the French language, culture, and character (1997: 75). The British project, by contrast, is *uneven pluralism*: that is, the pragmatic British expect immigrants to be loyal and law-abiding citizens, but they do not expect immigrants to 'become British' and they tolerate private cultivation of cultural differences as long as these do not threaten the British way of life (79–80). Finally, Melotti describes the German project as *the institutionalization of precariousness*, by which he means that despite the fact that Germany has within its borders more immigrants than any other European country, and began receiving immigrants at the end of the nineteenth century, its government continues to insist that Germany is not a country of immigrants. Immigrants were always considered 'guest workers', children born to guest workers are considered citizens of the country from which the worker came, and it still remains very difficult for guest workers or their German-born children to obtain German citizenship. (This contrasts with France, for example, where children of immigrants born on French soil automatically become French citizens.) A very different pattern can be found in Belgium, where the Dutch-speaking Flemings in the north and the French-speaking Walloons in the south enjoy considerable autonomy and the state's role is to protect the rights of each community in the public sphere. This system, known as *pillorization*, bears some similarity to the way separate religious communities were organized under the Ottoman Empire (Modood 1997: 22–3).

Coming to terms with increasing numbers of Muslims living in countries where Christianity has historically been dominant is a central theme in multicultural debates within Europe, as we saw in Chapters 7 and 13. Although all European states consider themselves secular in orientation, the relation between religion and state is far from uniform. France is unusual because of its strict legal separation between religion and state. In Britain, the combination of a secular outlook with state funding of the established Anglican Church has allowed citizens to support forms of religious inclusion that first involved state funding of Catholic schools for Irish immigrants and now involve state funding of Muslim schools for Muslim immigrants (Lewis 1997; Modood 1997). In Germany, where a secular outlook also combines with state-subsidized religious institutions, the state has devised curricula for elementary schools designed to teach all students about different religious traditions, including Islam, in ways that emphasize the possibility of harmonizing one's religious faith with one's obligations as a citizen. Although this approach may be seen as presumptuous or paternalistic, its supporters counter that its advantages

outweigh its costs. Perhaps as a result of their own history, many contemporary Germans have less faith than the British that a civic culture of religious tolerance will automatically lead to harmony without state intervention and less faith than the French in the existence of a separate secular sphere of society from which religion can be safely excluded (Schiffauer 1997).

These are, of course, thumbnail sketches of more complex attitudes and practices. But they illustrate the fact that there is no single 'European' approach to the challenges posed by immigration. In a way, each European state, with its own history and institutions, is experimenting with different ways of coping with the challenges of multiculturalism, and their failures and successes will influence the kinds of multicultural relations and institutions that develop in the twenty-first century. This is particularly significant in light of the fact that European nation-states have joined together in the European Union, a continent-wide superstate with 25 members. Reconciling the diverse interests and needs of member states poses enormous challenges for EU members, and multicultural issues are among them.

Many scholars and activists hope that solutions can be found that will involve extensions of social justice throughout the EU (e.g., Ben-Tovim 1997; Brewin 1997). But there is still a lot of work to be done, and no guarantees about the outcome. Modood points out, for example, that European multiculturalism requires supporting conceptions of citizenship that allow the 'right to assimilate' as well as conceptions of citizenship that allow the 'right to have one's "difference" . . . recognized and supported in the public and the private spheres'; multiculturalism must recognize that 'participation in the public or national culture is necessary for the effective exercise of citizenship' while at the same time defending the 'right to widen and adapt the national culture' (1997: 20). The potential and actual contradictions among some of these goals are apparent, but insofar as they are seen as necessary, the challenge becomes finding ways to move forward. And here, with no blueprint to follow, all parties find themselves involved in creating new cultural practices. Based on her experience in France, Dembour is convinced that 'we need to accept the discomfort of moving in-between, as a pendulum' (2001: 71–2). Modood agrees: 'There is indeed a tension here, and perhaps it can only be resolved in practice through finding and cultivating points of common ground between dominant and subordinate cultures, as well as new syntheses and hybridities. The important thing is that the burdens of change . . . are not all dependent on one party to this encounter' (1997: 20).

Anthropologists are inevitably drawn into these discussions, not only because they carry out research in the communities struggling for resolution but also because many of them are citizens of the societies whose future depends on the solutions that are implemented. As a result, theoretical debates in the field are intertwined with political debates in society, and scholars can disagree with one another just as political activists do. For example, Norwegian anthropologist Thomas Eriksen reports on the outcome of a formal debate organized by the Department of Anthropology at the University of Oslo in 1997, in which the thesis to be contested was the assertion that cultural freedom protects not only a group but also the rights of every individual within a group (Eriksen 2001: 144). 'Speaking from very different ethnographic horizons, the antagonists not only reached opposite conclusions but also failed to engage in a proper dialogue: they tended to depict each other . . . as hopeless Romantics and cynical modernists, respectively' (2001: 144). In the end, Eriksen observes, the debate raised the same kinds of issues and provoked the same kinds of responses and standoffs that can be found in the wider society. After the debate, the audience was invited to vote for the side they thought had made the best case. The results were 78 in favour of the motion, 75 against. This almost perfect standoff, Eriksen points out, is very different from what the outcome would likely have been 10 or 15 years earlier when there would have been 'almost certainly a massive "yes" vote . . . perhaps the tide will turn again' (145).

Thus, the struggles and dilemmas facing residents of Rione Monti are widespread across the new Europe. But the specifics of their situation, and the cultural resources at their disposal, have their own particularity. Thus, the traditionally left-wing Monti residents have resisted attempts by neo-fascist politicians to get them to turn against immigrant families in the neighbourhood. Still, they are unhappy with the location of the Ukrainian church in a building that overlooks the neighbourhood's central square because church-

Figure 14.5 Rione Monti is a neighbourhood in central Rome where long-time residents and new immigrants are negotiating new forms of relationships.

goers gather there twice a week, invading 'their' space (Herzfeld 2003: 4) (Figure 14.5). Herzfeld reports that the residents of Monti, like other Romans, claim not to be racist (which accords with Melotti's views of Italians in general) and that they seem less hostile to immigrants of colour than to Ukrainians. But Ukrainians are more numerous in Monti and more threatening because they look like local people but in fact are competing with local people for work and space in the neighbourhood (5). At the same time, the Monti code of politeness 'underlies the facility with which democratically inclined residents today construct a popular street democracy, a system of neighbourhood associations' (2). Currently, immigrants are not able to deploy this code, a fact that signals their outsider status and can lead to misunderstandings and bad feelings. If they could learn to use the code, however, fresh opportunities for political co-operation might be forged. This could be decisive, for the code of politeness is the foundation of local democratic processes and 'may also eventually be the only generally available means of denying access to manipulative party politics and land speculation alike' (6).

Anthropology and Human Rights

Recently, anthropologists have been involved in expanding the understanding of human rights and have participated in organizations for the defence of human rights. In particular, they have contributed to the recognition by human rights legal advocates that the collective rights of groups (such as Indigenous peoples) deserve as much attention as the rights of individuals. Ellen Messer observes that anthropologists have examined, and continue to examine, the

> contexts of human rights abuses to understand how the political economic conditions that create cultural customs such as infanticide, underfeeding of women and children, and other abuses of women might be improved and make the customs of less evident utility. They also continue to work with interpreters of local traditions, so that through persuasion and contextualization, and by drawing on the authority of multiple traditions, people might be empowered to improve human rights in their own lives. (1993: 24)

Perhaps one of the foremost anthropologically oriented organizations involved with human rights is Cultural Survival, founded in 1972 by anthropologists Pia Maybury-Lewis and David Maybury-Lewis and dedicated to helping Indigenous people and ethnic minorities deal as equals in their encounters with industrial society. Anthropologist Carolyn Nordstrom (1993) writes about the efforts of the Ministry of Education in Mozambique and the Mozambican Woman's Organization to begin programs to assist children and women traumatized, raped, displaced, and impoverished by the 16-year war in that country. She discusses how Indigenous healers have come to develop specialties in war trauma, 'to take the violence out of people', and are being brought into the national health care system.

Biological anthropologists, most notably Clyde Snow, have also contributed in an important way to the defence of human rights in the world. Snow is a consulting forensic anthropologist who is often called on by police departments, medical examiners, and other law enforcement officials to try to identify human remains and to determine the cause of death. He is helped in this task by his knowledge of

- human skeletal features to determine sex, age, and population subgroup; and
- the different ways trauma can affect the human skeleton.

In recent years, Snow has been involved in a number of international human rights cases. Beginning in 1984, he worked with the American Association for the Advancement of Science to help the Argentinian National Commission on Disappeared Persons to determine the fate of some of the more than 10,000 people who had vanished during the 'dirty war' waged by the Argentine military government against supposed subversives. Snow began his work in Argentina by training a team of medical and anthropology students in the techniques of forensic investigation, both skeletal and archaeological, and then helped them exhume and examine scores of the remains of the *desaparecidos* ('those who have disappeared'). By 1988, only 25 victims had been positively identified, but those identifications helped convict seven members of the former ruling junta and other high-ranking military and police officers (Huyghe 1988).

The Argentine team Snow trained has gone on to investigate sites of massacres in Guatemala, Bolivia, Panama, Iraq, and, most recently, the site of the massacre at El Mozote, El Salvador. Snow himself was in Chiapas in February 1994 to investigate the deaths of peasants following the Mexican army's battle with the Emiliano Zapata Liberation Army in early January (Figure 14.6). Snow states, 'There are human rights violations going on all around the world. But to me murder is murder, regardless of the motive. I hope that

Figure 14.6 Some applied anthropologists like Clyde Snow, shown here, use their knowledge and skills in skeletal identification.

we are sending a message to governments who murder in the name of politics that they can be held to account' (Huyghe 1988).

Paul Oldham and Miriam Frank (2008) consider the adoption of the UN's 2007 Declaration on the Rights of Indigenous Peoples. Declarations are important but

In Their Own Words

Into the Warp and Woof of Multicultural Worlds

Changes in the contemporary world are producing what anthropologist George Marcus calls 'transcultural "traditional" peoples', whose members live in many different places and whose sense of cultural identity involves a mix of many cultural elements.

The power of global cultural homogenization in the late twentieth century challenges the conventions and rationales by which anthropology has so far produced its knowledge of other cultures. The reorganization of the world economy through technological advances in communication, production processes, and marketing has thoroughly de-territorialized culture. For example, the Tongan Islanders of Polynesia that I studied in the early 1970s now constitute a diaspora of communities in locales around the Pacific Rim. As many, if not more, Tongans now live permanently in Australia, New Zealand, and the United States as in the islands themselves. One might fairly ponder where both the cultural and geographical centre of the Tongan people resides. Their identity is produced in many locales and through the mix of many cultural elements. And their conditions are similar to those of numerous other peoples that anthropologists have traditionally studied. It is no longer just the most powerful, large-scale, and most modern societies, such as the United States and Japan, that exist in international, transcultural science.

Among such transcultural 'traditional' peoples, levels of cultural self-consciousness and alternatives increase. The authenticity of performances, rituals, or apparently deep-seated norms like those of kinship cannot be merely assumed, either by locals or by visitors such as anthropologists. To some extent, media documentaries have absorbed anthropology's function of presenting vividly the lifeways of other cultures to Euro-American publics that themselves can no longer be considered as homogeneous or mainstream. And, finally, the subjects of anthropological study independently and articulately translate their own perspectives with sensitivity to the effects of different media.

Peoples who in particular have become classic anthropological subjects, such as the Samoans, Trobriand Islanders, Hopi, and Todas of India, know their status well, and have, with some ambivalence, assimilated anthropological knowledge about them as part of their sense of themselves. A recent example was the visit of a Toda woman to Houston. A trained nurse among her people, as well as a cultural broker, she was on tour in the United States giving talks about the Todas, of the sort that anthropologists might have given in past decades. By chance, she was visiting the home of a colleague just as a British documentary about the Todas appeared on the television—a documentary in which the visitor was featured prominently as the filmmaker's prime source of information. The visitor's comments as she watched the program along with my colleague did not much concern the details of Toda culture but rather dealt with the ironies of the multiple representations of her people—by herself, by anthropologists, and by the British Broadcasting Corporation.

The lesson of this story is compelling. The penetrations of a world economy, communications, and the effects of multiple, fragmented identities on cultural authenticity, once thought restricted to advanced modernity, have increased markedly among most local and regional cultures worldwide. They have thus engendered an ethnography in reverse among many peoples who not only can assimilate the professional idioms of anthropology but can relativize them among other alternatives and ways of knowledge. This does not mean that the traditional task of anthropology to represent distinctive and systematic cultural forms of life has been fundamentally subverted by its own subjects. Rather, anthropology's traditional task is now much more complicated, requiring new sensibilities in undertaking fieldwork and different strategies for writing about it.

Source: Marcus, George. 1990. 'Into the Warp and Woof of Multicultural Worlds', guest editorial in *Cultural Anthropology: A Perspective on the Human Condition*, eds Emily Schultz and Robert Lavenda, 2nd edn (St Paul: West), 254–5.

only so far as they become the road map for action, and they challenge us to consider the role that anthropology might play in promoting such human rights. For Canadians, this is poignant as we watch the process and outcome of the Indian Residential Schools Truth and Reconciliation Commission.

Awareness and Uncertainty

Why study anthropology? The second part of our answer is personal.

Studying cultural anthropology brings students into contact with different ways of life. It makes them aware of just how arbitrary their own understanding of the world is as they learn how other people have developed satisfying but different ways of living. In addition, if they are from Western countries that were responsible for colonialism and its consequences, it makes them painfully aware of just how much their own tradition has to answer for in the modern world.

Knowing and experiencing cultural variety gives rise, perhaps inevitably, to doubt. We come to doubt the ultimate validity of the central truths of our own cultural tradition, which have been ratified and sanctified by the generations who preceded us. We doubt because a familiarity with alternative ways of living makes the ultimate meaning of any action, of any object, a highly ambiguous matter. Ambiguity is part and parcel of the human condition. Human beings have coped with ambiguity from time immemorial by means of culture, which places objects and actions in contexts and thereby makes their meanings plain. This doubt can lead to anxiety, but it can also be liberating.

Freedom and Constraint

Why study anthropology? The third part of our response is, for want of a better word, humanistic.

All human beings live in culturally shaped worlds, enmeshed in webs of interpretation and meaning. It has been the particular task of anthropologists to go out into the world to bear witness to and record the vast creative diversity in world-making that has been the history of our species. In our lifetimes, we will witness the end of many of those ways of life—and if we are not careful, of all ways of life. This loss is tragic, for as these worlds disappear so too does something special about humanity: variety, creativity, and awareness of alternatives.

Our survival as a species, and our viability as individuals, depends on the possibility of choice, of perceiving and being able to act on alternatives in the various situations we encounter during our lives. If, as a colleague has suggested, human life is a minefield, then the more paths we can see and imagine through that minefield, the more likely we are to make it through—or at least to have an interesting time trying. As alternatives are destroyed, wantonly smashed, or thoughtlessly crushed, *our* own human possibilities are reduced. A small group of men and women have, for the last century, laboured in corners of the world, both remote and nearby, to write the record of human accomplishment and bring it back and teach it to others.

Surely our greatest human accomplishment is the creation of the sometimes austerely beautiful worlds in which we all live. Anthropologists have rarely given in to the romantic notion that these other worlds are all good, all life-enhancing, all fine or beautiful. They are not. Ambiguity and ambivalence are, as we have seen, hallmarks of the human experience. There are no guarantees that human cultures will be compassionate rather than cruel or that people will agree they are one or the other. There are not even any guarantees that our species will survive. But all anthropologists have believed that these are *human* worlds that have given those who have lived in them the ability to make sense out of their experiences and to derive meaning for their lives, that we are a species at once bound by our culture and free to change it.

This is a perilous and fearsome freedom, a difficult freedom to grasp and to wield. Nevertheless, the freedom is there, and in this dialectic of freedom and constraint lies our future. It is up to us to create it.

Chapter Summary

1. The discipline of anthropology is discussed as a challenging profession in today's world. The emphasis is on applied anthropology and what it contributes to contemporary solutions of social issues. The skill set acquired through anthropology is highlighted. Applied anthropologists do their work using holism, comparison, relativism, and a concern for particular cases.

2. Not everyone who studies anthropology goes on to work as an anthropologist. One of the challenges faced by people everywhere in the world at the beginning of the twenty-first century is that of citizenship in a complex, diverse, and difficult world. You can consider how the ideas and issues you have studied this semester can be applied, and you can anticipate your potential efficacy as a global citizen. Anthropology is not just an esoteric exercise. Regardless of your consideration of anthropology as a profession, it remains a guide for a way of living in the world in a state of reflexivity—a state of constant engagement and growth.

3. Recently, anthropologists involved in expanding the understanding of human rights have participated in organizations for the defence of human rights. In particular, they have contributed to the recognition by human rights legal advocates that the collective rights of groups (such as Indigenous peoples) deserve as much attention as the rights of individuals. Additionally, forensic anthropologists have worked to uncover evidence of genocides and ethnic cleansings in various parts of the world.

4. Cultural anthropology brings us into contact with different ways of life and challenges our awareness of just how arbitrary our own understanding of the world is as we learn how other people have developed satisfying but different ways of living.

5. In addition, anthropology helps us understand our place in and responsibility for the historical and present-day worlds of colonialism and postcolonialism. The consequences of colonialism resonate, and we can become aware of just how much the Western tradition has to answer for in the modern world.

6. Our survival as a species, and our viability as individuals, depends on the possibility of choice, of perceiving and being able to act on alternatives in the various situations we encounter during our lives.

Critical Thinking Questions

1. How would you describe the potential of medical anthropology to address various issues of concern in today's world?

2. Considering the 12 learnings that can be achieved from anthropology, as presented in the SUNY document, which have been the greatest challenge for you?

3. How can coming to understand the social knowledge or values based on an underlying, taken-for-granted cultural logic of another culture be of importance to you?

4. Why do you suppose anthropologists are particularly aware of the problems in applied work, the problems in trying to make people, or systems, change? What is it about anthropology that engenders such sensitivity?

5. How you would describe the ambiguity and ambivalence of the human experience in the sometimes austerely beautiful worlds in which we all live?

Suggested Readings

Canadian Heritage. 2001–2. *Canadian Arts, Culture, and Heritage: A Story Celebrating Our Diversity*, available at: <http://www.canadianheritage.gc.ca/multi/reports/ann01-2002/part4_e.cfm>. *A government of Canada website praising the virtues of multiculturalism.*

Lock, Margaret. 2001. 'The Tempering of Medical Anthropology: Troubling Natural Categories', *Medical Anthropology Quarterly* 15: 478–92. *A continuation of Lock's work on the relationship of emerging bio-scientific knowledge and associated technologies with the social, political, and moral order, and with the subjectivity of categories (typologies).*

Oldham, Paul, and Miriam Anne Frank. 2008. '"We the People…": The United Nations Declaration on the Rights of Indigenous Peoples', *Anthropology Today* 24, 2: 5–9. *The UN document of the rights of Indigenous people worldwide. Note that not all states have signed on!*

Rodman, William L. 1991. 'When Questions Are Answers: The Message of Anthropology, According to the People of Ambae', *American Anthropologist* 93, 2 (June): 421–34. *The story of a young man who established an important social movement in Ambae based on his allegorical interpretation of Rodman's questions in the New Hebrides archipelago.*

Salzman, Philip Carl. 1986. 'Is Traditional Fieldwork Outmoded?', *Current Anthropology* 27, 5 (Dec.): 528–30. *Challenges the view that research is the lone observer and calls anthropologists to adopt a team approach—this would include the 'informant' as the specialist as well.*

Wardlow, Holly. 2007. 'Men's Extramarital Sexuality in Rural Papua New Guinea', *American Journal of Public Health* 97, 6 (26 Apr.): 1006–14. *Considers the role of extramarital activity in the spread of HIV/AIDS.*

Warry, Wayne, S. Smith, and N. Johnson, eds. 1997. *Nurtured by Knowledge: Learning to Do Participatory Action Research* (New York/Ottawa: The Apex Press and the International Development Research Centre [IDRC Books]). *Discussion of PAR (Participatory Action Research), a methodology that enables people to take control of their lives through the integration of formal and informal knowledge and by using this integrated knowledge in a transformative way to challenge their assumed realities. Now that suggests reflexivity!*

Related Websites

Cultural Survival: http://www.culturalsurvival.org/
Indian Residential Schools Truth and Reconciliation Commission: http://www.trc-cvr.ca/indexen.html
INTSORMIL: http://www.ianr.unl.edu/INTSORMIL/

Muhammad Yunus: http://www.grameen-info.org/
Survival International: http://www.survival-international.org/
USAID: http://www.usaid.gov/

References

Abbas, Ackbar. 2002. 'Cosmopolitan Description: Shanghai and Hong Kong', in *Cosmopolitanism*, eds Carol A. Breckenridge et al. (Durham, NC: Duke University Press), 209–28.

Abley, Mark. 2005. *Spoken Here: Travels among Threatened Languages* (Mariner Books).

Abu-Lughod, Lila. 1991. 'Writing against Culture', in *Recapturing Anthropology*, ed. Richard Fox (Santa Fe, NM: SAR), 137–62.

———. 1995. 'The Objects of Soap Opera: Egyptian Television and the Cultural Politics of Modernity', in *Worlds Apart: Modernity through the Prism of the Local*, ed. Daniel Miller (London: Routledge), 109–210.

Adams, Richard Newbold. 1979. *Energy and Structure: A Theory of Social Power* (Austin: University of Texas Press).

Advameg Inc. 2008. 'Xikrin: Orientation', from World Culture Encyclopedia, available at: <http://www.everyculture.com/South-America/Xikrin-Orientation.html>.

Agar, Michael. 1996. *The Professional Stranger: An Informal Introduction to Ethnography*, 2nd edn (San Diego: Academic Press).

Alland, Alexander. 1977. *The Artistic Animal* (New York: Doubleday Anchor).

Allen, Catherine J. 1988. *The Hold Life Has: Coca and Cultural Identity in an Andean Community* (Washington, DC: Smithsonian Institution Press).

Allen, Theodore. 1994–97. *The Invention of the White Race*, 2 vols (London: Verso).

Allen, Timothy F.H., and T.W. Hoekstra. 1991. 'Role of Heterogeneity in Scaling of Ecological Systems under Analysis', *Ecological Heterogeneity (Ecological Studies)*, Vol. 86, eds J. Kolasa and S. Pickett (New York: Springer Verlag), 47–68.

Alonso, Ana María. 1994. 'The Politics of Space, Time, and Substance: State Formation, Nationalism, and Ethnicity', *Annual Review of Anthropology* 23: 379–405.

Alverson, Hoyt. 1978. *Mind in the Heart of Darkness* (New Haven: Yale University Press).

AAA (American Anthropological Association). 1998. *Code of Ethics*, available at: <http://www.aaanet.org/committees/ethics/ethcode.htm>.

Anderson, Benedict. 2002 [1992]. 'The New World Disorder', in *The Anthropology of Politics*, ed. Joan Vincent (Malden, MA: Blackwell), 261–70.

Anderson, Richard L. 1990. *Calliope's Sisters: A Comparative Study of Philosophies of Art* (Englewood Cliffs, NJ: Prentice-Hall).

Apfel, Roberta J., and Bennett Simon. 2000. 'Mitigating Discontents with Children in War: An Ongoing Psychoanalytic Inquiry', in *Cultures under Siege: Collective Violence and Trauma*, eds Antonius C.G.M. Robben and Marcelo M. Suárez-Orozco (Cambridge: Cambridge University Press), 102–30.

Appadurai, Arjun. 1990. 'Disjuncture and Difference in the Global Cultural Economy', in *Global Culture*, ed. Mike Featherstone (London: Sage), 295–310.

———. 2002. 'Grassroots Globalization and the Research Imagination', in *The Anthropology of Politics*, ed. Joan Vincent (Malden, MA: Blackwell), 271–84.

Asad, Talal, ed. 1973. *Anthropology and the Colonial Encounter* (London: Ithaca Press).

———. 2002. 'From the History of Colonial Anthropology to the Anthropology of Western Hegemony', in *The Anthropology of Politics*, ed. Joan Vincent (Malden, MA: Blackwell), 133–42.

———. 2003. *Formations of the Secular: Christianity, Islam, Modernity* (Palo Alto, CA: Stanford University Press).

Atwood, M. 1972. *Survival: A Thematic Guide to Canadian Literature* (Toronto: House of Anansi Press Ltd).

Bailey, A.G. 1969 [1937]. *The Conflict of European and Eastern Algonquian Cultures, 1504–1700*, 2nd edn (Toronto: University of Toronto Press).

Bailyn, Bernard. 1986. *The Peopling of British North America: An Introduction* (New York: Knopf).

Bakhtin, Mikhail. 1981. *The Dialogical Imagination* (Austin: University of Texas Press).

Ball, M.S., and G.W.H. Smith. 1992. 'Analyzing Visual Data', *Qualitative Research Methods* 24 (Newbury Park: Sage Publications).

Barad, Karen. 1999. 'Agential Realism: Feminist Interventions in Understanding Scientific Practices', in *The Science Studies Reader*, ed. Mario Biagioli (New York: Routlege), 1–11.

Barber, Benjamin R. 1995. *Jihad versus McWorld: How Globalism and Tribalism Are Reshaping the World* (New York: Times Books).

Basham, Richard. 1978. *Urban Anthropology* (Palo Alto: Mayfield).

Bashir, Halima. 2008. *Tears of the Desert: A Memoir of Survival in Darfur* (New York: One World).

Bauman, Zygmunt. 1989. *Modernity and the Holocaust* (Ithaca: Cornell University Press).

———. 1990. 'Modernity and Ambivalence', in *Global Culture*, ed. Mike Featherstone (London: Sage), 143–69.

Baxter, P.T.W. 1978. 'Boran Age Sets and Generation Sets: *Gada*, a Puzzle or a Maze?', in *Age, Generation, and Time*, eds P.T.W. Baxter and Uri Almagor (New York: St Martin's Press), 151–82.

———, and Uri Almagor, eds. 1978. *Age, Generation and Time* (New York: St Martin's Press).

Beals, Alan. 1962. *Gopalpur, A South Indian Village* (New York: Holt, Rinehart & Winston).

Bell, Sandra, and Simon Coleman, eds. 1999. 'The Anthropology of Friendship: Enduring Themes and Future Possibilities', in *The Anthropology of Friendship* (Oxford: Berg), 1–19.

Bellman, Beryl. 1984. *The Language of Secrecy* (New Brunswick, NJ: Rutgers University Press).

Belmonte, Thomas. 1978. *The Broken Fountain* (New York: Columbia University Press).

Ben-Tovim, Gideon. 1997. 'Why "Positive Action" Is "Politically Correct"', in *The Politics of Multiculturalism in the New Europe: Racism, Identity, and Community*, eds Tariq Modood and Pnina Werbner (Cambridge: Cambridge University Press), 209–22.

Benedict, Ruth. 1934. *Patterns of Culture* (New York: Houghton Mifflin).

Bernhardt, B., J. Ball, and J. Deby. 2007. 'Cross-cultural Interaction and Children's Speech Acquisition', in *The International Guide to Speech Acquisition*, ed. S. McLeod (Clifton Park, NY: Delmar), available at: <http://www.ecdip.org/dialects/index.htm>.

Berreman, Gerald D. 1962. *Behind Many Masks: Ethnography and Impression Management in a Himalayan Village* (Lexington, KY: Society for Applied Anthropology).

Betts, Wendy. 2008. Review in *Notes from the Windowsill*, available at: <http://www.armory.com/~web/gaybooks.html>.

Bickerton, Derek. 1981. *Roots of Language* (Ann Arbor, MI: Karoma).

Bigenho, Michelle. 2002. *Sounding Indigenous: Authenticity in Bolivian Music Performance* (New York: Palgrave).

Bishop, C.A. 1970. 'The Emergence of Hunting Territories among the Northern Ojibwa', *Ethnology* XI, 1: 1–15.

———. 1973. 'Ojibwa Cannibalism', IX International Congress of Anthropological and Ethnological Sciences (Chicago).

———. 1981. 'Northeastern Indian Concepts of Conservation and the Fur Trade: A Critique of Calvin Martin's Thesis', in *Indians, Animals and the Fur Trade*, ed. S. Krech III (Athens: University of Georgia Press), 39–58.

Blackwood, Evelyn, and Saskia E. Wieringa, eds. 1999. 'Preface', in *Female Desires: Same-sex Relations and Transgender Practices across Cultures* (New York: Columbia University Press), ix–xiii.

Blanchard, Kendall, and Alyce Cheska. 1985. *The Anthropology of Sport* (South Hadley, MA: Bergin & Garvey).

Bledsoe, Caroline. 1993. 'The Politics of Polygyny in Mende Education and Child Fosterage Transactions', in *Sex and Gender Hierarchies*, ed. Barbara Diane Miller (Cambridge: Cambridge University Press), 170–92.

Boaz, Noel T., and Linda Wolfe, eds. 1995. *Biological Anthropology: The State of the Science* (Bend, OR: International Institute for Human Evolutionary Research).

Bock, Philip, ed. 1994. *Psychological Anthropology* (Westport, CT: Praeger).

Bodenhorn, Barbara. 2000. '"He Used to Be My Relative": Exploring the Bases of Relatedness among Iñupiat of Northern Alaska', in *Cultures of Relatedness: New Approaches to the Study of Kinship*, ed. Janet Carsten (Cambridge: Cambridge University Press), 128–48.

Boesch-Ackermann, H., and C. Boesch. 1994. 'Hominization in the Rain Forest: The Chimpanzee's Piece of the Puzzle', *Evolutionary Anthropology* 3, 1: 9–16.

Bohannan, Paul, and Fred Plog, eds. 1967. *Beyond the Frontier* (Garden City, NY: Natural History Press).

Bowen, John. 2002. *Religions in Practice: An Approach to the Anthropology of Religion*, 2nd edn (Needham Heights, MA: Allyn & Bacon).

Bradburd, Daniel. 1998. *Being There: The Necessity of Fieldwork* (Washington, DC: Smithsonian Institution Press).

Brain, Robert. 1976. *Friends and Lovers* (New York: Basic Books).

Braroe, Niels. 1975. *Indian and White* (Stanford: Stanford University Press).

Breckenridge, Carol A., et al. 2002. 'Cosmopolitanisms', in *Cosmopolitanism* (Durham, NC: Duke University Press), 1–14.

Brenneis, Donald, and Ronald K.S. Macauley, eds. 1996. *The Matrix of Language* (Boulder, CO: Westview).

Brewin, Christopher. 1997. 'Society as a Kind of Community: Communitarian Voting with Equal Rights for Individuals in the European Union', in *The Politics of Multiculturalism in the New Europe: Racism, Identity, and Community*, eds Tariq Modood and Pnina Werbner (Cambridge: Cambridge University Press), 223–39.

Briggs, Jean. 1980. 'Kapluna Daughter: Adopted by the Eskimo', in *Conformity and Conflict: Readings in Cultural Anthropology*,

4th edn, eds J. Spradley and D. McCurdy (Glenview, IL: Scott Foresman), 44–62.

Bromberger, Christian. 1995. *Le match de football: Etnologie d'une passion partisane à Marseille, Naples et Turin* (Paris: Éditions de la maison des sciences de l'homme).

Broom, Leonard, et al. 1954. 'Acculturation: An Exploratory Formulation', *American Anthropologist* 56: 973–1000.

Burch Jr, Ernest S. 1970. 'Marriage and Divorce among the North Alaskan Eskimos', in *Divorce and After*, ed. Paul Bohannan (Garden City, NY: Doubleday), 152–81.

CIHR, NSERC, SSHRC (Canadian Institutes of Health Research, Natural Sciences and Engineering Research Council of Canada, Social Sciences and Humanities Research Council of Canada). 1998 (with 2000, 2002, and 2005 amendments). *Tri-council Policy Statement: Ethical Conduct for Research Involving Humans*, available at: <http://www.pre.ethics.gc.ca/english/policystatement/policystatement.cfm>.

Canadian Multiculturalism Act. 1988. Revised Statutes of Canada, 1985, c. 24 (4th Supp.), available at: <http://laws.justice.gc.ca/en/C-18.7/>.

CSSA (Canadian Sociology and Anthropology Association). 1994. *Statement of Professional Ethics*, available at: <http://www.csaa.ca/structure/Code.htm>.

Carsten, Janet, ed. 2000. 'Introduction: Cultures of Relatedness', in *Cultures of Relatedness: New Approaches to the Study of Kinship* (Cambridge: Cambridge University Press), 1–36.

Chance, John K. 1978. *Race and Class in Colonial Oaxaca* (Stanford: Stanford University Press).

Cheyfitz, E. 1991. *The Poetics of Imperialism: Translation and Colonization from the Tempest to Tarzan* (New York: Oxford University Press).

Chomsky, Noam. 1957. *Syntactic Structures* (The Hague: Mouton).

———. 1965. *Aspects of the Theory of Syntax* (Cambridge, MA: MIT Press).

Chrisjohn, R., S. Young, and M. Maraun. 1997. *The Circle Game: Shadows and Substance in the Indian Residential School Experience in Canada* (Penticton: Theytus Books Limited).

Clark, Gracia. 1994. *Onions Are My Husband* (Chicago: University of Chicago Press).

Clastres, Pierre. 1977. *Society against the State*, trans. Robert Hurley (New York: Urizen Books).

Cohen, I.B., ed. 1994. 'An Analysis of Interactions between the Natural and Social Sciences', *Boston Studies in the Philosophy of Science* 150 (Dordrecht: Kluwer), 1–99.

Cole, Michael. 1994. *Cultural Psychology: A Once and Future Discipline* (Cambridge, MA: Harvard University Press).

———, and Sylvia Scribner. 1974. *Culture and Thought: A Psychological Introduction* (New York: Wiley).

Collier, Jane, and Sylvia Yanagisako, eds. 1987. 'Toward a Unified Analysis of Gender and Kinship', in *Gender and Kinship: Essays Toward a Unified Analysis* (Stanford: Stanford University Press), 14–50.

Colloredo-Mansfeld, Rudi. 1999. *The Native Leisure Class: Consumption and Cultural Creativity in the Andes* (Chicago: University of Chicago Press).

Colson, Elizabeth. 1977. 'Power at Large: Meditation on "The Symposium on Power"', in *The Anthropology of Power: Ethnographic Studies from Asia, Oceania, and the New World*, eds R. Fogelson and R.N. Adams (New York: Academic Press), 375–86.

Comaroff, John, and Jean Comaroff. 1992. *Ethnography and the Historical Imagination* (Boulder, CO: Westview).

Conservation International. 2003. 'Kayapó Indigenous Territories: Preserving Ancestral Lands', *Conservation International Online*, available at: <http://www.conservation.org/xp/frontlines/2003/fall/features/parkprofiles/parkprofile5.xml>. Accessed 13 September 2003.

Cowan, Jane. 1990. *Dance and the Body Politic in Northern Greece* (Princeton: Princeton University Press).

———, Marie-Bénédicte Dembour, and Richard A. Wilson, eds. 2001. 'Introduction', in *Culture and Rights: Anthropological Perspectives* (Cambridge: Cambridge University Press), 1–26.

Crehan, Kate. 2002. *Gramsci and Cultural Anthropology* (Berkeley: University of California Press).

Crick, Malcolm. 1976. *Explorations in Language and Meaning: Towards a Semantic Anthropology* (New York: Wiley).

Csikszentmihalyi, Mihalyi. 1981. 'Some Paradoxes in the Definition of Play', in *Play and Context*, ed. Alyce Cheska (West Point: Leisure Press), 14–25.

D'Andrade, Roy G. 1992. 'Cognitive Anthropology', in *New Directions in Psychological Anthropology*, eds Theodore Schwartz, Geoffrey M. White, and Catherine A. Lutz (Cambridge: Cambridge University Press), 47–58.

———. 1995. *The Development of Cognitive Anthropology* (Cambridge: Cambridge University Press).

Daniel, E. Valentine. 1997. 'Suffering Nation and Alienation', in *Social Suffering*, eds Arthur Kleinman, Veena Das, and Margaret Lock (Berkeley: University of California Press), 309–58.

Danner, Mark. 1994. *The Massacre at El Mozote* (New York: Vintage).

Darnell, Regna. 2001. *Invisible Genealogies: A History of Americanist Anthropology* (Lincoln: University of Nebraska Press), 16–17.

Das, Veena, and Arthur Kleinman. 2000. 'Introduction', in *Violence and Subjectivity*, eds Veena Das et al. (Berkeley: University of California Press), 1–18.

Davis, Shelton. 1977. *Victims of the Miracle* (Cambridge: Cambridge University Press).

Deacon, Terrence W. 1997. *The Symbolic Species: The Co-evolution of Language and the Brain* (New York: Norton).

de Gobineau, A. 1967 [1915]. *The Inequality of Human Races*, trans. A. Collins with Introduction by O. Levy (New York: Howard Fertig).

Dembour, Marie-Bénédicte. 2001. 'Following the Movement of a Pendulum between Universalism and Relativism', in *Culture and Rights: Anthropological Perspectives*, eds Jane Cowan, Marie-Bénédicte Dembour, and Richard A. Wilson (Cambridge: Cambridge University Press), 26–79.

de Saussure, F. 1993. *Saussure's Third Course of Lectures in General Linguistics (1910–1911): From the Notebooks of Emile Constantin*, Language and Communication Series 12, trans. R. Harris and ed. E. Komatsu (Oxford: Pergamon).

De Vos, George, and Hiroshi Wagatsuma. 1966. *Japan's Invisible Race* (Berkeley: University of California Press).

Dods, R.R. 2003. 'Pondering the Wetland: Archaeology through the Lens of Myth and Metaphor in Northern Boreal Canada', *Journal of Wetland Archaeology* 3: 17–36 (Oxbow Books).

———. 2007. 'Pyrotechnology and Landscapes of Plenty in the Northern Boreal', in *The Archaeology of Fire: Understanding Fire as Material Culture*, eds D. Gheorghiu and G. Nash (Archaeolingua).

Dolgin, Janet. 1995. 'Family Law and the Facts of Family', in *Naturalizing Power*, eds Sylvia Yanagisako and Carol Delaney (New York: Routledge), 47–67.

Douglas, Mary. 1966. *Purity and Danger* (London: Routledge & Kegan Paul).

———, and Baron Isherwood. 1979. *The World of Goods: Towards an Anthropology of Consumption* (New York: Norton).

Dozier, E.P. 1960. 'The Pueblos of the Southwestern United States', *Journal of the Royal Anthropological Institute* 90: 146–160.

———. 1970. *The Pueblo Indians of North America* (New York: Holt, Rinehart & Winston).

Drewal, Margaret. 1992. *Yoruba Ritual* (Bloomington: Indiana University Press).

Driver, Harold E. 1961. *Indians of North America* (Chicago: University of Chicago Press).

Duranti, Alessandro. 1994. *From Grammar to Politics: Linguistic Anthropology in a Western Samoan Village* (Berkeley: University of California Press).

Eggan, F. 1950. *Social Organization of the Western Pueblos* (Chicago: University of Chicago Press).

Elliot, Alison. 1981. *Child Language* (Cambridge: Cambridge University Press).

Eriksen, Thomas Hylland. 2001. 'Between Universalism and Relativism: A Critique of the UNESCO Concept of Culture', in *Culture and Rights: Anthropological Perspectives*, eds Jane Cowan, Marie-Bénédicte Dembour, and Richard A. Wilson (Cambridge: Cambridge University Press), 127–48.

Errington, Shelly. 1998. *The Death of Authentic Primitive Art and Other Tales of Progress* (Berkeley: University of California Press).

Ervin, Alexander M. 1996. 'Collaborative and Participatory Research in Urban Social Planning and Restructuring: Anthropological Experiences from a Medium-sized Canadian City', *Human Organization* 55, 3: 324–33.

Escobar, Arturo. 1992. 'Culture, Economics, and Politics in Latin American Social Movements Theory and Research', in *The Making of Social Movements in Latin America*, eds Arturo Escobar and Sonia Alvarez (Boulder, CO: Westview), 62–85.

Etienne, Mona. 1980. 'Women and Men, Cloth and Colonization: The Transformation of Production–Distribution Relations among the Baule (Ivory Coast)', in *Women and Colonization: Anthropological Perspectives*, eds Mona Etienne and Eleanor Leacock (New York: Praeger), 270–93.

Evans, Mike. 2004. 'Ethics, Anonymity, and Authorship in Community Centred Research Or Anonymity and the Island Cache', *Pimatisiwin: A Journal of Aboriginal and Indigenous Community Health* 2, 1 (spring): 60–75.

Evans-Pritchard, E.E. 1951. *Kinship and Marriage among the Nuer* (Oxford: Oxford University Press).

———. 1963. *Social Anthropology and Other Essays* (New York: Free Press).

——— 1976 [1937]. *Witchcraft, Oracles, and Magic among the Azande*, abr. edn (Oxford: Oxford University Press).

Fagen, Robert. 1981. *Animal Play Behavior* (New York: Oxford University Press).

———. 1992. 'Play, Fun, and Communication of Well-being', *Play and Culture* 5, 1: 40–58.

Farmer, Paul. 2002 [1996]. 'On Suffering and Structural Violence: A View from Below', in *The Anthropology of Politics*, ed. Joan Vincent (Malden, MA: Blackwell), 424–37.

Feinman, Gary M., Kent G. Lightfoot, and Steadman Upham. 2000. 'Political Hierarchies and Organizational Strategies in the Puebloan Southwest', *American Antiquity* 65, 3 (July): 449–70.

Ferguson, James. 2002. 'The Anti-politics Machine', in *The Anthropology of Politics*, ed. Joan Vincent (Malden, MA: Blackwell), 399–408.

Fernandez, James W. 1977. 'The Performance of Ritual Metaphors', in *The Social Use of Metaphors*, eds J.D. Sapir and J.C. Crocker (Philadelphia: University of Pennsylvania Press).

———. 1980. 'Edification by Puzzlement', in *Explorations in African Systems of Thought*, eds Ivan Karp and Charles Bird (Bloomington: Indiana University Press), 44–69.

———. 1982. *Bwiti: An Ethnography of the Religious Imagination in Africa* (Princeton: Princeton University Press).

Firth, Raymond. 1984 [1936]. *We, the Tikopia* (Stanford: Stanford University Press).

Fischer, Michael M.J. 1999. 'Emergent Forms of Life: Anthropologies of Late or Postmodernities', *Annual Review of Anthropology* 28: 455–78.

Floating in the Air, Followed by the Wind. 1973. Film distributed by Indiana University Instructional Support Services. Produced by Michigan State University.

Foley, Douglas. 1989. *Learning Capitalist Culture: Deep in the Heart of Tejas* (Philadelphia: University of Pennsylvania Press).

Forge, Anthony. 1967. 'The Abelam Artist', in *Social Organization: Essays Presented to Raymond Firth*, ed. Maurice Freedman (London: Cass), 65–84.

Fortes, Meyer. 1950. 'Kinship and Marriage among the Ashanti', in *African Systems of Kinship and Marriage*, eds A.R. Radcliffe-Brown and Daryll Forde (Oxford: Oxford University Press).

———. 1953. 'The Structure of Unilineal Descent Groups', *American Anthropologist* 55: 25–39.

———, and E.E. Evans-Pritchard. 1940. *African Political Systems* (Oxford: Oxford University Press for the International African Institute).

Foucault, Michel. 1991. 'Governmentality', in *The Foucault Effect: Studies in Governmentality*, eds Graham Burchell, Colin Gordon, and Peter Miller (Chicago: University of Chicago Press), 87–104.

Fouts, Roger. 1997. *Next of Kin: What Chimpanzees Have Taught Me about Who We Are* (New York: William Morrow & Company).

———. 1999. *The Fateful Hoaxing of Margaret Mead: A Historical Analysis of Her Samoan Research* (Boulder, CO: Westview Press).

Fratkin, Elliot. 1997. 'Pastoralism: Governance and Development Issues', *Annual Review of Anthropology* 26: 235–61.

Friedman, J. 1994. *Cultural Identity and Global Process* (London: Sage).

———. 1997. 'Global Crises, the Struggle for Cultural Identity and Intellectual Porkbarrelling: Cosmopolitans versus Locals, Ethnics and Nationals in an Era of Dehegemonisation', in *Debating Cultural Hybridity: Multicultural Identities and the Politics of Anti-racism*, eds Pnina Werbner and Tariq Modood (London: Zed Books), 70–89.

Frye, N. 1971. *The Bush Garden: Essays on the Canadian Imagination* (Toronto: House of Anansi Press Ltd).

Gampel, Yoland. 2000. 'Reflections on the Prevalence of the Uncanny in Social Violence', in *Cultures under Siege: Collective Violence and Trauma*, eds Antonius C.G.M. Robben and Marcelo M. Suárez-Orozco (Cambridge: Cambridge University Press), 48–69.

Geertz, Clifford. 1973. *The Interpretation of Cultures* (New York: Basic Books).

Geertz, Hildred, and Clifford Geertz. 1975. *Kinship in Bali* (Chicago: University of Chicago Press).

Georges, Eugenia. 1990. *The Making of a Transnational Community: Migration, Development, and Cultural Change in the Dominican Republic* (New York: Columbia University Press).

Giddens, Anthony. 1979. *Central Problems in Social Theory* (Berkeley: University of California Press).

———. 1990. *The Consequences of Modernity* (Stanford: Stanford University Press).

Gilligan, Carol. 1982. *In a Different Voice* (Cambridge, MA: Harvard University Press).

Gillman, Neil. 1992. *Sacred Fragments: Recovering Theology for the Modern Jew* (New York: Jewish Publication Society).

Gilsenan, Michael. 1982. *Recognizing Islam: Religion and Society in the Modern Arab World* (New York: Pantheon).

Ginsburg, Faye, and Rayna Rapp, eds. 1995. *Conceiving the New World Order: The Global Politics of Reproduction* (Berkeley: University of California Press).

Gledhill, John. 1994. *Power and Its Disguises* (London: Pluto Press).

Gomes, Mercio. 1996. 'Indians and Brazil: Holocaust and Survival of a Native Population', unpublished translation of *Os indios e o Brasil*, 2nd edn (Petropolis: Editora Vozes).

Goody, Jack, and S. Tambiah. 1973. *Bridewealth and Dowry* (Cambridge: Cambridge University Press).

Gordon, Colin. 1991. 'Governmental Rationality: An Introduction', in *The Foucault Effect: Studies in Governmentality*, eds Graham Burchell, Colin Gordon, and Peter Miller (Chicago: University of Chicago Press), 1–52.

Gordon, Robert. 1992. *The Bushman Myth* (Boulder, CO: Westview).

Gottlieb, Alma. 1989. 'Witches, Kings, and the Sacrifice of Identity, Or the Power of Paradox and the Paradox of Power among the Beng of Ivory Coast', in *Creativity of Power: Cosmology and Action in African Societies*, eds W. Arens and Ivan Karp (Washington, DC: Smithsonian Institution Press), 245–72.

Goulet, Jean-Guy A. 1996. 'The "Berdache"/"Two-spirit": A Comparison of Anthropological and Native Constructions of Gendered Identities among the Northern Athapaskans', *Journal of the Royal Anthropological Institute* 2, 4 (Dec.): 683–701 (published by Royal Anthropological Institute of Great Britain and Ireland).

Gramsci, Antonio. 1971. *Selections from the Prison Notebooks*, trans. Q. Hoare and G.N. Smith (New York: International Publishers).

Greenwood, David, and William Stini. 1977. *Nature, Culture, and Human History* (New York: Harper & Row).

Gregory, Richard. 1981. *Mind in Science: A History of Explanations in Psychology and Physics* (Cambridge: Cambridge University Press).

———. 1983. 'Visual Perception and Illusions: Dialogue with Richard Gregory', in *States of Mind*, ed. Jonathan Miller (New York: Pantheon), 42–64.

Guneratne, Arjun. 2002. 'Caste and State', in *South Asian Folklore: An Encyclopedia*, eds Peter Claus and Margaret Mills (New York: Garland).

Gupta, Akhil, and James Ferguson, eds. 1997. 'Discipline and Practice: "The Field" as Site, Method, and Location in Anthropology', in *Anthropological Locations: Boundaries and Grounds of a Field Science* (Berkeley: University of California Press), 1–46.

Gutierrez Muñiz, Jose A., Josefina Lopez Hurtado, and Guillermo Arias Beatón. 1997. 'La educacion ambiental en el proceso docente educativo en las montañas de Cuba', available at: <http://www.monografias.com/trabajos11/eduamb/eduamb.shtml?monosearch>.

Hacking, Ian. 1991. 'How Should We Do the History of Statistics?', in *The Foucault Effect: Studies in Governmentality*, eds Graham Burchell, Colin Gordon, and Peter Miller (Chicago: University of Chicago Press), 181–96.

Hale, Charles. 1997. 'Cultural Politics of Identity in Latin America', *Annual Review of Anthropology* 26: 567–90.

Halperin, Rhoda. 1994. *Cultural Economics: Past and Present* (Austin: University of Texas Press).

Handelman, Don. 1977. 'Play and Ritual: Complementary Frames of Metacommunication', in *It's a Funny Thing, Humour*, eds A.J. Chapman and H. Foot (London: Pergamon), 185–92.

Hanks, William. 1996. *Language and Communicative Practices* (Boulder, CO: Westview).

Hann, Christopher. 2002. 'All Kulturvölker Now? Social Anthropological Reflections on the German–American Tradition', in *Anthropology Beyond Culture*, eds Richard Fox and Barbara J. King (Oxford: Berg), 259–76.

Hannerz, Ulf. 1996. *Transnational Connections: Culture, People, Places* (New York: Routledge).

Haraway, Donna. 1991. *Simians, Cyborgs and Women: The Reinvention of Nature* (New York: Routledge).

Harding, Sandra. 1991. *Whose Science? Whose Knowledge?: Thinking from Women's Lives* (Ithaca: Cornell University Press).

Harrison, Faye. 1995. 'The Persistent Power of "Race" in the Cultural and Political Economy of Racism', *Annual Review of Anthropology* 24: 47–74.

———. 1998. 'Introduction: Expanding the Discourse on "Race"', *American Anthropologist* 100, 3: 609–31.

Hartigan Jr, John. 1997. 'Establishing the Fact of Whiteness', *American Anthropologist* 99, 3: 495–504.

Harvey, David. 1990. *The Condition of Postmodernity* (Malden, MA: Blackwell).

Hastrup, Kirsten, and Peter Elsas. 1990. 'Anthropological Advocacy: A Contradiction in Terms?', *Current Anthropology* 31, 3 (June): 301–11.

Hedican, Edward J. 2000. *Applied Anthropology in Canada: Understanding Aboriginal Issues* (Toronto: University of Toronto Press).

Heider, Karl. 1979. *Grand Valley Dani* (New York: Holt, Rinehart & Winston).

Herdt, Gilbert, ed. 1994. 'Mistaken Sex: Culture, Biology, and the Third Sex in New Guinea', in *Third Sex, Third Gender* (New York: Zone Books), 419–45.

Herring, D.A. 1994. '"There Were Young People and Old People and Babies Dying Every Week": The 1918–1919 Influenza Pandemic at Norway House', *Ethnohistory* 41, 1: 73–105.

Herskovits, Melville. 1973. *Cultural Relativism*, ed. Frances Herskovits (New York: Vintage).

Herzfeld, Michael. 2001. *Anthropology: Theoretical Practice in Culture and Society* (Malden, MA: Blackwell Publishers).

———. 2003. 'Competing Diversities: Ethnography in the Heart of Rome', *Plurimundi* 3, 5: 147–54.

Hess, David J. 1997. *Science Studies: An Advanced Introduction* (New York: New York University Press).

Hill, Jane, and Judith Irvine. 1992. *Responsibility and Evidence in Oral Discourse* (Cambridge: Cambridge University Press).

Hockett, C.F. 1966. 'The Problems of Universals in Language', in *Universals of Language*, ed. J.H. Greenberg (Cambridge, MA: MIT Press), 1–29.

Holm, John. 1988. *Pidgins and Creoles: Theory and Structure*, Vol. 1 (Cambridge: Cambridge University Press).

Holy, Ladislav. 1996. *Anthropological Perspectives on Kinship* (London: Pluto Press).

Horton, Robin. 1982. 'Tradition and Modernity Re-visited', in *Rationality and Relativism*, eds M. Hollis and Steven Lukes (Cambridge, MA: MIT Press), 201–60.

Howell, Nancy. 1988. 'Health and Safety in the Fieldwork of North American Anthropologists', *Current Anthropology* 29, 5 (Dec.): 780–7.

Høygaard, A. 1941. *Studies on the Nutrition and Physio-pathology of Eskimos*. Skrifter utgitt av Det Norske Videnskaps-Akademi i Oslo. I. Mat.-Naturv. Klasse 1940, No. 9. Oslo: I Kommisjon Hos Jacob Dybwad.

Hudson, R.A. 1980. *Sociolinguistics* (Cambridge: Cambridge University Press).

Hunter, David, and Phillip Whitten, eds. 1976. *Encyclopedia of Anthropology* (New York: Harper & Row).

Hutnyk, John. 1997. 'Adorno at Womad: South Asian Crossovers and the Limits of Hybridity-talk', in *Debating Cultural Hybridity: Multicultural Identities and the Politics of Anti-racism*, eds Pnina Werbner and Tariq Modood (London: Zed Books), 106–36.

Huyghe, Patrick. 1988. 'Profile of an Anthropologist: No Bone Unturned', *Discover* (Dec.).

Hymes, Dell. 1972. 'On Communicative Competence', in *Sociolinguistics: Selected Readings*, eds J.B. Pride and J. Holmes (Baltimore: Penguin), 269–93.

Ignace, Ron, George Speck, and Renee Taylor. 1993. 'Some Native Perspectives on Anthropology and Public Policy', in *Anthropology, Public Policy and Native Peoples in Canada*, eds Noel Dyck and James B. Walram (Montreal and Kingston: McGill-Queen's University Press), 166–91.

Inda, Jonathan Xavier, and Renato Rosaldo, eds. 2002. 'Introduction: A World in Motion', in *The Anthropology of Globalization* (Malden, MA: Blackwell).

Ingold, Tim. 1983. 'The Significance of Storage in Hunting Societies', *Man* 18: 553–71.

———. 2000. *The Perception of the Environment: Essays on Livelihood, Dwelling and Skill* (London: Routledge).

Jourdan, Christine. 1991. 'Pidgins and Creoles: The Blurring of Categories', *Annual Review of Anthropology* 20: 187–209.

Kapferer, Bruce. 1983. *A Celebration of Demons* (Bloomington: Indiana University Press).

Karp, Ivan. 1978. *Fields of Change among the Iteso of Kenya* (London: Routledge & Kegan Paul).

———. 1986. 'Laughter at Marriage: Subversion in Performance', in *The Transformation of African Marriage*, ed. David Parkin (London: International African Institute).

———, and Martha B. Kendall. 1982. 'Reflexivity in Field Work', in *Explanation in Social Science*, ed. P. Secord (Los Angeles: Sage).

Kearney, M. 1995. 'The Local and the Global: The Anthropology of Globalization and Transnationalism', *Annual Review of Anthropology* 24: 547–65.

Keesing, Roger. 1982. *Kwaio Religion* (New York: Columbia University Press).

———. 1983. *'Elota's Story* (New York: Holt, Rinehart & Winston).

———. 1992. *Custom and Confrontation: The Kwaio Struggle for Cultural Autonomy* (Chicago: University of Chicago Press).

Keller, Evelyn Fox. 1997. 'Secrets of God, Nature, and Life', in *The Gender/Sexuality Reader*, eds Roger Lancaster and Micaela di Leonardo (New York: Routledge), 209–18.

Kelly, John D., and Martha Kaplan. 2001. *Represented Communities: Fiji and World Decolonization* (Chicago: University of Chicago Press).

Kenny, Michael G. 1999. 'A Place for Memory: The Interface between Individual and Collective History', *Comparative Studies in Society and History* 41, 3 (July): 420–37.

Knorr Cetina, Karin. 2000. *Epistemic Cultures* (Cambridge, MA: Harvard University Press).

Köhler, G. 1978. *Global Apartheid* (New York: Institute for World Order).

Kopytoff, Igor, and Suzanne Miers, eds. 1977. 'Introduction: African "Slavery" as an Institution of Marginality', in *Slavery in Africa* (Madison: University of Wisconsin Press), 3–84.

Kroeber, Alfred L. 1939. 'Cultural and Natural Areas of Native North America', *University of California Publications in American Archaeology and Ethnology* 38 (Berkeley: University of California Press).

Kuhn, Thomas. 1962. *The Structure of Scientific Revolutions*, 1st edn (Chicago: University of Chicago Press).

———. 1970. *The Structure of Scientific Revolutions* (Chicago: University of Chicago Press).

———. 1979. 'Metaphor in Science', in *Metaphor and Thought*, ed. Andrew Ortony (Cambridge: Cambridge University Press), 409–19.

Kumar, Nita. 1992. *Friends, Brothers, and Informants: Fieldwork Memoirs of Banaras* (Berkeley: University of California Press).

Kunitz, S.J. 1983. *Disease, Change and the Role of Medicine in the Navajo Experience* (Berkeley: University of California Press).

Kuper, Adam. 1982. *Wives for Cattle: Bridewealth and Marriage in Southern Africa* (London: Routledge & Kegan Paul).

———. 1999. *Culture: The Anthropologists' Account* (Cambridge, MA: Harvard University Press).

Labov, William. 1972. *Language in the Inner City: Studies in the Black English Vernacular* (Philadelphia: University of Pennsylvania Press).

Lakoff, George, and Mark Johnson. 1980. *Metaphors We Live By* (Berkeley: University of California Press).

Lancaster, Roger. 1992. *Life Is Hard* (Berkeley: University of California Press).

Langer, Lawrence L. 1997. 'The Alarmed Vision: Social Suffering and Holocaust Atrocity', in *Social Suffering*, eds Arthur Kleinman, Veena Das, and Margaret Lock (Berkeley: University of California Press), 47–65.

Laqueur, Thomas. 1990. *Making Sex* (Cambridge, MA: Harvard University Press).

Larkin, Brian. 2002. 'Indian Films and Nigerian Lovers: Media and the Creation of Parallel Modernities', in *The Anthropology of Globalization*, eds Jonathan Xavier Inda and Renato Rosaldo (Malden, MA: Blackwell), 350–78.

Lave, Jean. 1988. *Cognition in Practice* (Cambridge: Cambridge University Press).

Lee, Richard B. 1992a. 'Art, Science, or Politics? The Crisis in Hunter–Gatherer Studies', *American Anthropologist* 94: 31–54.

———. 1992b. *The Dobe Ju/'hoansi*, 2nd edn (New York: Holt, Rinehart & Winston).

———. 2002. *The Dobe Ju/'hoansi*, 3rd edn (Belmont, CA: Wadsworth).

Lever, Janet. 1983. *Soccer Madness* (Chicago: University of Chicago Press).

———. 1995. *Soccer Madness* (Prospect Heights, IL: Waverland Press).

Levi-Strauss, Claude. 1967 [1962]. *L'antropologie structurale* (Paris: Plon), trans. under the title *Structural Anthropology*, eds Claire Jacobson and Brooke Grundfest Schoepf (New York: Doubleday Anchor).

Levine, Nancy. 1980. 'Nyinba Polyandry and the Allocation of Paternity', *Journal of Comparative Family Studies* 11, 3: 283–8.

———. 1988. *The Dynamics of Polyandry: Kinship, Domesticity, and Population on the Tibetan Border* (Chicago: University of Chicago Press).

———, and Walter Sangree. 1980. 'Women with Many Husbands', *Journal of Comparative Family Studies* 11, 3.

Levinson, S.C. 1998. 'Studying Spatial Conceptualization across Cultures', in *Language, Space, and Culture*, ed. E. Danziger, special issue of *Ethos: Journal of the Society for Psychological Anthropology* 26, 1: 7–24.

Lewellen, Ted. 1983. *Political Anthropology* (South Hadley, MA: Bergin & Garvey).

Lewis, I.M. 1967. *A Pastoral Democracy: A Study of Pastoralism and Politics among the Northern Somali of the Horn of Africa* (London: Oxford University Press).

Lewis, Philip. 1997. 'Arenas of Ethnic Negotiations: Co-operation and Conflict in Bradford', in *The Politics of Multiculturalism in the New Europe: Racism, Identity, and Community*, eds Tariq Modood and Pnina Werbner (London: Zed Books), 126–46.

Lewontin, Richard, Steven Rose, and Leon J. Kamin. 1984. *Not in Our Genes* (New York: Pantheon).

Liebersohn, Harry. 1994. 'Discovering Indigenous Nobility: Tocqueville, Chamisso, and Romantic Travel Writing', *American Historical Review* 99, 3 (June): 746–66.

Linke, Uli. 1997. 'Gendered Difference, Violent Imagination: Blood, Race, Nation', *American Anthropologist* 99, 3: 559–73.

Little, Kenneth. 1967. *The Mende of Sierra Leone* (London: Routledge & Kegan Paul).

Lock, Margaret. 2001. 'The Tempering of Medical Anthropology: Troubling Natural Categories', *Medical Anthropology Quarterly* 15: 478–92.

Lukács, Georg. 1971. *History and Class Consciousness: Studies in Marxist Dialectics* (Cambridge, MA: MIT Press).

MacCormack, Carol P. 1980. 'Proto-social to Adult: A Sherbro Transformation', in *Nature, Culture, and Gender*, eds Carol MacCormack and Marilyn Strathern (Cambridge: Cambridge University Press), 95–118.

McGregor, G. 1985. *The Wacousta Syndrome* (Toronto: University of Toronto Press).

McPherson, Naomi. 2007. 'Myth Primogeniture and Long Distance Trade-friends in Northwest New Britain, Papua New Guinea', *Oceania* 77, 2 (July): 129–57.

Mafeje, A. 1976. 'The Problem of Anthropology in Historical Perspective: An Inquiry into the Growth of the Social Sciences', *Canadian Journal of African Studies* 10, 2: 307–33.

Malinowski, Bronislaw. 1944. *A Scientific Theory of Culture and Other Essays* (New York: Oxford University Press).

———. 1948 [1926]. *Magic, Science, and Religion, and Other Essays* (New York: Doubleday Anchor).

Malkki, Liisa. 1992. 'National Geographic: The Rooting of Peoples and the Territorialization of National Identity among Scholars and Refugees', *Cultural Anthropology* 7, 1: 24–44.

Mandler, George. 1975. *Mind and Emotion* (New York: Wiley).

———. 1983. 'The Nature of Emotion: Dialogue with George Mandler', in *States of Mind*, ed. Jonathan Miller (New York: Pantheon), 136–52.

Mann, Charles C. 2005. *1491: New Revelations of the Americas before Columbus* (New York: Random House).

Maquet, Jacques. 1970. 'Rwanda Castes', in *Social Stratification in Africa*, eds Arthur Tuden and Leonard Plotnicov (New York: Free Press).

Marcus, George. 1995. 'Ethnography in/of the World System: The Emergence of Multi-sited Ethnography', *Annual Review of Anthropology* 24: 95–117.

Marks, Jonathan. 1995. *Human Biodiversity* (New York: Aldine).

Marx, Karl. 1963. *The 18th Brumaire of Louis Bonaparte* (New York: International Publishers).

———. 1977 [1932]. 'The German Ideology', selections reprinted in *Karl Marx: Selected Writings*, ed. David McLellan (Oxford: Oxford University Press).

Mason, O.T. 1896. 'Influence of Environment upon Human Industries or Arts', in *Annual Review of the Smithsonian Institution of 1895* (Washington: Smithsonian Institution), 639–65.

———. 1902. *A Study of Industry among Primitive Peoples* (London: Walter Scott Publishing Co.), originally *The Origins of Invention: A Study of Industry among Primitive Peoples* (London: Walter Scott Publishing Co., 1895).

Matthiasson, John S. 1992. *Living on the Land: Northern Baffin Inuit Respond to Change* (Peterborough, ON: Broadview Press).

Mauss, Marcel. 2000 [1950]. *The Gift: The Form and Reason for Exchange in Archaic Societies* (New York: W.W. Norton).

Mead, George Herbert. 1934. *Mind, Self, and Society* (Chicago: University of Chicago Press).

Meisch, Lynn. 2002. *Andean Entrepreneurs: Otavalo Merchants and Musicians in the Global Arena* (Austin: University of Texas Press).

Melotti, Umberto. 1997. 'International Migration in Europe: Social Projects and Political Cultures', in *The Politics of Multiculturalism in the New Europe: Racism, Identity and Community*, eds Tariq Modood and Pnina Werbner (London: Zed Books), 73–92.

Merry, Sally Engle. 2001. 'Changing Rights, Changing Culture', in *Culture and Rights: Anthropological Perspectives*, eds Jane Cowan, Marie-Bénédicte Dembour, and Richard A. Wilson (Cambridge: Cambridge University Press), 31–55.

Messer, Ellen. 1993. 'Anthropology and Human Rights', *Annual Review of Anthropology* 22: 221–49.

Mignolo, Walter D. 2002. 'The Many Faces of Cosmo-polis: Border Thinking and Critical Cosmopolitanism', in *Cosmopolitanism*, eds Carol A. Breckenridge et al. (Durham, NC: Duke University Press), 157–87.

Miller, Daniel, ed. 1995. *Acknowledging Consumption: A Review of New Studies* (New York: Routledge).

———, and Don Slater. 2000. *The Internet: An Ethnographic Approach* (Oxford: Berg).

Miner, Horace. 1956. 'Body Ritual among the Nacirema', *American Anthropologist* 58, 3 (June): 503–7, available at: <http://www.msu.edu/~jdowell/miner.html>.

Minturn, Leigh. 1993. *Sita's Daughters* (Oxford/New York: Oxford University Press).

Miracle, Andrew. 1991. 'Aymara Joking Behavior', *Play and Culture* 4, 2: 144–52.

Mitra, Subrata. 1994. 'Caste, Democracy, and the Politics of Community Formation in India', in *Contextualizing Caste: Post-dumontian Approaches*, eds Mary Searle-Chatterjee and Ursula Sharma (Oxford: Blackwell Publishers/The Sociological Review), 49–71.

Modood, Tariq. 1997. 'Introduction: The Politics of Multiculturalism in the New Europe', in *The Politics of Multiculturalism in the New Europe: Racism, Identity, and Community*, eds Tariq Modood and Pnina Werbner (Cambridge: Cambridge University Press), 1–25.

Moll, Luis, ed. 1990. *Vygotsky and Education* (Cambridge: Cambridge University Press).

Montgomery, Heather. 2001. 'Imposing Rights? A Case Study of Child Prostitution in Thailand', in *Culture and Rights: Anthropological Perspectives*, eds Jane Cowan, Marie-Bénédicte Dembour, and Richard A. Wilson (Cambridge: Cambridge University Press), 80–101.

Morgan, L.H. 1871. *Systems of Consanguinity and Affinity of the Human Family* (Washington: Smithsonian Institute).

———. 1877. *Ancient Society: Researches in the Lines of Human Progress from Savagery through Barbarism to Civilization* (New York: Holt).

Morgan, Marcyliena. 1995. 'Theories and Politics in African American English', *Annual Review of Anthropology* 23: 325–45.

Morris, A. 1877. *The Treaties of Canada with the Indians of Manitoba and the North-West Territories, including the Negotiations on Which They Were Based, and Other Information Relating Thereto* (Toronto: Belford, Clarke & Co.).

Murphy, Robert, and Yolanda Murphy. 1974. *Women of the Forest* (New York: Columbia University Press).

Myerhoff, Barbara. 1974. *Peyote Hunt* (Ithaca: Cornell University Press).

Naiman, R.J., J.M. Melillo, and J.E. Hobbie. 1986. 'Ecosystem Alteration of Boreal Forest Streams by Beaver (*Castor Canadensis*)', *Ecology* 67, 5: 1254–69.

Nanda, Serena. 1994. 'Hijras: An Alternative Sex and Gender Role', in *Third Sex, Third Gender*, ed. Gilbert Herdt (New York: Zone Books), 373–417.

Nash, June. 1979. *We Eat the Mines, and the Mines Eat Us* (New York: Columbia University Press).

Nordstrom, Carolyn. 1993. 'Treating the Wounds of War', *Cultural Survival Quarterly* 17 (summer): 28–30.

O'Donnell, Guillermo, and Philippe Schmitter. 1986. *Tentative Conclusions about Uncertain Democracies* (Baltimore: Johns Hopkins University Press).

Odling-Smee, F.J. 1994. 'Niche Construction, Evolution and Culture', in *Companion Encyclopedia of Anthropology: Humanity, Culture, and Social Life*, ed. Tim Ingold (London: Routledge).

Oldham, Paul, and Miriam Anne Frank. 2008. '"We the People. . .": The United Nations Declaration on the Rights of Indigenous Peoples', *Anthropology Today* 24, 2: 5–9.

Ong, Aiwa. 2002 [1999]. 'The Pacific Shuttle: Family, Citizenship, and Capital Circuits', in *The Anthropology of Globalization*, eds Jonathan Xavier Inda and Renato Rosaldo (Malden, MA: Blackwell), 172–97.

Ortner, Sherry. 1973. 'On Key Symbols', *American Anthropologist* 75, 5: 1338–46.

———, ed. 1999. *The Fate of 'Culture': Geertz and Beyond* (Berkeley, CA: University of California Press).

Overholt, T.W., and J.B. Callicott. 1982. *Clothed-in-Fur and Other Tales: An Introduction to an Ojibwa World View* (Washington: University Press of America).

Oyama, Susan. 1985. *The Ontogeny of Information* (Cambridge: Cambridge University Press).

Parkin, David. 1984. 'Mind, Body, and Emotion among the Giriama', paper presented in *Humanity as Creator* lecture series (St Cloud State University).

Parsons, E.C. 1939. *Pueblo Hzdian Religion*, 2 vols (Chicago: University of Chicago Press).

Partridge, William L., ed. 1984. 'Training Manual in Development Anthropology', special publication of the American Anthropological Association and the Society for Applied Anthropology 17 (Washington, DC: American Anthropological Association).

Peletz, Michael. 1995. 'Kinship Studies in Late Twentieth-century Anthropology', *Annual Review of Anthropology* 24: 343–72.

Pickering, Andrew. 1995. *The Mangle of Practice: Time, Agency and Science* (Chicago: University of Chicago Press).

Pieterse, Jan Nederveen. 1995. 'Globalization as Hybridization', in *Global Modernities*, eds Mike Featherstone and Scott Lash (London: Sage).

Pike, Kenneth L. 1943. *Phonetics, a Critical Analysis of Phonetic Theory and a Technique for the Practical Description of Sounds* (Ann Arbor: University of Michigan Press).

———. 1967. *Language in Relation to a Unified Theory of the Structure of Human Behaviour* (The Hague: Mouton).

Poewe, Karla. 1989. 'On the Metonymic Structure of Religious Experiences: The Example of Charismatic Christianity', *Cultural Dynamics* 2, 4: 361–80.

Popper, K.R. 1979. *The Logic of Scientific Discovery* (London: Unwin Hyman).

Potts, Richard. 1996. *Humanity's Descent* (New York: Morrow).

Rabinow, Paul. 1977. *Reflections on Fieldwork in Morocco* (Berkeley: University of California Press).

Rainforest Foundation US. 2003. 'The Panará', *Rainforest Foundation US Online*, available at: <http://www.rainforestfoundation.org/1panara.html>. Accessed 13 September 2003.

Ray, A.J. 1976. 'Diffusion of Disease in the Western Interior of Canada, 1830–1950', *Geographical Review* 66, 2: 139–57.

Redfield, Robert, Ralph Linton, and Melville Herskovits. 1936. 'Memorandum for the Study of Acculturation', *American Anthropologist* 38: 149–52.

Reeves, Edward, Billie DeWalt, and Kathleen DeWalt. 1987. 'The International Sorghum/Millet Research Project', in *Anthropological Praxis*, eds Robert Wolfe and Shirley Fiske (Boulder, CO: Westview), 72–83.

Reeves-Ellington, Richard H. 1993. 'Using Cultural Skills for Co-operative Advantage in Japan', *Human Organization* 52, 2: 203–16.

Rezende, Claudia Barcellos. 1999. 'Building Affinity through Friendship', in *The Anthropology of Friendship*, eds Sandra Bell and Simon Coleman (Oxford: Berg), 79–97.

Ribeiro, Gustavo Lins. 1998. 'Cybercultural Politics: Political Activism at a Distance in a Transnational World', in *Cultures of Politics, Politics of Cultures: Re-visioning Latin American Social Movements*, eds Sonia E. Alvarez, Evelina Dagnino, and Arturo Escobar (Boulder, CO: Westview), 325–52.

Rich, E.E. 1961a. *The Hudson's Bay Company, 1670–1870: Vol. I, 1670–1763* (New York: Macmillan).

Richards, Audrey. 1954. *Chisungu* (London: Methuen).

Riddington, Robin. 1982. 'Technology, World View, and Adaptive Strategy in a Northern Hunting Society', *Canadian Review of Sociology and Anthropology* 19, 4: 469–81.

———. 1998. 'Coyote's Cannon: Sharing Stories with Thomas King', *American Indian Quarterly* 22, 3 (summer): 343–62.

Ringrose, Kathryn M. 1994. 'Living in the Shadows: Eunuchs and Gender in Byzantium', in *Third Sex, Third Gender*, ed. Gilbert Herdt (New York: Zone Books), 85–109.

Rogers, E.S., and M.B. Black. 1976. 'Subsistence Strategy in the Fish and Hare Period, Northern Ontario: The Weagomow Ojibwa, 1880–1920', *Journal of Anthropological Research* (SWJA) 32, 1: 1–43.

Ronan, Colin A., and Joseph Needham. 1978. *Shorter Science and Civilisation in China* (Cambridge: Cambridge University Press).

Rosaldo, Renato. 2008. 'Of Headhunters and Soldiers: Separating Cultural and Ethical Relativism', *Markkula Center for Applied Ethics*, available at: <http://www.scu.edu/ethics/publications/iie/v11n1/relativism.html>.

Roscoe, Will. 1994. 'How to Become a Berdache: Toward a Unified Analysis of Gender Diversity', in *Third Sex, Third Gender*, ed. Gilbert Herdt (New York: Zone Books), 329–72.

Rosen, Lawrence. 1984. *Bargaining for Reality: The Constructions of Social Relations in a Muslim Community* (Chicago: University of Chicago Press).

Rubin, Jeffrey W. 1997. *Decentering the Regime: Ethnicity, Radicalism, and Democracy in Juchitán, Mexico* (Durham, NC: Duke University Press).

Sabloff, Jeremy A. 2008. *Archaeology Matters: Action Archaeology in the Modern World* (Walnut Creek, CA: Left Coast Press, Inc.).

Sacks, Karen. 1979. *Sisters and Wives* (Urbana: University of Illinois Press).

Sahlins, Marshall. 1972. *Stone Age Economics* (Chicago: Aldine).

———. 1976a. *The Use and Abuse of Biology* (Ann Arbor: University of Michigan Press).

———. 1976b. *Culture and Practical Reason* (Chicago: University of Chicago Press).

———. 1995. *How 'Natives' Think: About Captain Cook for Example* (Chicago: University of Chicago Press).

Salzman, Philip Carl. 2002. 'On Reflexivity', *American Anthropologist* 104, 3: 805–13.

Sanjek, Roger. 1994. 'The Enduring Inequalities of Race', in *Race*, eds Steven Gregory and Roger Sanjek (New Brunswick, NJ: Rutgers University Press), 1–17.

Sapir, Edward. 1966 [1933]. *Culture, Language, and Personality*, ed. David Mandelbaum (Berkeley: University of California Press).

Schiffauer, Werner. 1997. 'Islam as a Civil Religion: Political Culture and the Organization of Diversity in Germany', in *The Politics of Multiculturalism in the New Europe: Racism, Identity, and Community*, eds Tariq Modood and Pnina Werbner (London: Zed Books), 147–66.

Schiller, Nina Glick, and Georges Fouron. 2002. 'Long-distance Nationalism Defined', in *The Anthropology of Politics*, ed. Joan Vincent (Malden, MA: Blackwell), 356–65.

Schneider, David. 1968. *American Kinship: A Cultural Account* (Englewood Cliffs, NJ: Prentice-Hall).

Schultz, Emily. 1984. 'From Pagan to Pullo: Ethnic Identity Change in Northern Cameroon', *Africa* 54, 1: 46–64.

———. 1990. *Dialogue at the Margins: Whorf, Bakhtin, and Linguistic Relativity* (Madison: University of Wisconsin Press).

Schwartzman, Helen. 1978. *Transformations: The Anthropology of Children's Play* (New York: Plenum).

Schwartzman, Steven. 1998. 'Success Story in Brazil: The Return of the Panará', *The Aisling Magazine*, available at: <http://www.aislingmagazine.com/Anu/articles/TAM23/Success.html>. Accessed 13 September 2003.

Scott, James C. 1985. *Weapons of the Weak* (New Haven: Yale University Press).

————. 1990. *Domination and the Arts of Resistance: Hidden Transcripts* (New Haven: Yale University Press).

Segalen, Martine. 1986. *Historical Anthropology of the Family* (Cambridge: Cambridge University Press).

Service, Elman R. 1975. *Origins of the State and Civilization: The Process of Cultural Evolution* (New York: Norton).

Shapiro, Robert. 2007. 'A Simpler Origin for Life', *Scientific American* 296 (June): 46–53.

Sharma, Ursula. 1999. *Caste* (Buckingham: Open University Press).

Shepherd, Gill. 1987. 'Rank, Gender, and Homosexuality: Mombasa as a Key to Understanding Sexual Options', in *The Cultural Construction of Sexuality*, ed. Pat Caplan (London: Tavistock), 240–70.

Shostak, Marjorie. 1981. *Nisa: The Life and Words of a !Kung Woman* (New York: Vintage Books).

Silverstein, Michael. 1976. 'Shifters, Linguistic Categories, and Cultural Description', in *Meaning in Anthropology*, eds Keith Basso and Henry Selby (Albuquerque: University of New Mexico Press), 11–55.

————. 1985. 'The Functional Stratification of Language and Ontogenesis', in *Culture, Communication, and Cognition: Vygotskian Perspectives*, ed. James Wertsch (Cambridge: Cambridge University Press), 205–35.

Smart, Alan. 1999. 'Expressions of Interest: Friendship and *Guanzi* in Chinese Societies', in *The Anthropology of Friendship*, eds Sandra Bell and Simon Coleman (Oxford: Berg), 119–36.

Smedley, Audrey. 1993. *Race in North America: Origin and Evolution of a Worldview* (Boulder, CO: Westview Press).

————. 1998. '"Race" and the Construction of Human Identity', *American Anthropologist* 100, 3: 690–702.

Smith, Mary G. 1981 [1954]. 'Introduction', in *Baba of Karo* (New Haven: Yale University Press).

Smith, Wilfred Cantwell. 1982. *Towards a World Theology* (Philadelphia: Westminster).

Solway, Jacqueline, and Richard Lee. 1990. 'Foragers, Genuine or Spurious: Situating the Kalahari San in History', *Current Anthropology* 31: 109–46.

Sontag, Susan. 2004. *Regarding the Pain of Others* (New York: Picador).

Spencer, Jonathan. 2000. 'On not Becoming a "Terrorist": Problems of Memory, Agency, and Community in the Sri Lankan Conflict', in *Violence and Subjectivity*, eds Veena Das, Arthur Kleinman, Mamphela Ramphele, and Pamela Reynolds (Berkeley: University of California Press), 120–40.

Spiro, Melford. 1977. *Kinship and Marriage in Burma: A Cultural and Psychodynamic Account* (Berkeley: University of California Press).

Starn, Orin. 1992. '"I Dreamed of Foxes and Hawks": Reflections on Peasant Protest, New Social Movements, and the *Rondas Campesinas* of Northern Peru', in *The Making of Social Movements in Latin America: Identity, Strategy, and Democracy*, eds Arturo Escobar and Sonia E. Alvarez, Series in Political Economy and Economic Development in Latin America (Boulder, CO: Westview), 89–111.

Statistics Canada. 2005a. 'Family Violence in Canada: A Statistical Profile', *The Daily* (14 July), available at: <http://www.statcan.gc.ca/daily-quotidien/050714/tdq050714-eng.htm>.

————. 2005b. *The Daily* (9 Mar.), available at: <http://www.statcan.ca/Daily/English/050309/d050309b.htm>.

Stewart, Charles, and Rosalind Shaw. 1994. *Syncretism/Anti-syncretism* (London: Routledge).

Strathern, Marilyn. 1972. *Women in between* (London: Academic Press).

————. 1992. *Reproducing the Future: Anthropology, Kinship, and the New Reproductive Technologies* (New York: Routledge).

Suárez-Orozco, Marcelo M., and Antonius C.G.M. Robben, eds. 2000. 'Interdisciplinary Perspectives on Violence and Trauma', in *Cultures under Siege: Collective Violence and Trauma* (Cambridge: Cambridge University Press), 1–41.

Sutton-Smith, Brian. 1992. 'Notes Towards a Critique of Twentieth-century Psychological Play Theory', in *Homo ludens: Der spielende Mensch*, Vol. 2, ed. Günther G. Bauer (München-Salzburg: Musikverlag Emil Katzbichler), 95–108.

Tannen, Deborah. 1990. *You Just Don't Understand: Women and Men in Conversation* (New York: Ballantine).

Tcherkézoff, Serge. 1998. 'Is Aristocracy Good for Democracy? A Contemporary Debate in Western Samoa', in *Pacific Answers to Western Hegemony: Cultural Practices of Identity Construction*, ed. Jürg Wassmann (Oxford: Berg), 417–34.

Tedlock, Barbara. 2005. *The Woman in the Shaman's Body: Reclaiming the Feminine in Religion and Medicine* (Random House).

Thomas, Nicholas. 1991. *Entangled Objects* (Cambridge, MA: Harvard University Press).

————. 1996. 'Cold Fusion', *American Anthropologist* 98: 9–25.

Thomsen, C.J. 1936 [1836]. *Ledetraad til Nordisk Oldkyndighed* (*A Guide to Northern Antiquities*) (Copenhagen).

Tollefson, Kenneth D. 1995. 'Potlatching and Political Organization among the Northwest Coast Indians', *Ethnology* 34, 1 (winter): 53–73.

Tonkinson, Robert. 1998. 'National Identity: Australia after Mabo', in *Pacific Answers to Western Hegemony: Cultural Practices of Identity Construction*, ed. Jürg Wassmann (Oxford: Berg), 287–310.

Tooker, Elisabeth. 1992. 'Lewis H. Morgan and His Contemporaries', *American Anthropologist* 94, 2: 357–75.

Trigger, B.D. 1975. 'Review of Culture and Nationality by A.G. Bailey', *American Anthropologist* 77, 3: 636–7.

Trigger, B.G. 1981. 'Ontario People and the Epidemics of 1634–1640', in *Indians, Animals, and the Fur Trade*, ed. S. Krech III (Athens: University of Georgia Press), 21–38.

Trouillot, Michel-Rolph. 1991. 'Anthropology and the Savage Slot: The Poetics and Politics of Otherness', in *Recapturing Anthropology*, ed. Richard Fox (Santa Fe, NM: SAR Press), 17–44.

————. 1994. 'Culture, Color and Politics in Haiti', in *Race*, eds Steven Gregory and Roger Sanjek (New Brunswick, NJ: Rutgers University Press), 149–74.

Turnbull, Colin. 1961. *The Forest People* (New York: Simon & Schuster).

Turner, Terence. 1989. 'Amazonian Indians Fight to Save Their Forest', *Anthropology Newsletter* 30, 3: 21–2.

Turner, Victor. 1969. *The Ritual Process* (Chicago: Aldine).

Tylor, E.B. 1958 [1871]. *Primitive Culture* (New York: Harper & Row).

Union of BC Indian Chiefs. 2008. 'First Nations Pressure Canada to Endorse the UN Declaration on the Rights of Indigenous Peoples' (12 Sept.), available at: <http://www.ubcic.bc.ca/News_Releases/UBCICNews09120801.htm>.

van den Berghe, Pierre. 1970. 'Race, Class, and Ethnicity in South Africa', in *Social Stratification in Africa*, eds Arthur Tuden and Leonard Plotnicov (New York: Free Press), 345–71.

van der Veer, Peter. 1997. '"The Enigma of Arrival": Hybridity and Authenticity in the Global Space', in *Debating Cultural Hybridity: Multicultural Identities and the Politics of Anti-racism*, eds Pnina Werbner and Tariq Modood (London: Zed Books), 90–195.

Van Gennep, Arnold. 1960. *The Rites of Passage* (Chicago: University of Chicago Press).

van Willigen, John. 1991. *Anthropology in Use: A Source Book on Anthropological Practice* (Boulder, CO: Westview).

Vincent, Joan, ed. 2002. 'Introduction', in *The Anthropology of Politics* (Malden, MA: Blackwell), 1–13.

Vogel, Susan M. 1997. *Baule: African Art, Western Eyes* (New Haven: Yale University Press).

Voloshinov, V.N. 1986 [1929]. *Marxism and the Philosophy of Language*, trans. Ladislav Matejka and I.R. Titunik (Cambridge, MA: Harvard University Press).

———. 1987 [1926]. 'Discourse in Life and Discourse in Art', in *Freudianism*, trans. and ed. I.R. Titunik in collaboration with Neil H. Bruss (Bloomington: Indiana University Press), 93–116.

Von Maltzahn, K.E. 1994. *Nature as Landscape: Dwelling and Understanding* (Montreal and Kingston: McGill-Queen's University Press).

Vonnegut Jr, Kurt. 1976. *Slapstick, or Lonesome No More!* (New York: Dell Publishing).

Vygotsky, Lev. 1978. *Mind in Society: The Development of Higher Psychological Processes* (Cambridge, MA: Harvard University Press).

Wallace, A.F.C. 1966. *Religion: An Anthropological View* (New York: Random House).

———. 1972. *The Death and Rebirth of the Seneca* (New York: Vintage).

Wallerstein, Immanuel. 1974. *The Modern World System* (New York: Academic Press).

Wardlow, Holly. 2007. 'Men's Extramarital Sexuality in Rural Papua New Guinea', *American Journal of Public Health* 97, 6 (26 Apr.): 1006–14.

Warner, W. Lloyd. 1936. 'American Caste and Class', *American Sociological Review* 42, 2: 234–7.

Waubageshig, ed. 1970. *The Only Good Indian: Essays by Canadian Indians* (Toronto: New Press).

Weiner, Annette. 1976. *Women of Value, Men of Renown* (Austin: University of Texas Press).

———. 1980. 'Stability in Banana Leaves: Colonization and Women in Kiriwina, Trobriand Islands', in *Women and Colonization: Anthropological Perspectives*, eds Mona Etienne and Eleanor Leacock (New York: Praeger), 270–93.

———. 1988. *The Trobrianders of Papua New Guinea* (New York: Holt, Rinehart & Winston).

Weinker, Curtis. 1995. 'Biological Anthropology: The Current State of the Discipline', in *Biological Anthropology: The State of the Science*, eds Noel T. Boaz and Linda Wolfe (Bend, OR: International Institute for Human Evolutionary Research).

Werbner, Pnina. 1997. 'Afterword: Writing Multiculturalism and Politics in the New Europe', in *The Politics of Multiculturalism in the New Europe: Racism, Identity, and Community*, eds Tariq Modood and Pnina Werbner (London: Zed Books), 261–7.

Weston, Kath. 1991. *Families We Choose* (New York: Columbia University Press).

———. 1995. 'Forever Is a Long Time: Romancing the Real in Gay Kinship Ideologies', in *Naturalizing Power*, eds Sylvia Yanagisako and Carol Delaney (New York: Routledge), 87–110.

Whorf, Benjamin. 1956. *Language, Thought, and Reality*, ed. John B. Carroll (Cambridge, MA: MIT Press).

Wilk, Richard. 1996. *Economies and Cultures* (Boulder, CO: Westview).

Williams, Brackette. 1989. 'A Class Act: Anthropology and the Race to Nation across Ethnic Terrain', *Annual Review of Anthropology* 18: 401–44.

Wilmsen, Edwin. 1989. *Land Filled with Flies: A Political Economy of the Kalahari* (Chicago: University of Chicago Press).

———. 1991. 'Pastoro-foragers to "Bushmen": Transformation in Kalahari Relations of Property, Production, and Labor', in *Herders, Warriors, and Traders: Pastoralism in Africa*, eds John G. Galaty and Pierre Bonte (Boulder, CO: Westview), 248–63.

Wilson, Monica. 1951. *Good Company* (Oxford: Oxford University Press).

Winn, Peter. 1992. *Americas* (New York: Pantheon).

Wissler, C. 1914. 'Material Cultures of the North American Indians', *American Anthropologist* 16: 447–505.

Witherspoon, Gary. 1975. *Navajo Kinship and Marriage* (Chicago: University of Chicago Press).

Wolcott, Harry F. 1999. *Ethnography: A Way of Seeing* (Walnut Creek, CA: AltaMira Press).

Wolf, Eric. 1969. *Peasant Wars of the Twentieth Century* (New York: Harper & Row).

———. 1982. *Europe and the People without History* (Berkeley: University of California Press).

———. 1994. 'Facing Power: Old Insights, New Questions', in *Assessing Cultural Anthropology*, ed. Robert Borofsky (New York: McGraw-Hill), 218–28.

Wolfe, Linda. 1995. 'Current Research in Field Primatology', in *Biological Anthropology: The State of the Science*, eds Noel T. Boaz and Linda Wolfe (Bend, OR: International Institute for Human Evolutionary Research), 149–67.

Woolard, Kathryn A. 1998. 'Introduction: Language Ideology as a Field of Inquiry', in *Language Ideologies: Practice and Theory*, eds Bambi Schieffelin, Kathryn Woolard, and Paul V. Kroskrity (New York: Oxford University Press), 3–47.

Woost, M.D. 1993. 'Nationalizing the Local Past in Sri Lanka: Histories of Nation and Development in a Sinhalese Village', *American Ethnologist* 20, 3: 502–21.

Yengoyan, A. 1986. 'Theory in Anthropology: The Demise of the Concept of Culture', *Comparative Studies in Society and History* 28, 2: 368–74.

Yuval-Davis, Nina. 1997. 'Ethnicity, Gender Relations and Multiculturalism', in *Debating Cultural Hybridity: Multicultural Identities and the Politics of Anti-racism*, eds Pnina Werbner and Tariq Modood (London: Zed Books), 193–208.

Credits

Photographic

Chapter 1 1.1, © iStockphoto.com/Vasiliki Varvaki; 1.4, © iStockphoto.com/Mel Bedggood; 1.5, courtesy of Roberta Robin Dods; 1.6, courtesy of Roberta Robin Dods; 1.7, National Anthropological Archives, Smithsonian Institution (OPPS NEG MNH 8298); 1.8, Scott Sady/tahoeLight.com; 1.10, © iStockphoto.com/Norbert Bieberstein; 1.11, © iStockphoto.com/Jeff Chevrier; 1.12, The Canadian Press/Tom Hanson. **Chapter 2** 2.1, © iStockphoto.com/Karel Gallas; 2.2L, courtesy of the Institute for Intercultural Studies, Inc., NY; 2.2R, courtesy of Naomi McPherson; 2.3, Ryan J. Cook; 2.4, © iStockphoto.com/Jeremy Edwards; 2.5, Peter Kelly; 2.6, © iStockphoto.com/John Woodworth. **Chapter 3** 3.1, UTA, Daniel Wilson, A1973-0026/517P(99)0003(IB001); 3.2, UTA, Thomas F. McIlwraith, A1978-0041/014(15); 3.3, Bud Glunz, NFB, Library and Archives Canada, PA-161446; 3.4, Archives of Manitoba; 3.5, © iStockphoto.com/poco_bw; 3.6, The Canadian Press/Fred Chartrand; 3.7, © Bettmann/Corbis; 3.8, courtesy of the Peabody Essex Museum, Salem, MA; 3.10, Arjun Guneratne. **Chapter 4** 4.1, © iStockphoto.com/Alex Jeffries; 4.3, © iStockphoto.com/Liz Leyden; 4.4, © iStockphoto.com/Solidago; 4.5, © iStockphoto.com/Marisa Allegra; 4.6, Don Smetzer, TravelUSA Stock Photos; 4.7, Radio Australia, <http://www.radioaustralia.net.au/>; 4.8, The Canadian Press/Toronto Star/Colin McConnell; 4.9, courtesy of Christine Schreyer. **Chapter 5** 5.5, © Wendy Stone/Corbis; 5.7, © iStockphoto.com/Imre Cikajlo; 5.8, © Gilles Peress/Magnum Photos; 5.9, LAC, PA-001024. **Chapter 6** 6.1, © iStockphoto.com/rest; 6.2, courtesy of Robert Lavenda; 6.3, The Canadian Press/AP Photo/Andre Penner; 6.4, © iStockphoto.com/Brian Brockman; 6.5, © iStockphoto.com/Bimarto Sasri; 6.6, The Canadian Press/Chuck Stoody; 6.7, from the collection of Michelle Bigenho; 6.8, © Fulvio Roiter/Corbis; 6.9, Susan Vogel, Prince Street Pictures, NY; 6.10, Rollout Photograph © Justin Kerr, K 555; 6.11, © iStockphoto.com/Lawrence Karn; 6.12, courtesy of Chris Hoddinott. **Chapter 7** 7.3, © iStockphoto.com/Robert Churchill; 7.4, © iStockphoto.com/Robert Churchill; 7.5, from Barbara Myerhoff, *Peyote Hunt*, © 1974 by Cornell University Press, reproduced with permission of the publisher; 7.6, from John L. Esposito et al., *World Religions Today*, 3rd edn, © 2009 by Oxford University Press. **Chapter 8** 8.1, © Roberto Escobar/EFE/Corbis; 8.3, reproduced with permission of the Kelowna Public Archives; 8.4, courtesy of John Wagner; 8.6, © iStockphoto.com/Paul Cowan; 8.7, from Statistics Canada, 'The Census of Canada', <www19.statcan.gc.ca/12/12_004-eng.htm>; 8.8, © Jeremy Horner/Corbis; 8.9, © iStockphoto.com/Chen How Sia; 8.10, Orin Starn. **Chapter 9** 9.1, Irven DeVore/Anthrophoto; 9.4, courtesy of the American Museum of Natural History Library, Image #411791; 9.5, courtesy of Robert Lavenda; 9.6, courtesy of Roberta Robin Dods; 9.7, by Carole-Anne Fooks of Australian Image Originals. **Chapter 10** 10.1, © Karan Kapoor/Corbis; 10.3, © Anthony Bannister, Gallo Images/Corbis; 10.6, © Alison Wright/Corbis; 10.8, courtesy of Naomi McPherson; 10.9, © iStockphoto.com/Henrik Jonsson; 10.10, courtesy of Robert Lavenda; 10.11, © Vanni Archive/Corbis. **Chapter 11** 11.1, courtesy of Roberta Robin Dods; 11.2, © STRINGER/INDIA/Reuters/Corbis; 11.4, The Canadian Press/Toronto Star; 11.5, courtesy of Robert Lavenda; 11.6, from Leigh Minturn, *Sita's Daughter's*, © 1993 by Oxford University Press; 11.7, © Victor Englebert; 11.8, courtesy of Robert Lavenda; 11.9, © Tomas Van Houtryve/Corbis; 11.10, Tom Cockrem. **Chapter 12** 12.1, © iStockphoto.com/Alberto Pomares; 12.2, © Shawn Baldwin/Corbis; 12.3, Tom Burnett Collection; 12.4, © iStockphoto.com/Richard Robinson; 12.5, Schalkwijk/Art Resource, NY; 12.7, © Matthew McKee, Eye Ubiquitous/Corbis; 12.9, © Reuters/Corbis; 12.10, © Reuters/Corbis. **Chapter 13** 13.1, © Ricardo Azoury/Corbis; 13.2, © Wendy Stone/Corbis; 13.3, courtesy of Robin Mouat; 13.4, © Bettmann/Corbis; 13.5, from Robert M. Bone, *The Regional Geography of Canada*, 4th edn, © 2008 by Oxford University Press; 13.6, courtesy of Daniel Lavenda; 13.7, © Micheline Pelletier/Corbis Sygma; 13.8, Lynn A. Meisch. **Chapter 14** 14.1, Andrea Wiley; 14.2, © iStockphoto.com/Dean Bergmann; 14.3, © iStockphoto.com/Grant Dougall; 14.4, © Nik Wheeler/Corbis; 14.5, courtesy of Robert Lavenda; 14.6, courtesy of Lilliana Nieto/Physicians for Human Rights.

Text and Illustrations

Chapter 1 p. 16, © 2001 by the University of Nebraska Press, reprinted with permission of the publisher. **Chapter 2** pp. 35–47, © 1977 by the University of California Press, reprinted with permission of the publisher; p. 42, published originally in *The Atlantic Monthly* (Mar. 1992) as an introduction to *Jihad vs McWorld* (Ballantine paperback, 1996), a volume that discusses and extends the themes of the original article. Benjamin R. Barber Distinguished Senior Fellow, Demos; Director, CivWorld and the author of many books including the classic *Strong Democracy* (1994), international best-seller *Jihad vs McWorld* (Times Books, 1995), and *Consumed: How Markets Corrupt Children, Infantilize Adults, and Swallow Citizens Whole*; p. 45, © 1999 by Annual Reviews, <www.annualreviews.org>, reprinted with permission of the publisher. **Chapter 5** pp. 98–117, © 1994 by Greenwood Publishing Group Inc., reprinted with permission of the publisher; pp. 103–4, reprinted with permission of the author; p. 109, © 1999 by the Society for Comparative Study of Society and History,

Index